The World of
PSYCHOANALYSIS

The World of
PSYCHOANALYSIS

EDITED BY G. B. LEVITAS

VOLUME TWO

George Braziller · *New York*

ACKNOWLEDGMENTS

The editor and publisher have made every effort to determine and credit the holders of copyright of the selections in this book. Any errors or omissions may be rectified in future volumes. The editor and publisher wish to thank the following for permission to reprint the material included in this anthology:

Basic Books, Inc.—for "Psychoanalysis" from *Character and Culture, The Collected Papers of Sigmund Freud,* Volume IV, ed. by Ernest Jones, Basic Books, 1959;—for "Family Romances" from *The Sexual Enlightenment of Children, The Collected Papers of Sigmund Freud,* Vol. V, ed. by Ernest Jones, Basic Books, 1959;—for extracts from *The Self in Transformation* by Herbert Fingarette, Basic Books, 1963;—and for an extract from *The Individual Psychology of Alfred Adler,* ed. and annotated by Heinz L. and Rowena R. Ansbacher, Basic Books, 1956. All selections reprinted by permission of the publisher.

Bollingen Foundation—for extracts from *The Archetypes and the Collective Unconscious* by C. G. Jung, tr. by R. F. G. Hull, Copyright © 1959 by Bollingen Foundation;—and for "Brother Klaus" from *Psychology and Religion: West and East* by C. G. Jung, tr. by R. F. G. Hull, Copyright © 1958 by Bollingen Foundation. Selections reprinted by permission of the publisher.

George Braziller, Inc.—for "Two Sheep" from *Snowman Snowman* by Janet Frame, Copyright © 1962, 1963 by Janet Frame. Reprinted by permission of the publisher.

Esquire, Inc.—for "I Look Out for Ed Wolfe" by Stanley Elkin, © 1962 by Esquire, Inc. Reprinted by permission of *Esquire Magazine.*

The Estate of Frieda Fromm-Reichmann—for an extract from "Psychiatric Aspects of Anxiety" by Frieda Fromm-Reichmann, as it appeared in *An Outline of Psychoanalysis,* ed. Clara Thompson, et al, Random House, Inc. Reprinted by permission of Mrs. Edward H. Gunst, Richmond, Virginia.

The Free Press of Glencoe, Inc.—for an extract from *The Criminal, The Judge, and The Public* by Franz Alexander and Hugo Staub, tr. by G. Zilboorg. Copyright 1956 by The Free Press, a Corporation, copyright 1931 by The Macmillan Company;—for an extract from *Dialogues With Mothers* by Bruno Bettelheim. Copyright © 1962 by The Free Press of Glencoe, Inc.;—for "The Themes of Work and Play in the Structure of Freud's Thought" from *Individualism Reconsidered* by David Riesman. Copyright © 1954 by The Free Press, a Corporation; —and for extracts from *The Informed Heart* by Bruno Bettelheim. Copyright © 1960 by The Free Press, a Corporation. All selections reprinted by permission of the publisher.

Harcourt, Brace & World, Inc.—for "Sex Education" from *A Harvest of Stories* by Dorothy Canfield. Copyright 1945, by Dorothy Canfield Fisher;—for extracts from *Man Against Himself* by Karl Menninger, copyright, 1938, by Karl Menninger;—and Leonard Woolf and The Hogarth Press for "An Unwritten Novel" from *A Haunted House and Other Stories* by Virginia Woolf, copyright, 1944, by Harcourt, Brace & World, Inc. All selections reprinted by permission of the publisher.

Harper & Row, Publishers, Inc.—for "Patterns in Neurotic Marriages" from

Divorce Won't Help by Edmund Bergler, Copyright 1948 by Edmund Bergler;— for "Identity and Adolescence" by Leo A. Spiegel and "The Role of Parents" by Anita Bell, both from *Adolescents,* ed. by Sandor Lorand and Henry I. Schneer. Copyright © 1961 by Hoeber Medical Division, Harper & Row, Publishers, Inc.; —and for extracts from *The Adventures of Tom Sawyer* by Mark Twain. All selections reprinted by permission of the publisher.

The Hogarth Press, Ltd.—for extracts from *The Psychoanalysis of Children* by Melanie Klein, tr. by Alix Strachey. Published by The Hogarth Press and The Institute of Psycho-Analysis as No. 22 in the International Psycho-Analytical Library, London. Reprinted by permission of The Hogarth Press, Ltd.

Holt, Rinehart and Winston, Inc. and The Society of Authors as the literary representative of the Estate of the late A. E. Housman, and Messrs. Jonathan Cape Ltd., publishers of A. E. Housman's *Collected Poems*—for "I did not lose my heart" from *The Collected Poems of A. E. Housman.* Copyright 1939, 1940, © 1965 by Holt, Rinehart and Winston, Inc. Reprinted by permission of the publishers.

Houghton Mifflin Co.—for "Epstein" from *Goodbye, Columbus* by Philip Roth, Copyright © 1959 by Philip Roth. Reprinted by permission of the publisher.

Indian Psychoanalytical Society—for "Rivalry and Envy Between Joseph and His Brothers" by Leon Grinberg, from *Samiksa, Journal of the Indian Psychoanalytic Society*, Vol. 17, No. 3, 1963. Reprinted by permission of the Indian Psychoanalytical Society.

International Universities Press, Inc.—for "The Relationship of Regressive Phenomena to the Aging Process" by Norman E. Zinberg from *Normal Psychology of the Aging Process* ed. by Norman E. Zinberg and Irving Kaufman. Copyright 1963 by International Universities Press, Inc. Reprinted by permission of Norman E. Zinberg and Irving Kaufman;—and The Hogarth Press Ltd. for "The Problem of Paul Morphy" from *Essays in Applied Psychoanalysis* by Ernest Jones, copyright 1964 by International Universities Press Inc.;—and George Allen & Unwin Ltd. for "The Group as a Regressive Force" from *The Unconscious Motives of War* by Alix Strachey. Selections reprinted by permission of the publisher.

The Julian Press, Inc.—for an extract from *One Little Boy* by Dorothy Baruch, copyright 1952 by Dorothy Baruch. Reprinted by permission of the publisher.

Alfred A. Knopf, Inc.—for an extract from *The Myth of the Birth of the Hero* by Otto Rank, tr. by F. Robbins and Smith Ely Jelliffee. Copyright 1932 by Alfred A. Knopf, Inc.;—and for "Should Wizard Hit Mommy?" by John Updike. Copyright © 1959 by John Updike. Originally appeared in *The New Yorker*. Reprinted from *Pigeon Feathers and Other Stories* by John Updike. Selections reprinted by permission of the publisher.

J. B. Lippincott Co.—for "Eighteenth Birthday" from *The Dignity of Night* by Klaus Roehler. Originally published under the title *Die Würde der Nacht,* copyright © 1958 by R. Piper & Co. Verlag, Munich. English tr. copyright © 1960 by Barrie & Rockliff (Barrie Books Ltd.), London. Revisions to the English trans., authorized by R. Piper and Co. Verlag, copyright © 1961 by J. B. Lippincott Co. Reprinted by permission of J. B. Lippincott Co.

Liveright Publishers, Inc. and The Hogarth Press, Ltd.—for an extract from *Beyond the Pleasure Principle* by Sigmund Freud, from The Standard Edition of *The Complete Psychological Works of Sigmund Freud,* ed. by James Strachey, Vol. XVIII. Reprinted by permission of the publishers.

Harold Matson Co., Inc.—for "The Invisible Boy" from *Golden Apples of the Sun* by Ray Bradbury. Copyright 1952 and 1953 by Ray Bradbury. Reprinted by permission of the Harold Matson Co.

Margaret Mead, Literary Executrix for the Estate of Ruth Benedict—for "Continuities and Discontinuities in Cultural Conditioning" by Ruth Benedict, as appeared in *Readings in Child Development* ed. by Martin and Stendler. Reprinted by permission of Margaret Mead.

William Morrow & Co., Inc.—for "Man with a Family" from *The Last Husband*

and Other Stories by William Humphrey, copyright 1949, 1950, 1951, 1952, 1953 by William Humphrey. Reprinted by permission of William Humphrey.

The New York Academy of Medicine—for "Psychoanalysis and the Study of the Creative Imagination" by Ernst Kris, from the *Bulletin of the New York Academy of Medicine,* Vol. 29, No. 4, April 1953, copyright by The New York Academy of Medicine. This was originally a Freud Lecture of the New York Psychoanalytic Institute. Reprinted by permission of the New York Academy of Medicine, The New York Psychoanalytic Institute and Dr. Marianne Kris.

W. W. Norton & Co. Inc.—for extracts from *Man's Search for Himself* by Rollo May. Copyright 1953 by W. W. Norton & Co., Inc.;—for an extract from *Neurosis and Human Growth* by Karen Horney. Copyright 1950 by W. W. Norton & Co., Inc.;—and for an extract from *Childhood and Society* by Erik H. Erikson. Copyright 1950 and © 1963 by W. W. Norton & Co., Inc. All selections reprinted by permission of the publisher.

Harold Ober Associates Inc.—for "Brother Death" from *Death in the Woods* by Sherwood Anderson. Copyright © 1926 by Eleanor Anderson. Reprinted by permission of Harold Ober Associates, Inc.

Ivan Obolensky, Inc.—for "Promise of Rain" from *Happy Families Are All Alike* by Peter Taylor. Copyright © 1959 by Ivan Obolensky, Inc. Reprinted by permission of the publisher.

Oxford University Press, Inc.—for "God's Grandeur" from *Collected Poems of Gerard Manley Hopkins.*

The Psychiatric Quarterly—for "Psychotherapeutic Evaluations of Birth-Trauma Analysis" by M. Lietaert Peerbolte from *The Psychiatric Quarterly,* Vol. 25, No. 4, Oct., 1951. Copyright by *The Psychiatric Quarterly.* Reprinted by permission of *The Psychiatric Quarterly* and M. Lietaert Peerbolte.

The Psychoanalytic Review—for "Buddhistic Training as an Artificial Catatonia" by Franz Alexander, from *The Psychoanalytic Review,* Vol. 18, No. 2, 1931;—and for "Phobias in Children" by Hanna N. Colm from *Psychoanalysis and The Psychoanalytic Review,* Fall, 1959. Selections reprinted by permission of *The Psychoanalytic Review.*

G. P. Putnam's Sons—for extracts from *What Life Should Mean to You* by Alfred Adler, Copyright 1931, 1958 by Raissa Adler. Reprinted by permission of the publisher.

Random House, Inc.—for "The Dare," Copyright 1949 by Budd Schulberg. Reprinted from *Some Faces in the Crowd* by Budd Schulberg;—for "The Chinese Cinderella" from *The Wisdom of China and India,* ed. by Lin Yutang. Copyright 1942 by Random House, Inc.;—for an extract from *Mind and Body* by Flanders Dunbar. Copyright 1947, 1955 by Flanders Dunbar;—for "I and My Chimney" from *The Complete Short Stories of Herman Melville,* ed. by Jay Leyda. Copyright 1949 by Random House, Inc.;—and Chatto and Windus Ltd. for an extract from "The Past Recaptured" by Marcel Proust. Copyright 1932 and renewed 1959 by Random House, Inc. Reprinted from *Remembrance of Things Past* by Marcel Proust.—and T. & T. Clark for an extract from *The City of God* by St. Augustine, tr. by Marcus Dods. All selections reprinted by permission of the publishers.

Idris Seabright—for her story, "Judgment Planet." © 1953 by Mercury Press, Inc. Reprinted from *The Magazine of Fantasy and Science Fiction,* July, 1953. Reprinted by permission of Mercury Press, Inc. and Idris Seabright.

James Still—for his story, "Mrs. Razor." Copyright, 1945, The Atlantic Monthly Company. Reprinted by permission of James Still.

The Viking Press, Inc.—for an extract from *The Dharma Bums* by Jack Kerouac. Copyright © 1958 by Jack Kerouac;—for "The Vigilante" from *The Long Valley* by John Steinbeck. Copyright 1936, 1964 by John Steinbeck;—for extracts from *Wayward Youth* by August Aichhorn. Copyright 1935 by The Viking Press, Inc.;—for an extract from *The Vital Balance* by Karl Menninger. Copyright © 1963 by Karl Menninger;—for "Araby" from *The Dubliners* by James Joyce. Copyright 1916 by B. W. Huebsch, Inc. All rights reserved;—and William

Heinemann Ltd. and Laurence Pollinger Ltd. on behalf of the author for "The Hint of an Explanation" from *Twenty-One Stories* by Graham Greene. Copyright 1949 by Graham Greene. All selections reprinted by permission of the publishers.

A. P. Watt & Son—for an extract from *The Bulpington of Blup* by H. G. Wells. Reprinted by permission of A. P. Watt & Son, Messrs. Hutchinson & Co. Ltd. and the Executors of the Estate of H. G. Wells.

George B. Wilbur—for "The Myth in Jane Austen" by Geoffrey Gorer, reprinted from *American Imago*, Vol. 2, No. 3, Sept. 1941. Copyright by George B. Wilbur;—for "On Origins of Hatred Toward Negroes" by Martin Reiser, reprinted from *American Imago*, Vol. 18, No. 2, Summer 1961. Copyright by George B. Wilbur. Selections reprinted by permission of George B. Wilbur.

The Williams & Wilkins Co.—for "The Psychodynamics of Suicide" by Herbert Hendin, *Journal of Nervous and Mental Disease*, Vol. 136, No. 3, March 1963, pp. 236-251. Copyright © 1963, The William & Wilkins Co., Baltimore, Md. A version of this article also appears in *Suicide in Scandinavia*, Doubleday Anchor, 1965. Reprinted by permission of the Williams & Wilkins Co. and Herbert Hendin.

The World Publishing Company—for "The Unconscious" by Hans Herma from *A Handbook of Psychoanalysis* ed. by Hans Herma and Gertrud M. Kurth. Copyright 1950 by The World Publishing Company. Reprinted by permission of the publisher.

T. C. Worsley—for his story, "The Sacred Table." Originally published in *Horizon*. Reprinted by permission of T. C. Worsley.

Yale University Press—for an extract from *Psychoanalysis and Religion* by Erich Fromm, copyright 1950 by Erich Fromm. Reprinted by permission of the publisher.

Contents

ix

BOOK THREE

THE ETERNAL WHEEL
The Cause and Effect of Man's Institutions

Once again Lewis Carroll echoes the unconscious and the primary process—this time with reference to old age. In the ambivalence towards the old, rejection is combined with sympathy. (This reflects a similar ambivalence towards the death of a loved one.) The numerous sexual symbols that appear in this poem all coalesce into one impression of frenetic rhythmic activity. Aimless rocking, dancing, jumping are often significant in tales of old age. They refer back consistently to sexual acts—and wistfully describe the attempts made by the shrinking ego to affirm its life in the face of impending death.

LEWIS CARROLL

The White Knight's Song

I'll tell thee everything I can;
    There's little to relate.
I saw an aged aged man,
    A-sitting on a gate.
"Who are you, aged man?" I said.
    "And how is it you live?"
And his answer trickled through my head,
    Like water through a sieve.

He said "I look for butterflies
    That sleep among the wheat:
I make them into mutton-pies,
    And sell them in the street.
I sell them unto men," he said,
    "Who sail the stormy seas;
And that's the way I get my bread—
    A trifle, if you please."

But I was thinking of a plan
  To dye one's whiskers green,
And always use so large a fan
  That they could not be seen.
So, having no reply to give
  To what the old man said,
I cried "Come, tell me how you live!"
  And thumped him on the head.

His accents mild took up the tale:
  He said "I go my ways,
And when I find a mountain-rill,
  I set it in a blaze;
And thence they make a stuff they call
  Rowland's Macassar-Oil—
Yet twopence-halfpenny is all
  They give me for my toil."

But I was thinking of a way
  To feed oneself on batter,
And so go on from day to day
  Getting a little fatter.
I shook him well from side to side,
  Until his face was blue:
"Come, tell me how you live," I cried,
  "And what it is you do!"

He said "I hunt for haddocks' eyes
  Among the heather bright,
And work them into waistcoat-buttons
  In the silent night.
And these I do not sell for gold
  Or coin of silvery shine,
But for a copper halfpenny,
  And that will purchase nine.

"I sometimes dig for buttered rolls,
  Or set limed twigs for crabs;
I sometimes search the grassy knolls
  For wheels of Hansom-cabs.

And that's the way" (he gave a wink)
    "By which I get my wealth—
And very gladly will I drink
    Your Honour's noble health."

I heard him then, for I had just
    Completed my design
To keep the Menai bridge from rust
    By boiling it in wine.
I thanked him much for telling me
    The way he got his wealth,
But chiefly for his wish that he
    Might drink my noble health.

And now, if e'er by chance I put
    My fingers into glue,
Or madly squeeze a right-hand foot
    Into a left-hand shoe,
Or if I drop upon my toe
    A very heavy weight,
I weep, for it reminds me so
Of that old man I used to know—
Whose look was mild, whose speech was slow,
Whose hair was whiter than the snow,
Whose face was very like a crow,
With eyes, like cinders, all aglow,
Who seemed distracted with his woe,
Who rocked his body to and fro,
And muttered mumblingly and low,
As if his mouth were full of dough,
Who snorted like a buffalo—
That summer evening long ago
    A-sitting on a gate.

Freud's concept of a death-wish pulses strongly beneath this touching narrative of a man who "accidentally" kills himself to escape the anguish of his guilt. The family romance, the relationship of the man with his own parents is etched in broad strokes. Only when he is placed in a situation of dependency that recalls the painful helplessness of his childhood does he make the final, resolute decision for death.

WILLIAM HUMPHREY

Man with a Family

1

She lifted the lid and peered in the churn to see if the butter had come. Straightening, she saw him round the corner, carrying one of his hands in the other as if he were afraid of spilling it. She dropped the dasher and ran to the door. He thrust out his hands as if she might know what to do with them. She reached for them, then drew back sharply and stood watching the blood fall on the doorsill. What was it now? As bad as the other times? He licked his lips, shook his head, then took his hand over and laid it on the table as if he meant to leave it there while he looked for something to patch it with.

From the range she brought a kettle of water and filled the washpan, testing it with her finger. As the blood swirled sluggishly through the water she sat tensely, brushing a wisp of hair back into her bun, wishing he would say something. She sighed and went to the bedroom and took a tattered pillowslip from the cedar chest. She bit a start in the cloth and rent it into bandage.

"Well," he sighed, "it was like this."

She sat down and turned her face up attentively, trying to look as she did when he told some favorite story, as if she had never heard it before, as if this was the first accident he ever had.

"I was plowing." He waited a second until she had him placed. He held his hands out, gripping the handles. She had it—there's Daisy, here's you and those are the reins around your neck.

"There was a big stone," he said, looking at the floor. She looked down at it with a frown. "But I didn't see it because it was covered. Now who would have thought of a stone in that south twenty?" he wanted to know, bristling a little, giving her a defiant look. She tried to show it was the last thing on earth that would have occurred to her. "In three years I never took more than a bucketful of stones out of that field. And they was all no bigger than your fist." She made a fist and laid it on the table; she honestly wanted to help him. "Smack!" he cried, trying desperately to steady the handles and straining his neck against the reins. She reached out to catch him and he caught himself a moment to remind her that she was at home churning butter, so she settled back and helplessly watched him flung over the handle bar, shoot out a hand to catch himself and rip it to the bone on the moldboard.

The story finished, Dan snorted, looking around him for some explanation, some reason for it, and she looked, too, glaring blamefully at the air around her. The story finished, Laura roused herself and realized suddenly that he would never get the cotton planted.

As he held out his hand for her to wrap Dan said apologetically, "I figure it was that last heavy frost pushed that stone up so high."

"I suppose," Laura sighed.

He gave a laugh to show how little his fault it was.

"What is it to laugh about?" she demanded.

They talked about other things driving home from the doctor's office but Laura couldn't help being a little suspicious. Surely he had been more careless than he admitted. In this past winter he had cut one thumb, twisted his knee, broken a rib, sprained an ankle and got a sliver of steel in his eye. To recall all that, why, who wouldn't be suspicious, and who wouldn't be aggravated with him? Of course he didn't do any of it on purpose and of course he was the one that suffered. When it reached the point where she just had to speak her mind about it, naturally she was not mad at him. But somebody had to insist he be more careful. She took her eyes from the road, trying to harden herself to speak plainly. Then she saw what he was hoping she wouldn't see, how much pain his hand was giving him and how carefully he was coddling it. She mumbled something about putting it inside his shirt and though he had heard her, he looked at the gasoline gauge and said he thought there was enough to get them home.

At four o'clock the school bus settled with a crunch before the gate and Harold came stamping in, yelling back from the door to friends and, without looking, flung his books on the table with a splash.

"What's he doing home?" He jerked a thumb toward Dan as he rifled the breadbox.

"He cut his hand," said Laura in a shooshing tone, trying to look a little respect into him.

He wanted to see. Laura said it might get infected. She added impressively, "It's got stitches."

"Stitches!" He gave Dan a look of respect. "Did it hurt much?" he asked.

"Lord, of course it hurt, silly!" Laura cried. "What do you think?"

He wanted to know how he did it.

"Oh," said Dan, "plowing. Hit a stone and fell against the moldboard." It sounded a little silly to tell it now and Harold looked as if he thought it did, too. "A big stone," he added.

"Why didn't you hold onto the handles?"

"What do you think I was doing, dancing a jig?"

"Here," said Laura. "Now you leave him alone. You go on out and play."

Harold drifted to the door and then wandered back. Coming close to Laura he said low, "You mean he's had another *accident*?"

There was rain every day for a week. Dan mended harness and puttered impatiently around the chicken yard. But rain could not have come at a better time, so he was not too downhearted. Laura was glad to have him home once she got used to the idea. She enjoyed shooing him out of the kitchen and showing him how to make fudge that always turned to sugar and had to be given to Daisy and reading the serial in the back numbers of the *Country Gentleman* aloud to him in the afternoons.

She finished milking on the third morning while he stood awkwardly by, then he grabbed the pail to take it to the house, took three steps and a corncob rolled under his foot, twisted his ankle and turned him end up in a puddle of milk. It was so funny they both rolled on the ground laughing but when he tried to get up she had to help him. But that was funny, too, and as she wrapped it up she said that pretty soon he would look like he had been hit by a truck and would need somebody to lead him around. He hobbled like an old, old man, but when Harold came home it would have been hard to tell he was limping even a little if she had not known it already.

Catching Harold's eyes on him, Dan decided to see what he could do with one hand about that old stump at the corner of the chicken yard that he had let stay there so long. He went over to it and spat on his hand, gave it a careless tug, then a heave, then nearly broke his back on it but it wouldn't budge. He looked around and decided to move that big stone he had let lay there for years, gave it a yank and it came loose. He raised it 'way above his head and threw it over the fence, then went casually back for his jumper, but Harold was gone. He looked back at it and had to admit it was not such a big stone at that.

2

Anxious as she was to have him get back, it did seem foolish for a man to think of planting cotton when his wife had to harness the mule. She was about ready to go to the field with him. Thank heaven, at least they were not that bad off yet, for the neighbors to see her walking behind a plow.

In low places in the fields, Laura thought, the ground would still be muddy. Neighbors who could afford to would stay home another couple of days; she hoped Dan didn't feel she was rushing him. She snapped the trace chains and settled Daisy's collar better. Dan gripped the handles and smiled at her.

As innocently as possible she said, "Now be careful, Dan," and he replied without resentment, "I will."

Laura might have canned a lot more peas but for looking up between every two she shelled, expecting to see him coming in with a limp or a drag or a stagger. Now that he had already lost so much time she feared he might be overcautious. Like Harold—leave him alone and he brought the milk in without spilling a drop, but just let him spill it once and then tell him to be careful not to, how much it cost and all, and he stumbled with it sure as the world.

A drummer came to the door and usually she simply couldn't turn one away, but today, as this one rounded the corner, she kicked over her bucket of pods, scared stiff, and almost slammed the door right in his face, he had given her such a scare. As the day passed she got jumpier. It was silly, she knew, but to think of any more delay in the planting made her run cold all over. Maybe she imagined it, but Harold looked around the place as if it surprised him, too, not to find Dan home with some ailment or other. She sent him out but he moped around the back door. Dan was late and to get Harold to bed and give herself something to do she gave him his supper early. He ate slowly while Laura fretted whether she ought to cook a supper of Dan's favorite things, or would that seem she was making an occasion of a day that ought to be passed over as nothing out of the ordinary?

Harold finished and went to the window. It was dark now and he sighed lumpily, "I wonder what happened?" Laura turned to snap something, but he was already in the bedroom and instead she sat down to cry when she heard Dan's step. If he noticed her red eyes he never let on and probably he didn't; he was blind tired. His arm was stiff and she guessed he had followed the plow bent double all day, one handle in the crotch of his arm to spare his hand.

As he got back into shape he came in less tired, able to sit up after supper and read a while, or try to read but not be able for watching Laura, seeing how worried she had been all day and how, through the evening, she tried to accustom herself to the notion that another day had been got past, able to see that something, something he couldn't just put his finger on, but something peculiar had settled down in his house, and what was even more peculiar, even harder to find words to suit, something that seemed to mean to stay. He felt left out of everything. It was as if he had gone away for a while and come back before he was expected. It was such a queer feeling and it wasn't helped any by looking up sometimes and seeing Laura and Harold standing together like a photograph he hadn't got into.

The way they looked at him! Like they had really had something different in mind, but he had come and they had used him and now they couldn't send him back. Did they? Maybe he imagined it; he wasn't feeling good, anyway. Maybe his mind was all tired and bent over, too. But what could you think when your own boy looked at you like a horse somebody was trying to sell too cheap, and when he went to bed was thirstier than ever before and kept having to go to the pot to see if you had managed to keep on your feet once you had him out of sight?

3

Laura's mama came over as soon as she sent word that the washing machine had come. It was Saturday and Dan had gone into town to buy groceries, but Harold was too interested in the machine to go with him. Laura's mama drove her buggy over early. She loved machinery and was proud of her daughter for owning the shiny, mysterious washing machine and being able to run it. She loved the noise and loved having to yell above it to make herself heard.

"You might get that thing to churn butter," she urged in a shout.

Harold was disgusted but Laura thought it might work and promised herself to try it. Now the grandmother wanted to shut it off and give it a rest and rest herself. She rubbed a finger over it as tenderly as over a sleeping baby.

"A thing like that must cost a heap of money," she said.

Laura swelled with pride. "I should think it does."

Her mama stood with her question on her face but the amount was almost too much for Laura to be proud of. She said, "We bought it on the installment plan, of course."

"Well," said her mama, as though she had been taken for some kind of a fool, as though she didn't know a fine piece of machinery when she saw it, "I never thought you could buy such a thing outright," and in fact she couldn't really see how they had made the down payment. "How much was it?" she asked hungrily and cocked her ear around to receive some astounding figure.

She looked ready not to resent the price but to admire it. Laura couldn't think of another woman anywhere around whose husband had spent so much money on her at one time, so she told. Her mother flinched as if somebody had suddenly blown in her ear. She had prepared herself for the limit; now her face turned sour and she looked at the washing machine with distaste. She thought she had raised a more sensible daughter and one not nearly so trifling. She had washed work-clothes and dirty diapers on her seventy-nine-cent washboard for forty-odd years and it was good enough for anybody. She began to take notice that Laura's dress had a hole under the arm and that Harold had on pants too small for him and needed a haircut. Well, she never thought she would see the day when Laura would let her family go to seed and put her man in debt for years because she was too lazy to wash his clothes, and she said as much.

Laura said, "Well, I don't know as it will keep him in debt all that long."

"However long it is, looks like you'll sure be ragged but clean."

"Well," said Laura, standing sharp, hands on her hips, "if I am it'll be no change from what I always was at home. Except maybe cleaner," and she turned the machine on with a clatter and stuffed it with practically every stitch the family owned.

Grandmother recalled the bag of candy she had brought and fished it out of her purse. She took one herself and called Harold over and gave him one.

Laura snapped off the washer and said, "Don't feed him that junk this near dinnertime."

"Let him have it," Grandmother insisted, and with a look at the washer, "I don't suppose he got much while you was saving up for that thing."

"I declare, Mama, I never thought I'd see the day," said Laura, "when you'd envy your own daughter a little comfort and not like to see her come up in life."

"Comfort," said her mama, "is for them as can afford it."

"Well, you just let me worry about affording it. And this is only the first. I mean to have a lot of nice things and I'm looking around now to decide what I'll get when the crop's in."

"Yes, I've seen a new player piano," her mama sighed, "and a new second-hand car come to our house and seen the men come and take them away when they was half paid for." She shot the bag of candy at the boy; it was giving her a toothache. "Probably the last you'll see for some time," she mumbled.

Harold looked at his mother to have this denied.

Laura snapped at him, "I reckon you get enough candy."

"I don't either," he appealed to his Granny. "I've never got enough candy in my whole life."

Laura sent him out the door with no buts about it. The old woman called after him, "You just come over to your Granny's. She's always got a little candy for her boy.

"You better send that thing back," she said. She was serious now. "You never know what's going to happen to keep it from getting paid for."

"You're just mad," said Laura, "that Dan wants me to have a few nice things when Papa never bought anything nice for you."

"Never mind that kind of talk. You just better get rid of it." She clamped her bonnet on and gave the washing machine a scampering look.

"I was going to say you could bring your wash over and use my new machine," said Laura, "and to show you how big I can be, you still can."

Her mama replied with a lift of her nose to show that she wouldn't be caught dead doing it, "No, thank you. Thank you just the same. I've come this far without it and I reckon my rub-board will see me the rest of my way. You as much as said I keep a dirty house. Besides we ain't got as much clothes as all that," and she gave Laura's wash-pile a look that said as plain as day: But it's a good deal more than you all have.

4

When the cotton was in the ground they all drew a deep breath. He was only a week or so behind with it, and then he started seeding his corn. That went so well that Dan spoke of taking off to go fishing. Laura looked forward to it and had it on her mind as she carried whey to the chickens. What a pity Harold was in school, she was thinking, when Dan came over the hill on Daisy.

Laura poured the whey in the trough and went out to meet him. He looked disgusted with something, so the fishing trip fizzled out.

"What happened?" she asked, holding the reins. Then she stooped under the mule's neck and she saw where Dan's leg dangled down and floated stiffly inside his bloody pants. Just above the knee his leg took a sickening jump to one side, like a pencil seen through a glass of water.

Laura crept out from under Daisy's head and started to look up, when she fainted. Dan slid off Daisy and got his good leg under him. But there he was stuck. He thought, Daisy might take it into her head any minute to make off for oats in the barn. Then what would he do? The nearest support was a fence post he could never reach. He couldn't possibly get on her back again. How long would she stand still? How long would it take Laura to come to? How long could he stand the sun without keeling over?

"Laura!" he shouted and Daisy shied. He licked the sweat from the corner of his mouth and called her more softly. Hanging around Daisy's neck, he inched his good leg out and gave her a shove, waited a second and when she didn't stir he kicked her. Laura, with a groan, rolled over and buried her face in the dirt. Dan could feel himself going and decided it would probably be best to fall a little to his left and forward.

Laura got propped on her elbows and shook herself down and got to her feet. Dan moaned as she tried to raise him. Maybe moving him would make things worse. She looked around, half-expecting someone to see the trouble she was having and come over to give her a hand. She went to the house and got a quilt. She wrapped him in it and started for the car to go to the neighbor's phone.

Laura's papa sat at the table and steadily cropped the shreds of his cigarette, his coffee saucered and blowed, being careful to swill it quietly, stiffly respectful, which consisted in not hearing anything that was said to him and looking as if, under the circumstances, words just didn't reach him, trying to keep his own two good legs out of sight and not look any too well himself. Laura's mama worked quietly over the stove and Harold sat in the corner he had hardly left all day, trying to make himself as small as possible, scared to death. He would not go into Dan's room and Laura didn't insist. The sight of him could only have made Dan feel worse.

Laura pulled her hands out of the bucket of plaster and scrubbed them thoughtfully in the washpan. She picked up the heavy bucket and her papa looked like he would offer to carry it but he had had his own reverses lately and too much must not be expected of him. He rubbed a hand along a tender kidney and looked wistfully away.

The doctor plastered the leg. "Well," he said, "we might have waited till a little more of the swelling went down, but I don't think it will matter too much."

It didn't matter much to Dan. He looked at the leg with only the top layer of his eyes. He brought himself up with a bitter sigh and said, "He says I'll be in bed six weeks," and gave Laura a long defiant stare.

She had already told herself it would be a long time but now her surprise showed and so did her pain. Dan's tone hurt her. He didn't have to throw it up to her like that. She hadn't asked.

"That at least," the doctor said. "What I said in fact was six to ten weeks." He gathered up his tools and laid them neatly in his bag, taking out a bottle of pills. "Give him these to sleep but never more than three a day. I'll come out every day for a week or so. I don't know just what time of day but I'll get here."

"What I don't know," said Dan, "is when you're going to get paid."

"Well, I'll worry about that."

Out in the kitchen the doctor washed his hands, rolled down his sleeves and drew on his coat while everyone watched. Laura's papa nodded sagely at his movements and her mama stopped setting the table to pat her hair in shape and smooth the ruffles of her dress.

"I wouldn't leave him too much alone," said the doctor. "Keep his mind occupied. Just don't make too much over it. Course you can't exactly act like nothing happened," he smiled broadly, "but remember, it could have been worse."

How? How could it have been any worse, Laura wanted to know. He said that to everybody without thinking. Her papa registered with a snort that he thought it was bad enough.

The doctor settled his things in his pocket and turned to the old man. "Well, John, how've you been coming along lately?"

It was no time to feel well when a doctor was talking to you free, so the old man dug out his cigarette and got ready to give details. "Well, when you get my age, you know, Doctor, ever' little thing—"

The doctor pulled up his watch and glanced at it impatiently. He has other calls to make, thought Laura with some surprise, other bones to set. She got a glimpse of her papa rubbing up his rheumatic knee as though to polish it for show. She saw the fright in Harold's eyes over all these broken bones and aching knees and cut hands. She saw her mother reach over and set the turnips aside to simmer and look at the doctor as though she would like to ask him to stay for a bite but was ashamed of what her daughter had to offer.

Laura slammed the door and buried her face in Dan's arm. He let her cry and then raised her to him. She hugged him and sobbed. He stroked her head gently and gently eased her back a little. She had shaken him and the pain in his leg was awful.

5

Mr. Johnson hung soggily on the barnyard fence while Dan stood stiff and uneasy before him, not knowing what to do with his hands that he was keeping respectfully out of his pockets. Not far away Mr. Johnson's car rested in the shade of a tree, with Mr. Johnson's wife in the front seat. Mr. Johnson took out his cigar, shot a stream of juice onto a flat stone and watched it sizzle.

"I ain't been mean, have I, Dan?"

"No, Mr. Johnson," Dan replied, "you been mighty patient and I appreciate it. But, Mr. Johnson . . ."

"Now, Dan," he interrupted, "you know as well as I do, not many men would have strung along with you as far as I have."

"I know it, Mr. Johnson. You been mighty patient."

"Well, these things just happen. I reckon everybody has a stretch like this some time or other." Mr. Johnson waved a large chunk of charity at him. "I don't want to be mean. I ain't forgot you done well here before all this begun to happen. I don't forget them things. But now, you see, prices is good. This here's a good piece of land and with proper work we'd have us a whopping big crop off of it. Everybody else is doing good this year. You got one of the best sixty acres in the county right here,

Dan, and you and me could both be making a killing if it was going right."

Mr. Johnson removed his big lazy Panama and mopped his forehead and the back of his neck with a sopping handkerchief. Dan shifted the weight from his aching leg slowly, trying not to wince. What was the good of all this? Why stand out here in the sun and jaw about it? He hadn't done it on purpose, for God's sake. Didn't he know it was a good year, and who stood to lose the most, him or Johnson?

"You've got a good head on you, Dan," Mr. Johnson was saying. "You ain't wild. You're about as settled a man for your age as I ever seen. I knew your papa and I could see his boy would make a good farmer. I just mean to say I got faith in you, Dan. But you can see the fix this puts me in."

Dan nodded wearily and followed Mr. Johnson's eyes down along the length of his stiff leg.

"Jesus, it ain't your fault. But it ain't mine, either." Mr. Johnson was getting hotter and his eye acknowledged an impatient stir from his wife.

"Well, I don't know what to say. We'll just have to let things go on like this for a while, I guess. I don't see nothing else we can do."

Neither did Dan. He stood helplessly, wishing Mr. Johnson would go on and not stop at those awkward spots.

"I can bring in a team and make another alfalfa cutting. And we might get a stand of soybeans if the weather holds. But if anything else happens, God help us. Dan, you just got to be more careful."

Careful! It made him so mad he heard the insides of his ears pop. Careful! He raised his head, raised a forefinger, raised his leg to set it out before him in a stance, then thanked the Lord for the pain it caused him. Johnson would never know how near he had come to a good round cussing.

Mr. Johnson turned to go. Reaching into his pocket he brought up a lighter for his guttering cigar. At a gesture Dan went closer. Mr. Johnson, with a show of lighting his cigar, slipped a bill into his hand and signaled his wife that he was coming, that only the lighting of his cigar was keeping him.

6

When Harold's summer vacation began Laura bent over backwards being nice to him. He'd been through so much, poor little fellow, had taken Dan's accident so serious and she had scrimped him on so many things he needed. Most of all she was ashamed of being sorry to have him home. She even refused to call him down when she knew he was bothering Dan with his racket. And Dan was being so nice, even softened her when once or twice she did fly off the handle at the boy.

Dan felt that his accident had done one good thing at least, brought him and Laura closer together than they had been since they were married, certainly a lot closer than they had been for a long time lately.

Not that he wasn't worried just about every minute. He worried over the look of things, what the neighbors were saying about Laura spading the vegetable garden and pitching manure out of the barn. They had seen her, all right, gone out of their ways to see her and he worried most over how she felt about the loss of her pride.

One Saturday after she had gone to town he found the washing machine gone. How she managed to get it into the car by herself he couldn't guess and didn't ask. Someday he would get her another one, meanwhile it wasn't as if it was any comedown. It wouldn't hurt her to wash a few clothes.

Laura said, "How did you do it?" glaring down at the boy. She was worn out with chopping kindling and he had been going like a wild Indian since the break of day. She would have to leave off her cooking and trying to get in a few strokes on the churn and trying to clean up the place that had got to looking like a pigsty and having to move Dan around to sweep under his feet with him sitting there like he didn't even know she was in the same room, much less trying to clean up where he was, have to break off and leave things to boil over and burn and come out to drag Harold down out of the mulberry tree or off the barn roof or out from under the house where all kinds of spiders and snakes were liable to get at him, a dozen times she'd had to come out and yell at him for something and now this cut thumb was the last straw.

"Drawing the knife towards you, I bet, weren't you?" He made her mad the way he stood there so hangdog and she had a mind to grab him and shake a little of the nonsense out of him. Didn't she have enough to do without this now and didn't anybody care even enough to look after their own selves? "How many times have I told you never to whittle towards yourself? Huh? How many times? Well, just march over to that washpan and daub it good with iodine."

He twisted his face up at her with a plea. "Couldn't I use monkey-blood just as good?"

Dan put his paper down with a rustle and the boy looked at him with a slow flush of accusation, his eyes coming to rest on the leg stretched

out under the table. He turned to Laura and began to whimper. She
snatched him a turn and gave him a little whack, warmed up to it and
gave him another.

"Stop it," said Dan. "He wasn't doing that a bit. I saw him and he
was cutting away from him."

Laura shut her arm off midway and turned the boy to face her. He
turned himself back and stared at Dan in bewilderment. Dan ducked
back into his paper and when Laura looked down at Harold she knew
instantly it was a lie. But what should she do? Not ask him and have
Dan shown up, or if he said it was so, why, she'd be just encouraging
him to lie. He started to tremble and she knew he was thinking the same
thing. Poor little fellow, what a fix to put him in. He shied away when
she tried to hug him. Dan put his paper down and cleared his throat and
limped to the door while they both stood and gaped at him. The thought
in Laura's mind scared her and made her ashamed. Her husband, the
father of her child, and for a minute she had stood there and just hated
him.

Harold knew how bad he always got to feeling after he told a fib, so
he thought Dan might use a little cheering up. He found him in the barn
and said, "You know, that was a pretty deep cut I got," thinking he
would give him a little company.

"It didn't look like much to me," said Dan.

"Yes, it was but I didn't cry a bit."

"Why should you have? It wasn't nothing but a scratch."

Harold thought deeply. "I'm not as big as you are and for my size it
was just about as much as your cut hand was for you." After a moment
he added gravely, "I don't think it needs stitches, though."

"You look like stitches," said Dan. "You couldn't even stand the
thought of a little iodine."

"Do you think I ought to lay off with it for a few days?" asked
Harold.

Why, the little smart aleck! Dan drew back his hand to fetch him a
good one, then let it fall. "Get out of here," he said, "and leave me
alone. And the next time I catch you whittling towards you I'll give you
such a whipping as you never had."

7

Dan had been on his feet about two weeks when Mr. Johnson brought
over a riding plow and an extra mule. Dan could not really make out

now, he knew it and had for a long time, but maybe he could keep from getting quite so far in the hole with some late-maturing truck crop. He had the land for it, three acres, black as coal.

"Now, Dan," Laura pumped herself up to begin, "I hope they won't be nothing else happen. And probably nothing will." Lord, what else could? "But you never can tell and it's better to be safe than sorry. I was thinking, what if something was to happen and you wasn't able to get home. Here you are now still in that cast, I mean, and so you ought to have some way of calling me. Just in case, you understand."

Dan nodded. He couldn't afford to seem mulish.

She looked at him to see if it was all right to go on. "Now they's an old cowbell hangs in the barn. Suppose we wrapped up the clapper and hung it on your plow, then, just in case—"

She stopped. He was hopping mad.

It made him madder every time he thought about it all day long and he wouldn't have spoken a word to her when he came home if he hadn't come with a big blue bruise like a windfallen plum over one eye where he had fallen off the plow seat and just laid there, unable to believe it, for half an hour. So he spoke just about a word and Laura didn't urge him to any more. Herself, she hadn't one. Next morning, without letting her see, he took the big brass cowbell off its hook in the barn, wrapped the clapper in a strip of burlap and hung it under the plow seat. It made him feel like a fool, like a clabber-headed heifer that jumped fences, but when he reached down to yank the thing off and throw it in a ditch the blood pounded in the knot over his eye and he left it.

He plowed along and tried to forget it was there, but it might just as well have been strung around his neck. He couldn't be mad at her, she meant well and he was past pretending she didn't have reason for fear. He had got to feeling like he ought to have a bell, not to call anybody to him, but to warn them he was coming and they'd all better hide so they wouldn't catch whatever it was he had. People already looked at him like they would rather he didn't come too close, like he had caught something nasty, not to be spoken of. He didn't imagine it, no more than he imagined the look on Mr. Johnson's face the last time he was over, like he just couldn't see how a man could change overnight and go so completely to the dogs, shaking his head as much as to say, I don't see how you could do it, a man with a wife and family. Then again, half-awake in the morning, aching all over and dreading the clang of the alarm, he would see a long row of backs all turned his way and hear sniggers, "You know, he ain't no good to his wife any more. Ain't been for months. So just keep your eye on her for the next little spell."

He knew people talked about how tacky he dressed them, too, her and Harold. It looked like every dress she owned had a way of coming out at the seams under the arms and though he knew she had a lot to do, it did seem she could keep her things mended a little better. Not that she left those holes there to make him feel bad, but she ought to have seen they did.

Then her mama and papa would come over and the old woman would sit with her nose stiff and her eyes loose, looking behind and under and atop things as if what she saw before her, bad as it was, wasn't bad enough, and she was sure they had worse things hid away. And the old man would sit and rub his belly, ducking his head, pumping up a good long belch that rumbled like an indoor toilet, letting everybody know what a good dinner he had left home on and how little he looked forward to getting here for his supper.

The old man was the only one didn't think he had a nasty case of something. He just thought he was lazy and he had a sly steady look for him: I know what you're up to, tried it myself, but hell, they's a point to stop at and you passed it long ago.

And now, even Daisy, turning round with a long disappointed look at him. He pulled the team up, thinking he would eat, but he couldn't get a bite down.

He thought how Laura's mama shook her head over Harold every time she laid eyes on him. Dan couldn't see anything wrong with him. Kids were supposed to be a little dirty and wear old clothes around home. But to her he was such a pitiful sight, maybe he was just closing his eyes to all that was wrong with the boy.

He thought how long he had let that twenty-dollar bill Mr. Johnson slipped him stay in the cupboard, how he vowed to go over and give it right back the very next day but hadn't got around to it somehow, and instead come to say he'd let it lay there and never use it and return the very same one when he had enough for sure never to need it, and then, how he had turned it over to Laura and away it had gone. Gone fast, too, and he wondered was Laura really being careful of her spending. How he had stood around hemming and hawing and looking far-off when Mr. Johnson came again, waiting for him to slip him another, and then being mad when he didn't. Being mad when you didn't get charity—that was a pretty low comedown.

He leaned back against the tree, worn out, his leg thumping with pain, and let the team stray off down the fence-row. He lay down to rest a while but the sun shifted and bored through the branches as if it wanted to get a look at him. He tried to doze but he could hear that cowbell ringing in his head. Each of his hurts came back to him and he tried to recall the day it happened, hoping to remember something that might seem to deserve such punishment. The details of his troubles began crawling up over the edges of his mind and grew thick, like a gathering swarm of bees. It was not his family nor the people on the street—he was the one who had changed. Other men had troubles but they were separate and unconnected, each came and stung and went on. Something was wrong with a man when they came and did their hurt and then stayed, waiting for the next, until they'd eaten him hollow. He didn't have any troubles any more, he just had one big trouble. For a moment that gave him a sad thrill. He had been marked out. But why? He started to raise himself to see if the answer didn't lie somewhere near at hand, and halfway up was caught and held by the thought that nobody knew why, nobody could tell him. He lay back heavily and said aloud, "I probably have it all coming to me." It made him sad that he couldn't remember whatever he had done to deserve it.

They sat down to supper with Harold quiet and cautious. He had been punished for something and Dan felt like being sure he had deserved it. "What's wrong with him?" he asked.

Laura looked at Harold, waiting for him to speak up and declare how bad he had been and just what he had got for it. "He got a spanking," she said. Harold squirmed. Laura straightened him up with a look and said, "He got hisself a bell and went around ringing it all day. I asked him a hundred times to stop it but he wouldn't. I was jumping out of my skin all day long every five minutes thinking it was you and something bad had happened."

Dan threw his knife on his plate with a clatter. "Jesus Christ! Did you have it on your mind every minute that I was going to sound off on that damn thing!"

Laura bounced in her seat as if he had hit her; a slow hard pinch started in around the edges of her eyes. "Well, yes," she said, picking out all the bruises and breaks and bumps up and down him, "I did!"

8

Dan sat hunched up on the front porch, wandering wearily back and forth between the two minds he had about everything. He had sat there, just breathing, ever since they left, and now it was hard to believe that in the house behind his back anything had happened for years, or again, it seemed something had happened all right, the last thing that ever would, and now the house lay dead. Laura, she was down behind the barn, crying, he supposed, and one minute he would reckon he ought to stir himself and go out and try to comfort her, and the next minute figure he had just better keep out of her sight—not rousing himself to do either and not caring the next minute one way or the other, just wishing he could keep out of his own sight.

She was only going to take the boy over to her place until Laura had a little more time to spare him, the grandmother said, and Laura had taken no exception, even agreed with a tired nod that she hadn't given him much time of late and that Harold looked it every bit. It was not time she hadn't given him—though she hadn't given him that, either—and she knew it wasn't time or attention that his grandmother was thinking he needed. The old woman looked the boy over, tallying all the hollow spots that a few square meals would fill out. Her man was torn—strutting around throwing it up to Dan that he couldn't support his only child, pleased that *he* could, had figured for years that sooner or later he would have to, then suddenly fearing they might get to thinking he was better able to do it than he wanted them to think. Then he would pull a thin face to show how pinched he was going to be with his new responsibility.

Laura had followed them out to the buggy, wanting to say, We'll have you back soon, Harold, don't you worry. And afraid he would act as if that were the only thing that worried him. Suddenly she wanted to tell him that it wasn't any of her doing, that she wasn't that way, that there wasn't anything wrong with her—because he did look at her as though, since she was staying behind, the same thing must be wrong with her. Instead, settling him on the seat, not thinking, she said, "Drive careful, Papa."

She watched them move away and, turning, shoved the gate shut and watched it fall back in exhaustion. Walking up the path her words scraped dryly in her mind: Be careful, Papa. Be careful, careful, be careful. She came to the front steps and stood looking at Dan as she would at an old no-good hound dog lolling on the porch, then turned and walked around the house.

9

That three acres of truck was not going to make a stand; they both saw that and so did Mr. Johnson. He hadn't got it in early enough and hadn't been able to work it like he should have, it had been too hot and dry or too cold and damp and it never got proper spraying and the bugs got at it and it wasn't a very good piece of land anyway and if anybody needed any more reason, well, it was his, and that ought to be enough.

They clung as long as they could, holding out against what they knew without saying was their only alternative. But a day came when the last piece of salt pork spread its weak stain through the last pot of beans, when the flour barrel was turned end up and dusted out on a newspaper, when you could just about see the blue flowers right through the pancakes on your plate, then, as if he had timed it to the last mouthful, Laura's papa pulled up outside the limp gate in his sway-backed wagon behind his draughty mules and sat up on the high spring seat looking down as though he might have revived things no end just by spitting on that ruined soil and wouldn't do it—which was a lie; he was so dried up himself he couldn't have brought up a nourishing spit. His face looked eroded and was covered with a maze of capillaries like exposed roots. On top of this a tangle of dry hair drifted like tumbleweed.

Behind him, piled among their battered belongings, Laura and Dan rode away without a backward glance.

He was hard up all right, Laura's papa, always had been, always would be, but his actual condition was never so low as you'd guess from the meal he gave them that first night. You would have thought he expected a bill collector for company. And he was upset that Laura's mama had put on such a good expensive-looking dress to welcome her daughter home and he found a way to remark two or three times about it being her only one. What it was was her very best guinea hen print and she sat puffed up in it all evening as if she had an egg but wouldn't lay it. As her husband offered the Lord his thanks for this and all His blessings—with a look at Dan—a scandalized look sneaked out of the corner of the old woman's eye and stole upward. She wanted Him and the others as well to know she hadn't forgot having had more in her day to thank Him for.

Dan guessed he'd never had more and they were all, it seemed, anxious to assure him that he never had. It looked as if her family had not only known him all his life but known him better than anyone else, better than he knew himself. They could recall accidents he had had and bring them clearly back to him, things he hadn't thought of for years, and now he supposed he had deliberately tried to forget them and had run for years from admitting this mark that was set on him, it seemed, the day he was born—and rolled out of his crib and got a knot on his head, the old man swore, and swore not to be mean, but you could tell from the look on his face, in genuine astonishment, it all added together so perfectly.

So perfectly it left not a minute's doubt in the mind of any of them that he was an absolute leper. Laura got tired of seeing him take it without any fight, but his time was taken up. Something would poke him awake in the morning, urge him to gulp down his coffee, so he could get started doing nothing and thinking nothing, and the effort of it had him worn out by evening. Everything everybody said or did was meant in some way for him, he felt, but it all had so little to do with him. Sometimes he felt like speaking up and getting in a dig himself at himself when they were all having such a good time running him down.

Laura believed he wasn't taking his position seriously enough. Instead of resenting her folks' charity as she had at first, she had come to feel they were being pretty nice to do all they had and that Dan might be decent enough to be grateful. He wasn't. They were getting their money's worth; they hadn't had anybody they could take as much out on in a long time. He had given them something more in common than they could ever have agreed upon amongst them. The bunch of them got along together now like fingers in a mitten.

At first Laura was always prophesying rain. If her papa was kept home then Dan wouldn't feel quite so bad that he wasn't out working. When it did rain she would pray for it to clear and get the old man back to the fields and out of the house where he couldn't torment Dan. The old man had the same problem rain or shine: Ought he to let them know how well the crops were coming for him—compared to *some* he could mention—or let them know what a lean winter they were in for around his table? He chose always to look worn to a frazzle; whichever way it turned out he had done his share and more.

Dan didn't care whether it rained or shone and he could see before long that Laura wasn't so worried one way or the other any more. Even with all she had to put up with from her mama, complaining about her cooking and the way she cleaned house and the grease she left around the sink and the way Harold dirtied his overalls so fast, with all that, Laura couldn't forget that she wasn't out forking hay or shaking out sods, couldn't feel any other way except that that was over now and she had come back home.

On the morning he was killed Dan woke earlier, struck with the thought he'd sooner spend the day with the old man than with the women. He went out to work a month before the date the doctor had set. He had expected it, but still it hurt when Laura didn't even try to stop him. She had seen him limp for so long she'd forgot there was a time when he didn't, couldn't believe a time might ever come when he wouldn't. He'd gone out too early before and the leg hadn't healed but it probably wouldn't have, anyway, and if it had something else as bad would have happened, if not worse.

How funny it was, Dan thought, that he didn't mind the old man now. It was clear that the old man despised him, and so it was no surprise to see that cowbell Laura had made him carry on Johnson's place hung under the mower that the old man meant for him to use. What did surprise Dan was that he didn't care. The old man stood by itching for a quarrel over it; Dan didn't have the energy.

He started in at one corner of the field and mowed three laps around. The steady clatter of the machine soothed him. With some surprise he had about decided that nothing out of the way was likely to happen when, near the end of his fourth time around, the mower bumped over a rock and he was thrown in front of the blade. The pointed runners held him spitted and the mules, taking fright, dragged him fifty feet before the spikes tore out and rolled over him.

He fought hard against coming to and half-conscious he knew he was badly hurt. He thought of what it was going to be like, dragging in bloody from head to toe, and he said to himself: Why can't I really have a good one once and for all and get it over with? He opened his eyes and looked at himself in disgust. Now, he thought, I'm going to catch hell sure enough. He started poking around in him for the strength to get up, but a wave of pain and sadness bent his will like the wind coming over the grass. If only he could just lie there and not have to go. But supposing they found him like this—that would be worse than if he dragged himself in. He tried to rise. But the grass came up cool and crisp, rustling like a fresh bedsheet, and tucked him in. What shall I dream about, he asked, and heard himself answer: You're already dreaming.

Then a voice like Mr. Johnson's said, "Are you going to lie there all day?" "No, sir, I'm going to get right up now and support my family."

He rolled over and groaned and opened his eyes. He could see the team a little ways off and was thankful for that bell hanging there. It cheered him so he got to his elbows and once he had he took a look at himself and laughed. If he could do that then he damned sure wasn't going to ring that bell. It would just be giving the old man too much to crow about. He looked again and wondered if he could have reached the bell anyhow, for there it went dancing all over the field.

Then Dan watched himself get up, get the bell and begin swinging it with all his might, pointing at the body on the ground as though he wanted everybody to come see what he had gone and done with himself now.

Of all the fantasies that underlie suicide or attempted suicide, the most persistent may be the desire for death as a punishment. In this story of an eighteen-year-old girl, the theme of guilt and expiation is quite clear.

KLAUS ROEHLER

Eighteenth Birthday

1

The front door slammed. Herr and Frau Hopp walked briskly toward the garage. Their car was out. Kibus waited at the driveway gate. He held it open. The car backed slowly into the street. Frau Hopp called to Kibus through the car window: "Don't you leave the house! You've got school tomorrow." Kibus nodded. Herr and Frau Hopp drove past the house without looking back. Kibus pushed the gate shut. He looked hesitantly around him. He waved to Justine, who was standing at the window of her room. Then he sauntered down the street.

Justine switched on the light. She sat down on the bed. She took a razor blade from her pencil box and held it gingerly between the index finger and thumb of her right hand. She extended her left forearm palm upward on the stool next to her bed. Bending forward, she began to scrape off the skin over the artery. She worked in silence, her breath the only sound in the room. As the bits of skin peeled off, she blew them on to the stool. The night-blue tracery of veins throbbed under the blade. It mustn't bleed. A circle of raw flesh in the parchment of the skin. With her eyebrow pencil Justine drew a black line around it. She extended it around her wrist like the strap of a watch. Red. Black. She put figures inside the circle. Three, six, nine, twelve. It hadn't bled.

2

All parents had names. Justine's parents were named Hopp. Herr Hopp was a traveling salesman—not one of those poor stiffs who spend all day hunched over the steering wheel of a little car, shabby, harassed, peddling their wares with a desperate affability: with Herr Hopp everything was large, roomy and well kept-up—his house, his car, his wife. Herr Hopp sold office machines. He spent a lot of money on his children. He said to Justine: "Remember one thing, my girl, when you go getting married: the first few years you can live on love, after that it takes money."

Frau Hopp: she was an excellent cook.

Kibus: the name of Justine's brother. He was two years her junior and wanted to play the trumpet in a jazz band.

Ulses: the name of Justine's boy-friend. They were in the same class at school.

Teachers, male and female: Justine had them because she went to school.

Acquaintances: Justine had acquaintances, as everyone does, with whom she exchanged remarks from time to time about the weather, the movies and clothes—with whom she made conversation, as everyone makes conversation with acquaintances.

Herr Hopp: Frau Hopp: Kibus: Ulses: school—that was Justine's world. When asked her age Justine said: "Almost eighteen and the end isn't in sight."

3

It was summer, but it could just as well have been winter or spring or autumn or some season unrecorded in the calendar. Each day was the spitting image of the one before it; their idiot similarity made you doubt the competence as well as the good intentions of the Creator.

The day began in the morning with school, but what problems does an education solve: it merely grazes the surface, the educators are salaried functionaries waiting out their pensions They only concern themselves with problems the solutions to which are contained in the syllabus. In the afternoon Justine helped around the house, "the family" always means work, leafed through fashion magazines, read, went swimming, played tennis with Ulses, it was summer, after all, sometimes there was company, friends of Frau Hopp, and Justine had to make coffee. But what was the point of it all? In the evening Justine was allowed to go downtown, to the theater or a movie, or to go dancing with Ulses. But what was it all for? Or, Herr and Frau Hopp suddenly became family-conscious: they all had to play cards, Herr Hopp, with the joviality of the successful businessman, broke out a bottle of wine, and they all sloshed around dispiritedly in the lukewarm puddle of affection long gone stale.

So the week went by and the calendar inexorably decreed that the seventh day should be a day of rest, designated in red letters. But rest for what, if you had no religion? Justine prayed only: "Dear God, if you do exist: make it rain on Sunday." Mostly, however, it didn't rain, it was summer, after all, and people who have the money and a car spend their Sundays in the country. Herr Hopp was on the road all week, as his business required, and he liked to pass his Sundays in the bosom of his family.

On Sundays Daddy is mine.

So Herr Hopp routed his family out of bed at the crack of dawn and into the car, and the family festival was enacted on a wide screen with Nature as a backdrop. The car zoomed along on the Autobahn, radio on full blast, later they parked in some picturesque spot, a meadow with woods, spread blankets, and ate what they had brought, after the meal the Hopp couple stretched out in the sun and went to sleep. Justine and Kibus were left to their own devices. What were they to do with a wood, which they hadn't asked for? And how far would they have to go to be out of earshot of the radio? Countless Hopp families had invaded the countryside, and the noise from their loudspeakers drowned out the song of the birds. Then what good were the trees? Justine felt herself lost in a desert, Kibus her helpless shadow, and that any attempt to get out was meaningless, her whole life was a prison.

In the evening, driving home on the overcrowded highways, she felt this sense of meaninglessness even more sharply. Grotesque visions assailed her: Justine cast out, lost and forgotten in the middle of the road, and surrounding her innumerable Hopps in their cars, reeking of gasoline and spitting dust, silently pointing their fingers at her. But the endless stream of vehicles, lined up bumper to bumper, sent Herr and Frau Hopp into a state of mutual elation. They drew each other's and their children's attention to this long procession of turning wheels, they felt themselves a part of the power that had conquered the highway, and their share in the victory gave them the right to rejoice and to feel a sense of moral superiority. The boredom of Sunday had been put to flight: great was the triumph, in the fading light the armies were returning to their camps, battered, covered with dust, fenders dented, and the number of dead by the roadside was too insignificant by comparison with the victorious millions to arouse any serious concern.

Justine sat back in her corner, her feet drawn up under her, and Kibus made faces out the window.

4

There were days when Justine was overcome with disgust at the thought of going home after school. She knew she was expected; and just this feeling of *being expected* was capable of causing her actual physical discomfort.

"I hate the street we live on," she told Ulses. "I hate the garden, I hate the house. Frau Hopp's in the kitchen this minute, either she's in a bad mood because she's had to keep my lunch warm, or she's had a good day and will get chummy, while I'm eating, asking me what it was like at school and whether I'm in love with you. What can I tell her? She only wants to know whether I'm in love with you because she's afraid you might get me pregnant."

"Shush," said Ulses. "Don't say such things."

"If she only knew it, I can't stand babies," said Justine. "But you're not supposed to admit that, are you?"

"Of course not," replied Ulses.

"I'm not going home," said Justine.

"But I'm hungry," Ulses said.

"We could hook something to eat," said Justine.

"Not a bad idea," Ulses said.

They took a streetcar to the center of town. It was very hot, the awnings were down over the shop windows, the heat decomposed all the smells, the revolving doors of the department stores spat gusts of cool air into the faces of passersby. Justine stopped in front of a delicatessen.

"Does it have to be on the main street?" Ulses asked.

"It's more dangerous here," Justine replied. It was a corner store with a large plate-glass window on two sides. Next to a post was a tank with fish in it. Beside this boxes of fruit. "You stay by the door and keep a lookout," Justine went on. "If I'm spotted, I'll run, and you stand there and trip them. O.K.?"

"Sure," Ulses answered. "Watch yourself!"

Justine went into the store. She held her school bag tight with both hands. The clerks behind the counter were all busy. Justine turned her back on them and, holding the open bag in front of her with her left hand, approached the tank of fish. In the box next to the tank were oranges. Ulses nodded encouragement from behind the plate-glass window while Justine, keeping her eyes on the fish in their prison, groped with her right hand for oranges. The shopping noises behind her fell into a trough of silence, only a soft murmur persisted, Ulses' face was enormous behind the glass, the street was still. Justine touched the oranges.

Suddenly it was a glorious feeling to be afraid. Her body was almost paralyzed, she could feel nothing any longer in heart head leg arm, but a strange contraction in the region of the stomach, a grumbling and a pumping and a throbbing, a pang of pleasure and at the same time a searing, soothing pain, and a lump filling her throat like a cork. Justine did not dare swallow

had the conversation died down?

had the theft been discovered?

but then Ulses' face appeared again behind the glass, and Justine hastily slipped two oranges into her bag, "Can I help you?" she suddenly heard a clerk just behind her, "No thank you," Justine mumbled, without knowing whether the girl had actually been speaking to her, and started moving toward the door, how heavy her feet were how long the way, outside stood Ulses, Justine grabbed him by the hand and started to run, and dragged him with her down the street to the next crossing, and not until they reached a side street did they stop.

The town. It grew on Justine like a movie shot that, starting from a point in the farthest distance, expands quickly until it fills the whole screen and commands our attention. Ulses looked around. "Nobody's following us," he said. Justine laughed. How wonderful to be alive the danger was overcome a great victory a triumph of liberty there was an opening in the cage. Justine had broken out, if I spread my arms I can fly—but nobody had taught her how to fly and she could only flap her wings wildly.

"Two oranges," she cried and opened the bag. "And the world hasn't come to an end. I have committed a theft, and what has changed? Nothing!"

"Not so loud!" said Ulses.

"I can thumb my nose at the whole lousy world!"

"Don't shout!" Ulses said. "People are looking at us."

"I'm a thief, a thief, a thief!"

"We were lucky," Ulses said.

"I'd like to see the look on that clerk's face when she finds out the oranges are missing."

"Probably no one will count them," said Ulses.

5

On the glass door of the living room, which led into the hall, moved the silhouettes of Herr and Frau Hopp and Kibus. Justine sat on the sofa. No point in closing your eyes. The voices in the hall could still be heard.

"You said this afternoon I could go out," said Kibus.

"I said nothing of the kind," replied Frau Hopp.

"When I asked you, you said yes."

"In any event, I do not want you to leave the house again," said Herr Hopp.

"But Mama gave her permission!"

"I did nothing of the kind," cried Frau Hopp.

"But I promised to be there, you must let me go."

"You shouldn't have promised," said Frau Hopp.

"But you gave me permission!" cried Kibus.

"That will do," said Herr Hopp. "I see no need for your hanging around downtown at night."

"It's not hanging around," returned Kibus. "There's a jazz concert at the Town Hall."

"You're staying at home," said Frau Hopp. "You've got school to-morrow."

"What a dirty trick!" cried Kibus and stamped his foot. "Just because Mama is in a bad mood I'm not allowed to go."

"Another word and there'll be trouble," said Herr Hopp. "Go to your room."

For a moment there was silence in the hall. Through the glass door Justine watched Herr Hopp; he stood at the foot of the staircase, opposite the living-room door, and pointed upward with outstretched arm. Frau Hopp and Kibus could not be seen.

"Let me past," Justine heard Kibus say.

"What's the matter with you?" said Frau Hopp. "That's no way to speak to your mother!"

"I don't care. I want out of here."

"That does it," cried Herr Hopp, leaving his position by the staircase. "Go to your room this minute."

"No," said Kibus.

The voices of Herr and Frau Hopp and Kibus came now from the vicinity of the front door, an excited and exasperated babble of argument, Kibus' voice, broken and shaken by sobs, piping shrilly above the heavy thunderclouds of Herr Hopp's bellowing, Justine couldn't understand a word, in the frame of the glass door the back of Herr Hopp's head and shoulders appeared, vanished again, and reappeared abruptly with Kibus, who was hitting about him wildly and being slowly maneuvered backward by Herr Hopp to the foot of the stairs. Bringing up the rear was Frau Hopp, who gave Kibus a shove whenever Herr Hopp succeeded for a moment in pinioning his arms. Justine listened to the panting of the combatants, she couldn't help laughing, but it hurt her and brought her no relief.

Suddenly Kibus managed to free himself. Justine saw him dash up the stairs and out of her field of vision. "Look out!" shouted Herr Hopp, and something heavy landed on the stone flags of the hall. A dull thud and the clatter of broken pottery.

"You leave my flowerpots alone!" shouted Frau Hopp.

"Come up and make me!" Kibus shouted back and hurled the rest of her flowerpots from the second-story banisters down into the hall.

"I'll call the police," shouted Frau Hopp.

"Don't forget to give your full name and address," Kibus shouted back.

The telephone was in the hall. Justine could hear Frau Hopp dialing. Herr Hopp ran up the stairs once Kibus had smashed all the flowerpots.

"Is this the police?" screamed Frau Hopp. "Hello, I want the police!"

A door slammed on the second floor. The noise shook the house. The key turned twice in the lock.

"Send an officer at once," shouted Frau Hopp. "Our son is throwing flowerpots at us."

Herr Hopp came back down the stairs.

"It's not a joke," shouted Frau Hopp indignantly into the receiver. "I'll report you!" Herr Hopp flashed past the glass door of the living room.

"H-o-p-p," shouted Frau Hopp. "That's it, Hopp."

Herr Hopp reached the telephone. "Thank you," Justine heard him say. "The matter is under control." He put down the receiver. "Kibus has locked himself in his room," Herr Hopp informed his wife.

Justine got up as steps approached the door. Frau Hopp opened it. She was all eyes: two big, round eyes starting angrily from their sockets, which seemed not to register Justine's presence. "I've had enough for one day," said Frau Hopp. "You go to your room too!" She turned and went out again into the hall, leaving the door open behind her. Herr Hopp had begun to sweep up the mess of earth, plants and broken pottery.

Justine escaped from the living room by way of the French windows. She went around the house through the garden. She waited outside the front door until the light in the hall went out. Then she opened the door softly, took off her shoes and tiptoed through the dark hall past the brightly lit door of the living room to which Herr and Frau Hopp had retired, raced upstairs and locked herself in her room.

6

The Hopps had gone out again. They led a very active social life. Justine had retired with Kibus and Ulses to the bar Herr and Frau Hopp had had built in the basement of the house. Long-legged bar stools stood in front of the gleaming curve of the bar, indirect lighting had been installed, and there were wooden benches along the walls with small black kidney-shaped tables. On the wall opposite the bar Justine had hung a poster advertising stockings, a girl dangling a shapely leg and underneath

THE STOCKING THAT YOU LOVE TO WEAR
MUST THE NAME OF ARWA BEAR.

Kibus and Ulses were sitting at the bar, elbows on the cool, reflecting chrome surface. Ulses was smoking. Justine was standing behind the bar. She had parted her hair in the middle and plaited it into two short, bristly pigtails. Her mouth was heavily lipsticked. The black pullover she was wearing left her shoulders bare and was cut very low. "Eyes front," she said to Ulses. Ulses sucked at his cigarette, leaned over the bar and blew smoke down her neck. "Shall I leave?" asked Kibus. Justine applied her lips firmly to Ulses' forehead. "Now you're branded," she said. Kibus was putting on records, the voices of the gods he worshiped:
Basin Street Blues

Jungle Drums
Tia Juana
Burgundy Street Blues
Black Bottom Stomp:
Existence lost its sting in the soft melancholy of the blues, its pain was drowned like a wasp in cider.

Justine raised her glass. "To Herr and Frau Hopp's not coming back before dawn!" They drank. "What is the most beautiful thing in the world?" asked Justine.

"A trumpet," answered Kibus.

"You," Ulses said.

"Shall I go get my trumpet?" asked Kibus.

"Don't you dare," Ulses said.

"The most beautiful thing on earth is the sky above it," said Justine.

"Shall I leave?" asked Kibus.

"I'd like to be alone for a whole month," Justine went on, "lying in the grass and staring at the sky. Everything would be so quiet I could hear the clouds when they collide with each other. I would give every cloud a name according to the face it happened to be wearing at the moment. Every cloud has a different face, you know."

"Now," interrupted Kibus, "I really have to go get my trumpet."

"And me?" Ulses asked. "What about me?"

"You could come along after the first couple of weeks," Justine replied. "You too," she said to Kibus.

"But without your trumpet," Ulses said.

"Baabaadoodeeleedaa hoo-ver," Kibus tooted. "Whisky, please."

He drank it and shuddered. "Awful-tasting stuff," he said.

"Spit it out," said Ulses.

"A trumpeter has to drink whisky," retorted Kibus. "Shtshtshtsh baadaa deedaadeeleedeedaadood hoo-ver."

"Don't drink so much," Ulses told Justine. "You know you can't hold it."

"I'm trying to do myself in," replied Justine.

"Nonsense," said Ulses.

"I'll blow my trumpet over your grave," said Kibus.

"When I'm thirty I'm going to commit suicide because I never want to become like Herr and Frau Hopp."

"Suicide is immoral," said Kibus. "Dee-dee-dee-hoo. Shtsh-shtsh-shtsh-hoo. Baadeelaadeedaa-hoo-oo. Deedeeloodeedeebaadaa-baadaa-hoohohoo-ho-hoo-hoo-ver."

Justine had seated herself on a stool behind the bar. Her face hung low over her drink, from which she was taking tiny sips through a straw. When she leaned forward a little, she touched Ulses' forehead. "Women who drink," said Kibus, "give birth to idiot children. Bee-baa-deelaa-daadood." Ulses took Justine's straw between thumb and index finger and squashed it. "Stop," he said.

"I'm not even allowed to do myself in."

"No," said Ulses.

"Brute," said Justine.

"All right, go ahead, be a drunk," said Ulses.

"Thanks," replied Justine.

"One step forward, one step back; cyanide and all goes black," sang Kibus.

"The stocking that you love to wear, must the name of Arwa bear," croaked Justine.

"Here's to you," cried Kibus. "We don't want to be like our parents."

"Not so loud," Ulses said.

"No, shout," said Justine. "Shout as loud as you can."

"Hoo-ver," shouted Kibus.

"Quiet," Ulses said.

"Hurrah!" cried Justine. "Everybody up."

They all climbed onto their bar stools, holding hands for balance, and bumping their heads on the ceiling. "Let's sing a round," said Justine. "Ready, set, go. We-don't-want-to-be-like-our-parents!"

"One step forward, one step back; cyanide and all goes black," Ulses broke in.

"Baa-bee-lee-daa-dood-hoo-ver," Kibus tooted.

"We-don't-want-to-be-like-our-parents!"

"With a shoe from Kall you pass them all."

"Baa-bee-lee-daa-dood-hoo-ver."

"We-don't-want-to-be-like-our-parents!"

"And now let's go, to Gebhardt and Co!"

"Baa-bee-lee-daa-dood-hoo-ver."

"We-don't-want-to-be-like-our-parents!"

7

Parents.

When you were little they made a big fuss over you.

Little children are so cute.

Or was it only that you were too young to appreciate just how little your parents really cared about you? Not, of course, that Herr and Frau Hopp had in any way neglected their parental duties.

I shall bring up my child to be a
useful member of society

And so one day the training began:

You must not cut
potatoes with a knife
Speak only when spoken to
Education is
a preparation for life
Be careful with your allowance
Help your mother
You must know how to
Cookcleanmend
Beware of
Men they are bad
They only want one thing from you

"Is Daddy bad?" Justine had asked.

"Good gracious, what put that into your head?" exclaimed Frau Hopp.

"What did Daddy want from you?"

"Daddy," said Frau Hopp, "was an exception. Don't ask so many questions."

Life flowed on in the shadow of your parents. But suddenly, I don't know how it happened, Justine thought, suddenly you are all alone, a certain Frau Hopp claims she is your mother and a certain Herr Hopp your father. Were they really still your father and mother? Had they ever been? Herr Hopp was mostly on the road, earning the money that Frau Hopp needed to run the house. Frau Hopp kept a model house, and her children were part of it. When there were visitors Kibus and Justine were handed around as if they were sandwiches and cakes, Kibus had such broad shoulders, and Justine had such a good figure and was so pretty, and the fact that she really owed all this to an oversight on their part was not mentioned on these occasions by Herr and Frau Hopp.

Justine remembered standing, her hair still in braids, outside the glass door of the living room, about to go in and say good night to her parents, the door was ajar, and Herr and Frau Hopp were chatting in tones of good-natured indolence about their children. "It wasn't my fault," Frau Hopp had said, assuming that tone of mixed familiarity and innuendo with which respectable married couples discuss the affairs of the bedroom, and Herr Hopp had replied: "I didn't want to become a father so soon."

"If you'd only taken precautions," said Frau Hopp.

"We'd had so little time to ourselves," Herr Hopp continued. "Justine could perfectly well have waited a while."

"I didn't want her that soon," said Frau Hopp. "She ruined my waist-line in the first year of marriage."

"We just had bad luck," Herr Hopp said.

"Never mind, fatso," said Frau Hopp and laughed. "We didn't get caught the second time. With Kibus you said: 'Now for a son!' Do you remember?"

Justine had never forgotten this conversation. After she had come to understand the indirect language of grownups its full meaning dawned on her. She felt superior to Kibus in that at least there had been no deliberate intention in her case, still it was rather embarrassing to owe your existence to an oversight. How many children had been dumped on their own Hopps in this haphazard way? What if Herr Hopp had taken precautions on that occasion? There would have been no Justine! Really, she thought, bringing children into the world is a wretched busi-ness, there ought to be a law against it. People inconsiderately pursue their own pleasure, and when a child is the accidental consequence they are just as inconsiderate toward it. And for that you're supposed to love your parents? They bring you into the world, thought Justine, and then they go off and leave you there. Or were you supposed to give Herr and Frau Hopp credit for their sporadic and clumsy attempts to restore your confidence in them? A child is not a dog you can whistle for whenever you want him, Justine thought.

What did parents have to offer their children anyway?

Children become a nuisance when they start asking questions to which you have found no answers yourself. Isn't it enough to have given them a good start in life? Hadn't you achieved something: house, car, property? Oughtn't children to be grateful for that? What more did they expect? What could be more pleasant than to explore in imagina-tion all the possibilities opened up by Herr Hopp's money?

In the evening the active man..
needs relaxation..

Movies, the theater, having a good time, sitting in the midst of people of your own kind in the crowded shop windows of a disinfected world, giving parties, going to parties. Traveling. What were the children supposed to do in the meantime? A solitary person is always in bad company.

8

A week before Justine's eighteenth birthday Herr and Frau Hopp flew to Paris. Frau Hopp needed a change of air and scene, and people who can afford it make a habit of flying to Paris for a day or two now and then: *See Paris in summer*. Kibus, Justine and the car were left behind. Herr and Frau Hopp promised to be back in time for the birthday. Justine waited in vain. When she came home from school there was only a telegram: *Many happy returns. Arriving late afternoon. Mummy and Daddy*.

"As far as I'm concerned they can stay away as long as they like," said Justine to Kibus. "Celebrating my birthday with Herr and Frau Hopp is silly anyway. It's only another reminder that they brought me into the world."

"Maybe their flight was grounded," said Kibus. "Or Daddy may have had some last-minute business."

"What's the difference?" Justine said. "Do you think I'd come all the way home just because somebody was having a birthday? That's just silly family sentimentality."

"I'll do the dishes for you today," said Kibus.

After lunch they lay in the garden. Kibus read. Justine stared at the sky. So this is my birthday. Trees. Sky. Clouds. Blue sky flashing through a green susurration of leaves. Every cloud has a different face. Justine began to give them names. A fat gray cloud with a big blue eye in its forehead she christened Frau Hopp. From the depths of the sky a white caterpillar came creeping up with a tiny metallic head that reflected the sun and penetrated Frau Hopp's eye. She was blinded instantly and the wind then gave her another form. Justine sighed. Not even the sky had anything to offer. I didn't ask to be born! But what was the use of grumbling? Parents could do anything. Why shouldn't they bring children into the world? And what difference did it make whether it was by chance or on purpose? Yet did you have a right to live if an oversight was the cause of your being here? Did living under such circumstances make any sense at all? Oversight or no oversight, thought

Justine, what difference is there between life and death if you're always going to be alone? Kibus and Ulses can't help me. Those who have received no answers have none to give.

Now was a good time. Kibus had fallen asleep over his book. Justine rose stealthily. She went and got the car key that lay on the desk in Herr Hopp's study and went into the garage. I really ought to say good-by to Kibus. But that was silly sentimentality. Or shouldn't Ulses get at least a note? Justine hesitated, then shut the door firmly behind her. How silly to leave a farewell note!

It was very hot in the garage. The leather upholstery was roasting in the heat, there was a strong smell of gasoline and rubber. The smell of Sunday outings. Justine sat at the wheel. She started the engine. She inhaled deeply. Let's hope it's over soon. The running engine made the car vibrate gently. Justine closed her eyes. How pleasant to die gently.

Suddenly Kibus was standing by the car. The bright light flooding in through the open door of the garage hurt Justine's eyes.

"Going for a ride?" Kibus said.

"Brute," said Justine. "They won't even let you die in peace."

"I was having a nice nap," said Kibus. "But the engine woke me up." He took the key out of the ignition and put it in his pocket. "Come on," he said. "It's hot in here."

"Give me back the key," said Justine.

"Next time," answered Kibus, "don't forget to shut the garage windows. If you leave them open you can keep the engine running for years without anything happening."

Justine got out of the car. Kibus was right: the garage windows were open. Justine felt like a fool over having forgotten to shut them. "Let's play badminton," Kibus suggested.

"No," said Justine. "I'm going down to the bar." She spent the whole afternoon there. Toward evening she phoned Ulses. "Hello," she said. "I just wanted to tell you I'm feeling marvelous. You can come and celebrate my birthday now. I'm feeling mar-vel-ous!"

9

Ulses was there in half an hour. Kibus let him in.

"She's plastered," he said.

"I could tell that on the telephone," Ulses replied. "Aren't your parents back yet?"

"No," said Kibus.

"Why did you let her drink?" asked Ulses.

"What was I supposed to do?" Kibus replied. "She just shut herself up in the bar."

"Where is she now?" asked Ulses.

"In the kitchen," Kibus answered.

Justine was standing in front of the refrigerator, on top of which she had spread out bread, butter, sausage, and pickles. "My last meal," she declared as Kibus and Ulses came in. She washed her hands under the faucet, dried them elaborately and went up to Ulses. "Evening," she said. "You haven't given me a birthday kiss yet."

"Why didn't you call me earlier?" Ulses asked.

"Would you have been any help?" said Justine.

"I wouldn't have let you have anything to drink," Ulses said.

"Yes, teacher," said Justine. "How about a kiss?"

"Your breath reeks with pickles," Kibus said.

"Better leave us alone," Ulses said to Kibus.

"I'll be in the garden," said Kibus and went out.

Justine went back to the refrigerator. "Want anything to eat?" she asked.

"No thanks," Ulses said.

"That wasn't necessary," Justine said. "I was talking to the refrigerator."

"Don't be childish," retorted Ulses. "You look terrible. It makes me sick to look at you."

"Leave me alone," Justine said. "I just want to do myself in."

She turned her back on Ulses and began eating again. Outside it grew slowly dark. From the trees in the garden a wind sprang up, wafting a cool breeze through the open window. "In case you're interested," said Justine suddenly, "I didn't get drunk just because Herr and Frau Hopp are away. I don't give a damn about them." She sliced at her pickle, impaled a piece on the fork and flourished it above her head. "We-don't-want-to-be-like-our-parents," she chanted.

"You'll be sick if you go on eating pickles," said Ulses, and took the fork away from her.

"Vomiting is the best answer to life," retorted Justine. "After all, you've got to do something."

"Why did you have to drink?" Ulses asked.

"Because I like it and because it's bad for me," Justine answered. "Anything else you want to know?"

"Why won't you let anyone help you?" Ulses asked.

"You can't help me," replied Justine. "But I love you all the same."

She put her arms around his neck. Her mouth tasted of pickles. Ulses felt uncomfortable. Justine held on to him tightly, a dark whirlpool was eddying to and fro at the back of her brain, suddenly it began to spin like a top and drag her down with it. No longer able to stand up, she let herself go. Softly, her body glided down into the abyss, at the same time, oddly, her head began to rise, to free itself from the anchoring body and to soar upwards, leaving the torso far below. Ulses held her tight. He had to grip very tightly to hold on to her at all. Justine opened her eyes. Head and body were joined again, they had whizzed together from above and from below and met in the vicinity of the stomach. The impact was extremely violent.

"Oooh," groaned Justine. "I feel awful."

"I'll carry you up to your room," said Ulses.

"Too late," Justine said.

She headed for the sink by the refrigerator. Ulses was still holding her. She began to vomit, and he turned on the faucet. Justine was very heavy. "Do it again!" Ulses ordered. "Stick your finger down your throat."

"What a dirty trick," groaned Justine. "What a dirty trick." Ulses rinsed out the sink. There was an acid smell of alcohol and pickles. "Feel better?" he asked.

"A little," Justine replied.

She was trembling and sticky all over with sweat. Ulses dabbed at her face with his handkerchief, wiped her mouth clean and maneuvered her over to the window. "Take a deep breath," he said. Justine inhaled deeply. "How do you feel now?" Ulses asked. "Feel like doing it again?" Justine shook her head.

"Then I'll carry you upstairs," Ulses said.

"I don't want to go on living," Justine said.

"That comes from being sick," Ulses replied. "Sleep on it first."

As he picked her up, he saw that she was crying. He pressed her head against his shoulder. "It's all over now," he said.

"It'll never be over," replied Justine. "There's no end in sight. I don't want to live any more."

"Just because you had a little too much to drink?" Ulses asked.

"Nobody gives a damn about me," Justine answered. "Not even those damned Hopps show up for my birthday. Nobody will have anything to do with me. I'm a thief. I'm a pig. I've been sick. You're staying with a . . ."

Ulses put his hand over her mouth. "Never mind about me," he said.

"I don't want to live any more," Justine cried.

It sounded self-pitying, but really it was a battle cry, she needed a flesh-and-blood antagonist, and as Ulses was the only suitable object within her reach, Justine gripped him tighter than ever, sinking her teeth savagely in the lapel of his jacket in an effort to hold back her tears, but it was no use, she could no longer control herself, sobs shook her and she drummed with both fists on Ulses' back so that he had to steady himself to keep from falling over. "What a dirty trick," sobbed Justine. "Even on your birthday they leave you all alone. I'm fed up. It isn't fair to leave you all alone on your birthday. It just isn't fair," she cried, underlining every word with a blow of her fist on Ulses' back. "I wish I were dead."

"You're all mixed up," said Ulses. He felt helpless. All he could do was hold on to Justine, and when she had calmed down somewhat he wiped her face with his handkerchief and mopped at his collar which was soggy with tears. Justine swayed. "I'm going to be sick again," she said.

10

This time it was only a thin white watery liquid which did not smell. Afterwards Justine felt so washed out and miserable and weak that the sobbing stopped of its own accord. Ulses carried her up to her room. He dumped her on the bed and went back to the kitchen to clear away the remains of the meal. While he was washing his hands Kibus came in from the garden.

"How is she?" he asked.

"Better," Ulses replied. "She's got it out of her system."

"You'd better hurry," said Kibus. "My parents will be coming soon."

"I won't be long," Ulses replied.

"I'll keep a lookout at the gate," Kibus said. "Give the patient my sympathies."

"Thanks," replied Ulses.

Justine had switched off the light in her room. Outside the summer night was bright and warm. From her bed Justine could see the sky. It was cloudless. Ulses sat down beside her. "You ought to try to sleep now," he said.

"I can't go to bed like this," Justine said. "I have to undress first.

Herr and Frau Hopp would see that something is wrong. Will you get my pyjamas?"

"Where are they?" Ulses asked.

"In the closet," Justine replied.

"Shall I draw the curtains?" Ulses asked.

"Am I so ugly?" Justine said.

It wasn't easy to undress her. She was dazed with alcohol and exhausted with weeping, and it was a slow and clumsy process, undoing all the unfamiliar hooks and buttons of her clothing. He was glad when she was finally under the covers. Only her head peeped out. There were deep shadows under her eyes. The rhythm of sobbing could still be heard in her short, adenoidal inhalations. "Don't go," Justine said. Ulses kissed her on the forehead. "You don't have to be afraid to kiss me on the mouth," Justine said. "I'm not as weak as all that. Or am I so repulsive?"

"Sometimes," said Ulses, "you are very stupid."

Hearing Kibus coming up the stairs he got up and tiptoed to the door. "Quiet," he said. "I think Justine's asleep."

"You'll have to go," Kibus whispered. "They'll be here any minute."

"I'm wide awake," Justine said. "Please stay."

"There'll be an awful row if they find Ulses here," Kibus objected.

"I don't want to be alone," Justine said. Ulses sat down on the bed again. "Please be sensible," he said. "You can see I can't stay."

"You can hide in the closet when they come," Justine pleaded.

"I'll see you in the morning after class," Ulses said.

"You can stand it till tomorrow morning," Kibus put in. Justine began to cry again. Her hands emerged from under the blanket and took hold of Ulses'. "You can hide in the closet."

"You'll go to sleep right away when I've gone," Ulses replied. "You're terribly tired."

"You must go," Kibus said.

"I can't get to sleep unless you're here," Justine said.

"Kibus'll be with you," Ulses replied.

"I'll knock on the wall later," Kibus said.

"I don't want to be alone," Justine repeated.

"Christ, don't make such a fuss," Kibus said.

"What'll your parents think if they come and find me sitting on your bed at this hour of the night?" Ulses asked.

"You'll be in the closet," Justine pleaded.

"But you can see I can't stay," cried Ulses

"You really must go now," Kibus said.

Ulses got up. Justine let go of his hand and the sobbing started again. Kibus ran to the window. "I hear a car," he said. "It's stopping in front of our gate. Quick, Ulses! You've still got time to get out through the garden."

"Our car's in the garage," Justine said.

"It's a taxi," said Kibus from the window.

Ulses kissed Justine. "Please be sensible," he said. He went to the door. Justine buried her head in the pillow. "Hurry up," said Kibus.

He took Ulses downstairs into the living room and let him out through the French windows into the garden. Ulses crossed the garden, keeping his head well down, swung himself over the fence and hid behind some bushes. The taxi started up again, turned, and accelerated away down the street past Ulses.

11

House garden fence bushes. The leaves swished against Ulses' clothes. Parting the branches in order to see better he noticed the bright green of the leaves' veins. The indifferent brightness of dead fish floating belly up on the surface of a stream. Gradually Ulses became accustomed to the strange nocturnal brightness. The moon was the night's distended, glassy eye. Crickets chirped, knocking at the wall of silence surrounding Ulses, forcing themselves on his ear yet without distracting his attention.

The lights in the living room went on. Ulses ducked. First came Frau Hopp. She sat down on the sofa. Then came Herr Hopp. He switched on the floor lamp by the sofa. He turned out the other light. He sat himself down in an armchair. Ulses could now see only the heads of Herr and Frau Hopp. Kibus' room was dark. Justine's room was dark. Herr and Frau Hopp had taken a trip. They had returned. Kibus was awake. Justine was awake. What did Herr and Frau Hopp care about them?

The active man
needs relaxation
See Paris in summer
Hadn't you achieved
something: house car property?
After that it takes money
Children become a nuisance when they
start asking questions to which
you have found
no answers yourself

The broad, dazzling bright picture window of the living room. Before it the veranda. Herr Hopp rose. He strode up and down the room. He looked out into the garden. He sat down again. Ulses bent down. He picked up a stone. Justine was still awake. Ulses threw the stone. The breaking glass shattered the silence into a thousand pieces. Frau Hopp jumped up from the sofa. Ulses threw another stone. The light went on in Kibus' room. The light went on in Justine's room. The light went on in the house next door. Somewhere a dog, roused from its slumbers, began to bark. Herr Hopp ran out into the garden. Pieces of glass crunched under his shoes as he hurried across the veranda. Ulses broke through the bushes and kept to the shadow of the fence, then raced across the street, and ran until he reached the woods, which began some distance beyond the street. Here, under the protection of the trees, he threw himself on the ground, dug his fingers into the warm rustling pine-needle cushion of the forest floor, and the strain, excitement and despair of the last few hours found release in a dry sob.

Book Three

THE ETERNAL WHEEL:
The Cause and Effect of Man's Institutions

In applying the findings of psychoanalysis to the study of human institutions, one must always remember that institutions do not necessarily behave like individuals, that they function on their own level and that events that occur within them can be explained in their own terms. In other words, we can seek for the source of war in economics or politics or history—without resorting to psychology.

Yet, to ignore completely the contributions that psychoanalysis can make to the study of human institutions is to turn one's back on an enormous body of information about human behavior. The pretense that the unconscious has no meaning on an institutional level is as damaging to the growth of human knowledge as is the opposite attempt to reduce everything to unconscious sources.

Anthropologists who have tried to develop theories of cultural character have relied heavily on psychoanalytic data to describe which particular human institutions may lead to the development of a particular kind of personality. Their findings point to the fact that most character development takes place in the nursery. Why is one group warlike and another peace-loving? Why does one group of people submit to authority while another rebels constantly against it? Partial answers to these questions may be found in a study of the institutions set up by a country to deal with its government and its economic structure, or in its more subtle techniques for education and child-raising. But the study of human institutions cannot tell us what motivates people to create them. For this we must have psychoanalytic tools. For example, we might wish to understand why a nation consistently elects to be ruled by dictators. A study of its institutions will probably reveal a desire to submit to authority. In an individual, such desire for submission usually indicates a poorly integrated super-ego or conscience and an inability to handle the anxiety created by guilt. Like the child who needs a parent to tell him, "NO," such a culture may be so afraid of its own potential for destruction or of its own guilt that it must have a "father" on whom it can lean.

Naturally, a scheme such as I have described is a gross oversimplification: numerous forces are at work in any society that may confound any simplistic explanation. Yet, dominant motifs do appear in human institutions and we are justified in trying to isolate them, in trying to unearth the conditions under which they flourish. The application of psychoanalytic data gleaned from the study of the individual to the behavior of groups and institutions is, therefore, as valid an endeavor as the study of economic or political or social motives—and it deserves as much consideration.

1 · Education

Although psychoanalysis is, in its broadest sense, an educational process, psychoanalytic writers have largely ignored the problems posed by learning theory in constructing their models of human behavior. The lack is a peculiar one in light of the fact that the learning of healthier behavior is the final goal of all psychoanalytic therapies. Most of our current educational theories, as they apply to our schools, have tended to ignore psychoanalytic findings and concentrate instead on the discoveries of clinical psychologists about automatic responses to stimuli and the simpler response mechanisms of the lower animals. The most talked-about discoveries in education today are, as a consequence, the development of teaching machines that take advantage of our barely understood functional researches in physical and glandular responses to the learning situation.

The situation was not always thus: thirty years ago, the progressive education movement was the dominant movement on the educational scene and its concern was largely with freeing the psychic mechanism of emotional "blocks" to learning. Without knowledge of the learning mechanism, however, the progressive movement floundered badly: its theories of freedom led to excesses that proved as damaging as the previous repressive practices of an earlier day. Today we are still searching to uncover the techniques by which emotional factors can be used to help the educational process. The material in the following section offers a few simple explanations of the effect of the emotions on the learning process, as well as an examination of some of the areas that need to be explored if our search for ways to teach useful and creative behavior is to be successful.

The manner in which cultural institutions may affect emotional behavior is described by Ruth Benedict. Our culture demands traits in our adults that are given no opportunity to develop by our child-raising institutions. We enjoin women to enjoy sexual pleasure in marriage, for example, but forbid them the necessary sexual freedom that might make achievement of the pleasure more likely. The failure of many of our educational processes may result from discontinuities in conditioning—discontinuities that force people to develop compromises in the form of behavior that maintains attitudes developed with approval during a child's formative years.

In making a plea for alterations in our social institutions Ruth Benedict is not denying psychoanalytic theory, but simply asking that institutions be created which, like those of many primitive people, would reduce the strain caused by our inability "to put off childish things."

RUTH BENEDICT

Continuities and Discontinuities in Cultural Conditioning

All cultures must deal in one way or another with the cycle of growth from infancy to adulthood. Nature has posed the situation dramatically: on the one hand, the new born baby, physiologically vulnerable, unable to fend for itself, or to participate of its own initiative in the life of the group, and, on the other, the adult man or woman. Every man who rounds out his human potentialities must have been a son first and a father later and the two roles are psychologically in great contrast; he must first have been dependent upon others for his very existence and later he must provide such security for others. This discontinuity in the life cycle is a fact of nature and is inescapable. Facts of nature, however, in any discussion of human problems, are ordinarily read off not at their bare minimal but surrounded by all the local accretions of behavior to which the student of human affairs has become accustomed in his own culture. For that reason it is illuminating to examine comparative material from other societies in order to get a wider perspective on our own special accretions. The anthropologist's role is not to question the facts of nature, but to insist upon the interposition of a middle term between "nature" and "human behavior"; his role is to analyse that term, to document local man-made doctorings of nature and to insist that these doctorings should not be read off in any one culture as nature itself. Although it is a fact of nature that the child becomes a man, the way in which this transition is effected varies from one society to another, and no one of these particular cultural bridges should be regarded as the "natural" path to maturity.

From a comparative point of view our culture goes to great extremes in emphasizing contrasts between the child and the adult. The child is sexless, the adult estimates his virility by his sexual activities; the child must be protected from the ugly facts of life, the adult must meet them without psychic catastrophe; the child must obey, the adult must command this obedience. These are all dogmas of our culture, dogmas which in spite of the facts of nature, other cultures commonly do not share. In spite of the physiological contrasts between child and adult these are cultural accretions.

It will make the point clearer if we consider one habit in our own culture in regard to which there is not this discontinuity of conditioning. With the greatest clarity of purpose and economy of training, we achieve our goal of conditioning everyone to eat three meals a day. The baby's training in regular food periods begins at birth and no crying of the child and no inconvenience to the mother is allowed to interfere. We gauge the child's physiological make-up and at first allow it food oftener than adults, but, because our goal is firmly set and our training consistent, before the child is two years old it has achieved the adult schedule. From the point of view of other cultures this is as startling as the fact of three-year-old babies perfectly at home in deep water is to us. Modesty is another sphere in which our child training is consistent and economical; we waste no time in clothing the baby and in contrast to many societies where the child runs naked till it is ceremonially given its skirt or its pubic sheath at adolescence, the child's training fits it precisely for adult conventions.

In neither of these aspects of behavior is there need for an individual in our culture to embark before puberty, at puberty or at some later date upon a course of action which all his previous training has tabued. He is spared the unsureness inevitable in such a transition.

The illustration I have chosen may appear trivial, but in larger and more important aspects of behavior, our methods are obviously different. Because of the great variety of child training in different families in our society, I might illustrate continuity of conditioning from individual life histories in our culture, but even these, from a comparative point of view, stop far short of consistency and I shall therefore confine myself to describing arrangements in other cultures in which training which with us is idiosyncratic, is accepted and traditional and does not therefore involve the same possibility of conflict. I shall choose childhood rather than infant and nursing situations not because the latter do not vary strikingly in different cultures but because they are nevertheless more circumscribed by the baby's physiological needs than is its later training. Childhood situations provide an excellent field in which to illustrate the range of cultural adjustments which are possible within a universally given, but not so drastic, set of physiological facts.

The major discontinuity in the life cycle is of course that the child who is at one point a son must later be a father. These roles in our society are strongly differentiated; a good son is tractable, and does not assume adult responsibilities; a good father provides for his children and should not allow his authority to be flouted. In addition the child must be sexless so far as his family is concerned, whereas the father's sexual role is primary in the family. The individual in one role must revise his behavior from almost all points of view when he assumes the second role.

I shall select for discussion three such contrasts that occur in our culture between the individual's role as child and as father: I. responsible–non-responsible status role, II. dominance-submission, III. contrasted sexual role. It is largely upon our cultural commitments to these three contrasts that the discontinuity in the life cycle of an individual in our culture depends.

I. RESPONSIBLE–NON-RESPONSIBLE STATUS ROLE

The techniques adopted by societies which achieve continuity during the life cycle in this sphere in no way differ from those we employ in our uniform conditioning to three meals a day. They are merely applied to other areas of life. We think of the child as wanting to play and the adult as having to work, but in many societies the mother takes the baby daily in her shawl or carrying net to the garden or to gather roots, and adult labor is seen even in infancy from the pleasant security of its position in close contact with its mother. When the child can run about it accompanies its parents still, doing tasks which are essential and yet suited to its powers, and its dichotomy between work and play is not different from that its parents recognize, namely the distinction between the busy day and the free evening. The tasks it is asked to perform are graded to its powers and its elders wait quietly by, not offering to do the task in the child's place. Everyone who is familiar with such societies has been struck by the contrast with our child training. Dr. Ruth Underhill tells me of sitting with a group of Papago elders in Arizona when the man of the house turned to his little three-year-old granddaughter and asked her to close the door. The door was heavy and hard to shut. The child tried, but it did not move. Several times the grandfather repeated, "Yes, close the door." No one jumped to the child's assistance. No one took the responsibility away from her. On the other hand there was no impatience, for after all the child was small. They sat gravely waiting till the child succeeded and her grandfather gravely thanked her. It was assumed that the task would not be asked of her unless she could perform it, and having been asked the responsibility was hers alone just as if she were a grown woman.

The essential point of such child training is that the child is from infancy continuously conditioned to responsible social participation while at the same time the tasks that are expected of it are adapted to its capacity. The contrast with our society is very great. A child does not make any labor contribution to our industrial society except as it competes with an adult; its work is not measured against its own strength and skill but against high-geared industrial requirements. Even when we praise a child's achievement in the home we are outraged if such praise is interpreted as being of the same order as praise of adults. The child is praised because the parent feels well disposed, regardless of whether the task is well done by adult standards, and the child acquires no sensible standard by which to measure its achievement. The gravity of a Cheyenne Indian family ceremoniously making a feast out of the little boy's first snowbird is at the furthest remove from our behavior. At birth the little boy was presented with a toy bow, and from the time he could run about serviceable bows suited to his stature were specially made for him by the man of the family. Animals and birds were taught him in a graded series beginning with those most easily taken, and as he brought in his first of each species his family duly made a feast of it, accepting his contribution as gravely as the buffalo his father brought. When he finally killed a buffalo, it was only the final step of his childhood conditioning, not a new adult role with which his childhood experience had been at variance.

The Canadian Ojibwa show clearly what results can be achieved. This tribe gains its livelihood by winter trapping and the small family of father, mother and children live during the long winter alone on their great frozen hunting grounds. The boy accompanies his father and brings in his catch to his sister as his father does to his mother; the girl prepares the meat and skins for him just as his mother does for her husband. By the time the boy is 12, he may have set his own line of traps on a hunting territory of his own and return to his parent's house only once in several months—still bringing the meat and skins to his sister. The young child is taught consistently that it has only itself to rely upon in life, and this is as true in the dealings it will have with the supernatural as in the business of getting a livelihood. This attitude he will accept as a successful adult just as he accepted it as a child.[3]

II. DOMINANCE-SUBMISSION

Dominance-submission is the most striking of those categories of behavior where like does not respond to like but where one type of behavior stimulates the opposite response. It is one of the most prominent ways in which behavior is patterned in our culture. When it obtains between classes, it may be nourished by continuous experience; the difficulty in its use between children and adults lies in the fact that an individual conditioned to one set of behavior in childhood must adopt the opposite as an adult. Its opposite is a pattern of approximately identical reciprocal behavior, and societies which rely upon continuous conditioning characteristically invoke this pattern. In some primitive cultures the very terminology of address between father and son, and more commonly, between grandfather and grandson or uncle and nephew, reflects this attitude. In such kinship terminologies one reciprocal expresses each of these relationships so that son and father, for instance, exchange the same term with one another, just as we exchange the same term with a cousin. The child later will exchange it with his son. "Father–son," therefore, is a continuous relationship he enjoys throughout life. The same continuity, backed up by verbal reciprocity, occurs far oftener in the grandfather–grandson relationship or that of mother's brother–sister's son. When these are "joking" relationships, as they often are, travellers report wonderingly upon the liberties and pretensions of tiny toddlers in their dealings with these family elders. In place of our dogma of respect to elders such societies employ in these cases a reciprocity as nearly identical as may be. The teasing and practical joking the grandfather visits upon his grandchild, the grandchild returns in like coin; he would be led to believe that he failed in propriety if he did not give like for like. If the sister's son has right of access without leave to his mother's brother's possessions, the mother's brother has such rights also to the child's possessions. They share reciprocal privileges and obligations which in our society can develop only between age mates.

From the point of view of our present discussion, such kinship conventions allow the child to put in practice from infancy the same forms of behavior which it will rely upon as an adult; behavior is not polarized into a general requirement of submission for the child and dominance for the adult.

It is clear from the techniques described above by which the child is conditioned to a responsible status role that these depend chiefly upon arousing in the child the desire to share responsibility in adult life. To achieve this little stress is laid upon obedience but much stress upon approval and praise. Punishment is very commonly regarded as quite outside the realm of possibility, and natives in many parts of the world have drawn the conclusion from our usual disciplinary methods that white parents do not love their children. If the child is not required to be submissive, however, many occasions for punishment melt away; a variety of situations which call for it do not occur. Many American Indian tribes are especially explicit in rejecting the ideal of a child's submissive or obedient behavior. Prince Maximilian von Wied who visited the Crow Indians over a hundred years ago describes a father's boasting about his young son's intractability even when it was the father himself who was flouted; "He will be a man," his father said. He would have been baffled at the idea that his child should show behavior which would obviously make him appear a poor creature in the eyes of his fellows if he used it as an adult. Dr. George Devereaux tells me of a special case of such an attitude among the Mohave at the present time. The child's mother was white and protested to its father that he must take action when the child disobeyed and struck him. "But why?" the father said, "He is little. He cannot possibly injure me." He did not know of any dichotomy according to which an adult expects obedience and a child must accord it. If his child had been docile he would simply have judged that it would become a docile adult—an eventuality of which he would not have approved.

Child training which brings about the same result is common also in other areas of life than that of reciprocal kinship obligations between child and adult. There is a tendency in our culture to regard every situation as having in it the seeds of a dominance-submission relationship. Even where dominance-submission is patently irrelevant we read in the dichotomy, assuming that in every situation there must be one person dominating another. On the other hand some cultures, even when the situation calls for leadership, do not see it in terms of dominance-submission. To do justice to this attitude it would be necessary to describe their political and especially their economic arrangements, for such an attitude to persist must certainly be supported by economic mechanisms that are congruent with it. But it must also be supported by—or what comes to the same thing, express itself in—child training and familial situations.

III. CONTRASTED SEXUAL ROLE

Continuity of conditioning in training the child to assume responsibility and to behave no more submissively than adults is quite possible in terms of the child's physiological endowment if his participation is suited to his strength. Because of the late development of the child's reproductive organs continuity of conditioning in sex experience presents a difficult problem. So far as their belief that the child is anything but a sexless being is concerned, they are probably more nearly right than we are with an opposite dogma. But the great break is presented by the universally sterile unions before puberty and the presumably fertile ones after maturation. This physiological fact no amount of cultural manipulation can minimize or alter, and societies therefore which stress continuous conditioning most strongly sometimes do not expect children to be interested in sex experience until they have matured physically. This is striking among American Indian tribes like the Dakota; adults observe great privacy in sex acts and in no way stimulate children's sexual activity. There need be no discontinuity, in the sense in which I have used the term, in such a program if the child is not taught anything it has to unlearn later. In such cultures adults view children's experimentation as in no way wicked or dangerous but merely as innocuous play which can have no serious consequences. In some societies such play is minimal and the children manifest little interest in it. But the same attitude may be taken by adults in societies where such play is encouraged and forms a major activity among small children. This is true among most of the Melanesian cultures of Southeast New Guinea; adults go as far as to laugh off sexual affairs within the prohibited class if the children are not mature, saying that since they cannot marry there can be no harm done.

It is this physiological fact of the difference between children's sterile unions and adults' presumably fertile sex relations which must be kept in mind in order to understand the different mores which almost always govern sex expression in children and in adults in the same culture. A great many cultures with preadolescent sexual license require marital fidelity and a great many which value premarital virginity in either male or female arrange their marital life with great license. Continuity in sex experience is complicated by factors which it was unnecessary to consider in the problems previously discussed. The essential problem is not whether or not the child's sexuality is consistently exploited—for even where such exploitation is favored in the majority of cases the child must seriously modify his behavior at puberty or at marriage. Continuity in sex expression means rather that the child is taught nothing it must unlearn later. If the cultural emphasis is upon sexual pleasure the child who is continuously conditioned will be encouraged to experiment freely and pleasurably, as among the Marquesans;[1] if emphasis is upon reproduction, as among the Zuni of New Mexico, childish sex proclivities will not be exploited for the only important use which sex is thought to serve in his culture is not yet possible to him. The important contrast with our child training is that although a Zuni child is impressed with the wickedness of premature sex experimentation he does not run the risk as in our culture of associating this wickedness with sex itself rather than with sex at his age. The adult in our culture has often failed to unlearn the wickedness or the dangerousness of sex, a lesson which was impressed upon him strongly in his most formative years.

DISCONTINUITY IN CONDITIONING

Even from this very summary statement of continuous conditioning the economy of such mores is evident. In spite of the obvious advantages, however, there are difficulties in its way. Many primitive societies expect as different behavior from an individual as child and as adult as we do, and such discontinuity involves a presumption of strain.

Many societies of this type however minimize strain by the techniques they employ, and some techniques are more successful than others in ensuring the individual's functioning without conflict. It is from this point of view that age-graded societies reveal their fundamental significance. Age-graded cultures characteristically demand different behavior of the individual at different times of his life and persons of a like age-grade are grouped into a society whose activities are all oriented toward the behavior desired at that age. Individuals "graduate" publicly and with honor from one of these groups to another. Where age society members are enjoined to loyalty and mutual support, and are drawn not only from the local group but from the whole tribe as among the Arapaho, or even from other tribes as among the Wagawaga of Southeast New Guinea, such an institution has many advantages in eliminating conflicts among local groups and fostering intratribal peace. This seems to be also a factor in the tribal military solidarity of the similarly organized Masai of East Africa. The point that is of chief interest for our present discussion however is that by this means an individual who at any time takes on a new set of duties and virtues is supported not only by a solid phalanx of age mates but by the traditional prestige of the organized "secret" society into which he has now graduated. Fortified in this way, individuals in such cultures often swing between remarkable extremes of opposite behavior without apparent psychic threat. For example, the great majority exhibit prideful and non-conflicted behavior at each stage in the life cycle even when a prime of life devoted to passionate and aggressive head hunting must be followed by a later life dedicated to ritual and to mild and peaceable civic virtues.[2]

Our chief interest here, however, is in discontinuity which primarily affects the child. In many primitive societies such discontinuity has been fostered not because of economic or political necessity or because such discontinuity provides for a socially valuable division of labor, but because of some conceptual dogma. The most striking of these are the Australian and Papuan cultures where the ceremony of the "Making of Man" flourishes. In such societies it is believed that men and women have opposite and conflicting powers, and male children, who are of undefined status, must be initiated into the male role. In Central Australia the boy child is of the woman's side and women are tabu in the final adult stages of tribal ritual. The elaborate and protracted initiation ceremonies of the Arunta therefore snatch the boy from the mother, dramatize his gradual repudiation of her. In a final ceremony he is reborn as a man out of the men's ceremonial "baby pouch." The men's ceremonies are ritual statements of a masculine solidarity, carried out by fondling one another's *churingas,* the material symbol of each man's life, and by letting out over one another blood drawn from their veins. After this warm bond among men has been established through the ceremonies, the boy joins the men in the men's house and participates in tribal rites.[4,5] The enjoined discontinuity has been tribally bridged.

West of the Fly River in southern New Guinea there is a striking development of this Making of Men cult which involves a childhood period of passive homosexuality. Among the Keraki,[6] it is thought that no boy can grow to full stature without playing the role for some years. Men slightly older take the active role, and the older man is a jealous partner. The life cycle of the Keraki Indians includes, therefore, in succession, passive homosexuality, active homosexuality and heterosexuality. The Keraki believe that pregnancy will result from postpubertal passive homosexuality and see evidences of such practices in any fat man whom even as an old man, they may kill or drive out of the tribe because of their fear. The ceremony that is of interest in connection with the present discussion takes place at the end of the period of passive homosexuality. This ceremony consists in burning out the possibility of pregnancy from the boy by pouring lye down his throat, after which he has no further protection if he gives way to the practice. There is no technique for ending active homosexuality, but this is not explicitly tabu for older men; heterosexuality and children however are highly valued. Unlike the neighboring Marindanim who share their homosexual practices, Keraki husband and wife share the same house and work together in the gardens.

I have chosen illustrations of discontinuous conditioning where it is not too much to say that the cultural institutions furnish adequate support to the individual as he progresses from role to role or interdict the previous behavior in a summary fashion. The contrast with arrangements in our culture is very striking, and against this background of social arrangements in other cultures the adolescent period of *Sturm und Drang* with which we are so familiar becomes intelligible in terms of our discontinuous cultural institutions and dogmas rather than in terms of physiological necessity. It is even more pertinent to consider these comparative facts in relation to maladjusted persons in our culture who are said to be fixated at one or another preadult level. It is clear that if we were to look at our social arrangements as an outsider, we should infer directly from our family institutions and habits of child training that many individuals would not "put off childish things"; we should have to say that our adult activity demands traits that are interdicted in children, and that far from redoubling efforts to help children bridge this gap, adults in our culture put all the blame on the child when he fails to manifest spontaneously the new behavior or, overstepping the mark, manifests it with untoward belligerence. It is not surprising that in such a society many individuals fear to use behavior which has up to that time been under a ban and trust instead, though at great psychic cost, to attitudes that have been exercised with approval during their formative years. Insofar as we invoke a physiological scheme to account for these neurotic adjustments we are led to overlook the possibility of developing social institutions which would lessen the social cost we now pay; instead we elaborate a set of dogmas which prove inapplicable under other social conditions.

NOTES

[1] Ralph Linton, class notes on the Marquesans.

[2] Henry Elkin, manuscript on the Arapaho.

[3] LANDES, RUTH. *The Ojibway Woman.* New York: Columbia Univ. Press, 1938.

[4] ROHEIM, GÉZA. Psychoanalysis of primitive cultural types. *Int. J. Psychoanal.,* 1932, 13:1–224.

[5] SPENCER, B., and GILLEN, F. J. *The Arunta.* New York: Macmillan, 1927.

[6] WILLIAMS, FRANCIS E. *Papuans of the Trans-Fly.* London: Oxford, 1936.

The use of a conflict situation to induce catharsis has many implications, both practical and theoretical, for education theory. In the following article August Aichhorn describes how a form of "attack" therapy works to release repressed emotions, induce catharsis and finally helps effect the transference necessary for a successful re-educative process.

AUGUST AICHHORN

The Training School
FROM *Wayward Youth*

It is often necessary to take a youth out of his environment and to put him into an institution in order to treat his dissocial behavior. We would not see all that psychoanalysis has to contribute to re-education if we studied only individual cases of delinquency and did not go into the reformatories where numbers of dissocial children are brought together. We know that psychoanalysis offers great therapeutic possibilities in the treatment of individual cases. How can it help us in the institution? We shall find that here also the psychoanalytically trained worker is better equipped for his task than the worker without this training.

How can we apply psychoanalytic theory in the organization of a training school? In most institutions, the children live in groups in charge of a counsellor. This matter of grouping is of first importance. In the older type of institution the groups are for the most part composed of children with varying pathological conditions; this can serve only to aggravate the condition of the individual child. It is self-evident that we cannot do educational work with such a group; we can maintain control only through use of force. This may be one of the reasons why, in correctional institutions, it seems difficult to forgo corporal punishment.

In more modern institutions, two efforts are being made: (1) to separate the children into the smallest possible groups, and (2) to compose these groups in such a way that the group life will favorably influence the behavior difficulties. For practical reasons it is impossible to assign a worker to each individual, nor should this be the aim of the organization. Re-education in an institution is and must remain a group training, which should be adapted to meet the special needs of delinquents. It is easy to understand why those who actually work with youth prefer small groups whereas the administration wishes to operate with large groups for reasons of economy. With the severest cases, even the administration will realize the advantages of a small group. I do not mean to say that grouping is considered an important matter in all institutions. There are many old institutions that have changed their names but are dominated exclusively by an economic policy. It is out of the question to expect any psychoanalytic understanding in these institutions.

The children in our institution were separated originally according to sex, and whether or not they had finished school. Otherwise they were left in groups which they had happened to join on arrival. Very soon, however, the management of these groups became so difficult that something had to be done. Since corporal punishment was ruled out from the beginning, we moved difficult individual cases about until we found a group where they could adjust themselves. The first grouping therefore arose out of these practical difficulties. There was one exception. One group consisted of those cases excluded from all other groups. Our experience and the intuitive judgment of some of our workers soon enabled us to place the children in a suitable group shortly after their admission.

By means of this grouping we brought fairly similar children together. The frequent recurrence of typical peculiarities within the group impressed the counsellor, who thus became aware of them and was enabled to devise methods suitable to these children. He could apply the same methods more effectively in such a group because it was homogeneous. Thus the children in the group found the most favorable conditions for their development and treatment, and the groups were therapeutically as well as economically advantageous.

What I have related of this grouping system is not for the sake of giving you a ready-made sample, but of showing you how the form was evolved in response to our practical needs. No psychoanalytic theory was involved in this plan. As I have pointed out, we followed an economic principle. Grouping is most effective when the mere living together has a favorable influence on the dissocial behavior. The question then becomes: "Which types of dissocial behavior are most favorably influenced by living together in such a group?"

From the psychoanalytic point of view, the manifest character of the delinquency is not important, but rather the psychic mechanisms which motivate the dissocial behavior. We must find out in each case what these motives are before we can group the pupils in such a way that they will have a favorable influence on each other and thus be made fit to return to society. Psychoanalysis will help us more in the problem of grouping when it has uncovered these underlying mechanisms in a great number of cases of delinquency. However, we must not confuse this application of psychoanalytic knowledge with the actual psychoanalytic treatment of a delinquent. We refer here only to ways in which psycho-analytical application can help us in diagnosis.

The problem of grouping is not solved merely by bringing children together in the expectation that the interaction of their psychic mechanisms will operate therapeutically. Conditions other than those of the personality of the individual pupils must be considered. I refer to those external conditions which in general constitute the *milieu*. Not only are the companions with whom he lives important to the dissocial child, but also the material world around him; not only the *milieu* of the group but also the institution as a whole.

Let us consider the conditions in the old type of reformatory and in the new training school. In the former, we are struck by the surly, shut-in reaction of the inmates. Everywhere we meet a cautious, distrustful, antagonistic attitude. No one looks us straight in the eye. The usual happy overflowing of youthful good spirits is entirely absent. What cheerfulness there is to be seen strikes us as sad. Real joy in living expresses itself quite differently. We can hardly restrain a shudder at the dammed-up hate we feel in these young people. This antagonism finds no solution in the institution but is condensed and stored up for later discharge against society.

The superintendent of such an institution once called my attention to wash basins that had been in use for twenty years. He was proud of the fact that they had remained so long undamaged and still shone like new. In the dormitories the beds stood in a row, twenty-five on each side, like rows of soldiers, not an inch out of line. The covers were all folded at correct right angles and fell like a plumb-line. Everywhere was the same meticulous order. When we consider how hard it is to make most children orderly at all, we know what constant discipline is necessary to maintain such military order as this. If it is difficult for normal children to be neat, how much harder is it for dissocial children! They could not conform to the demands of society outside. Can we expect to socialize them through such methods?

Now for the other type of institution. If you had come to our training school on a particularly good day you would have found something like the following: Before you reached the grounds of the institution you might have met a local inhabitant complaining loudly that the delinquents, instead of being locked up and marched out in a line to go walking, were allowed to run around in the neighborhood, that they could come and go at will through unlocked doors and gates. He is on his way to complain to the superintendent because some boys, who were scuffling on their way home, had broken one of his windows. You cannot see me at once because a policeman is waiting for me. From my office you hear the excited voice of a gardener complaining that he cannot have the boys coming into his orchard. I invite you to come in with the policeman and let you hear the account of what happened the day before. Two boys made a fire in the woods and cooked a trout that was obviously caught in a near-by brook, a thing forbidden by law. The policeman is no more than out of the room and we are on the point of making a round of the institution when the cook bursts in in great excitement to say that she had made just the right number of dumplings and five have disappeared. Maybe you will decide to forgo further inspection of the institution.

Is it better to have such a state of affairs in a training school or should one really depend on lock and key? In the consultation room of the clinic the worker accepts the misconduct of the delinquent and in the beginning does not interfere with it but awaits the time when a change comes of itself. We can see no reason why the procedure should be different in the institution just because there are more cases and the difficulties are greater.

It is characteristic of the delinquent that he possesses little capacity for repressing instinctual impulses and for directing energy away from primitive goals. He is thus unable to achieve what is considered by society a normal ethical code. The great majority of children in need of retraining come into conflict with society because of an unsatisfied need for tenderness and love in their childhood. We therefore find in them a proportionately increased thirst for pleasure and for primitive forms of instinctual gratification. They lack inhibitions and they have a strong, though distorted, craving for affection. If the delinquency is to be cured rather than repressed, we must meet these needs even though at first this seems futile to so-called "understanding people."

As a matter of fact, the work in our institution was misunderstood. Anxious, timid people were horrified, the neighbors were angry, and every time anything went wrong there was a great outcry. However, we did not let ourselves be misled. We utilized the daily conflict to achieve an educational purpose. We assured these youths of our interest and affection in an environment calculated to please them, made use of the love thus won from them to retrieve a neglected part of their development, i.e., the transition from their earlier unreal world of self-indulgence to one of reality. . . .

The cure of delinquency is fundamentally a problem of libido; that is to say, the most important thing is the child's feeling for the counsellor or, more generally, for the people of his environment. This we must recognize in institutional care. I have already explained how we try to direct the children's feelings toward us, to stabilize these feelings, and to make use of them. In spite of all our efforts, however, our institution was not a paradise and we often had conflicts and ugly moods. It was especially noticeable in those groups directed by women that a bad mood in the leader would communicate itself to the children, who in turn reacted unfavorably, until the situation became intensified to the point of open conflict. At that time I had no understanding of the cathartic effect of talking things over, but I did notice how the mood of the whole group changed with the mood of the teacher. Through repeated conferences and talks with individual workers, in which we often touched on personal matters, I succeeded gradually in building up a friendly and confidential relationship with my co-workers. This in turn reacted on our charges so that finally the same feeling-tone dominated the whole establishment. We sacrificed none of our authority but we had taken away the children's fear of us and replaced it with their confidence.

The mechanism of the transference as explained by psychoanalysis showed me later how we had accomplished our results. It showed me also why it is so easy to talk about training children, whereas we learn what to do only from experience. What succeeds with one teacher can be a total failure with another. I consider that successful work in an institution without a strong bond of feeling between the superintendent and personnel is impossible. I cannot conceive that a dissocial youth can be re-educated without a strong, positive feeling for the people in his environment. The attitude of the worker toward the leader determines of itself the relationship between the worker and the child.

At this point, it seems important to warn you against a too hasty application of what we have learned. The temptation is great to apply conclusions which are suitable for dissocial children to the education of normal children. Although deep and far-reaching relationships exist between the training of the two groups, we are not ready to say with assurance where they coincide. Among our charges we find border-line cases and transitional states approaching neurosis and psychosis. Here our work touches the field of psychiatry. We also find border-line cases of delinquent children that approach the normal. In such cases, we concern ourselves with the family, with educational work done by child-welfare groups, and with movements for young people. Our main work, however, must always develop along separate lines.

We found that the cases in our institution came almost without exception from families where the home situation was disturbed, broken up, or disharmonious, regardless of the deeper underlying causes of their delinquency. It seems as if the shocks which the individual receives from society are endurable only when he finds a haven, which in our society the family normally offers. Given such a haven, the expressions of his instincts are held within bounds acceptable to society. When this is lacking, the equilibrium of these unstable individuals is all the more easily thrown out of balance.

These disturbances of equilibrium bring about lasting effects which must be treated by social re-education when they take the form of dissocial behavior. The methods used in influencing these dissocial children, especially at first, must differ essentially from the education of normal children.

Let us return to the institution. We know that the character and intensity of the child's libidinal ties to the objects of his earliest environment determine the course of his later life. This agrees with our belief that our success in the treatment of delinquency is to be attributed to the fact that we influenced the later development of the libido in the direction of sublimation and compensation. . . .

In a case of stealing within the institution I did not rely on my intuition but deliberately created the situation I needed. This case will illustrate again how the worker must free himself from all stereotyped methods.

About this time, I read Dr. Rank's book, *Das Inzestmotiv in Dichtung und Sage* (The Incest Motive in Poetry and Saga), in which he introduces the Aristotelian theory of catharsis. It occurred to me that we might use the conflict situation of our charges to introduce catharsis; that is, we could make the boy the hero of the drama. The first opportunity for trying this seemed to be a conflict over stealing.

We had an eighteen-year-old boy who had been expelled from a military school for stealing from his comrades and who had stolen at home and elsewhere. After he had been with us for several months, I put him in charge of the tobacco shop. The employees each contributed a certain amount to buy their tobacco in common. I told the cashier to keep an eye on the boy without letting him know and to report to me when any money was missing. Four weeks later, he reported that about half the sum taken in weekly was missing. This seemed to be the right moment to expose the boy to an emotional shock in order to bring about catharsis, although I had no clear idea how I was going to do this. Since I wanted to gain a little time I told the cashier to send the boy to me in the afternoon without telling him that anything was wrong. The boy came while I was still undecided what to do. I wished to keep him with me for a while, so I proposed that he help me dust my books and put them in order. What should I do? I must proceed in such a way that the situation would develop around the boy himself, so that his anxiety once aroused would become so intense as to be unbearable. The instant he realized that the catastrophe of exposure was unavoidable, his anxiety must be turned into an emotional outburst. This sudden change of affect would make him accessible to treatment.

The "drama" was played as follows. We began our work. I inquired how he was getting along and gradually we approached the topic of the tobacco shop. "How much do you take in each week?" He mentioned a certain sum. We continued to dust the books. After a pause, "Does the money always come out right?" A hesitating "Yes" of which I took no further notice. After another pause, "When do you have the most trade?" "In the morning." Then still later, "I must look in on you some time and go over your cash drawer." The boy was getting more restless all the time, but I ignored it, went on working and kept coming back to the tobacco shop. When I felt that I had intensified his uneasiness sufficiently I suddenly brought the crisis to a head. "Well, when we get through here I'll go and take a look at your cash." We had been working together for about an hour and a quarter. He stood with his back to me, took a book from the shelf, and suddenly let it fall. Then I took cognizance of his excitement. "What's the matter?" "Nothing." "*What's wrong with your cash?*" His face became distorted with anxiety, and he stammered out the sum. Without saying a word I gave him this amount. He looked at me with an indescribable expression on his face and was about to speak. I would not let him talk because I felt that my action must have time to take effect and so I sent him away with a friendly gesture. About ten minutes later, he came back and laid the money on the table, saying "Let them lock me up. I don't deserve your help—I'll only steal again." He was greatly excited and was sobbing bitterly. I let him sit down and I began to talk to him. I did not preach, but listened sympathetically to what he poured out, his thievery, his attitude toward his family and to life in general, and everything that troubled him. The emotion gradually receded, relieved by the weeping and talking. Finally I gave the money back to him, saying that I did not believe he would steal again; that he was worth that much to me. I said, too, that it was not a present, that he could smoke less and pay it back gradually. So that no one should know about this, however, he had better put the money back in the cash drawer. I told the cashier that the amount had been returned and that he need take no notice of the affair. In the course of the next two months, the money was actually returned.

It is not improbable that the contrast in emotion from fear to relief brought about the solution. Practically the treatment was effective; in the short time he stayed with us, he conducted himself well. Later he was employed as a draughtsman in a furniture factory and acquitted himself creditably. In this case, we had succeeded in arousing a strong emotion in him and in making use of it in his retraining. We must wait for further experience with this method to see in which cases it is applicable as a special technique.

We must take it for granted that some young people will steal in an institution. Some people will regard it as regrettable that stealing takes place in an institution and others will think it absurd to make use of stealing in a boy's retraining as in the above case.

After such a solution of a conflict, a very intensive transference sets in that is important for the further course of the retraining but that endangers the results if the worker does not see to it that this emotional relationship is later dissolved. It is easy to see how such an intense tie to the worker can be the cause of jealousy and how this, in turn, can motivate further dissocial behavior. The transference is the most important aid in our work but it can have undesirable consequences if we do not understand the mechanisms involved.

The remedial treatment of the individual can begin only when the transference is established, whether this be in the consultation room or in the institution. Re-education, however, is not achieved through words, admonition, scolding, or punishment, but through what the child actually experiences. Through the *milieu* we created in our institution and through our type of leadership, we had opportunities every day to give the children experiences the deep effect of which helped to relieve their dissocial behavior. Often we made use of the mood of the moment or created a situation to produce the desired mood. Sometimes we used bandit adventure stories, which the dissocial love, to secure a foothold for further educational work. I can give you no general directions how to proceed. Every educator must work out the details of his own technique. If he possesses the capacity for this work, he can learn through observation, experience, and earnest study of the problems. It is certainly true that you cannot make an educator out of every personality. A great deal of harm can be done by the dilettante in this work as well as by the professional worker who is not endowed for this task. . . .

We find that the question of whether the dissocial should be treated with severity, as in the old style institution, or with gentleness, as in the modern one, does not meet the real problem at all. These two methods arise out of opposed emotional attitudes to the delinquent and do not take into consideration the fact that one type can be influenced and made socially acceptable through severity, another through gentleness, and that a third responds to neither one of these methods; and that the usual educational methods are in general ineffective. Why is this?

Socially acceptable behavior is preserved by means of the ego-ideal, which frees normal conscious feelings of guilt. With the delinquent this does not obtain. These feelings are either repressed, weak, or non-existent. If the ego-ideal is excessively severe, as in the border-line neurotic cases with dissocial features, the worker achieves therapeutic results through being kind and gentle and reducing his demands on the child. If the delinquent is an uninhibited primitive type who has not learned to adjust himself to reality because the restrictions placed on his instincts were too slight, the worker must begin with increased demands. Thus every type of delinquency requires a special type of treatment. In all cases, however, the treatment must concern itself with the further development of the ego-ideal, and we must put the question thus: how can we direct social retraining in order to bring about corrections of character in the individual?

I cannot close . . . without once more stressing the great importance of the personality of the workers in this field. You have seen that a character change in the delinquent means a change in his ego-ideal. This occurs when new traits are taken over by the individual. The source of these traits is the worker himself. He is the important object with whom the dissocial child or youth can retrieve the defective or non-existent identification and with whom he can experience all the things in which his father failed him. With the worker's help, the youth acquires the necessary feeling relation to his companions which enables him to overcome the dissocial traits. The word "father-substitute," so often used in connection with remedial education, receives its rightful connotation in this conception of the task.

What helps the worker most in therapy with the dissocial? The transference! And especially what we recognize as the positive transference. It is, above all, the tender feeling for the teacher that gives the pupil the incentive to do what is prescribed and not to do what is forbidden. The teacher, as a libidinally charged object for the pupil, offers traits for identification that bring about a lasting change in the structure of the ego-ideal. This in turn effects a change in the behavior of the formerly dissocial child. We cannot imagine a person who is unsocial as a worker in this field. We assume therefore that the ego-ideal of the child will be corrected through the worker's help in bringing him to a recognition of the claims of society and to participation in society. Our work differs from that of the psychoanalyst in that we use the transference to accomplish an entirely different task. In the analysis of neurotic patients, the transference must be used, not for temporary improvement, but to give the patient strength to complete a special piece of work, to change unconscious material into conscious material and thereby to bring about a permanent change in his whole being. In remedial training we cannot be content with transient results which rise from the emotional tie of the dissocial boy or girl to the worker. We must succeed, as in psychoanalysis, in bringing the wayward youth under the influence of the transference to a definite achievement. This achievement consists in a real character change, in the setting up of a socially directed ego-ideal, that is, in the retrieving of that part of his development which is necessary for a proper adjustment to society.

"The Sacred Table" sensitively explores a rarely studied relationship between teacher and pupil. It reveals much about the process of education and the nature of the sexual conflicts that are frequently the source of a student's inability to learn. The story also reflects a peculiarly familiar discontinuity in our culture. We encourage a relationship between mother and son that can only result in infantile dependency; then we expect the child to be able to free himself of his mother so that he can take his place as a mature adult. We wish him to "put off childish things" when childish things are his only security.

T. C. WORSLEY

The Sacred Table

Mrs. Moroney was the sort of woman who went straight to the point, even when the point was an unpleasant one. At the very beginning of her first interview with the prospective tutor, she held her finger on the pulse of the problem.

"It's not," she said, "that I particularly want the boy to be interested in my sort of thing" (and it was perfectly clear that this was just what she did want) "if only he was interested in *something*."

She kept returning to this, to her young son's listlessness, all the time that she was walking round her special room displaying to him her "things." She moved about, touching a jug, edging forward a chair, adding the animation of her pleasure in them to the lights that glowed in the woods and flickered across the coloured porcelain. Spread across the sacred table, her special treasure, were some William Morris stuffs and a portfolio of drawings, which she came back to handle lovingly, caressingly, her restlessness stilled and centered round them.

"Philip seems to care about nothing any longer," she deplored. "Nothing. If only he liked rugger, it would be something." But not, the prospective tutor felt, very much.

625

"Why on earth," she went on, picking up and fingering the stuff, "why on earth should he keep running away from school to us, only to be bored to extinction when he gets here? It isn't that he appreciates his home any more," and she picked up the stuff and the drawings which her Philip no longer cared about and put them tenderly away.

It was on the strength of his unprompted admiration for that table when he first came into the room that the tutor—so he later felt—had been finally engaged. His academic qualifications were not striking, his "experience" non-existent. His application in answer to an advertisement in *The Times* had been the result of a sudden whim, prompted in part by a temporary financial embarrassment. Six guineas a week for three months, all found, had been tempting; and having no very clear notion of what a tutorship entailed except that he wouldn't allow it to be exacting, he had looked forward to a spell of heavy reading. He took himself seriously, if not his duties.

But the household caught his interest from the outset. When he first approached the Edwardian villa on the outskirts of the little country town, his heart had sunk as his imagination ran too easily forward to a vision of stuffy domesticity, of insipid suety meals, of long evenings during which he might be made the victim of B.B.C. variety or the reminiscences of a retired planter. Mrs. Moroney herself had been a first hint of the unusual. Vague and restless, in her faded Pre-Raphaelite shades, she had all the same struck him as decided. She knew what she wanted even if it was not plainly formulated. She was the one that counted, too. Mr. Moroney was not to be consulted. He was never to come much into the picture, was always to remain a background figure who nursed some powerful disease in the privacy of his workshop emerging only to preside in silence over meals and long summer evenings. A large heavy man with a blunt wedgelike face, he had made some surrender to her, of golf probably, and his bridge and his clubs, and, in an outside shed, he manufactured endless small boxes inlaid with mother o' pearl, which he turned on a number of small lathes; they piled up, these boxes, endlessly under his indefatigable industry—to become Christmas presents for friends and relations or to decorate numberless stalls in numberless bazaars for numberless more or less good causes. They were anyhow a success; the demand always seemed to exceed his supply and gave him no rest from his chipping and turning and his endless treadle.

Mr. Moroney was soon dismissed to his "work," being given time only for a hand-shake after which the prospective tutor was conducted for the interview to Mrs. Moroney's special room. This came as a second surprise after the Edwardian exterior, and the shapeless colourless parlourmaid who had answered the old-fashioned bell. The sacred table made its immediate impression of light dignity and elegant poise. It was featured: the room was arranged towards it: everything else was there to heighten its effect. It was also a kind of Test. The tutor saw, so soon as he had remarked on it approvingly to Mrs. Moroney, that he had "passed." He was as good as engaged.

But the interest soon shifted from Mrs. Moroney's "things," which were not so remarkable except in the lively pleasure she had from them. The Moroneys were only mediumly well-to-do and she couldn't—apart from the table—go in for rarities. No, the interest was in the sad queer little story of her only son, Philip, and in what she wanted from him in relation to this boy; and whether he would be able to help her get it— whether, even, it was desirable that he should if he could.

What it was that she wanted soon became clear:

"You see, Philip wasn't always like this, by any manner of means," she told him. "Before he went to school he bubbled with life and vitality and energy. . . . And he was so unusual. He had the liveliest interest in all my things, and, besides, one special interest of his own. It was by an accident that I discovered his passion for dancing. I used to play to him every evening and one day quite on his own, quite spontaneously, he began to dance. He was only six, but I can't tell you how beautifully he felt the music. And I was always careful about choosing it. From the very first I'd always made sure that he only came in contact with the best—music, books, stuff, everything. So I insisted from the first when he started dancing that it should be in keeping with the best. Not that there was much need to insist. He had a natural taste from the beginning . . . in everything he touched. He'd seize up a scarf and a shawl and combine them always in just the right balance of tone. But it was danc- ing that became almost our life. I've never liked potted music, but I did buy a gramophone and chose the records carefully, so that he should dance to every sort of thing—and always he gave this beautiful inter- pretation of the quality. Later he used to act for me—scenes from Shakespeare and, oh, one thing and another. He knew acres and acres of The Plays by heart . . . I wasn't going to let him go to school too early. They go away from home much too soon nowadays, don't you agree? Of course when you see some of their homes——! But if a boy has a home where——well, hadn't he much better benefit by it as long as possible instead of being plunged into the barbarity of a boys' school? Wasn't I right?"

The tutor could only assent.

"His father wanted him packed off to some beastly seminary at eight and a half. He thought I was molly-coddling him. But of course I wasn't. There's nothing molly-coddling about Shakespeare and dancing, is there? His father couldn't be expected to understand. But I kept to my plan. I was going to be quite sure; sure that the foundation was solid before I risked it being broken up. By the time he was ten I thought it was all right. By then he really 'knew.' I felt it as safe to let him choose as to choose myself. That was the moment. He could go to school and learn what he had to."

Mrs. Moroney took another restless turn round the room before she went on with her story. He had gone to school, and he had positively enjoyed it. That was what was so extraordinary. He'd got on surprisingly well. He'd learnt quickly and come out top in his classes. He'd shown a great aptitude for—of all things!—cricket. She was almost as pleased as her husband, who was thoroughly delighted with these signs of ordinariness. She felt completely justified. She had never believed there need be any division between art and life. Of course his taste and his art didn't interfere with the ordinary pursuits. They helped. She hadn't been surprised that he was outstripping his companions. It was what she had expected.

Then, for no reason, without any warning, with no preparatory tears, fuss, or outward signs, he ran away. He walked out of the school one night and found himself a train and turned up at the house at midnight. He could give no explanation. He was not "upset." He didn't know in the least why he had done it. The school could provide no clue. After a week—a week in which he mooched aimlessly about the house and countryside, he volunteered to go back. And after six weeks he ran away again. It was the same pattern. No explanation, no tears, no fuss. But—and this was the trouble—no animation. All the enthusiasm, all the spontaneity, all the precious responsiveness, had abruptly vanished. The boy didn't want to do anything. He was stuck, like a clock that had gone wrong, and no manner of shaking could set him off again.

He went back to school once more, only to run away once more. Doctors were consulted and proved expensively unhelpful. The school refused to take any further responsibility. They recommended her to find a tutor.

"You must bring him alive again," was Mrs. Moroney's final instruction to the newly engaged tutor. "I don't mind how you do it. I don't care what form it takes. I shouldn't even object—" and this was evidently the proof of her despair—"if he starts to like rugger. But bring him alive. Get him interested in *something*, I don't mind what."

But when she went on to give a hint about *interesting* ruins and a church with an antiquarian interest within bicycle reach, the tutor saw which way her mind was moving. Without quite knowing why, dimly foreseeing a possible need for desperate remedies without so much as having yet seen the child, "I should have to have a quite free hand," he suddenly found it necessary to insist.

"Naturally," she answered quickly; too quickly. The tutor felt that she hadn't really listened.

"I might have to do—well, anything."

"Do what you like." But he still felt that she didn't really mean it. Yet he began to enjoy the situation. He felt he had, at twenty-three, some sort of power which he could use. But he had to ensure himself absolutely in advance.

"You'll have to surrender the final responsibility to me."

She gave him one careful look. "Of course," she said. "I won't interfere. You must completely take him on."

2

He didn't meet the boy that day. He was left to wonder what he was like during the three days they gave him to collect his belongings from London. As he talked the thing over with his friends, the smattering of psychological phrases and technical terms which everyone has at their tongue's end nowadays were invoked to help him. It was generally decided that the parents were the culprits and that it would be them rather than the boy he would have to straighten out. The tutor was too interested in himself and his own future to be very objective about it; but he was intrigued by the situation, and he felt, without anything much to justify the feeling, that just because he was himself a young man full of vigour and life and interests, he must therefore be able to help. He contrasted himself—all youth and hope and expectation—with something that he thought of, in recollection, as "anti-life" in Mrs. Moroney. Vitality she had, yet somehow it was muffled; interests she had, yet somehow they were blunted; passion she had, yet somehow it was withheld. Passion, interest, vitality—they were more his than hers. Both of them claimed them, but her claim was not valid; his own, just because he was twenty-three, was. Above all—and it was why he had intuitively felt it essential to press the point—she had never really intended to give him a free hand. There was something quite definite she reserved.

What, on the other hand, it was that he so wanted a free hand over, he didn't in the least know; and his first meeting with the boy, when he came back from London, didn't in the least clear it up. If he had hoped that anything in the boy's manner would be suggestive, he was soon disappointed.

Philip Moroney was twelve, a slight, well-made boy, who stood regarding the tutor amiably but without friendliness. The hazel which lay like an undercoat beneath a warm complexion paled off, the tutor observed, into whiteness above the cheek-bones. He didn't look very well. Mrs. Moroney effected an introduction between pupil and master and left them together, facing each other across the sacred table. It was a moment for which the tutor had almost consciously not prepared himself. Faced with it now, he really didn't know how to begin. What did one, what on earth did one, say to even a normal boy of twelve? Two openings alone insisted on obtruding themselves, and either was hopelessly tactless. The questions that came uppermost were: "Why *did* you run away?" and then much more insistently, "What do you think of your mother?" He asked the first in sheer despair to avoid asking the second. The boy shrugged his shoulders as much as to say, how should *he* know, and then surprised the tutor, after a pause, by offering a suggestion.

"To get equal with them?"

The tutor didn't make much of that. Equal with whom and for what? But he wasn't going to lose a chance.

"It was the best thing you could do."

The child looked puzzled. "But it doesn't work."

The tutor felt a renewal of power: "We'll try and make it."

"No, it won't work," the boy repeated.

"We'll find something," the tutor said, and from that moment was determined that he would. "What about a walk?" and, the boy assenting, they went off for a stroll in the flat Essex country before dinner. But conversation was desultory. No opening through which to approach the main question presented itself. Nor did any for the next three weeks.

But the time passed amicably at least. Lessons were arranged for the morning, more to keep the child occupied than in any hope of getting anything learnt. For the enthusiasm which his mother had described him so vividly as possessing was now quite dormant, so much so that the tutor began to wonder if it hadn't only existed in her imagination. The boy listlessly did what he was told, learnt his lessons with a dull obedience, unprotestingly walked or cycled in the afternoon; he took his lead obediently from the tutor, grateful, it appeared, to have someone to make up his mind for him, since he had none of his own to make up.

Mrs. Moroney watched and waited. Mr. Moroney chipped and twiddled in his outside shed. The tutor discovered no clue.

He looked for it first, as his friends had suggested, in the mother. He observed her carefully, and, in the evenings, when the boy was asleep—he slept mercifully early and late—tried to draw her out by artful questions. She was quite shrewd enough to parry him with equally artful evasions. He learnt a good deal about Chinese painting and the origins and development of brown lustre. But about herself he learned nothing. She was a discreet reticent woman who liked nothing so much as sharing her enthusiasms, and nothing so little as displaying her feelings. Her son she treated with a brusque affection, being very punctilious about his manners and appearance. He would be sent away from table for the faintest indication of dirty finger-nails and reprimanded for the slightest indication of childish greed. He took such reproofs with a sort of weary docility, just as he accepted her morning and evening kiss with an air of resigned patience.

But if, in the three weeks, the tutor felt himself no nearer a solution, he counted it as something that he was gaining the boy's confidence. He rather wished sometimes that he belonged to the earlier generation of his own schoolmasters who had still been sure enough of their ground to pick out a goal—house matches, prefectship, something of that sort—and had driven their charges roughshod towards it. He himself was acutely conscious of knowing only enough to know that the human machine was excessively delicate and that a false suggestion or a clumsy question might be enough to delay recovery. He bided his time, deciding, as his only point of policy, to try to give an impression that whatever in the world the lad was up to would have his unreserved approval.

Not that the boy seemed to be up to anything in particular. The first sign he gave of any feeling was so small and so negative that the tutor made little of it. It happened during the fourth week when one day he interrupted their mechanical translating of Sophocles to digress a little on the life of the Greeks. He felt it was up to him—that Mrs. Moroney would especially consider it up to him—to waken the boy's interest in Greek art. He approached it circuitously, picturing in modern terms the life of a Greek boy. Philip listened obediently to the first part of his description, but the moment he reached art in the shape of describing a chorus by Pindar in praise of a victorious athlete, the tutor noticed an obstinate expression shut down the boy's face. It was, anyhow, a sign of *something*; it was better than the docile attention which was all the boy gave him as a rule. The tutor continued as if he noticed nothing:

"And in the evening there would be a dinner, with the victor gar-landed as guest of honour, and some of the other boys would dance to the song which Pindar had composed. The boy himself might have danced too—"

Philip broke his pencil with a quiet snap. He had hung his head and his body was tensed to resist taking in what the tutor was saying; the tutor pushed on:

"Boys in those days danced as naturally as today they play cricket. They were all trained in it from childhood. Quite early on they—"

In the rudest voice the boy interrupted:

"This is very dull. Let's go on translating."

The tutor was disconcerted. He'd quite expected an outburst but somehow, against all reason, was a little nettled to hear his efforts described as dull.

"If you find it dull, by all means. I was trying to make it interesting."

His pique evidently affected Philip. "I didn't mean you were dull," he said, and it was plainly an apology.

"What *did* you mean, I wonder?"

But that was too big a question. "Let's go on translating."

It was the first time anyhow that the boy had wanted to translate. But the tutor pressed the point:

"You mean dancing's dull?"

The child looked miserable and cornered. He turned away his head. "Let's go on translating," he finally repeated, bringing the repetition out from some depth of misery.

They went on translating.

His pique, the tutor noted, had made its effect. That gave him at least some kind of weapon, although it was one that he instinctively felt he must be extremely sparing in the use of. But it was from this incident that things began to happen. The boy took to following him around. Previously he had been quite content to be left on his own, and had only given the tutor his company at the prescribed times, or at the tutor's express suggestion. Now he began to attach himself whenever he could. It was part of the arrangement with Mrs. Moroney that the tutor was to have to himself the interval between tea and dinner, and it was his usual practice to go to his own room to read. One day the boy sought him out there; he opened the door shyly and said, "Do you mind if I come in? I'll be quite quiet," and he settled himself noiselessly at the window and stared out of it, his handsome little face cupped in his hands, his elbows propped up on the sill. He didn't apparently want anything from the tutor except his presence, and when the tutor began speaking, the boy rebuked him:

"You go on with what you're doing. I don't want to disturb you." It was solemn and grown up and touching. The tutor had the feeling that the child, in his demonstrated silence, was offering some kind of sacrifice that it would be offending to refuse. All the same he felt an awkwardness in going on reading his law books with that grave, speechless, staring boy sitting in the window waiting.

With half an hour to spare before dinner, he announced that he would take a bath; and the boy not responding or stirring he undressed; just as he was getting into his dressing-gown the boy turned and spoke.

"How old are you?"

"Twenty-three. Why?"

"You're terrifically strong, aren't you?"

The tutor felt so curiously complimented that he had to deprecate. "Oh, I don't know about that."

"Yes, you are," the boy said, "terrifically."

The tutor turned and looked at Philip. "Well, you know, so are you for your age."

"Not as strong as you," Philip said, turning back to the window.

"You soon will be," the tutor said.

For one moment the boy's face lighted up. "Do you think I will?" It was the long-awaited moment of returned excitement and it died the very moment that it flared. "No, I won't. I can't be."

"Of course you can be and you will." But the boy had presented his back again and cupped his chin in his hands and was staring out on to the small neat lawn.

All the same Mrs. Moroney noticed a change in the boy that evening and the next day. It was slight but discernible.

"Something's stirring," she said to the tutor. "I don't know how you've managed it, but something's moving, don't you notice it?"

"Don't expect too much," the tutor was prompted to answer, "and above all don't watch all the time."

For Mrs. Moroney, although she took no overt interest in the child's progress, never so much as asking what they were doing or how they were getting on, was all the time, the tutor had been feeling, present with her eyes; all the time she was out shopping or paying visits or going up to London, all the time she was dusting, rearranging, quietly reading, her eyes, he felt, were following them expectantly, in their lessons, on their walks, so that he had even contemplated suggesting that he and the boy should go away on their own. He had just before this hinted at the possibility and found Mrs. Moroney obstinately hostile. But he kept the idea up his sleeve in case it might be wanted.

The next evening, after Mrs. Moroney had, at luncheon, announced her intention of being out to tea, the boy turned up again at the tutor's room and installed himself in the same position at the window. The tutor after the merest welcome went on reading, but watched Philip covertly from behind his book. The boy had picked up a pencil and notebook from the window-sill and had begun scribbling. Presently his face tightened into concentration and the small tongue stuck out between the lips in the effort of doing something precise and difficult. He was drawing, his face and hand screwed tight; then there was a relaxation: the pencil travelled freely and wildly in circles round the paper, gathering momentum, speed and strength, as the circles decreased in diameter towards a centre, and on that centre it was struck down in a sudden burst of violence, slashing across and across, till it tore the centre out.

The boy turned round with a sudden friendly grin:

"You wouldn't like to come out and play cricket? I've got a ball and some things in the shed."

Surprised and delighted, the tutor agreed. Stumps were found and pitched on the narrow lawn between the house and the poplar trees. The tutor's suggestion that a soft ball would be best—he had put it on the ground of the windows—had been rejected, and a new fresh jumping enthusiasm easily over-rode his objections. He had persuaded the boy to bat presuming his refusal to be prompted by politeness. But he found him to be a bad bat, alternately absurdly over-cautious, when he would step back and cover his wicket, allowing anything a fraction wide to go past and bang against the shed door—or wildly rash, when he would shut his eyes and swipe, missing completely each time—mercifully, for the tutor felt that Mrs. Moroney would turn out to be very unindulgent in respect to her windows, especially the long fragile French window which guarded so inadequately her special room. The boy soon got tired of his ineffectual efforts and called out "Now let me bowl!"

Then the tutor saw why. Without being an expert he could tell that the boy had a fine natural left-hand action, graceful, easy and by no means slow. He bowled, for his age, fast, too fast for the tutor who, without pads, found that his shins were in constant danger from balls that swung in nastily and late. He had, if he wasn't to retire hurt, to give all his attention to the bowling for the first over or two. Only then could he take notice of the fact that the boy was a changed person, that he had a confident smile, held himself erect and was thoroughly enjoying show-ing off to his tutor his graceful run, his lithe and smooth swing. He began, as small boys commonly do, to bowl faster and faster; but unlike most small boys did not allow himself to become correspondingly wild. He bowled with a deliberate precision at the tutor's body and hardly for a single ball was it out of danger. All the same, in an interval the tutor, out of the inveterate habit of instructors, advised the boy to control his speed. "Length, not pace," was a maxim that returned to him from his own schooldays. Philip, he noticed, did not respond favourably, and when they resumed, he started off at his fastest and seemed intent on proving that he could bowl faster yet.

After only five or six balls, the tutor's wicket was spread flat; and then from behind the bowler came an unexpected clap. The tutor looked up: the boy turned round: there was Mrs. Moroney who had returned from her tea, standing, head on one side, in her flowing clothes, decorously applauding. The animation faded from the boy's face, and when the tutor set up the wicket again and threw the ball back to him, he let it drop, put his hands in his pockets and announced:

"I'm tired."

"Do go on, do go on," his mother called out. "I want to see you hit for a sixer." The tutor saw Philip wince at the word, and when he obediently picked up the ball and started bowling it was with a desultory indolence which was nothing like his real style. The tutor pulled up the stumps and called out to her:

"We're too tired. We've been going a long time," and the game was abandoned.

Up till then he had been thinking Mrs. Moroney remarkably sensible: having reconciled herself to there being no intimacy between herself and her son, she had never tried to invent it. But the cricket evidently per-suaded her that a basis for it had now returned. Instead of talking at dinner, as she usually did, on indifferent topics to him or to her husband, she tried now to draw the boy in. She introduced cricket as a subject and didn't seem to see that the child squirmed. When she asked him a question about school—a subject that hadn't in four weeks been men-tioned—he didn't answer. She repeated her question:

"What was the name of that nice master you used to talk about, the one who admired your bowling?"

Philip went on eating. Mrs. Moroney looked at the tutor, as if for support, but he too pretended to be intent on his food.

Mr. Moroney made a sudden descent into action:

"Answer your mother when she speaks to you, can't you? You've a tongue in your head."

But the boy didn't speak.

"Answer your mother or clear off to bed." And the boy put down knife and fork, stood up, pushed in his chair and walked, with a dignity the tutor couldn't help admiring, out of the door. He didn't even slam it behind him.

When the tutor returned that night to his room, he picked up the notebook in which the boy had been scribbling and turned to the page. It was difficult to make anything out among the scrawl and scribble. It looked as if, beneath the circles, the leaf pattern of a William Morris paper had been copied. But whatever had been drawn in the centre of the page had been utterly obliterated by the last fierce onslaught.

3

There was no more cricket for the next three or four days, not till Mrs. Moroney announced one day at breakfast that she and her husband were going up to Town for the day, and would not be back until late in the evening. But during those days the tutor noticed a distinct advance in his pupil; he was becoming more ordinary. Instead of walking warily, circumspectly, almost daintily, he kicked about with his shoes: he would run on ahead: he thought nothing of arguing, disputing, scuffling even with his tutor; Mrs. Moroney had to reprove him several times for kicking, idly, the wainscoting or the door. He was taking an interest in his lessons, especially as the tutor now conducted them, talking with him about things more than teaching. There was a big illustrated book of Athenian pottery which Mrs. Moroney had said the boy used to enjoy and which the tutor had at the beginning, with no sort of result, tried to interest him in. Now Philip demanded it as the foundation of his lessons, delighting in the athletes, the warriors, the great gods, the battle pieces, the trussed-up sacrificial victims. He wanted them all explained and expanded, and it was noticeable to the tutor that he seemed to identify himself always with the most muscle-bound figure in any frieze. There was one plate that particularly fascinated, of a youth dancing, a heavily built young man who seemed to be stamping in a grinning triumph, wearing a helmet and greaves and shaking a spear. The boy didn't seem able to believe that he was dancing. "But he looks so fierce," he kept saying. "But he looks so fierce—" and then he added—"and happy."

"Is there any reason why dancing shouldn't be fierce—and happy?" the tutor asked, watching the boy's head bent in concentrated delight over the terra-cotta plate, as if he were retracing every line and stamping it on his memory. He was murmuring expressions of wonder and surprise as another boy might at an engine or an aeroplane. Finally he wound up with:

"Whew! That's something like dancing, isn't it?"

The wickets were put up again that evening. The boy bowled delightedly for three-quarters of an hour. As before, his bowling got faster and faster towards the end, but this time also wilder and wilder. The tutor thought it time to make an end. But Philip pleaded for one more over.

"Just six of my special, please!"

The tutor giving in to the plea, the boy went back for a slightly longer run, made a special show of ferocity, ran fast up to the wicket and then, instead of bowling, drew back his arm and threw the ball with all his strength straight at the tutor's head. The tutor ducked sharply and called out "Here, steady!" and when he recovered his balance, he saw that the boy was standing stock still, white in the face, as if scared out of his wits. Acting instinctively, the tutor made a joke of it.

"You'll have to be careful, young man, you don't know your own strength."

The boy was still standing uncertain and a bit dazed, as if he was horrified at what he had done; the ball had rebounded off the shed door and lay in the middle of the pitch; the tutor went over and picked it up and threw it to the boy, but he simply let it fall without moving.

"Come on, give me your six specials, but not as special as that last."

Philip turned round and put his hands in his pockets: "I don't want to play any more."

The tutor went and picked up the ball, took it across and forced it into the boy's hands. For the first time in a month he spoke with a firmness which wasn't to be denied: "You're going to take this and bowl me six more before we knock off. Here you are."

The tutor went back and took up his stance; he saw the boy walk back irresolutely and then lollop up to the wicket to bowl the feeblest kind of ball at him. But the second one was a little more in the boy's real style; the third quite in it; and, by the time he had bowled a couple of overs, he was back again in his best mood, self-confident, skilful and smilingly showing off. When they had finished, he ragged the tutor and began a fight with him. He escaped from his grasp and pranced across the lawn. He seized a stump and, holding it as a spear, imitated the young dancer on the Greek plate, stamping, twisting and turning, in a pirouette that was more violent than classical.

The tutor was surprised to find Mrs. Moroney in the drawing-room when he had packed the boy off to have a bath. She had come back early and turned towards him now from the window.

"I've been watching you two," she said coldly.

"But did you see him dance?" The tutor was too excited to notice her coolness.

"Dance?" She turned back to the window: "I saw him capering like a guttersnipe."

The tutor was dashed, but he persisted: "He's coming alive."

"He's getting very rough, I've noticed. Don't you think you indulge him too much? Personally I think you should start being a little stricter."

The tutor was young enough to find his temper insufficiently under control. He said nothing for a moment or two and then: "You gave me a free hand, you remember."

"Within reason," she now emended. "We don't want to turn him into a hooligan."

"You wanted him alive, and you didn't care how," he reminded her.

But she wasn't listening. "You didn't know Philip before," she continued with her thoughts. "So I suppose it's not unnatural for you to expect him to turn into any other noisy scrapping little boy. But Philip was never like that. Never. Even his father, who wouldn't have so much minded, recognized that. He takes after me."

The tutor considered that. He was wondering whether he should tell her about Philip's renewed interest in the Greek figures. But instead he spoke deliberately:

"If you started interfering, I don't know what would happen. I'm not sure that I know what will, if you don't. But I think it may be what you want."

"And what *do* you think I want?" she suddenly turned round to face him with.

"That he should be free—free from whatever it is that damped him down," the tutor tried to recall her to her original purpose.

"Fighting and throwing balls at people—is that the way you hope to do it?"

"Wait and see," he pleaded, catching up his temper in deference to a loyalty to the boy's interests. "Please wait and see."

"I'm not sure that I've quite the confidence that I had," she said going past him without looking him full in the face.

In the subsequent days Mrs. Moroney began throwing in her weight, and in so exasperating a manner that it became unbearable for the tutor. She nagged and fussed and interfered. She wanted to hear what they had been learning and criticized the choice. She made suggestions of her own as if she wanted now to enter their life on level terms. She took to playing on the piano, in the evenings, the pieces to which Philip had danced as a child and recalled, as she played, the way he had responded to them. She took to coming over in the mornings "to join in their reading" and suggested that she might reasonably be invited to accompany them on their walks. She was impervious both to the tutor's disapproval and to the boy's hostility, expressed now in a more active sentiment of dislike. He was no longer accepting her, and, if the hostility had not yet reached the stage of action or even of speech, it was abundantly clear to the tutor in looks and grimaces behind her back, in turnings away and sulky silences, in stampings and kickings when she had left.

The tutor was impossibly placed. If he was to be even superficially loyal to her, he couldn't be loyal to the boy; if he was to be loyal to the boy, he couldn't even superficially put up with her interference; and, as he felt committed to the boy's recovery, not hers, he worked himself more and more into a suppressed temper with her. So far was she from giving him his free hand, she was threatening to undo all he felt he had, even if unconsciously, done. He would have to have it out with her he felt one evening, after a particularly unnecessary piece of nagging at tea. She was really impossible; he'd have to tell her so straight. Her sensitiveness didn't evidently extend to other people's feelings: hints and indications were lost on her. There was only one thing to do and that was to have it straight out; and the cumulative effect of her general impossibility was to make him feel that having it out might well lead to a flaming row—and he really rather hoped it would; he knew what he would say.

He went downstairs thoroughly worked up for it. But he couldn't find her in the house. He went out into the garden and there, from one of the potting sheds, he heard sounds which drew his attention; it sounded as if someone was crying. It was a long dark shed, and when he came and stood at the side of the door, he made out his pupil at the far end, intent apparently on some private purpose which the tutor felt justified in watching. The boy's left arm was stretched out, holding something on the angle of a low shelf and the wall, and this something, the tutor, as his eyes became accustomed to the dark, saw to be a cat. The boy was holding it roughly by its neck and was forcing it down on its back while it cried and hissed and fought and whimpered. This was the crying that had drawn his attention and it was caused, he finally forced himself to realize, by the boy's holding in his right hand a lighted cigarette which he kept bringing up towards its face and eyes, so that he was singeing the fur.

The tutor's first and natural instinct to interfere was, for some reason that he had no time to analyse, held back. He was to justify it later by reminding himself that interference would have been Mrs. Moroney's immediate reaction, and it was therefore by definition wrong. But at the time he was simply stuck there, silent and gaping, and increasingly involved. It simply struck him that this playing of the cigarette up towards the cat's face wasn't enough; they must go further; it must really be hurt. So identified was he with the boy that he was sweating, as the boy must have been sweating, his head was buzzing, as the boy's must have been buzzing, he was working himself up as the boy was visibly working himself up, jabbing the cigarette nearer and nearer, until suddenly with a grunt he took the decision and plunged the glowing end into the soft neck. The cat squealed and the boy, letting go with his left hand, hit it, swinging off his balance; the terrified animal shrunk back, and in an onset of fury the boy hit at it with both hands till it streaked away, howling, down the shed and out of the door past the tutor. The boy was after it, throwing something—a flower pot—and he too dashed towards the door past the tutor who put out his arms and caught him into them. The child was shaking and breathing in quick violent snorts through his nostrils.

"Steady," said the tutor. "Steady. It's well away by now." . . . .

The boy struggled and panted and then sagged against the young man's arms, turning his back, still panting. The tutor not knowing what to say, said nothing; he just hoped by his grip on the boy's shoulders to communicate his own share in the guilt. They stood for some minutes like that, and then the tutor turned the boy round and giving his cheek a friendly slap said:

"Come on, let's go and have a bath before dinner."

The speed with which the child's moods could change had several times surprised the tutor. The boy insisted on his going and talking to him while he had his bath; and he chattered now and splashed and laughed as if he had no connection with the concentrated figure at the end of the long dark potting shed.

That night Mrs. Moroney, after dinner, went as usual to the piano.

This evening, the tutor noticed, the boy was not resisting. He was rest-less, his legs were moving, his hands fluttering; and then he got up and went out. Mrs. Moroney hadn't noticed, she went on playing. It was a mazurka, slavonic, romantic. The tutor was not yet quite reassured about the boy and he thought it best to keep an eye on him. Mrs. Moroney's special room was next door to the drawing room and it was in there that he found Philip. The music easily penetrated and the boy was standing in his steel-tipped shoes on the very centre of the sacred table; at the tutor's entrance he burst into a dance. It was the dance of the young warrior on the Attic plate; the boy was alive and grinning; he was triumphant. He spun and twisted, leapt and stamped, and the deli-cate surface of the wood tore and splintered; it creaked and cracked—but it held. The music was approaching its finale, and the dance—while the tutor simply watched—gathered strength and violence, until with the last chords, the boy attempted an *entrechat* and failed to come down in the centre of the table. As the music stopped he landed on one leaf which gave beneath his weight. He threw himself into the tutor's arms, panting and laughing and crying out:

"That was something like a dance, that was. That was something like a dance."

4

There was less awkwardness than there might have been about the tutor's departure—which took place the following day—because he made the arrangements exclusively with Mr. Moroney. Mrs. Moroney was, in the circumstances, remarkably restrained, but she was too grieved to act. Mr. Moroney's dash-in with a metaphorical uplifted cane had been intercepted by the tutor; he took the blame on himself and, quietly in the study, persuaded the husband that if the boy went back to school he would make a first-class left-handed bowler.

The good-bye between boy and tutor was quite unemotional; even, the tutor thought, a little surprisingly so. He felt at Philip's nonchalant "So long!" that he less than ever understood children. The boy talked all the way to the station about his school, his friends there, and the one particularly nice master who admired his bowling; he was dying to get back. The tutor stepped into his compartment and shut the door. The boy waited as the train gathered speed, and the last the tutor saw of him was a small sturdy figure with hands in pockets, apparently whistling a tune and idly kicking a piece of clinker.

In the following excerpt from Oliver Twist *Charles Dickens
displays, once again, an acute sensitivity to psychological
mechanisms. Here Fagin, using exactly the same methods of
catharsis and transference as Aichhorn, ironically teaches his
young charges to steal.*

CHARLES DICKENS

FROM *Oliver Twist*

Oliver reached the stile at which the by-path terminated; and once
more gained the high-road. It was eight o'clock now. Though he was
nearly five miles away from the town, he ran, and hid behind the hedges,
by turns, till noon: fearing that he might be pursued and overtaken.
Then he set down to rest by the side of the milestone, and began to
think, for the first time, where he had better go and try to live.

The stone by which he was seated, bore, in large characters, an in-
timation that it was just seventy miles from that spot to London. The
name awakened a new train of ideas in the boy's mind. London!— that
great large place!—nobody—not even Mr. Bumble—could ever find
him there! He had often heard the old men in the workhouse, too, say
that no lad of spirit need want in London; and that there were ways of
living in that vast city, which those who had been bred up in country
parts had no idea of. It was the very place for a homeless boy, who must
die in the streets unless some one helped him. As these things passed
through his thoughts, he jumped upon his feet, and again walked forward.

He had diminished the distance between himself and London by full
four miles more, before he recollected how much he must undergo ere
he could hope to reach his place of destination. As this consideration
forced itself upon him, he slackened his pace a little, and meditated
upon his means of getting there. He had a crust of bread, a coarse shirt,
and two pairs of stockings, in his bundle. He had a penny too—a gift of
Sowerberry's after some funeral in which he had acquitted himself more

than ordinarily well—in his pocket. 'A clean shirt,' thought Oliver, 'is a very comfortable thing; and so are two pairs of darned stockings; and so is a penny; but they are small helps to a sixty-five miles' walk in winter time.' But Oliver's thoughts, like those of most people, although they were extremely ready and active to point out his difficulties, were wholly at a loss to suggest any feasible mode of surmounting them; so, after a good deal of thinking to no particular purpose, he changed his little bundle over to the other shoulder, and trudged on.

Oliver walked twenty miles that day; and all that time tasted nothing but the crust of dry bread, and a few draughts of water, which he begged at the cottage-doors by the road-side. When the night came, he turned into a meadow; and, creeping close under a hay-rick, determined to lie there, till morning. He felt frightened at first, for the wind moaned dismally over the empty fields: and he was cold and hungry, and more alone than he had ever felt before. Being very tired with his walk, however, he soon fell asleep and forgot his troubles.

He felt cold and stiff, when he got up next morning, and so hungry that he was obliged to exchange the penny for a small loaf, in the very first village through which he passed. He had walked no more than twelve miles, when night closed again. His feet were sore, and his legs so weak that they trembled beneath him. Another night passed in the bleak damp air, made him worse; when he set forward on his journey next morning, he could hardly crawl along.

He waited at the bottom of a steep hill till a stage-coach came up, and then begged of the outside passengers; but there were very few who took any notice of him: and even those told him to wait till they got to the top of the hill, and then let them see how far he could run for a halfpenny. Poor Oliver tried to keep up with the coach a little way, but was unable to do it, by reason of his fatigue and sore feet. When the outsides saw this, they put their halfpence back into their pockets again, declaring that he was an idle young dog, and didn't deserve anything; and the coach rattled away and left only a cloud of dust behind.

In some villages, large painted boards were fixed up: warning all persons who begged within the district, that they would be sent to jail. This frightened Oliver very much, and made him glad to get out of those villages with all possible expedition. In others he would stand about the inn-yards, and look mournfully at every one who passed: a proceeding which generally terminated in the landlady's ordering one of the post-boys who were lounging about, to drive that strange boy out of the place, for she was sure he had come to steal something. If he begged at a farmer's house, ten to one but they threatened to set the dog on him; and when he showed his nose in a shop, they talked about the beadle—which brought Oliver's heart into his mouth,—very often the only thing he had there, for many hours together.

In fact, if it had not been for a good-hearted turnpike-man, and a benevolent old lady, Oliver's troubles would have been shortened by the very same process which had put an end to his mother's; in other words, he would most assuredly have fallen dead upon the king's highway. But the turnpike-man gave him a meal of bread and cheese; and the old lady, who had a shipwrecked grandson wandering barefoot in some distant part of the earth, took pity upon the poor orphan, and gave him what little she could afford—and more—with such kind and gentle words, and such tears of sympathy and compassion, that they sank deeper into Oliver's soul, than all the sufferings he had ever undergone.

Early on the seventh morning after he had left his native place, Oliver limped slowly into the little town of Barnet. The window-shutters were closed; the street was empty; not a soul had awakened to the business of the day. The sun was rising in all its splendid beauty; but the light only served to show the boy his own lonesomeness and desolation, as he sat, with bleeding feet and covered with dust, upon a door-step.

By degrees, the shutters were opened; the window-blinds were drawn up; and people began passing to and fro. Some few stopped to gaze at Oliver for a moment or two, or turned round to stare at him as they hurried by; but none relieved him, or troubled themselves to inquire how he came there. He had no heart to beg. And there he sat.

He had been crouching on the step for some time: wondering at the great number of public-houses (every other house in Barnet was a tavern, large or small), gazing listlessly at the coaches as they passed through, and thinking how strange it seemed that they could do, with ease, in a few hours, what it had taken him a whole week of courage and determination beyond his years to accomplish: when he was roused by observing that a boy, who had passed him carelessly some minutes before, had returned, and was now surveying him most earnestly from the opposite side of the way. He took little heed of this at first; but the boy remained in the same attitude of close observation so long, that Oliver raised his head, and returned his steady look. Upon this, the boy crossed over; and walking close up to Oliver, said,

'Hullo, my covey! What's the row?'

The boy who addressed this inquiry to the young wayfarer, was about his own age: but one of the queerest looking boys that Oliver had ever seen. He was a snub-nosed, flat-browed, common-faced boy enough; and as dirty a juvenile as one would wish to see; but he had about him all the airs and manners of a man. He was short of his age: with rather bow-legs, and little, sharp, ugly eyes. His hat was stuck on the top of his head so lightly, that it threatened to fall off every moment—and would have done so, very often, if the wearer had not had a knack of every now and then giving his head a sudden twitch, which brought it back to its old place again. He wore a man's coat, which reached nearly to his heels. He had turned the cuffs back, half-way up his arm, to get his hands out of the sleeves: apparently with the ultimate view of thrusting them into the pockets of his corduroy trousers; for there he kept them. He was, altogether, as roystering and swaggering a young gentleman as ever stood four feet six, or something less, in his bluchers.

'Hullo, my covey! What's the row?' said this strange young gentleman to Oliver.

'I am very hungry and tired,' replied Oliver: the tears standing in his eyes as he spoke. 'I have walked a long way. I have been walking these seven days.'

'Walking for sivin days!' said the young gentleman. 'Oh, I see. Beak's order, eh? But,' he added, noticing Oliver's look of surprise, 'I suppose you don't know what a beak is, my flash com-pan-i-on.'

Oliver mildly replied, that he had always heard a bird's mouth described by the term in question.

'My eyes, how green!' exclaimed the young gentleman. 'Why, a beak's a madgst'rate; and when you walk by a beak's order, it's not straight forerd, but always agoing up, and nivir a coming down agin. Was you never on the mill?'

'What mill?' inquired Oliver.

'What mill! Why, *the* mill—the mill as takes up so little room that it'll work inside a Stone Jug and always goes better when the wind's low with people, than when it's high acos then they can't get workmen. But come,' said the young gentleman; 'you want grub, and you shall have it. I'm at low-watermark myself—only one bob and a magpie; but, *as* far *as* it goes, I'll fork out and stump. Up with you on your pins There! Now then! Morrice!'

Assisting Oliver to rise, the young gentleman took him to an adjacent chandler's shop, where he purchased a sufficiency of ready-dressed ham and a half-quartern loaf, or, as he himself expressed it, 'a fourpenny bran!' The ham being kept clean and preserved from dust, by the ingenious expedient of making a hole in the loaf by pulling out a portion of the crumb, and stuffing it therein. Taking the bread under his arm, the young gentleman turned into a small public-house, and led the way to a tap-room in the rear of the premises. Here, a pot of beer was brought in, by direction of the mysterious youth; and Oliver, falling to, at his new friend's bidding, made a long and hearty meal, during the progress of which, the strange boy eyed him from time to time with great attention.

'Going to London?' said the strange boy, when Oliver had at length concluded.

'Yes.'

'Got any lodgings?'

'No.'

'Money?'

'No.'

The strange boy whistled; and put his arms into his pockets, as far as the big coat-sleeves would let them go.

'Do you live in London?' inquired Oliver.

'Yes. I do when I'm at home,' replied the boy. 'I suppose you want some place to sleep in to-night, don't you?'

'I do, indeed,' answered Oliver. 'I have not slept under a roof since I left the country.'

'Don't fret your eyelids on that score,' said the young gentleman. 'I've got to be in London to-night; and I know a 'spectable old genelman as lives there, wot'll give you lodgings for nothink, and never ask for the change—that is, if any genelman he knows interduces you. And don't he know me? Oh, no! Not in the least! By no means. Certainly not!'

The young gentleman smiled, as if to intimate that the latter fragments of discourse were playfully ironical; and finished the beer as he did so.

This unexpected offer of shelter was too tempting to be resisted; especially as it was immediately followed up, by the assurance that the old gentleman referred to, would doubtless provide Oliver with a comfortable place without loss of time. This led to a more friendly and confidential dialogue; from which Oliver discovered that his friend's name was Jack Dawkins, and that he was a peculiar pet and *protégé* of the elderly gentleman before mentioned.

Mr. Dawkins's appearance did not say a vast deal in favour of the comforts which his patron's interest obtained for those whom he took under his protection; but, as he had a rather flighty and dissolute mode of conversing, and furthermore avowed that among his intimate friends he was better known by the *sobriquet* of 'The Artful Dodger,' Oliver concluded that, being of a dissipated and careless turn, the moral precepts of his benefactor had hitherto been thrown away upon him. Under this impression, he secretly resolved to cultivate the good opinion of the old gentleman as quickly as possible; and, if he found the Dodger incorrigible, as he more than half suspected he should, to decline the honour of his farther acquaintance.

As John Dawkins objected to their entering London before night-fall, it was nearly eleven o'clock when they reached the turnpike at Islington. They crossed from the Angel into St. John's Road; struck down the small street which terminates at Sadler's Wells Theatre; through Exmouth Street and Coppice Row; down the little court by the side of the work-house; across the classic ground which once bore the name of Hockley-in-the-Hole; thence into Little Saffron Hill; and so into Saffron Hill the Great; along which the Dodger scudded at a rapid pace, directing Oliver to follow close at his heels.

Although Oliver had enough to occupy his attention in keeping sight of his leader, he could not help bestowing a few hasty glances on either side of the way, as he passed along. A dirtier or more wretched place he had never seen. The street was very narrow and muddy, and the air was impregnated with filthy odours. There were a good many small shops; but the only stock in trade appeared to be heaps of children, who, even at that time of night, were crawling in and out at the doors, or screaming from the inside. The sole places that seemed to prosper amid the general blight of the place, were the public-houses; and in them, the lowest order of Irish were wrangling with might and main. Covered ways and yards, which here and there diverged from the main street, disclosed little knots of houses, where drunken men and women were positively wallowing in filth; and from several of the door-ways, great ill-looking fellows were cautiously emerging, bound, to all appearance, on no very well-disposed or harmless errands.

Oliver was just considering whether he hadn't better run away, when they reached the bottom of the hill. His conductor, catching him by the arm, pushed open the door of a house near Field Lane; and, drawing him into the passage, closed it behind them.

'Now, then!' cried a voice from below, in reply to a whistle from the Dodger.

'Plummy and slam!' was the reply.

This seemed to be some watchword or signal that all was right; for the light of a feeble candle gleamed on the wall at the remote end of the passage; and a man's face peeped out, from where a balustrade of the old kitchen staircase had been broken away.

'There's two on you,' said the man, thrusting the candle farther out, and shading his eyes with his hand. 'Who's the t' other one?'

'A new pal,' replied Jack Dawkins, pulling Oliver forward.

'Where did he come from?'

'Greenland. Is Fagin upstairs?'

'Yes, he's a sortin' the wipes. Up with you!' The candle was drawn back, and the face disappeared.

Oliver, groping his way with one hand, and having the other firmly grasped by his companion, ascended with much difficulty the dark and broken stairs: which his conductor mounted with an ease and expedition that showed he was well acquainted with them. He threw open the door of a back-room, and drew Oliver in after him.

The walls and ceiling of the room were perfectly black with age and dirt. There was a deal table before the fire: upon which were a candle, stuck in a ginger-beer bottle, two or three pewter pots, a loaf and butter, and a plate. In a frying-pan, which was on the fire, and which was secured to the mantelshelf by a string, some sausages were cooking; and standing over them, with a toasting-fork in his hand, was a very old shrivelled Jew, whose villainous-looking and repulsive face was obscured by a quantity of matted red hair. He was dressed in a greasy flannel gown, with his throat bare; and seemed to be dividing his attention between the frying-pan and the clothes-horse, over which a great number of silk handkerchiefs were hanging. Several rough beds made of old sacks, were huddled side by side on the floor. Seated round the table were four or five boys, none older than the Dodger, smoking long clay pipes, and drinking spirits with the air of middle-aged men. These crowded about their associate as he whispered a few words to the Jew; and then turned round and grinned at Oliver. So did the Jew himself, toasting-fork in hand.

'This is him, Fagin,' said Jack Dawkins; 'my friend, Oliver Twist.'

The Jew grinned; and, making a low obeisance to Oliver, took him by the hand, and hoped he should have the honour of his intimate acquaintance. Upon this, the young gentlemen with the pipes came round him, and shook both his hands very hard—especially the one in which he held his little bundle. One young gentleman was very anxious to hang up his cap for him; and another was so obliging as to put his hands in his pockets, in order that, as he was very tired, he might not have the trouble of emptying them, himself, when he went to bed. These civilities would probably have been extended much farther, but for a liberal exercise of the Jew's toasting-fork on the heads and shoulders of the affectionate youths who offered them.

'We are very glad to see you, Oliver, very,' said the Jew. 'Dodger, take off the sausages; and draw a tub near the fire for Oliver. Ah, you're a-staring at the pocket-handkerchiefs! eh, my dear. There are a good many of 'em, ain't there? We've just looked 'em out, ready for the wash; that's all, Oliver; that's all. Ha! ha! ha!'

The latter part of this speech, was hailed by a boisterous shout from all the hopeful pupils of the merry old gentleman. In the midst of which they went to supper.

Oliver ate his share, and the Jew then mixed him a glass of hot gin-and-water: telling him he must drink it off directly, because another gentleman wanted the tumbler. Oliver did as he was desired. Immediately afterwards he felt himself gently lifted on to one of the sacks; and then he sunk into a deep sleep.

It was late next morning when Oliver awoke, from a sound, long sleep. There was no other person in the room but the old Jew, who was boiling some coffee in a saucepan for breakfast, and whistling softly to himself as he stirred it round and round, with an iron spoon. He would stop every now and then to listen when there was the least noise below: and when he had satisfied himself, he would go on, whistling and stirring again, as before.

Although Oliver had roused himself from sleep, he was not thoroughly awake. There is a drowsy state, between sleeping and waking, when you dream more in five minutes with your eyes half open, and yourself half conscious of everything that is passing around you, than you would in five nights with your eyes fast closed, and your senses wrapt in perfect unconsciousness. At such times, a mortal knows just enough of what his mind is doing, to form some glimmering conception of its mighty powers, its bounding from earth and spurning time and space, when freed from the restraint of its corporeal associate.

Oliver was precisely in this condition. He saw the Jew with his half-closed eyes; heard his low whistling; and recognised the sound of the spoon grating against the saucepan's sides: and yet the self-same senses were mentally engaged at the same time, in busy action with almost everybody he had ever known.

When the coffee was done, the Jew drew the sauce-pan to the hob.

Standing, then, in an irresolute attitude for a few minutes, as if he did not well know how to employ himself, he turned round and looked at Oliver, and called him by his name. He did not answer, and was to all appearance asleep.

After satisfying himself upon this head, the Jew stepped gently to the door: which he fastened. He then drew forth: as it seemed to Oliver, from some trap in the floor: a small box, which he placed carefully on the table. His eyes glistened as he raised the lid, and looked in. Dragging an old chair to the table, he sat down; and took from it a magnificent gold watch, sparkling with jewels.

'Aha!' said the Jew, shrugging up his shoulders, and distorting every feature with a hideous grin. 'Clever dogs! Clever dogs! Staunch to the last! Never told the old parson where they were. Never peached upon old Fagin! And why should they? It wouldn't have loosened the knot, or kept the drop up, a minute longer. No, no, no! Fine fellows! Fine fellows!'

With these, and other muttered reflections of the like nature, the Jew once more deposited the watch in its place of safety. At least half a dozen more were severally drawn forth from the same box, and surveyed with equal pleasure; besides rings, brooches, bracelets, and other articles of jewellery, of such magnificent materials, and costly workmanship, that Oliver had no idea, even of their names.

Having replaced these trinkets, the Jew took out another: so small that it lay in the palm of his hand. There seemed to be some very minute inscription on it; for the Jew laid it flat upon the table, and, shading it with his hand, pored over it, long and earnestly. At length he put it down, as if despairing of success; and leaning back in his chair, muttered:

'What a fine thing capital punishment is! Dead men never repent; dead men never bring awkward stories to light. Ah, it's a fine thing for the trade! Five of 'em strung up in a row, and none left to play booty, or turn white-livered!'

As the Jew uttered these words, his bright dark eyes, which had been staring vacantly before him, fell on Oliver's face; the boy's eyes were fixed on his in mute curiosity; and although the recognition was only for an instant—for the briefest space of time that can possibly be conceived —it was enough to show the old man that he had been observed. He closed the lid of the box with a loud crash; and, laying his hand on a bread knife which was on the table, started furiously up. He trembled very much though; for even in his terror, Oliver could see that the knife quivered in the air.

'What's that?' said the Jew. 'What do you watch me for? Why are you awake? What have you seen? Speak out, boy! Quick—quick! for your life!'

'I wasn't able to sleep any longer, sir,' replied Oliver, meekly. 'I am very sorry if I have disturbed you, sir.'

'You were not awake an hour ago?' said the Jew, scowling fiercely on the boy.

'No! No, indeed!' replied Oliver.

'Are you sure?' cried the Jew: with a still fiercer look than before: and a threatening attitude.

'Upon my word I was not, sir,' replied Oliver, earnestly. 'I was not, indeed, sir.'

'Tush, tush, my dear!' said the Jew, abruptly resuming his old manner, and playing with the knife a little, before he laid it down; as if to induce the belief that he had caught it up, in mere sport. 'Of course I know that, my dear. I only tried to frighten you. You're a brave boy. Ha! ha! you're a brave boy, Oliver.' The Jew rubbed his hands with a chuckle, but glanced uneasily at the box, notwithstanding.

'Did you see any of these pretty things, my dear?' said the Jew, laying his hand upon it after a short pause.

'Yes, sir,' replied Oliver.

'Ah!' said the Jew, turning rather pale. 'They—they're mine, Oliver; my little property. All I have to live upon, in my old age. The folks call me a miser, my dear. Only a miser; that's all.'

Oliver thought the old gentleman must be a decided miser to live in such a dirty place, with so many watches; but, thinking that perhaps his fondness for the Dodger and the other boys, cost him a good deal of money, he only cast a deferential look at the Jew, and asked if he might get up.

'Certainly, my dear, certainly,' replied the old gentleman. 'Stay. There's a pitcher of water in the corner by the door. Bring it here; and I'll give you a basin to wash in, my dear.'

Oliver got up; walked across the room; and stooped for an instant to raise the pitcher. When he turned his head, the box was gone.

He had scarcely washed himself, and made everything tidy, by emptying the basin out of the window, agreeably to the Jew's directions, when the Dodger returned: accompanied by a very sprightly young friend, whom Oliver had seen smoking on the previous night, and who was now formally introduced to him as Charley Bates. The four sat down, to breakfast, on the coffee, and some hot rolls and ham which the Dodger had brought home in the crown of his hat.

'Well,' said the Jew, glancing slyly at Oliver, and addressing himself to the Dodger, 'I hope you've been at work this morning, my dears?'

'Hard,' replied the Dodger.

'As Nails,' added Charley Bates.

'Good boys, good boys!' said the Jew. 'What have *you* got, Dodger?'

'A couple of pocket-books,' replied that young gentleman.

'Lined?' inquired the Jew, with eagerness.

'Pretty well,' replied the Dodger, producing two pocket-books; one green, and the other red.

'Not so heavy as they might be,' said the Jew, after looking at the insides carefully; 'but very neat and nicely made. Ingenious workman, ain't he, Oliver?'

'Very, indeed, sir,' said Oliver. At which Mr. Charles Bates laughed uproariously; very much to the amazement of Oliver, who saw nothing to laugh at, in anything that had passed.

'And what have you got, my dear?' said Fagin to Charley Bates.

'Wipes,' replied Master Bates; at the same time producing four pocket-handkerchiefs.

'Well,' said the Jew, inspecting them closely; 'they are very good ones, very. You haven't marked them well, though, Charley; so the marks shall be picked out with a needle, and we'll teach Oliver how to do it. Shall us, Oliver, eh? Ha! ha! ha!'

'If you please, sir,' said Oliver.

'You'd like to be able to make pocket-handkerchiefs as easy as Charley Bates, wouldn't you, my dear?' said the Jew.

'Very much indeed, if you'll teach me, sir,' replied Oliver.

Master Bates saw something so exquisitely ludicrous in this reply, that he burst into another laugh; which laugh, meeting the coffee he was drinking, and carrying it down the wrong channel, very nearly terminated in his premature suffocation.

'He is so jolly green!' said Charley when he recovered, as an apology to the company for his unpolite behaviour.

The Dodger said nothing, but he smoothed Oliver's hair over his eyes, and said he'd know better, by and by; upon which the old gentleman, observing Oliver's colour mounting, changed the subject by asking whether there had been much of a crowd at the execution that morning? This made him wonder more and more; for it was plain from the replies of the two boys that they had both been there; and Oliver naturally wondered how they could possibly have found time to be so very industrious.

When breakfast was cleared away; the merry old gentleman and the two boys played at a very curious and uncommon game, which was performed in this way. The merry old gentleman, placing a snuff-box in one pocket of his trousers, a note-case in the other, and a watch in his waistcoat pocket, with a guard-chain round his neck, and sticking a mock diamond pin in his shirt: buttoned his coat tight round him, and putting his spectacle-case and handkerchief in his pockets, trotted up and down the room with a stick, in imitation of the manner in which old gentlemen walk about the streets any hour in the day. Sometimes he stopped at the fire-place, and sometimes at the door, making believe that he was staring with all his might into shop-windows. At such times, he would look constantly round him, for fear of thieves, and would keep slapping all his pockets in turn, to see that he hadn't lost anything, in such a very funny and natural manner, that Oliver laughed till the tears ran down his face. All this time, the two boys followed him closely about: getting out of his sight, so nimbly, every time he turned round, that it was impossible to follow their motions. At last, the Dodger trod upon his toes, or ran upon his boot accidentally, while Charley Bates stumbled up against him; and in that moment they took from him, with the most extraordinary rapidity, snuff-box, note-case, watch-guard, chain, shirt-pin, pocket-handkerchief, even the spectacle-case. If the old gentleman felt a hand in any one of his pockets, he cried out where it was; and then the game began all over again.

When this game had been played a great many times, a couple of young ladies called to see the young gentlemen; one of whom was named Bet, and the other Nancy. They wore a good deal of hair, not very neatly turned up behind, and were rather untidy about the shoes and stockings. They were not exactly pretty, perhaps; but they had a great deal of colour in their faces, and looked quite stout and hearty. Being remarkably free and agreeable in their manners, Oliver thought them very nice girls indeed. As there is no doubt they were.

The visitors stopped a long time. Spirits were produced, in consequence of one of the young ladies complaining of a coldness in her inside; and the conversation took a very convivial and improving turn. At length, Charley Bates expressed his opinion that it was time to pad the hoof. This, it occurred to Oliver, must be French for going out; for, directly afterwards, the Dodger, and Charley, and the two young ladies, went away together, having been kindly furnished by the amiable old Jew with money to spend.

'There, my dear,' said Fagin. 'That's a pleasant life, isn't it? They have gone out for the day.'

'Have they done work, sir?' inquired Oliver.

'Yes,' said the Jew; 'that is, unless they should unexpectedly come across any, when they are out; and they won't neglect it, if they do, my dear, depend upon it. Make 'em your models, my dear. Make 'em your models,' tapping the fire-shovel on the hearth to add force to his words; 'do everything they bid you, and take their advice in all matters—especially the Dodger's, my dear. He'll be a great man himself, and will make you one too, if you take pattern by him.—Is my handkerchief hanging out of my pocket, my dear?' said the Jew, stopping short.

'Yes, sir,' said Oliver.

'See if you can take it out, without my feeling it: as you saw them do, when we were at play this morning.'

Oliver held up the bottom of the pocket with one hand, as he had seen the Dodger hold it, and drew the handkerchief lightly out of it with the other.

'Is it gone?' cried the Jew.

'Here it is, sir,' said Oliver, showing it in his hand.

'You're a clever boy, my dear,' said the playful old gentleman, patting Oliver on the head approvingly. 'I never saw a sharper lad. Here's a shilling for you. If you go on, in this way, you'll be the greatest man of the time. And now come here, and I'll show you how to take the marks out of the handkerchiefs.'

Oliver wondered what picking the old gentleman's pocket in play, had to do with his chances of being a great man. But, thinking that the Jew, being so much his senior, must know best, he followed him quietly to the table, and was soon deeply involved in his new study.

For many days Oliver remained in the Jew's room, picking the marks out of the pocket-handkerchiefs, (of which a great number were brought home,) and sometimes taking part in the game already described: which the two boys and the Jew played, regularly, every morning. At length, he began to languish for fresh air, and took many occasions of earnestly entreating the old gentleman to allow him to go out to work with his two companions.

Oliver was rendered the more anxious to be actively employed, by what he had seen of the stern morality of the old gentleman's character. Whenever the Dodger or Charley Bates came home at night, empty-handed, he would expatiate with great vehemence on the misery of idle and lazy habits; and would enforce upon them the necessity of an active life, by sending them supperless to bed. On one occasion, indeed, he even went so far as to knock them both down a flight of stairs; but this was carrying out his virtuous precepts to an unusual extent.

At length, one morning, Oliver obtained the permission he had so eagerly sought. There had been no handkerchiefs, to work upon, for two or three days, and the dinners had been rather meagre. Perhaps these were reasons for the old gentleman's giving his assent; but, whether they were or no, he told Oliver he might go, and placed him under the joint guardianship of Charley Bates, and his friend the Dodger.

The three boys sallied out; the Dodger with his coat-sleeves tucked up, and his hat cocked, as usual; Master Bates sauntering along with his hands in his pockets; and Oliver between them, wondering where they were going, and what branch of manufacture he would be instructed in, first.

The pace at which they went, was such a very lazy, ill-looking saunter, that Oliver soon began to think his companions were going to deceive the old gentleman, by not going to work at all. The Dodger had a vicious propensity, too, of pulling the caps from the heads of small boys and tossing them down areas; while Charley Bates exhibited some very loose notions concerning the rights of property, by pilfering divers apples and onions from the stalls of the kennel sides, and thrusting them into pockets which were so surprisingly capacious, that they seemed to undermine his whole suit of clothes in every direction. These things looked so bad, that Oliver was on the point of declaring his intention of seeking his way back, in the best way he could; when his thoughts were suddenly directed into another channel, by a very mysterious change of behaviour on the part of the Dodger.

They were just emerging from a narrow court not far from the open square in Clerkenwell, which is yet called, by some strange perversion of terms, 'The Green'; when the Dodger made a sudden stop; and, laying his fingers on his lip, drew his companions back again, with the greatest caution and circumspection.

'What's the matter?' demanded Oliver.

'Hush!' replied the Dodger. 'Do you see that old cove at the book-stall?'

'The old gentleman over the way?' said Oliver. 'Yes, I see him.'

'He'll do,' said the Dodger.

'A prime plant,' observed Master Charley Bates.

Oliver looked from one to the other, with the greatest surprise; but he was not permitted to make any inquiries; for the two boys walked stealthily across the road, and slunk close behind the old gentleman towards whom his attention had been directed. Oliver walked a few paces after them; and, not knowing whether to advance or retire, stood looking on in silent amazement.

The old gentleman was a very respectable-looking personage, with a powdered head and gold spectacles. He was dressed in a bottle-green coat with a black velvet collar; wore white trousers; and carried a smart bamboo cane under his arm. He had taken up a book from the stall, and there he stood, reading away, as hard as if he were in his elbow-chair, in his own study. It is very possible that he fancied himself there, indeed; for it was plain, from his abstraction, that he saw not the book-stall, nor the street, nor the boys, nor, in short, anything but the book itself: which he was reading straight through: turning over the leaf when he got to the bottom of a page, beginning at the top line of the next one, and going regularly on, with the greatest interest and eagerness.

What was Oliver's horror and alarm as he stood a few paces off, looking on with his eyelids as wide open as they would possibly go, to see the Dodger plunge his hand into the old gentleman's pocket, and draw from thence a handkerchief! To see him hand the same to Charley Bates; and finally to behold them, both, running away round the corner at full speed!

In an instant the whole mystery of the handkerchiefs, and the watches, and the jewels, and the Jew, rushed upon the boy's mind. He stood, for a moment, with the blood so tingling through all his veins from terror, that he felt as if he were in a burning fire; then, confused and frightened, he took to his heels; and, not knowing what he did, made off as fast as he could lay his feet to the ground.

This was all done in a minute's space. In the very instant when Oliver began to run, the old gentleman, putting his hand to his pocket, and missing his handkerchief, turned sharp round. Seeing the boy scudding away at such a rapid pace, he very naturally concluded him to be the depredator; and, shouting 'Stop thief!' with all his might, made off after him, book in hand.

But the old gentleman was not the only person who raised the hue-and-cry. The Dodger and Master Bates, unwilling to attract public attention by running down the open street, had merely retired into the very first doorway round the corner. They no sooner heard the cry, and saw Oliver running, than, guessing exactly how the matter stood, they issued forth with great promptitude and, shouting 'Stop thief!' too, joined in the pursuit like good citizens.

Although Oliver had been brought up by philosophers, he was not theoretically acquainted with the beautiful axiom that self-preservation is the first law of nature. If he had been, perhaps he would have been prepared for this. Not being prepared, however, it alarmed him the more; so away he went like the wind, with the old gentleman and the two boys roaring and shouting behind him.

'Stop thief! Stop thief!' There is a magic in the sound. The tradesman leaves his counter, and the car-man his wagon; the butcher throws down his tray; the baker his basket; the milk-man his pail; the errand-boy his parcels; the school-boy his marbles; the paviour his pickaxe; the child his battledore. Away they run, pell-mell, helter-skelter, slap-dash: tearing, yelling, screaming, knocking down the passengers as they turn the corners, rousing up the dogs, and astonishing the fowls: and streets, squares, and courts, re-echo with the sound.

'Stop thief! Stop thief!' The cry is taken up by a hundred voices, and the crowd accumulate at every turning. Away they fly, splashing through the mud, and rattling along the pavements: up go the windows, out run the people, onward bear the mob, a whole audience desert Punch in the very thickest of the plot, and, joining the rushing throng, swell the shout, and lend fresh vigour to the cry, 'Stop thief! Stop thief!'

'Stop thief! Stop thief!' There is a passion for *hunting something* deeply implanted in the human breast. One wretched breathless child, panting with exhaustion; terror in his looks: agony in his eyes; large drops of perspiration streaming down his face; strains every nerve to make head upon his pursuers; and as they follow on his track, and gain upon him every instant, they hail his decreasing strength with still louder shout, and whoop and scream with joy. 'Stop thief!' Ay, stop him for God's sake, were it only in mercy!

Stopped at last! A clever blow. He is down upon the pavement; and the crowd eagerly gather round him: each new comer, jostling and struggling with the others to catch a glimpse. 'Stand aside!' 'Give him a little air!' 'Nonsense! he don't deserve it.' 'Where's the gentleman?' 'Here he is, coming down the street.' 'Make room there for the gentleman!' 'Is this the boy, sir!' 'Yes.'

Oliver lay, covered with mud and dust, and bleeding from the mouth, looking wildly round upon the heap of faces that surrounded him, when the old gentleman was officiously dragged and pushed into the circle by the foremost of the pursuers.

'Yes,' said the gentleman, 'I am afraid it is the boy.'

'Afraid!' murmured the crowd. 'That's a good 'un!'

'Poor fellow!' said the gentleman, 'he has hurt himself.'

'*I* did that, sir,' said a great lubberly fellow, stepping forward; 'and preciously I cut my knuckle agin' his mouth. *I* stopped him, sir.'

The fellow touched his hat with a grin, expecting something for his pains; but, the old gentleman, eyeing him with an expression of dislike, looked anxiously round, as if he contemplated running away himself: which it is very possible he might have attempted to do, and thus have afforded another chase, had not a police officer (who is generally the last person to arrive in such cases) at that moment made his way through the crowd, and seized Oliver by the collar.

'Come, get up,' said the man, roughly.

'It wasn't me indeed, sir. Indeed, indeed, it was two other boys,' said Oliver, clasping his hands passionately, and looking round. 'They are here somewhere.'

'Oh, no, they ain't,' said the officer. He meant this to be ironical, but it was true besides; for the Dodger and Charley Bates had filed off down the first convenient court they came to. 'Come, get up!'

'Don't hurt him,' said the old gentleman, compassionately.

'Oh no, I won't hurt him,' replied the officer, tearing his jacket half off his back, in proof thereof. 'Come, I know you; it won't do. Will you stand upon your legs, you young devil?'

Oliver, who could hardly stand, made a shift to raise himself on his feet, and was at once lugged along the streets by the jacket-collar, at a rapid pace. The gentleman walked on with them by the officer's side; and as many of the crowd as could achieve the feat, got a little ahead, and stared back at Oliver from time to time. The boys shouted in triumph; and on they went.

2 · Religion

When Sigmund Freud wrote "The Future of an Illusion" he touched off a battle between psychoanalysis and religion that has been raging ever since. Freud looked at religion and saw it simply as a reflection of the child's relationship to his parents. Man's helpless nature, he said, leads him to create a protector, an all-powerful father who is omniscient and omnipresent. Like a real father this creation is both loved and feared, and submission to His will is a prerequisite for man's existence.

Unfortunately, in laying out his scheme Freud indicated that man's relationship to God, like his relationship to his parents, was often neurotic. Religion, in fact, was not only a fantasy projected from the mind of man, but it contained in its rituals all kinds of obsessional and destructive traits. Religion, Freud insisted, had not really succeeded in making men happier; it only served to confirm him in his neurotic beliefs. This being so, Freud suggested that man should relinquish the fantasy of God and seek elsewhere for happiness.

There were many good reasons why Freud should have seen religion in this particular light. His own strict upbringing and his relation to his father led him to project onto religion ideas that reflect simply his own subjective point of view.

Other analysts were not raised as Freud had been. Jung in particular was always aware of another power in man. Jung's own childhood visions had brought him into contact with religious experiences, and as a doctor, he frequently observed that his patients produced images with religious content. He concluded that man was by nature religious and that some neuroses could only be understood in terms of this regard for the religious or numinous principle. It was Jung *who began to explore the relationship between the symbolism of the unconscious and Christianity—as well as other religions. Jung's conclusions were the exact opposite of Freud's: he saw neurosis as a disturbance in the unconscious; this unconscious was not a* tabula rasa *but contained traces of evolutionary processes just as the body shows traces of its growth from fish to mammal. Jung saw the object of psychoanalysis as essentially spiritual in nature: it was to put men in touch once again with this life-giving source of energy which he called the archetype.*

Although current psychoanalytic theory tends to side largely with Freud in his analysis of religion as a projection of man's wishes, it also is less doctrinaire in dismissing the need for faith, and it is less optimistic than Freud who had hoped to find a substitute for religion in scientific theories.

*Jung's espousal of the religious or spiritual nature of man
did not make him any friendlier to dogma than was Sigmund
Freud. The church's unwillingness to reconcile the human
potential for evil with its potential for good had led, he believed, to a rejection of the basic principles of life. Evil as
represented by the devil is rejected. This unwillingness of the
church to recognize the power of unconscious forces as part
of human nature has been constantly thwarted by the church's
own visionaries. It is these mystics whom Jung celebrated.*

C. G. JUNG

Brother Klaus[1]

Before me lies a little book by Father Alban Stoeckli on the Visions
of the Blessed Brother Klaus.[2] Let the reader not be alarmed. Though a
psychiatrist takes up his pen, it does not necessarily mean that he is
going to set about this venerable figure with the profane instrument of
psychopathology. Psychiatrists have committed enough sins already and
have put their science to the most unsuitable uses. Nothing of the kind
is to happen here: no diagnosis or analysis will be undertaken, no significant hints of pathological possibilities will be dropped, and no attempt will be made to bring the Blessed Nicholas of Flüe anywhere near
a psychiatric clinic. Hence it must seem all the stranger to the reader
that the reviewer of the book is a physician. I admit this fact is difficult
to explain to anyone who does not know my unfashionable view on visions and the like. In this respect I am a good deal less sophisticated and
more conservative than the so-called educated public, whose philosophical perplexity is such that it sighs with relief when visions are equated
with hallucinations, delusional ideas, mania, and schizophrenia, or whatever else these morbid things may be called, and are reduced to the right
denominator by some competent authority. Medically, I can find nothing
wrong with Brother Klaus. I see him as a somewhat unusual but in no
wise pathological person, a man after my own heart: my brother Klaus.
Rather remote, to be sure, at this distance of more than four hundred

years, separated by culture and creed, by those fashionable trifles which we always think constitute a world. Yet they amount to no more than linguistic difficulties, and these do not impede understanding of the essentials. So little, in fact, that I was able to converse, in the primitive language of inward vision, with a man who in every way was even further removed from me than Brother Klaus—a Pueblo Indian, my friend Ochwiabiano ("Mountain Lake"). For what interests us here is not the historical personage, not the well-known figure at the Diet of Stans,[3] but the "friend of God," who appeared but a few times on the world stage, yet lived a long life in the realms of the soul. Of what he there experienced he left behind only scant traces, so few and inarticulate that it is hard for posterity to form any picture of his inner life.

It has always intrigued me to know what a hermit does with himself all day long. Can we still imagine a real spiritual anchorite nowadays, one who has not simply crept away to vegetate in misanthropic simplicity? A solitary fellow, like an old elephant who resentfully defies the herd instinct? Can we imagine a normal person living a sensible, vital existence by himself, with no visible partner?

Brother Klaus had a house, wife, and children, and we do not know of any external factors which could have induced him to become a hermit. The sole reason for this was his singular inner life; experiences for which no merely natural grounds can be adduced, decisive experiences which accompanied him from youth up. These things seemed to him of more value than ordinary human existence. They were probably the object of his daily interest and the source of his spiritual vitality. It sounds rather like an anecdote from the life of a scholar who is completely immersed in his studies when the so-called "Pilgrim's Tract"[4] relates: "And he [Brother Klaus] began to speak again and said to me, 'If it does not trouble you, I would like to show you my book, in which I am learning and seeking the art of this doctrine.' And he brought me a figure, drawn like a wheel with six spokes." So evidently Brother Klaus studied some mysterious "doctrine" or other; he sought to understand and interpret the things that happened to him. That the hermit's activity was a sort of study must also have occurred to Gundolfingen,[5] one of the oldest writers on our subject. He says: "Did he not likewise learn in that High School of the Holy Ghost the representation of the wheel, which he caused to be painted in his chapel, and through which, as in a clear mirror, was reflected the entire essence of the Godhead?" From the same "High School" he derived "his kindness, his doctrine, and his science."

Here we are concerned with the so-called Trinity Vision, which was of the greatest significance for the hermit's inner life. According to the oldest reports, it was an apparition of light, of surpassing intensity, in the form of a human face. The firsthand reports make no mention of a "wheel." This seems to have been a subsequent addition for the purpose of clarifying the vision. Just as a stone, falling into calm water, produces wave after wave of circles, so a sudden and violent vision of this kind has long-lasting after-effects, like any shock. And the stranger and more impressive the initial vision was, the longer it will take to be assimilated, and the greater and more persevering will be the efforts of the mind to master it and render it intelligible to human understanding. Such a vision is a tremendous "irruption" in the most literal sense of the word, and it has therefore always been customary to draw rings round it like those made by the falling stone when it breaks the smooth surface of the water.

Now what has "irrupted" here, and wherein lies its mighty "impression"? The oldest source, Wölflin's biography,[6] narrates the following on this score:

All who came to him were filled with terror at the first glance. As to the cause of this, he himself used to say that he had seen a piercing light resembling a human face. At the sight of it he feared that his heart would burst into little pieces. Overcome with terror, he instantly turned his face away and fell to the ground. And that was the reason why his face was now terrible to others.

This is borne out by the account which the humanist Karl Bovillus (Charles de Bouelles) gave to a friend in 1508 (some twenty years after the death of Brother Klaus):

I wish to tell you of a vision which appeared to him in the sky, on a night when the stars were shining and he stood in prayer and contemplation. He saw the head of a human figure with a terrifying face, full of wrath and threats.[7]

So we shall not go wrong in surmising that the vision was terrifying in the extreme. When we consider that the mental attitude of that age, and in particular that of Brother Klaus, allowed no other interpretation than that this vision represented God himself, and that God signified the *summum bonum,* Absolute Perfection, then it is clear that such a vision must, by its violent contrast, have had a profound and shattering effect, whose assimilation into consciousness required years of the most strenuous spiritual effort. Through subsequent elaboration this vision then became the so-called Trinity Vision. As Father Stoeckli rightly conjectures, the "wheel" or circles were formed on the basis of, and as parallels to, the illustrated devotional books that were read at the time. As mentioned above, Brother Klaus even seems to have possessed such a book himself. Later, as a result of further mental elaboration, there were added the spokes of the wheel and the six secondary circles, as shown in the old picture of the vision in the parish church at Sachseln.

The vision of light was not the only one which Brother Klaus had. He even thought that, while still in his mother's womb, he had seen a star that outshone all others in brightness, and later, in his solitude, he saw a very similar star repeatedly. The vision of light had, therefore, occurred several times before in his life. Light means illumination; it is an illuminating idea that "irrupts." Using a very cautious formulation, we could say that the underlying factor here is a considerable tension of psychic energy, evidently corresponding to some very important unconscious content. This content has an overpowering effect and holds the conscious mind spellbound. The tremendous power of the "objective psychic" has been named "demon" or "God" in all epochs with the sole exception of the recent present. We have become so bashful in matters of religion that we correctly say "unconscious," because God has in fact become unconscious to us. This is what always happens when things are interpreted, explained, and dogmatized until they become so encrusted with man-made images and words that they can no longer be seen. Something similar seems to have happened to Brother Klaus, which is why the immediate experience burst upon him with appalling terror. Had his vision been as charming and edifying as the present picture at Sachseln, no such terror would ever have emanated from it.

"God" is a primordial experience of man, and from the remotest times humanity has taken inconceivable pains either to portray this baffling experience, to assimilate it by means of interpretation, speculation, and dogma, or else to deny it. And again and again it has happened, and still happens, that one hears too much about the "good" God and knows him too well, so that one confuses him with one's own ideas and regards them as sacred because they can be traced back a couple of thousand years. This is a superstition and an idolatry every bit as bad as the Bolshevist delusion that "God" can be educated out of existence. Even a modern theologian like Gogarten[8] is quite sure that God *can only be good.* A good man does not terrify me—what then would Gogarten have made of the Blessed Brother Klaus? Presumably he would have had to explain to him that he had seen the devil in person.

And here we are in the midst of that ancient dilemma of how such visions are to be evaluated. I would suggest taking every genuine case at its face value. If it was an overwhelming experience for so worthy and shrewd a man as Brother Klaus, then I do not hesitate to call it a true and veritable experience of God, even if it turns out not quite right dogmatically. Great saints were, as we know, sometimes great heretics, so it is probable that anyone who has immediate experience of God is a little bit outside the organization one calls the Church. The Church itself would have been in a pretty pass if the Son of God had remained a law-abiding Pharisee, a point one tends to forget.

There are many indubitable lunatics who have experiences of God, and here too I do not contest the genuineness of the experience, for I know that it takes a complete and a brave man to stand up to it. Therefore I feel sorry for those who go under, and I shall not add insult to injury by saying that they tripped up on a mere psychologism. Besides, one can never know in what form a man will experience God, for there are very peculiar things just as there are very peculiar people—like those, for instance, who think that one can make anything but a conceptual distinction between the individual experience of God and God himself. It would certainly be desirable to make this distinction, but to do so one would have to know what God is in and for himself, which does not seem to me possible.

Brother Klaus's vision was a genuine primordial experience, and it therefore seemed to him particularly necessary to submit it to a thorough dogmatic revision. Loyally and with great efforts he applied himself to this task, the more so as he was smitten with terror in every limb so that even strangers took fright. The unconscious taint of heresy that probably clings to all genuine and unexpurgated visions is only hinted at in the Trinity Vision, but in the touched-up version it has been successfully eliminated. All the affectivity, the very thing that made the strongest impression, has vanished without a trace, thus affording at least a negative proof of our interpretation.

Brother Klaus's elucidation of his vision with the help of the three circles (the so-called "wheel") is in keeping with age-old human practice, which goes back to the Bronze Age sun-wheels (often found in Switzerland) and to the mandalas depicted in the Rhodesian rock-drawings. These sun-wheels may possibly be paleolithic; we find them in

Mexico, India, Tibet, and China. The Christian mandalas probably date back to St. Augustine and his definition of God as a circle. Presumably Henry Suso's notions of the circle, which were accessible to the "Friends of God," were derived from the same source. But even if this whole tradition had been cut off and no little treatise with mandalas in the margin had ever come to light, and if Brother Klaus had never seen the rose-window of a church, he would still have succeeded in working his great experience into the shape of a circle, because this is what has always happened in every part of the world and still goes on happening today.[9]

We spoke above of heresy. In Father Stoeckli's newly found fragment describing the vision, there is another vision which contains an interesting parallelism. I put the two passages side by side for the sake of comparison:

There came a handsome majestic man through the palace, with a shining colour in his face, and in a white garment. And he laid both arms on his shoulders and pressed him close and thanked him with all the fervent love of his heart, because he had stood by his son and helped him in his need.

There came a beautiful majestic woman through the palace, also in a white garment. . . . And she laid both arms on his shoulders and pressed him close to her heart with an overflowing love, because he had stood so faithfully by her son in his need.

It is clear that this is a vision of God the Father and Son, and of the Mother of God. The palace is heaven, where "God the Father" dwells, and also "God the Mother." In pagan form they are unmistakably God and Goddess, as their absolute parallelism shows. The androgynity of the divine Ground is characteristic of mystic experience. In Indian Tantrism the masculine Shiva and the feminine Shakri both proceed from Brahman, which is devoid of qualities. Man as the son of the Heavenly Father and Heavenly Mother is an age-old conception which goes back to primitive times, and in this vision the Blessed Brother Klaus is set on a par with the Son of God. The Trinity in this vision—Father, Mother, and Son—is very undogmatic indeed. Its nearest parallel is the exceedingly unorthodox Gnostic Trinity: God, Sophia, Christ. The Church, however, has expunged the feminine nature of the Holy Ghost, though it is still suggested by the symbolic dove.

It is nice to think that the only outstanding Swiss mystic received, by

God's grace, unorthodox visions and was permitted to look with unerring eye into the depths of the divine soul, where all the creeds of humanity which dogma has divided are united in *one* symbolic archetype. As I hope Father Stoeckli's little book will find many attentive readers, I shall not discuss the Vision of the Well, nor the Vision of the Man with the Bearskin, although from the standpoint of comparative symbolism they offer some very interesting aspects—for I do not want to deprive the reader of the pleasure of finding out their meaning by himself.

NOTES

[1] [In 1947 Nicholas of Flüe, "Bruder Klaus," was canonized by Pope Pius XII and declared patron saint of Switzerland.—EDITORS.]

[2] [*Die Visionen des seligen Bruder Klaus* (Einsiedeln, 1933).—EDITORS.]

[3] [The Diet of Stans was a meeting in 1481 of representatives of the Swiss cantons at which disputes between the predominantly rural and the predominantly urban cantons were regulated, and as a result of which—largely through the intervention of Nicholas—Fribourg and Solothurn became members of the Confederation. Cf. *Cambridge Medieval History*, VII, p. 210.—EDITORS.]

[4] *Ein nutzlicher und loblicher Tractat von Bruder Claus und einem Bilger* (Nürnberg, 1488). The actual author is anonymous, according to Robert Durrer, *Bruder Klaus.*

[5] Heinrich Gundolfingen (Gundelfingen or Gundelfinger), *c.* 1444–90, priest and professor of humanistic studies at the University of Fribourg, knew Klaus probably around the year 1480, and wrote his biography.

[6] Heinrich Wölflin, also called by the Latin form Lupulus, born 1470, humanist and director of Latin studies at Bern.

[7] *Ein gesichte Bruder Clausen ynn Schweytz und seine deutunge* (Wittenberg, 1528), p. 5. Cited in Stoeckli, p. 34.

[8] [Friedrich Gogarten (b. 1887), recently professor of systematic theology at Göttingen; author of *Die Kirche in der Welt* (1948).—EDITORS.]

[9] More on this in Zimmer, *Myths and Symbols in Indian Art and Civilization,* and Wilhelm, *The Secret of the Golden Flower,* together with my commentary.

Herbert Fingarette's discussion of the relation between the mystic steps toward self-forgetfulness and the process of psychoanalysis points up the startling similarities as well as the differences between these two ways of developing human potentiality. Though it is important to recognize that belief in God may simply be a projection of man's wishes and desires onto an all-powerful being, it is equally important for us to be aware of the psychic wisdom of religious systems that provide structured outlets for conflict. The idea of mystic selflessness and the concept of psychological maturity prove, on examination, to have much in common.

HERBERT FINGARETTE

Mystic Selflessness

FROM *The Self in Transformation*

The acceptance of guilt and the assumption of responsibility lead to a new mode of spiritual existence. We have seen that this involves a reorganization of psychic structure and function, a transformation of the Self and of the relationships with the world. In practice, only a limited area of life and of the psyche are thus transformed. There are always unexplored areas remaining into which one could, at least in principle, extend the arena of insight, responsibility, and transformation. Moreover, the phaselike retrogression and progression of the "working-through" process is a lengthy and yet a necessary labor if the areas already opened up are to be made secure and if they are to be cultivated so that the new roots grow deep. Psychoanalysis, as Freud said, is terminated in practice but is interminable in principle.[1] And so it is with all spiritual knowledge and transformation. . . .

From the standpoint of his own personal achievement rather than communication with others or helping them, the central task of the mystic is that of achieving an unusually strong ego within an unusually well-integrated personality. This implies maximal ego-autonomy and neutralization of drives, and it implies minimal conflict, anxiety, and defense. If, for the moment, we consider the self to be the same as character in Reich's[2] sense—the relatively enduring defensive "armor" —then the mystic aims at minimal defensive-armor and hence the "death" of such a self. The process of achieving a mature personality with an extreme minimum of defensive character armor ordinarily involves major (and stormy) personality reorganization. The soul-racking death which leads to blissful "rebirth" is the death of the subjectively experienced, anxiety-generated "self" perception; it is the emergence into the freedom of introspective "self-forgetfulness" of the psychically unified self.

It is now appropriate to test the metapsychological hypotheses presented up to this point by developing their implications and determining whether they are consistent with a reasonably broad sample of the language and phenomena of mysticism. Such an examination will show, I believe, the validity of these suggestions. It will also reveal the need for important amplifications of the psychological analysis. These amplifications will, in effect, show how the more traditional psychoanalytic interpretations of mysticism are to be integrated with the present one to form a more comprehensive view in which the interrelations of ego and id are exhibited.

. . . [Both the psychoanalytic patient] and the mystic are trying to express that introspected difference in the quality of experience correlated with the metapsychological shift from anxiety and defense to sublimation and ego-syntonic experience. On this basis one can see the naturalness of denying any "striving." The very word "compulsion," used by Freud in connection with characteristic symptoms of defense against anxiety, is of a piece with such words as "bondage," "attachment," "striving." This peculiar subjective sense of pressure, of need, of not-to-be-brooked desire is in sharp contrast to the subjective experience associated with anxiety-free cathexes. The latter we naturally express as "freedom," especially freedom of inner initiative ("free will"). We have here an experience which, as Knight points out,[3] needs to be distinguished carefully from the deceptive subjective sense of "freedom" associated with certain other types of psychological conditions. This deceptive sense of "freedom" occurs in the child during flights of fantasy; it is also reported by the person who, unconsciously driven by intense defiance, carries out criminal, libertinist, or other spurious acts of "independence." I call this a deceptive sense of freedom because freedom includes much more than merely subjective feelings. Furthermore, it is possible, though not easy, to distinguish introspectively the genuine subjective experience of freedom from the spurious one.

For the child and the neurotically rebellious person to be able to introspect the distinction between the "mature" and the "immature" subjective sense of freedom requires, as we know, long and arduous self-exploration and self-transformation. Nevertheless, from the theoretician's and the trained observer's standpoint, the distinction can be made relatively easily with the aid of the appropriate psychological distinctions and techniques. "Absence of anxiety, of irrational doubt, and of those inhibitions and restrictions which paralyze both choice and action"[4] are the negative indicators of the mature sense of freedom. The ability to make effective, ego-syntonic choices is among the positive criteria.

For the relatively mature person, minor decisions are made with an unqualified subjective sense of freedom. In connection with weighty decisions in life, there is the more complex feeling that one is free and yet that, in terms of one's integrity, "one can do no other."[5]

This latter point of Knight's, and our own discussion of choice . . . show that the subjective experience of one who is psychologically mature is naturally described in terms of the mystic paradox of complete freedom coexisting with utter passivity. As a person of thoroughgoing psychological integrity, it is true that "one can do no other"; but in thus doing, while not consciously concerned with "self," one gives expression to a unified and accepted self, an undivided and effective will. "The truth is that the more ourselves we are, the less self is in us."[6] This is precisely the way "emotionally mature, well-integrated persons" feel their activity to be.[7]

Mature individuals, says Knight, have achieved a harmonious integration of the instinctual drives, the superego standards and restrictions, the ego perceptions and discriminative faculties, and the real possibilities offered by the environment.[8] Thus they are at once perceptive and yet, as was noted earlier, "self-forgetful." "Desire flows into the mind of the seer, but he is never disturbed."[9]

In describing generally those who have failed to achieve such an ideally strong ego and well-integrated personality, Knight's language is sharply reminiscent of the language of the Eastern mystics when they talk about *maya* and *samsara*, the world of birth-and-death in which the unenlightened live. Persons who have failed to achieve such harmonious integration, says Knight, meet with obstacles whose nature they do not understand (ignorance), or they are driven by "intense defiance or greed or hostile impulses."[10] Ignorance, pride, lust, and hatred—here is the universally acknowledged "syndrome" associated by mystics with the disease of self-ishness. The psychoanalytic explanation of neuroses is analogous. Unsublimated libido and aggression (lust, hatred, and greed) result in distorted, fantasy-colored experiences ("ignorance," "illusion"). The general traits of self-ishness and conflictful experience thus being established as parallel, it now is appropriate to consider more specific notions found in mysticism.

"Freedom from striving" and "acceptance," key notions of the mystic, are often misinterpreted to mean systematic refusal to take the initiative, consistent absence of goals of any sort, submissiveness. This the unenlightened read into the words in spite of the evidence before their eyes that those who best exemplify mystic enlightenment are people who obviously do take the initiative, who clearly execute well-organized, purposive behavior, and who have indeed modified the world. The misinterpretation is encouraged by the fact that, not uncommonly, those who are *trying to achieve* enlightenment go through a phase of submissiveness.

In order to obviate this particular misunderstanding the mystic must eventually qualify his remarks. He must confess that he *does* have desires and does not merely "submit." He thus admits that the natural way of expressing the matter is unfortunately ambiguous. His language originally suggests a *loss*, an absence, a "giving up." He now tries to suggest that the aspect of his experience in question involves neither sense of presence nor of loss, neither a sense of striving *nor* of surrender. Hence he says that, in truth, what he speaks of is *beyond* "desire" or "no-desire"; it is beyond "freedom" or "bondage." What he really wishes to express is the fact that feelings of these kinds, one way or another, simply do not exist. He tries, tentatively, to speak of Nothingness[11] or *Sunyata*. Yet to speak of *Nothingness* suggests mere emptiness or absence—a gap. Yet life, in truth, is *full*. Worst of all: in the moment of speaking of experience "beyond desire," he lies, for in order to make the point he must make reference to the category of desire and thus he is no longer "beyond" desire!

If only the audience would *see*—there is only one way of taking his language consistently with the facts. But, of course, the audience does not, *will not,* see. Like the patient in psychoanalytic therapy, the mystic's disciple, too, must be ready for the insight or else the interpretation will meet not merely with blank ignorance but with positive resistance. The context of anxiety is then substituted, and all the words are taken in a foolish, paradoxical, or positively hurtful sense.

The mystic says:

> When striving and gaining are balanced, nothing remains,
> Aimless striving is quite different. . . .[12]

In the same spirit the psychoanalyst says: defensive equilibria consist of pitting one set of inner demands against another, thus warding off dangerous impulses by an inner stalemate. Such equilibria are basically self-defeating; they produce ever higher levels of tensions. Ego-syntonic activity is "quite different"—it is genuinely gratifying. The "aimlessness" of the mystic thus refers always to the absence of *inner* aims, i.e., the aims of repression. The mystic language is a language of subjective experience—it does not have to do in the first instance with "external" aims, obviously an inevitable part of life. The confusion arises because our "external" aims—jobs, love conquests, cars—are so often the rationalizations of inner defensive aims. It is in the latter sense of "aim" that the enlightened are aimless. Thus the mystic may well acknowledge that he enjoys food, friends, kindred, honor, and comfort provided he is not anxiously dependent upon them, unable to cope with their opposites.[13] Thus, in a fundamental sense aimless and open to experience, the enlightened pursue and enjoy whatever concrete aims seem appropriate.

Closely related to the absence of striving, of aimlessness, are the phenomena which the mystic describes as "no-discrimination," "no-perception," "no-sensation," "no-thought." If our hypothesis is correct, we should expect that what he is denying is the compulsive, obsessive, acutely self-conscious focusing of attention upon our feelings and our perceptions, our theoretical distinctions and logical proofs. What the mystic decries is, in terms of the psychological conditions which are associated with it, the neurotic drive to achieve security by fitting all experience into a firm, clear, and neat logical system within which one can then manipulate the elements in an absolutely regularized way.

On the other hand, according to our psychological analysis, we should expect that sensing, perceiving, thinking, discriminating are essential functions within the enlightened life, but that they are used unselfconsciously, uncompulsively, and flexibly in accordance with the integrity of the individual and the demands of the real environmental situation. They are *used*; they do not dominate.

> [The enlightened] use their sense organs when occasion requires,
> But the concept of "using" does not arise.[14]

Consistent with our inference is the mystic's statement that enlightened meditation is "[observing] things in the phenomenal world, yet [dwelling] in emptiness." Perception *is* present, but it comes as it will to a mind that is "empty," i.e., without compulsive, stereotyped modes of perceiving and thinking.

One way of putting the matter is in terms of the Buddhist notion of "abiding." It is the (neurotically rigid) abiding with specific thoughts or sensations that is the mark of the unenlightened.

> In action Prajna [the wisdom of enlightenment] is everywhere present, yet it "sticks" nowhere. What we have to do is to so purify the mind that the six aspects of consciousness (sight, sound, smell, taste, touch, mentation) in passing through their six sense-gates will neither be defiled by nor attached to their six sense-objects. . . . *To refrain from thinking of anything, in the sense that all mental activity is suppressed, is to be Dharma-ridden; this is an extremely erroneous view.*[15] [Italics added]

To suppose that Nirvana is the "mere stopping of discrimination" is to commit the error typical of the philosopher (who takes everything in its abstract, theoretical sense) as distinguished from the person with genuine mystic insight.[16]

The previous discussion makes it clear—and it is consistent with our psychoanalytic theses—that when we speak of enlightenment, we are not talking of an existence divorced from the "everyday world." On the contrary, it consists of life within this world. Zen, says one of the great Zen masters, "is your everyday mind."[17] "Birth-and-death (i.e., our everyday world) and Nirvana are not separate from one another."[18]

> This world is the Buddha-world
> Within which enlightenment may be sought.
> To seek enlightenment by separating from this world
> Is as foolish as to search for a rabbit's horn.[19]

At the same time we confidently infer from the psychological analysis what mystic literature also suggests at times: that so far as the subjective feel of life goes, there is in some sense a "world" of difference between that of enlightenment and that of birth-and-death. How can one distinguish the subtle but profound difference between these "worlds" in terms of a subjective language? This difference may be reported as, for example, action in which one "remains poised in the tranquility of the Atman."[20] It is an "inner light" which does not flicker while the every-day life goes on.[21] It is that engagement in the world of joys and sorrows which Eckhart compares with the door which swings back and forth while the hinge at the center remains fixed and solid.[22] It is the life of the Bodhisattvas who are "joyous in heart but ever grieved over the sight of suffering beings. . . ."[23] It is the "inner stillness" which is the "joy of Brahman, which words cannot express and the mind cannot reach . . . free from fear."[24] It is "the inaction that is in action."[25] It transforms the experienced world with its coming. In the poetic language of Indian mysticism,

> . . . there will be music; not only music made by human lips and played by human hands on various instruments, but there will be music among the grass and shrubs and trees, and in mountains and towns and palaces and hovels; much more will there be music in the hearts of those endowed with sentiency.[26]

In Knight's more prosaic clinical terminology, the free man is one with "feelings of well-being, of self-esteem, of confidence, of inner satisfaction based on successful use of one's energies for achievement that promotes the best interests of one's fellow men as well as one's own."[27] This language is a remarkable parallel to another expressive mystic report which I shall now quote. I trust the reader will tolerate my esthetically inexcusable interpolations.

> Free from the domination of words you will be able to establish your-selves where there will be a "turning about" in the deepest seat of consciousness by means of which you will attain self-realisation of Noble Wisdom and be able to enter into all the Buddha-land and assemblies. There you will be stamped with the stamp of the powers, self-command, the psychic faculties, and will be endowed with wisdom and the power of the ten inexhaustible vows. . . . There you will shine without effort like the moon, the sun, the magic wishing-jewel, and at every stage will view things as being of perfect oneness with yourself, uncontaminated by any self-consciousness. Seeing that all things are like a dream [i.e., seeing that your life has been lived until now in the neurotic fan-

tasy-world] you will be able to enter into the stage of the Tathagatas and be able to deliver discourses on the Dharma to the world of beings in accordance with their needs [i.e., in the manner of therapeutic interventions or the well-timed advice of the wise layman rather than formal lectures or general theories] and be able to free them from all dualistic notions and false discriminations.[28]

We know that neither Knight nor the writer of the Lankavatara Sutra intend us to understand that the enlightened one is a "self-satisfied," neurotically dedicated "do-gooder." We know that for the one who seeks enlightenment to "hold in his mind any arbitrary conceptions about kindness"[29] would be a gross mistake. "Kindness, after all, is only a word and charity should be spontaneous and self-less."[30] Put negatively and in psychoanalytic terms, doing well by others is not the outcome of a moralistic program of "altruistic" action rationalizing narcissism or other neurotic gratifications. Likewise the *thought* that one has attained "Highest Perfect Wisdom" or that one is on the way there is evidence that one is *mistaken*. One who *is* confident does not have a conscious feeling of confidence; one who is wise does not consciously think to himself that he is wise. Those who have such thoughts or feelings reveal that, perturbed by anxiety and doubts, they have had to react with reassurances to themselves.

The enlightened one is, therefore, not only an unassuming and "ordinary" person (as well as an extraordinary one), he is in many ways "more ordinary" than most people. He is not overly proud, not driven by ambition, not prone to keeping up with the Joneses, not given to disingenuous logical or theoretical disquisitions. He tends to shun words. He suffers, enjoys, knows pain and pleasure, but he is not driven and dominated by these. Sensual without being sensualist, he is also aware of his ills without being hypochondriacal. "He does not call attention to himself."[31]

At the same time there are ways in which he clearly stands apart: "I alone am dark . . . blown adrift . . . intractable and boorish."[32] Such a person does not always quite fit because, while he may often conform, he is not a conformist. He will even at times appear "ruthless."[33] For when the ordinary ways conflict with his own integrity, when realism calls for breaking through sentimentality, when life has shattered the old façades, he acts accordingly. His ruthlessness is kindliness in the same way as the parent's realistic discipline may be kinder than a guilt-motivated "permissiveness."

In the last analysis, then, the mystic way is a "simple" and "obvious" way—for those who will open their eyes. For the mystic experience is not the achievement of any finally fixed state of mind or any universal doctrine at all. It is the liberation from neurotic fixation and dogma of all kinds.

> Right views are called "transcendental,"
> Erroneous views are called "worldly,"
> But when all views, both right and erroneous, are discarded,
> Then the essence of Wisdom manifests itself.[34]

This is the emptiness of a mind which is thoroughly open to the world. As Hui-neng says, it is the "voidness" which can be filled.[35] It is not mere "vacuity" or idealessness. Bergson has spoken in this connection of the "open soul."[36]

Dwelling in such a (psychic) "emptiness," our life is full, but not full of our repetitive fantasies. It is pervaded by an elusive but profound sense of joy. How natural then to express this pervasive "peace" as an aspect of the presence of God. But then God becomes the "atmosphere" of life rather than an object within life. " 'God,' said St. Augustine, 'is the Country of the soul'; 'its Home,' says Ruysbroeck."[37] The mystic God is "nothingness" in the sense that God is not an object of contemplation; He is the realm within which all objects exist. It is Emptiness which, in Christian language, appears as the "poverty of the spirit" which is an ultimate joy. Poverty here is not to be identified with asceticism or moral masochism; it is absence of pretense, absence of anxious dependence or "clinging," "openness" to life. God is perceived as a radical "inner stillness." The psychological condition of this perception is, according to our hypothesis, the growth of personality beyond anxiety and intrapsychic conflict to primarily conflict-free integrity.

> One must achieve this unself-consciousness by means of transformed knowledge. *This* ignorance does not come from lack of knowledge but rather it is from knowledge that one may achieve this ignorance.[38]

Eckhart here means to distinguish, on the one hand the naïveté of the unsocialized child, or of the neurotic who *will* not learn, and on the other hand the humility and spontaneity of the person who uses his learned skills and his knowledge as a means of *meeting* life in its novelty instead of insisting that life conform to his stereotyped nursery fantasies.

To achieve this simplicity is, as we know, the most arduous struggle, the most radical and intricate operation which we need to perform in our lives. "The Great Way is right before your eye, but difficult to see."[39]

It follows from the thesis we have presented that there are likely to be significant similarities between the ways in which the mystic and the psychoanalytic patient achieve "enlightenment." To review this aspect of the matter briefly will help illuminate and validate our theses. As I have said before, there are, of course, substantial differences between the mystic and psychoanalytic "ways." However, with the exception of the last portions of this chapter, I am concerned with stressing the similarities.

Lao-tse says:

> *Yet by seizing on the way that was*
> *You can ride the things that are new.*
> *For to know what once there was, in the Beginning,*
> *This is called the essence of the Way.*[40]

The literal meaning of Lao-tse's term translated above as "essence" is "main-thread." One could not put Freud's views better than to say that the main-thread by means of which one masters the present is the thread which leads to the past. We cannot do more than note here that the Chinese reference to the past has a double meaning which parallels Freud's treatment of the psychologically significant past. For Lao-tse refers in his verse both to the archetypal or archaic past and to the past of the individual's personal history.

Freud provides us with detailed classifications of the various typical roots of our present psychic troubles. The mystic, however, usually provides us either with very concrete, personal, and hence idiosyncratic accounts, or else he offers very broad but suggestive generalizations. The mystic's fundamental generalizations are remarkably reminiscent of some of Freud's basic postulates. Hui-neng tells us that

> *When neither hatred nor love disturb the mind,*
> *Serene and restful is our sleep.*[41]

We know from Freud that the image is perfectly apt. Provided one interprets "hatred" and "love" as unsublimated aggressive and libidinal instinctual drives, one hardly needs to change a word to consider the verse as a basic psychological truth. Likewise we could consider the following verse in the Bhagavad-Gita as an almost word for word analysis, according to Freud, of the roots of neurotic self-deception in current unresolved libidinal and aggressive conflicts and the unconscious fantasies connected with them:

> *When a man lacks lust and hatred,*
> *His renunciation does not waver.*
> *He neither longs for one thing*
> *Nor loathes its opposite:*
> *The chains of his delusion*
> *Are soon cast off.*[42]

The total picture that we get of the state of existence of man prior to entering upon the path of Enlightenment is expressed in the great Eastern image of the wheel of birth-and-death. Lust, anger, and ignorance bind man ever more tightly to the wheel of suffering. This is the very model of the self-harassed and self-driven neurotic.

How can we control such behavior? More important yet, how can we break away from the wheel entirely? The Buddhist formula is threefold. At the most primitive level, the rules of morality, if strictly adhered to, help to prevent *actions* leading to bad Karma. As a second step, mental and moral concentrated effort help to *suppress* the *thoughts* and *feelings* which lie behind such actions. But to get to the root, to eradicate the source of such thoughts, feelings, and actions, what is needed is insight. It is, in practice, the proper concurrent use of all three which can lead, step by step, to broader and deeper insight with eventual liberation from the wheel.[43] *Perfect* enlightenment seems to be a mythic ideal in mysticism. The ever-present potential in real life for still further deepening insight is expressed in the concept of the stages of enlightenment.

This picture of successive rebirths in Samsara eventuating ideally in release from Karma and the achievement of Nirvana is a wonderful image which parallels in the essential psychological aspects the process of psychoanalytic therapy. We start with neurotic behavior and experience (Samsara). The neurotic, motivated by unresolved instinctual conflict (lust and anger), unwittingly ignorant, creates his own half fantasy experience (the illusory world of Maya). This world provides temporary gratification at the cost of increasing enslavement to the very anxieties and conflicts which are so painful. Thus the neurotic is ever more tightly bound to the wheel. Social codes, repressions, and suppression can, however, keep the actions and thoughts within some control. But the move toward maturity requires insight. Yet psychoanalytic insight takes place not in a vacuum or all at once: it proceeds (ideally) by limited and partial insights in a setting of substantial social conformity (no acting-out) and continuing suppression and repression (no "wild analysis"; careful timing and dosage in therapeutic interventions). The "complete" analysis is a theoretical ideal ("Buddha-hood"). As for the "medium" within which enlightening communication takes place:

> . . . the way of instruction presented by the Tathagatas is not based on assertions and refutations by means of words and logic. . . .[44]
>
> If I should tell you that I had a system of Dhyana to transmit to others, I would be deceiving you. What I try to do to my disciples, is to liberate them from their own bondage, by such devices as each case requires. . . .[45]
>
> As circumstances arise, [the enlightened] take appropriate action; they give suitable answers according to the varying temperaments of their questioner.[46]

That is to say, liberation is achieved as a way of life and by means of "pragmatic," not theoretical communication, communication oriented to the immediate context and the particular person. It is not a question of proving or disproving theories. Likewise, the psychoanalytic therapist, as a *therapist*, is not primarily concerned with establishing the truth of some general theory; he is concerned to provide specific interventions which enable the patient to *undergo the experience* with concurrent insight.

When Hui-neng says that "they give suitable answers," he is speaking of responding "therapeutically," not of giving the person directions as to how to live his life. Tai-tz'u Huang-chung, the Zen teacher, said: "I do not know how to make answers; I only know where diseases are."[47] This is analogous to the analyst's task which, according to Freud, is to "unmask the roots," not "to play the part of prophet, saviour, and redeemer to the patient . . . but to give the patient's ego *freedom* to choose one way or the other."[48] (And the parallel to the later teachings of Wittgenstein is evident to those familiar with the latter.)

The manner of the psychoanalyst is, ideally, that of the Bodhisattva: one "who practice[s] compassion but [is not given up to petty kindness

. . .] practice[s] indifference but never cease[s] benefitting others."[49] This is a clear description of important aspects of the ideal therapeutic relationship.

The actual occasion of insight (out of which decisions flow spontaneously) involves a peculiar shifting of mental gears, as it were.

Suzuki says: "In our religious life, passivity comes as the culmination of strenuous activity; passivity without this preliminary condition is sheer inanity. . . ."[50]

The activity leading up to enlightenment is imbued with a "spirit of inquiry" requiring that we pursue the advice of the master: "Ask of your self, inquire into your self, pursue your self, investigate within your self. . . ."[51]

At the moment preceding *satori*, the Zen enlightenment, we are like a man at the "edge of a precipice."[52] It is a moment of uneasiness, despair, death. At this point, by "letting go," the disciple is awakened as from a stupor.

The characteristic terms for this moment of enlightenment are "one bursting cry," "the bursting of the bag," "a sudden snapping," "a sudden bursting," and so on.[53] It is difficult to avoid recalling the comparable phrases used to characterize insight experience in Western terminology, phrases such as the "Aha! experience," or, in the simple formula of Greenson's patient, "Bong!"[54]

The sense of passive receptiveness in the ultimate phase of mystic enlightenment appears to occur characteristically in all the mystics.[55]

From the psychoanalytic side, Kris[56] has discussed the relation between insight and passivity at length, and he concludes one such discussion by asserting that

The maturing of thought, the entry into awareness from preconsciousness to consciousness tend to be experienced as derived from outside, as passively received, not as actively produced. The tendency toward passive reception takes various shapes and forms, appears under the guise of various modalities, but the subjective experience remains one of reception.[57]

Kris holds that in the creative solution of problems as distinguished from mere fantasy gratification, there is a feeling of satisfaction as well as mere relief.

We might amplify slightly as follows. The "letting go" is the cessation of defensive "striving." The joy is associated psychologically with the sudden availability of the energy previously expended in the repressive process, energy which is now freed by the "creative" solution of the problem but would not be by a neurotic "solution." In the neurotic "solution" the diminished anxiety accounts for the sense of relief, but there is no "joy" because the neurotic solution requires the energies of repressive countercathexes.

This combination of felt passivity and heightened joy at the moment of insight is a characteristic mark of mystic enlightenment. This, as a part of the characteristic behavior and affect patterns of the mystic, is important evidence that the mystic enlightenment of which we speak is, psychologically, a creative solution of a problem rather than merely regressive fantasy gratification.

Kris, in the course of the discussion of insight and passivity cited above, introduces a number of closely connected issues which are appropriately introduced here in our discussion of mysticism. These issues pertain to the specific fantasy and symbolic content of the mystical experiences. They lead to that major amplification of the psychoanalytic theses with which I shall terminate the present discussion.

In spite of the fact that I am not primarily concerned in this chapter with what I shall call broadly the symbolism of mysticism but rather with mystic "selflessness," it remains the case that symbolism in mysticism is so pervasive as to require some comment. I must at least indicate how what I have said up to this point is consistent with the symbolic aspects of mysticism. For this purpose I propose to confine the discussion to the ubiquitous symbols of "oneness" in mystic writings. This will, in turn, lead us back in a new way to the more traditional, id-oriented formulations of the psychological conditions of mystic experience.

The all-engulfing sense of Oneness, the loss of distinction between self and object, is frequently asserted in both Eastern and Christian mysticism to be of the essence of the experience of enlightenment. This aspect of mystic experience has been commented upon by a number of psychoanalytic writers including Freud himself.

Freud's suggestion[58] was that this "oceanic feeling" of oneness, of ineffable ecstasy, is a concomitant of regression to the primal unity with the mother, a unity in which there were yet no ego boundaries and in which gratification was direct and complete. As Lewin says, the experience is felt as *known*, as more certain than anything, because it is the closest we come to what is primal, immediate, unquestioned experience as distinguished from experience mediated by concepts and the subject-object distinction.[59] It represents the primitive narcissistic trust in sensory experience.[60]

It is, of course, essential to recall that the frequently quoted erotic and often orgastic language of a number of the Christian mystics is not interpreted psychoanalytically as a symptom of "genital" orgasm in the psychological sense. Rather what is meant is that the experience, while intensely *libidinal* and orgastic, is on the earliest infantile oral level, the level of primal unity through incorporation.

There is no doubt that the images and the language of the mystics strongly suggest feelings of total gratification and of omnipotence ("A snap of the fingers, and eight thousand gates of the teaching are established").[61] There is no doubt that, at crucial stages along the mystic way, at least momentary trance or ecstasy states occur. This, according to Lewin,[62] is to be expected if we associate the subjective experience with regression to infantile narcissistic gratification at the mother's breast—for this is a state culminating in ecstasy-sleep.

Although the mother-image pervades religious and mystical literature, Lao-tse's language is most explicit and sharp:

> ... the Doorway of the Mysterious Female
> Is the base from which Heaven and Earth sprang.
> It is there within us all the while;
> Draw upon it as you will, it never runs dry.[63]
>   ... wherein I most am different from men
> Is that I prize no sustenance that comes not from the Mother's breast.[64]

The views of Freud and Lewin as to the psychological conditions of the mystic experience are clearly quite different from those I have developed in the earlier sections of this discussion. I have stressed that the experience of loss of self and of the loss of the sense of subject-object relations is in fact loss of a certain kind of anxiety-generated self-consciousness; it is, as such, creative rather than regressive movement. Specifically, it results from ego-syntonic conflict resolution, drive neutralization (sublimation), and consequent absence of anxiety and defense. Furthermore, the sense of joy and power associated with this mode of experience was interpreted, psychologically, as the characteristic result of realistic problem solutions rather than (regressive) fantasy gratifications. The more typical psychoanalytic interpretations just cited, however, imply that this sense of joy and power is, in contrast to what Kris's thesis seems to imply, a result of deeply regressive fantasy gratification. I wish to show now how these two contrasting interpretations are complementary rather than incompatible. *Indeed it is the very fusion of the two processes which constitutes the characteristic psychological condition of the mystic experience.*

The crux of the problem is touched if we follow Kris's well-known development of the psychoanalytic theory of creativity in terms of "regression in the service of the ego." Kris states:

> This relationship between creativity and passivity exemplifies once more one of the leading theses of this presentation: the integrative functions of the ego include self-regulated regression and permit a combination of the most daring intellectual activity with the experience of passive receptiveness.[65]

The implication of such a view is that, in "regression in the service of the ego," it is the movement toward maturity rather than the concurrent regression which is psychodynamically primary. The appropriateness of this conception as applied to the regressive aspects of mysticism needs now to be shown.

We have already seen that the mystic is one who "returns to the Beginning" in order to "ride the present." We have held that this is analogous to the psychoanalytic exploration of the past as inherent in current self-exploration and re-creation. The return to the Beginning is in essential respects an uncovering of infantile history and a reintegration of the personality on the basis of the insights achieved. We must expect, then, that in the course of following the Way, the mystic would become subjectively aware of, and would more or less frequently act out, many of the fantasies and feelings associated with the various infantile stages of development in his own life. This, in turn, means that the mystic's history would be filled with the language—and frequently the symptomatology—of infantile conflicts. We would expect, ideally, that he would eventually uncover the earliest infantile memories, the most archaic fantasies and feelings. Such a thoroughgoing self-exploration and stripping off of the defensive character "armor" is bound to be a dramatic and long drawn-out struggle. We should not be surprised if, frequently, the motivation sufficient to continue such a painful effort is a threatening sense of personal disintegration on a massive scale as the only alternative to success. Such a struggle, while not inevitable, should be relatively common among mystics.[66]

Thus regressive symptomatology is of the essence of the movement toward maturity. This is precisely the case with psychoanalytic self-exploration. What makes the process in both cases essentially *pro*gressive when successful rather than *re*gressive is the fact that the fundamental context is established by the ego in its movement toward increasing integrity and strength. This may, perhaps be more evident in psychoanalytic theory which is characterized by the systematic attempt to maintain continuously the "splitting of the ego" into the "observing," realistic ego as well as the regressive ego. The mystic (and the creative artist?) may be supposed at times to take the more radical—and risky—step of a more total ego regression, a more total reliving of the old conflicts in the course of creating new, ego-syntonic solutions.

There is a second way in which regression enters the mystic experience: it is inherent not only in the stages leading to enlightenment but in the "enlightenment" experience itself. In the most advanced stage of mystic experience, it is true, the pathological symptomatology, trances, and visions are finally superseded by highly ego-syntonic behavior. Such mature gratifications produce, as has been noted earlier, a subjective experience which is without anxious self-consciousness, without compulsive intellectualization or defensive striving. But the strength of ego and the radicalness of the self-exploration implicit in achieving such enlightenment justify certain further assumptions. We may suppose that such persons have retained, far more than most, a significant degree of accessibility to infantile fantasies and a tolerance of partial instinct gratification within a context of essentially mature behavior. Infantile fantasy and partial instinct gratification would therefore not dominate current experience and make it *anti*realistic, but they would be less rigidly repressed, more ego-syntonic.

Thus the selflessness of anxiety-free experience would be "deepened" and "colored" by the quite different but now complementary selflessness of the primal fantasy. The sense of joy and power generated by conflict-free functioning would have the ecstatic "overtones" of the fantasies of primal gratification and omnipotence. The core of reality perception would be enlivened and enriched by the peripheral but compatible illusions associated with residual partial instinct gratifications. This process is, in effect, no more than a broadening and deepening of processes we know to be characteristic of our "everyday" life,[67] whether the latter involves doing arithmetic, eating dinner, or experiencing sexual orgasm.

We are now in a position to suggest in general terms the lines along which we should differentiate mystic experiences, one from another and also from other related types of experience.

What I have outlined as a psychological schema of the mystic way is an idealized and oversimplified structure. For example, the experience of enlightenment is not a self-identical, permanent, and total experience. Mystic literature often seems to suggest this just as psychoanalytic literature often seems to suggest the goal of being "finally and completely analyzed." In both cases, whenever the issue is at the focus of attention, it is clear that such suggestions do not do justice to the facts: there are, after all, many varieties of enlightenment and "degrees" of enlightenment; the scope of enlightenment is limited, its persistence under stress variable. Such variation is found as well in psychoanalysis, *mutatis mutandis.*

In psychological language, we can express such differences from individual mystic to individual mystic in terms of such matters as the relative balance of regressive fantasy and realism, the specific content of the fantasies which predominate, the strength of the ego, and the scope of the conflict-free area of the latter. The differing linguistic patterns, philosophic-religious trends, and, more broadly, the cultural traditions which contribute to the total experience provide a basis for differentiating types of mysticism. These differentiating factors are not "frills" on an underlying psychological "reality." Importance depends upon purposes and these are, for many purposes, at least as important or more important than the psychological factors common to the various kinds of mystic experience. Their analysis, involving humanistic, historical, and scientific studies of varied sorts is, of course, in the highest degree complex.

Similar considerations hold with regard to the relation of mysticism and psychoanalysis. The psychoanalytic patient's experience is patently different in many important respects from the mystic's. This is in many ways obvious, in others not; but such a discussion is beyond the scope of this chapter.

A final question remains. Are we suggesting that, while the mystical experience is not identical with the psychoanalytic process, it is still, after all, only a "subjective" experience and therefore not a "genuine" revelation of or union with God?

Extended discussion here of such issues is not appropriate. Nevertheless, at least brief comment is required.

The burden of what I have said is, of course, not that there is no union with God in the mystic's experience; it is rather that I am saying there *is* union with God, "dwelling in" God. To let go of this is to let go of the essence. But to suppose that union with God or dwelling in God is union with a substantial person, or existence in a definite place, is naïve. For the mystic tells us—and it is essential to listen seriously to him— that he is not concerned with a sensual or substantial being, nor is the "place" in which he dwells a physical or quasi-physical place having measurable dimensions.

Let us consider an analogous situation. The experience of "three-dimensional space" in a painting is not an experience of physical three-dimensional space. Nor is it an "illusion," for no one is deceived by it. It is an *obviously* different experience from that of three-dimensional physical space. Still, in certain ways, it is sufficiently reminiscent of the physical space experience so that we borrow physical space *language* in talking of it. We call it "esthetic space"—a phrase which perhaps over-emphasizes the (limited) similarity. Esthetic space certainly exists, however, and it is no more a mystery than any other perception. To call it an "illusion" or "subjective" is to attack a straw man—as if the artist had ever said or intended us to think that it was *literally* the same as three-dimensional physical space! If one takes it to be physical space, one *is* deluded, of course. But taken as it is, it is a genuine and distinct phenomenon in nature having for some persons its own intrinsic and special value. Just so, the mystical experience of God is illusion only if it is taken naïvely to be what the mystic constantly insists that it is not: a logically impossible, quasi-physical or mental union with a quasi-substantial being who has quasi-human traits.

There is no way of *verbally* communicating about the experience of esthetic space except by means of the potentially misleading analogies with physical space. Just as this esthetic language of space misleads, so the mystic language of personification misleads and suggests a kind of mysterious anthropomorphism.

Not everyone perceives the drama inherent in the forms of esthetic space. Those who do not may feel comfortable calling art an illusion. Such persons find in esthetic space only that trivial value which consists in supposing that it is the product of ingenious technique intended to deceive, having no intrinsic interest other than as deception. But for some persons the perception of esthetic space is, in and of itself, of momentous significance; it establishes a world of its own. And for some, needless to say, the same is true of the experience of spiritual illumination and the apprehension of the divine.

REFERENCES:

[1] FREUD, S. "Analysis Terminable and Interminable," in *Collected Papers,* Basic Books, New York, 1958, V, pp. 316–357.
[2] REICH, W. *Character-Analysis,* Orgone Institute Press, New York, 1949, Chap. IV.

[3] KNIGHT, R. P. "Determinism, 'Freedom,' and Psychotherapy," in *Psychoanalytic Psychiatry and Psychology*, Knight, R. P., and Friedman, C. R., eds., International University Press, New York, 1954, p. 372.

[4] *Loc. cit.*

[5] *Loc. cit.*

[6] ECKHART. *Writings and Sermons*, Blakney, R. B., trans., Harper & Bros., New York, 1957, p. 17.

[7] KNIGHT, R. P. *Op. cit.*, p. 372.

[8] *Ibid.*, p. 376.

[9] *Bhagavad-Gita*, Prabhavananda & Isherwood, Co., trans., New American Library, New York, 1954, p. 43.

[10] KNIGHT, R. P. *Op. cit.*, p. 378.

[11] ECKHART. *Op. cit.*, pp. 227, 232.

[12] SENZAK, N., and MCCANDLESS, R. *Buddhism and Zen*, Philosophical Library, New York, 1956, p. 55.

[13] ECKHART. *Op. cit.*, p. 25.

[14] GODDARD, D. *A. Buddhist Bible*, E. P. Dutton & Co., New York, 1938, p. 546.

[15] *Ibid.*, p. 519.

[16] *Ibid.*, p. 352.

[17] SUZUKI, D. T. *Essays in Zen Buddhism* (Second Series), p. 276.

[18] GODDARD, D. *Op. cit.*, p. 324.

[19] *Ibid.*, p. 521.

[20] *Bhagavad-Gita*, p. 52.

[21] ECKHART. *Op. cit.*, pp. 246–247.

[22] *Ibid.*, p. 87.

[23] SUZUKI, D. T. *Essays in Zen Buddhism* (Third Series), p. 116.

[24] *Upanishads*, Prabhavananda and Manchester, F., trans., New American Library, New York, 1957, p. 58.

[25] *Bhagavad-Gita*, p. 52.

[26] GODDARD, D. *Op. cit.*, pp. 38–39.

[27] KNIGHT, R. P. *Op. cit.*, p. 372.

[28] GODDARD, D. *Op. cit.*, pp. 318–319.

[29] *Ibid.*, p. 91.

[30] *Ibid.*, pp. 521–522.

[31] *Tao Te Ching*, in *The Way and Its Power*, Waley, A., The Macmillan Co., New York, 1956, p. 143.

[32] *Ibid.*, pp. 168–169.

[33] *Ibid.*, p. 147.

[34] GODDARD, D. *Op. cit.*, pp. 521–522.

[35] *Ibid.*, p. 514.

[36] BERGSON, H. *The Two Sources of Morality and Religion*, Doubleday Anchor, New York, 1954, p. 38.

[37] UNDERHILL, E. *Mysticism*, Meridian Books, New York, 1957, p. 420.

[38] ECKHART. *Op. cit.*, p. 107.

[39] SUZUKI, D. T. *Essays in Zen Buddhism* (Third Series), p. 46.

[40] *Tao Te Ching*, p. 159.

[41] GODDARD, D. *Op. cit.*, p. 521.

[42] *Bhagavad-Gita*, pp. 56–57.

[43] THITTILA, M. T. U. "The Fundamental Principles of Theravada Buddhism," in *The Path of the Buddha*, Morgan, K. W., ed., Ronald Press, New York, 1956, pp. 107–108.

[44] GODDARD, D. *Op. cit.*, p. 284.

[45] *Ibid.*, p. 549.

[46] *Ibid.*, p. 550.

[47] SUZUKI, D. T. *Essays in Zen Buddhism* (Third Series), p. 55.

[48] FREUD, S. *Ego & Id*, p. 72.

[49] SUZUKI, D. T. *Essays in Zen Buddhism* (Third Series), p. 116.

[50] ————.*Essays in Zen Buddhism* (Second Series), p. 276.

[51] *Ibid.*, p. 127.

[52] *Ibid.*, p. 98.

[53] *Ibid.*, pp. 117–118.

[54] GREENSON, R. R. "On Boredom," *JAP 1:7*–21 (1953).

[55] UNDERHILL, E. *Op. cit.*, p. 412.

[56] KRIS, E. *Psychoanalytic Explorations in Art*, International Universities Press, New York, 1952.

[57] *Ibid.*, p. 318.

[58] FREUD, S. *Civilization and Its Discontents*, Chap. I.

[59] LEWIN, B. D. *The Psychoanalysis of Elation*, W. W. Norton & Co., New York, 1950, p. 149.

[60] *Ibid.*, p. 150.

[61] SENZAKI, N., and MCCANDLESS, R. *Op. cit.*, p. 61.

[62] LEWIN, B. D. *Op. cit.*, p. 150.

[63] *Tao Te Ching*, p. 149.

[64] *Ibid.*, p. 169.

[65] KRIS, E. *Op. cit.*, p. 318.

[66] BOISEN, A. T. *Exploration of the Inner World*, Harper & Bros., New York, 1936.

[67] SPERLING, O. E. "Illusion, Naïve and Controlled," *Psychoanalytic Quarterly* 20:204–214 (1951).

Erich Fromm's analysis of Western religion recognizes the Jungian conflict on an entirely different level. Fromm divides religion into two types—one promotes the neurotic attachment of the child for his family by allowing him to indulge a dependence on God, the Father; and the other is the humanistic religion which recognizes the unconscious sources of religious beliefs and sees God as the best projection of man's wishes and desires.

ERICH FROMM

Some Types of Religious Experience

FROM *Psychoanalysis and Religion*

Any discussion of religion is handicapped by a serious terminological difficulty. While we know that there were and are many religions outside of monotheism, we nevertheless associate the concept religion with a system centered around God and supernatural forces; we tend to consider monotheistic religion as a frame of reference for the understanding and evaluation of all other religions. It thus becomes doubtful whether religions without God like Buddhism, Taoism, or Confucianism can be properly called religions. Such secular systems as contemporary authoritarianism are not called religions at all, although psychologically speaking they deserve this name. We simply have no word to denote religion as a general human phenomenon in such a way that some association with a specific type of religion does not creep in and color the concept. For lack of such a word I shall use the term religion in these chapters, but I want to make it clear at the outset that I understand by religion *any system of thought and action shared by a group which gives the individual a frame of orientation and an object of devotion.*

There is indeed no culture of the past, and it seems there can be no culture in the future, which does not have religion in this broad sense of our definition. . . .

The thesis that the need for a frame of orientation and an object of devotion is rooted in the conditions of man's existence seems to be amply verified by the fact of the universal occurrence of religion in history. This point has been made and elaborated by theologians, psychologists, and anthropologists, and there is no need for me to discuss it any further. I only want to stress that in making this point the adherents of traditional religion have often indulged in a fallacious bit of reasoning. Starting out with so broad a definition of religion as to include every possible religious phenomenon, their concept has remained associated with monotheistic religion, and thus they proceed to look upon all non-monotheistic forms as precursors of or deviations from the "true" religion and they end demonstrating that the belief in God in the sense of the Western religious tradition is inherent in man's equipment.

The psychoanalyst whose "laboratory" is the patient and who is a participant observer of another person's thoughts and feelings is able to add another proof to the fact that the need for some frame of orientation and object of devotion is inherent in man. In studying neuroses he discovers that he is studying religion. It was Freud who saw the connection between neurosis and religion; but while he interpreted religion as a collective childhood neurosis of mankind, the statement can also be reversed. We can interpret *neurosis as a private form of religion,* more specifically, as a regression to primitive forms of religion conflicting with officially recognized patterns of religious thought.

One can look at a neurosis from two aspects. One can focus on the neurotic phenomena themselves, the symptoms and other specific difficulties in living which the neurosis produces. The other aspect is not concerned with the positive as it were, with the neurosis, but with the negative, the failure of the neurotic individual to accomplish the fundamental aims of human existence, independence and the ability to be productive, to love, to think. Anyone who has failed to achieve maturity and integration develops a neurosis of one kind or another. He does not "just live," unbothered by this failure, satisfied to eat and drink, sleep and have sexual satisfaction and do his work; if this were the case then indeed we would have the proof that the religious attitude, while perhaps desirable, is not an intrinsic part of human nature. But the study of man shows that this is not so. If a person has not succeeded in integrating his energies in the direction of his higher self, he canalizes them in the direction of lower goals; if he has no picture of the world and his position in it which approximates the truth, he will create a picture which is illusory and cling to it with the same tenacity with which the religionist believes in his dogmas. Indeed, "man does not live by bread alone." He has only the choice of better or worse, higher or lower, satisfactory or destructive forms of religions and philosophies.

What is the religious situation in contemporary Western society? It resembles in curious fashion the picture which the anthropologist gets in studying the religion of the North American Indians. They have been converted to the Christian religion but their old pre-Christian religions have by no means been uprooted. Christianity is a veneer laid over this old religion and blended with it in many ways. In our own culture monotheistic religion and also atheistic and agnostic philosophies are a thin veneer built upon religions which are in many ways far more "primitive" than the Indian religions and, being sheer idolatry, are also more incompatible with the essential teaching of monotheism. As a collective and potent form of modern idolatry we find the worship of power, of success and of the authority of the market; but aside from these collective forms we find something else. If we scratch the surface of modern man we discover any number of individualized primitive forms of religion. Many of these are called neuroses, but one might just as well call them by their respective religious names: ancestor worship, totemism, fetishism, ritualism, the cult of cleanliness, and so on.

Do we actually find ancestor worship? Indeed, ancestor worship is one of the most widespread primitive cults in our society and it does not alter its picture if we call it, as the psychiatrist does, neurotic fixation to father or mother. Let us consider such a case of ancestor worship. A beautiful, highly talented woman, a painter, was attached to her father in such a way that she would refuse to have any close contact with men; she spent all her free time with her father, a pleasant but rather dull gentleman who had been widowed early. Aside from her painting, nothing but her father was of any interest to her. The picture she gave of him to others was grotesquely different from reality. After he died she committed suicide and left a will stipulating only that she was to be buried by his side.

Another person, a very intelligent and gifted man, highly respected by everyone, led a secret life completely devoted to the worship of his father who, viewed most charitably, could be described as a shrewd go-getter, interested solely in acquiring money and social prestige. The son's picture of the father was, however, that of the wisest, most loving, and devoted parent, ordained by God to show him the right way to live; the son's every action and thought was considered from the standpoint of whether his father would approve or not, and since in real life his father had usually disapproved, the patient felt "out of grace" most of the time and frantically attempted to regain his father's approval even many years after his father had died.

The psychoanalyst tries to discover the causes of such pathological attachments and hopes to help the patient to free himself from such crippling father worship. But we are not interested here in the causes or in the problem of cure but in the phenomenology. We find a dependency on a father enduring with undiminished intensity many years after the parent's death, which cripples the patient's judgment, renders him unable to love, makes him feel like a child, constantly insecure and frightened. This centering one's life around an ancestor, spending most of one's energy in his worship, is not different from a religious ancestor cult. It gives a frame of reference and a unifying principle of devotion. Here too is the reason the patient cannot be cured by simply pointing out the irrationality of his behavior and the damage he does to himself. He often knows this intellectually in one compartment of himself, as it were, but emotionally he is completely devoted to his cult. Only if a profound change in his total personality occurs, if he becomes free *to* think, *to* love, *to* attain a new focus of orientation and devotion, can he be free *from* the slavish devotion to his parent; only if he is capable of adopting a higher form of religion can he free himself from his lower form.

Compulsive neurotic patients exhibit numerous forms of private ritual. The person whose life is centered around the feeling of guilt and the need for atonement may choose a washing compulsion as the dominant ritual of his life; another whose compulsion is exhibited in thinking rather than actions will have a ritual which forces him to think or say certain formulas which are supposed to avert disaster and others which are supposed to guarantee success. Whether we call these neurotic symptoms or ritual depends on our point of view; in substance these symptoms *are* rituals of a private religion.

Do we have totemism in our culture? We have a great deal—although the people suffering from it usually do not consider themselves in need of psychiatric help. A person whose exclusive devotion is to the state or his political party, whose only criterion of value and truth is the interest of state or party, for whom the flag as a symbol of his group is a holy object, has a religion of clan and totem worship, even though in his own eyes it is a perfectly rational system (which, of course, all devotees to any kind of primitive religion believe). If we want to understand how systems like fascism or Stalinism can possess millions of people, ready to sacrifice their integrity and reason to the principle, "my country, right or wrong," we are forced to consider the totemistic, the religious quality of their orientation.

Another form of private religion, very widespread although not dominant in our culture, is the religion of cleanliness. The adherents of this religion have one major standard of value according to which they judge people—cleanliness and orderliness. The phenomenon was strikingly apparent in the reaction of many American soldiers during the last war. Often at odds with their political convictions, they judged allies and enemies from the standpoint of this religion. The English and the Germans ranked high, the French and Italians low in this scale of values. This religion of cleanliness and orderliness is, in substance, not too different from certain highly ritualistic religious systems which are centered around the attempt to get rid of evil by cleansing rituals and to find security in the strict performance of ritualistic orderliness.

There is one important difference between a religious cult and neurosis which makes the cult vastly superior to the neurosis as far as the satisfaction gained is concerned. If we imagine that the patient with his neurotic fixation to his father lived in a culture where ancestor worship is generally practiced as a cult, he could share his feelings with his fellow men rather than feel himself isolated. And it is the feeling of isolation, of being shut-out, which is the painful sting of every neurosis. Even the most irrational orientation if it is shared by a considerable body of men gives the individual the feeling of oneness with others, a certain amount of security and stability which the neurotic person lacks. There is nothing inhuman, evil, or irrational which does not give some comfort provided it is shared by a group. The most convincing proof for this statement can be found in those incidents of mass madness of which we have been and still are witnesses. Once a doctrine, however irrational, has gained power in a society, millions of people will believe in it rather than feel ostracized and isolated.

These ideas lead to an important consideration concerning the function of religion. If man regresses so easily into a more primitive form of religion, have not the monotheistic religions today the function of saving man from such regression? Is not the belief in God a safeguard against falling back into ancestor, totem, or golden-calf worship? Indeed, this would be so if religion had succeeded in molding man's character according to its stated ideals. But historical religion has capitulated before and compromised with secular power again and again. It has been concerned far more with certain dogmas rather than with the practice of love and humility in everyday life. It has failed to challenge secular power relentlessly and unceasingly where such power has violated the spirit of the religious ideal; on the contrary, it has shared again and again in such violations. If the churches were the representatives not only of the words but of the spirit of the Ten Commandments or of the Golden Rule, they could be potent forces blocking the regression to idol worship. But since this is an exception rather than the rule, the question must be asked, not from an antireligious point of view but out of concern for man's soul: Can we trust religion to be representative of religious needs or must we not separate these needs from organized, traditional religion in order to prevent the collapse of our moral structure?

In considering an answer to this question we must remember that no intelligent discussion of the problem is possible as long as we deal with religion in general instead of differentiating between various types of religion and religious experience. It would far transcend the scope of this chapter to attempt a review of all types of religion. Even to discuss only those types which are relevant from the psychological standpoint cannot be undertaken here. I shall therefore deal with only one distinction, but one which in my opinion is the most important, and which cuts across nontheistic and theistic religions: that between *authoritarian* and *humanistic* religions.

What is the principle of authoritarian religion? The definition of religion given in the *Oxford Dictionary,* while attempting to define religion as such, is a rather accurate definition of authoritarian religion. It reads: "[Religion is] recognition on the part of man of some higher unseen power as having control of his destiny, and as being entitled to obedience, reverence, and worship."

Here the emphasis is on the recognition that man is controlled by a higher power outside of himself. But this alone does not constitute authoritarian religion. What makes it so is the idea that this power, because of the control it exercises, is *entitled* to "obedience, reverence and worship." I italicize the word "entitled" because it shows that the reason for worship, obedience, and reverence lies not in the moral qualities of the deity, not in love or justice, but in the fact that it has control, that is, has power over man. Furthermore it shows that the higher power has a right to force man to worship him and that lack of reverence and obedience constitutes sin.

The essential element in authoritarian religion and in the authoritarian religious experience is the surrender to a power transcending man. The main virtue of this type of religion is obedience, its cardinal sin is disobedience. Just as the deity is conceived as omnipotent or omniscient, man is conceived as being powerless and insignificant. Only as he can gain grace or help from the deity by complete surrender can he feel strength. Submission to a powerful authority is one of the avenues by which man escapes from his feeling of aloneness and limitation. In the act of surrender he loses his independence and integrity as an individual but he gains the feeling of being protected by an awe-inspiring power of which, as it were, he becomes a part.

In Calvin's theology we find a vivid picture of authoritarian, theistic thinking. "For I do not call it humility," says Calvin, "if you suppose that we have anything left. . . . We cannot think of ourselves as we ought to think without utterly despising every thing that may be supposed an excellence in us. This humility is unfeigned submission of a mind over-whelmed with a weighty sense of its own misery and poverty; for such is the uniform description of it in the word of God."[1]

The experience which Calvin describes here, that of despising everything in oneself, of the submission of the mind overwhelmed by its own poverty, is the very essence of all authoritarian religions whether they are couched in secular or in theological language.[2] In authoritarian religion God is a symbol of power and force, He is supreme because He has supreme power, and man in juxtaposition is utterly powerless. . . .

That early Christianity is humanistic and not authoritarian is evident from the spirit and text of all Jesus' teachings. Jesus' precept that "the kingdom of God is within you" is the simple and clear expression of nonauthoritarian thinking. But only a few hundred years later, after Christianity had ceased to be the religion of the poor and humble peasants, artisans, and slaves (the *Am haarez*) and had become the religion of those ruling the Roman Empire, the authoritarian trend in Christianity became dominant. Even so, the conflict between the authoritarian and humanistic principles in Christianity never ceased. It was the conflict between Augustine and Pelagius, between the Catholic Church and the many "heretic" groups and between various sects within Protestantism. The humanistic, democratic element was never subdued in Christian or in Jewish history, and this element found one of its most potent expressions in the mystic thinking within both religions. The mystics have been deeply imbued with the experience of man's strength, his likeness to God, and with the idea that God needs man as much as man needs God; they have understood the sentence that man is created in the image of God to mean the fundamental identity of God and man. Not fear and submission but love and the assertion of one's own powers are the basis of mystical experience. *God is not a symbol of power over man but of man's own powers.*

Thus far we have dealt with the distinctive features of authoritarian

and humanistic religions mainly in descriptive terms. But the psychoanalyst must proceed from the description of attitudes to the analysis of
their dynamics, and it is here that he can contribute to our discussion
from an area not accessible to other fields of inquiry. The full understanding of an attitude requires an appreciation of those conscious and,
in particular, unconscious processes occurring in the individual which
provide the necessity for and the conditions of its development.

While in humanistic religion God is the image of man's higher self, a
symbol of what man potentially is or ought to become, in authoritarian
religion God becomes the sole possessor of what was originally man's:
of his reason and his love. The more perfect God becomes, the more
imperfect becomes man. He *projects* the best he has onto God and thus
impoverishes himself. Now God has all love, all wisdom, all justice—
and man is deprived of these qualities, he is empty and poor. He had
begun with the feeling of smallness, but he now has become completely
powerless and without strength; all his powers have been projected onto
God. This mechanism of projection is the very same which can be
observed in interpersonal relationships of a masochistic, submissive
character, where one person is awed by another and attributes his own
powers and aspirations to the other person. It is the same mechanism
that makes people endow the leaders of even the most inhuman systems
with qualities of superwisdom and kindness.[3]

When man has thus projected his own most valuable powers onto
God, what of his relationship to his own powers? They have become
separated from him and in this process he has become *alienated* from
himself. Everything he has is now God's and nothing is left in him. *His
only access to himself is through God.* In worshiping God he tries to get
in touch with that part of himself which he has lost through projection.
After having given God all he has, he begs God to return to him some of
what originally was his own. But having lost his own he is completely at
God's mercy. He necessarily feels like a "sinner" since he has deprived
himself of everything that is good, and it is only through God's mercy or
grace that he can regain that which alone makes him human. And in
order to persuade God to give him some of his love, he must prove to
him how utterly deprived he is of love; in order to persuade God to
guide him by his superior wisdom he must prove to him how deprived he
is of wisdom when he is left to himself.

But this alienation from his own powers not only makes man feel
slavishly dependent on God, it makes him bad too. He becomes a man
without faith in his fellow men or in himself, without the experience of

his own love, of his own power of reason. As a result the separation between the "holy" and the "secular" occurs. In his worldly activities man acts without love, in that sector of his life which is reserved to religion he feels himself to be a sinner (which he actually is, since to live without love is to live in sin) and tries to recover some of his lost humanity by being in touch with God. Simultaneously, he tries to win forgiveness by emphasizing his own helplessness and worthlessness. Thus the attempt to obtain forgiveness results in the activation of the very attitude from which his sins stem. He is caught in a painful dilemma. The more he praises God, the emptier he becomes. The emptier he becomes, the more sinful he feels. The more sinful he feels, the more he praises his God—and the less able is he to regain himself.

Analysis of religion must not stop at uncovering those psychological processes within man which underly his religious experience; it must proceed to discover the conditions which make for the development of authoritarian and humanistic character structures, respectively, from which different kinds of religious experience stem. Such a sociopsychological analysis goes far beyond the context of these chapters. However, the principal point can be made briefly. What people think and feel is rooted in their character and their character is molded by the total configuration of their practice of life—more precisely, by the socioeconomic and political structure of their society. In societies ruled by a powerful minority which holds the masses in subjection, the individual will be so imbued with fear, so incapable of feeling strong or independent, that his religious experience will be authoritarian. Whether he worships a punishing, awesome God or a similarly conceived leader makes little difference. On the other hand, where the individual feels free and responsible for his own fate, or among minorities striving for freedom and independence, humanistic religious experience develops. The history of religion gives ample evidence of this correlation between social structure and kinds of religious experience. Early Christianity was a religion of the poor and downtrodden; the history of religious sects fighting against authoritarian political pressure shows the same principle again and again. Judaism, in which a strong anti-authoritarian tradition could grow up because secular authority never had much of a chance to govern and to build up a legend of its wisdom, therefore developed the humanistic aspect of religion to a remarkable degree. Whenever, on the other hand, religion allied itself with secular power, the religion had by necessity to become authoritarian. The real fall of man is his alienation from himself, his submission to power, his turning against himself even though under the guise of his worship of God.

NOTES

[1] Johannes Calvin, *Institutes of the Christian Religion* (Presbyterian Board of Christian Education, 1928), p. 681.

[2] See Erich Fromm, *Escape from Freedom* (Farrar & Rinehart, 1941), pp. 141 ff. This attitude toward authority is described there in detail.

[3] Cf. the discussion about symbiotic relationship in *Escape from Freedom*, pp. 158 ff.

*Brother Klaus (in a preceding article by Jung) rings a
strange bell of recollection. Where has there been such a man
before? "All who came to him were filled with terror at the
first glance. As to the cause of it, he himself used to say
that he had seen a piercing light resembling a human face . . .
Overcome with terror, he instantly turned his face away and
fell to the ground. And that was the reason his face was
terrible to others."*

*The resemblance between Hawthorne's Minister in his
black veil, and the terrible face of Brother Klaus is too striking to be missed. Quite obviously, the vision of absolute perfection is a vision of the unconscious—in which evil and
good together appear in one terrifying symbol.*

NATHANIEL HAWTHORNE

The Minister's Black Veil

The sexton stood in the porch of Milford meeting-house, pulling
busily at the bell-rope. The old people of the village came stooping along
the street. Children, with bright faces, tripped merrily beside their parents, or mimicked a graver gait, in the conscious dignity of their Sunday
clothes. Spruce bachelors looked sidelong at the pretty maidens, and
fancied that the Sabbath sunshine made them prettier than on week
days. When the throng had mostly streamed into the porch, the sexton
began to toll the bell, keeping his eye on the Reverend Mr. Hooper's
door. The first glimpse of the clergyman's figure was the signal for the
bell to cease its summons.

"But what has good Parson Hooper got upon his face?" cried the
sexton in astonishment.

All within hearing immediately turned about, and beheld the semblance of Mr. Hooper, pacing slowly his meditative way towards the
meeting-house. With one accord they started, expressing more wonder
than if some strange minister were coming to dust the cushions of Mr.
Hooper's pulpit.

699

"Are you sure it is our parson?" inquired Goodman Gray of the sexton.

"Of a certainty it is good Mr. Hooper," replied the sexton. "He was to have exchanged pulpits with Parson Shute, of Westbury; but Parson Shute sent to excuse himself yesterday, being to preach a funeral sermon."

The cause of so much amazement may appear sufficiently slight. Mr. Hooper, a gentlemanly person, of about thirty, though still a bachelor, was dressed with due clerical neatness, as if a careful wife had starched his band, and brushed the weekly dust from his Sunday's garb. There was but one thing remarkable in his appearance. Swathed about his forehead, and hanging down over his face, so low as to be shaken by his breath, Mr. Hooper had on a black veil. On a nearer view it seemed to consist of two folds of crape, which entirely concealed his features, except the mouth and chin, but probably did not intercept his sight, further than to give a darkened aspect to all living and inanimate things. With this gloomy shade before him, good Mr. Hooper walked onward, at a slow and quiet pace, stooping somewhat, and looking on the ground, as is customary with abstracted men, yet nodding kindly to those of his parishioners who still waited on the meeting-house steps. But so wonderstruck were they that his greeting hardly met with a return.

"I can't really feel as if good Mr. Hooper's face was behind that piece of crape," said the sexton.

"I don't like it," muttered an old woman, as she hobbled into the meeting-house. "He has changed himself into something awful, only by hiding his face."

"Our parson has gone mad!" cried Goodman Gray, following him across the threshold.

A rumor of some unaccountable phenomenon had preceded Mr. Hooper into the meeting-house, and set all the congregation astir. Few could refrain from twisting their heads towards the door; many stood upright, and turned directly about; while several little boys clambered upon the seats, and came down again with a terrible racket. There was a general bustle, a rustling of the women's gowns and shuffling of the men's feet, greatly at variance with that hushed repose which should attend the entrance of the minister. But Mr. Hooper appeared not to notice the perturbation of his people. He entered with an almost noiseless step, bent his head mildly to the pews on each side, and bowed as he passed his oldest parishioner, a white-haired great-grandsire, who occupied an arm-chair in the centre of the aisle. It was strange to observe how slowly this venerable man became conscious of something singular in the appearance of his pastor. He seemed not fully to partake of the prevailing wonder, till Mr. Hooper had ascended the stairs, and showed himself in the pulpit, face to face with his congregation, except for the black veil. That mysterious emblem was never once withdrawn. It shook with his measured breath, as he gave out the psalm; it threw its obscurity between him and the holy page, as he read the Scriptures; and while he prayed, the veil lay heavily on his uplifted countenance. Did he seek to hide it from the dread Being whom he was addressing?

Such was the effect of this simple piece of crape, that more than one woman of delicate nerves was forced to leave the meeting-house. Yet perhaps the pale-faced congregation was almost as fearful a sight to the minister, as his black veil to them.

Mr. Hooper had the reputation of a good preacher, but not an energetic one: he strove to win his people heavenward by mild, persuasive influences, rather than to drive them thither by the thunders of the Word. The sermon which he now delivered was marked by the same characteristics of style and manner as the general series of his pulpit oratory. But there was something, either in the sentiment of the discourse itself, or in the imagination of the auditors, which made it greatly the most powerful effort that they had ever heard from their pastor's lips. It was tinged, rather more darkly than usual, with the gentle gloom of Mr. Hooper's temperament. The subject had reference to secret sin, and those sad mysteries which we hide from our nearest and dearest, and would fain conceal from our own consciousness, even forgetting that the Omniscient can detect them. A subtle power was breathed into his words. Each member of the congregation, the most innocent girl, and the man of hardened breast, felt as if the preacher had crept upon them, behind his awful veil, and discovered their hoarded iniquity of deed or thought. Many spread their clasped hands on their bosoms. There was nothing terrible in what Mr. Hooper said, at least, no violence; and yet, with every tremor of his melancholy voice, the hearers quaked. An unsought pathos came hand in hand with awe. So sensible were the audience of some unwonted attribute in their minister, that they longed for a breath of wind to blow aside the veil, almost believing that a stranger's visage would be discovered, though the form, gesture, and voice were those of Mr. Hooper.

At the close of the services, the people hurried out with indecorous confusion, eager to communicate their pent-up amazement, and conscious of lighter spirits the moment they lost sight of the black veil.

Some gathered in little circles, huddled closely together, with their mouths all whispering in the centre; some went homeward alone, wrapt in silent meditation; some talked loudly, and profaned the Sabbath day with ostentatious laughter. A few shook their sagacious heads, intimating that they could penetrate the mystery; while one or two affirmed that there was no mystery at all, but only that Mr. Hooper's eyes were so weakened by the midnight lamp, as to require shade. After a brief interval, forth came good Mr. Hooper also, in the rear of his flock. Turning his veiled face from one group to another, he paid due reverence to the hoary heads, saluted the middle aged with kind dignity as their friend and spiritual guide, greeted the young with mingled authority and love, and laid his hands on the little children's heads to bless them. Such was always his custom on the Sabbath day. Strange and bewildered looks repaid him for his courtesy. None, as on former occasions, aspired to the honor of walking by their pastor's side. Old Squire Saunders, doubtless by an accidental lapse of memory, neglected to invite Mr. Hooper to his table, where the good clergyman had been wont to bless the food, almost every Sunday since his settlement. He returned, therefore, to the parsonage, and, at the moment of closing the door, was observed to look back upon the people, all of whom had their eyes fixed upon the minister. A sad smile gleamed faintly from beneath the black veil, and flickered about his mouth, glimmering as he disappeared.

"How strange," said a lady, "that a simple black veil, such as any woman might wear on her bonnet should become such a terrible thing on Mr. Hooper's face!"

"Something must surely be amiss with Mr. Hooper's intellects," observed her husband, the physician of the village. "But the strangest part of the affair is the effect of this vagary, even on a sober-minded man like myself. The black veil, though it covers only our pastor's face, throws its influence over his whole person, and makes him ghostlike from head to foot. Do you not feel it so?"

"Truly do I," replied the lady; "and I would not be alone with him for the world. I wonder he is not afraid to be alone with himself!"

"Men sometimes are so," said her husband.

The afternoon service was attended with similar circumstances. At its conclusion, the bell tolled for the funeral of a young lady. The relatives and friends were assembled in the house, and the more distant acquaintances stood about the door, speaking of the good qualities of the deceased, when their talk was interrupted by the appearance of Mr. Hooper, still covered with his black veil. It was now an appropriate emblem. The clergyman stepped into the room where the corpse was laid, and bent over the coffin, to take a last farewell of his deceased parishioner. As he stooped, the veil hung straight down from his forehead, so that, if her eyelids had not been closed forever, the dead maiden might have seen his face. Could Mr. Hooper be fearful of her glance, that he so hastily caught back the black veil? A person who watched the interview between the dead and living, scrupled not to affirm, that, at the instant when the clergyman's features were disclosed, the corpse had slightly shuddered, rustling the shroud and muslin cap, though the countenance retained the composure of death. A superstitious old woman was the only witness of this prodigy. From the coffin Mr. Hooper passed into the chamber of the mourners, and thence to the head of the staircase, to make the funeral prayer. It was a tender and heart-dissolving prayer, full of sorrow, yet so imbued with celestial hopes, that the music of a heavenly harp, swept by the fingers of the dead, seemed faintly to be heard among the saddest accents of the minister. The people trembled, though they but darkly understood him when he prayed that they, and himself, and all of mortal race, might be ready, as he trusted this young maiden had been, for the dreadful hour that should snatch the veil from their faces. The bearers went heavily forth, and the mourners followed, saddening all the street, with the dead before them, and Mr. Hooper in his black veil behind.

"Why do you look back?" said one in the procession to his partner.

"I had a fancy," replied she, "that the minister and the maiden's spirit were walking hand in hand."

"And so had I, at the same moment," said the other.

That night, the handsomest couple in Milford village were to be joined in wedlock. Though reckoned a melancholy man, Mr. Hooper had a placid cheerfulness for such occasions, which often excited a sympathetic smile where livelier merriment would have been thrown away. There was no quality of his disposition which made him more beloved than this. The company at the wedding awaited his arrival with impatience, trusting that the strange awe, which had been gathered over him throughout the day, would now be dispelled. But such was not the result. When Mr. Hooper came, the first thing that their eyes rested on was the same horrible black veil, which had added deeper gloom to the funeral, and could portend nothing but evil to the wedding. Such was its immediate effect on the guests that a cloud seemed to have rolled duskily from beneath the black crape, and dimmed the light of the candles. The bridal pair stood up before the minister. But the bride's cold fingers quivered in the tremulous hand of the bridegroom, and her deathlike paleness caused a whisper that the maiden who had been buried a few hours before was come from her grave to be married. If ever another wedding were so dismal, it was that famous one where they tolled the wedding knell. After performing the ceremony, Mr. Hooper raised a glass of wine to his lips, wishing happiness to the new-married couple in a strain of mild pleasantry that ought to have brightened the features of the guests, like a cheerful gleam from the hearth. At that instant, catching a glimpse of his figure in the looking-glass, the black veil involved his own spirit in the horror with which it overwhelmed all others. His frame shuddered, his lips grew white, he spilt the untasted wine upon the carpet, and rushed forth into the darkness. For the Earth, too, had on her Black Veil.

The next day, the whole village of Milford talked of little else than Parson Hooper's black veil. That, and the mystery concealed behind it, supplied a topic for discussion between acquaintances meeting in the street, and good women gossiping at their open windows. It was the first item of news that the tavern-keeper told to his guests. The children babbled of it on their way to school. One imitative little imp covered his face with an old black handkerchief, thereby so affrighting his playmates that the panic seized himself, and he well-nigh lost his wits by his own waggery.

It was remarkable that of all the busybodies and impertinent people in the parish, not one ventured to put the plain question to Mr. Hooper, wherefore he did this thing. Hitherto, whenever there appeared the slightest call for such interference, he had never lacked advisers, nor shown himself averse to be guided by their judgment. If he erred at all, it was by so painful a degree of self-distrust, that even the mildest censure would lead him to consider an indifferent action as a crime. Yet, though so well acquainted with this amiable weakness, no individual among his parishioners chose to make the black veil a subject of friendly remonstrance. There was a feeling of dread, neither plainly confessed nor carefully concealed, which caused each to shift the responsibility upon another, till at length it was found expedient to send a deputation of the church, in order to deal with Mr. Hooper about the mystery, before it should grow into a scandal. Never did an embassy so ill discharge its duties. The minister received them with friendly courtesy, but became silent, after they were seated, leaving to his visitors the whole burden of introducing their important business. The topic, it might be supposed, was obvious enough. There was the black veil swathed round Mr.

Hooper's forehead, and concealing every feature above his placid mouth, on which, at times, they could perceive the glimmering of a melancholy smile. But that piece of crape, to their imagination, seemed to hang down before his heart, the symbol of a fearful secret between him and them. Were the veil but cast aside, they might speak freely of it, but not till then. Thus they sat a considerable time, speechless, confused, and shrinking uneasily from Mr. Hooper's eye, which they felt to be fixed upon them with an invisible glance. Finally, the deputies returned abashed to their constituents, pronouncing the matter too weighty to be handled, except by a council of the churches, if, indeed, it might not require a general synod.

But there was one person in the village unappalled by the awe with which the black veil had impressed all beside herself. When the deputies returned without an explanation, or even venturing to demand one, she, with the calm energy of her character, determined to chase away the strange cloud that appeared to be settling round Mr. Hooper, every moment more darkly than before. As his plighted wife, it should be her privilege to know what the black veil concealed. At the minister's first visit, therefore, she entered upon the subject with a direct simplicity, which made the task easier both for him and her. After he had seated himself, she fixed her eyes steadfastly upon the veil, but could discern nothing of the dreadful gloom that had so overawed the multitude: it was but a double fold of crape, hanging down from his forehead to his mouth, and slightly stirring with his breath.

"No," said she aloud, and smiling, "there is nothing terrible in this piece of crape, except that it hides a face which I am always glad to look upon. Come, good sir, let the sun shine from behind the cloud. First lay aside your black veil: then tell me why you put it on."

Mr. Hooper's smile glimmered faintly.

"There is an hour to come," said he, "when all of us shall cast aside our veils. Take it not amiss, beloved friend, if I wear this piece of crape till then."

"Your words are a mystery, too," returned the young lady. "Take away the veil from them, at least."

"Elizabeth, I will," said he, "so far as my vow may suffer me. Know, then, this veil is a type and a symbol, and I am bound to wear it ever, both in light and darkness, in solitude and before the gaze of multitudes, and as with strangers, so with my familiar friends. No mortal eye will see it withdrawn. This dismal shade must separate me from the world: even you, Elizabeth, can never come behind it!"

"What grievous affliction hath befallen you," she earnestly inquired, "that you should thus darken your eyes forever?"

"If it be a sign of mourning," replied Mr. Hooper, "I, perhaps, like most other mortals, have sorrows dark enough to be typified by a black veil."

"But what if the world will not believe that it is the type of an innocent sorrow?" urged Elizabeth. "Beloved and respected as you are, there may be whispers that you hide your face under the consciousness of secret sin. For the sake of your holy office, do away this scandal!"

The color rose into her cheeks as she intimated the nature of the rumors that were already abroad in the village. But Mr. Hooper's mildness did not forsake him. He even smiled again—that same sad smile, which always appeared like a faint glimmering of light, proceeding from the obscurity beneath the veil.

"If I hide my face for sorrow, there is cause enough," he merely replied; "and if I cover it for secret sin, what mortal might not do the same?"

And with this gentle, but unconquerable obstinacy did he resist all her entreaties. At length Elizabeth sat silent. For a few moments she appeared lost in thought, considering, probably, what new methods might be tried to withdraw her lover from so dark a fantasy, which, if it had no other meaning, was perhaps a symptom of mental disease. Though of a firmer character than his own, the tears rolled down her cheeks. But, in an instant, as it were, a new feeling took the place of sorrow: her eyes were fixed insensibly on the black veil, when, like a sudden twilight in the air, its terrors fell around her. She arose, and stood trembling before him.

"And do you feel it then, at last?" said he mournfully.

She made no reply, but covered her eyes with her hand, and turned to leave the room. He rushed forward and caught her arm.

"Have patience with me, Elizabeth!" cried he, passionately. "Do not desert me, though this veil must be between us here on earth. Be mine, and hereafter there shall be no veil over my face, no darkness between our souls! It is but a mortal veil—it is not for eternity! O! you know not how lonely I am, and how frightened, to be alone behind my black veil. Do not leave me in this miserable obscurity forever!"

"Lift the veil but once, and look me in the face," said she.

"Never! It cannot be!" replied Mr. Hooper.

"Then farewell!" said Elizabeth.

She withdrew her arm from his grasp, and slowly departed, pausing at

the door, to give one long shuddering gaze, that seemed almost to penetrate the mystery of the black veil. But, even amid his grief, Mr. Hooper
smiled to think that only a material emblem had separated him from
happiness, though the horrors, which it shadowed forth, must be drawn
darkly between the fondest of lovers.

From that time no attempts were made to remove Mr. Hooper's black
veil, or, by a direct appeal, to discover the secret which it was supposed
to hide. By persons who claimed a superiority to popular prejudice, it
was reckoned merely an eccentric whim, such as often mingles with the
sober actions of men otherwise rational, and tinges them all with its own
semblance of insanity. But with the multitude, good Mr. Hooper was
irreparably a bugbear. He could not walk the street with any peace of
mind, so conscious was he that the gentle and timid would turn aside to
avoid him, and that others would make it a point of hardihood to throw
themselves in his way. The impertinence of the latter class compelled
him to give up his customary walk at sunset to the burial ground; for
when he leaned pensively over the gate, there would always be faces
behind the gravestones, peeping at his black veil. A fable went the
rounds that the stare of the dead people drove him thence. It grieved
him, to the very depth of his kind heart, to observe how the children fled
from his approach, breaking up their merriest sports, while his melancholy figure was yet afar off. Their instinctive dread caused him to feel
more strongly than aught else, that a preternatural horror was interwoven with the threads of the black crape. In truth, his own antipathy to
the veil was known to be so great, that he never willingly passed before a
mirror, nor stooped to drink at a still fountain, lest, in its peaceful
bosom, he should be affrighted by himself. This was what gave plausi-
bility to the whispers, that Mr. Hooper's conscience tortured him for
some great crime too horrible to be entirely concealed, or otherwise than
so obscurely intimated. Thus, from beneath the black veil, there rolled a
cloud into the sunshine, an ambiguity of sin or sorrow, which enveloped
the poor minister, so that love or sympathy could never reach him. It
was said that ghost and fiend consorted with him there. With self-
shudderings and outward terrors, he walked continually in its shadow,
groping darkly within his own soul, or gazing through a medium that
saddened the whole world. Even the lawless wind, it was believed, respected his dreadful secret, and never blew aside the veil. But still good
Mr. Hooper sadly smiled at the pale visages of the worldly throng as
he passed by.

Among all its bad influences, the black veil had the one desirable effect, of making its wearer a very efficient clergyman. By the aid of his mysterious emblem—for there was no other apparent cause—he became a man of awful power over souls that were in agony for sin. His converts always regarded him with a dread peculiar to themselves, affirming, though but figuratively, that, before he brought them to celestial light, they had been with him behind the black veil. Its gloom, indeed, enabled him to sympathize with all dark affections. Dying sinners cried aloud for Mr. Hooper, and would not yield their breath till he appeared; though ever, as he stooped to whisper consolation, they shuddered at the veiled face so near their own. Such were the terrors of the black veil, even when Death had bared his visage! Strangers came long distances to attend service at his church, with the mere idle purpose of gazing at his figure, because it was forbidden them to behold his face. But many were made to quake ere they departed! Once, during Governor Belcher's administration, Mr. Hooper was appointed to preach the election sermon. Covered with his black veil, he stood before the chief magistrate, the council, and the representatives, and wrought so deep an impression, that the legislative measures of that year were characterized by all the gloom and piety of our earliest ancestral sway.

In this manner Mr. Hooper spent a long life, irreproachable in outward act, yet shrouded in dismal suspicions; kind and loving, though unloved, and dimly feared; a man apart from men, shunned in their health and joy, but ever summoned to their aid in mortal anguish. As years wore on, shedding their snows above his sable veil, he acquired a name throughout the New England churches, and they called him Father Hooper. Nearly all his parishioners, who were of mature age when he was settled, had been borne away by many a funeral: he had one congregation in the church, and a more crowded one in the churchyard; and having wrought so late into the evening, and done his work so well, it was now good Father Hooper's turn to rest.

Several persons were visible by the shaded candlelight, in the death chamber of the old clergyman. Natural connections he had none. But there was the decorously grave, though unmoved physician, seeking only to mitigate the last pangs of the patient whom he could not save. There were the deacons, and other eminently pious members of his church. There also, was the Reverend Mr. Clark, of Westbury, a young and zealous divine, who had ridden in haste to pray by the bedside of the expiring minister. There was the nurse, no hired handmaiden of death, but one whose calm affection had endured thus long in secrecy, in solitude, amid the chill of age, and would not perish, even at the long dying hour. Who, but Elizabeth! And there lay the hoary head of good

Father Hooper upon the death pillow, with the black veil still swathed about his brow, and reaching down over his face, so that each more difficult gasp of his faint breath caused it to stir. All through life that piece of crape had hung between him and the world: it had separated him from cheerful brotherhood and woman's love, and kept him in that saddest of all prisons, his own heart; and still it lay upon his face, as if to deepen the gloom of his darksome chamber, and shade him from the sunshine of eternity.

For some time previous, his mind had been confused, wavering doubtfully between the past and the present, and hovering forward, as it were, at intervals, into the indistinctness of the world to come. There had been feverish turns, which tossed him from side to side, and wore away what little strength he had. But in his most convulsive struggles, and in the wildest vagaries of his intellect, when no other thought retained its sober influence, he still showed an awful solicitude lest the black veil should slip aside. Even if his bewildered soul could have forgotten, there was a faithful woman at his pillow, who, with averted eyes, would have covered that aged face, which she had last beheld in the comeliness of manhood. At length the death-stricken old man lay quietly in the torpor of mental and bodily exhaustion, with an imperceptible pulse, and breath that grew fainter and fainter, except when a long, deep, and irregular inspiration seemed to prelude the flight of his spirit.

The minister of Westbury approached the bedside.

"Venerable Father Hooper," said he, "the moment of your release is at hand. Are you ready for the lifting of the veil that shuts in time from eternity?"

Father Hooper at first replied merely by a feeble motion of his head; then, apprehensive, perhaps, that his meaning might be doubtful, he exerted himself to speak.

"Yea," said he, in faint accents, "my soul hath a patient weariness until that veil be lifted."

"And is it fitting," resumed the Reverend Mr. Clark, "that a man so given to prayer, of such a blameless example, holy in deed and thought, so far as mortal judgment may pronounce; is it fitting that a father in the church should leave a shadow on his memory, that may seem to blacken a life so pure? I pray you, my venerable brother, let not this thing be! Suffer us to be gladdened by your triumphant aspect as you go to your reward. Before the veil of eternity be lifted, let me cast aside this black veil from your face!"

And thus speaking, the Reverend Mr. Clark bent forward to reveal the mystery of so many years. But, exerting a sudden energy, that made all the beholders stand aghast, Father Hooper snatched both his hands from beneath the bedclothes, and pressed them strongly on the black veil, resolute to struggle, if the minister of Westbury would contend with a dying man.

"Never!" cried the veiled clergyman. "On earth, never!"

"Dark old man!" exclaimed the affrighted minister, "with what horrible crime upon your soul are you now passing to the judgment?"

Father Hooper's breath heaved; it rattled in his throat; but with a mighty effort, grasping forward with his hands, he caught hold of life, and held it back till he should speak. He even raised himself in bed; and there he sat, shivering with the arms of death around him, while the black veil hung down, awful, at that last moment, in the gathered terrors of a lifetime. And yet the faint, sad smile, so often there, now seemed to glimmer from its obscurity, and linger on Father Hooper's lips.

"Why do you tremble at me alone?" cried he, turning his veiled face round the circle of pale spectators. "Tremble also at each other! Have men avoided me, and women shown no pity, and children screamed and fled, only for my black veil? What, but the mystery which it obscurely typifies, has made this piece of crape so awful? When the friend shows his inmost heart to his friend; the lover to his best beloved; when man does not vainly shrink from the eye of his Creator, loathsomely treasuring up the secret of his sin; then deem me a monster, for the symbol beneath which I have lived, and die! I look around me, and, lo! on every visage a Black Veil!"

While his auditors shrank from one another, in mutual affright, Father Hooper fell back upon his pillow, a veiled corpse, with a faint smile lingering on the lips. Still veiled, they laid him in his coffin, and a veiled corpse they bore him to the grave. The grass of many years has sprung up and withered on that grave, the burial stone is moss-grown, and good Mr. Hooper's face is dust; but awful is still the thought that it mouldered beneath the Black Veil!

No recounting of a Saint's life could indicate more clearly the sexual and unconscious nature of a particular religious belief than this perverse tale of incest, parricide, guilt and expiation.

GUSTAVE FLAUBERT

The Legend of Saint Julian the Hospitaller

1

Julian's father and mother dwelt in a castle built on the slope of a hill, in the heart of the woods.

The towers at its four corners had pointed roofs covered with leaden tiles, and the foundation rested upon solid rocks, which descended abruptly to the bottom of the moat.

In the courtyard, the stone flagging was as immaculate as the floor of a church. Long rain-spouts, representing dragons with yawning jaws, directed the water towards the cistern, and on each window-sill of the castle a basil or a heliotrope bush bloomed, in painted flower-pots.

A second enclosure, surrounded by a fence, comprised a fruit-orchard, a garden decorated with figures wrought in bright-hued flowers, an arbour with several bowers, and a mall for the diversion of the pages. On the other side were the kennel, the stables, the bakery, the wine-press and the barns. Around these spread a pasture, also enclosed by a strong hedge.

Peace had reigned so long that the portcullis was never lowered; the moats were filled with water; swallows built their nests in the cracks of the battlements, and as soon as the sun shone too strongly, the archer who all day long paced to and fro on the curtain, withdrew to the watch-tower and slept soundly.

Inside the castle, the locks on the doors shone brightly; costly tapestries hung in the apartments to keep out the cold; the closets overflowed with linen, the cellar was filled with casks of wine, and the oak chests fairly groaned under the weight of money-bags.

In the armoury could be seen, between banners and the heads of wild beasts, weapons of all nations and of all ages, from the slings of the Amalekites and the javelins of the Garamantes, to the broad-swords of the Saracens and the coats of mail of the Normans.

The largest spit in the kitchen could hold an ox; the chapel was as gorgeous as a king's oratory. There was even a Roman bath in a secluded part of the castle, though the good lord of the manor refrained from using it, as he deemed it a heathenish practice.

Wrapped always in a cape made of fox-skins, he wandered about the castle, rendered justice among his vassals and settled his neighbours' quarrels. In the winter, he gazed dreamily at the falling snow, or had stories read aloud to him. But as soon as the fine weather returned, he would mount his mule and sally forth into the country roads, edged with ripening wheat, to talk with the peasants, to whom he distributed advice. After a number of adventures he took unto himself a wife of high lineage.

She was pale and serious, and a trifle haughty. The horns of her head-dress touched the top of the doors and the hem of her gown trailed far behind her. She conducted her household like a cloister. Every morning she distributed work to the maids, supervised the making of preserves and unguents, and afterwards passed her time in spinning, or in embroidering altar-cloths. In response to her fervent prayers, God granted her a son!

Then there was great rejoicing; and they gave a feast which lasted three days and four nights, with illuminations and soft music. Chickens as large as sheep, and the rarest spices were served; for the entertainment of the guests, a dwarf crept out of a pie; and when the bowls were too few, for the crowd swelled continuously, the wine was drunk from helmets and hunting-horns.

The young mother did not appear at the feast. She was quietly resting in bed. One night she awoke, and beheld in a moonbeam that crept through the window something that looked like a moving shadow. It was an old man clad in sackcloth, who resembled a hermit. A rosary dangled at his side and he carried a beggar's sack on his shoulder. He approached the foot of the bed, and without opening his lips said: "Rejoice, O mother! Thy son shall be a saint."

She would have cried out, but the old man, gliding along the moonbeam, rose through the air and disappeared. The songs of the banqueters grew louder. She could hear angels' voices, and her head sank back on the pillow, which was surmounted by the bone of a martyr, framed in precious stones.

The following day, the servants, upon being questioned, declared, to a man, that they had seen no hermit. Then, whether dream or fact, this must certainly have been a communication from heaven; but she took care not to speak of it, lest she should be accused of presumption.

The guests departed at daybreak, and Julian's father stood at the castle gate, where he had just bidden farewell to the last one, when a beggar suddenly emerged from the mist and confronted him. He was a gipsy—for he had a braided beard and wore silver bracelets on each arm. His eyes burned and, in an inspired way, he muttered some disconnected words: "Ah! Ah! thy son!—great bloodshed—great glory—happy always—an emperor's family."

Then he stooped to pick up the alms thrown to him, and disappeared in the tall grass.

The lord of the manor looked up and down the road and called as loudly as he could. But no one answered him! The wind only howled and the morning mists were fast dissolving.

He attributed his vision to a dullness of the brain resulting from too much sleep. "If I should speak of it," quoth he, "people would laugh at me." Still, the glory that was to be his son's dazzled him, albeit the meaning of the prophecy was not clear to him, and he even doubted that he had heard it.

The parents kept their secret from each other. But both cherished the child with equal devotion, and as they considered him marked by God, they had great regard for his person. His cradle was lined with the softest feathers, and a lamp representing a dove burned continually over it; three nurses rocked him night and day, and with his pink cheeks and blue eyes, brocaded cloak and embroidered cap, he looked like a little Jesus. He cut all his teeth without even a whimper.

When he was seven years old his mother taught him to sing, and his father lifted him upon a tall horse, to inspire him with courage. The child smiled with delight, and soon became familiar with everything pertaining to charges. An old and very learned monk taught him the Gospel, the Arabic numerals, the Latin letters, and the art of painting delicate designs on vellum. They worked in the top of a tower, away from all noise and disturbance.

When the lesson was over, they would go down into the garden and study the flowers.

Sometimes a herd of cattle passed through the valley below, in charge of a man in Oriental dress. The lord of the manor, recognising him as a merchant, would despatch a servant after him. The stranger, becoming confident, would stop on his way and after being ushered into the castle-hall, would display pieces of velvet and silk, trinkets and strange objects whose use was unknown in those parts. Then, in due time, he would take leave, without having been molested and with a handsome profit.

At other times, a band of pilgrims would knock at the door. Their wet garments would be hung in front of the hearth and after they had been refreshed by food they would relate their travels, and discuss the uncertainty of vessels on the high seas, their long journeys across burning sands, the ferocity of the infidels, the caves of Syria, the Manger and the Holy Sepulchre. They made presents to the young heir of beautiful shells, which they carried in their cloaks.

The lord of the manor very often feasted his brothers-at-arms, and over the wine the old warriors would talk of battles and attacks, of war-machines and of the frightful wounds they had received, so that Julian, who was a listener, would scream with excitement; then his father felt convinced that some day he would be a conqueror. But in the evening, after the Angelus, when he passed through the crowd of beggars who clustered about the church-door, he distributed his alms with so much modesty and nobility that his mother fully expected to see him become an archbishop in time.

His seat in the chapel was next to his parents, and no matter how long the services lasted, he remained kneeling on his *prie-dieu*, with folded hands and his velvet cap lying close beside him on the floor.

One day, during mass, he raised his head and beheld a little white mouse crawling out of a hole in the wall. It scrambled to the first altar-step and then, after a few gambols, ran back in the same direction. On the following Sunday, the idea of seeing the mouse again worried him. It returned; and every Sunday after that he watched for it; and it annoyed him so much that he grew to hate it and resolved to do away with it.

So, having closed the door and strewn some crumbs on the steps of the altar, he placed himself in front of the hole with a stick. After a long while a pink snout appeared, and then the whole mouse crept out. He struck it lightly with his stick and stood stunned at the sight of the little, lifeless body. A drop of blood stained the floor. He wiped it away hastily with his sleeve, and picking up the mouse, threw it away, without saying a word about it to anyone.

All sorts of birds pecked at the seeds in the garden. He put some peas in a hollow reed, and when he heard birds chirping in a tree, he would approach cautiously, lift the tube and swell his cheeks; then, when the little creatures dropped about him in multitudes, he could not refrain from laughing and being delighted with his own cleverness.

One morning, as he was returning by way of the curtain, he beheld a fat pigeon sunning itself on the top of the wall. He paused to gaze at it; where he stood the rampart was cracked and a piece of stone was near at hand; he gave his arm a jerk and the well-aimed missile struck the bird squarely, sending it straight into the moat below.

He sprang after it, unmindful of the brambles, and ferreted around the bushes with the litheness of a young dog.

The pigeon hung with broken wings in the branches of a privet hedge.

The persistence of its life irritated the boy. He began to strangle it, and its convulsions made his heart beat quicker, and filled him with a wild, tumultuous voluptuousness, the last throb of its heart making him feel like fainting.

At supper that night, his father declared that at his age a boy should begin to hunt; and he arose and brought forth an old writing-book which contained, in questions and answers, everything pertaining to the pastime. In it, a master showed a supposed pupil how to train dogs and falcons, lay traps, recognise a stag by its fumets, and a fox or a wolf by footprints. He also taught the best way of discovering their tracks, how to start them, where their refuges are usually to be found, what winds are the most favourable, and further enumerated the various cries, and the rules of the quarry.

When Julian was able to recite all these things by heart, his father made up a pack of hounds for him. There were twenty-four greyhounds of Barbary, speedier than gazelles, but liable to get out of temper; seventeen couples of Breton dogs, great barkers, with broad chests and russet coats flecked with white. For wild-boar hunting and perilous doublings, there were forty boarhounds as hairy as bears.

The red mastiffs of Tartary, almost as large as donkeys, with broad backs and straight legs, were destined for the pursuit of the wild bull. The black coats of the spaniels shone like satin; the barking of the setters equalled that of the beagles. In a special enclosure were eight growling bloodhounds that tugged at their chains and rolled their eyes, and these dogs leaped at men's throats and were not afraid even of lions.

All ate wheat bread, drank from marble troughs, and had high-sounding names.

Perhaps the falconry surpassed the pack; for the master of the castle, by paying great sums of money, had secured Caucasian hawks, Babylonian sakers, German gerfalcons, and pilgrim falcons captured on the cliffs edging the cold seas, in distant lands. They were housed in a thatched shed and were chained to the perch in the order of size. In front of them was a little grass-plot where, from time to time, they were allowed to disport themselves.

Bag-nets, baits, traps and all sorts of snares were manufactured.

Often they would take out pointers who would set almost immediately; then the whippers-in, advancing step by step, would cautiously spread a huge net over their motionless bodies. At the command, the dogs would bark and arouse the quails; and the ladies of the neighbourhood, with their husbands, children and hand-maids, would fall upon them and capture them with ease.

At other times they used a drum to start hares; and frequently foxes fell into the ditches prepared for them, while wolves caught their paws in the traps.

But Julian scorned these convenient contrivances; he preferred to hunt away from the crowd, alone with his steed and his falcon. It was almost always a large, snow-white, Scythian bird. His leather hood was ornamented with a plume, and on his blue feet were bells; and he perched firmly on his master's arm while they galloped across the plains. Then Julian would suddenly untie his tether and let him fly, and the bold bird would dart through the air like an arrow. One might perceive two spots circle around, unite, and then disappear in the blue heights. Presently the falcon would return with a mutilated bird, and perch again on his master's gauntlet with trembling wings.

Julian loved to sound his trumpet and follow his dogs over hills and streams, into the woods; and when the stag began to moan under their teeth, he would kill it deftly, and delight in the fury of the brutes, which would devour the pieces spread out on the warm hide.

On foggy days, he would hide in the marshes to watch for wild geese, otters and wild ducks.

At daybreak, three equerries waited for him at the foot of the steps; and though the old monk leaned out of the dormer-window and made signs to him to return, Julian would not look around.

He heeded neither the broiling sun, the rain nor the storm; he drank spring water and ate wild berries, and when he was tired, he lay down under a tree; and he would come home at night covered with earth and blood, with thistles in his hair and smelling of wild beasts. He grew to be like them. And when his mother kissed him, he responded coldly to her caress and seemed to be thinking of deep and serious things.

He killed bears with a knife, bulls with a hatchet, and wild boars with a spear; and once, with nothing but a stick, he defended himself against some wolves, which were gnawing corpses at the foot of a gibbet.

One winter morning he set out before daybreak, with a bow slung across his shoulder and a quiver of arrows attached to the pummel of his saddle. The hoofs of his steed beat the ground with regularity and his two beagles trotted close behind. The wind was blowing hard and icicles clung to his cloak. A part of the horizon cleared, and he beheld some rabbits playing around their burrows. In an instant, the two dogs were upon them, and seizing as many as they could, they broke their backs in the twinkling of an eye.

Soon he came to a forest. A woodcock, paralysed by the cold, perched on a branch, with its head hidden under its wing. Julian, with a lunge of his sword, cut off its feet, and without stopping to pick it up, rode away.

Three hours later he found himself on the top of a mountain so high that the sky seemed almost black. In front of him, a long, flat rock hung over a precipice, and at the end, two wild goats stood gazing down into the abyss. As he had no arrows (for he had left his steed behind), he thought he would climb down to where they stood; and with bare feet and bent back he at last reached the first goat and thrust his dagger below its ribs. But the second animal, in its terror, leaped into the precipice. Julian threw himself forward to strike it, but his right foot slipped, and he fell, face downward and with outstretched arms, over the body of the first goat.

After he returned to the plains, he followed a stream bordered by willows. From time to time, some cranes, flying low, passed over his head. He killed them with his whip, never missing a bird. He beheld in the distance the gleam of a lake which appeared to be of lead, and in the middle of it was an animal he had never seen before, a beaver with a black muzzle. Notwithstanding the distance that separated them, an arrow ended its life and Julian only regretted that he was not able to carry the skin home with him.

Then he entered an avenue of tall trees, the tops of which formed a triumphal arch to the entrance of a forest. A deer sprang out of the thicket and a badger crawled out of its hole, a stag appeared in the road, and a peacock spread its fan-shaped tail on the grass—and after he had slain them all, other deer, other stags, other badgers, other peacocks, and jays, blackbirds, foxes, porcupines, polecats, and lynxes, appeared; in fact, a host of beasts that grew more and more numerous with every step he took. Trembling, and with a look of appeal in their eyes, they gathered around Julian, but he did not stop slaying them; and so intent was he on stretching his bow, drawing his sword and whipping out his knife, that he had little thought for aught else. He knew that he was hunting in some country since an indefinite time, through the very fact of his existence, as everything seemed to occur with the ease one experiences in dreams. But presently an extraordinary sight made him pause.

He beheld a valley shaped like a circus and filled with stags which, huddled together, were warming one another with the vapour of their breaths that mingled with the early mist.

For a few minutes, he almost choked with pleasure at the prospect of so great a carnage. Then he sprang from his horse, rolled up his sleeves, and began to aim.

When the first arrow whizzed through the air, the stags turned their heads simultaneously. They huddled closer, uttered plaintive cries, and a great agitation seized the whole herd. The edge of the valley was too high to admit of flight; and the animals ran around the enclosure in their efforts to escape. Julian aimed, stretched his bow and his arrows fell as fast and thick as raindrops in a shower.

Maddened with terror, the stags fought and reared and climbed on top of one another; their antlers and bodies formed a moving mountain which tumbled to pieces whenever it displaced itself.

Finally the last one expired. Their bodies lay stretched out on the sand with foam gushing from the nostrils and the bowels protruding. The heaving of their bellies grew less and less noticeable, and presently all was still.

Night came, and behind the trees, through the branches, the sky appeared like a sheet of blood.

Julian leaned against a tree and gazed with dilated eyes at the enormous slaughter. He was now unable to comprehend how he had accomplished it.

On the opposite side of the valley, he suddenly beheld a large stag, with a doe and their fawn. The buck was black and of enormous size; he had a white beard and carried sixteen antlers. His mate was the color of dead leaves, and she browsed upon the grass, while the fawn, clinging to her udder, followed her step by step.

Again the bow was stretched, and instantly the fawn dropped dead, and seeing this, its mother raised her head and uttered a poignant, almost human wail of agony. Exasperated, Julian thrust his knife into her chest, and felled her to the ground.

The great stag had watched everything and suddenly he sprang forward. Julian aimed his last arrow at the beast. It struck him between his antlers and stuck there.

The stag did not appear to notice it; leaping over the bodies, he was coming nearer and nearer with the intention, Julian thought, of charging at him and ripping him open, and he recoiled with inexpressible horror. Bur presently the huge animal halted, and, with eyes aflame and the solemn air of a patriarch and a judge, repeated thrice, while a bell tolled in the distance:

"Accursed! Accursed! Accursed! some day, ferocious soul, thou wilt murder thy father and thy mother!"

Then he sank on his knees, gently closed his lids and expired.

At first Julian was stunned, and then a sudden lassitude and an immense sadness came over him. Holding his head between his hands, he wept for a long time.

His steed had wandered away; his dogs had forsaken him; the solitude seemed to threaten him with unknown perils. Impelled by a sense of sickening terror, he ran across the fields, and choosing a path at random, found himself almost immediately at the gates of the castle.

That night he could not rest, for, by the flickering light of the hanging lamp, he beheld again the huge black stag. He fought against the obsession of the prediction and kept repeating: "No! No! No! I cannot slay them!" and then he thought: "Still, supposing I desired to?—" and he feared that the devil might inspire him with this desire.

During three months, his distracted mother prayed at his bedside, and his father paced the halls of the castle in anguish. He consulted the most celebrated physicians, who prescribed quantities of medicine. Julian's illness, they declared, was due to some injurious wind or to amorous desire. But in reply to their questions, the young man only shook his head. After a time, his strength returned, and he was able to take a walk in the courtyard, supported by his father and the old monk.

But after he had completely recovered, he refused to hunt.

His father, hoping to please him, presented him with a large Saracen sabre.

It was placed on a panoply that hung on a pillar, and a ladder was required to reach it. Julian climbed up to it one day, but the heavy weapon slipped from his grasp, and in falling grazed his father and tore his cloak. Julian, believing he had killed him, fell in a swoon.

After that, he carefully avoided weapons. The sight of a naked sword made him grow pale, and this weakness caused great distress to his family.

In the end, the old monk ordered him in the name of God, and of his forefathers, once more to indulge in the sports of a nobleman.

The equerries diverted themselves every day with javelins and Julian soon excelled in the practice.

He was able to send a javelin into bottles, to break the teeth of the weather-cocks on the castle and to strike door-nails at a distance of one hundred feet.

One summer evening, at the hour when dusk renders objects indistinct, he was in the arbour in the garden, and thought he saw two white wings in the background hovering around the espalier. Not for a moment did he doubt that it was a stork, and so he threw his javelin at it.

A heart-rending scream pierced the air.

He had struck his mother, whose cap and long streamers remained nailed to the wall.

Julian fled from home and never returned.

2

He joined a horde of adventurers who were passing through the place.

He learned what it was to suffer hunger, thirst, sickness and filth. He grew accustomed to the din of battles and to the sight of dying men. The wind tanned his skin. His limbs became hardened through contact with armour, and as he was very strong and brave, temperate and of good counsel, he easily obtained command of a company.

At the outset of a battle, he would electrify his soldiers by a motion of his sword. He would climb the walls of a citadel with a knotted rope, at night, rocked by the storm, while sparks of fire clung to his cuirass, and molten lead and boiling tar poured from the battlements.

Often a stone would break his shield. Bridges crowded with men gave way under him. Once, by turning his mace, he rid himself of fourteen horsemen. He defeated all those who came forward to fight him on the field of honour, and more than a score of times it was believed that he had been killed.

However, thanks to Divine protection, he always escaped, for he shielded orphans, widows, and aged men. When he caught sight of one of the latter walking ahead of him, he would call to him to show his face, as if he feared that he might kill him by mistake.

All sorts of intrepid men gathered under his leadership, fugitive slaves, peasant rebels, and penniless bastards; he then organized an army which increased so much that he became famous and was in great demand.

He succoured in turn the Dauphin of France, the King of England, the Templars of Jerusalem, the General of the Parths, the Negus of Abyssinia and the Emperor of Calicut. He fought against Scandinavians covered with fish-scales, against negroes mounted on red asses and armed with shields made of hippopotamus hide, against gold-coloured Indians who wielded great, shining swords above their heads. He conquered the Troglodytes and the cannibals. He travelled through regions so torrid that the heat of the sun would set fire to the hair on one's head; he journeyed through countries so glacial that one's arms would fall from the body; and he passed through places where the fogs were so dense that it seemed like being surrounded by phantoms.

Republics in trouble consulted him; when he conferred with ambassadors, he always obtained unexpected concessions. Also, if a monarch behaved badly, he would arrive on the scene and rebuke him. He freed nations. He rescued queens sequestered in towers. It was he and no other that killed the serpent of Milan and the dragon of Oberbirbach.

Now, the Emperor of Occitania, having triumphed over the Spanish Mussulmans, had taken the sister of the Caliph of Cordova as a concubine, and had had one daughter by her, whom he brought up in the teachings of Christ. But the Caliph, feigning that he wished to become converted, made him a visit, and brought with him a numerous escort. He slaughtered the entire garrison and threw the Emperor into a dungeon, and treated him with great cruelty in order to obtain possession of his treasures.

Julian went to his assistance, destroyed the army of infidels, laid siege to the city, slew the Caliph, chopped off his head and threw it over the fortifications like a cannon-ball.

As a reward for so great a service, the Emperor presented him with a large sum of money in baskets; but Julian declined it. Then the Emperor, thinking that the amount was not sufficiently large, offered him three quarters of his fortune, and on meeting a second refusal, proposed to share his kingdom with his benefactor. But Julian only thanked him for it, and the Emperor felt like weeping with vexation at not being able to show his gratitude, when he suddenly tapped his forehead and whispered a few words in the ear of one of his courtiers; the tapestry curtains parted and a young girl appeared.

Her large black eyes shone like two soft lights. A charming smile parted her lips. Her curls were caught in the jewels of her half-opened bodice, and the grace of her youthful body could be divined under the transparency of her tunic.

She was small and quite plump, but her waist was slender.

Julian was absolutely dazzled, all the more since he had always led a chaste life.

So he married the Emperor's daughter, and received at the same time a castle she had inherited from her mother; and when the rejoicings were over, he departed with his bride, after many courtesies had been exchanged on both sides.

The castle was of Moorish design, in white marble, erected on a promontory and surrounded by orange-trees.

Terraces of flowers extended to the shell-strewn shores of a beautiful bay. Behind the castle spread a fan-shaped forest. The sky was always blue, and the trees were swayed in turn by the ocean-breeze and by the winds that blew from the mountains that closed the horizon.

Light entered the apartments through the incrustations of the walls. High, reed-like columns supported the ceiling of the cupolas, decorated in imitation of stalactites.

Fountains played in the spacious halls; the courts were inlaid with mosaic; there were festooned partitions and a great profusion of architectural fancies; and everywhere reigned a silence so deep that the swish of a sash or the echo of a sigh could be distinctly heard.

Julian now had renounced war. Surrounded by a peaceful people, he remained idle, receiving every day a throng of subjects who came and knelt before him and kissed his hand in Oriental fashion.

Clad in sumptuous garments, he would gaze out of the window and think of his past exploits; and wish that he might again run in the desert in pursuit of ostriches and gazelles, hide among the bamboos to watch for leopards, ride through forests filled with rhinoceroses, climb the most inaccessible peaks in order to have a better aim at the eagles, and fight the polar bears on the icebergs of the northern sea.

Sometimes, in his dreams, he fancied himself like Adam in the midst of Paradise, surrounded by all the beasts; by merely extending his arm, he was able to kill them; or else they filed past him, in pairs, by order of size, from the lions and the elephants to the ermines and the ducks, as on the day they entered Noah's Ark.

Hidden in the shadow of a cave, he aimed unerring arrows at them; then came others and still others, until he awoke, wild-eyed.

Princes, friends of his, invited him to their meets, but he always refused their invitations, because he thought that by this kind of penance he might possibly avert the threatened misfortune; it seemed to him that the fate of his parents depended on his refusal to slaughter animals. But he suffered because he could not see them, and his other desire was growing well-nigh unbearable.

In order to divert his mind, his wife had dancers and jugglers come to the castle.

She went abroad with him in an open litter; at other times, stretched out on the edge of a boat, they watched for hours the fish disport themselves in the water, which was as clear as the sky. Often she playfully threw flowers at him or nestling at his feet she played melodies on an old mandolin; then, clasping her hands on his shoulder, she would inquire tremulously: "What troubles thee, my dear lord?"

He would not reply, or else he would burst into tears; but at last, one day, he confessed his fearful dread.

His wife scorned the idea and reasoned wisely with him: probably his father and mother were dead; and even if he should ever see them again, through what chance, to what end, would he arrive at this abomination? Therefore, his fears were groundless, and he should hunt again.

Julian listened to her and smiled, but he could not bring himself to yield to his desire.

One August evening when they were in their bedchamber, she having just retired and he being about to kneel in prayer, he heard the yelping of a fox and light footsteps under the window; and he thought he saw things in the dark that looked like animals. The temptation was too strong. He seized his quiver.

His wife appeared astonished.

"I am obeying you," quoth he, "and I shall be back at sunrise."

However, she feared that some calamity would happen. But he reassured her and departed, surprised at her illogical moods.

A short time afterwards, a page came to announce that two strangers desired, in the absence of the lord of the castle, to see its mistress at once.

Soon a stooping old man and an aged woman entered the room; their coarse garments were covered with dust and each leaned on a stick.

They grew bold enough to say that they brought Julian news of his parents. She leaned out of the bed to listen to them. But after glancing at each other, the old people asked her whether he ever referred to them and if he still loved them.

"Oh! yes!" she said.

Then they exclaimed:

"We are his parents!" and they sat themselves down, for they were very tired.

But there was nothing to show the young wife that her husband was their son.

They proved it by describing to her the birthmarks he had on his body. Then she jumped out of bed, called a page, and ordered that a repast be served to them.

But although they were very hungry, they could scarcely eat, and she observed surreptitiously how their lean fingers trembled whenever they lifted their cups.

They asked a hundred questions about their son, and she answered each one of them, but she was careful not to refer to the terrible idea that concerned them.

When he failed to return, they had left their château; and had wandered for several years, following vague indications but without losing hope.

So much money had been spent at the tolls of the rivers and in inns, to satisfy the rights of princes and the demands of highwaymen, that now their purse was quite empty and they were obliged to beg. But what did it matter, since they were about to clasp again their son in their arms? They lauded his happiness in having such a beautiful wife, and did not tire of looking at her and kissing her.

The luxuriousness of the apartment astonished them; and the old man, after examining the walls, inquired why they bore the coat-of-arms of the Emperor of Occitania.

"He is my father," she replied.

And he marvelled and remembered the prediction of the gipsy, while his wife meditated upon the words the hermit had spoken to her. The glory of their son was undoubtedly only the dawn of eternal splendours, and the old people remained awed while the light from the candelabra on the table fell on them.

In the heyday of youth, both had been extremely handsome. The mother had not lost her hair, and bands of snowy whiteness framed her cheeks; and the father, with his stalwart figure and long beard, looked like a carved image.

Julian's wife prevailed upon them not to wait for him. She put them in her bed and closed the curtains; and they both fell asleep. The day broke and outdoors the little birds began to chirp.

Meanwhile, Julian had left the castle grounds and walked nervously through the forest, enjoying the velvety softness of the grass and the balminess of the air.

The shadow of the trees fell on the earth. Here and there, the moonlight flecked the glades and Julian feared to advance, because he mistook the silvery light for water and the tranquil surface of the pools for grass. A great stillness reigned everywhere, and he failed to see any of the beasts that only a moment ago were prowling around the castle. As he walked on, the woods grew thicker, and the darkness more impenetrable. Warm winds, filled with enervating perfumes, caressed him; he sank into masses of dead leaves, and after a while he leaned against an oak-tree to rest and catch his breath.

Suddenly a body blacker than the surrounding darkness sprang from behind the tree. It was a wild boar. Julian did not have time to stretch his bow, and he bewailed the fact as if it were some great misfortune. Presently, having left the woods, he beheld a wolf slinking along a hedge.

He aimed an arrow at him. The wolf paused, turned his head and quietly continued on his way. He trotted along, always keeping at the same distance, pausing now and then to look around and resuming his flight as soon as an arrow was aimed in his direction.

In this way Julian traversed an apparently endless plain, then sandhills, and at last found himself on a plateau that dominated a great stretch of land. Large flat stones were interspersed among crumbling vaults; bones and skeletons covered the ground, and here and there some mouldy crosses stood desolate. But presently, shapes moved in the darkness of the tombs, and from them came panting, wild-eyed hyenas. They approached him and smelled him, grinning hideously and disclosing their gums. He whipped out his sword, but they scattered in every direction and continuing their swift, limping gallop, disappeared in a cloud of dust.

Some time afterwards, in a ravine, he encountered a wild bull, with threatening horns, pawing the sand with his hoofs. Julian thrust his lance between his dewlaps. But his weapon snapped as if the beast were made of bronze; then he closed his eyes in anticipation of his death. When he opened them again, the bull had vanished.

Then his soul collapsed with shame. Some supernatural power destroyed his strength, and he set out for home through the forest. The woods were a tangle of creeping plants that he had to cut with his sword, and while he was thus engaged, a weasel slid between his feet, a panther jumped over his shoulder, and a serpent wound itself around an ash-tree.

Among its leaves was a monstrous jackdaw that watched Julian intently, and here and there, between the branches, appeared great, fiery sparks as if the sky were raining all its stars upon the forest. But the sparks were the eyes of wild-cats, owls, squirrels, monkeys and parrots.

Julian aimed his arrows at them, but the feathered weapons lighted on the leaves of the trees and looked like white butterflies. He threw stones at them; but the missiles did not strike, and fell to the ground. Then he cursed himself, and howled imprecations, and in his rage he could have struck himself.

Then all the beasts he had pursued appeared, and formed a narrow circle around him. Some sat on their hind-quarters, while others stood at full height. And Julian remained among them, transfixed with terror and absolutely unable to move. By a supreme effort of his will-power, he took a step forward; those that perched in the trees opened their wings, those that trod the earth moved their limbs, and all accompanied him.

The hyenas strode in front of him, the wolf and the wild boar brought up the rear. On his right, the bull swung its head and on his left the serpent crawled through the grass; while the panther, arching its back, advanced with velvety footfalls and long strides. Julian walked as slowly as possible, so as not to irritate them, while in the depth of the bushes he could distinguish porcupines, foxes, vipers, jackals, and bears.

He began to run; the brutes followed him. The serpent hissed, the malodorous beasts frothed at the mouth, the wild boar rubbed his tusks against his heels, and the wolf scratched the palms of his hands with the hairs of his snout. The monkeys pinched him and made faces, the weasel rolled over his feet. A bear knocked his cap off with its huge paw, and the panther disdainfully dropped an arrow it was about to put in its mouth.

Irony seemed to incite their sly actions. As they watched him out of the corners of their eyes, they seemed to meditate a plan of revenge, and Julian, who was deafened by the buzzing of the insects, bruised by the wings and tails of the birds, choked by the stench of animal breaths, walked with outstretched arms and closed lids, like a blind man, without even the strength to beg for mercy.

The crowing of a cock vibrated in the air. Other cocks responded; it was day; and Julian recognised the top of his palace rising above the orange-trees.

Then, on the edge of a field, he beheld some red partridges fluttering around a stubble-field. He unfastened his cloak and threw it over them like a net. When he lifted it, he found only a bird that had been dead a long time and was decaying.

This disappointment irritated him more than all the others. The thirst for carnage stirred afresh within him; animals failing him, he desired to slaughter men.

He climbed the three terraces and opened the door with a blow of his fist; but at the foot of the staircase, the memory of his beloved wife softened his heart. No doubt she was asleep, and he would go up and surprise her. Having removed his sandals, he unlocked the door softly and entered.

The stained windows dimmed the pale light of dawn. Julian stumbled over some garments lying on the floor and a little further on, he knocked against a table covered with dishes. "She must have eaten," he thought; so he advanced cautiously towards the bed which was concealed by the darkness in the back of the room. When he reached the edge, he leaned over the pillow where the two heads were resting close together and stooped to kiss his wife. His mouth encountered a man's beard.

He fell back, thinking he had become crazed; then he approached the bed again and his searching fingers discovered some hair which seemed to be very long. In order to convince himself that he was mistaken, he once more passed his hand slowly over the pillow. But this time he was sure that it was a beard and that a man was there! a man lying beside his wife!

Flying into an ungovernable passion, he sprang upon them with his drawn dagger, foaming, stamping and howling like a wild beast. After a while he stopped.

The corpses, pierced through the heart, had not even moved. He listened attentively to the two death-rattles, they were almost alike, and as they grew fainter, another voice, coming from far away, seemed to continue them. Uncertain at first, this plaintive voice came nearer and nearer, grew louder and louder and presently he recognised, with a feeling of abject terror, the bellowing of the great black stag.

And as he turned around, he thought he saw the spectre of his wife standing at the threshold with a light in her hand.

The sound of the murder had aroused her. In one glance she understood what had happened and fled in horror, letting the candle drop from her hand. Julian picked it up.

His father and mother lay before him, stretched on their backs, with gaping wounds in their breasts; and their faces, the expression of which was full of tender dignity, seemed to hide what might be an eternal secret.

Splashes and blotches of blood were on their white skin, on the bed-clothes, on the floor, and on an ivory Christ which hung in the alcove. The scarlet reflection of the stained window, which just then was struck by the sun, lighted up the bloody spots and appeared to scatter them around the whole room. Julian walked toward the corpses, repeating to himself and trying to believe that he was mistaken, that it was not possible, that there are often inexplicable likenesses.

At last he bent over to look closely at the old man and he saw between the half-closed lids, a dead pupil that scorched him like fire. Then he went over to the other side of the bed, where the other corpse lay, but the face was partly hidden by bands of white hair. Julian slipped his finger beneath them and raised the head, holding it at arm's length to study the features, while, with his other hand he lifted the torch. Drops of blood oozed from the mattress and fell one by one upon the floor.

At the close of the day, he appeared before his wife, and in a changed voice commanded her first not to answer him, not to approach him, not even to look at him, and to obey, under the penalty of eternal damnation, every one of his orders, which were irrevocable.

The funeral was to be held in accordance with the written instructions he had left on a chair in the death-chamber.

He left her his castle, his vassals, all his worldly goods, without keeping even his clothes or his sandals, which would be found at the top of the stairs.

She obeyed the will of God in bringing about his crime, and accordingly she must pray for his soul, since henceforth he should cease to exist.

The dead were buried sumptuously in the chapel of a monastery which it took three days to reach from the castle. A monk wearing a hood that covered his head followed the procession alone, for nobody dared to speak to him. And during the mass, he lay flat on the floor with his face downward and his arms stretched out at his sides.

After the burial, he was seen to take the road leading into the mountains. He looked back several times, and finally passed out of sight.

He left the country and begged his daily bread on his way.

He stretched out his hand to the horsemen he met in the roads, and humbly approached the harvesters in the fields; or else remained motionless in front of the gates of castles; and his face was so sad that he was never turned away.

Obeying a spirit of humility, he related his history to all men, and they would flee from him and cross themselves. In villages through which he had passed before, the good people bolted the doors, threatened him, and threw stones at him as soon as they recognised him. The more charitable ones placed a bowl on the window-sill and closed the shutters in order to avoid seeing him.

Repelled and shunned by everyone, he avoided his fellow-men and nourished himself with roots and plants, stray fruits and shells which he gathered along the shores.

Often, at the bend of a hill, he could perceive a mass of crowded roofs, stone spires, bridges, towers and narrow streets, from which arose a continual murmur of activity.

The desire to mingle with men impelled him to enter the city. But the gross and beastly expression of their faces, the noise of their industries and the indifference of their remarks, chilled his very heart. On holidays, when the cathedral bells rang out at daybreak and filled the people's hearts with gladness, he watched the inhabitants coming out of their dwellings, the dancers in the public squares, the fountains of ale, the damask hangings spread before the houses of princes; and then, when night came, he would peer through the windows at the long tables where families gathered and where grandparents held little children on their knees; then sobs would rise in his throat and he would turn away and go back to his haunts.

He gazed with yearning at the colts in the pastures, the birds in their nests, the insects on the flowers; but they all fled from him at his approach and hid or flew away. So he sought solitude. But the wind brought to his ears sounds resembling death-rattles; the tears of dew reminded him of heavier drops, and every evening, the sun would spread blood in the sky, and every night, in his dreams, he lived over his parricide.

He made himself a hair-cloth lined with iron spikes. On his knees, he ascended every hill that was crowned with a chapel. But the unrelenting thought spoiled the splendour of the tabernacles and tortured him in the midst of his penances.

He did not rebel against God, who had inflicted his action, but he despaired at the thought that he had committed it.

He had such a horror of himself that he took all sorts of risks. He rescued paralytics from fire and children from the waves. But the ocean scorned him and the flames spared him. Time did not allay his torment, which became so intolerable that he resolved to die.

One day, while he was stooping over a fountain to judge of its depth, an old man appeared on the other side. He wore a white beard and his appearance was so lamentable that Julian could not keep back his tears. The old man also was weeping. Without recognising him, Julian remembered confusedly a face that resembled his. He uttered a cry; for it was his father who stood before him; and he gave up all thought of taking his own life.

Thus weighted down by his recollections, he travelled through many countries and arrived at a river which was dangerous, because of its violence and the slime that covered its shores. Since a long time nobody had ventured to cross it.

The bow of an old boat, whose stern was buried in the mud, showed among the reeds. Julian, on examining it closely, found a pair of oars and hit upon the idea of devoting his life to the service of his fellow-men.

He began by establishing on the bank of the river a sort of road which would enable people to approach the edge of the stream; he broke his nails in his efforts to lift enormous stones which he pressed against the pit of his stomach in order to transport them from one point to another; he slipped in the mud, he sank into it, and several times was on the very brink of death.

Then he took to repairing the boat with débris of vessels, and afterwards built himself a hut with putty and trunks of trees.

When it became known that a ferry had been established, passengers flocked to it. They hailed him from the opposite side by waving flags, and Julian would jump into the boat and row over. The craft was very heavy, and the people loaded it with all sorts of baggage, and beasts of burden, who reared with fright, thereby adding greatly to the confusion. He asked nothing for his trouble; some gave him left-over victuals which they took from their sacks or worn-out garments which they could no longer use.

The brutal ones hurled curses at him, and when he rebuked them gently they replied with insults, and he was content to bless them.

A little table, a stool, a bed made of dead leaves and three earthen bowls were all he possessed. Two holes in the wall served as windows. On one side, as far as the eye could see, stretched barren wastes studded here and there with pools of water; and in front of him flowed the greenish waters of the wide river. In the spring, a putrid odour arose from the damp sod. Then fierce gales lifted clouds of dust that blew everywhere, even settling in the water and in one's mouth. A little later swarms of mosquitoes appeared, whose buzzing and stinging continued night and day. After that, came frightful frosts which communicated a stone-like rigidity to everything and inspired one with an insane desire for meat. Months passed when Julian never saw a human being. He often closed his lids and endeavored to recall his youth;—he beheld the courtyard of a castle, with greyhounds stretched out on a terrace, an armoury filled with valets, and under a bower of vines a youth with blond curls, sitting between an old man wrapped in furs and a lady with a high cap; presently the corpses rose before him, and then he would throw himself face downward on his cot and sob:

"Oh! poor father! poor mother! poor mother!" and would drop into a fitful slumber in which the terrible visions recurred.

One night he thought that some one was calling to him in his sleep. He listened intently, but could hear nothing save the roaring of the waters.

But the same voice repeated: "Julian!"

It proceeded from the opposite shore, a fact which appeared extraordinary to him, considering the breadth of the river.

The voice called a third time: "Julian!"

And the high-pitched tones sounded like the ringing of a church-bell.

Having lighted his lantern, he stepped out of his cabin. A frightful storm raged. The darkness was complete and was illuminated here and there only by the white waves leaping and tumbling.

After a moment's hesitation he untied the rope. The water presently grew smooth and the boat glided easily to the opposite shore, where a man was waiting.

He was wrapped in a torn piece of linen; his face was like a chalk mask, and his eyes were redder than glowing coals. When Julian held up his lantern he noticed that the stranger was covered with hideous sores; but notwithstanding this, there was in his attitude something like the majesty of a king.

As soon as he stepped into the boat, it sank deep into the water, borne downward by his weight; then it rose again and Julian began to row.

With each stroke of the oars, the force of the waves raised the bow of the boat. The water, which was blacker than ink, ran furiously along the sides. It formed abysses and then mountains, over which the boat glided, then it fell into yawning depths where, buffeted by the wind, it whirled around and around.

Julian leaned far forward and, bracing himself with his feet, bent backwards so as to bring his whole strength into play. Hail-stones cut his hands, the rain ran down his back, the velocity of the wind suffocated him. He stopped rowing and let the boat drift with the tide. But realising that an important matter was at stake, a command which could not be disregarded, he picked up the oars again; and the rattling of the tholes mingled with the clamourings of the storm.

The little lantern burned in front of him. Sometimes birds fluttered past it and obscured the light. But he could distinguish the eyes of the leper who stood at the stern, as motionless as a column.

And the trip lasted a long, long time.

When they reached the hut, Julian closed the door and saw the man sit down on the stool. The species of shroud that was wrapped around him had fallen below his loins, and his shoulders and chest and lean arms were hidden under blotches of scaly pustules. Enormous wrinkles crossed his forehead. Like a skeleton, he had a hole instead of a nose, and from his bluish lips came breath which was fetid and as thick as mist.

"I am hungry," he said.

Julian set before him what he had, a piece of pork and some crusts of coarse bread.

After he had devoured them, the table, the bowl, and the handle of the knife bore the same scales that covered his body.

Then he said: "I thirst!"

Julian fetched his jug of water and when he lifted it, he smelled an aroma that dilated his nostrils and filled his heart with gladness. It was wine; what a boon! but the leper stretched out his arm and emptied the jug at one draught.

Then he said: "I am cold!"

Julian ignited a bundle of ferns that lay in the middle of the hut. The leper approached the fire and, resting on his heels, began to warm himself; his whole frame shook and he was failing visibly; his eyes grew dull, his sores began to break, and in a faint voice he whispered:

"Thy bed!"

Julian helped him gently to it, and even laid the sail of his boat over him to keep him warm.

The leper tossed and moaned. The corners of his mouth were drawn up over his teeth; an accelerated death-rattle shook his chest and with each one of his aspirations, his stomach touched his spine. At last, he closed his eyes.

"I feel as if ice were in my bones! Lay thyself beside me!" he commanded. Julian took off his garments; and then, as naked as on the day he was born, he got into the bed; against his thigh he could feel the skin of the leper, and it was colder than a serpent and as rough as a file.

He tried to encourage the leper, but he only whispered:

"Oh! I am about to die! Come closer to me and warm me! Not with thy hands! No! with thy whole body."

So Julian stretched himself out upon the leper, lay on him, lips to lips, chest to chest.

Then the leper clasped him close and presently his eyes shone like stars; his hair lengthened into sunbeams; the breath of his nostrils had the scent of roses; a cloud of incense rose from the hearth, and the waters began to murmur harmoniously; an abundance of bliss, a superhuman joy, filled the soul of the swooning Julian, while he who clasped him to his breast grew and grew until his head and his feet touched the opposite walls of the cabin. The roof flew up in the air, disclosing the heavens, and Julian ascended into infinity face to face with our Lord Jesus Christ, who bore him straight to heaven.

And this is the story of Saint Julian the Hospitaller, as it is given on the stained-glass window of a church in my birthplace.

The mystic experience referred to and described by Herbert Fingarette takes on another dimension in Stefan Zweig's story of a man's transfiguration. As no scientific tract could, this story paints a haunting picture of the impact of a mystic experience and its psychic significance. Its hero's description of his awe and wonder enforces the pictures of growth offered by the mystic as well as by the patient who has completed psychoanalytic treatment.

STEFAN ZWEIG

Transfiguration

In the autumn of 1914, Baron Friedrich Michael von G., an officer in a dragoon regiment, was killed in action at Rawaruska. Among the papers in his desk at home was found a sealed packet which contained the following story. The relatives of the deceased, judging by the title and by a fugitive glance at the text, regarded it as a first attempt at fiction, and handed it over to me for examination, with authority to publish it if I thought fit. My own belief is that it is not a work of fiction at all, but an account of actual experiences. I therefore publish it as a human document, making neither alterations nor additions, but concealing the author's identity.

It suddenly occured to me to-day that I should like to write an account of my experiences during that queer night, so that I might be able to survey the whole course of events in their natural sequence. Ever since this fancy seized me, I have been dominated by an inexplicable impulse to pen the record of my adventures, although I doubt whether I shall find it possible to give an adequate impression of the strangeness of the occurrences. I have no artistic talent, no practice as a writer. My only attempts at authorship have been one or two humorous trifles written during my school days. I do not even know whether a special technique has been worked out in such matters; whether the aspirant to authorship can be taught the best way of producing a coherent account of the succession of outward things and their simultaneous reflexion in the mind. I am even dubious whether I shall be able to fit the meaning to the word and the word to the meaning, and thus to secure the balance which has always seemed to me characteristic of the style of the successful novelist. However, I am writing only for myself, and with no thought of making intelligible to others what I myself find it difficult enough to understand. My aim is merely to settle accounts, as it were, with certain happenings in which I was strongly interested and by which I was greatly moved—to look upon these happenings as objectively as possible. I have never told the story of the incidents to any of my friends. I was withheld from doing so, partly by my doubt whether I could make them understand the essence of what occurred, and partly because I was a little ashamed at having been so profoundly affected by a chance happening. The whole thing was no more than a petty experience. And yet, even as I write these words I realise how difficult it is for the prentice hand to choose the right words; I understand how much ambiguity is implicit in the simplest syllables. When I describe the experience as "petty," of course I mean this only in a relative sense, in contrast with the mighty and dramatic experiences in which whole nations and manifold destinies are involved; and I also use the term in a temporal sense, seeing that all the adventures I am going to relate took place within six hours. Nevertheless, for me personally, this experience, however petty, insignificant, and unimportant from a detached and general viewpoint, was so momentous that even to-day—four months after that queer night—I am still burning with it, and burning to tell the story. Daily and hourly I turn over the details in my mind, for that night has become, as it were, the axis of my whole existence; everything I do and say is unconsciously determined by it; I think of nothing else; I am always trying to recapitulate its sudden happenings, and thus to ensure my grasp of them. Indeed, I now realise what was still hidden from me when I took up my pen ten minutes ago, that my sole object in writing this account of the incidents is that I may hold them fast, may have them so to speak concretised before me, may again enjoy their rehearsal at once emotionally and intellectually. I was quite wrong when I said that I wanted to settle accounts with these memories by writing them down. The fact is that I want to have a livelier picture of what was all-too-fugitive at the time when it was lived through; I want a warm and breathing picture of them, which will make them real to me for ever. Not, indeed, that I am afraid for a moment of forgetting that sultry afternoon, or the queer night that followed. I need no memento, no milestones to mark my course during those hours. Like a sleep-walker, I move with an assured tread through those memories, whether of the day or of the night; I see the most trivial details with the clarity proper to the heart rather than to our fallible intellectual memory. I could sketch on this paper the outline of every leaf in the green, spring landscape; and now, in autumn, I can still fancy myself smelling the soft and pollen-laden odour of the chestnut blossoms. If, therefore, I write this record, and thus recapitulate those hours, I do so, not in fear lest I should forget them, but in sheer delight at the recapitulation. And when I attempt to describe the exact succession of events, I shall have to keep a tight hand on myself, for whenever I recall them I am seized with a kind of intoxication, an ecstasy of feeling, so that I find it hard to steady the flow of memories, and to keep the incidents from becoming merged in a motley confusion. So passionate, still, are my impressions when I recall that day, June 8, 1913, on which I took a cab. . . .

Once more I feel the need to curb my pen, for I am startled when I note the ambiguity of words. Now that for the first time I am trying to give a connected account of what took place, I realise how hard it is to give a fixed presentation of that perpetual flux we call life. I wrote that "I" did so and so, that "I" took the cab on June 8, 1913. But the very pronoun is ambiguous, for I have long ceased to be the "I" of that eighth of June, although only four months have passed since then; although I live in the house that used to belong to that "I," sit at his desk, and hold his pen in my hand. I have long since become distinguished from the man of that day, and above all on account of the experiences I am about to describe. I see him from without, dispassionately and with an alien eye. I can describe him as I might describe a friend or companion of whom I knew a great deal, but who was an essentially different entity from myself—one of whom I could speak, one whom I could praise or blame, without feeling for a moment that he had once belonged to me.

The man I then was differed but little either in externals or internals from other members of his class—from the people who, without any overweening sense of pride, are wont to think of themselves as "good society." I was thirty-five years old. My parents died shortly before I came of age, and had left me fairly well off, so that there was no question of my having to earn a livelihood or of having to carve out a career for myself. Their death thus relieved me of the need for making a decision which had been worrying me a good deal. I had just finished my university studies, and it had become incumbent on me to choose a profession. Family connexions, and my own leanings towards a tranquil, secure, and meditative life, had made it likely that I should enter the higher civil service; but I was my parents' sole heir, and I found that my means would now enable me to lead an independent existence and to gratify all my wishes. I had never been troubled with ambition, so I decided to spend a few years seeing life, and to defer the possibility of taking up some more active occupation should any prove sufficiently enticing. Ultimately, I remained content with this life of watching and waiting, for I found that, since my wishes were modest, I coveted nothing I was not able to get. In the easy and pleasant life of Vienna, which excels all other capitals in the charm of its promenades, its opportunities for idle contemplation, its elegance, and its artistry—all combining to form a life which seems a sufficient end in itself—, I forgot to think of more strenuous activities. I enjoyed all the pleasures open to a rich, good-looking, and unambitious young man of family: the harmless tension of mild gambling, sport, travel, and the like. But soon I began to supplement this sort of existence by the cultivation of artistic tastes. I collected rare glass, not so much out of a special fondness for it, as because it was easy to acquire connoisseurship in this restricted field. I adorned the walls of my rooms with Italian engravings in the rococo style, and with landscapes of the Canaletto school, sometimes getting them from dealers, and sometimes buying them at auctions where I luxuriated in the gentle excitement of the bidding. I made a point of attending performances of good music, and frequented the studios of our best painters. Nor were successes with women lacking to round off my experience. In this field, likewise, impelled by the collector's secret urge (which ever denotes the lack of sufficient occupation), I enjoyed many memorable hours, and gradually became a true connoisseur. On the whole, my time was well filled, and my life seemed a satisfying one. I grew increasingly fond of this lukewarm and easy-going atmosphere of days that were always interesting and never agitating; and I was rarely moved by any new desires, for, in these peaceful surroundings, trifles brought me sufficient joy. The successful choice of a necktie, the purchase of a fine book, a motoring excursion, or an hour with a woman, would brim the measure of my happiness. An especial delight to me was the fact that my existence resembled a suit perfectly cut by an English tailor, in that there was nothing unduly striking about it. I believe my friends liked me well enough and were always glad to see me. Most of my acquaintances regarded me as a lucky fellow.

I really cannot remember whether this man of an earlier day whom I have been trying to describe, also regarded himself as a lucky fellow; for now when, thanks to my crucial experience, I demand of every feeling that it shall have a deeper and more adequate significance, the appraisement of my earlier feelings has become almost impossible. But I am certain that I was not unhappy in those days. Practically all my wishes were gratified, all my claims on life fulfilled. But the very fact that I was accustomed to get all I wanted, and to make no further demands of fate, had as its inevitable sequel the growth of a sense that life was rather a flaccid affair. Unconscious, or half-realised, longings were at work. Not genuine wishes, but the wish for wishes; the desire to have stronger, less perfectly controlled, more ambitious, and less readily satisfied desires; the longing to live more fully, and perhaps also the longing to suffer. By too admirably designed a technique, I had cleared all resistances out of my path, and the lack of resistances was sapping my vitality. I noticed that desire stirred in me less often and less vigorously; that a sort of stagnation had ensued in my feelings; that I was suffering (how can I best phrase it?) from a spiritual impotence, from an incapacity to grasp life with all the ardour of passion. Let me mention some little signs which first brought this lack home to me. I noticed that I often had no inclination to go to the theatre to see some noted performance; that I would order books about which every one was talking, and then leave them uncut for weeks; and that though I continued, mechanically, to enrich my collections of glass and pictures, I no longer troubled to find the proper place for new acquisitions, and no longer felt any particular pleasure when I at length happened upon some object of which I had long been in search.

But the first time when I became fully aware of this transitional and slight decline in mental energy is still clearly present to my mind. It was in the summer. Simply from that strange disinclination to exert myself, and from the failure to be attracted by any new possibility, I had remained in Vienna. At this juncture I received a letter from a woman with whom I had been on intimate terms for three years, and with whom I honestly believed myself to be in love. The epistle was long and impassioned—it ran to fourteen pages. She told me that she had recently made the acquaintance of a man who had become all in all to her. She intended to marry him in the autumn, and must therefore break off relationships with me. She had no thought of regretting the experiences we had shared; the memory of them was a delight to her; the thought of me would accompany her in her new marriage as the sweetest thought of her life hitherto; she hoped that I would forgive her for this sudden decision. After the circumstantial opening, she went on to adjure me not to despise her, and not to suffer at being thus cast off. I was to make no attempt to hold her back, nor was I to do anything foolish as far as I myself was concerned. I was to seek consolation elsewhere; I was to write to her instantly, for she would be consumed with anxiety until she heard from me. In a pencilled postscript she added: "Don't do anything rash! Understand and forgive!"

The first time I read this letter, I was simply surprised at the news. But when I reread it, I became aware of a certain sense of shame, which, as I realised its meaning, rapidly increased to a feeling of positive alarm. For I could not detect within myself any of those strong and natural sentiments which my mistress had anticipated. There was not a trace of them. Her communication had caused me no pain. I had not felt angry with her, nor had I dreamed for a moment of any act of violence against either her or myself. Such coldness was so strange that it could not but frighten me. I was to lose one who had been my intimate for many years; a woman whose warm, soft body I had clasped in my arms, and whose gentle breathing I had rejoiced to hear when she lay beside me at night—but nothing stirred in me at the news, I had no impulse to resist, no longing to reassert my conquest. My emotions showed not a sign of that which her instincts had led her to expect as a matter of course from a real man. This was the first thing to make me fully alive to the process of stagnation within me. Or, I might be said to be drifting, rudderless, on the surface of a stream. I knew that there was something dead, something corpse-like, about this coldness. There was not, as yet, the foul odour of corruption; but there was the hopeless apathy of waning life, the apathy of the moment that precedes bodily death and the consequent obvious decay.

Thenceforward I began to watch this remarkable stagnation of feeling, as a patient watches the progress of his disease. Shortly afterwards, one of my men friends died. An intimate of my childhood's days passed out of my life for ever. At the graveside I asked myself whether I was truly a mourner, whether I felt any active sense of loss. There was no such feeling. I seemed to be made, as it were, of glass; to be something through which things became visible, without forming part of it. However earnestly, on this and similar occasions, I might strive to feel, however excellent the reasons I might bring forward to convince myself that I ought to feel, there was no response from within. Men were lost to me, women came and went; and I was myself moved by these movements as little as one who sits in a room is moved by raindrops on the

window-pane. There was a transparent partition between me and the
immediate things of life, a partition which I had not the strength to
shatter.

Nevertheless, this clear realisation brought, in the long run, no anxiety in its train; for, as I have already explained, I was indifferent even to
the things that touched me closely. Sorrow itself was no longer sharp
enough. My spiritual lack was no more perceptible to my associates,
than the sexual impotence that is revealed only in the intimate hour is
perceptible to a man's ordinary associates. In social life, I often aroused
astonishment by an artificial fervour, by a parade of emotional interest
designed to conceal my inward apathy. To all appearance, I continued
to live the old, easy-going, unhampered life. Weeks and months slipped
away, and the months slowly lengthened into years. One morning I
noticed in the glass that my temples were tinged with grey, and I realised
that my youth was preparing to take flight. But what others term
"youth" had departed from me long ere this. The loss of youth was not
particularly distressing to me, for I had not valued it immoderately. I
had no special interest even in myself.

Thanks to this apathy, my days became more and more monotonous,
despite all outward differences in occupation and incident. They followed one another in an undistinguished series, growing and then fading
like the leaves on a tree. Nor was there any distinguishing mark about
the beginning of the day I am about to describe. It seemed one just like
another. That morning, June 8, 1913, I had got up rather late, for a
lingering memory of my school-days always inclined me to lie abed on
Sunday morning. After I had had my tub and had glanced at the newspapers, I was lured out-of-doors by the warmth of the day. As usual, I
strolled down Graben, nodding to acquaintances and exchanging a word
with one here and there. I dropped in at a friend's house to luncheon. I
had no engagements that afternoon, for I liked to keep Sunday afternoon free, and to dispose of it when the time came as fancy might
dictate. When I left my friend's house and crossed the Ringstrasse, I had
a lively sense of the beauty of the sunlit town, and was delighted with its
charm that afternoon in early summer. Everyone looked cheerful.
People were rejoicing in the Sundayfied aspect of the gay thoroughfare; I
was myself struck by many of the details, and especially by the contrast
of the spreading green foliage with the asphalt of the pavement. Although I walked this way almost every day, the sight of the crowd in its
Sunday best came upon me as a surprise, and involuntarily I began to
long for more verdure, more brightness, and an even more diversified

colouring. I felt a curiosity to see the Prater, where now at the close of spring and the beginning of summer the great trees stood like rows of giant green-liveried footmen on either side of the main alley way thronged with carriages—the huge trees silently proffering their white blossoms to the smartly dressed loiterers. Being wont to yield to such trivial impulses, I hailed the first cab that passed, and told the driver to take me to the Prater.

"To the races, Herr Baron?" he asked with polite alacrity.

This reminded me that to-day was, indeed, a fashionable race-day, when all Vienna would turn up to the show. "That's queer!" I thought, as I stepped into the cab. "A few years ago I could not possibly have forgotten that this was race-day!"

My forgetfulness made me realise, like an invalid who has to move an aching limb, the full significance of the apathy with which I was afflicted.

The main avenue was almost empty when we arrived. The racing must have begun some time before. Instead of the usual throng of carriages, there were only a few isolated cabs rattling along at top speed. My coachman turned half-round on his box to ask whether he, too, should whip up. But I told him to drive quietly, as I was in no hurry. I had seen too many races and racecourse frequenters to care whether I arrived early or late. In my lethargic mood I enjoyed the gentle swaying of the cab, which gave me the sensation of being cradled in a ship. Driving slowly, I could get a better view of the lovely chestnut blossoms, from which the petals were dropping here and there to become the sport of the breeze, in whose warm eddies they were tossed for a while until they fell to join those that already flecked the ground with white. It was agreeable to me to close my eyes and breathe this spring atmosphere, and to feel that there was no reason for pressing onwards towards the goal. I was disappointed when the cab drew up at the entrance to the racecourse. I was half inclined to turn back, and to be content with another hour's cradling, this pleasant afternoon. But here I was at my destination. A confused uproar came from the course, like the noise of a sea surging within the enclosure. The crowd from which this noise came was not yet visible to me; and involuntarily I was reminded how at Ostend, when one is walking from the lower part of the town up any of the little side alleys leading to the esplanade, one can already feel the bite of salt in the air and hear the murmur of the sea before being greeted by the view over the grey expanse where the waves thunder on the shore.

The uproar showed that a race was actually being run, but between me and the course was a motley crowd shaken as if by a convulsion. All the phases of the race were betrayed by the varying moods of the onlookers. This particular race must now be well advanced. The horses could no longer be galloping in a bunch, but must be strung out along the course, with a keen competition for the lead; those who were watching that which I could not see were giving tongue in their excitement to the name of this horse or that. The direction of their heads showed me which part of the track was now the centre of interest, for all had their eyes fixed upon a spot to me invisible. The cries from thousands of throats united into a single clamour growing ever louder, filling the whole place and rising into the impassive heaven. I looked more closely at the faces of a few individuals. They were distorted, almost frenzied; eyes were fixed and gleaming, lips compressed, chins thrust out, nostrils working. To me, a dispassionate observer, the sight of this uncontrolled intoxication was at once ludicrous and horrible. On a bench nearby was standing a smartly dressed man, whose face was doubtless amiable as a rule, but now he looked like one possessed by the devil. He was thrashing the air with his walking stick, as if flogging a horse, and his whole body was imitating the movements of a man riding hell-for-leather. His heels beat rhythmically on the bench as if he were rising in stirrups, and with the stick in his right hand he continued to flog the void, while in his left hand he was gripping a white betting slip. Everywhere I saw these white slips; they showed up like flecks of foam upon the noisy flood. Now several horses must be passing the curve neck and neck, for their names were thundered like battle-cries by various groups of persons who would have been overwhelmed by their delirious excitement but for this outlet in shouting.

Amid the frenzied uproar I was as unmoved as a rock amid the breakers, and I find it difficult to give a precise account of my sensations. Preeminently, no doubt, I was struck by the utter absurdity of so much excitement, was inspired with ironical contempt for the vulgarity with which it was displayed. But I had unwillingly to admit that there was a spice of another feeling, that I was not free from envy of such ardency of passion, and of the vigorous life which the passion disclosed. What, I wondered, could stir me like this? What could throw me into a fever of excitement, could make my body burn, could force me to utter such involuntary shouts? I could not think of any sum of money that could move me so keenly, or of any woman who could stir my feelings to such a pitch. There was nothing in the world that could thus fire my dead emotions. If a pistol were at my head, a moment before the trigger was pulled, my heart would not throb as the hearts of these thousands and tens of thousands were throbbing because of a handful of money.

But now one of the horses must have been close to the winning post, for from a myriad throats came, even louder, the cry of one name, the sound breaking at last into a roar. The band began to play, and the throng scattered. One of the races was over, one of the contests decided, and the tension relaxed into a lively animation. What had a moment before been an ardent integration of passion, broke up into groups of individuals, laughing, talking, and hurrying to and fro. The mask of maniacal excitement gave place to a tranquil expression. Social groups were crystalised out of the undifferentiated mass which, so recently, had been united by the passion for sport. I recognised acquaintances, and exchanged greetings with them, but most of those present were strangers to me and to one another, and they contemplated one another civilly but indifferently. The woman appraised one another's new dresses; the men looked ardently at the women; the well-bred curiosity, which is the chief occupation of the idle rich class, was at work once more; people sampled one another in point of smartness, and looked to see who was present and who had stayed away. Though they had but just recovered from their frenzy they were now in doubt whether this interlude or the racing itself was the main purpose of their social encounter. I strolled through the crowd, well pleased to breathe its atmosphere, for it was, after all, the atmosphere of my own daily life; I enjoyed the aroma of smartness that emanated from this kaleidoscopic medley—but still more enjoyable was the gentle breeze from the meadows and the woods which from time to time stirred the white muslin dresses of the women. Some of my acquaintances wanted to talk to me; Diana, the pretty actress, beckoned to me from where she was sitting; but I paid no heed. I did not want to converse with these fashionable folk. It would have bored me to see myself in their mirror. All I desired was to study the spectacle of life, to watch the excitements of the hour—for, to the non-participant, the excitement of others is the most agreeable of spectacles.

A couple of handsome women passed me, and I looked at them with bold eyes (though inwardly unmoved by desire), amused to note in them mingling of embarrassment at being thus regarded and pleasure at attracting my attention. In reality, they had no particular charm for me. It merely gratified me to simulate an interest, and to arouse their interest, for with me as with so many whose passions are lukewarm, my chief erotic enjoyment was to arouse warmth and uneasiness in others rather than to feel the stirring of my own blood. Thus, as I walked up and down the enclosure, I glanced at the women and received their glances in return, with no sentiment beneath the surface of things, and but mildly titillated by the sheer pleasure of the sport.

Even this palled on me ere long. I passed the same people again and again, and grew weary of their faces and their gestures. Seeing a vacant chair, I sat down. A fresh turmoil was beginning to animate the concourse, a restlessness was increasingly apparent among those who passed by. Obviously a new race was about to begin. This mattered nothing to me. I sat musing, and watched the smoke-wreaths from my cigarette, watched them disperse as they rose into the blue sky. Now came the real beginning of that unprecedented experience which still influences my life. I know the exact instant, for it happened that I had just looked at my watch. The hands, as I saw, glancing lackadaisically, were exactly over one another; it was just after a quarter past three on that afternoon of June 8, 1913. I was looking at the white dial, immersed in childish contemplation of this triviality, when behind me I heard the laughter of a woman, the bright and somewhat agitated laughter I so dearly love in women—laughter that issues from the burning bush of voluptuousness. I had an impulse to turn my head that I might see this woman whose vocalised sensuality had broken in upon my careless reverie like a white pebble thrown into the dark waters of a stagnant pool; but I controlled the desire. An inclination for a harmless psychological experiment, one I was fond of performing, held the impulse in check. I did not wish to look at this laughing woman yet; I wanted to set my imagination to work upon her, to equip her in my fancy with a face, a mouth, a neck, a swelling breast. I wanted to picture the whole living and breathing woman.

She was close behind me. Her laugh ended, she began to talk. I listened attentively. She spoke with a slight Hungarian accent, quickly and vivaciously, enunciating the vowels with a rich intonation like that of a singer. It amused me to fit the speech into my fancy picture, to add this to all the other details. I gave her dark hair and dark eyes; a rather large and sensuously curved mouth with strong and very white teeth; a small and finely chiselled nose, but with wide, sensitive nostrils. On her left cheek I gave her a patch. In one hand she carried a riding switch, and flicked her skirt with it as she laughed. She continued to speak, and each word served to enrich my fancy picture with a new detail. She must have small and virginal breasts; she must be wearing a dark green dress fastened with a diamond clasp, and a light-coloured hat with a white plume. The picture grew plainer and plainer, and I felt as if this stranger woman, invisible behind my back, must be brightly imaged in the pupils of my eyes. But I would not turn around. Some stirrings of desire were interwoven with my vision. I closed my eyes and waited, certain that when I opened them and turned to look at her, the reality would confirm my fancy.

At this moment, she stepped forward. Involuntarily I opened my eyes—and was extremely annoyed. It was all wrong. Everything was different, maliciously different, from my fancy picture. She was wearing a white gown instead of a green; was not slender, but deep of bosom and broad of hip; there was not a sign, on her plump cheeks, of the patch I had expected; the hair that showed from beneath her helmet-shaped hat was auburn instead of black. None of the details were right; but she was handsome, strikingly so; and yet, my psychologist's vanity being pricked, I was loath to admit the fact. I looked at her almost malevolently; and yet, in spite of myself, I recognised her wanton charm, perceived the attractive animalism of her firm but soft contour. Now she laughed aloud once more, showing her strong white teeth, and it was plain to me that her ardent and sensuous laughter was in keeping with the pervading luxuriance of her aspect. Everything about her was vehement and challenging; her well-rounded figure; the way she thrust out her chin when she laughed; her penetrating glance; her imperious nose; the hand with which she held her sunshade firmly planted on the ground. Here was elemental femininity, primal energy, deliberate witchery, a beacon of voluptuousness made flesh. Standing beside her was a dapper and somewhat wizened army officer, who was talking to her in emphatic tones. She listened to him, smiled, laughed, made the appropriate responses. But this was mere by-play. The whole time she was drinking in her surroundings eagerly. She drew the notice, the smiles, of all who passed by, and especially of the males among them. Her restless glance wandered over the grand stand, lighting up from time to time as she recognised an acquaintance; then, still listening smilingly and yet indifferently to her companion, she gazed to right and to left. But her eyes never lighted on me, for I was hidden from her by her squire. This piqued me. I rose to my feet, but still she did not see me. I moved nearer—now she was looking back at the grand stand. Resolutely I stepped quite close, raised my hat, and offered her my chair. She glanced at me in some surprise; her eyes twinkled; her lips formed themselves into a caressive smile. With a laconic word of thanks, she accepted the chair, but did not sit down. She merely rested her shapely hand on the back of the chair, thus leaning forward slightly, to show off her figure to better advantage.

Annoyance at my false anticipations had been forgotten. I thought only of the little game I was playing with this woman. I moved back to the wall of the grand stand, to a spot from which I could look at her freely without attracting too much notice. She became aware of the fixity of my gaze and turned a little towards me, but inconspicuously, as if it had been a chance movement; not repelling my mute advances; answering them occasionally in a non-committal way. Unceasingly her eyes roved from point to point; nothing held her attention longer than a moment. Did she smile with any special meaning when her glance rested on me? I could not feel sure, and the doubt irritated me. In the intervals, when the flashlight of her errant gaze met mine, her expression seemed full of promise; and yet she indiscriminately countered the interest of everyone else in like manner, simply, it would seem, to gratify her coquetry; just as at the same time she appeared to be giving due heed to her friend's conversation. There was something saucy in this ostentation. Was she a confirmed flirt? Was she stirred by a surplus of animal passion? I drew a step nearer, for I had been infected by her sauciness. I no longer looked her in the eyes, but deliberately appraised the outlines of her form. She followed the direction of my glance, and showed no sign of embarrassment. A smile fluttered round the corners of her mouth, as if at some observation of the chattering officer, and yet I felt sure that the smile was really an answer to me. Then, when I was looking at her foot as it peeped from beneath her white dress, she, too, looked down carelessly, and a moment later, as if by chance, lifted the foot and rested it on the rung of the chair, so that, through the slit of her directoire skirt, her leg was exposed to the knee. At this moment, the smile with which she looked at her companion seemed to have an ironical or quizzical flavour. It was obvious that she was playing with me as unconcernedly as I with her. The boldness and subtlety of her technique aroused in me an admiration that was not free from dislike; for while, with a deceitful furtiveness, she was displaying to me the charms of her body, she was fully responsive to the whispered conversation of her gallant—was playing with us both at once. I was soured, for I detested in others this cold and calculating sensuality, precisely because I was aware of its incestuous kinship to my own conscious apathy. None the less, my senses were stirred, though perhaps more by aversion than by desire. Impudently I came still nearer, and looked at her with frank brutality. "I want you,

you pretty animal," was the message of my unveiled eyes; and involuntarily my lips must have moved, for she smiled somewhat contemptuously, turning her head away and letting her skirt drop over the exposed limb. But, a moment later, her dark and sparkling eyes had resumed their tireless roving. She was my match; she was as cool as I. We were both playing with an alien fire, which was nothing more than painted flame, but was pretty to look at. This sport was a pleasant pastime to while away a dull hour.

Suddenly the alertness of her expression vanished; the sparkle in her eyes was dimmed. Though she continued to smile, an irritable fold appeared at the corner of her mouth. I followed the direction of her glance, to see a short, thickset man, whose clothes hung untidily on him, hastening towards her. His face was moist with hurry and excitement, and he was nervously mopping it with his handkerchief. Since his hat was awry, one could see that he was almost bald. (I pictured to myself that beneath this hat his scalp was beaded with sweat, and my gorge rose against the man.) In his bejewelled hand was a sheaf of betting-slips. He was bursting with excitement. Paying no heed to his wife, he began to talk loudly to the officer in Hungarian. Obviously, he was a devotee of the race-course, probably a horse-dealer in a good way of business, for whom this sport was his one ecstasy, a substitute for the sublime. His wife must have murmured some hint to him (she was manifestly annoyed at his coming, and her elemental self-confidence had vanished), for he straightened his hat, laughed jovially, and clapped her on the shoulder with good-humoured affection. She bent her brows angrily, enraged by this conjugal familiarity, which was peculiarly vexatious to her in the presence of the officer and perhaps still more in mine. Her husband apparently said a word of excuse, and then went on speaking in Hungarian to the officer, who answered with a complaisant smile. Subsequently, the new-comer took his wife's arm, fondly and perhaps a trifle humbly. It was plain to me that his public display of intimacy was galling to her, and I could not quell a sense of enjoyment at witnessing her humiliation, which aroused in me a feeling of amusement tinged with loathing. But in a moment she recovered her equanimity, and, while gently pressing her husband's arm to her side, she shot a sarcastic glance at me, as if to say: "Look, I am his, not yours." I was both enraged and repelled. I had an impulse to turn on my heel and walk away, to show her that the wife of such a vulgarian had no further interest for me. And yet her lure was too powerful. I stood my ground.

At that moment came the signal for the start, and instantly the chat-

tering crowd was seized as if by a general contagion. Everyone rushed
forward to the railings. I restrained myself forcibly from being carried
away by this rush, for I wished to remain close by the woman. Perhaps
there might be an opportunity for a decisive interchange of looks, a
handclasp, or some other advance, and I therefore stubbornly made my
way towards her through the scurrying throng. At the very same instant,
her fat spouse was hastening in the opposite direction, in search of a
good place on the grand stand. Thus moved by conflicting impulses, we
came into collision with such violence that his hat was dislodged and fell
to the ground. The betting-slips that were stuck in the band were shaken
out and scattered over the turf, looking like red, blue, yellow, and white
butterflies. He stared at me, and mechanically I was about to apologise.
But a malicious imp closed my lips, and made me look at him provoca-
tively without saying a word. For a brief space he endured my gaze,
though unsteadily, his face flushing with vexation. But soon he wilted.
With an expression of alarm which almost moved me to pity, he turned
his face away, appeared of a sudden to remember his betting-slips, and
stopped to recover them and to pick up his hat. His wife, furious at what
had happened, looked at me scornfully, and I saw with a secret pleasure
that she would have liked to slap my face. I continued to stand with a
nonchalant air, looking on with a smile and making no motion to help
the corpulent fellow who was groping about in search of his betting-
slips. In his stooping posture, his collar stood away from his neck like
the feathers of a ruffled hen; a roll of fat projected from the red nape; he
coughed asthmatically each time he bent forward. The ludicrous spectacle forced another smile from me, and the wife could hardly contain
her anger. She was pale now instead of red; at length I had made her
show genuine feeling—one of hatred, of untamed wrath. I should have
liked to prolong this spiteful scene indefinitely, to go on enjoying thus
callously the spectacle of his laborious attempts to retrieve his betting-
slips. A whimsical devil seemed to have taken possession of me, was
giggling in my throat, and longing to burst out into open laughter. I
wanted to prod the grovelling mass of flesh with my stick. Never could I
remember having been so overpowered with malice as now when I was
triumphing at the humiliation of this audacious woman.

But by this time the poor wretch fancied he had recovered nearly all
his slips. Really, he had overlooked one of them, a blue one, which had
been carried farther than the rest, and lay on the ground just in front of
me. He was still peering about with his short-sighted eyes, squinting
through the eyeglasses that had slipped down his perspiring nose, when

the spirit of mischief moved me to prolong his misery, and I slyly covered the blue slip with my foot, so that it would be impossible for him to find it while I maintained the same posture. He went on hunting for it, grunting to himself as he counted and recounted the coloured strips of paper in his hand. Certainly there was still one missing! Amid the growing tumult he was bent on returning to the search, when his wife, who with a savage expression was evading my quizzical glance, could no longer bridle her impatience.

"Lajos!" she called to him suddenly and imperiously.

He started like a horse at the sound of the bugle. Once again he looked searchingly at the ground. I seemed to feel the hidden slip tickling the sole of my foot, and I could hardly refrain from open derision. Then he turned submissively to his wife, who with ostentatious haste led him away to join the tumultuous crowd.

I stayed where I was without the slightest inclination to follow them. As far as I was concerned, the incident was closed. The feeling of erotic tension had given place to an agreeable serenity. My excitement had quite passed away, so that nothing remained beyond a healthy satiety after my sudden outbreak of impishness—nothing, beyond an almost arrogant satisfaction with the success of my coup. In front of me the spectators were closely packed, stirred with increasing excitement. In a dirty, black wave they were pressing on the railings, but I was bored with the races, and had no inclination to look at this one. I might as well go home. As I moved to put this thought into execution, I uncovered the blue slip which by now I had forgotten. Picking it up, I toyed with it my fingers, uncertain what to do with it. I had a vague thought of restoring it to "Lajos," for this would give me an excellent chance of making his wife's acquaintance. However, I instantly realised that she was of no further interest to me, that the fire of this adventure had cooled, and that I had relapsed into my customary indifference. A combative exchange of glances with Lajos' wife had been quite enough for me; the thought of sharing a woman with that gross creature was unappetising; I had enjoyed a transient titillation of the senses, and this had been succeeded by a feeling of agreeable relaxation.

Taking possession of the abandoned chair, I sat down at ease and lighted a cigarette. The little flame of passion had flickered out. Once again I was listless; the renewal of old experiences offered no charm. Idly watching the smoke-wreaths, I thought of the promenade at Meran where, two months earlier, I had sat looking at the waterfall. At Meran, too, there had been a continuous roar that left me unaffected, an un-

meaning sound had passed athwart the silence of the blue-tinted landscape. Now the passion of sport was attaining a fresh climax. The foam
of fluttering parasols, hats, and handkerchiefs rose above the black wave
of humanity. The voices of the throng condensed once more into a single
cry. I heard one name, shouted exultantly or desparingly from thousands of throats: "Cressy! Cressy! Cressy!" Once again the noise ceased
abruptly, as when a violin-string snaps. The band began to play, and the
crowd to break up into groups once more. The numbers of the leading
horses were displayed on the board, and half-unconsciously I glanced at
them. The winner's number was seven. Mechanically I looked down at
the blue slip in my hand. On this, likewise, was a seven.

I could not but laugh. The worthy Lajos had backed the winner! My
fit of spleen had actually robbed the fat husband of his money. The
sense of impishness revived; it would be interesting to learn how much
my stirring of jealousy had cost him. For the first time I scrutinised the
betting-slip attentively. It was for twenty crowns, and for a "win," not
simply for a "place." If the odds had been heavy, the slip might now be
worth a good deal of money. Following the urge of curiosity, I joined
the crowd of those who were hurrying towards the pay desk. I took my
stand in the queue and soon reached the window. When I presented my
ticket, two prompt and bony hands (I could not see the paying-clerk's
face) thrust across nine twenty-crown notes in exchange.

At this moment, when the money was actually offered me, the laughter stuck in my throat. I felt extremely uncomfortable, and involuntarily
drew away my hands for a moment, lest I should touch another man's
money. I should really have preferred to leave the blue bank-notes lying
on the counter, but hard on my heels were other winners, eager to
handle their gains. What could I do but reluctantly pick up the notes?
They seemed to burn my fingers as if they had been blue flames, and I
should have liked to shake off the hand that held them. I suddenly
realised the ignominy of my position. The jest had become deadly earnest; had developed into something quite incompatible with my position
as a man of honour, a gentleman, an officer in the reserve. I hesitated to
give what I had done its true name. The notes in my hand were not
simply treasure trove; they had been obtained by fraud, they were stolen
money.

There was a clamour of talk all round me, as the people streamed up
to the paying-clerk's window and passed on with their winnings. I stood
motionless, still holding the unwelcome notes. What had I better do?
The first and most obvious thought was to seek out the real winner, to

make my excuses, and hand over the money. But how could I do this? Above all, it would be impossible under the eyes of the officer who was the wife's companion. There would be a scandal which would certainly cost me my commission as a lieutenant in the reserve: for even if it might be supposed that I had accidentally picked up the betting slip, to draw the real owner's winnings had been a dishonourable act. My next idea was to crumple the notes into a ball and throw them away, but in such a crowd someone was sure to see what I did, and the act would arouse suspicion. Yet I could not dream of keeping the money; or of putting it into my note-case until I could give it away to some suitable recipient. From childhood onwards I had had impressed upon me a keen sense of what was fitting in money matters, and the handling of these notes was as unpleasant to me as the wearing of a dirty shirt would have been. Somehow, anyhow, and quickly, I must get rid of the contaminated pieces of paper. Looking around me in hopeless perplexity, in vain search for a hiding place or for some unwatched possibility for disposal, I noticed that a new line had formed of persons on the way to the window. This time, those in the queue were holding, not betting-slips, but banknotes. Here was the way out of my difficulty! Chance had brought me this money, and I would commit it to the winds of chance once again; I would thrust it into the greedy maw of that window which was now ceaselessly swallowing up new stakes in the form of silver coin and notes. Yes, yes, there was the path of deliverance.

Impetuously I pressed forward towards the window. Now there were only two backers in front of me. The first was already at the totalisator when it occurred to me that I did not know the names of any of the horses. I listened to the conversation of those standing near me.

"Are you going to back Ravachol?" asked one of another.

"Rather," came the answer.

"Don't you think Teddy has a good chance?" enquired number one.

"Teddy? Not an earthly!" replied number two. "Teddy's no good. You take my tip."

I grasped at the casual information. Teddy was no good; Teddy could not possibly win. All right, I would back Teddy. I threw down the money, and backed for a win the horse whose name I had just heard for the first time. In exchange for my notes, I received nine red-and-white slips. Even these were disagreeable to handle, but they did not burn my fingers as the greasy notes had done.

I drew a breath of relief, feeling now almost carefree. I had got rid of the money, had shaken off the unpleasant results of my adventure. The matter had become once more what it had been at the outset, a mere joke. I returned to my chair, lighted another cigarette, and blew smoke-rings with renewed content. But this mood did not last. I was restless, got up, walked about, and then sat down again. My agreeable reveries were over. A feeling of nervous irritability had taken possession of me. At first I thought it must be because I dreaded a fresh encounter with Lajos and his wife—but how could they dream that the new slips were really theirs? Nor was it the restlessness of the crowd which disturbed me. Indeed, I found myself watching the passers-by to see if there were any movement towards the barrier. I stood up again and again to look for the flag which is hoisted at the beginning of each race. Yes, I was certainly impatient. I had been seized by the fever of expectancy. I was looking forward to the race which was to close the unseemly incident for ever. A man came by with a bundle of sporting papers. I beckoned to him, bought one, began to search its columns, and, amid a jungle of strange jargon and tipsters' hints, I at length discovered "Teddy," learned the names of his jockey and his owner, and was informed that his colours were red-and-white. Why should these details interest me? Angrily crumpling the newspaper, I threw it away, stood up, and sat down again. Suddenly I had grown hot; I wiped my face; my collar seemed too tight. Was the race never going to begin?

At last the bell sounded. The crowd rushed to the railings, and to my extreme annoyance I found that this bell thrilled me as an alarm thrills one who is awakened by it from sleep. I jumped up so eagerly that I overturned the chair, and I hastened—nay, I ran—forward into the crowd, gripping my betting-slips tightly. I was terrified lest I should be too late, lest I should miss something of the utmost importance. Roughly shouldering my way through, I reached the barrier, and seized a chair on which a lady was about to seat herself. She was an acquaintance, Countess W., and her amazed and angry expression made me aware of my bad manners and my frenzy. But with a mixture of shame and defiance I ignored her, and leapt on to the chair in order to watch the field.

In the far distance, across the turf, I could see the eager horses, with difficulty kept in line by the little jockeys on their backs, who from here looked like multicoloured puppets. I tried to make out the colours of my own fancy, but my eyes were untrained to this sport. Everything flickered strangely under my gaze, and I could not distinguish the red-and-white. Now the bell rang for the second time; and, like seven coloured arrows shot from a single bow, the horses sped along the course. It must be a wonderful sight for those who can contemplate it unmoved, with a purely aesthetic pleasure; for those who can watch the slender race-horses in the gallop which seems almost as free as a bird's flight. But I recked naught of this. My one longing was to make out my own horse, my own jockey; and I cursed myself because I had not brought my field-glasses. Though I tried my hardest, I could discern nothing beyond a flying clump of coloured insects. At length the shape of this clump began to alter; at the curve, it assumed the form of a wedge, point foremost, while one or two stragglers were tailing off from the base of the wedge. The race was fiercely contested. Three or four of the galloping beasts were still in a bunch, now one and now another head and neck in front of the rest. Involuntarily I drew myself up to my full height, as if by this imitative and passionate tension I might hope to lend them an added speed.

The excitement of those around me was increasing. The habitués of the race-course must have been able to recognise the colours at the curve, for the names of some of the horses began to detach themselves from the confused shouting. Close by me, one of the onlookers was wringing his hands in his excitement. Now a horse forged a little ahead, and this man stamped, shouting with a raucous and triumphant voice:

"Ravachol! Ravachol!"

The colours worn by the jockey on the leading horse were blue, and I was furious that the animal I had backed was not to the front. The strident shouts of my neighbour, "Ravachol! Ravachol!" became more and more offensive to me. I was enraged, and should have liked to aim my fist at the great black cavity of his yelling mouth. I trembled in my wrath. From moment to moment I felt more capable of some preposterous action. But one of the other horses was pressing the leader hard. Perhaps it was Teddy, perhaps, perhaps—and the hope aroused new ardour. Looking at the jockey's arm as it moved rhythmically, I fancied that the sleeve was red. It might be red; it must be red! Why did not the rascal use his switch more vigorously? His mount had nearly overhauled the leader! Half a head more. Why Ravachol? Ravachol? No, not Ravachol! Not Ravachol! Teddy! Teddy! Go it, Teddy!

Suddenly I pulled myself together. Who was that shouting "Teddy! Teddy!" It was I shouting. In the very midst of my passion, I was startled at myself. I tried to maintain my self-command, and for a moment a sense of shame overpowered my excitement. But I could not tear away my eyes, for the two horses were still neck and neck, and it really must be Teddy that was thus overhauling the accursed Ravachol, the Ravachol I loathed with all my might—for from everywhere there now came a roar of "Teddy! Teddy!" The clamour infected me, after my brief moment's awakening. Teddy must win, must win. Now, in very truth, he was leading by a span; then by two; then by a head and neck. At this moment the bell rang, and there was an explosive shout of jubilation, despair, and anger. For an instant, the longed-for name seemed to fill the heavens. Then the uproar passed, and from somewhere came the strains of music.

I was hot, I was dripping with sweat, my temples were throbbing wildly, when I stepped down from the chair. I had to sit for a while, till the swimming in my head abated. An ecstasy such as I had never known before took possession of me; an idiotic delight at the answer Fate had given to my challenge. Vainly did I try to persuade myself that I had not wanted the horse to win, that my sole desire had been to lose the money. I put no trust in my own persuasion, and I soon became aware of an overmastering impulse. I felt drawn in a particular direction, and I knew whither this impulse led me. I wanted to see the concrete results of my victory; I wanted the money in palpable form; to feel the blue bank-notes, lots of them, crackling between my fingers. A strange, an alien, an evil lust had taken possession of me, and I no longer had any feeling of shame to prevent my yielding to it. I hurried to the pay-desk. Unceremoniously I thrust myself forward among those who were awaiting their turn at the window, elbowing other impatient winners aside, possessed by the urge to get the money into my hands.

"Bounder!" muttered one of those I had pushed out of my way.

I heard the insult, but ignored it in the fever of my impatience. At length I was at the window, and my fingers closed greedily upon a blue bundle of notes. I counted them over with tremulous exultation. My winnings amounted to six hundred and forty crowns. I snatched up the bundle and left the window.

My first thought was to venture my winnings once more, to multiply them enormously. Where was my sporting paper? Oh, bother, I had thrown it away! I looked round for the chance of buying another, only to notice, to my stupefaction and alarm, that every one was streaming towards the exit, that the windows of the pay-desks were closed, that the flags were being furled. The day's sport was over. The last race had been run. For a second or two I stood rigid. Then a fierce anger surged up in me, aroused by a keen sense of injustice. It seemed so unfair that when all my nerves were aquiver, and when the blood was rushing through my veins with a vigour I had not known for years, the game should be played out. But I could not cheat myself into the belief that I had made a mistake, for the crowd grew ever thinner, and broad stretches of trampled turf had become visible amid the few remaining loiterers. Gradually realising the absurdity of my tense expectation, I, too, moved towards the exit. An obsequious attendant sprang forward. I gave him the number of my cab. He bawled it through his hands, and in an instant my driver whipped forward from the waiting throng. I told him to drive slowly down the main avenue. My excitement was on the wane, was being replaced by an agreeable lassitude. I wanted to rehearse the whole scene in my thoughts.

At this moment another cab drove past. I glanced at it without thinking, but promptly turned my eyes away, for in it were the woman and her corpulent husband. They did not notice me. But at sight of them I was overcome by a disagreeable choking sensation, as if I had been found out. Their nearness made me uneasy.

The cab moved along quietly on its rubber-tyred wheels, in line with the others. The brightly coloured dresses of the women made these cabs look like flower-laden boats sailing down a canal with green banks bordered on either side by chestnut trees. The air was balmy, the first breath of the evening coolness was wafted across the dust. But the agreeable pensiveness came no more; the sight of the man I had swindled had disturbed me, had blown upon my ardours like a chill draught. With sobered senses I reviewed the episode, and found it impossible to understand my own actions. How could I, an officer and a gentleman, have done such a thing? Without the pressure of any need, I had appropriated another's money, and had done it with a zest which put my behaviour beyond the possibility of excuse. I, who an hour before had never transgressed the bounds of good form, had now actually become a thief. As if desiring to frighten myself, I passed judgment on myself by muttering, in time with the rhythm of the horses' hoofs:

"Thief! Thief! Thief! Thief!"

How shall I describe the strange thing that now befell? It seems so inexplicable, so amazing, and yet I am convinced that my memory of it is perfectly accurate. Every instant of my feeling, every pulse of my thought, during that brief period, comes back to me with supernatural clearness. Hardly any other happening throughout my thirty-five years of life is so vivid. Yet I scarcely dare to record in black and white the absurd succession, the preposterous seesaw, of my sensations. I do not know if any imaginative writer or any psychologist could depict them in logical order. All I can do is to sketch the sequence faithfully.

I was muttering to myself "thief, thief, thief." Then came a sort of strange pause, a vacant interval, as it were, in which nothing happened; in which—how hard it is to explain—I merely listened, listened inwardly. I had formulated the charge against myself, and now it was time for the accused to answer the charge. I listened, therefore, but nothing happened. I had expected that this name of "thief" would frighten me like the crack of a whip, would overwhelm me with intolerable shame; but there was no such response. I waited patiently for a few minutes, leaning over myself so to speak that I might watch the better (for I was convinced that there must be something astir beneath this obdurate silence). Feverishly expectant, I waited for the echo, for the cry of disgust, indignation, despair, that must inevitably follow so grave an accusation. Nothing! There was no answer! Once more I repeated to myself "thief, thief"; quite loud this time, in the hope of awakening my conscience, which seemed to be rather hard of hearing. Still there was no answer. Suddenly, in a lightning flash of awareness, I realised that I was only trying to feel ashamed, but was not in the least ashamed; that somewhere in the secret recesses of my being I was proud, was elated, because of my crazy deed.

How could this be? I was now positively afraid of myself, and tried to ward off the unexpected realisation; but the feeling I have attempted to describe was overwhelming, irresistible. There was no shame, no indignation, no self-contempt. This current of strong feeling was joy, intoxicating delight, which flamed up in me because I realised that during those few minutes I had for the first time been genuinely alive once more after the lapse of many years. I rejoiced to know that my feelings had merely been paralysed, and were not utterly dead; that somewhere beneath the smooth surface of my indifference, volcanic passion must still be raging; and that this afternoon, touched by the magic wand of chance, the volcano had erupted. In me, in me too, in this fragment of the living universe that passed by my name, there still glowed the mysterious and essential fire of our mortal life, which breaks forth from time to time in the vigorous pulses of desire. I too lived, was alive, was a human being with evil and ardent lusts. A door had been thrust open by the storm of this passion; an abyss had been riven in me, and with a voluptuous giddiness I gazed into the unknown profound with a sense of terror and delight. By degrees, while the cab gently conveyed my entranced body on its way through the respectable concourse, I climbed down step by step into the depths of the human within me, incredibly alone in this silent descent, lighted on my way by the flaring torch of my newly enkindled consciousness. What time a thousand others were laughing and chattering around me, I was seeking within myself the human being I had so long lost sight of, was traversing years in the magical course of reflection. Long buried memories surged up from the cobwebbed recesses of my mind. I recalled that, in my school days, I had stolen another boy's pocket-knife, and remembered how, while I watched him hunting everywhere in vain and asking all his comrades if they had seen his knife, I had been animated with the same impish joy I had felt this afternoon. Now, at length, I could understand the strange intensity of some of my love experiences; could understand that my passion had only been distorted but had never been completely suppressed, by the social illusion, by the dominant ideal of gentility. Deeply hidden within me, as within others, there had continued to flow all the time the hot current of life. Yes, I had lived, and yet had not dared to live; I had kept myself in bondage, and had hidden myself from myself. But now the repressed energy had broken loose; life, teeming with ineffable power, had carried me away. I knew that I was still alive. With the blissful confusion of the woman who first feels her child quicken within her, I perceived the reality, the irrefragable truth, of life germinating within me. I felt (I am almost ashamed to use the expression) that I, the man who had been fading and dying, was blossoming anew; I felt the red blood coursing through my veins, and that in these fresh blossoms there would grow unknown fruits both sweet and bitter. The miracle of Tannhäuser's blossoming staff had come to pass in me—on a racecourse amid the tumult of a thousand idlers. I had begun to feel once again. The dry staff was sprouting, was thrusting forth buds.

From a passing carriage a man hailed me, shouting my name—obviously I had failed to see his first and quieter salutation. I was furious at being roused out of the agreeable state of self-absorption, the profoundest reverie I had ever experienced. But a glance at my acquaintance recalled me to my ordinary self; it was my friend Alfons, an intimate of my school days, now public prosecutor. The thought flashed through my mind: "This man who greets you so cordially has now power over you; you would be at his mercy if he knew what you had done. Did he know, it would be his duty to hale you out of this cab, to tear you away from your comfortable existence, to have you kept behind bars for several years, in company with the scum of life, with those other thieves who have only been brought to the sordid pass of prison by the lash of necessity."

But this was no more than a momentary uneasiness. The thought was promptly transformed into an ardent feeling, a fantastic and impudent pride, which made me sample almost scornfully the people within my range of vision: "If you only knew, the friendly smile with which you greet me as one of yourselves would be frozen on your lips, and you would contemptuously give me the cut direct. But I have been beforehand with you. This afternoon I broke away from your cold and petrified world in which I was one of the wheels running noiselessly in the great machine, one of the idle wheels. I have plunged into an unknown abyss; and in this one hour of the plunge I have lived more fully than in all the sheltered years in your circle. I do not belong to you any more, I am no longer one of your set; I may be on the heights or in the depths, but never shall I return to the dead levels of your philistine comfort. For the first time I have felt all the thrill that man can feel in good and in evil; but you will never know where I have been, will never understand me. Never will you be able to pluck the heart out of my mystery!"

How can I describe all that I felt while I was thus driving, to outward appearance a man of fashion, quietly exchanging greetings with those of his own order! For while my larval form, the semblance of the man that had been, continued thus to recognise sometime acquaintances—within me there was surging so intoxicating a music that I had to keep a tight rein on myself lest I should shout in my exultation. There was such an uprush of emotion that it aroused a sense of bodily distress. Like one who is gasping for want of air, I pressed my hand on my heart and sensed its painful throbbing. But pain and pleasure, alarm, disgust, or concern, were not isolated and detached feelings. They were integrally fused, so that the sum of my sensations was that I lived and breathed and felt. It was the simplest and most primitive of feelings, one that I had not experienced for ages, and it went to my head like wine. Not for a single instant during my thirty-five years had I had such an ecstatic sense of being alive.

My driver pulled up the horses, and the cab stopped with a jerk. Turning on the box, the man asked me whether I wanted to drive home. Emerging from my reverie, I glanced up and down the avenue, astonished to note how long I had been dreaming, how the intoxication of my senses had swallowed up the hours. Night had fallen; the tree-tops were whispering in the breeze; the cool air was fragrant with the scent of the chestnut blossoms. The silvery moon could be glimpsed through the foliage. It was impossible to return home, impossible to go back into my customary world. I paid the driver. As I was counting out his fare, the touch of the bank-notes sent a kind of electric shock running up my arm; there were still vestiges of the larval personality, which could feel ashamed. My dying gentlemanly conscience still stirred within me, but none the less the touch of the stolen money was agreeable, and I was spendthrift in my delight. The cabman was so effusive in his thanks, that I could not but smile as I thought: "If you only knew!" He whipped up his horse and drove off. I looked after the cab as from shipboard a voyager will look back upon the receding shores of a land where he has spent happy days.

For a little while I stood musing. Then I strolled across towards the Sacher Garden, where it was my wont to dine after driving in the Prater. No doubt this was why the cabman had pulled up where he did. But when my hand was on the bell of the garden gate of this fashionable open-air restaurant, I had a counter-impulse. I did not want to go back into the familiar world. The idle chatter of my social equals would dispel this wonderful, this mysterious fermentation—would tear me away from the sparkling magic of my afternoon adventure.

From somewhere in the distance came snatches of music, and the crazy sounds drew me, as everything with a lure in it drew me that day. My mood made it delightful to follow chance currents. There was an extraordinary fascination in thus drifting amid the crowd. I fermented with the fermenting mass; all my senses were stirred by the acrid fumes of mingled dust, tobacco, human breath, and human sweat. Everything which till recently, till yesterday, had seemed to me vulgar and plebeian, and consequently repulsive, everything which I had been sedulously trained to avoid, had now become the goal of instinctive desire, as if for the first time I realised my own kinship with the animal, the impulsive, and the ordinary. Here, in the purlieus of the city, among common soldiers, servant girls and vagabonds, I found myself inexplicably at ease. I breathed this new air exultantly; rubbing shoulders with the crowd was pleasant; and with voluptuous curiosity I waited to learn whither my drifting would lead me. As I drew nearer to the Wurstel Prater, the blare of the brass band grew louder; it coalesced with the monotonous sound of orchestrions playing harsh polkas and riotous waltzes, with strange noises from the booths, outbursts of coarse laughter and drink-sodden yells. Through the trees I caught sight of the roundabouts whirling amid their crazy lights. I drank in the whole tumult. The cascade of noises, the infernal medley, was grateful to me, lulled me. I watched the girls on the switchback, their skirts blown out by the wind; heard them screaming in a way characteristic of their sex at each swoop of the car. There were butcher's lads roaring with laughter at the Try-your-Strength machine; touts standing at the doors of the booths, making monkey-like gestures, and doing their best to shout down the noise of the orchestrions. All this mixed confusedly with the manifold movements and clamours of the crowd, drunken with the cheap intoxication of the brass band, the flashing lights, and its own warm tumultuousness. Now that I had been awakened, I was able to enter into the life of these others, to share in the ardours of the great city, in its riot of Sunday amusement, its animal-like and nevertheless healthy and impulsive enjoyments. Through my contact with this tumultuous life, with these hot and passionate bodies, some of their fervour was transmitted to myself. My nerves were toned up by the acrid aroma; my senses wantoned amid the tumult; I had that intangible but sensuous ecstasy which is inseparable from every strong pleasure. Never before, perhaps, had I thus been in touch with the crowd, had I thus grasped humanity-at-large as a massed power from which pleasure could flow into my own separate personality. The barriers had been broken down, so that my own individual circulation was now connected up with the blood current of this wider world. I was seized with a new longing to overthrow the last obstacles between myself and this wider life; I was filled with an ardent desire for conjugation with this warm and strange and teeming humanity. With a man's lust I lusted after the flesh of this titanic body; and with a woman's lust I was ready to accept all its caresses and to respond to its every lure. Yes, at length I realised it, I loved and I longed to be loved as when I had been a boy first growing into manhood. I craved for life; for union with the laughing and breathing passion of these others, to be bone of their bone and flesh of their flesh. Enough to be small and nameless in the medley, an infusorian in the slime of the world, one tiny fragment of vigorous life among the myriads. Enough, so long as I was in and of that life, moving with others in the circle, no longer shot away like an arrow animated with an isolated energy and moving towards some heaven of separateness.

I am well aware that I was drunk. All the influences of the environment were at work in my blood: the clanging of the bells of the roundabouts; the lascivious laughter of the women when gripped by their male companions; the chaos of music; the rustling of the garments. My fingertips and temples were throbbing. I had a fierce urge to speak, to break the silence of many hours. Never had I such a longing for human intercourse, as here among this surging crowd, of whom nevertheless I was not yet one. I was like a man dying of thirst upon the ocean. The torment of my own separateness increased moment by moment, while I watched strangers, who were strangers also to one another, coalescing into groups and breaking up again like globules of quicksilver. I was filled with envy when I saw young fellows making girls' acquaintance in one moment, and walking arm-in-arm with them the next. A word while on the roundabout, a glance in passing, sufficed; the strangers entered into conversation, and perhaps separated after a minute or two; but meanwhile there had been a union, an intercourse of thoughts and feelings, such as my soul craved.

Here was I, a man at home in the best society, with a certain reputation as a conversationalist, one who knew all the rules of the social game—yet I was timid and abashed, was afraid to accost a buxom servant wench lest she should laugh at me. I lowered my eyes when anyone glanced at me, eager though I was to begin a talk. My desires were far from clear to me, but of one thing I was convinced, that I could no longer endure to be alone, consumed by my own fever. Still, no one greeted me, all passed by unheeding. Once a lad came near me, a boy about twelve years old in ragged clothes; his eyes shone with the reflex of the lamps as he stared longingly at the whirling wooden horses. There he stood open-mouthed. Having no money to pay for a ride, he was perforce content with the next best thing, with enjoying the shrieks and laughter of the fortunate riders. I constrained myself to walk up to him and ask (why did my voice tremble and my tone ring false?):

"Wouldn't you like to have a ride?"

He stared up at me, took fright (why? why?), flushed scarlet, and fled without a word. Not even a bare-footed urchin would accept a little pleasure from me. There must be something extraordinarily repellent about me—such was my thought. What else could account for my inability to become one with the crowd; for the way in which, amid the turbulent waters, I was detached as a droplet of oil?

But I would not give in; I could no longer bear to be alone. My feet were burning in my dusty patent-leather shoes; my throat was parched. Looking to right and left through gaps in the crowd, I could see islets of green on which there were tables decked with red cloths. Here, on wooden benches and chairs, tradespeople were seated, drinking beer and smoking cigars. This seemed attractive. Strangers hobnobbed here, and there was comparative quiet amid the turmoil. I went to one of these oases, and scrutinised the groups till I spied a table at which there were five persons—a fat, stocky workman, his wife, two merry girls, and a little boy. Their heads wagged in time with the music, they were chaffing one another and laughing, and their cheerful faces were good to see. I raised my hat, touched a chair, and asked if I might sit down. Instantly their laughter was frozen, and there was a moment's pause in which each of them seemed to be waiting for one of the others to answer. Then the mother, though discountenanced, murmured:

"If you please."

I sat down, with the feeling that my arrival had put an end to their unconstraint. A deadly silence now brooded over the table. I did not dare to raise my eyes from the red check tablecloth, on which salt and pepper had been freely spilled; but I realised that they must all be eyeing me stealthily, and it occurred to me (too late!) that my appearance was quite out of keeping with a beer garden of this character. My smartly-cut suit, my tall hat, the pearl pin in my dove-grey necktie, the general odour of luxury I exhaled, had sufficed to dig between me and my table-companions a chasm across which they glared at me with confusion and hostility. The silence of the five made it ever more impossible for me to raise my eyes. Shame forbade my leaving the place I had taken, so I sat there despairingly counting and recounting the checks on the tablecloth. Great was my relief when the waiter at length brought me my beer in a thick and heavy glass. At length I could move, and as I drank I could look at my companions furtively. Yes, I was the centre of all their eyes; and their expression, though not one of positive hatred, betrayed immeasurable estrangement. They knew me for an interloper into their dull world. With the instinct of their class they felt that I was in search of something which did not belong to my own surroundings. Not from love, not from longing, not from simple pleasure in waltzes or in beer, not in search of the placid enjoyments of the day of rest, could I have come to this resort. They felt that I must have been impelled by some desire beyond the range of their understanding, and they mistrusted me, as the youngster had mistrusted my offer to pay for his ride on the roundabout, as the thousand nameless frequenters of this place of merrymaking mistrusted my unfamiliar appearance, manners, and mode of speech. Yet I felt sure that if I could only happen upon a cordial, straightforward, and genuinely human way of opening up a conversation, the father or the mother would answer me, the daughters would giggle approvingly, and I should be able to take the boy with me to one of the shooting galleries, or to enjoy whatever sport might best please him. In five or ten minutes I should be delivered from myself, should be breathing the frank atmosphere of familiar converse, should be accepted as a desirable acquaintance—but the words I wanted were undiscoverable; I was stifled by false shame; and I sat among these simple folk wearing a hang-dog expression as if I were a criminal, tormented by the sense that my unwelcome presence was spoiling the last hour of their Sunday. In this formidable silence I atoned for all the years of careless arrogance in which without a glance I had passed thousands of such tables, millions upon millions of my brother human beings, concerned only with success in my own smart circle. I perceived that the way leading to unrestrained converse with them in this hour of my need, had been walled up from my side.

Thus I, who had hitherto been a free man, sat humbly with bowed head, counting and recounting the checks on the cloth, until the waiter came that way again. I settled up, left most of my beer, and uttered a civil farewell. The response was friendly, but not unmixed with astonishment. I knew, without looking, that, directly my back was turned, directly the foreign body had been removed, the round of cheerful talk would be resumed.

Again I threw myself into the maelstrom of the crowd—more eagerly this time and more despairingly. The press had become less dense under the black canopy of the trees, nor was there so great a throng where the big roundabout cast its glare; but in the darker parts of the square, along the edges, there seemed to be as many people as ever. The deep roar of the pleasure-seekers had broken up into a number of distinct smaller sounds, though these were fused into one from time to time when the music raged furiously as if in an attempt to summon back the seceders. New elements were conspicuous in the crowd. The children, with their air-balloons, paper windmills, and streamers, had been taken home, and the family parties had disappeared. Some of those who remained were uproariously drunk; vagabonds on the prowl were conspicuous in the side alleys; during the hour in which I had been glued to the table in the beer-garden, this remarkable world had changed considerably for the worse. But the stimulating aroma of rascality and danger was more congenial to me than the atmosphere of working-class respectability had been. The instinct that had awakened in me was in tune with the like tensions of those I was not contemplating. I seemed to see myself reflected in the slouching demeanour of these questionable shapes, these outcasts of society. Like myself, they were in search of some vivid adventure, some swift excitement. I positively envied the ragged prowlers, envied them for their lack of restraint. For there I stood leaning against one of the pillars of the roundabout, longing to break the spell of silence, to free myself from the torment of loneliness, and yet incapable of movement or word. I stood and stared across the square, across the brilliantly lighted open space, into the darkness on the other side, expectantly scrutinising every one who drew near. But none would meet my gaze. All looked at me with chill indifference. No one wanted me, no one would set me free.

How can I attempt to describe or explain what must sound like lunacy? Here was I, a man of education, rich and independent, at home in the best society of the capital—and that night I stood for a whole hour beside one of the pillars of a giddy-go-round, listening to twenty, forty, a hundred repetitions of the same waltz, the same polka, and watching the revolutions of the same idiotic horses of carved and painted wood—while an obdurate defiance, a determination to await the magic turn of fate, kept me rooted to the spot. I know that my conduct was absurd, but my torment during that hour was an expiation. And what I was expiating was not my theft, but the dull vacancy of my life prior to that afternoon. I had sworn to myself that I would not leave the spot until a sign had been vouchsafed that fate had set me free.

As the hour passed, the merry-making gradually came to an end. In one booth after another the lamps were extinguished, so that the darkness seemed to advance like a flood. The island of light where I was standing grew ever more isolated. In alarm I glanced at my watch. Another quarter of an hour and the garish wooden horses would cease to turn, the red and green lamps dangling from their foreheads would be switched off, and the blaring orchestrion would be silenced. Then I should be in the dark, alone in the murmuring night, outcast and forlorn. More and more uneasily I looked across the darkling square, traversed now only at intervals by a couple hastening homewards or by one or two reeling roisterers. But opposite me in the deep shadow there lurked a restless and stimulating life. When a man passed by, I could hear, emerging from this darkness, a whispered invitation. If, in answer, the passer-by turned his head, a woman's voice would speak more distinctly, and sometimes a woman's laugh was borne to me on the breeze. Little by little these dwellers in the darkness, growing bolder, began to invade the lighted square, but vanished instantly if the spiked helmet of a policeman loomed anywhere within sight. Directly the constable had passed on his round, the prowling shadows returned, and now, when they ventured farther into the light, I could make out plainly enough the ultimate scum that remained from the current of busy human life. They were prostitutes of the lowest class, those who have no homes to which they can take their customers, those who sell themselves for a trifle in any dark corner, harried by the police, harried by hunger, and harried by their own bullies, continually hunted and continually on the prowl for prey. Like hungry hounds they nosed their way across the lighted square towards anything masculine, towards any late straggler who might be tempted to satiate his lust for a crown or two. The money would buy a hot drink and a morsel of food at a coffee-stall, and would help to keep the life in them until its flicker should be extinguished in hospital or gaol.

Here was the very scum, the last spume, of the sensual flood of this Sunday crowd. With immeasurable horror I watched these wolfish forms slinking out of the gloom. But even in my horror there was an elemental pleasure, for in this tarnished mirror I could see vestiges of my own forgotten past. Here was a morass through which I had myself made my way in earlier years, and its phosphorescent marsh-lights were glowing anew in my senses. I recalled the days of adolescence, when my eye would rest on such figures at these with a mixture of alarm and eagerness; and I recalled the hour when I had first followed such a woman up a damp and creaky stair. Suddenly, as if illumined by a lightning-flash I saw in sharp relief every detail of that forgotten hour: the insipid oleograph over the woman's bed, the mascot she wore round her neck; and I remembered the ardour of yore, tinged with loathing and also with the pride of budding manhood. With a clarity of vision that was new to me I realised why sympathy with these outcasts was stirring within me. The instinct that had roused me to my crime of the afternoon made me feel my kinship with these hungry marauders. The pocket-book with the stolen money in it seemed to burn my breast where I carried it. I felt that across there in the darkness were human creatures, breathing and speaking, who wanted something of others, perhaps of me—of me who only waited to give himself, who was filled with a yearning for his fellows. At length I understood what drives men to such women. Seldom, indeed, are they driven merely by the urge of the senses. The main motive is dread of solitude, of the terrible feeling of aloofness which severs us one from another, and which I for the first time had fully realised that day. I recalled when I had last experienced it, though more dully. It had been in England, in Manchester, one of those towns hard as iron, roaring under grey skies with the noise of an underground railway, but where the visitor is apt to experience the chill of utter loneliness. I had passed three weeks there, staying with relatives, spending my evenings in bar-rooms, music-halls, and like places, always in search of the warmth of human companionship. One evening, I encountered such a woman, whose gutter English I could scarcely understand. Almost unawares, I found myself with her. I drank laughter from a strange mouth. A warm body was close to me, warm and soft. The cold, black town had vanished; the gloomy, thunderous abode of solitude was no longer there. In their stead was a fellow creature, an unknown woman, who waited for all comers, and could bring deliverance. I breathed freely once more, I discerned the brightness of life even in this iron cage. How precious to the lonely, to those who are prisoned within themselves, is this knowledge that after all they can find relief, that there is something to which they can cling, though it be something worn and besmirched. This is what I had forgotten during that hour of unspeakable loneliness. I had forgotten that out there in the darkness there were still those ready to give the uttermost in exchange for a trifling coin—which is assuredly too small a return for that which they bestow with their eternal readiness to give the great gift of human companionship.

The orchestrion of the roundabout by which I was standing began once more. This was the last turn; the last time the circling light would flash out into the dark before the Sunday passed into the drab weekdays. But there were very few riders; the tired woman at the receipt of custom was counting up the day's takings, and the odd man was standing by with a hook ready to pull down the noisy shutters directly the round was finished. But I still stood leaning against the post, looking across the empty square—empty except for the prowling figures I have described. Like me, they were expectant; and yet between them and me was a barrier of estrangement I could not cross. Now one of them must have noticed me, for she sidled past me, and from beneath my lowered eyelids I took in every detail of her appearance. She was a small woman, crippled by rickets, hatless, wearing a tawdry outfit, and down-at-heel dancing shoes, the whole probably bought at an old-clothes shop, and since then much worsened by the rough usage incidental to her trade. She stopped close at hand, and looked at me with a wheedling expression, and a smile of invitation that showed her bad teeth. I could hardly breathe. I feigned not to see her, and yet could not tear away my eyes. As if hypnotised, I realised that a human being was coveting me, was wooing me, that at length with a word or a gesture I could put an end to my hateful loneliness, to my tormenting sense of being an outcast. But I could not say the word or make the sign; I was as wooden as the post beside which I was standing. Nevertheless, while the tune of the roundabout dragged wearily to its close, even my impotence was suffused with pleasure because of the near presence of this woman who wooed me. I closed my eyes for a moment to enjoy the magnetic lure of invitation from a fellow creature.

The merry-go-round stopped turning, and therewith the waltz wheezed out into silence. I opened my eyes to perceive that the woman had begun to move away. Obviously she was tired of soliciting a wooden image. I was alarmed, and turned cold of a sudden. Why had I let her go, the one human being that had made advances to me on this amazing night? Behind me the lights were switched off, and the steel rollers were clattering down into their sockets. The revels were over.

Suddenly—how shall I describe the ferment within me? Suddenly I was overwhelmed with the longing that this bedraggled and rickety little prostitute would turn her head that I might speak to her. Not that I was too proud to follow her (my pride had been stamped into the dust, and had been replaced by feelings quite new to me); I was too irresolute. I stood there yearning that this poor little wretch would turn once more and favour me with her look of invitation.

And, she turned. Almost mechanically, she glanced over her shoulder. The release of tension must have been plainly manifest in my eyes, for she stopped to watch me. Then, turning half round, she beckoned with a movement of the head, beckoned me towards the darker site of the square. At length the hideous spell that had held me rigid was lifted. I was again able to move, and I nodded assent.

The invisible treaty had been signed. In the faint light she walked across the square, looking back from time to time to see if I was following her. And I followed. I was drawn along in her wake. She slackened her pace in an alley between the booths, and there I overtook her.

For a few seconds she looked me up and down with suspicion. Something about me made her doubtful—my timidity, and the contrast between my appearance and the place in which she found me. But after this brief hesitation, she pointed along the alley, which towards the end was black as pitch, saying:

"Let's go down there. It's quite dark behind the circus."

I could not answer. The horrible commonness of this encounter struck me dumb. I should have liked to buy myself off with a crown or two and a word of excuse, but my will had no power over my actions. I felt as one feels on a toboggan, sweeping round a curve leading to a precipitous descent, when a sense of fear is pleasantly fused with the exhilaration of speed, so that, instead of trying to hold back, one surrenders to the delight of the plunge. Thus I could not hold back, and perhaps no longer even wished to do so. When she pressed up against me, I took her involuntarily by the arm. It was very thin—not a woman's arm, but that of an undersized child—and when I felt it through her flimsy sleeve, I was overwhelmed with pity for this poor little fragment of down-trodden humanity which the night had tossed into my path.

We crossed the dimly lighted street and entered a little wood where the tree tops brooded over an evil-smelling darkness. I noticed that she half turned to look back as we entered, and that she did the same thing a few paces farther on. Even though I seemed paralysed as I slipped into this sordid adventure, my senses were keenly awake. With a lucidity which nothing could escape, I percieved that a shadow was following us along the edge of the path, and I could hear a stealthy footstep. The situation was clear to me in a flash. I was to be lured into an out-of-the-way spot, where the girl and her bully would have me at their mercy. With the marvellous insight which comes in moments betwixt life and death, I weighed up the chances. There was still time to get away. We were close to the main road, for I could hear the sound of a tram-car. A cry of a whistle would bring help. Thus I turned over in my mind all the possibilities of flight or rescue.

Strangely enough, however, the danger of my position inflamed my ardour instead of cooling it. To-day I find it difficult to account for the absurdity of my behaviour. Even as I moved onwards, I knew that I was needlessly putting my head into a noose; but the anticipation thrilled me. Something repulsive awaited me, perhaps deadly peril. Loathsome was the thought of the base issues in which I was becoming involved. But in my then mood of intoxication, even the menace of death exercised a sinister lure. What drove me forwards? Was I ashamed to show the white feather, or was I simply weak? I think, rather, that the ruling passion was a desire to taste the very dregs of life, a longing to stake my whole existence upon one cast. That was why, though fully aware of all the risks I was running, I went on into the wood arm-in-arm with the wench who had no physical attractions, and who regarded me only as a pigeon for her and her companion to pluck. I must play out the play which had begun with my crime on the racecourse, must play it to the end, even if the fall of the curtain should be death.

After a few more paces, she stopped and looked back yet again. Then she glanced at me expectantly, and said:

"Well, how much are you going to give me?"

Ah, yes, I had forgotten that aspect of the matter. But her question did not sober me. Far from it. I was so glad to be able to give riotously. Searching my pockets, I poured into her extended hand all the silver I had with me and two or three crumpled notes. Now there happened something so remarkable that it warms my heart when I think of it.

Perhaps the girl was amazed at my largesse; perhaps, in my spendthrift gesture, there was something quite new to her. Anyhow, she stepped back a pace, and through the thick, evil-smelling obscurity I could feel that her eyes were fixed on mine with astonished enquiry. At length I could enjoy what I had been craving for all the evening. Someone was concerned with me as an individual; for the first time I had become really alive to someone in this new world. The fact that it was an outcast among outcasts, a derelict who hawked her poor worn body in the darkness and never even saw the buyer's face—that this was the creature who now looked questioningly at me and was trying to understand what sort of human being I might be—served only to intensify my strange exaltation. She drew closer to me, not now in professional fulfilment of the task for which she had been paid, but animated, I believe, by an unconscious sense of gratitude, by a feminine desire for a caressive contact. Once more I took her by the emaciated arm; I felt the touch of her frail twisted body; and I pictured to myself what her life had been and was. I thought of the foul lodging in some slum, where from early morning till noon she had to snatch what sleep she could amid a noisy rabble of children. I pictured the souteneur who would knock her about; the drunken wretches who would be her usual clients; her life in the lock hospital; the workhouse infirmary in which she would end her days. Touched with infinite compassion, I stooped, and, to her amazement, kissed her.

At this moment there was a rustling behind me, and a fallen branch snapped. There was a guffaw; then a man spoke.

"Caught you in the act! Thought I should!"

Before I saw them, I knew who they were. I had not forgotten that I was being spied upon, and all the time I had been expecting this intervention. A figure became visible to me, and then a second; two savage-looking louts. There were more chuckles, and then:

"At your dirty tricks here in public. A gentleman, too, if you please! But we'll make him squeal."

I stood unmoved. My temples throbbed, but I was quite free from anxiety, and merely waited to see what would happen. Now I was indeed in the depths. At last would come the climax towards which I had been drifting.

The girl had started away from me, but not to join the men. She stood between us, and apparently the part assigned to her was not altogether congenial. The louts were obviously discomfited by my indifference. They looked at one another in perplexity, wondering why I did not betray any anxiety, or beg to be let off. At last one of them cried in a menacing tone:

"Aha! he's got nothing to say."

The other stepped up to me, and spoke imperatively:

"You must come with us to the station."

Still I made no answer. Then the man near me touched me on the shoulder, and gave me a little push.

"Step it," he said.

I did as I was bid, making no attempt to resist. Of course I was well aware that these fellows must be much more afraid of the police than I was, and that I could ransom myself for a few crowns; but I wanted to savour all the horrible humours of the situation. Slowly and mechanically I moved in the direction they indicated.

But this patient acceptance of the position, this willingness to return to the light, confounded my tormentors.

"Hist! Hist!"—they exchanged signals, and then began to speak with forced loudness.

"Better let the beggar go," said one of the two, a pock-marked shrimp of a man.

The other assumed a tone of stricter morality:

"No, no, that won't do. If he were a poor devil of our sort, without a morsel to line his belly with, they'd lock him up fast enough. We can't let our fine gentleman go scot free."

Through the words and the tone breathed an awkward invitation that I should begin bargaining. The criminal in me understood the criminal in them. I knew that they wanted to cow me, and that they themselves were cowed by my ready compliance. There was a dumb contest between myself and the two. How glorious it was! In imminent danger, in this filthy grove, dogged by a couple of bullies and a whore, I felt for the second time within twelve hours the magical charm of hazard—but this time the stake was higher, the stake was life itself. I surrendered wholly to the strange sport, awaiting the cast of the dice.

"Ah, there's a copper," said one of the men. "Our fine gentleman will have a jolly time of it. They won't give him less than a week in quod."

This was intended to alarm me, but I could hear that the speaker was far from sure of himself. I walked on confidently towards the lamp, where in actual fact I could see the gleaming spike of a policeman's helmet. Twenty paces, and we should reach him. The men behind me had nothing more to say. They were already lagging, and in a moment, I was sure, they would vanish into the darkness. They would slip back into their own world, embittered by their failure, and would perhaps wreak their anger upon the unhappy drab. The game was finished, and once more that day I was a winner. Just before reaching the bright circle of light cast on the ground by the street lamp, I turned, and for the first time looked into the faces of the two bullies. Their eyes betrayed both vexation and shame. They stood there cowed, ready for instant flight. Their power was at an end; the tables were turned, and they had good cause to be afraid of me.

At this instant, however, I was overcome by a feeling of immense sympathy, of brotherly sympathy for these two fellows. After all, what had they wanted of me, the two hungry loafers? What had they wanted of me, the overfed parasite? Two or three paltry crowns! They might have throttled me there in the gloomy wood, might have robbed me and murdered me. Yet they had merely tried, in clumsy fashion, to frighten me into handing over some of my loose silver. How could I dare, I who had been a thief from sheer caprice, who had become a criminal because I wanted a thrill, how could I dare to torment the poor devils? In my turn, I was ashamed because I had played with their fears. Now, at the last moment, when I had escaped from their toils, I would soothe the disappointment which was so obvious in their hollow eyes.

With an abrupt change of front, I went up to one of then, and simulated anxiety as I said:

"Why do you want to hand me over to the police? What do you expect to get out of it? Perhaps I shall be put in prison for a few days, perhaps not. Will you be any the better off? Why should you wish to do me harm?"

They stared at me in hopeless perplexity. Anything else they might have been prepared for, a denunciation, a threat, before which they would have cringed like dogs; but they did not know what to make of my yielding at the eleventh hour. At length one of them answered, not menacingly, but as if in self-exculpation:

"Justice must take its course. We are only doing our duty."

Plainly this was a stock phrase, conned for such occasions. But this time there was no spirit in it. Neither of them ventured to look at me. They waited. I knew what they were waiting for. They wanted me to beg for mercy, and then to offer them money.

I can recall the whole scene perfectly, and can remember every detail of my own feelings. I know, therefore, that malice prompted me to keep them on tenterhooks, in order that I might enjoy their discomfiture the more. But I constrained my will, for I knew that it behoved me to set their anxieties at rest. I began, therefore, to play a little comedy of terror, imploring them not to denounce me. I saw how embarrassed were these inexperienced blackmailers, and I felt that I must break down the barrier of silence between us.

At length I came to the words in expectation of which their mouths had been watering.

"I will give you . . . I will give you a hundred crowns."

All three of them were startled, and looked at one another in amazement. They had never expected such a sum at this stage, when they had given the game up for lost. But after a while the pock-marked man with the shifty eyes, plucked up heart a little. He made two unsuccessful attempts to break the spell. At last, and shamefacedly, he managed to get out the words:

"Make it two hundred, Guv'nor."

"Drop it, can't you," the girl suddenly broke in. "You can be jolly glad if he gives you anything at all. He hardly touched me. It's really a bit too thick."

She was furious, and my heart sang within me. Someone sympathised with me, interceded for me. Kindness rose out of the depths; there was an obscure craving for justice in this blackmailer's hussy. It was like a cordial to me. I could not play with them any longer, could not torment them in their fear and their shame.

"All right," I said, "two hundred crowns."

They made no answer. I took out my note-case. I opened it slowly and ostentatiously. It would have been easy for any one of them to snatch it and be off. But they looked timidly away. Between them and me there was a secret bond; no longer a struggle for mastery, but an understanding, mutual confidence, a human relationship. I detached two notes from the stolen bundle, and handed them to the nearest of the bullies.

"Thank you, Sir," he said in spite of himself, and turned to go.

It was plain that he felt how absurd it was to thank me for a blackmailer's gains. He was ashamed of himself for doing so, and I was sorry for him in his shame. I did not want him to feel shame before me, for I was a man of his own kidney; I was a thief just as much as he; I, too, was a coward and a weakling. His humiliation distressed me, and I wanted to restore his self-respect. I refused, therefore, to accept his thanks.

"It is my place to thank you," I replied, marvelling at my tone of genuine conviction. "If you had given me in charge I should have been ruined. I should have had to blow my brains out, and you would not have been any the richer. This is the best way out of the difficulty. Well, I shall take that turning to the right, and no doubt you'll be going in the opposite direction. Good-night!"

There was a moment's hesitation. Then one of the men said good-night, then the other, and last of all the girl, who had kept back in the shadows. These parting words were charged with a genuine sentiment of goodwill. Their voices showed me that they had in some sort taken a fancy to me, and that they would never forget the episode. It would recur to their minds some day in penitentiary or hospital. Something had gone from me into them, and would live on in them; I had given them something. The joy of this giving was the most poignant feeling I had ever experienced.

I walked on alone towards the gate leading out of the Prater. My sense of oppression had been wholly lifted. The trees whispered to me, and I loved them. The stars shone down on me, and I rejoiced in their luminous greeting. Voices raised in song were audible in the distance; they were singing for me. Everything was mine, now that I had broken the shell in which I had been confined. The joy of giving, the joy of prodigality, united me with the world-all. "How easy," I thought, "to give joy and win joy! We need merely raise the sluices, and then from man to man the living current flows, thundering from the heights into the depths and foaming from the depths upward into the infinite."

When I reached the exit from the Prater, I caught sight of an old woman sitting near the cab-stand—a hawker, wearily bent over her petty wares. She had some dusty cakes on her stall, and a little fruit. No doubt she had been there since morning to earn a few pence. "Why should you not enjoy yourself as well as I?" I thought, so I chose a cake and handed her a note. She started to fumble for the change, but I waved it away. She trembled with delight and astonishment, and began to pour out expressions of gratitude. Disregarding these, I went up to the horse which stood drooping between the shafts of her itinerant stall and offered him the cake. He nuzzled me in friendly fashion, as if he too would like to say thank you. Thereupon I was filled with the longing to dispense more pleasure, to learn more fully how easy it is to kill cares and diffuse cheerfulness with the aid of a few silver coins or some printed pieces of coloured paper. Why were there no beggars about? Where were the children who would like to have the air-balloons which that morose, white-haired, old fellow was limping home with? He had a huge bundle of them tied to strings, and had obviously had a poor day's custom. I accosted him:

"Give me those balloons."

"Penny each," he said dubiously, for he could not believe that a well-dressed idler would want to buy his coloured air-balloons at midnight.

"I'll take the lot," I said, and gave him a ten-crown note.

He positively staggered in his amazement, and then held out the cord to which the whole bundle was fastened. I felt the pull of it on my fingers. The balloons were longing for freedom, longing to fly skyward. Why should they not do what they wanted? I loosed the cord, and they rose like great tinted moons. People ran up laughing from all directions; pairs of lovers turned up out of the darkness; the cabmen cracked their whips, and called to one another as they pointed to the air-balloons sailing over the tree-tops and the roofs. Everyone made merry over my prank.

Why had I never known how easy it is and how enjoyable to give others pleasure? Once more the notes in my wallet began to burn me, they plucked at my fingers like the cord that had held the balloons; they, too, wanted to fly away into the unknown. I took them all out, not only the ones I had stolen from Lajos, but all the others I had with me, for I no longer recognised any difference between them, no longer felt that some of them were stained with crime. There they were, ready for any one who wanted them. I went across to a street sweeper who was listlessly cleaning up the deserted street. He fancied I was going to ask him the way, and looked at me surlily. Laughing, I offered him a twenty-crown note. He stared uncomprehendingly, but at length took the note, and waited to know what I wanted of him.

"Buy whatever you like with it," I said, and went on my way.

I peered in all directions, looking for some one who might ask a gift of me. Since no one did so, I had to make the offers. A prostitute accosted me, and I gave her a note. I handed two to a lamplighter. One I threw in at the area window of a bakery. Thus I made my progress, leaving a trail of surprise, gratitude, and delight.

At last I began to throw the notes here, there, and everywhere—in the street, on the steps of a church. I smiled to think how the old apple-woman who had a stall there would find the hundred crowns in the morning and would praise God for the windfall. Some poor student, or maidservant, or workman would pick up the notes with the same feeling of wonder and delight that animated me while scattering them abroad.

When I had got rid of the last of them, I felt incredibly lighthearted, almost as if I could fly, and I enjoyed a sense of freedom such as I had never before known. Towards the street, the sky, the houses, I had a new feeling of kinship. Never, up till now, even in the most ardent moments of my existence, had I felt the reality of all these things so strongly—that they were alive and I was alive, and that the life in them and in me was the same life, the great and mighty life that can never be overfilled with happiness—the life that only one who loves and one who gives can understand.

I had one last moment of uneasiness. It was when I had turned the latchkey in my door and I glimpsed the dark entry to my own rooms. Suddenly there came over me a rush of anxiety lest this should be a re-entry into my earlier life, now that I was going back into the familiar dwelling, was about to get into the familiar bed, to resume associations with all the things from which, that night, I had been able to break away. The one thing needful was that I should not again become the man I had been; that I should no longer be the gentleman of yesterday, the slave of good form, who was unfeeling, and lived apart from the world. Better to plunge into the abysses of crime and horror, so long as I could be truly alive! I was utterly tired out, and yet I dreaded sleep, for I was afraid that during sleep the fervour, the sense of new life, would vanish. I dreaded lest the whole experience should prove as fugitive as a dream.

But I woke next morning in a cheerful mood, to find that the current of new feeling was still vigorous. Four months have passed since then, and there has been no return of the old stagnation. The amazing elation of that day, when I left all the traditional paths of my world to launch forth into the unknown, plunging into the abysses of life, giddy with speed, and intoxicated with delight—this climax of ardour is, indeed, over. Yet in all my hours since then I have never ceased to feel renewed pleasure in life. I know that I have been reborn, with other senses, responsive to other stimuli, and animated with a clearer consciousness. I cannot venture to judge whether I am a better man, but I know that I am a happier one. Life had grown cold and unmeaning; but now it has acquired a meaning, one for which I can find no other name than the very word "Life." I have thrown off artificial restraints, for the rules and conventions of the society in which I was brought up have ceased to bind me. I am no longer ashamed either before others or before myself. Such words as honour, crime, and vice have grown hollow-sounding, and I find it distasteful to use them. My vital impetus comes from the power which I first recognised on that wonderful night. I do not know whither it is driving me: perchance towards a new abyss, towards what others call vice or crime; perchance towards something sublime. I neither know nor care to know. For I believe that he only is truly alive who does not seek to probe the mystery of the future.

Of one thing I am sure, that I have never loved life more keenly; and

I know that whoever is indifferent to any of the forms and modes of life, commits a crime (the only crime there is!). Since I have begun to understand myself, I understand enormously better all that goes on around me. The covetous glances of someone gazing in at a shop window can move me profoundly; the gambols of a dog can fill me with enthusiasm. I am interested in everything; nothing is indifferent to me. In the newspaper, which I used barely to glance at, I now read a hundred items with zest. Books which used to bore me, now make a strong appeal. The strangest thing is that I can talk to my fellow human beings about other matters than those which form the substance of what, in good society, is termed "conversation." My manservant, who has been with me for seven years, interests me, and I often have a talk with him. The porter of the flats, whom I used to pass unheeding as if he had been one of the door-posts, told me the other day about the death of his little girl, and the recital moved me more than I have ever been moved by one of Shakespeare's tragedies. It would seem, too, though in outward semblance I still live the old life of respectable boredom, that the change in me must be obvious to others. People greet me far more cordially than of old; three times last week a strange dog came and fawned on me in the street. My friends look at me with affectionate pleasure, as one looks at a person who is convalescent from illness, and tell me that I have grown younger.

Have I grown younger? All I know is that I have only just begun to live. Oh, I know, too, of the every-day illusion. I know how apt people are to think that all their past has been error and preparation. Doubtless it is arrogant to take a cold pen into my warm, living hand, and to write upon the dry paper that at length I am really alive. But even if it be an illusion, it is the first illusion that has made me happy, the first that has warmed my blood and unlocked my senses. If I sketch here the miracle of my awakening, I do it for myself alone, though I know it all better than words can describe. I have not spoken of the matter to any of my friends: they never knew how dead I had become; they will never guess how my life has blossomed afresh. Nor am I perturbed by the thought that death's hand may suddenly be laid upon this living life of mine, and that these lines may be read by other eyes. Those who have never known the magic of such an hour as I have described, will understand just as little as I could have understood six months ago how the fugitive and almost inconsequent happenings of one afternoon and evening could so have touched my life to flame. The thought of such a reader does not shame me, for he will not understand what I have written. But one who understands, will not judge, and will have no pride. Before him I shall not be ashamed. Whoever has found himself, can never again lose anything in this world. He who has grasped the human in himself, understands all mankind.

"The Hint of an Explanation" carries us back, via a ritual that has come down through the centuries, to a primitive fantasy of cannibalism. In this story a boy is tempted into an act against God. At the last minute he refuses to participate in the act, but he commits instead the crime of eating the Host by himself. As a grown man, he has become a priest— are we correct in assuming that he has surrendered his earthly pleasures as expiation for his sin of parricide?

GRAHAM GREENE

The Hint of an Explanation

A long train journey on a late December evening, in this new version of peace, is a dreary experience. I suppose that my fellow traveller and I could consider ourselves lucky to have a compartment to ourselves, even though the heating apparatus was not working, even though the lights went out entirely in the frequent Pennine tunnels and were too dim anyway for us to read our books without straining our eyes, and though there was no restaurant car to give at least a change of scene. It was when we were trying simultaneously to chew the same kind of dry bun bought at the same station buffet that my companion and I came together. Before that we had sat at opposite ends of the carriage, both muffled to the chin in overcoats, both bent low over type we could barely make out, but as I threw the remains of my cake under the seat our eyes met, and he laid his book down.

By the time we were half-way to Bedwell Junction we had found an enormous range of subjects for discussion; starting with buns and the weather, we had gone on to politics, the government, foreign affairs, the atom bomb, and, by an inevitable progression, God. We had not, however, become either shrill or acid. My companion, who now sat opposite me, leaning a little forward, so that our knees nearly touched, gave such an impression of serenity that it would have been impossible to quarrel with him, however much our views differed, and differ they did profoundly.

I had soon realized I was speaking to a Catholic, to someone who believed—how do they put it?—in the omnipotent and omniscient Deity, while I was what is loosely called an Agnostic. I have a certain intuition (which I do not trust, founded as it may well be on childish experiences and needs) that a God exists, and I am surprised occasionally into belief by the extraordinary coincidences that beset our path like the traps set for leopards in the jungle, but intellectually I am revolted at the whole notion of such a God who can so abandon his creatures to the enormities of Free Will. I found myself expressing this view to my companion, who listened quietly and with respect. He made no attempt to interrupt: he showed none of the impatience or the intellectual arrogance I have grown to expect from Catholics; when the lights of a wayside station flashed across his face that had escaped hitherto the rays of the one globe working in the compartment, I caught a glimpse suddenly of—what? I stopped speaking, so strong was the impression. I was carried back ten years, to the other side of the great useless conflict, to a small town, Gisors in Normandy. I was again, for a moment, walking on the ancient battlements and looking down across the grey roofs, until my eyes for some reason lit on one grey stony "back" out of the many, where the face of a middle-aged man was pressed against a windowpane (I suppose that face has ceased to exist now, just as I believe the whole town with its medieval memories has been reduced to rubble). I remembered saying to myself with astonishment, "That man is happy—completely happy." I looked across the compartment at my fellow traveller, but his face was already again in shadow. I said weakly, "When you think what God—if there is a God—allows. It's not merely the physical agonies, but think of the corruption, even of children. . . ."

He said, "Our view is so limited," and I was disappointed at the conventionality of his reply. He must have been aware of my disappointment (it was as though our thoughts were huddled as closely as ourselves for warmth), for he went on, "Of course there is no answer here. We catch hints . . ." and then the train roared into another tunnel and the lights again went out. It was the longest tunnel yet; we went rocking down it, and the cold seemed to become more intense with the darkness like an icy fog (perhaps when one sense—of sight—is robbed of sensation, the others grow more sensitive). When we emerged into the mere grey of night and the globe lit up once more, I could see that my companion was leaning back on his seat.

I repeated his last words as a question, "Hints?"

"Oh, they mean very little in cold print—or cold speech," he said, shivering in his overcoat. "And they mean nothing at all to a human being other than the man who catches them. They are not scientific evidence—or evidence at all for that matter. Events that don't, somehow, turn out as they were intended—by the human actors I mean, or the thing behind the human actors."

"The thing?"

"The word Satan is so anthropomorphic."

I had to lean forward now; I wanted to hear what he had to say. I am—I really am, God knows—open to conviction.

He said, "One's words are so crude, but I sometimes feel pity for that thing. It is so continually finding the right weapon to use against its Enemy and the weapon breaks in its own breast. It sometimes seems to me so—powerless. You said something just now about the corruption of children. It reminded me of something in my own childhood. You are the first person—except for one—that I have thought of telling it to, perhaps because you are anonymous. It's not a very long story, and in a way it's relevant."

I said, "I'd like to hear it."

"You mustn't expect too much meaning. But to me there seems to be a hint. That's all. A hint."

He went slowly on, turning his face to the pane, though he could have seen nothing real in the whirling world outside except an occasional signal lamp, a light in a window, a small country station torn backwards by our rush, picking his words with precision. He said, "When I was a child they taught me to serve at Mass. The church was a small one, for there were very few Catholics where I lived. It was a market town in East Anglia, surrounded by flat, chalky fields and ditches—so many ditches. I don't suppose there were fifty Catholics all told, and for some reason there was a tradition of hostility to us. Perhaps it went back to the burning of a Protestant martyr in the sixteenth century—there was a stone marking the place near where the meat stalls stood on Wednesdays. I was only half aware of the enmity, though I knew that my school nickname of Popey Martin had something to do with my religion, and I had heard that my father was nearly excluded from the Constitutional Club when he first came to the town.

"Every Sunday I had to dress up in my surplice and serve Mass. I hated it—I have always hated dressing up in any way (which is funny when you come to think of it), and I never ceased to be afraid of losing my place in the service and doing something which would put me to ridicule. Our services were at a different hour from the Anglican, and as our small, far-from-select band trudged out of the hideous chapel the whole of the townsfolk seemed to be on the way past to the proper church—I always thought of it as the proper church. We had to pass the parade of their eyes, indifferent, supercilious, mocking; you can't imagine how seriously religion can be taken in a small town, if only for social reasons.

"There was one man in particular; he was one of the two bakers in the town, the one my family did not patronize. I don't think any of the Catholics patronized him because he was called a free-thinker—an odd title, for, poor man, no one's thoughts were less free than his. He was hemmed in by his hatred—his hatred of us. He was very ugly to look at, with one wall-eye and a head the shape of a turnip, with the hair gone on the crown, and he was unmarried. He had no interests, apparently, but his baking and his hatred, though now that I am older I begin to see other sides of his nature—it did contain, perhaps, a certain furtive love. One would come across him suddenly sometimes on a country walk, especially if one were alone and it was Sunday. It was as if he rose from the ditches, and the smear of chalk on his clothes reminded one of the flour on his working overalls. He would have a stick in his hand and stab at the hedges, and if his mood were very black he would call out after one strange abrupt words like a foreign tongue—I know the meaning of those words, of course, now. Once the police went to his house because of what a boy said he'd seen, but nothing came of it except that the hate shackled him closer. His name was Blacker and he terrified me.

"I think he had a particular hatred of my father—I don't know why. My father was manager of the Midland Bank, and it's possible that at sometime Blacker may have had unsatisfactory dealings with the bank; my father was a very cautious man who suffered all his life from anxiety about money—his own and other people's. If I try and picture Blacker now I see him walking along a narrowing path between high windowless walls, and at the end of the path stands a small boy of ten—me. I don't know whether it's a symbolic picture or the memory of one of our encounters—our encounters somehow got more and more frequent. You talked just now about the corruption of children. That poor man was preparing to revenge himself on everything he hated—my father, the Catholics, the God whom people persisted in crediting—and that by corrupting me. He had evolved a horrible and ingenious plan.

"I remember the first time I had a friendly word from him. I was passing his shop as rapidly as I could when I heard his voice call out with a kind of sly subservience as though he were an under servant.

'Master David,' he called, 'Master David,' and I hurried on. But the next time I passed that way he was at his door (he must have seen me coming) with one of those curly cakes in his hand that we called Chelsea buns. I didn't want to take it, but he made me, and then I couldn't be other than polite when he asked me to come into his parlour behind the shop and see something very special.

"It was a small electric railway—a rare sight in those days, and he insisted on showing me how it worked. He made me turn the switches and stop and start it, and he told me that I could come in any morning and have a game with it. He used the word 'game' as though it were something secret, and it's true that I never told my family of this invitation and of how, perhaps twice a week those holidays, the desire to control that little railway became overpowering, and looking up and down the street to see if I were observed, I would dive into the shop."

Our larger, dirtier, adult train drove into a tunnel and the light went out. We sat in darkness and silence, with the noise of the train blocking our ears like wax. When we were through we didn't speak at once and I had to prick him into continuing. "An elaborate seduction," I said.

"Don't think his plans were as simple as that," my companion said, "or as crude. There was much more hate than love, poor man, in his make-up. Can you hate something you don't believe in? And yet he called himself a free-thinker. What an impossible paradox, to be free and to be so obsessed. Day by day all through those holidays his obsession must have grown, but he kept a grip; he bided his time. Perhaps that thing I spoke of gave him the strength and the wisdom. It was only a week from the end of the holidays that he spoke to me on what concerned him so deeply.

"I heard him behind me as I knelt on the floor, coupling two coaches. He said, 'You won't be able to do this, Master David, when school starts.' It wasn't a sentence that needed any comment from me any more than the one that followed. 'You ought to have it for your own, you ought,' but how skilfully and unemphatically he had sowed the longing, the idea of a possibility. . . . I was coming to his parlour every day now; you see, I had to cram every opportunity in before the hated term started again, and I suppose I was becoming accustomed to Blacker, to that wall-eye, that turnip head, that nauseating subservience. The Pope, you know, describes himself as 'the servant of the servants of God,' and Blacker—I sometimes think that Blacker was 'the servant of the servants of . . .,' well, let it be.

"The very next day, standing in the doorway watching me play, he began to talk to me about religion. He said, with what untruth even I recognized, how much he admired the Catholics; he wished he could believe like that, but how could a baker believe? He accented 'a baker' as one might say a biologist, and the tiny train spun round the gauge O track. He said, 'I can bake the things you eat just as well as any Catholic can,' and disappeared into his shop. I hadn't the faintest idea what he meant. Presently he emerged again, holding in his hand a little wafer. 'Here,' he said, 'eat that and tell me. . . .' When I put it in my mouth I could tell that it was made in the same way as our wafers for communion—he had got the shape a little wrong, that was all—and I felt guilty and irrationally scared. 'Tell me,' he said, 'what's the difference?'

" 'Difference?' I asked.

" 'Isn't that just the same as you eat in church?'

"I said smugly, 'It hasn't been consecrated.'

"He said, 'Do you think, if I put the two of them under a microscope, you could tell the difference?'

"But even at ten I had the answer to that question. 'No,' I said, 'the—accidents don't change,' stumbling a little on the word 'accidents' which had suddenly conveyed to me the idea of death and wounds.

"Blacker said with sudden intensity, 'How I'd like to get one of your ones in my mouth—just to see. . . .'

"It may seem odd to you, but this was the first time that the idea of transubstantiation really lodged in my mind. I had learned it all by rote; I had grown up with the idea. The Mass was as lifeless to me as the sentences in *De Bello Gallico;* communion a routine like drill in the school-yard, but here suddenly I was in the presence of a man who took it seriously, as seriously as the priest whom naturally one didn't count— it was his job. I felt more scared than ever.

"He said, 'It's all nonsense, but I'd just like to have it in my mouth.'

" 'You could if you were a Catholic,' I said naïvely.

"He gazed at me with his one good eye, like a Cyclops. He said, 'You serve at Mass, don't you? It would be easy for you to get at one of those things. I tell you what I'd do—I'd swap this electric train for one of your wafers—consecrated, mind. It's got to be consecrated.'

" 'I could get you one out of the box,' I said. I think I imagined that his interest was a baker's interest—to see how they were made.

" 'Oh, no,' he said, 'I want to see what your God tastes like.'

" 'I couldn't do that.'

" 'Not for a whole electric train, just for yourself? You wouldn't have any trouble at home. I'd pack it up and put a label inside that your dad could see: "For my bank manager's little boy from a grateful client." He'd be pleased as punch with that.'

"Now that we are grown men it seems a trivial temptation, doesn't it? But try to think back to your own childhood. There was a whole circuit of rails there on the floor at our feet, straight rails and curved, and a little station with porters and passengers, a tunnel, a footbridge, a level crossing, two signals, buffers, of course—and, above all, a turntable. The tears of longing came into my eyes when I looked at the turntable. It was my favorite piece—it looked so ugly and practical and true. I said weakly, 'I wouldn't know how.'

"How carefully he had been studying the ground! He must have slipped several times into Mass at the back of the church. It would have been no good, you understand, in a little town like that, presenting himself for communion. Everybody there knew him for what he was. He said to me, 'When you've been given communion you could just put it under your tongue a moment. He serves you and the other boy first, and I saw you once go out behind the curtain straight afterwards. You'd forgotten one of those little bottles.'

" 'The cruet,' I said.

" 'Pepper and salt.' He grinned at me jovially, and I—well, I looked at the little railway which I could no longer come and play with when term started. I said, 'You'd just swallow it, wouldn't you?'

" 'Oh, yes,' he said. 'I'd just swallow it.'

"Somehow I didn't want to play with the train any more that day. I got up and made for the door, but he detained me, gripping my lapel. He said, 'This will be a secret between you and me. Tomorrow's Sunday. You come along here in the afternoon. Put it in an envelope and post it me. Monday morning the train will be delivered bright and early.'

" 'Not tomorrow,' I implored him.

" 'I'm not interested in any other Sunday,' he said. 'It's your only chance.' He shook me gently backwards and forwards. 'It will always have to be a secret between you and me,' he said. 'Why, if anyone knew they'd take away the train and there'd be me to reckon with. I'd bleed you something awful. You know how I'm always about on Sunday walks. You can't avoid a man like me. I crop up. You wouldn't ever be safe in your own house. I know ways to get into houses when people are asleep.' He pulled me into the shop after him and opened a drawer. In the drawer was an odd looking key and a cut-throat razor. He said, 'That's a master key that opens all locks and that—that's what I bleed people with.' Then he patted my cheek with his plump floury fingers and said, 'Forget it. You and me are friends.'

"That Sunday Mass stays in my head, every detail of it, as though it had happened only a week ago. From the moment of the Confession to the moment of Consecration it had a terrible importance; only one other Mass has ever been so important to me—perhaps not even one, for this was a solitary Mass which would never happen again. It seemed as final as the last Sacrament when the priest bent down and put the wafer in my mouth where I knelt before the altar with my fellow server.

"I suppose I had made up my mind to commit this awful act—for, you know, to us it must always seem an awful act—from the moment when I saw Blacker watching from the back of the church. He had put on his best black Sunday clothes and, as though he could never quite escape the smear of his profession, he had a dab of dried talcum on his cheek, which he had presumably applied after using that cut-throat of his. He was watching me closely all the time, and I think it was fear— fear of that terrible undefined thing called bleeding—as much as covetousness that drove me to carry out my instructions.

"My fellow server got briskly up and, taking the paten, preceded Father Carey to the altar rail where the other communicants knelt. I had the Host lodged under my tongue: it felt like a blister. I got up and made for the curtain to get the cruet that I had purposely left in the sacristy. When I was there I looked quickly round for a hiding place and saw an old copy of the *Universe* lying on a chair. I took the Host from my mouth and inserted it between two sheets—a little damp mess of pulp. Then I thought: perhaps Father Carey has put out the paper for a particular purpose and he will find the Host before I have time to remove it, and the enormity of my act began to come home to me when I tried to imagine what punishment I should incur. Murder is sufficiently trivial to have its appropriate punishment, but for this act the mind boggled at the thought of any retribution at all. I tried to remove the Host, but it stuck clammily between the pages, and in desperation I tore out a piece of the newspaper and, screwing the whole thing up, stuck it in my trousers pocket. When I came back through the curtain carrying the cruet my eyes met Blacker's. He gave me a grin of encouragement and unhappiness—yes, I am sure, unhappiness. Was it perhaps that the poor man was all the time seeking something incorruptible?

"I can remember little more of that day. I think my mind was shocked and stunned, and I was caught up too in the family bustle of Sunday. Sunday in a provincial town is the day for relations. All the family are at home, and unfamiliar cousins and uncles are apt to arrive, packed in the back seats of other people's cars. I remember that some crowd of the kind descended on us and pushed Blacker temporarily out of the foreground of my mind. There was somebody called Aunt Lucy, with a loud hollow laugh that filled the house with mechanical merriment like the sound of recorded laughter from inside a hall of mirrors, and I had no opportunity to go out alone even if I had wished to. When six o'clock came and Aunt Lucy and the cousins departed and peace returned, it was too late to go to Blacker's, and at eight it was my own bed-time.

"I think I had half forgotten what I had in my pocket. As I emptied my pocket the little screw of newspaper brought quickly back the Mass, the priest bending over me, Blacker's grin. I laid the packet on the chair by my bed and tried to go to sleep, but I was haunted by the shadows on the wall where the curtains blew, the squeak of furniture, the rustle in the chimney, haunted by the presence of God there on the chair. The Host had always been to me—well, the Host. I knew theoretically, as I have said, what I had to believe, but suddenly, as someone whistled in the road outside, whistled secretively, knowingly, to me, I knew that this which I had beside my bed was something of infinite value—something a man would pay for with his whole peace of mind, something that was so hated one could love it as one loves an outcast or a bullied child. These are adult words, and it was a child of ten who lay scared in bed, listening to the whistle from the road, Blacker's whistle, but I think he felt fairly clearly what I am describing now. That is what I meant when I said this Thing, whatever it is, that seizes every possible weapon against God, is always, everywhere, disappointed at the moment of success. It must have felt as certain of me as Blacker did. It must have felt certain too of Blacker. But I wonder, if one knew what happened later to that poor man, whether one would not find again that the weapon had been turned against its own breast.

"At last I couldn't bear that whistle any more and got out of bed. I opened the curtains a little way, and there right under my window, the moonlight on his face, was Blacker. If I had stretched my hand down, his fingers reaching up could almost have touched mine. He looked up at me, flashing the one good eye, with hunger—I realize now that near-success must have developed his obsession almost to the point of madness. Desperation had driven him to the house. He whispered up at me. 'David, where is it?'

"I jerked my head back at the room. 'Give it me,' he said. 'Quick. You shall have the train in the morning.'

"I shook my head. He said, 'I've got the bleeder here, and the key. You'd better toss it down.'

" 'Go away,' I said, but I could hardly speak for fear.

" 'I'll bleed you first and then I'll have it just the same.'

" 'Oh, no, you won't,' I said. I went to the chair and picked it—Him —up. There was only one place where He was safe. I couldn't separate the Host from the paper, so I swallowed both. The newsprint stuck like a prune skin to the back of my throat, but I rinsed it down with water from the ewer. Then I went back to the window and looked down at Blacker. He began to wheedle me. 'What have you done with it, David? What's the fuss? It's only a bit of bread,' looking so longingly and pleadingly up at me that even as a child I wondered whether he could really think that, and yet desire it so much.

" 'I swallowed it,' I said.

" 'Swallowed it?'

" 'Yes,' I said. 'Go away.'

"Then something happened which seems to me now more terrible than his desire to corrupt or my thoughtless act: he began to weep—the tears ran lopsidedly out of the one good eye and his shoulders shook. I only saw his face for a moment before he bent his head and strode off, the bald turnip head shaking, into the dark. When I think of it now, it's almost as if I had seen that Thing weeping for its inevitable defeat. It had tried to use me as a weapon, and now I had broken in its hands and it wept its hopeless tears through one of Blacker's eyes."

The black furnaces of Bedwell Junction gathered around the line. The points switched and we were tossed from one set of rails to another. A spray of sparks, a signal light changing to red, tall chimneys jetting into the grey night sky, the fumes of steam from stationary engines—half the cold journey was over, and now remained the long wait for the slow cross-country train. I said, "It's an interesting story. I think I should have given Blacker what he wanted. I wonder what he would have done with it."

"I really believe," my companion said, "that he would first of all have put it under his microscope—before he did all the other things I expect he had planned."

"And the hints," I said. "I don't quite see what you mean by that."

"Oh, well," he said vaguely, "you know for me it was an odd beginning, that affair, when you come to think of it," but I never should have known what he meant had not his coat, when he rose to take his bag from the rack, come open and disclosed the collar of a priest.

I said, "I suppose you think you owe a lot to Blacker."

"Yes," he said, "you see, I am a very happy man."

Gerard Manley Hopkins was a member of a strict religious order, and his poetry is admired both for its stunning Christian imagery and a rare ecstasy that proceeds from his unique invention of a poetic meter called sprung rhythm.

Interestingly, Hopkin's religious devotion is underscored in each of his poems by a strong sense of ambivalence towards his God. The constant threat of abandonment that Erikson has perceived as dominant fear of the ego, is nowhere more evident than in this poetry. Submission to God the father and fear of Him alternates with the childish fantasy of safety through the intercession of the mother. "The Holy Ghost over the bent / World broods with warm breast . . ."

GERARD MANLEY HOPKINS

God's Grandeur

The world is charged with the grandeur of God.
It will flame out, like shining from shook foil;
It gathers to a greatness, like the ooze of oil
Crushed. Why do men then now not reck his rod?
Generations have trod, have trod, have trod;
And all is seared with trade; bleared, smeared with toil;
And wears man's smudge and shares man's smell: the soil
Is bare now, nor can foot feel, being shod.

And for all this, nature is never spent;
There lives the dearest freshness deep down things;
And though the last lights off the black West went
Oh, morning, at the brown brink eastward, springs—
Because the Holy Ghost over the bent
World broods with warm breast and with ah! bright wings.

3 · Work and Play

The meaning of work to the individual and its function in society, while they are not necessarily the same, do converge at one point: they serve to channel the aggressive drives of the individual into socially acceptable and generally useful forms of behavior.

Work may also enhance both skill and creativity to become not merely a method of displacing aggression, but a drive in itself by which man achieves satisfaction and fulfillment of his full human potential.

Such a positive attitude towards work has been largely buried in the Western world by the Puritan association of work with guilt. Man labors to expiate the sin he committed in the Garden of Eden. Work is a punishment for his crimes. Play, as would be expected, is not permissible as long as man carries his guilt with him. With its wistful recall of the auto-erotic behavior of the child, play is what is left to man of that pre-Oedipal heaven before sexual conflict reared its ugly head. But in our industrial view of things, such play—like all auto-erotic behavior—is forbidden and shameful. Those who play rather than work are viewed with mistrust and often hatred by our puritan world, which considers the achievement of heaven-on-earth incompatible with its work-a-day ideals. It is, of course, no accident that the word for childbirth is labor; nor that all creative activity is expected to take place on a bed of pain.

Thus our reaction to art and to the artist is highly ambivalent: he is a man who plays at his work.

Ordinary men profess admiration for the artist; but they hate and envy his unique ability to "regress"—to play, and emerge from his play without the shame and guilt ordinarily attached to such activities.

791

Problems of work and play have been accentuated in our society by the rapid development of automation. If we are no longer able to provide man with work, how will we channel his aggressive drives? Will we continue a trend, obvious in our marriage manuals, to transfer the compulsive, drive-reducing nature of work into the areas formerly regarded as play?

This section offers some interesting observations on work and play by writers keenly aware of our tendency to turn play into work; and by artists who know that human happiness is a process, not an end in itself. Truly creative work partakes of the nature of play while work motivated solely by a desire to expiate guilt becomes a meaningless activity that in the end may create more guilt and tension than it displaces. If automation should turn us into machines, then the guilt aroused by our meaningless work may turn against society and destroy it. If, on the other hand, automation successfully blurs the distinction between work and play, man has two choices: he may turn his play into compulsive, driven work, or he may finally achieve that creative self-fulfillment of which he dreams, by becoming in his turn an artist, whose life's work is the molding and shaping of his own potential.

*Our attitudes toward work and play reveal the full extent
of human feelings of guilt for the imaginary crimes committed
in the unconscious. The Western world has been dominated
by the Puritan conception of work as a punishment for the
commission of Original Sin.*

*Play on the other hand, recalls to us the dangerous erotic
world of childhood. Riesman's examination of Freud's attitudes toward work and play raises serious questions as to how
our society will weather the storms of automation: will we
be able to occupy our leisure with play without being consumed by guilt and without displacing the anger and fear
now absorbed by work onto less socially desirable objects?*

DAVID RIESMAN

Themes of Work and Play in Freud's Thought

The process of incorporating Freud's thought into our living heritage
of social and humanistic studies has moved bewilderingly fast, especially
in America. But incorporation, as always with great thinkers, has been
partial. There has been a tendency, among Freud's medical followers, to
"empiricize" him, to forget about his philosophical interests and outlook
in order to get on with the clinical job. Among nonspecialists, however,
it is this philosophical side of Freud's thought that has often been most
influential. In generally accepting it at face value without an effort to
refer it back to its base in Freud's own experience, people have neglected the very kind of reference he taught us to make. In my opinion,
it is not possible to separate his technique from his cultural outlook and
setting. It is sometimes said that he was a therapist and medical man in
his earlier writings and a gloomy and speculative philosopher in his later
writings. But we must be wary of such dichotomies by which, for many,
the "good" Freud is separated from the "bad" Freud as, by similar
measures, the "good" early Comte is separated from the "bad" later
Comte, or the "good" Marx of *The German Ideology* from the "bad"
Marx of the *Manifesto* or *Capital*. Though of course there are important

differences in emphases, these men are of a piece—this, too, Freud would teach us—and their earlier writings contain the germs of the later views.

I have sought to establish this wholeness of the man in the light of certain important themes in Freud's philosophic and social outlook, by examining some of the implications of his early writings, making particular use of his own reported dreams. The later explicit statements in such writings as *Civilization and Its Discontents* or *The Future of an Illusion*[1] often merely confirm and elaborate a position that can be inferred from the "Dora" history, for instance, or from the book on dreams. I have, so far as possible, avoided coming into contact with biographical material or gossip about Freud, in order to see what the works themselves, so bravely revealing, have to say.

For my purposes here, it is not of very great importance to decide at what point Freud's writings reveal him as a unique person—reveal, that is, his own deep affective involvement in an idea—and at what point he simply speaks, without much affect or individuation, in terms stereotypical of the general attitude of the era.[2] Certainly, his utilitarian and Philistine attitudes toward work and play were both central to his own view of life and a dominant note in his cultural environment. But what really matters for us is that by virtue of his greatness—by virtue, too, of the fact that he was on the whole a liberator of men—Freud has succeeded in imposing on a later generation a mortgage of reactionary and constricting ideas that were by no means universally held even in his own epoch. Like so many original thinkers, he was ambivalent; he provides the texts for the partialities of incorporation, and for contradictory life paths and social policies.[3]

In this essay, I deal with Freud's basic attitudes to work and to play. They were formed in a society that was primarily job-minded; they circulate today in an American society that has much more chance to be leisure-minded and play-minded. While my preoccupation is with the social and cultural implications, it will I think be clear that the more technical contributions of Freud—for instance, his theory of dream interpretation, or his concept of the analytic transference—were to a very considerable degree shaped by his class and cultural outlook. This, of course, does not mean that the contributions are wrong; rather it helps us understand them, and puts us on the lookout for unsuspected pitfalls of ideological bias that may be hidden beneath questions of technique.

WORK: FREEDOM OR NECESSITY

Freud viewed work as an inescapable and tragic necessity. Although he was no student of population problems, he implicitly agreed with Malthus' gloomy conclusion that men would be forever caught between the drives of hunger and sex—lucky to be one jump ahead of starvation. And sex, too, was for Freud a realm of necessity. He saw it, not as presenting men with a problem to be solved, nor with a game to be played, nor, coupled with love, as a road to human closeness and intimacy, but rather as a "teleological" prime mover, charged with the task of socializing and civilizing men and thus preserving the species. Sex could fulfill this task because of its ability to bribe with an elemental pleasure and to appease with an elemental release. Work was, then, the means by which the species maintains itself while performing its endless procreative mission.

This outlook, heavily influenced by Puritanism, took shape in the early nineteenth century, in part as a reaction against the views of utopian visionaries—men such as Condorcet, Godwin, and Owen—who envisaged the possibility that, beyond this realm of necessity, might lie a realm of freedom where work had social meaning and where the economy would be our servant, not our master.

Needless to say, men are producing animals and must work in order to live. Moreover, it is altogether likely, men being the creatures they are and work being what it is, that some drudgery will continue to be associated with it. The question of the meaning of work, of how it is experienced, is primarily a cultural problem; and cultures differ enormously in the way work is interpreted in their value scheme. In some, work is not sharply differentiated from other aspects of life. It may be viewed as fulfilling religious duties; it may have the pleasurable variety, creativeness, and interpersonal texture which is associated with some kinds of farming, or artisanship, art, or science. It may be viewed in other ways. Only, probably, in our Western industrial culture, has work in fact the features Freud attaches to it: it is sharply set off against love, against pleasure, against consumption, against almost every sort of freedom. Only here is it a curse for most people, mitigated as such, often enough, not by its own nature, but by the fear of boredom, which can be even greater than the irksomeness of toil.

In the nineteenth century, dominated by scarcity economics and Malthusian fears, work could nevertheless be given the rational meaning of the avoidance of hunger. And hunger and gain (ambition) could be viewed as the self-evident motives of a market economy, the former operating on the poor, the latter on the well-to-do.[4] In the mid-twentieth century, in the countries of the Industrial Revolution and especially in America, it is likely that with very little human toil a full abundance can be assured to all inhabitants as the result of the machine technology. But although the result has already been a great lowering in the hours of work and vast improvement in physical conditions, work itself is still subjectively felt as a duty, without meaning in its own terms. This is most striking evidence of the fact that the pattern of a culture can disguise, even distort, the inescapable problem of work. Neither the basic physiological drive of hunger, nor the basic equipment of production—man's brain and eyes and hands—instruct him in what meaning, what pattern, he shall give to work, any more than the basic drive of sex, and its genital equipment, tell him what meaning, what pattern, he shall give to love.

It is, as I shall try to show, the more pessimistic, middle-class, nineteenth-century attitudes that are reflected and elaborated in Freud's thought. I shall consider, first, his view of the "real," the workaday world, including his view of his own role in it, and, second, his attitude toward the subordinated world of play.

THE WORKADAY WORLD

Freud, like so many scientists of a system-building cast of mind, was always in search of simplifying dichotomies, of polar opposites. As the "self" was the opposite of the "other," as the pleasure principle and the reality principle—or Eros and Thanatos—divided life between them, so the workaday world with its productive machinery, its markets, its other economic processes, was sharply marked off from the play world, the world of fantasy and gratification. The former world Freud took for granted as he found it; he reserved his insight and his unconventionality largely for the latter.

Freud regarded the world of business and professional life—of all areas where hunger and gain were alleged to hold sway—as unquestionably real. The views of critics such as Veblen or Thurman Arnold who see the mythical or fantastic elements of business enterprise,[5] are foreign to his mode of thought. It did not seem to occur to him that much work was obsessive busywork, that businessmen often fled into work to avoid women, or that the seeming pursuit of business self-interest might be the sheerest rationalization for activities that were quite differently motivated. To be sure, the European businessman is more of an "economic man" than his American counterpart; his compartmentalization of work, separate from home and from play, is more complete; he *does* seek gain as his principal end, rather than friends, prestige, or an agenda. Nevertheless, Freud's attitude toward the work that men do in their occupations was almost that of a behaviorist who does not probe into motives.

Indeed, Freud concluded his book on dreams on the qualifiedly behaviorist note that "actions, above all, deserve to be placed in the front rank" in judging human character, since the dark and demonic psychic forces he had been describing had usually only the most limited consequences in the real, that is, the workaday, world.[6] In the same volume, Freud described the dream experiments of his colleague Dr. Schrötter, and concluded: "Unfortunately, the value of this important investigation was diminished by the fact that Dr. Schrötter shortly afterwards committed suicide."[7] There was no note of sympathy or grief for this human tragedy: what mattered to Freud was the work and not the man. Such behavioristic views seem to be a reflection of the psychology of a market economy: it does not matter what men think or how they feel, but only that, overtly, they react "appropriately" to the stimuli of hunger and gain.

Middle-Class Conventions Concerning Work

Freud's friends and patients, mainly upper-middle-class folk, were not supposed to be motivated by the spur of hunger, but by the hope of gain. Freud knew penury as a youth—financial needs drove him out of the laboratory and into practice—but it was still the penury of the rising student, not of the destitute proletarian. He assumed that the individualistic motives of getting on in the world, the desires of fame and success, were perfectly "natural"; it did not occur to him that they might be culturally stimulated or produced, let alone that they might be in themselves neurotic drives. While he was apt to minimize the extent of his own ambition, it did not trouble him to avow his wish to be a full professor, to be famous, to be "an authority." With the exception of the cases where he had personal experience of bigotry or incompetence, he rather easily assumed that his teachers such as Brücke or Meynert were "great masters," entitled to "veneration";[8] there was nothing unreal about their attainments and position. And, just as he assumed without question the conventions about greatness, he also assumed the other conventions of the workaday world—for instance, about the great importance of priority in scientific work. In one of his dreams he is anxious to "give Professor N. due credit for his diagnosis."[9]

The Playboy Classes

Three social groups seemed to Freud to be immune to the demands of the workaday world. These were the aristocrats, who needed only to be born in order to be fed;[10] the professional artists and writers, who were privileged not only to live in the play world of illusion but to draw from it the realities of fame and fortune;[11] and the monks and priests.[12]

The artist, as Freud viewed him, had the gift of being able to sell his daydreams, his fantasy productions, even his megalomania, on the market; he could appeal to the hidden dreams and desires of his audience who responded by bestowing on him the admiration he could not have won in direct economic or sexual competition. The artist, moreover, was free from the arduous conventions of the scientist; by his gift, he could obtain a release from what others have to do and gain as direct an access to truth as to the hearts of mankind. While for the scientist, too—such as Freud—dreams and fancies might be real data, he must work and not play with them in order to make a profit.[13] But he must on no account "waste" his talents; Freud found Leonardo da Vinci infantile when, instead of turning his powers to account, he employed them in ephemeral toys and antic jests.[14] In a different vein, he also found Leonardo's passion for investigation neurotic: where one investigates the universe (instead of acting on it, or moving one's fellowmen by great art), one obviously misses real values for which a normal person would strive.[15] Naturally Freud applied to his own work a similarly conventional judgment: what helped him to cure patients was "real"; all else was "speculation."[16]

While, however, the artist had a privileged position in the native ease with which he won success, he remained, in Freud's eyes, a mere decoration upon the economic and political processes which mattered in the workaday world. Freud, the middle-class patron of the theater and collector of figurines, wrote of art as a monarch might speak of his court jester: "Art is almost always harmless and beneficent, it does not seek to be anything else but an illusion. Save in the case of a few people who are, one might say, obsessed by Art, it never dares to make any attacks on the realm of reality."[17] Freud's attitude toward Count Thun, the aristocratic "do-nothing" Prime Minister of Austria, was not very different: he, too, was a "privileged idler."[18]

Work as the Man's World

Only in one respect did Freud deal with success as anything but an obvious, self-evident goal which justifies the expenditure of immense efforts: he observed that in daydreams men seek to throw their laurels at the feet of beautiful women. Does it follow from this that the real world, too, was in Freud's eyes subordinate to sex? The question raises all sorts of ambiguities. On one level, Freud saw men's libidinal drives, coupled in various harnesses with their aggressive ones, as the source of all their productions: work was a channeling and sublimation of these drives. But on another level, the nighttime sphere of sex was clearly subsidiary to the daytime sphere of work, of accomplishment in the real world. For one thing, in Freud's eyes the man of potency and means, unintimidated by cultural taboos, would have no difficulty in finding appropriate sexual outlets. Achievement—making a dent in the world—this was the problem. Indeed, women were only trophies, to be tied, metaphorically, at the conqueror's wheel: they were a by-product, pleasant enough, of his achievement, but only incidentally an aim.

The workaday world then was clearly a man's world. Speaking again of Leonardo, Freud referred to his "manly creative power" prior to his homosexual, reflective and investigative stage;[19] Freud's attitude toward Hamlet's indecision expressed a quite similar judgment. This "man's" world was threatened, not only by homosexual tendencies, but by an excessive, uncautious interest in women. In connection with one of his dreams, Freud tells us his fear that his sons' talents will be "ruined by women," just as the great Lassalle was killed in a duel over a lady.[20]

The place of women in this man's world was rather like that assigned to them in Veblen's ironic *The Theory of the Leisure Class*.[21] Their very narcissism makes them desirable objects of display; their role is to be fed, tended, exhibited. But they must remain tractable in their gilded cage, and neither lure men to failure by giving them syphilis or otherwise draining their work potential, nor, above all, enter the world of men as competitors.[22] Indeed, any effort of a woman to take part in the real world, in any capacity other than consumer of goods and libido, was interpreted as a desire to make up for her lack of a penis, the organ of power and creativeness. So strong were Freud's psychoanalytic rationalizations of the conventional Victorian—or, as Veblen would hold, predatory—attitude toward women, that they still impress many psychoanalysts, even women psychoanalysts.[23] Freud seems to have coped with the inconsistency, from his viewpoint, of his own daughter's entry upon analytic work by assigning to women analysts the field of child-analysis—very much as women in industrial management today are assigned the job of handling the morale problems, not of men and women, but of women only.

MAN'S NATURAL LAZINESS AND THE FUTILITY OF SOCIALISM

The grimness of today's workaday world, as Freud saw and accepted it, is so great that it is understandable that men should exhibit signs of laziness, as if to justify the charge that they would not turn a hand without the spur of hunger and gain. It is not surprising therefore to find Freud falling in with the hoary argument which seeks to derive the futility of socialism from the observed laziness of the working class.[24]

The Passive Paradise

This attitude Freud expressed in his interpretation of the myth of the Garden of Eden, which he saw as meaning that man longed for the idyllic idleness of the womb, or of childhood—the next best in dependent passivity. But man was driven by his "original sin"—apparent in the sexual aggressive Oedipus complex—to violate the conditions under which he might be taken care of in carefree bliss. Forced out of Paradise, he had ever after to work in the world, as sign and as penance; only in illusion could he momentarily return. Freud, who was accustomed to overturn many myths and see through them, accepted this myth as a historical truth, or rather as a primitive anticipation of the Victorian conviction that "life is real, life is earnest." A similar view is implicit in Freud's theory that man, as child and primitive, passed through a stage of belief in the omnipotence of thought. This magical thinking, in which wishes are automatically gratified, as they almost are for the infant, seemed to Freud to constitute one part of the charm of Paradise; men give it up for reality thinking only under the pressure of frustration and pain. "If wishes were horses, beggars would ride"—or, more accurately, would fly. By a word, men would annihilate bothersome rivals, as Freud actually did in one of his most striking dreams.[25] The intensity of wishes and their violent ability to propel a dream thus arise from the fact that wish fulfillment was once effortless, and that men never become reconciled to a workaday world in which this is no longer so. Freud assumed that men do not grow psychically, that nothing new happens to them in the course of development which might lead them to desire activity for its own sake.

Thus Freud had no doubt whatever that man needs to be driven into reality, by an angry God or his earthly deputies. Children, he felt, naturally did not want to grow up; they must be forcibly socialized, forcibly adapted to reality.[26] Parents who fail early to acquaint the child with pain, with what he must expect from the world, will create neurotics, recusants to their workaday tasks. Freud had no faith in his own children's talents as self-realizing, and he enjoined upon his wife the "training" by which these would be husbanded.[27]

In all this, I feel that Freud patronizes infancy and childhood. Even small infants seem to want to explore the universe—and not only in search of food and sex. Children—though, of course, like all of us, they have moments of regression—often are stifled in their wish to grow up, to accept responsibility and arduous tasks, by adult authorities who underestimate them. Conversely, adults and children too, forced to work at a pace that is not their own, react by rejecting work, in fantasy if not in feather-bedded fact.

FREUD'S ATTITUDE TOWARD HIS OWN WORK

Freud's very definition of pleasure as release of physiological tension contains, in capsulated form, the essence of his attitude toward work. Even though he might, under certain conditions, regard work as a sublimatory release of tensions which are sexual in origin—which permits him on occasion to speak of "intellectual pleasures"—still he viewed these as only a poor second best, purchased through a stunting of the primary, libidinal releases.[28] But if pleasure is release of tension, then toil—ordinarily the opposite of release—is by definition arduous. Nevertheless, despite the elaborateness of Freud's physiological and metapsychological explanations, despite all his talk about pleasure principle and reality principle, we must not forget the cultural setting: How could he as a self-respecting Victorian admit that his work was anything else but a chore? To speak of his job, as Americans today often do—usually with like conventionality—as "good fun," would hardly befit a practitioner of the Harley Streets of the world; we need merely remind ourselves of the unspeakable boredom from which even the most exciting case could hardly rescue the languorous Sherlock Holmes.

The Slave of Science

Freud's work, as I read his own account of it, seems to me of the very greatest intellectual interest; beside such detective work, even that of Sherlock Holmes is pallid and limited. But Freud seems to have found—or at least admitted to—almost no pleasure in it; on the contrary, his writings are full of references to his weariness, to the arduousness, rather than the ardor, of his unique intellectual adventure. "It is a habit of mine to run up two or three steps at a time"[29]—how blithely he speaks of "habit" rather than symptom when it is himself he is describing. His hurried days were almost incredible: ten or twelve hours of analysis—made especially anxious by the novelty of the task and the dangerously isolated position of the therapist—followed by writing up his notes on his cases;[30] then working far into the night on his writing, lectures, and correspondence; at night, writing and interpreting his frequent dreams, sometimes pages in length—only *once* did he not make "careful notes" on a dream;[31] finally rousing himself in the morning with the greatest effort to begin another weary round.[32] Even when he suffered from the most painful boils, he refused to rest from "my peculiarly strenuous work"[33] until ordered to by the doctor. And of course in later life, his agonizing cancer of the throat gave him no excuse to slow the pace of his labor. Like other middle-class, self-made, self-driven men, he could only relax at the conventional times: on his vacation, or at the parties to which he infrequently went. He said of himself, characteristically, after a summer evening's lecture: "I was tired; I took not the least pleasure in my difficult work, and longed to get away from this rummaging in human filth. . . ."[34] But even on vacation Freud could not abandon his vocation. Just as he "amused" himself by examining starfish on his first visit to the Irish Sea at the age of 19[35]—how different his preoccupations from those of James Joyce by the Irish Sea—so he drove himself even in his beloved Italy, like any harried tourist.[36] Though he reproaches himself or permits himself to be reproached for his hobbies,[37] as for his other "vices" such as smoking which did not directly contribute to his work, he did in fact manage to turn most of his "play" to economic account, like a cook who saves her leftovers for a stew. He enjoyed jokes—and collected them for a book on wit; he loved Michelangelo—and wrote a long analysis of his Moses statue; his wide reading of novels and poetry was automatically and unaffectedly ransacked for analytic clues. So in fact, nothing was "wasted"—nothing, that is, but Freud, who took for himself Claude Bernard's motto, *"Travailler comme une bête."*

In return for his Spartan zeal, Freud allowed himself to take pride in his conscientiousness, especially in cases involving no admixture of interest, like the twice-a-day injections he gave a cranky old lady;[38] while he scolded those "spoilt" gentlemen, the devout, who "had an easier time of it with their revelation."[39] And, indeed, the Sisyphus task of science, endlessly pursuing truth, becomes for Freud the very core of his personal philosophy of life.[40] Nevertheless, while Freud would agree with Spinoza that "the joy by which the drunkard is enslaved is altogether different from the joy which is the portion of the philosopher,"[41] still he would have insisted that there is little joy, but much enslavement, in the philosopher's quest.

"Per Ardua ad Astra"

In one very important respect Freud's Puritan attitude toward work in general and to his own work in particular had a profound influence on the whole psychoanalytic method. For he assumed as a matter of course that any answer to which one came without arduous toil must be wrong. It was this feeling, that truth must cost something if it is to be worth anything, which, among other factors, led Freud to feel that the more farfetched and "difficult" the solution, the more probable its correctness. Thus, despite his reference, which we have earlier quoted, to the successful "intuitions" of his admired Goethe and Helmholtz, he distrusted intuition in psychoanalysis. Repeatedly he attacked the "intuitive" method of dealing with dream symbolism.[42] Moreover, not only in dream interpretation but in all his work, Freud played down the role of intuition, just as he distinguished between mere "speculation" and real scientific work. Again and again he referred to himself as a sobersided, meticulous investigator, who never jumps to conclusions but constantly acknowledges his dependence in observation and theory on "the real external world."[43] Understanding is the reward, not of the gifts of genius, but of the "expenditure of effort."[44] Undoubtedly, Freud expended tremendous effort, but of course it is not only this which led him to his genuine innovations. While he accused intuition of arbitrariness, the very logical and often pedestrian rigor of his own treatment of symbols led repeatedly to highly arbitrary, indeed quite fanatical, constructions. But, of course, these were "work"; they did not spring from an alerted but at the same time unstrenuous "listening" for what the symbol was attempting to convey, but rather from a forceful, categorical insistence that the symbol surrender its meaning to Freud's intransigence. Perhaps his relative disregard for his own imaginative gifts was not only a defense against the critical pettifogging researchers of his day, but also a rationalization of his envy for those whom he considered still greater geniuses such as Goethe, who appeared to him to have had an easier, sunnier path.

Every so often, however, Freud did refer to his pleasure in mastering difficulties.[45] But, like most political conservatives, he did not assume that men generally could share his own loftier motivations.[46] Among Puritans such a hierarchy of toilsomeness is not uncommon. Compare the statement of Mrs. Gromyko: "Oh, Andrei does work hard, yet not as hard as Mr. Vishinsky, and even that is not so hard as Mr. Molotov works."[47]

Freud's Own Dreamwork

A single, magnificent example illustrates Freud's method, and at the same time these limitations. In his famous "Dream of the Botanical Monograph," Freud says:

> I have written a monograph on a certain plant. The book lies before me; I am just turning over a folded coloured plate. A dried specimen of the plant, as though from a herbarium, is bound up with every copy.[48]

His associations to the dream were manifold and revealing. Among other things, Freud noted an association to his own monograph on the coca plant. He has told us elsewhere of his frustration because he did not become known as the discoverer of the anesthetic properties of cocaine, the reason being that he let a friend continue the research so that he (Freud) might take time out to become engaged to his future wife.[49] He also made reference to the fact that his wife often remembered to bring his "favourite flower"—the artichoke—from the market where she diligently shopped, while he was less "thoughtful" of her, seldom bringing her flowers.[50] The artichoke reminds him of a childhood scene where he tore up a book containing "coloured plates" and of his later fondness for collecting books; he reproaches himself, both for this expensive hobby and for the "one-sidedness" of his *Gymnasium* studies, which had led him close to failing his botany examintion.[51] In sum, after pages and pages of examining separately each dream detail, he permits himself in his analysis a slight awareness of his "thoughtlessness" toward his wife, of envy and grandiose ambition, and a memory of destructiveness, safely remote in childhood and in any case blamed upon his father. The worst thing he can say about himself is that he has expensive and distracting hobbies! In fact, he calls the childhood memory itself a " 'screen or concealing memory' for my subsequent bibliophilia."[52] A curious "screen" in which he concealed the amiable and redeeming veniality of a hobby for collecting books behind the less amiable vice of destroying them—perhaps the vice of destructiveness itself! But play—that is, preoccupations and hobbies, especially if expensive, not directly advancing one in one's profession—did appear to Freud as sinful.[53]

In his associations to the dream, Freud pushed aside his unconscious recognition of what the dream was about and disregarded the significance of flowers as a symbol. Instead, he tore the dream word-from-word like the leaves of an artichoke; he viewed the dream not as a *Gestalt* but in a series of concentric verbal associations. I would like to suggest another possible interpretation of the dream, on a fairly obvious symbolic level. Freud seems to have been aware in the dream that flowers—a symbol which he elsewhere recognizes as plainly sexual[54]—do not speak to him; his love has become "a dried specimen of the plant, as though from a herbarium. . . ." Is it not also correct to assume that he is unconsciously aware that he has sacrificed his wife's love to his ambition—that *this* is screened by the mild and yet symbolic charge he elsewhere makes against her that, but for his devotion to her, he would be famed as the discoverer of cocaine? Indeed, he scarcely permits himself to realize that he is readier to buy himself a monograph—he speaks of his "fondness for . . . possessing books"[55]—than to buy flowers for his wife; this, although the dream commentary refers to his seeing at a bookseller's on the previous day a monograph on the cyclamen, his wife's favorite flower.[56] (His wife has, in fact, become "puffy," like a stuffed animal, while Mrs. "Gardener," whom he met the night before, is still "blooming," presumably from Mr. "Gardener's" care.)[57] Flowers are, by their very nature, a symbol of emotional feeling, even waste; in the act of "possessing" them, they dry up; the artichoke, on the other hand, is not a real extravagance—it is edible. Yet there is more than "possessing" involved; Freud has imprisoned love within the covers of an illustrated monograph; he has crushed it; in penetrating to the heart of the artichoke, he has a lifeless specimen in his hand. I strongly suspect that the mild scene of childhood destructiveness, which Freud treats as screening his bibliophilia and, on a deeper level, his sexual curiosity, actually conceals the way in which his own life and that of those around him is torn by his almost total incapacity for love and spontaneity—this is his true "one-sidedness." It is like the Irish Sea, which means little more to him than the examination of a starfish and the recollection of its Latin name.

Dreamwork and Entropy

The concept of dreamwork attributes to the process of dream formation the same economics of affect which Freud employed in the process of dream interpretation. He writes, "We take pains to dream only in connection with such matters as have given us food for thought during the day";[58] that is, the dreamwork is the processing plant which prepares the material with an eye to the driving wishes behind it, the inspection of the censor, and the economical and convenient packaging of the imagery. Behind this concept, there lies again the assumption of man's laziness. If we had our way, Freud is saying, we would not even dream; we would lie in the blissful fetal state. But our wishes, and external stimuli also, prevent this; these create tensions in our otherwise flaccid state of rest; the *purpose* of the dreamwork is to release this tension and thus, by permitting us to go on sleeping, to restore us to the workless state. As Freud divided his year between his workaday months and his vacation period, so he divided the day between the waking tensions and the night's release. But this is not the only way to live! A vacation may be restful, though strenuous, if it lends variety and enjoyment to life; likewise, sleep is not merely the opposite of waking tension. In fact, recent studies have shown that restful slumber is accompanied by frequent changes of position; motionless sleep is not nearly so refreshing. Dreaming, too, is assumed to be an almost continuous process, of which the dreamer is only occasionally aware.

This feeling of Freud's that he needed to explain the fact of having a dream and to find the energy source for the amount of "work" involved, misled him in at least two ways. It was one factor in his insistence that every dream represents a—probably libidinal—wish fulfillment, the wish being the primal source of energy; this insistence led him to over-elaborate explanations of those dreams, such as anxiety dreams, judgment dreams, and so on, which did not appear to fit his formula. Secondly, it made him suspicious of dreams which, by their baroque imagery, their eloquent speeches, or other luxuriance, seemed to have required much "work"; since work is unnatural to man, this effort must hide something, must cover up a most forbidden thought. Thus, when Freud recalls in a dream the formula for trymethylamin, he takes this as "evidence of a great effort on the part of my memory,"[59] and goes off accordingly on a long, interpretative search.

This attitude toward effort pushed Freud toward overinterpretation in his analytic thinking generally. Being a strenuously effortful man, his thoughts and dreams, even without further elaboration on his part, would naturally tend to be complicated and far-flung. Moreover, Freud's work drive compelled him to go beyond even his initial reaction, toward sometimes overintricate structures of thought—the *Moses* book is a final and brilliant testament of this obsession which was at the same time part of the drive which made him great and courageous. And yet, concealed beneath all this work, is it possible that Freud is occasionally "playing" with us, and with himself? Is it not likely that, outwardly denying himself any playfulness or frivolity as doctor and scientist, he may have unwittingly sublimated his play impulses, so that they can be glimpsed only in an "unnecessary" metaphor, a finespun interpretation of a dream, a tenuous reconstruction of history?

However that may be, it would seem an important task to track down in Freud's more technical writings some of the overinterpretations that may have resulted from his attitude toward effort. Here all I can do is to indicate some of the implications of this attitude. It seems clear that Freud, when he looked at love or work, understood man's physical and psychic behavior in the light of the physics of entropy and the economics of scarcity. For him, life was not self-renewing, or self-producing; he viewed the process of life as drawing on the given natal store, as on a bank account. Hence, for him, effort, expenditure, was problematical: it needed to be explained; something must lie behind it.

One views dreams quite differently if one holds a different view of the nature of life itself. If one thinks that growth is characteristic of life, that life can unfold unsuspected potentialities and resources, one feels that it is not *effort* that needs to be explained—that is life itself—but the *absence* of effort. Then it is the absence which appears pathological. So, if one comes upon a dream which is rich in invention and the use of symbolic expression, or which exhibits indignation, or judgment, or wit, or other human faculties which one appreciates in waking life, one will not feel that this is strange and that the dream must *necessarily* be about something altogether different. Any dream ordinarily requires interpretation, but its prima facie opacity need not be due to a censorship over malign or outrageous wishes; the necessity for interpretation may result from the fact that symbolic expression is simply a different language, often a more abundant one than the dreamer allows himself in waking life.[60] Or it may be due to the fact that the memories called up in the dream have not been pigeonholed into the dreamer's organized, waking categories and thus appear with a freshness and intensity of experience which he may have had as a child.[61]

THE WORLD OF PLAY

Already, in order to talk about the world of work as Freud saw it I have had to picture in contrast the opposing world of play. For, indeed, Freud saw these two worlds as sharply separated as was the *Aussee* where he spent vacations from the urban Vienna where he did his analytic work. Freud's world of play, as we shall see, is a world of children, of artists, and, only surreptitiously, of adults—that is, those adults who are real men and not idlers or escapists.

The Nursery Years

Freud regarded childhood as an autoerotic haven where all one's pleasures are within reach. Nor is there any conflict between the drives of hunger and sex: "Love and hunger meet at the mother's breast." Soon, moreover, the child discovers the pleasures of onanism; these, too, require no work, not even the labor of object choice. But this cannot go on; Freud writes:

> This age of childhood, in which the sense of shame is unknown, seems a paradise when we look back upon it later, and paradise itself is

nothing but the mass-phantasy of the childhood of the individual. This is why in paradise men are naked and unashamed, until the moment arrives when shame and fear awaken; expulsion follows, and sexual life and cultural development begin. Into this paradise dreams can take us back every night. . . .[62]

But this view of childhood as not subject to the laws of the adult world of reality was only one side of Freud's position. He noticed that children liked to play at being grown up, and indeed wished to grow up;[63] and he had a clear vision, unusual for his epoch, of the terrors, phobias, and conflicts which beset even the most protected child. Unlike most adults, he did not condescend to the battles and nightmares of the nursery; these he accepted as real. And with his usual pessimistic sense, he observed that "the excited play of children often enough culminates in quarrelling and tears."[64] Thus he saw the child as more adult, and the adult as more child, than was the conventional opinion.

This contradiction in Freud's thought can be reconciled if one observes that he saw through the current myths regarding "the innocents of the nursery" only insofar as sex and aggression or matters related to them were concerned—and, obviously, this was no small achievement but one of his most decisive contributions. He saw, clearly enough, the sexual elements in children's play, the onanist practices, the animistic fantasies.[65] But he was at one with his adult generation in looking down on play in general as childish; he did not entirely grasp its reality testing and reality expanding functions, its nature as a part or an aspect of preparation for human adult existence, any more than he respected the creative functions of the playful moods which he criticized in Leonardo's life.

Indeed, even to talk about "functions" when discussing play runs the risk of catching us in an anthropological or psychoanalytic functionalism which means that human freedom is limited to being "unfunctional" —a privilege, paradoxically, most relevant to human existence when seemingly most irrelevant, as many great teachers of mankind have understood.

Play and Foreplay

This divorce between work and play which sharply separates the world of the adult from the world of the child is not reconciled by maturity. Rather, once the genital stage is reached, play becomes at-

tached primarily to the sexual function and continues in an underground, often unconscious existence. In his utilitarian attitude toward
sex, Freud was much interested in what he called "foreplay," the preliminary stages of lovemaking. Foreplay seemed to him a kind of come-on
which tempted couples onto the path of biological fulfillment; by its
tension-heightening nature, it seemed to violate the pleasure principle
and to demand ejaculative release. By this ambiguity, it impelled otherwise reluctant people to comply with the "laws of propagation."[66] (The
term "foreplay" itself seems to carry its own linguistic self-contradic-
tion: if it is play for a purpose, it is robbed of most of its spontaneous,
amiable, frivolous, or tender playfulness.) In other words, just as Freud
"allowed himself" his book-collecting and other hobbies for their recrea-
tive functions, so he "allowed" mankind this apparent frivolity of foreplay for its procreative functions: in both cases, pleasure is not really
free, it merely baits the trap. After intercourse, so Freud felt, there is
sadness; after play, one pays by sorrow and work.

Dreams and Daydreams as Play

Fantasy and art are among the secondary and derivative efforts of
mankind to obtain sexual pleasure; they constitute a kind of bargain
basement, in which a need of pleasure is sublimated—no other pleasure
could equal direct sexual pleasure in Freud's view—in return for a
modification in the ensuing pain. The discovery of this *ersatz,* inexpen-
sive pleasure is made by the child, Freud argued, in the form of a
hallucinatory wish fulfillment, a kind of mirage in which the hungry
infant, for instance, can persuade himself that he is being fed.[67] In later
life, the adult can restore this state in dreams and daydreams.

Freud perhaps tended to exaggerate the extent to which one can
actually escape reality, unless one is crazy, by means of these fantasies.
For although he is correct in believing that in the passive state one can
afford wishes which would endanger one in real life, by the same token
one diminishes one's satisfaction: somehow one realizes that "it's only a
dream"[68] or a daydream—and that it will never come to pass. Moreover, our individual and cultural imagination sets limits to wishes; they
are often as poverty-stricken as that of the woman in the famous tale,
which Freud quotes, who used the first of her three fairy wishes to
procure some sausages which she had smelled next door.[69] The "damned
wantlessness of the poor," against which Lassalle protested, is not
dissipated when they sleep.[70]

My conclusion here is that Freud was romantic about dreams, as he was about more overt sexual life. By his insistence that underneath the manifest dream there must lie a wish, and that this wish, in an adult, would have a dark, luxuriant, and forbidden quality, he avoided seeing how flat and conventional, how sorrowful and anxious, many dreams actually are. There is, for example, little that is wish-fulfilling in his own "Dream of the Botanical Monograph." Actually the censorhip, to which he himself called attention, is not so easily evaded as he supposed; the most daring and therefore frightening wishes do not even exist in our unconscious, let alone rebel in the night against the dictation of the censorship.

But though there is a romantic element in Freud's view of the dream, this did not prevent him from subjecting it, like every other psychic performance, to the laws of scarcity economics. One dreams, he says, in order to continue sleeping, for otherwise the ungratified wish or outside stimulus, would wake one—one continues sleeping, of course, to prepare for the labor of the following day.[71] Thus the dream represents an elaborate compromise, a deal between the psychic forces: with the censorship relaxed by sleep, the repressed wishes are able to go in search of pleasure, using the thought residues of the day, but at the same time the dreamwork "binds the unconscious excitation and renders it harmless as a disturber . . . of sleep," while satisfying through displacement and other devices of evasion the censorship's one open eye. This involves, Freud writes, a lesser "outlay of . . . work, than to hold the unconscious in check throughout the whole period of sleep."[72]

Art as Play and Display

So far, I have been discussing the play world in its private aspects, to which one has access principally in sexual "play" and in dreams. There is also a public play world; it has virtually the same economy as that of the dream. It is built on fairy tales[73] and other folk myths, on wit, and on art.

The artist's job is that of giving public expression to his private fantasies, fantasies which others may share; his work is others' play. Moreover, art, as Freud viewed it, is not bound by the rules of the workaday world—it is free. Like religion, the other great operator in the play world of illusion, it can dissolve the dichotomies of human existence; it can deny the fact of death, or, as in the Greek and Egyptian sculptures which fascinated Freud, it can unite man and woman.[74] The pleasure in art is, as one would expect, partly Oedipal and rebellious sexuality, partly narcissism, in which both artist and audience identify with the hero. Licit gratification of illicit wishes is secured by these projections.

The relative thinness of the role assigned by Freud to art is surprising, in view of the amount of attention which he gave the subject both in his own writings and in his "hobbies." Of art as critic of society, as transcending the given cultural divisions and definitions of work and play, as conscious creator of new values, Freud does not speak. His own tastes in art seem to have been conventional for his time, place, and class. Like so many nineteenth-century bourgeois, he admired the Renaissance, perhaps finding in it an age less cramped than his own. His great hero was Goethe, regarded as a late Renaissance figure. He seems to have had little taste for music. Though he admired Ibsen, who was also a defier of sexual convention in his writings, he was not in general interested in "modern art." But it is modern art which has most strongly rebelled against being a plaything for rich patrons; sometimes it has done so by its very "ugliness" according to accepted patterns. Moreover, Freud paid little attention to the formal problems of art, being primarily concerned with its psychological causes and effects; when he thought about form at all, he said that the problem was insoluble.[75] Thus, his attitude toward art, as well as his taste, was conventional: by assigning it to the world of play, of regression, of sex, he patronized it, as a sober, cultivated bourgeois should. Perhaps one could say that he viewed it, as a modern city planner views a zoo or park, as a territory zoned off from the workaday world, which is there to delight but not to be taken with full seriousness.[76]

The Play of Words

Somewhat the same attitude governs Freud's view of wit. He saw the role of language as a reality instrument in a way that could hardly have been done before the development of his theory of dreams. For by means of words, one delays gratifications and tests reality experimentally before, so to speak, setting foot in it. Though the infant, like the primitive, uses them as magic handles, in his phase of thought omnipotence they nevertheless become tools, not pleasures. By their nature, moreover, they are logical, unautistic: they relate us to the world and to the other people in it; only children and lovers are permitted a private language. But even here, in this instrument of communication, there is a domain reserved for pleasure: this is wordplay or wit. At one point in his dream theory, he speaks of comical effects as a "surplus" which is discharged by laughter;[77] wit is, indeed, the theater and poetry of the poor. But the pleasure which Freud found in wit is not only that of release of the tensions of obedience to the laws of language;[78] it is also that of direct rebellion. While he collected for study jokes and stories of Jewish humor, he enjoyed also the richness of its satiric and sardonic elements.[79] And even the sexual elements which Freud emphasized in his analysis of wit are not only pleasurable in their own right, but in their rejection of convention. Freud, so meticulously clean as a physician, was quite "rebelliously" fond of "dirty" stories, just as he enjoyed spitting on the stairs of an old lady patient whom he detested.[80]

CONCLUSION

I have indicated that Freud's ascetic rationalistic dichotomy between work and play, and the very limited role he assigned the latter, belong to the work morality of nineteenth-century Europe—to the years when the advancing industrial revolution had still not shown its potentialities for drastically shortening labor and expanding leisure horizons. The chances are, moreover, that Freud went much further in the direction of asceticism, of eliminating "waste," than did most of the members of his class and culture: he actually did what it was only their ideal to do. But when one looks at contemporary American attitudes toward work and play, one cannot be too critical of Freud—one can, indeed, see much in his view that is refreshing. Thus he never adopted the notion that work and play must alike be "fun"—and, more particularly, fun with people. This notion forces men in the American upper-middle class to merge the spheres of work and play, often without advantage to either. An anxious gregariousness and concern for the expression of appropriate consumer tastes can permeate a business or professional conference as easily as a cocktail party. To a degree, Americans have substituted fun morality for work morality. But this, among other things, makes it difficult to admit that one is tired: one has not done enough to "deserve" it. Conversely, one tends to exploit his vacations not, as Freud did—when he was not traveling or climbing mountains—by doing productive work, but by seeking to train oneself for advances in status or in the solution of vexing interpersonal problems.

I can put my point another way by saying that there are certain advantages to making fun and play surreptitious—even sinful. For then play is less apt to be socially guided, less apt to be compulsively gregarious. Freud's view of play as a kind of underground in adult life protects it—gives it some of the same chaotic freedom that the carnival provides in Catholic countries. As against this, the contemporary social focus on recreation sometimes tends to leave no room either for whorehouses or for underground passages of any sort; everything must be out in the open. And while in a utopian society this would not be so bad, today it often means that play is exploited in fact—as it was for Freud in principle—for physical and psychic hygiene.

Indeed, Freud's own account, in a somewhat distorted version, is one of the factors which has shaped this modern view. Many women, for instance, indulge in sexual play not because they seek pleasure but because they have been told, and told themselves, that repression is bad. Men justify their vacations on the ground that they "owe it to themselves." Emancipated parents are anxious if their children do not masturbate, lest they become neurotic. Men who have stomach trouble feel that they must "relax," must have more fun, to avoid further psychosomatic disorder—the give-away clue of psychic imperfection. And those men who cannot play are robbed, both by cultural developments and by the loss of psychological innocence Freud helped bring about, of the older defenses provided for them in a work-oriented society. So it turns out that, under the guise of fun and play, we remain today almost as truly ascetic as Freud, often enough without the very real satisfactions which—in spite of himself and in spite of his views as to the supremacy of sexual pleasure—he derived from his intellectually demanding and adventurous work. The threat of work today is not that it is arduous, but—in the some ways far worse fact—that it is boring and without meaning.

As against this, Freud, despite his skepticisms and reservations, had no doubt that work was worthwhile and that scientific work, whatever its uncanny "primal" sources in sexual or aggressive drives, had its own logic, its own convention, and its own tradition. Moreover, while he was a utilitarian in his attitude toward play, and in a way toward life in general, he was actually much less of a utilitarian about science than many of his successors. The pursuit of truth was for him self-justifying: man had every right to penetrate the secrets of nature without giving an account of himself to academic, priestly, democratic, or other moralizing authority. Although he thought the truth would set men free, he was, nevertheless, far from the mood of many "policy oriented" researchers today, who hedge their curiosity about by all sorts of expediential considerations and concern for various good causes. One of the things that makes Freud such perennially exhilarating reading is the sense of the "play of the mind" that he communicates.

It may be a long time before middle-class people in America will feel themselves free to play when they are not free to really work—if their work has degenerated into sociability or feather-bedding. Those who are excluded from meaningful work are, by and large, excluded from meaningful play—women and children, to a degree, excepted. The kind of passionate fondness and excitement about his work that Freud had, although he would seldom admit this to himself, is also a good base from which to learn to play. And people have to learn to play—or stop unlearning; in this enterprise they are faced with the whole long tradition of the driving and driven men who created Western industrial society, Western political organization, and Western scientific thought, including psychoanalysis.

Perhaps it is time now for the analysts, and for other social scientists, to pay more attention to play, to study blockages in play in the way that they have studied blockages in work and sexuality. Yet, in studying play, one must be aware of the ambiguities that haunt play, be aware of the elusiveness and privacy that are its main defenses. We have far to go before we move to a new integration of work and play unreservedly superior to the Freudian dichotomies—an integration allowing us more work in work and more play in play.

NOTES

¹ *Civilization and Its Discontents* develops, *inter alia*, certain themes set forth in " 'Civilized' Sexual Morality and Modern Nervousness," *Collected Papers* 2:76, published in 1908, and the Clark University lectures of the following year.

² To decide this question, in each specific case, could be often highly speculative and difficult. Problems of the same sort arise when one seeks to interpret contemporary interview material, at least of a nonpsychoanalytic sort. These one must always ask: Does what the respondent reports say much about him as an individual, or is it mainly testimony—and, of course, that he gives this testimony says something about him—to the norm of his group, his social class, or the group or class to which he aspires? In Freud's case, we have the advantage of his reported dreams and associations, and many stray remarks, which it is sometimes possible to reinterpret by use of the method he discovered.

³ See Erich Fromm, "Individual and Social Origins of Neurosis," *Amer. Sociological Rev.* (1944) 9:380; reprinted in Clyde Kluckhohn and Henry A. Murray, eds., *Personality in Nature, Society, and Culture.*

⁴ Cf. Karl Polanyi, *The Great Transformation.*

⁵ See, for example, Thorstein Veblen, *The Theory of Business Enterprise;* Thurman Arnold, *The Folklore of Capitalism.*

⁶ Freud, "The Interpretation of Dreams," in *The Basic Writings of Sigmund Freud,* p. 548.

⁷ Reference footnote 6; p. 386.

⁸ Reference footnote 6; pp. 407, 409, 417. For a disavowal of ambition, see p. 219, and cf. pp. 257, 446.

⁹ Reference footnote 6; p. 333.

¹⁰ See Freud's dream of Count Thun (reference footnote 6; p. 415).

¹¹ "A kindly nature has bestowed upon the artist the capacity to express in artistic productions his most secret psychic feelings hidden even from himself, which powerfully grips outsiders, strangers to the artist, without their knowing whence this emotivity comes." Freud, *Leonardo da Vinci,* p. 84.

¹² See, for example, Freud, "A Neurosis of Demoniacal Possession in the Seventeenth Century," in *Collected Papers* 4:436; see especially pp. 470–471.

¹³ However, even a scientist may sometimes be lucky; thus Freud writes: "From the reports of certain writers who have been highly productive, such as Goethe and Helmholtz, we learn, rather, that the most essential and original part of their creations came to them in the form of inspirations, and offered itself to their awareness in an almost completed state." Freud, reference footnote 6; p. 543.

¹⁴ Reference footnote 11; p. 108.

¹⁵ Reference footnote 11; pp. 42–43.

¹⁶ Freud, *A New Series of Introductory Lectures on Psychoanalysis,* pp. 207, 218.

¹⁷ Reference footnote 16; p. 219.

¹⁸ See Freud's dream of Count Thun (reference footnote 6; p. 415).

¹⁹ Reference footnote 11; p. 115.

²⁰ Reference footnote 6; pp. 333–334. Freud does not see that Lassalle was lured to his death, not by feminine wiles, but by his highly ambivalent ambition for social status and fear of social humiliation. The plebeian Jewish Lassalle, despite his leftist views, was moved by the unconscious wish to prove his patent of nobility; therefore, his real "folly" lay precisely in acceptance of the motives and outlook which Freud took as the highest, most realistic wisdom. Cf. George Brandes, *Ferdinand Lassalle.*

²¹ Veblen, *The Theory of the Leisure Class.*

²² "We say also of women that their social interests are weaker than those of men, and that their capacity for the sublimation of their instincts is less." Reference footnote 16; p. 183.

²³ Cf., for example, Helene Deutsch, *The Psychology of Women,* Vol. I, Chapters 7 and 8.

²⁴ Reference footnote 16; p. 246. Freud found socialism impossible on other grounds as well, namely man's natural aggressiveness, which departs somewhat from the conservative Malthusian pattern; but aggressiveness, too, comes down, though only in part, to the scarcity of possessions and men's desire to seize them from each other, rather than to work for them.

²⁵ Reference footnote 6; p. 406. Freud says in the introduction to the second edition of the book on dreams that many of the dreams reported were connected with the poignant and emotionally significant period of his father's death.

²⁶ Reference footnote 16; p. 201.

²⁷ Reference footnote 6; p. 333.

²⁸ Reference footnote 11; p. 46.

²⁹ Reference footnote 6; p. 290.

³⁰ Reference footnote 6; p. 197.

³¹ Reference footnote 6; p. 349.

³² Reference footnote 6; p. 210.

³³ See Freud's dream of not working; reference footnote 6; pp. 284-285.

³⁴ Reference footnote 6; p. 441.

³⁵ Reference footnote 6; p. 475.

36 Reference footnote 6; p. 414. Freud speaks of wearing out his brother "by rushing him too quickly from place to place, and making him see too many beautiful things in a single day."

37 See the dream of the botanical monograph; reference footnote 6; p. 243.

38 Reference footnote 6; pp. 204, 206 *et seq.*

39 Reference footnote 16; p. 237.

40 Reference footnote 16; pp. 236–238.

41 *The Philosophy of Spinoza,* edited by Joseph Ratner, p. 245.

42 For example, reference footnote 6; pp. 369, 371, 374, 401.

43 Reference footnote 16; p. 239.

44 Reference footnote 16; p. 238.

45 For example, reference footnote 6; p. 275n.

46 *Civilization and Its Discontents;* reference footnote 1; pp. 24–25.

47 *Time,* August 18, 1947; p. 25.

48 Reference footnote 6; p. 241.

49 Freud, *An Autobiographical Study,* pp. 23–25.

50 Reference footnote 6; p. 242.

51 Reference footnote 6; pp. 243, 323.

52 Reference footnote 6; p. 243.

53 In speaking of the absence of affect in this dream, Freud writes that the dream "corresponds to a passionate plea for my freedom to act as I am acting, to arrange my life as seems right to me, and to me alone." Reference footnote 6; p. 439. But the "freedom" he refers to is that of his collecting mania, against the reproaches of his own conscience and those of his even more puritanical friends like the eye specialist, Dr. Koenigstein, who had told him the evening before that he was "too absorbed" in his hobbies. Reference footnote 6; p. 243. He reproaches himself: for not inventing cocaine, for "neglect" of botany; but he answers, "I am entitled to freedom for, after all, I am conscientious and have made some good monographic studies." Thus, he assumes that he must justify not driving himself 100 per cent—"allowing himself," as he says, some small vices. By his standard, even his meager vacations from the workaday world were sinful, especially where he "missed something," such as the cocaine discovery, as a result. Reference footnote 6; p. 268.

54 Reference footnote 6; pp. 382–383.

55 Reference footnote 6; p. 243.

56 Reference footnote 6; p. 241.

57 Reference footnote 6; p. 245.

58 Reference footnote 6; p. 245.

59 Reference footnote 6; p. 203.

60 I have leaned heavily on Erich Fromm's lectures on dream interpretation. See his article, "The Nature of Dreams," *Scientific Amer.* (1949) 180:44.

61 See Ernest Schachtel, "On Memory and Childhood Amnesia," *Psychiatry* (1947) 10:1; also Evelyn T. Riesman, "Childhood Memory in the Painting of Joan Miró," *Etc.,* (1949) 6:160.

62 Reference footnote 6; p. 294.

63 Reference footnote 11; p. 107.

64 Reference footnote 6; p. 315.

65 See, however, his discussion of children's food wishes and disappointments; reference footnote 6; p. 214.

66 The phrase is from Freud's *Leonardo da Vinci;* reference footnote 11; p. 70.

67 Reference footnote 6; pp. 509–510.

68 This phrase is from Freud's "The Interpretation of Dreams"; reference footnote 6; p. 513.

69 Reference footnote 6; p. 520n.

70 In a recent *Fortune* poll, a cross-section of the American people was asked what income they would like to have, if there were no limits to their demands. The average person gave a figure less than 25 per cent above what he was at the

moment making; the mean figure was less than $4,000. See "Portrait of the American People," *Fortune* (1947) 35:10.

⁷¹ Reference footnote 6; pp. 518–519.

⁷² Anxiety dreams do not seem to fit in this economy, and their explanation caused Freud no end of trouble. He finally concluded that anxiety is the response of that part of the dreamer's psyche which is displeased by the forbidden wish; this part, at least, is pleased by the suffering the anxiety occasions, which is felt as punishment. Reference footnote 6; p. 520; Freud, *A General Introduction to Psychoanalysis*, p. 192.

⁷³ Freud had the genius to see that fairy tales were *"nichts für Kinder,"* that they had an adult meaning though one which the adults did not permit themselves to see. He applied to them the same interpretative process he had used on dreams; he analyzed their symbolism; he tried to see what really happens in them beneath their decorative screen. He found it typical that the heroine, for example Cinderella, marries the prince; he took the status striving, as well as the sexual, even incest, elements, as "real"; naturally, every girl would want to marry a prince and lead the do-nothing life of an aristocrat. Reference footnote 6; p. 371. Moreover he held that in fairy tales we commit the Oedipal offenses; we are the "great criminals"; we indulge in the totem feast, with its sacrilege. All this gives us pleasure whose true nature, like that of dream, is concealed from us by its apparently harmless, innocent garb.

⁷⁴ Reference footnote 11; p. 96.

⁷⁵ Reference footnote 11; p. 120.

⁷⁶ See Freud's remarks on the uselessness of beauty, including parks, in *Civilization and Its Discontents;* reference footnote 1; pp. 54–55.

⁷⁷ Reference footnote 6; p. 538.

⁷⁸ Reference footnote 6; p. 332n.

⁷⁹ Freud, *Wit and Its Relation to the Unconscious;* pp. 164 *et seq.*

⁸⁰ Reference footnote 6; pp. 269, 272, 291.

*The obsessional nature of some occupations can be clearly
traced to unresolved neurotic conflicts of childhood. Ernest
Jones' case history of Paul Morphy, a famous chess player,
shows quite clearly how his choice of a profession was determined by an unsatisfactory resolution of an early Oedipal
complex. The Morphy story has a literary counterpart in the
recent novel by Vladimir Nabokov,* The Defense. *Nabokov
explores the same problems of guilt, obsession and expiation,
and uses a chess player and chess game to delineate the
underlying sexual themes.*

ERNEST JONES

The Problem of Paul Morphy[1]

Paul Morphy was born at New Orleans on June 22, 1837; he had a
sister six and half years older than himself, one two and a quarter years
younger, and a brother two and a half years older.[2] His father was a
Spaniard by nationality, but of Irish descent; his mother was of French
extraction.

When Paul was ten years old his father, who was himself no mean
player, taught him chess. In a year or two he proved himself the superior
of his elder brother Edward, his father, his mother's father, and his
father's brother who was at that time the chess king of New Orleans. A
game is preserved which, according to an eye-witness, he is said to have
played victoriously against his uncle on his twelfth birthday while blind-
folded. At the same age he played against two masters of international
renown who happened to be in New Orleans at the time. One of these
was the famous French player Rousseau, with whom he played some
fifty games, winning fully nine-tenths. The other was the Hungarian
master Loewenthal, one of the half-dozen greatest living players; of the
two games played the young Paul won one and the other was drawn.
After this period, little serious chess was played for some eight years
while he was pursuing his studies; his father allowed him to play occasionally on Sundays, but with the exception of Judge Meek, the Presi-

dent of the American Chess Congress, against whom he played and won six games when he was seventeen years old, he encountered only much inferior opponents. His uncle had by then left New Orleans for the West, Rousseau was otherwise absorbed, and Paul's brother, father, and grandfather had abandoned chess when he was in his teens, so the statement that has been made is probably true that in these years he never met anyone to whom he could not give a rook, consequently no one from whose play he could learn anything. In 1851 the first International Chess Tournament had taken place, at which Anderssen emerged as victor, and in 1857, when Morphy was just twenty years old, one was held in New York. He easily gained the first place, losing only one game out of seventeen, and during his stay in New York played a hundred games with the best players there, losing only five of them. In circumstances which will engage our attention presently, he visited London and Paris in the following year and his prodgious feats there read like a fairy tale. He not only defeated every champion he could induce to meet him, including Anderssen himself, but also gave several astounding exhibitions of simultaneous blindfold play against eight picked players, winning the large majority of the games. Towards the end of his stay in Paris he defeated blindfold the whole of the Versailles Chess Club playing in consultation. On his return to New Orleans he issued a challenge to play anyone in the world at odds. On receiving no response to this he declared his career as a chess player—which had lasted barely eighteen months, comprising actually only six months of public play—finally and definitely closed.

Of the actual quality of Morphy's play we shall have something to say later, but for the moment it will suffice to say that many of the most competent judges have pronounced him to have been the greatest chess player of all time. After his extraordinarily premature retirement he took up the practice of law, his father's profession, but although he possessed much skill in the work he was unsuccessful in practice. He gradually relapsed into a state of seclusion and introversion which culminated in unmistakable paranoia. At the age of forty-seven he died suddenly of 'congestion of the brain', presumably apoplexy, as his father had before him.

The evident problem arises of what relation, if any, his tragic neurosis bore to the supreme activities of his life, activities for which his name will always be remembered in the world of chess. It was popularly believed that the excessive preoccupation had affected his brain, but his biographers, who were naturally chess enthusiasts and zealous for the credit of their beloved pursuit, asserted with conviction that this was in no way responsible. Nevertheless, with our present knowledge we should find it impossible to believe that there was not some intimate connection between the neurosis, which is necessarily concerned with the kernel of the personality, and the superb efforts of sublimation which have made Morphy's name immortal. In contemplating this problem, let us begin with some reflections on the nature of the sublimation in question.

The slightest acquaintance with chess shows one that it is a play-substitute for the art of war, and indeed it has been a favourite recreation of some of the greatest military leaders, from William the Conqueror to Napoleon. In the contest between the opposing armies the same principles of both strategy and tactics are displayed as in actual war, the same foresight and powers of calculation are necessary, the same capacity for divining the plans of the opponent, and the rigour with which decisions are followed by their consequences is, if anything, even more ruthless. More than that, it is plain that the unconscious motive actuating the players is not the mere love of pugnacity characteristic of all competitive games, but the grimmer one of father-murder. It is true that the original goal of capturing the king has been given up, but from the point of view of motive there is, except in respect of crudity, no appreciable change in the present goal of sterilizing him in immobility. The history of the game and the names for it are of confirmatory interest here. Authorities seem to be agreed that the game originated in India, passed from there to Persia, whose Arabian conquerors transmitted it to Europe nearly a thousand years ago. Its first name, from which all others are derived, was the Sanscrit one of *chaturanga,* literally four members. This was also the Indian word for 'army', probably because of the four components of elephants, chariots, horse, and foot. The old Persians shortened the name from *chaturanga* to *chatrang* and their Arabian successors, having neither the initial nor the final sound of this word in their language, modified it into *shatranj.* When it re-emerged into later Persian the unconscious must have been at work, for it had by then been shortened to *Schah,* an assimilation having evidently taken place with the Persian *Shah*-King; 'chess' thus means the royal game, or the game of kings. *Shah-mat,* our 'check-mate', German 'Schachmatt', French 'échec et mat', means literally 'the king is dead'. At least so the Arabian writers on chess thought, and most European authors copy them in this. Modern Orientalists, however, are of opinion that the word 'mat' is of Persian, and not of Arabian, origin, and that 'Shah-mat' means 'the king is paralysed, helpless, and defeated'. Again, from the point of view of the king it makes very little difference.

In the Middle Ages an interesting innovation was introduced into the rules of chess which deserves incidental mention. By the side of the king stands another piece who was originally his counsellor, Persian *firz* (Turkish *vizier*). As his main occupation was supposed to be, not fighting, but advising and defending, he was in action the weakest piece on the board, his only move being one square diagonally. In the Middle Ages he gradually changed his sex, thus passing through the same evolution as the Holy Ghost, and came to be known as the regina, dame, queen, and so on. It is not known why this happened. It was suggested by Freret, an eighteenth-century writer on chess, that a confusion must have arisen between the words 'fierge', the French for *firz*, and 'vierge'. It has more generally been thought that as this used to be the only piece for which a pawn could be exchanged on reaching the eighth square, when it was sometimes called 'un pion damé', this circumstance led to its being given the same name as the French one for draughts, *i.e. dames*. About the middle of the fifteenth century this change in sex was followed by a great increase in power, so that the piece is now stronger than any other two together. Whatever may be the truth, therefore, about the linguistic speculations I have just mentioned, it will not surprise the psycho-analyst when he learns the effect of the change: it is that in attacking the father the most potent assistance is afforded by the mother (=queen.)

It is perhaps worth remarking further that the mathematical quality of the game gives it a peculiar anal-sadistic nature. The exquisite purity and exactness of the right moves,[3] particularly in problem work, combine here with the unrelenting pressure exercised in the later stages which culminates in the merciless *dénouement*. The sense of overwhelming mastery on the one side matches that of unescapable helplessness on the other. It is doubtless this anal-sadistic feature that makes the game so well adapted to gratify at the same time both the homosexual and the antagonistic aspects of the son-father contest. In these circumstances it will be understood that a serious match places a considerable strain on psychical integrity and is likely to reveal any imperfections of character development. All games are apt at times to be marred by unsportsmanlike behaviour, *i.e.* by the sublimation undergoing a regression to its asocial origins, but with chess the strain is exceptionally great and is complicated by the circumstance that a specially high standard of correct demeanour is exacted.

It is interesting to compare with these psychological considerations some historical data on the way in which the game has been variously received by religious authorities. Van der Linde and Murray, the two greatest authorities on the history of chess, discuss sympathetically the Indian tradition that the game was invented by the Buddhists. It is certainly suggestive that the first mention of it occurs in connection with a stronghold of Buddhists. According to their ideas, war and the slaying of one's fellow-men, for any purpose whatever, is criminal, and the punishment of the warrior in the next world will be much worse than that of the simple murderer; hence—so runs the story—they invented chess as a substitute for war. In this they would appear to have anticipated William James's suggestion of providing war-like substitutes, one quite in accord with the psycho-analytical doctrine of the displacement of affects. In a similar vein St. J. G. Scott narrates a Burmese story to the effect that chess was invented by a Talaing queen who was passing fond of her lord and hoped by this distraction to keep him out of war. Ambivalence runs through the whole story, however, for the view has also been put forward that chess was invented by a Chinese mandarin, Han-sing, who wanted to amuse his soldiers when in winter quarters. A Ceylon legend has it that the game was invented by Ravan, the wife of the King of Lanka, in order to distract that monarch when his metropolis was being besieged. On the other hand, about the year 1000, a puritanical regent of Egypt, usually known as Mansar, issued an edict forbidding chess. In mediaeval times chess became widely popular, and the ecclesiastical attitude towards it appears to have been mainly negative. The statutes of the church of Elna, for example, lay down that clergy indulging in chess shall be *ipso facto* excommunicated. At the end of the twelfth century the Bishop of Paris forbade the clergy even to have a chess-board in their houses; in 1212 the Council of Paris condemned it utterly; and, some forty years later, St. Louis, the pious King of France, imposed a fine on whoever should play the game. John Huss, when in prison, deplored having played at chess and thereby run the risk of being subject to violent passions.

In returning to the problem of Paul Morphy I shall begin with giving some description of his personal attributes and the characteristics of his play. In appearance he was small, only five feet four in height, with preternaturally small hands and feet, a slim, graceful figure, and a 'face like a young girl in her teens' (F. M. Edge). Falkbeer, who knew him, observed that he appeared younger than he really was, adding: 'One would certainly have taken him rather for a schoolboy on his vacation than for a chess adept who had crossed the Atlantic for the express purpose of defeating, one after another, the most eminent players the world then knew'. He had a very pleasing manner and a delightful smile.

His demeanour was strikingly modest. On only two occasions was he known to invite anyone to play with him, and, with an uncanny intuition, he chose for these exceptions the two men, Staunton and Harrwitz, who were to exercise such a baleful influence on his life. He bore himself, even in the unpleasant controversy we shall presently relate, with the greatest courtesy and dignity. While playing he was very impassive, with his eyes fixed steadfastly on the board; opponents got to know that whenever he looked up, which he did without any exultation, it meant he could foresee the inevitable end. His patience seemed inexhaustible; Edge, his first biographer, records having watched the famous Paulsen spend and hour or two over a single move while Morphy sat calmly looking on without the slightest movement of uneasiness. He seemed insensitive to fatigue, and I will recall a story which illustrates his powers of endurance as well as two other features: his astounding memory —which, incidentally, he possessed also for music—and his capacity for sensorial imagery, a quality which links chess players with musicians and mathematicians. It is narrated by Edge, who was at the time acting as his secretary, and concerns an exhibition he was giving when just twenty-one at the Café de la Régence in Paris, then the Mecca of chess players from all over the world. He played blindfold eight games simultaneously against powerful opponents who, incidentally, were freely helped by advice from a crowd of expert players. It was seven hours before the first of them was defeated and the match lasted ten consecutive hours, during the whole of which time Morphy abstained from taking either food or even water. At the close there was a scene of terrific excitement, and Morphy had the greatest difficulty in extricating himself from the ovation in the streets and escaping to his hotel. There he slept well, but at seven in the morning he called his secretary and dictated to him every move in all the games, at the same time discussing with him the possible consequences of hundreds of hypothetical variations. It will be agreed that only a mind working with exceptional ease could have accomplished such an astounding feat. Nor was it an isolated achievement sustained by excitement. There are few more exhausting occupations than serious chess, and the number of those who can continue for more than three or four hours on end without feeling the strain is not very great. Yet Morphy has been known to play continuously from nine in the morning until midnight on many successive days without his play weakening in the least and without his showing any signs of fatigue. In psycho-analytical terms this must signify a very exceptional level of sublimation, for a psychological situation of such a degree of freedom can only mean that there is no risk of its stimulating any unconscious conflict or guilt.

It is not easy to describe Morphy's qualities as a player in other than general terms without presupposing a knowledge of chess technique. I hope that the generalizations I shall venture on will be in some measure trustworthy; we possess, at all events, ample data on which to found generalizations, for there survive some four hundred of Morphy's games, and an extensive literature has grown up of critical comments subsequent authorities have made on the individual moves.

To begin with, there are different styles of chess which depend partly on the temperament and aim of the player and partly on the conditions under which he is playing. Speaking very roughly, it depends on whether one sets more store on winning or on not losing. In tournaments, for instance, where defeats are heavily penalized, it may pay to aim at a few victories and a number of draws rather than at more victories but more defeats. The two extremes are represented by a slashing but risky attack on the one hand and a tediously defensive stone-walling on the other. Naturally the ideal player combines the best from each attitude. He spends some time in fortifying his army, not so much for defensive reasons as to get them into the strongest position from which to deliver an attack. A player may excel in either of these activities, or his fortifying may have an almost purely defensive aim in which any opportunity for an attack comes rather as a piece of luck. In chess there are—if we omit the recent 'hyper-modern' play—two well-known styles, known as the combinational and the positional, which are sometimes said to correspond with the romantic and the classical temperaments respectively. At the period we are concerned with, about the middle of the last century, only the former existed and, indeed, the latter is essentially the product of the last fifty years. The main difference between the two methods, at least in its extreme form, may be likened to that between a cleverly designed attack in battle and a steady siege. The aim of the combinational method is to plan a skilful grouping of the pieces to make a co-ordinated onslaught on the king, whereas that of the positional method is the more cautious—but in the end sounder—one of gradually building up a fortified position and taking advantage of the slightest weakness in the opponent's position, wherever this may happen to be.

Now Morphy certainly possessed in the highest degree the gifts necessary for a master of combinational play, those of foresight, calculation, and power of divining his opponent's intentions. Some of his games are masterpieces in this respect which have rarely been equalled and, indeed, the popular impression of his style among chess players is that of vehement and victorious onslaught. One would therefore have anticipated with assurance that someone possessing such gifts, and whose brilliant performances were at such an early age, would have owed his success to an unusual genius in the qualities of intuition and adventurousness that might naturally be expected to appeal to youth. Yet the interesting thing is, and one that throws a good deal of light on Morphy's psychology, that he passed beyond this style and, in fact, ranks as the first pioneer of positional play—though it was Steinitz who later developed the principles of it. It was a fortunate coincidence that the only player in history whose genius in combinational play has equalled Morphy's was not only just at that time at the height of his career, but actually met Morphy in combat: I refer to Anderssen, till that moment the foremost player of the day and virtually the world's champion—though this title was not formally employed till a decade later. Murray says of the two men: 'Both were players of rare imaginative gifts, and their play has never been equalled for brilliance of style, beauty of conception, and depth of design. In Morphy these qualities blazed forth from sheer natural genius; in Anderssen they were the result of long practice and study.' Reti, in his *Modern Ideas in Chess,* has instructively explained that Morphy's famous victory over Anderssen was due, not to greater brilliance in the sense just indicated, but to his establishing the method of brilliance on a basis of the more mature positional play. It must have been a memorable scene to witness this slim youth overpowering the huge, burly Teuton of forty, not in the traditional fashion of the young hero overcoming a giant by more audacious imagination—for in this quality they were equally matched and equally unsurpassable—but by more mature depth of understanding. The interest of this observation for our purpose is the indication it gives that in Morphy's mind chess must have signified a fully adult activity, and success in it the serious occupation of a man rather than the rebellious ambition of a boy. I shall submit later that being shaken in this matter was one of the factors that led to his mental catastrophe.

Morphy was master of all aspects of the game in such a high degree, and was so free of mannerisms and individual peculiarities of style, that it is not easy to single out any particular characteristics. Chess, it is true, like all other games, is replete with unconscious symbolism. One could, for instance, comment on the skill he showed in attacking the king from behind or in separating the opposing king and queen; the latter, by the way, is illustrated in the first of his games ever recorded, which was played against his own father. But such details are not to our purpose, for pre-eminence in chess depends on a broad synthesis of exceptional qualities rather than on skill in any particular device or method. Careful consideration of the whole of Morphy's manner of play yields, I think, the indubitable conclusion that the outstanding characteristic he exhibited in it was an almost unbelievably supreme *confidence*. He knew, as if it was a simple fact of nature, that he was bound to win, and he quietly acted on this knowledge. When the Americans who had seen him play prophesied that, on meeting any European champion, he would, in the manner of Andrea del Sarto to Raphael, 'bring the sweat into that brow of his', chess players in Europe scoffed at the prediction as mere American bombast, and the only question in their minds was whether it was worth their leaders' while to play such a youngster. To anyone who knows what years of assiduous practice and rich experience go to attaining any degree of prowess in chess, nothing could seem more utterly unlikely than that a beginner embarking on this arduous path, as Paul Morphy was, should have the career he actually did on reaching Europe. Yet before he left his native town he calmly predicted his coming victories with the completest assurance. Such presumption might reasonably be regarded as megalomania were it not for the awkward fact that it was justified. On his return home, far from being flushed with pride, he remarked that he had not done so well as he should have, and in a sense this also was true, for when playing on a few occasions in a state of indisposition he was guilty of some weak moves that fell below his usual standard of play and even cost him a few games. It is not surprising that, endowed with such confidence in his powers, his play was marked by a boldness and even audacity in his moves that give at first the impression of being over-adventurous, and perhaps even of hazarding risks, until one perceives the sureness of the calculation behind them. His intrepidity was naturally more manifest when he had to do with relatively inferior players. Here he could behave with apparent recklessness, extravagantly flinging away one after another of his pieces until, with an unsuspected movement, his small remaining force would suddenly deliver the *coup de grace*; on one such occasion he achieved the extraordinary feat of effecting a mate by simply castling. His boldness and his sense of how important position is in chess-playing are shown in two other characteristics for which he is well known: the extent to which he appreciated the value of developing the pieces early and continuously, and his willingness to make sacrifices to gain a better position. There is a story, perhaps apocryphal, that when he was a child he was so eager to bring his pieces forward that he regarded his pawns as a nuisance to be got rid of as soon as possible: how different from the great Philidor, who had declared pawns to be the very soul of chess! It is, at all events, quite fitting that the name 'Morphy opening' in chess has been attached to the following device. What is called the Muzio opening is characterized by a bold attack in which a knight is sacrificed in the fifth move so as to obtain what is believed to be a commensurate advantage in position. In the Morphy opening the same tactics are followed up by sacrificing a bishop also, so that it is sometimes known by the name of 'double Muzio'. Very few people indeed are to be found confident enough of their attack to be able to risk such grave initial losses. Even the defence named after him, the Morphy defence to the Ruy Lopez opening, one which is so valuable as to have been elaborated since into some twenty named variations, is the most aggressive of the manifold defences to this opening.

With Morphy, chess sense, if one may use such an expression, was far more innate than acquired. He had read a good deal, but gave away the book as soon as he had looked through it. He said himself that no author had been of much value to him, and that 'he was astonished at finding various positions and solutions given as novel—certain moves producing certain results, etc., for that he had made the same deductions himself, as necessary consequences' (Edge). MacDonnell, who watched his play in London, wrote later of it in his *Chess Life-Pictures*: 'I fancy he always discerned the right move at a glance, and only paused before making it partly out of respect for his antagonist and partly to certify himself of its correctness, to make assurance doubly sure, and to accustom himself to sobriety of demeanour in all circumstances'. The following story raises the whole question of the method employed in mental calculation. In the famous seventeenth move in the Four Knights' game with Paulsen on November 8, 1857, Morphy offered to exchange his queen for his opponent's bishop. Paulsen was naturally suspicious of a trap and carefully investigated the possibilities. After pondering on the situation for more than an hour, and detecting no trap, he accepted the offer and after eleven more moves had to resign. Years afterwards, Steinitz carried out a full analysis of the situation and maintained as a result of it that the future possibilities in the game were far too numerous and complicated for it to be conceivable that any human brain could calculate and predict them. It so happened that an onlooker had asked Morphy after the game was over whether he had been able to foresee the end of it from his famous move; to the question he returned the enigmatic answer: 'I knew it would give Paulsen a deal of trouble'. Steinitz was doubtless right in his conclusion so far as consciousness is concerned, but one wonders whether the so-called intuitive chess does not imply a special power of pre-conscious calculation. The experiments Milne Bramwell carried out showed that the subconscious capacity for arithmetical calculation, as tested in hypnosis, far exceeds the conscious capacity, and the same may well hold good for the computation of chess moves.

We may take it that this remarkable combination of capacity and confidence could not occur unless it was a direct representative of the main stream of the libido and was providing the best possible solution of any conflicts in the deepest trends of the personality. It follows that anything interfering with such an indispensable expression [of] the personality would be likely gravely to endanger its integrity, and so indeed events proved. Our knowledge of the unconscious motivation of chess-playing tells us that what it represented could only have been the wish to overcome the father in an acceptable way. For Morphy, the conditions necessary for its acceptability were essentially three: that the act in question should be received in a friendly manner; that it should be ascribed to worthy motives; and that it should be regarded as a serious and grown-up activity. We shall see that each of these conditions was grossly violated on his fateful visit to Europe and shall try to trace the mental consequences of this. It is no doubt significant that Morphy's soaring odyssey into the higher realms of chess began just a year after the—unexpectedly sudden—death of his father,[4] which had been a great shock to him, and we may surmise that his brilliant effort of sublimation was, like Shakespeare's *Hamlet* and Freud's *Traumdeutung,* a reaction to this critical event.

I shall now consider the critical period of Morphy's life in more detail, and for this purpose shall find it necessary, in the first place, to introduce to those of you who are not conversant with the history of chess some of the most prominent figures of the day in that world. Six of these need to be mentioned in this context: four of them became friendly admirers of Morphy, the other two set him a psychological problem to which he was not equal.

First in order of time was Loewenthal, whom Morphy had already successfully encountered when a child. Loewenthal had made further progress since then, and in the Birmingham tournament that took place during Morphy's visit to England, in which the latter did not participate, he won the first place, although both Staunton and Saint-Amant were

also competitors. In a match arranged between the two, Morphy decisively beat him, and Loewenthal became a firm friend and admirer,
taking his side in the unfortuante controversy to which we shall presently have to refer. He foretold that, after Morphy's games were published—a task which he himself successfully undertook later—the chess
world would rank him above all other players living or dead. The stakes
in the Loewenthal match were £100, and after winning, Morphy immediately presented Loewenthal with some furniture costing £120 for a
new house he was taking. We shall repeatedly have occasion to note how
fastidious Morphy was over the subject of money. Before he left America, for instance, when the New Orleans Chess Club offered to subscribe
money to enable him to participate in the Birmingham tournament, he
had refused—not wishing to travel as a professional chess player. Next
comes Paulsen, an American, famous at that time for his amazing exhibitions in blindfold chess and later for winning two matches against
Anderssen as well as for his important contributions to chess theory. He
was Morphy's only serious rival at the New York tournament, and, from
reading a couple of his published games he predicted on that occasion
that Morphy would beat him; just before the tournament they played
three games, blindfold, of which Morphy won two and drew one.
Paulsen also became a devoted friend of Morphy. Saint-Amant was at
that time the foremost player in France. He did not play any single-
handed games with Morphy, but lost five and drew two of seven consultation games against him. He also became a fervent admirer, and said of
his blindfold play that it was enough to make the bones of Philidor and
La Bourdonnais rattle in their grave, without doubt the handsomest
compliment a Frenchman could pay. The genial Anderssen we have
already met. He was the best player living and was generally recognized
to be the world's champion until his defeat by Steinitz some years later;
he obtained a prize at each of the twelve tournaments he took part in
and won the first place in seven of them. Mongredien, the president of
the London Chess Club, said of him that he was, 'except Morphy, the
most splendid and chivalrous player whom I have ever encountered',
and his treatment of Morphy certainly confirms this estimate of him.
Although his colleagues brought the greatest possible pressure to bear to
prevent his impairing German prestige by going abroad to play a match
with a youngster of no official standing, and in spite of his having no
opportunity to practise beforehand, Anderssen made no excuses but
travelled to Paris to meet his fate at Morphy's hands. Reproached
afterwards for not having played so brilliantly as he had in his famous

match with Dufresne, he made the generous rejoinder: 'No, Morphy wouldn't let me'.

Morphy's relations with these four men contrast sadly with his experiences of the two who will next concern us. Of these the more important was Staunton, and to explain his significance for Morphy a word must be said about the position he occupied. He was a man with a greater prestige than his tournament record would lead one to suppose. It is true that, by his victory over Saint-Amant, Horwitz, and Harrwitz in the 'forties, he could claim to be considered the leading player in the world, but he was not able to sustain this position, being beaten, for instance, in the London tournament of 1851 and the Birmingham one of 1858. He was, however, a great analyst; and the standard text-book that he wrote, together with his position as one of the first chess editors, made him the *doyen* of the English, if not of the European, chess world. In the middle of the last century England was easily paramount in chess, and perhaps this contributed to the reasons that made Morphy select Staunton as the antagonist he most wanted to meet; it was the wish to play against Staunton that was his main motive in crossing the Atlantic. In psychoanalytical language we may say that Staunton was the supreme father *imago* and that Morphy made the overcoming of him the test case of his capacity to play chess, and unconsciously of much else besides. A piece of evidence is extant which goes to show that this choice of father *imago* was far from being a recent one. At the age of fifteen Morphy had been presented with a copy of the games played at the first International Tournament of 1851, of which Stunton was the secretary. He took it on himself to write on the title-page: 'By H. Staunton, Esq., author of the *Handbook of Chess, Chess-Player's Companion,* etc. (and some devilish bad games)'. After Morphy's victory at the New York tournament some enthusiasts mooted the possibility of a European champion coming to America to play him. On hearing of this Staunton published a deprecatory paragraph in his weekly chess column and remarked that 'the best chess players in Europe are not chess professionals but have other and more serious avocations'. To hint that Morphy's chess was either a juvenile pastime or else a means of making money were innuendoes that must have wounded him to the quick, for there is ample evidence that he was morbidly sensitive to either suggestion. His New Orleans friends nevertheless issued a challenge to Staunton to come to America, which he not unnaturally refused, dropping, however, a broad hint that Morphy would find him at his disposal were he to come to Europe. Morphy crossed four months later, and, on being introduced to

Staunton, at once asked him for a game. Staunton pleaded an engagement and followed this by a course of such ungentlemanly behaviour as
to be explicable only on the score of neurotic apprehension; it was in
fact said of him that he suffered from what was called 'nervous irritability'. For three months, during his stay in England and after, Morphy
endeavoured, in the most dignified manner, to arrange a match, to which
Staunton replied with a series of evasions, postponements, broken promises, and pretexts that his brain 'was overtaxed by more important
pursuits'—not that the latter prevented him from participating in the
Birmingham tournament in the very same month. Foiled in his hopes
Morphy laid the whole matter before Lord Lyttelton, the President of
the British Chess Association, who made a sympathetic reply, and the
matter rested at that. During this time, however, Staunton kept up in his
chess column a steady fire of criticism of the man he avoided meeting,
depreciating his play, hinting that he was a monetary adventurer, and so
on. One sentence may be quoted from Morphy's final letter to him:
'Permit me to repeat what I have invariably declared in every chess
community I have had the honour of entering, that I am not a professional player—that I never wished to make any skill I possess the means
of pecuniary advancement'.[5] The whole episode led to an acrimonious
wrangle in the chess world in which the large majority supported
Morphy, and subsequent opinion almost unanimously regards Staunton's behaviour as totally unworthy of him. The effect on Morphy was
immediate, and it showed itself in a strong revulsion against chess. As
Sergeant, Morphy's latest and best biographer, writes, 'Morphy sickened
of chess tactics—off the board. Is there any wonder?'

Towards the end of this episode Morphy crossed to Paris, where he at
once approached Harrwitz, *le roi de la Régence*. This gentleman also
does not appear in an amiable light in his dealings with Morphy, which
were marked by morbid vanity and a total lack of chivalry (Sergeant).
We need not go into the sordid details, which have been fully described
by Edge, but the upshot was that Harrwitz withdrew from the match
when he was being decisively beaten. Morphy at first refused to accept
the stake, a sum of 290 francs, but on its being represented to him that
other people would lose money unless his victory was officially sealed in
this way, he assented, but devoted the sum towards defraying Anderssen's travelling expenses to Paris. Morphy's neurosis increased after this,
and it was only temporarily abrogated by the pleasant episode of the
match with Anderssen, the final flare-up of his chess fever.

Something should now be said about the reception Morphy's successes met with, for they were of such a kind as to raise the question whether his subsequent collapse may not have been influenced through his perhaps belonging to the type that Freud has described under the name of *Die am Erfolge scheitern* (those wrecked by success). I alluded earlier to the scene at the Café de la Régence on the occasion of the brilliant *tour de force* when Morphy successfully encountered eight strong players at once when blindfold; it was so tumultuous that soldiers ran up in the expectation that there was another revolution. Morphy became the lion of Parisian society, was entertained everywhere, politely allowed himself to be defeated at chess by duchesses and princesses, and finally left France in a blaze of glory, the culmination of which was a banquet at which his bust, made by a famous sculptor, was presented to him crowned with a laurel wreath. His reception on his return to New York, where patriotic fervour was added to the other enthusiasms, may well be imagined. It was widely felt that this was the first time in history in which an American had proved himself, not merely the equal, but the superior of any representative in his field drawn from the older countries, so that Morphy had added a cubit to the stature of American civilization. In the presence of a great assembly in the chapel of the University he was presented with a testimonial consisting of a chessboard with mother-of-pearl and ebony squares and a set of men in gold and silver; he also received a gold watch, on which coloured chesspieces took the place of the numerals. An incident that occurred at this presentation may be mentioned as illustrating Morphy's sensitiveness. Colonel Mead, the chairman of the reception committee, alluded in his speech to chess as a profession, and referred to Morphy as its most brilliant exponent. 'Morphy took exception to being characterized as a professional player, even by implication, and he resented it in such a way as to overwhelm Colonel Mead with confusion. Such was his mortification at this untoward event that Colonel Mead withdrew from further participation in the Morphy demonstration' (Buck). At the Union Club of New York he was presented with a silver wreath of laurels. He then proceeded to Boston, where a banquet was given in his honour at which were present, among others, Agassiz, Oliver Wendell Holmes, Longfellow, and Lowell; in a speech at this banquet Quincey made the witty remark: 'Morphy is greater than Caesar, because he came and without seeing conquered'. Shortly after this he was presented with a golden crown in Boston.

Adulation of this degree showered on a young man of twenty-one inevitably imposes a severe strain on his mental integrity, and one may well ask whether it did not play some part in the tragedy that followed. In this connection I should like to quote an interesting passage from the obituary notice written years later by Morphy's boyhood friend Maurian. Maurian ascribes the revulsion against chess—which, by the way, he does not associate with the subsequent mental derangement—to the completeness of Morphy's success, but in quite the opposite sense to that we have just indicated. He writes: 'Paul Morphy was never so passionately fond, so inordinately devoted to chess as is generally believed. An intimate acquaintance and long observation enables us to state this positively. His only devotion to the game, if it may be so termed, lay in his ambition to meet and to defeat the best players and great masters of this country and of Europe. He felt his enormous strength, and never for a moment doubted the outcome. Indeed, before his first departure for Europe he privately and modestly, yet with perfect confidence, predicted to us his certain success, and when he returned he expressed the conviction that he had played poorly, rashly—that none of his opponents should have done so well as they did against him. But, this one ambition satisfied, he appeared to have lost all interest in the game.'

Before attempting to answer the question just raised, I think it well to finish the story itself and give some account of the later mental developments. On settling down in New Orleans, Morphy's intention was to devote himself to the profession of law, of which he had an excellent knowledge. He found, however, that his now unwelcome fame as a chess player prevented people from taking him seriously as a lawyer, and this injustice preyed greatly on his mind. Buck, who had the assistance of Morphy's relatives in compiling the story of his later years, states that 'he became enamoured of a wealthy and handsome young lady in New Orleans and informed a mutual friend of the fact, who broached the subject to the lady; but she scorned the idea of marrying "a mere chess-player" '.

Within a year or two of his establishing himself in what he intended to be his serious permanent profession, the Civil War broke out, and Morphy was faced with the prospect of a real war interfering with his endeavour to substitute a peaceful occupation for his pastime of mock war.[6] His reaction was characteristic of the man who had built his mental integrity on converting hostile intentions into friendly ones—he hastened to Richmond, and in the midst of hostilities applied for a *diplomatic* appointment. This was refused, and soon after his return to New Orleans, his mother-town, it was captured by the Federal enemy. The Morphy family fled on a Spanish warship to Cuba, thence to

Havana, Cadiz, and Paris. He spent a year in Paris and then returned to Havana until the war was over.

Already at that time his mental state could not have been at all satisfactory, for within a couple of years of returning to New Orleans his mother persuaded him to spend eighteen months in Paris, his third visit there, in the hope that the change of environment would restore him. His aversion to chess was by now so complete that he did not go near the scenes of his former triumphs.

Before long there manifested itself unmistakable evidence of paranoia. He imagined himself persecuted by people who wished to render his life intolerable. His delusions centred on the husband of his elder sister, the administrator of his father's estate, who he believed was trying to rob him of his patrimony. He challenged him to a duel, and then brought a law-suit against him, spending his time for years in preparing his case; in court it was easily shown that his accusations were quite baseless. He also thought that people, particularly his brother-in-law, were trying to poison him, and for a time refused to take food except at the hands of his mother or his (younger, unmarried) sister. Another delusion was that his brother-in-law and an intimate friend, Binder, were conspiring to destroy his clothes, of which he was very vain, and to kill him; on one occasion he called in the latter's office and unexpectedly assaulted him. He was given to stopping and staring at every pretty face in the street, which I should ascribe to feminine identification. He was also passionately fond of flowers. I will quote one habit from this time, on which, however, I am unable to throw any light. During a certain period, according to his niece's account, he had a mania for striding up and down the verandah declaiming the following words: 'Il plantera la bannière de Castille sur les murs de Madrid au cri de Ville gagnée, et le petit Roi s'en ira tout penaud'. It sounds like a quotation, but, if so, I have not been able to trace it, nor can I explain the allusion. His mode of life was to take a walk every day, punctually at noon and most scrupulously attired, after which he would retire again until the evening when he would set out for the opera, never missing a single performance. He would see no one except his mother, and grew angry if she ventured to invite even intimates to the house. Two years before his death he was approached for his permission to include his life in a projected biographical work on famous Louisianians. He sent an indignant reply, in which he stated that his father, Judge Alonzo Morphy, of the High Court of Louisiana, had left at his death the sum of 146,162 dollars and 54 cents, while he himself had followed no profession and had nothing to do with biography. His talk was constantly of his father's fortune, and the mere mention of chess was usually sufficient to irritate him.

The problem we have set ourselves at the outset is: what relation did Morphy's chess career bear to his later mental disorder? Sergeant is at pains to demonstrate that mere preoccupation with chess could not be held responsible, and every medical and psychological expert can only confirm this opinion. His summary of the pathogeny of the disorder is so clear as to merit full quotation. 'Firstly, Morphy had some reason to be disgusted with, not chess, but chess-masters, whom he found of a very different character from himself. He set out, very young, generous, and high-spirited, recognizing, as he said himself, no incentive but reputation, and met not fellow-knights but tortuous acrobats of the pen, slingers of mud, and chess-sharpers. Granted he also met very decent gentlemen such as Anderssen, Loewenthal, and the majority of the leading amateurs in London and Paris. But the mean wounds inflicted by the other sort did not readily heal. Secondly, he always kept himself pure from any taint (as he rightly or wrongly imagined it to be) of professionalism in chess, yet was constantly being, if not called, at least looked on as a professional. And, lastly, he was ambitious in the career he had chosen for himself in life, and, failing in that through an unfortunate combination of circumstances, laid the blame upon chess. The disappointed ambition was assuredly a cause of Morphy's sad fate. . . . A supersensitive nature like his was ill-fitted to stand such trials.' How much Morphy strove to conceal his wound from himself may be seen from the following passage from his speech at the presentation made to him on his return to New York: 'Of my European tour, I will only say that it has been pleasant in almost every respect. Of all the adversaries encountered in the peaceful jousts of the checkered field, I retain a lively and agreeable recollection. I found them gallant, chivalrous and gentlemanly, as well as true votaries of the kingly pastime.'

Let me put the problem in another way. Was Morphy's mental derangement brought on by his very success or by his failure and disappointment? Was his situation that of Browning's Pictor Ignotus, from whom the approach of supreme fame brought forth the cry:

"The thought grew frightful, 'twas so wildly dear!"?

Did he say to himself, like Andrea:

"Too live the life grew, golden and not grey,
And I'm the weak-eyed bat no sun should tempt
Out of the grange whose four walls make this world"?

Did he withdraw from the world with the disdainful consolation:

"At least no merchant traffics in my heart"?

Couched in more psychological language, was Morphy affrighted at his own presumptuousness when the light of publicity was thrown on it? Freud has pointed out that the people who break under the strain of too great success do so because they can endure it only in imagination, not in reality. To castrate the father in a dream is a very different matter from doing it in reality. The real situation provokes the unconscious guilt in its full force, and the penalty may be mental collapse.

I do not think the full explanation can lie here. We have to remember that in the aim most vital to Morphy he had not succeeded, but failed. We have seen how Staunton must have been to him the arch *imago,* and he had not managed to bring him to book. It was all very well to have shown himself to be the best player in the world, with a good presumption that he could have defeated Staunton also. But the cold fact remains that this arch-opponent eluded him. The dreaded father was not merely still at large, but had himself shown signs of unmistakable hostility. Morphy's aim had miscarried of dealing with this repressed hostility towards his father—and the fear of his father's towards him—by converting this into a friendly homosexual encounter. The following consideration gives, I think, a hint that Morphy himself was partly conscious of the failure of his aim. When he returned to New York he declared he would not play any American again except at odds, and this was doubtless justified in the circumstances. But when, a few weeks later, he reached the safety of his home in New Orleans he issued a challenge to play anyone in the world at odds of pawn and move, the only instance in his whole chess career of his probably over-estimating his powers.[7] I read this as indicating a psychological compensation for the underlying sense of having failed, and the anxiety this must have stirred in his unconscious.

There was, however, more than this. When Staunton eluded him he did so in a way that must have suggested to a sensitive person, as Morphy assuredly was, that his aim was accused of being a disreputable one. We know that mental integrity rests essentially on moral integrity, that mental stability can exist only so long as there is guiltlessness. It is impossible that Morphy could have displayed the capacities he did had not his gifts and mental functioning been free to be wholly concentrated on the tasks he set them. But this was so only as long as he could be relieved from any possibility of the counter-forces in his unconscious being stirred. He was at the mercy of anything that might do this. I have pointed out earlier how abnormally sensitive he was to any hint that his aims might not be received in a friendly manner, *i.e.* that they might be treated as if they were unfriendly themselves; to any suggestion that they did not proceed from the purest incentives, and particularly to the possibility of their being tainted by mercenary motives; and to any attitude that betrayed disdain for their juvenile nature.[8] Staunton bitterly wounded him in each of these three respects. His treatment of him was certainly the reverse of friendly—it is hardly an exaggeration to call it scurrilous; he practically accused him of being a penniless adventurer; and he finally avoided him on the plea that he had more serious, *i.e.* grown-up, matters to attend to. In the face of these accusations Morphy's heart failed him, he succumbed and abandoned the wicked path of his chess career. It was as if the father had unmasked his evil intentions and was now adopting a similarly hostile attitude towards him in turn. What had appeared to be an innocent and laudable expression of his personality was now being shown to be actuated by the most childish and ignoble of wishes, the unconscious impulses to commit a sexual assault on the father and at the same time to maim him utterly: in short, to 'mate' him in both the English and the Persian senses of that word. Obedient to his actual father's wishes he now engaged in the grown-up profession of law and discarded what he had been told was the childish preoccupation of chess.[9] But it was too late: his 'sins' pursued him. In the two things that comprise manhood, a serious career among men and the love of women, his chess past dogged and thwarted him. He was never able to escape from the 'sins' of youth and to take his place among the world of men. Little wonder that his abandonment of chess became increasingly complete, until he loathed the very name of it. The only recourse left to him in attempting to deal with his burden of guilt was to project it. In the delusions of being poisoned and robbed we recognize the oral-and-anal-sadistic phantasies projected on to his sister's husband. His homosexual friendliness to men had broken down, and the antagonism underlying it lay exposed. This emerged in the direction of his brother-in-law, evidently a substitute for his brother, while the last anecdote of his life related above shows how he clung to the exaltation and veneration of his father, to whom was reserved the patriarchal privilege of 'making money'.

Perhaps a general conclusion emerges from contemplating this tragic story. It would seem to afford some clue to the well-recognized association between genius and mental instability. It may well be that Morphy's case is a general one. Genius is evidently the capacity to apply unusual gifts with intense, even if only temporary, concentration. I would suggest that this, in its turn, depends on a special capacity for discovering conditions under which the unconscious guilt can be held in complete abeyance. This is doubtless to be connected with the well-known rigour, the sincerity, and the purity of the artistic conscience. It is purchased, however, at the cost of the psychical integrity being at the mercy of any disturbance of these indispensable conditions. And that would appear to be the secret of 'artistic sensitiveness'.

The story also lends itself to a discussion of some important psycho-analytical considerations which I have scarcely time here to adumbrate.

It will have been noticed that, for the sake of simplicity, I have throughout referred to Morphy's gifts as a mark of his capacity for sublimation, and the question may well be asked whether this is a just description of a disguised way of gratifying hostile, *e.g.* parricidal, impulses. In answer I would admit that the impulses behind the play are ultimately of a mixed nature, but the essential process seems to me to be a libidinal one. I conceive that the parricidal impulses were 'bound' by an erotic cathexis, actually a homosexual one, and that this in its turn was sublimated. The enormous value of the process to Morphy's mental health is evident from the considerations adduced above, and this I take to be an example of an important general law, namely, that the process of sublimation has ultimately a defensive function.[10] By discharging id energy along a deflected path, and particularly by transforming a sexualized aggressivity, it protects against the dangers to the ego which we know to proceed from excessive accumulation of that energy.

Finally, it is worth pointing out that when one speaks clinically of the 'breakdown of a sublimation' one really means the cessation of its defensive function. Morphy could play chess as well after as before his mental failure, as may be seen from his occasional games with Maurian; in most such cases, perhaps in all, the actual capacity acquired in the sublimating process remains intact in itself. What is lost is the ability to use this talent as a means of guarding against overwhelming id impulses, and this is really what patients are fearing when they express the anxiety lest 'psycho-analysis will take their sublimations away from them'.[11]

NOTES

[1] Read before the British Psycho-Analytical Society, November 19, 1930. Published in the *International Journal of Psycho-Analysis*, January 1931.

2 As the dates of their birth are not given in any of the biographies, I may use-
fully mention them here: Mahrina, February 5, 1830; Edward, December 26, 1834;
Paul, June 22, 1837; Helena, October 21, 1839.

3 Chess may well be called the art of the intellect.

4 This occurred on November 22, 1856.

5 F. M. Edge, *Exploits and Triumphs of Paul Morphy,* 1859.

6 In the discussion of this essay Dr. Bryan and Miss Searl attached great importance to the effect of this episode on Morphy's mind, and I am inclined to
agree with them; it may even have been the precipitating cause of the psychosis,
as the London experiences certainly were of the neurosis.

7 Against this, I admit, the fact might be brought forward that no less a master
than Saint-Amant had maintained that "Paul Morphy must in future give odds to
every opponent."

8 How beautifully Morphy "moralized" the pastime may be observed in the
following passage from the speech already cited: "It is not only the most delightful
and scientific, but the most moral of amusements. Unlike other games in which
lucre is the end and aim of the contestants, it recommends itself to the wise, by
the fact that its mimic battles are fought for no prize nor honour. It is eminently
and emphatically the philosopher's game. Let the Chess board supersede the card
table and a great improvement will be visible in the morals of the community."

9 To quote again from the speech mentioned above: "Chess never has been and
never can be aught but a recreation. It should not be indulged in to the detriment
of other and more serious avocations—should not absorb or engross the thoughts
of those who worship at its shrine, but should be kept in the background, and
restrained within its proper provinces. As a mere game, a relaxation from the
severe pursuits of life, it is deserving of high commendation."

10 Dr. Glover expressed a similar conclusion in his recent paper before this
Society [British Psycho-Analytical Society]: "Sublimation, Substitution and Social
Anxiety," October, 1930.

11 The original material on which this essay is based can mostly be traced
through the bibliographical references given in the *Encyclopaedia Britannica*
(11th and 14th editions), and P. W. Sergeant's *Morphy's Games of Chess* (1921).
I am greatly indebted to Mr. Sergeant for his courtesy in placing at my disposal
much unpublished material, including the manuscript of another forthcoming book
by him on Paul Morphy. I am also obliged to Paul Morphy's niece, Mrs. Morphy-
Voitier, of New Orleans, for kindly furnishing me with much useful information
about him and the family.

In order to be play, an activity has to be free. Today, much of our play, as indicated in Riesman's article, has taken on the characteristics of compulsion generally found in work. Like work, the compulsive need to play expresses a profound sense of guilt, and as in the story that follows, may lead to a desire for death as the ultimate expiation.

BUDD SCHULBERG

The Dare

Paul Maxwell was staring out across the light-green sea. He was watching a small white outboard plowing up the water some hundred yards off the end of the pier. Skimming along behind in a golden blur was a water-skier. It was one of those things, Paul was thinking, for which you remember a vacation day when you're back in the city grind, the color of the sea sparkling green as champagne, the busy sound of the little outboard motor and its foamy white wake, and behind, the lithe human figure balanced gracefully on water skis that seemed to be flying over the surface of the sea.

Paul rose, and leaned on the railing of the pier to watch the sport. Only then did the yellow-brown halter above the deep-tan midriff inform him of the sex of the skier. Suddenly the outboard skidded to a daring turn and seemed to head directly toward him. It raced forward until he was sure it was too late to turn away. But in a last-moment swing of the stick, the small boat veered to safety by inches. But the girl behind, flying toward the pier—how could *she* possibly veer in time? It didn't seem real that anything so free, so perfect could come to such a brutal ending, but in his mind's panic he was already diving in to grope under water for the broken body. Then, close enough to Paul for him to see the smile on her face—more than a smile, a look of exhilaration—she calmly leaned out from her skis, in the opposite direction from what Paul would have thought logical, and shot away from the pier, streaking around the boat in a sweeping arc before coming back into position behind it again.

841

Twice more the boat and the skier made passes at the pier that seemed to make collision inevitable. But Paul was not to be taken in again and watched in fascination instead of panic as boat and girl dared themselves to see how close to the pier they could come without crashing into it.

"That first time I really thought they had it, General," Paul said to a little hard nut of a Cuban who looked as if he had been put in to bake and left too long. The General, who took care of renting boats and beach equipment, had won his rank in a now-forgotten South American war.

"Oh, that's Gerry Lawford. She's crazy." He said it as if everybody already knew it.

"What kind of crazy?" Paul asked, as he always did about words that had lost their original cutting edge.

"Real crazy," the General said. "Bats in the belfry crazy."

Paul did not have to ask the Cuban to enlarge on this. In these two weeks he had come to know the General.

"Always doing crazy things. Like last year, she tried to sail a dinghy to Cuba all by herself. The Coast Guard had to fish her out of the drink about thirty miles out. That crazy enough for you?"

Paul liked the story. Not being an adventurer himself, he always felt drawn to those who were.

"Who is she? Where'd she come from?"

"Oh, Gerry's been around Key West for years." The General's grin was an amiable slit in the burnt crust of his face. "Calls herself a fugitive from Palm Beach. Her folks have a big home up there. Real rich people, own a perfume business or something. 'Bout ten years ago they had her all set for one of those ritzy Palm Beach weddings. Supposed to marry a Prince Somebody-or-other. He's still around there, married to an automobile heiress. But anyway, the afternoon of the wedding, Gerry showed up down here. Came into this bar where I was working at the time. It's gone now. Just about all the old places are gone. Anyway, this girl Gerry, I'm telling you about. I can still remember what she said. 'Let him marry one of my sisters. They go in for that stuff. And he doesn't care which one it is as long as it comes equipped with a checkbook.'

"Well, the old checkbook wasn't much good to Gerry after she landed here. Old man cut her off without a cent. But it didn't seem to bother Gerry none. She just went on having one hell of a good time."

"But what'd she do? How'd she get by?" Paul was interested in things like this. In the dark hours he always wondered how he'd manage if he suddenly lost his knack for commercial illustrating.

The General considered a moment. "Gerry did—well, she just sort of did things nobody else could get away with. For a while she was a mate on a charter boat. I know that's a hell of a job for a girl, but somehow Gerry talked Red Merritt into it. Then she got on this WPA Artists' Project they had down here when things got so bad the whole town hadda go on relief. She paints real good when she feels like it. Then she came into some money—a trust fund or something the old man couldn't touch. She bought herself a sloop and just sailed around the islands until the money was gone. The kind of person Gerry is, you never have to worry about her and money. Last year she was a crew member in the yacht race to Havana. Her boat won and she stayed over in Havana with the millionaire and his wife who owned it. They staked her to five hundred dollars at the Casino and she came back here last fall with enough dough for the year." The General chuckled. "Even a year for Gerry."

Somebody had come up to rent a rowboat and the General was climbing agilely over the side to pull one toward the landing. While Paul had been listening to the General his eyes had been panning with the outboard and the tanned figure that soared in its wake. Now the boat was idling and Paul watched how the girl handed the skis up over the side and began swimming in toward the pier. She swam, as Paul had already come to expect her to, a capable Australian crawl, and he was fully prepared to believe that she had been a Woman's AAU free-style champion, maybe even an Olympic winner. For even before he had looked into her face, Paul was ready to accept her as one of those special people who perform the most amazing feats without breaking stride and for whom the improbable is merely routine.

He was watching her intently, at the same time trying to disguise the directness of his stare by occasionally glancing past her toward the outboard driver who was easing the boat toward shore. She scampered up the ladder to the pier, swinging herself up over the edge acrobatically. As he watched her lift her arms to shake the water from her shining hair, the image stuck vividly in his mind: the tall, glistening, honey-brown figure with its long, smooth muscular symmetry, and the wet, gleaming face with the surprising Asiatic cast to the eyes.

He studied her movements with a professional appraisal intensified by the challenge a man always feels when he comes unexpectedly into the presence of a woman who attracts him. But, a shy man in his manners, he would have let her go silently if she hadn't looked up from shaking her head clear to grin at him. There was no flirtation in it, he could see, no hint of coyness. It was just the sudden *hello* one person flashes to another when they're on the edge of the sea, when the sun is warming them and they're both caught up in that sense of exquisite well-being of a tropical island's winter day.

"How long have you been doing that?" he heard himself saying.

"The skiing?" Her voice was pitched low, charged with excess energy, and the water was still shining on her face. "I think I was born on those things. At least I can't even remember learning how to do it."

He knew everything she had done—all the crazy things—she had always done. She was one of those naturals.

"You make it look so easy."

"It is, for some people. I've seen others try for a month and never even get up out of the water."

She gave a little laugh that Paul would remember.

The driver of the outboard was climbing up onto the pier now and Paul was just wondering what he could say that would leave things open to further possibilities instead of closing them. But she solved his problem in the most casual way: "If you're on the beach around ten tomorrow, come out and try it." She paused, appraising him. "Are you good at things?"

"Well, what kind of . . . ?"

"Oh, you know, regular skiing, skating, diving," and then she added for fun, "tightrope walking, high trapeze . . ."

"Oh, sure," he replied. "Remember that fellow who crossed Niagara Falls on a high wire. . . ?"

She laughed, and her lips, still moistened with sea water, made him think of the blood-red bougainvillaea after a sudden shower.

"Probably see you tomorrow then," she said, and he watched as she strode down the pier with another man. For that was the way it already seemed to him. Even though an unromantic little voice of reason told him this was just one of those vacation reveries. The other man was young, tall, handsomely made, tanned to a color that comes with years of moving in the sun rather than carefully exposing oneself to it for two or three weeks a year. With that sense of inferiority that city men have when confronted by the masculine great outdoors, Paul had to admit to himself that this bronze Adonis, this sun god, was the perfect match for her. They were the two glorified figures in the cigarette ads, the bathing-suit displays. Good God, he should know them—for ten years he had made his living drawing them!

That evening, for the first time since he had come South, he put on his white linen suit, feeling a little foolish as he fussed with the bow an extra minute to get the ends even and checked the general effect in the full-length mirror of the bathroom door. Then he walked down to the Beach Club dance. His sense of foolishness, of a recapturing of college-prom excitement, increased as he saw the couples swaying slowly together in the open patio while the orchestra played what every orchestra seemed to be playing this season, "Because You're Mine . . ."

Gerry Lawford, who came skimming out of the sun and across the sparkling sea, did she really exist? Paul wondered. Or was she merely a city bachelor's sun-struck dream? And even if he were to find her here, what good would it do him if she were dancing in the arms of the sun god?

Then he saw her, all yellow gold, her hair swept up into a crown of jet topped by a single flaming hibiscus. Paul watched as the tired strains of a worn-out hit tune were finally abandoned for a samba. With her cigarette-ad partner, Gerry danced it as a professional would have, or, perhaps better, as an inspired amateur, with a wild enthusiasm that made all the other dancers on the floor appear to be not so much dancing as pushing each other around.

Paul wondered what it would feel like to dance with her, and whether cutting in was a breach of Club etiquette, and while he wondered the music stopped and Gerry and her cigarette ad were on their way from the patio to the parking lot. Paul had no idea how nakedly his eyes must have been following them until the General, now doubling as a buffet waiter, mumbled to him. "That's the way she always is—comes in for one dance, maybe two, then she's off again, always on the move."

"Think they'll be back, General?"

The General chuckled. Gerry and her restless ways obviously served him as entertainment. "A crazy one like that, who knows? Right now she's probably on her way to the casino at the Casa Marina. Win a thousand, lose a thousand, who knows where she'll wind up tonight? Maybe flying to Cuba. Maybe trolling around the Keys with a kicker."

The General was amused. But Paul, with nothing to go on but a romantic imagination that was working overtime, knew he had to go on to the casino.

He walked around the tables until he found her at the craps layout. There were only a few people playing, so it was easy to edge in behind her. "Hi," she said when she saw him, as if it were perfectly natural that he should be there, "bet with me. I'm hot."

She had the dice and her point rolled ten. The odds were with the house, but she bet a hundred on herself and made the point on her third roll. Paul had backed her for five. She made three more passes, dragging all her winnings until she had run a hundred up to almost three thousand. Betting with her each time, but conservatively, Paul was around fifty ahead. The reckless way she played seemed to mock his conservatism and he felt suddenly depressed, as if this was a surer sign than any he had had before that this was a will o' the wisp.

She was still running the game, the dice doing everything she asked of them, when she suddenly lost interest. "I'm going to cash these in. Let's play roulette."

At the roulette table Paul watched with an amazement lined with admiration as she plunged on hunches, betting the limit on single numbers, all or nothing, 35-1, while he was putting five on red or black or settling for the short odds on groups of numbers. The wheel wasn't rolling for her and in less than ten minutes she had managed to throw away the big win she had taken from the other table. It hadn't been money at all, just little colored chips to fling across a board.

"That's tough luck," Paul said. "You should have quit when you were out there in front."

"Oh, what difference does it make?" Gerry said. "I'd just as soon lose it as win it."

That was beyond him, that kind of recklessness, that kind of wildness. Maybe that's why it attracted him so strongly. "Time for a drink," she said, and she led him into the bar, full of laughter, full of hell, full of something Paul had never had to cope with before and he remembered the General's answer, "What kind of crazy—bats in the belfry crazy." Well, what kind was that? It came in all sizes, from you and me to the straitjacket and the chair.

She drank the way he had seen her do all these other things, doubles, fast, ready to go further than anybody else, closer to the pier. And then, as abruptly as she had lost interest in the dance, the dice, she said, "Oh, the hell with this drinking. Who wants to go swimming?"

The cigarette ad, who had been at the bar when they reached it, said, "Oh, God, that again? I gave up moonlight swimming about the time I had my first hangover. Once a season holds me fine."

Paul was wondering if he could make his voice sound casual enough when he said it. "I'll go swimming with you."

"Swell. Are you a good swimmer?"

"Oh, good enough to paddle around."

"I feel like swimming tonight. I think I could swim to Cuba tonight."

Remembering the General's joke about Gerry and her impulsive night flights, Paul wondered about that last one. He wondered too if her escort was objecting to this improvised shift in the evening's pairing. Paul even started to mutter something about it, but the sun god was ahead of him. "Good God, I'm glad she's found a sucker she can entice into those inky waters. Otherwise I might have had to go myself."

Paul and Gerry sat on the end of the Club pier. The water was black and uninviting as it sloshed up under the pilings. It should have been moonlight, Paul was thinking.

"I never win long shots," he was saying. "And this afternoon, when I first saw you out there, it was an easy hundred to one against our ending up alone together like this."

"I like people who are ready to do things without planning them ahead," she said.

"Isn't Bob the ready kind?" he asked, meaning the sun god left standing on his clay feet at the hotel bar.

"Oh, Bob . . ." The way his name trailed off told practically everything. "Bob is something like me. Only he isn't quite up to me. So he bores me. And anyway, I like people who do something. All Bob did was inherit money. He . . ." Then she swung the rudder on the conversation. "What're we talking about Bob for? Bob's always around to talk about. How about you? You aren't just a rich kid. I know you do something."

"Eleven months a year I'm a commercial artist. A pretty good one. The other month, I go away somewhere, Tehuantepec last year, Key West this time, and try to paint for myself. A sailor rowing in Central Park. Awful one-sided compromise."

"But better than nothing," she said, and they talked a little about painting, nothing too flossy, about actual techniques, and the local problems with light and dampness, and the things she said were more businesslike and practical than he would have expected.

"You must have been painting a long time," he said. That WPA thing was a long way back now.

"I don't really paint," she said. And then after a moment of silence, "I don't do anything."

"But I thought you didn't like people who don't do anything?" Paul said. He had meant it for banter.

"Maybe I don't like myself."

Then, abruptly finished with the conversation, she said, "The hell with it. Let's swim."

He saw her poise for a moment on the edge and then arch and knife cleanly into the dark water. He plunged in after her, expecting to tread water and splash around in the dark. But she was already moving off from the pier, her head bent low into the choppy sea as she executed her rapid crawl. Paul, an average swimmer, had to exert himself to keep up with her. Before they were fifty strokes out from the pier, this swim had taken on a disconcerting quality. When they passed the first marker a hundred yards beyond the landing Paul knew this was no hilarious midnight escapade. There was an intensity about this swim out toward a dark, far horizon that made Paul realize he had gone beyond his depth into waters measured in other ways than merely in fathoms.

The sea water poured down his throat when he gasped for breath and his body ached to turn back. But he feared doing this might lose everything he had gained this evening, this strange, wonderful girl, this water-gypsy who had risen for him out of the sea. Yet there was a limit to his endurance and he was beginning, for the first time in his life, to reach the edges of it. His stomach tightened with the panicky feeling that his next stroke would double him up in a cramp of exhaustion. Alone with all the salt water, he was going to have to swallow his pride and turn back, slowly work his way into shore. Just then Gerry's face bobbed up close to his.

"Hello," she said. She looked fresh and impish, and the sight of her so close to him revived him a little.

"I'm hungry," she announced. "Let's go back."

His stomach felt too full of ocean water for an appetite, but when he finally managed to get back to the pier and climbed up beside Gerry he was suddenly exhilarated. Of course he was hungry. He was starved. He had kept up with Gerry Lawford, crazy Gerry Lawford, and he was ready for anything.

They went skipping down Duval Street, actually skipping like a couple of crazy kids, and when they reached the all-night Cuban place, they both had two helpings of black beans and yellow rice, washed down with beer Gerry drank from the bottle. "An oral regression to infancy," she called it, and they both laughed. They were laughing at things that were funny only to them and Paul felt sorry for anyone who didn't have a Gerry Lawford in his life. The years before Gerry fell away to a flat, arid desert of monotony.

He walked her back to her hotel, the Southernmost House, it was called, an intriguing Victorian mansion of towers and great porches that dominated the point where the Atlantic met the Gulf. He stopped in for a nightcap at the old oak bar that looked out on the sea, and when they paused for a moment on the great balcony and listened to the waves, the night and what they had made of it suddenly gave him the courage, and he kissed her, feeling the recklessness, the restlessness passing from her lips to his. Then, with her kind of suddenness, she broke away.

"Let's go conching in the morning. Call for me early—say between eight and nine. I'll show you how the real conchs do it."

Her door closed him off from her so suddenly that he was left with the effect of her having vanished from his side in some metaphysical way. He could almost have believed this hadn't happened at all and that their evening had been simply an extension of his daydream. He walked back slowly to his hotel with his mind still flooded with the vision of that afternoon's golden sweep across the sunlit sea.

Every morning since he had come to Key West, Paul had slept late, counting that one of his chief vacation pleasures. But this next morning he was up in time to see the clouds opening up for the early sun to pour through. Even the pelicans were still asleep, drifting idly in small groups, rocking gently with the tide. Paul pulled on some ducks and a sport shirt and went down to the beach. Suddenly, as if by signal, all the pelicans rose together and went flapping out to sea on some urgent pelican business. Paul realized this was the first day since he had come to Key West that he was really alive. He thought about Gerry, and, for the first time, about her always being with him. The only trouble was, he couldn't quite see her in his tailored New York apartment. It was a little like bringing home to captivity some wild bird whose home is the open sea. He was in love with her, though, in a way he had not imagined a man of his temperament could be.

He walked down the beach to the Southernmost and when he didn't find her on the downstairs porch, he went up and knocked on her door.

"Come on in, Paul," she called, and he entered to find her in white ducks with the legs rolled up to her knees, and an old sweatshirt. But somehow these had the effect of heightening rather than smothering her beauty. She was squatting on the floor finishing a hurried water color. Strangely, it was the scene Paul had been watching from the beach, the pelicans rising in formation from the rose water of the morning sea. It was done in swift, fluid strokes, and the rose color was redder, stronger than it had been. The peace and tranquillity of the scene that had impressed Paul on the beach was translated into disturbing colors and broken lines. Thumbtacked on the walls were half a dozen other seascapes, all blurs and sudden strokes of color, suggesting rather than representing, all catching some of the recklessness and vitality that Gerry brought to everything she did.

"These are all yours?" It wasn't really a question, merely an opener.

"Just splashing around."

"But they're damn good."

"My God, Paul, I was only playing. Don't look so serious."

"But they're—they're big league. You should do something with them."

"I will, darling. I'll give them to you."

She jumped up, and with a little mock curtsey handed Paul the one she had just finished. "To remember me by." She laughed.

He took the picture, beginning to say something serious, trying to make it sound not too pompous, but she cut him off. "Hell with it. Let's go conching."

They walked down the street to the Negro "beach," a narrow, rocky promontory where the rowboats were pulled up. They carried the one they were going to use out over the rocks and pushed off. She showed him how to pole it, and then, when they were out a little way, she said, "Let's see if we can catch ourselves some crawfish first." He held the boat for her while she poised the long three-pronged spear over the surface and peered down through the single fathom of light-green water to the edge of the shoal at the bottom. Suddenly the spear shot into the water and when she pulled it up the prongs were fastened to a small speckled brown lobster. Paul tried it after that but even after he spied one on the bottom, the deceptive angle of the spear beneath the surface made him overshoot the target. It was much harder than it looked.

She tried it again, and when she brought up a larger one, lost interest in the spear.

"Conching's more fun," Gerry said. "I'll show you how we dive for them." Fixing a large circular glass to her eyes, she dived nimbly over the side. Paul was fascinated to watch her glide down through the twinkling green water to the rocks below. Watching her move along the bottom with slow-motion grace, he was reminded again of his earlier vision of her as a mermaid called up from the depths by his imagination.

But just then she popped up through the surface, crying, "Eureka!" triumphantly holding up a good-sized Queen conch.

She slithered over into the boat and handed Paul the goggles. "I know what let's do. Let's see who can stay down the longest." She said it as a child might, as a spur-of-the-moment dare. But Paul, remembering last night's swim, feared it might develop into more of an ordeal.

"But we haven't got a watch, Gerry."

"Oh, we can count, one-and-two-and . . ." She gave him the beat. "Oh, come on. It's beautiful down there. It's fun to stay down."

Paul adjusted the goggles, inhaled until his temples began to pound, and dived. As Gerry had promised, he found himself enveloped in a shimmering green world more beautiful than he had imagined. He gripped a rock at the bottom to hold himself from rising and groped along, pleased with his unfolding ability to measure up to Gerry's adventures. He wondered how much time had passed. He had begun keeping track but a large octopus that turned out to be a massive undersea growth had frightened him off his count. Water was slowly seeping in under the rubber rims of the goggles and his eyes were beginning to smart. Then his ears were aching and he had a sense of being squeezed within green walls that were pressing down and in and up at him. He thought he saw a conch a few feet ahead of him, but that was too far now. His lungs were ready to explode. Why, a man could die, die down here to prove something. But what? What did it mean to Gerry? He was shooting up toward the surface now, flailing his arms with mounting frenzy as he wondered if he could make it in time.

Then his head was above water at last and he was breathing, breathing, that first and last of luxuries.

"Ninety-three," Gerry called. "Paul, I'm proud of you." The praise, the smile, the warm camaraderie completely erased his choking panic of a moment before.

"Now count for me . . ." She could hardly wait to get the goggles on and be over the side again. She was gone in a swift little dive that hardly disturbed the calm surface.

Fifty . . . He could see her gliding leisurely along the bottom. Seventy-five . . . ninety . . . Soon she had passed his record and he waited for her to pop to the surface, chortling over her triumph. But she was staying down. One hundred . . . one hundred-and-twenty-five . . . He peered down anxiously. She wasn't moving any longer. Just seemed to be sitting there—the mermaid again—at home on the bottom of the sea. One hundred-and-fifty . . . sixty . . . seventy-five . . . And this count slower than seconds—that was three minutes! The pulse of panic began to thump in his throat. No one could stay down that long . . . Suddenly he remembered those nightmare stories of giant shellfish that clamp down on a swimmer's hands . . . Somewhere he had read how a Marine had been lost that way in the South Pacific . . .

In this same moment he dived, reached her, groped for her and they shot up to the surface together.

"Gerry—Gerry—are you all right?"

"Of course." She laughed. "I was just getting ready to come up. How high did you count?"

"One hundred-and-seventy-five."

"Dare me to stay down for two hundred?"

"Frankly," Paul said, "I've had enough diving for one morning. You won't be satisfied till the Coast Guard drags the bottom for you."

"Okay," she said, completely unconcerned. "Do you like conch? The couple who run the Southernmost are friends of mine. We can take these right in their kitchen and start working on them. I lived on these things one season down here when you could've turned me upsidedown and shaken me and never found a nickel."

That day Paul felt as if he were gliding through life on skis the way Gerry had skimmed the surface of the sea. The lunch on the sun porch of the Southernmost, the walk through town to the fishing docks; the long talk on the beach; the cocktails at sunset, the fun of drinking together and the marvelous sense of growing intimacy; and finally the moonlight dance in the patio and Gerry Lawford, this crazy, unpredictable, magical girl, in his arms at last. His lips were against her golden cheeks and even the smell of her was of some fresh wild berry that one finds on the hills. Later tonight, or perhaps tomorrow, he would ask her. He was already trying it, phrasing it, like a stage bit player with one line to perfect: Gerry, you said you never turn down a dare. So, I dare you to marry me.

The song was still "Because You're Mine," only this time Paul was much more tolerant of its sentimentality. Her lips were brushing his ear—his skin tingled with the pleasure of it—she was going to kiss him. Only instead, she was whispering, "Darling, feel like going swimming? Let's go swimming again."

"Gerry," he said. "I'm still water-logged. Why don't we skip it tonight?"

"I want to go swimming," she said. "At night I love to go swimming."

"Baby, I—I just can't tonight. I love you. I'm lost in you. I want to marry you. But if we start swimming out tonight, you know what'll happen, you'll dare me to see which one of us can swim out the farthest. I'll bust a gut trying to keep up with you and . . ."

"All right, don't swim with me. I'll swim alone. I like to swim alone."
She was glaring at him and the wildness was a new kind, and he thought
he knew for the first time what the General meant.

"Gerry, why get so angry? Tonight let's just dance and have some
drinks. Maybe tomorrow night we can swim."

"I don't want you to swim with me," she said. "I'm going swimming
alone. I'm going now."

For a moment Paul considered following her. But then he thought,
she's high-strung, she can't stay up at that pitch all the time without
having these moods. I'll let her work her way out of it and send her
flowers in the morning. By lunch time she'll be thinking up some new
crazy stunt and daring me to follow.

The next morning Paul reverted and slept late. When he went downstairs to breakfast, everyone was talking about it. The Coast Guard was
still searching for the body, he heard people say. But she was such a
wonderful swimmer, he heard people say. She was always such a happy-
go-lucky, such a high-spirited girl, it doesn't seem possible she'd do a
thing like that, he heard people say.

He walked slowly out to the edge of the point and looked across the
sea. The sun was high and the waters were smooth. He had no idea how
long he had stood there, or when the truth first flashed for him, but when
it did he was sure he had known it from that first moment of fear and
wonder when she had seemed bent on crashing into the pier. It was so
simple now. Gerry's courage had been fool's gold, not really courage
at all. Only the wish to die. When he cupped his hands to light a
cigarette he saw how they were trembling. He stood a long time that
morning at the sea wall.

By the time the sun was lowering toward the horizon, the first shock
was easing off into a kind of numb submission, a sense of inevitability,
of having entered for a few stolen moments into a shadow-world. For he
was no longer sure whether Gerry Lawford and their first day, their
second, and their last, had really happened. Or whether a mermaid, a
water-gypsy, turned mortal for a day, had merely swum home to the
green depths out of which she had come.

"Our Lady's Juggler" is a story about work and play disguised with religious symbols. It suggests the connection between work, play, and the sexual and aggressive drives. The equation of play with erotic fantasies is made quite clear in the reaction of the monks to the juggler's performance before the Virgin. While they work to please her without success, he plays, and achieves the fulfillment of his and their unconscious desire to possess the mother.

ANATOLE FRANCE

Our Lady's Juggler

1

In the days of King Louis there was a poor juggler in France, a native of Compiègne, Barnaby by name, who went about from town to town performing feats of skill and strength.

On fair days he would unfold an old worn-out carpet in the public square, and when by means of a jovial address, which he had learned of a very ancient juggler, and which he never varied in the least, he had drawn together the children and loafers, he assumed extraordinary attitudes, and balanced a tin plate on the tip of his nose. At first the crowd would feign indifference.

But when, supporting himself on his hands face downwards, he threw into the air six copper balls, which glittered in the sunshine, and caught them again with his feet; or when throwing himself backwards until his heels and the nape of the neck met, giving his body the form of a perfect wheel, he would juggle in this posture with a dozen knives, a murmur of admiration would escape the spectators, and pieces of money rain down upon the carpet. Nevertheless, like the majority of those who live by their wits, Barnaby of Compiègne had a great struggle to make a living.

Earning his bread in the sweat of his brow, he bore rather more than his share of the penalties consequent upon the misdoings of our father Adam.

Again, he was unable to work as constantly as he would have been willing to do. The warmth of the sun and the broad daylight were as necessary to enable him to display his brilliant parts as to the trees if flower and fruit should be expected of them. In winter time he was nothing more than a tree stripped of its leaves, and as it were dead. The frozen ground was hard to the juggler, and, like the grasshopper of which Marie de France tells us, the inclement season caused him to suffer both cold and hunger. But as he was simple-natured he bore his ills patiently.

He had never meditated on the origin of wealth, nor upon the inequality of human conditions. He believed firmly that if this life should prove hard, the life to come could not fail to redress the balance, and this hope upheld him. He did not resemble those thievish and miscreant Merry Andrews who sell their souls to the devil. He never blasphemed God's name; he lived uprightly, and although he had no wife of his own, he did not covet his neighbour's, since woman is ever the enemy of the strong man, as it appears by the history of Samson recorded in the Scriptures.

In truth, his was not a nature much disposed to carnal delights, and it was a greater deprivation to him to forsake the tankard than the Hebe who bore it. For whilst not wanting in sobriety, he was fond of a drink when the weather waxed hot. He was a worthy man who feared God, and was very devoted to the Blessed Virgin.

Never did he fail on entering a church to fall upon his knees before the image of the Mother of God, and offer up this prayer to her:

"Blessed Lady, keep watch over my life until it shall please God that I die, and when I am dead, ensure to me the possession of the joys of paradise."

2

Now on a certain evening after a dreary wet day, as Barnaby pursued his road, sad and bent, carrying under his arm his balls and knives wrapped up in his old carpet, on the watch for some barn where, though he might not sup, he might sleep, he perceived on the road, going in the same direction as himself, a monk, whom he saluted courteously. And as they walked at the same rate they fell into conversation with one another.

"Fellow traveller," said the monk, "how comes it about that you are clothed all in green? It is perhaps in order to take the part of a jester in some mystery play?"

"Not at all, good father," replied Barnaby. "Such as you see me, I am called Barnaby, and for my calling I am a juggler. There would be no pleasanter calling in the world if it would always provide one with daily bread."

"Friend Barnaby," returned the monk, "be careful what you say. There is no calling more pleasant than the monastic life. Those who lead it are occupied with the praises of God, the Blessed Virgin, and the saints; and, indeed, the religious life is one ceaseless hymn to the Lord."

Barnaby replied—

"Good father, I own that I spoke like an ignorant man. Your calling cannot be in any respect compared to mine, and although there may be some merit in dancing with a penny balanced on a stick on the tip of one's nose, it is not a merit which comes within hail of your own. Gladly would I, like you, good father, sing my office day by day, and especially, the office of the most Holy Virgin, to whom I have vowed a singular devotion. In order to embrace the monastic life I would willingly abandon the art by which from Soissons to Beauvais I am well known in upwards of six hundred towns and villages."

The monk was touched by the juggler's simplicity, and as he was not lacking in discernment, he at once recognized in Barnaby one of those men of whom it is said in the Scriptures: Peace on earth to men of good will. And for this reason he replied—

"Friend Barnaby, come with me, and I will have you admitted into the monastery of which I am Prior. He who guided St. Mary of Egypt in the desert set me upon your path to lead you into the way of salvation."

It was in this manner, then, that Barnaby became a monk. In the monastery into which he was received the religious vied with one another in the worship of the Blessed Virgin, and in her honour each employed all the knowledge and all the skill which God had given him.

The prior on his part wrote books dealing according to the rules of scholarship with the virtues of the Mother of God.

Brother Maurice, with a deft hand copied out these treatises upon sheets of vellum.

Brother Alexander adorned the leaves with delicate miniature paintings. Here were displayed the Queen of Heaven seated upon Solomon's throne, and while four lions were on guard at her feet, around the nimbus which encricled her head hovered seven doves, which are the seven gifts of the Holy Spirit, the gifts, namely, of Fear, Piety, Knowledge, Strength, Counsel, Understanding, and Wisdom. For her companions she had six virgins with hair of gold, namely, Humility, Prudence, Seclusion, Submission, Virginity, and Obedience.

At her feet were two little naked figures, perfectly white, in an attitude of supplication. These were souls imploring her all-powerful intercession for their soul's health, and we may be sure not imploring in vain.

Upon another page facing this, Brother Alexander represented Eve, so that the Fall and the Redemption could be perceived at one and the same time—Eve the Wife abased, and Mary the Virgin exalted.

Furthermore, to the marvel of the beholder, this book contained presentments of the Well of Living Waters, the Fountain, the Lily, the Moon, the Sun, and the Garden enclosed of which the Song of Songs tells us, the Gate of Heaven and the City of God, and all these things were symbols of the Blessed Virgin.

Brother Marbode was likewise one of the most loving children of Mary.

He spent all his days carving images in stone, so that his beard, his eyebrows, and his hair were white with dust, and his eyes continually swollen and weeping; but his strength and cheerfulness were not diminished, although he was now well gone in years, and it was clear that the Queen of Paradise still cherished her servant in his old age. Marbode represented her seated upon a throne, her brow encircled with an orb-shaped nimbus set with pearls. And he took care that the folds of her dress should cover the feet of her, concerning whom the prophet declared: My beloved is as a garden enclosed.

Sometimes, too, he depicted her in the semblance of a child full of grace, and appearing to say, "Thou art my God, even from my mother's womb."

In the priory, moreover, were poets who composed hymns in Latin, both in prose and verse, in honour of the Blessed Virgin Mary, and amongst the company was even a brother from Picardy who sang the miracles of Our Lady in rhymed verse and in the vulgar tongue.

3

Being a witness of this emulation in praise and the glorious harvest of their labours, Barnaby mourned his own ignorance and simplicity.

"Alas!" he sighed, as he took his solitary walk in the little shelterless garden of the monastery, "wretched wight that I am, to be unable, like my brothers, worthily to praise the Holy Mother of God, to whom I have vowed my whole heart's affection. Alas! alas! I am but a rough man and unskilled in the arts, and I can render you in service, blessed Lady, neither edifying sermons, nor treatises set out in order according to rule, nor ingenious paintings, nor statues truthfully sculptured, nor verses whose march is measured to the beat of feet. No gift have I, alas!"

After this fashion he groaned and gave himself up to sorrow. But one evening, when the monks were spending their hour of liberty in conversation, he heard one of them tell the tale of a religious man who could repeat nothing other than the Ave Maria. This poor man was despised for his ignorance; but after his death, there issued forth from his mouth five roses in honour of the five letters of the name Mary (Marie), and thus his sanctity was made manifest.

Whilst he listened to this narrative Barnaby marvelled yet once again at the loving kindness of the Virgin; but the lesson of that blessed death did not avail to console him, for his heart overflowed with zeal, and he longed to advance the glory of his Lady, who is in heaven.

How to compass this he sought but could find no way, and day by day he became the more cast down, when one morning he awakened filled full with joy, hastened to the chapel, and remained there alone for more than an hour. After dinner he returned to the chapel once more.

And, starting from that moment, he repaired daily to the chapel at such hours as it was deserted, and spent within it a good part of the time which the other monks devoted to the liberal and mechanical arts. His sadness vanished, nor did he any longer groan.

A demeanour so strange awakened the curiosity of the monks.

These began to ask one another for what purpose Brother Barnaby could be indulging so persistently in retreat.

The prior, whose duty it is to let nothing escape him in the behaviour of his children in religion, resolved to keep a watch over Barnaby during his withdrawals to the chapel. One day, then, when he was shut up there after his custom, the prior, accompanied by two of the older monks, went to discover through the chinks in the door what was going on within the chapel.

They saw Barnaby before the altar of the Blessed Virgin, head downwards, with his feet in the air, and he was juggling with six balls of copper and a dozen knives. In honour of the Holy Mother of God he was performing those feats, which aforetime had won him most renown. Not recognizing that the simple fellow was thus placing at the service of the Blessed Virgin his knowledge and skill, the two old monks exclaimed against the sacrilege.

The prior was aware how stainless was Barnaby's soul, but he concluded that he had been seized with madness. They were all three preparing to lead him swiftly from the chapel, when they saw the Blessed Virgin descend the steps of the altar and advance to wipe away with a fold of her azure robe the sweat which was dropping from her juggler's forehead.

Then the prior, falling upon his face upon the pavement, uttered these words—

"Blessed are the simple-hearted, for they shall see God."

"Amen!" responded the old brethren, and kissed the ground.

Like "Our Lady's Juggler," this, too, is a story about a man whose work seems to be play. Hawthorne's equation of creativity with play recalls the ability of the artist to regress and return. But Hawthorne is also aware of the relation between guilt and work, and the function of work in displacing aggression. He has personified work in the figure of an obviously aggressive blacksmith. His suggestion that the rhythmic process of creation is what gives pleasure thinly disguises a sexual theme.

NATHANIEL HAWTHORNE

The Artist of the Beautiful

An elderly man, with his pretty daughter on his arm, was passing along the street, and emerged from the gloom of the cloudy evening into the light that fell across the pavement from the window of a small shop. It was a projecting window; and on the inside were suspended a variety of watches, pinchbeck, silver, and one or two of gold, all with their faces turned from the streets, as if churlishly disinclined to inform the wayfarers what o'clock it was. Seated within the shop, sidelong to the window, with his pale face bent earnestly over some delicate piece of mechanism on which was thrown the concentrated lustre of a shade lamp, appeared a young man.

"What can Owen Warland be about?" muttered old Peter Hovenden, himself a retired watchmaker, and the former master of this same young man whose occupation he was now wondering at. "What can the fellow be about? These six months past I have never come by his shop without seeing him just as steadily at work as now. It would be a flight beyond his usual foolery to seek for the perpetual motion; and yet I know enough of my old business to be certain that what he is now so busy with is no part of the machinery of a watch."

"Perhaps, father," said Annie, without showing much interest in the question, "Owen is inventing a new kind of timekeeper. I am sure he has ingenuity enough."

"Poh, child! He has not the sort of ingenuity to invent anything better than a Dutch toy," answered her father, who had formerly been put to much vexation by Owen Warland's irregular genius. "A plague on such ingenuity! All the effect that ever I knew of it was to spoil the accuracy of some of the best watches in my shop. He would turn the sun out of its orbit and derange the whole course of time, if, as I said before, his ingenuity could grasp anything bigger than a child's toy!"

"Hush, father! He hears you!" whispered Annie, pressing the old man's arm. "His ears are as delicate as his feelings; and you know how easily disturbed they are. Do let us move on."

So Peter Hovenden and his daughter Annie plodded on without further conversation, until in a by-street of the town they found themselves passing the open door of a blacksmith's shop. Within was seen the forge, now blazing up and illuminating the high and dusky roof, and now confining its lustre to a narrow precinct of the coal-strewn floor, according as the breath of the bellows was puffed forth or again inhaled into its vast leathern lungs. In the intervals of brightness it was easy to distinguish objects in remote corners of the shop and the horseshoes that hung upon the wall; in the momentary gloom the fire seemed to be glimmering amidst the vagueness of unenclosed space. Moving about in this red glare and alternate dusk was the figure of the blacksmith, well worthy to be viewed in so picturesque an aspect of light and shade, where the bright blaze struggled with the black night, as if each would have snatched his comely strength from the other. Anon he drew a white-hot bar of iron from the coals, laid it on the anvil, uplifted his arm of might, and was soon enveloped in the myriads of sparks which the strokes of his hammer scattered into the surrounding gloom.

"Now, that is a pleasant sight," said the old watchmaker. "I know what it is to work in gold; but give me the worker in iron after all is said and done. He spends his labor upon a reality. What say you, daughter Annie?"

"Pray don't speak so loud, father," whispered Annie, "Robert Danforth will hear you."

"And what if he should hear me?" said Peter Hovenden. "I say again, it is a good and a wholesome thing to depend upon main strength and reality, and to earn one's bread with the bare and brawny arm of a blacksmith. A watchmaker gets his brain puzzled by his wheels within a wheel, or loses his health or the nicety of his eyesight, as was my case, and finds himself at middle age, or a little after, past labor at his own trade and fit for nothing else, yet too poor to live at his ease. So I say once again, give me main strength for my money. And then, how it takes the nonsense out of a man! Did you ever hear of a blacksmith being such a fool as Owen Warland yonder?"

"Well said, Uncle Hovenden!" shouted Robert Danforth from the forge, in a full, deep, merry voice, that made the roof reëcho. "And what says Miss Annie to that doctrine? She, I suppose, will think it a genteeler business to tinker up a lady's watch than to forge a horseshoe or make a gridiron."

Annie drew her father onward without giving him time for reply.

But we must return to Owen Warland's shop, and spend more meditation upon his history and character than either Peter Hovenden, or probably his daughter Annie, or Owen's old schoolfellow, Robert Danforth, would have thought due to so slight a subject. From the time that his little fingers could grasp a penknife, Owen had been remarkable for a delicate ingenuity, which sometimes produced pretty shapes in wood, principally figures of flowers and birds, and sometimes seemed to aim at the hidden mysteries of mechanism. But it was always for purposes of grace, and never with any mockery of the useful. He did not, like the crowd of school-boy artisans, construct little windmills on the angle of a barn or watermills across the neighboring brook. Those who discovered such peculiarity in the boy as to think it worth their while to observe him closely, sometimes saw reason to suppose that he was attempting to imitate the beautiful movements of Nature as exemplified in the flight of birds or the activity of little animals. It seemed, in fact, a new development of the love of the beautiful, such as might have made him a poet, a painter, or a sculptor, and which was as completely refined from all utilitarian coarseness as it could have been in either of the fine arts. He looked with singular distaste at the stiff and regular processes of ordinary machinery. Being once carried to see a steam-engine, in the expectation that his intuitive comprehension of mechanical principles would be gratified, he turned pale and grew sick, as if something monstrous and unnatural had been presented to him. This horror was partly owing to the size and terrible energy of the iron laborer; for the character of Owen's mind was microscopic, and tended naturally to the minute, in accordance with his diminutive frame and the marvellous smallness and delicate power of his fingers. Not that his sense of beauty was thereby diminished into a sense of prettiness. The beautiful idea has no relation to size, and may be as perfectly developed in a space too minute for any but microscopic investigation as within the ample verge that is measured by the arc of the rainbow. But, at all events, this characteristic minuteness in his objects and accomplishments made the world even more incapable than it might otherwise have been of appreciating Owen Warland's genius. The boy's relatives saw nothing better to be done—as perhaps there was not—than to bind him apprentice to a watchmaker, hoping that his strange ingenuity might thus be regulated and put to utilitarian purposes.

Peter Hovenden's opinion of his apprentice has already been expressed. He could make nothing of the lad. Owen's apprehension of the professional mysteries, it is true, was inconceivably quick; but he altogether forgot or despised the grand object of a watchmaker's business, and cared no more for the measurement of time than if it had been merged into eternity. So long, however, as he remained under his old master's care, Owen's lack of sturdiness made it possible, by strict injunctions and sharp oversight, to restrain his creative eccentricity within bounds; but when his apprenticeship was served out, and he had taken the little shop which Peter Hovenden's failing eyesight compelled him to relinquish, then did people recognize how unfit a person was Owen Warland to lead old blind Father Time along his daily course. One of his most rational projects was to connect a musical operation with the machinery of his watches, so that all the harsh dissonances of life might be rendered tuneful, and each flitting movement fall into the abyss of the past in golden drops of harmony. If a family clock was intrusted to him for repair,—one of those tall, ancient clocks that have grown nearly allied to human nature by measuring out the lifetime of many generations—he would take upon himself to arrange a dance or funeral procession of figures across its venerable face, representing twelve mirthful or melancholy hours. Several freaks of this kind quite destroyed the young watchmaker's credit with that steady and matter-of-fact class of people who hold opinion that time is not to be trifled with, whether considered as the medium of advancement and prosperity in this world or preparation for the next. His custom rapidly diminished—a misfortune, however, that was probably reckoned among his better accidents by Owen Warland, who was becoming more and more absorbed in a secret occupation which drew all his science and manual dexterity into itself, and likewise gave full employment to the characteristic tendencies of his genius. This pursuit had already consumed many months.

After the old watchmaker and his pretty daughter had gazed at him out of the obscurity of the street, Owen Warland was seized with a fluttering of the nerves, which made his hand tremble too violently to proceed with such delicate labor as he was now engaged upon.

"It was Annie herself!" murmured he. "I should have known it, by this throbbing in my heart, before I heard her father's voice. Ah, how it throbs! I shall scarcely be able to work again on this exquisite mechanism to-night. Annie! dearest Annie! thou shouldst give firmness to my heart and hand, and not shake them thus; for if I strive to put the very spirit of beauty into form and give it motion, it is for thy sake alone. O throbbing heart, be quiet! If my labor be thus thwarted, there will come vague and unsatisfied dreams which will leave me spiritless to-morrow."

As he was endeavoring to settle himself again to his task, the shop door opened and gave admittance to no other than the stalwart figure which Peter Hovenden had paused to admire, as seen amid the light and shadow of the blacksmith's shop. Robert Danforth had brought a little anvil of his own manufacture, and peculiarly constructed, which the young artist had recently bespoken. Owen examined the article and pronounced it fashioned according to his wish.

"Why, yes," said Robert Danforth, his strong voice filling the shop as with the sound of a bass viol, "I consider myself equal to anything in the way of my own trade; though I should have made but a poor figure at yours with such a fist as this," added he, laughing, as he laid his vast hand beside the delicate one of Owen. "But what then? I put more main strength into one blow of my sledge hammer than all that you have expended since you were a 'prentice. Is not that the truth?"

"Very probably," answered the low and slender voice of Owen. "Strength is an earthly monster. I make no pretensions to it. My force, whatever there may be of it, is altogether spiritual."

"Well, but, Owen, what are you about?" asked his old schoolfellow, still in such a hearty volume of tone that it made the artist shrink, especially as the question related to a subject so sacred as the absorbing dream of his imagination. "Folks do say that you are trying to discover the perpetual motion."

"The perpetual motion? Nonsense!" replied Owen Warland, with a movement of disgust; for he was full of little petulances. "It can never be discovered. It is a dream that may delude men whose brains are mystified with matter, but not me. Besides, if such a discovery were possible, it would not be worth my while to make it only to have the secret turned to such purposes as are now effected by steam and water power. I am not ambitious to be honored with the paternity of a new kind of cotton machine."

"That would be droll enough!" cried the blacksmith, breaking out into such an uproar of laughter that Owen himself and the bell glasses on his workboard quivered in unison. "No, no, Owen! No child of yours will have iron joints and sinews. Well, I won't hinder you any more. Good night, Owen, and success, and if you need any assistance, so far as a downright blow of hammer upon anvil will answer the purpose, I'm your man."

And with another laugh the man of main strength left the shop.

"How strange it is," whispered Owen Warland to himself, leaning his head upon his hand, "that all my musings, my purposes, my passion for the beautiful, my consciousness of power to create it,—a finer, more ethereal power, of which this earthly giant can have no conception,—all, all, look so vain and idle whenever my path is crossed by Robert Danforth! He would drive me mad were I to meet him often. His hard, brute force darkens and confuses the spiritual element within me; but I, too, will be strong in my own way. I will not yield to him."

He took from beneath a glass a piece of minute machinery, which he set in the condensed light of his lamp, and, looking intently at it through a magnifying glass, proceeded to operate with a delicate instrument of steel. In an instant, however, he fell back in his chair and clasped his hands, with a look of horror on his face that made its small features as impressive as those of a giant would have been.

"Heaven! What have I done?" exclaimed he. "The vapor, the influence of that brute force,—it has bewildered me and obscured my perception. I have made the very stroke—the fatal stroke—that I have dreaded from the first. It is all over—the toil of months, the object of my life. I am ruined!"

And there he sat, in strange despair, until his lamp flickered in the socket and left the Artist of the Beautiful in darkness.

Thus it is that ideas, which grow up within the imagination and appear so lovely to it and of a value beyond whatever men call valuable, are exposed to be shattered and annihilated by contact with the practical. It is requisite for the ideal artist to possess a force of character that seems hardly compatible with its delicacy; he must keep his faith in himself while the incredulous world assails him with its utter disbelief; he must stand up against mankind and be his own sole disciple, both as respects his genius and the objects to which it is directed.

For a time Owen Warland succumbed to this severe but inevitable test. He spent a few sluggish weeks with his head so continually resting in his hands that the towns-people had scarcely an opportunity to see his countenance. When at last it was again uplifted to the light of day, a cold, dull, nameless change was perceptible upon it. In the opinion of

Peter Hovenden, however, and that order of sagacious understandings who think that life should be regulated, like clockwork, with leaden weights, the alteration was entirely for the better. Owen now, indeed, applied himself to business with dogged industry. It was marvellous to witness the obtuse gravity with which he would inspect the wheels of a great old silver watch; thereby delighting the owner, in whose fob it had been worn till he deemed it a portion of his own life, and was accordingly jealous of its treatment. In consequence of the good report thus acquired, Owen Warland was invited by the proper authorities to regulate the clock in the church steeple. He succeeded so admirably in this matter of public interest that the merchants gruffly acknowledged his merits on 'Change; the nurse whispered his praises as she gave the potion in the sick-chamber; the lover blessed him at the hour of appointed interview; and the town in general thanked Owen for the punctuality of dinner time. In a word, the heavy weight upon his spirits kept everything in order, not merely within his own system, but wheresoever the iron accents of the church clock were audible. It was a circumstance, though minute, yet characteristic of his present state, that, when employed to engrave names or initials on silver spoons, he now wrote the requisite letters in the plainest possible style, omitting a variety of fanciful flourishes that had heretofore distinguished his work in this kind.

One day, during the era of this happy transformation, old Peter Hovenden came to visit his former apprentice.

"Well, Owen," said he, "I am glad to hear such good accounts of you from all quarters, and especially from the town clock yonder, which speaks in your commendation every hour of the twenty-four. Only get rid altogether of your nonsensical trash about the beautiful, which I nor nobody else, nor yourself to boot, could ever understand,—only free yourself of that, and your success in life is as sure as daylight. Why, if you go on in this way, I should even venture to let you doctor this precious old watch of mine; though, except my daughter Annie, I have nothing else so valuable in the world."

"I should hardly dare touch it, sir," replied Owen, in a depressed tone; for he was weighed down by his old master's presence.

"In time," said the latter,—"in time, you will be capable of it."

The old watchmaker, with the freedom naturally consequent on his former authority, went on inspecting the work which Owen had in hand at the moment, together with other matters that were in progress. The artist, meanwhile, could scarcely lift his head. There was nothing so antipodal to his nature as this man's cold, unimaginative sagacity, by contact with which everything was converted into a dream except the densest matter of the physical world. Owen groaned in spirit and prayed fervently to be delivered from him.

"But what is this?" cried Peter Hovenden abruptly, taking up a dusty bell glass, beneath which appeared a mechanical something, as delicate and minute as the system of a butterfly's anatomy. "What have we here? Owen! Owen! there is witchcraft in these little chains, and wheels, and paddles. See! with one pinch of my finger and thumb I am going to deliver you from all future peril."

"For Heaven's sake," screamed Owen Warland, springing up with wonderful energy, "as you would not drive me mad, do not touch it! The slightest pressure of your finger would ruin me forever."

"Aha, young man! And is it so?" said the old watchmaker, looking at him with just enough of penetration to torture Owen's soul with the bitterness of worldly criticism. "Well, take your own course; but I warn you again that in this small piece of mechanism lives your evil spirit. Shall I exorcise him?"

"You are my evil spirit," answered Owen, much excited,—"you and the hard, coarse world! The leaden thoughts and the despondency that you fling upon me are my clogs, else I should long ago have achieved the task that I was created for."

Peter Hovenden shook his head, with the mixture of contempt and indignation which mankind, of whom he was partly a representative, deem themselves entitled to feel towards all simpletons who seek other prizes than the dusty one along the highway. He then took his leave, with an uplifted finger and a sneer upon his face that haunted the artist's dreams for many a night afterwards. At the time of his old master's visit, Owen was probably on the point of taking up the relinquished task; but, by this sinister event, he was thrown back into the state whence he had been slowly emerging.

But the innate tendency of his soul had only been accumulating fresh vigor during its apparent sluggishness. As the summer advanced he almost totally relinquished his business, and permitted Father Time, so far as the old gentleman was represented by the clocks and watches under his control, to stray at random through human life, making infinite confusion among the train of bewildered hours. He wasted the sunshine, as people said, in wandering through the woods and fields and along the banks of streams. There, like a child, he found amusement in chasing butterflies or watching the motions of water insects. There was something truly mysterious in the intentness with which he contemplated these living playthings as they sported on the breeze or examined the structure of an imperial insect whom he had imprisoned. The chase of butterflies was an apt emblem of the ideal pursuit in which he had spent so many golden hours; but would the beautiful idea ever be yielded to his hand like the butterfly that symbolized it? Sweet, doubtless, were these days, and congenial to the artist's soul. They were full of bright conceptions, which gleamed through his intellectual world as the butterflies gleamed through the outward atmosphere, and were real to him, for the instant, without the toil, and perplexity, and many disappointments of attempting to make them visible to the sensual eye. Alas that the artist, whether in poetry, or whatever other material, may not content himself with the inward enjoyment of the beautiful, but must chase the flitting mystery beyond the verge of his ethereal domain, and crush its frail being in seizing it with a material grasp. Owen Warland felt the impulse to give external reality to his ideas as irresistibly as any of the poets or painters who have arrayed the world in a dimmer and fainter beauty, imperfectly copied from the richness of their visions.

The night was now his time for the slow progress of re-creating the one idea to which all his intellectual activity referred itself. Always at the approach of dusk he stole into the town, locked himself within his shop, and wrought with patient delicacy of touch for many hours. Sometimes he was startled by the rap of the watchman, who, when all the world should be asleep, had caught the gleam of lamplight through the crevices of Owen Warland's shutters. Daylight, to the morbid sensibility of his mind, seemed to have an intrusiveness that interfered with his pursuits. On cloudy and inclement days, therefore, he sat with his head upon his hands, muffling, as it were, his sensitive brain in a mist of indefinite musings; for it was a relief to escape from the sharp distinctness with which he was compelled to shape out his thoughts during his nightly toil.

From one of these fits of torpor he was aroused by the entrance of Annie Hovenden, who came into the shop with the freedom of a customer, and also with something of the familiarity of a childish friend. She had worn a hole through her silver thimble, and wanted Owen to repair it.

"But I don't know whether you will condescend to such a task," said she, laughing, "now that you are so taken up with the notion of putting spirit into machinery."

"Where did you get that idea, Annie?" said Owen, starting in surprise.

"Oh, out of my own head," answered she, "and from something that I heard you say, long ago, when you were but a boy and I a little child. But come; will you mend this poor thimble of mine?"

"Anything for your sake, Annie," said Owen Warland,—"anything, even were it to work at Robert Danforth's forge."

"And that would be a pretty sight!" retorted Annie, glancing with imperceptible slightness at the artist's small and slender frame. "Well; here is the thimble."

"But that is a strange idea of yours," said Owen, "about the spiritualization of matter."

And then the thought stole into his mind that this young girl possessed the gift to comprehend him better than all the world besides. And what a help and strength would it be to him in his lonely toil if he could gain the sympathy of the only being whom he loved! To persons whose pursuits are insulated from the common business of life—who are either in advance of mankind or apart from it—there often comes a sensation of moral cold that makes the spirit shiver as if it had reached the frozen solitudes around the pole. What the prophet, the poet, the reformer, the criminal, or any other man with human yearnings, but separated from the multitude by a peculiar lot, might feel, poor Owen felt.

"Annie," cried he, growing pale as death at the thought, "how gladly would I tell you the secret of my pursuit! You, methinks, would estimate it rightly. You, I know, would hear it with a reverence that I must not expect from the harsh, material world."

"Would I not? to be sure I would!" replied Annie Hovenden, lightly laughing. "Come; explain to me quickly what is the meaning of this little whirligig, so delicately wrought, that it might be a plaything for Queen Mab. See! I will put it in motion."

"Hold!" exclaimed Owen, "hold!"

Annie had but given the slightest possible touch, with the point of a needle, to the same minute portion of complicated machinery which has been more than once mentioned, when the artist seized her by the wrist with a force that made her scream aloud. She was affrighted at the convulsion of intense rage and anguish that writhed across his features. The next instant he let his head sink upon his hands.

"Go, Annie," murmured he; "I have deceived myself, and must suffer for it. I yearned for sympathy and thought, and fancied, and dreamed that you might give it me; but you lack the talisman, Annie, that should admit you into my secrets. That touch has undone the toil of months and the thought of a lifetime! It was not your fault, Annie; but you have ruined me!"

Poor Owen Warland! He had indeed erred, yet pardonably; for if any human spirit could have sufficiently reverenced the processes so sacred in his eyes, it must have been a woman's. Even Annie Hovenden, possibly, might not have disappointed him had she been enlightened by the deep intelligence of love.

The artist spent the ensuing winter in a way that satisfied any persons who had hitherto retained a hopeful opinion of him that he was, in truth, irrevocably doomed to inutility as regarded the world, and to an evil destiny on his own part. The decease of a relative had put him in possession of a small inheritance. Thus freed from the necessity of toil, and having lost the steadfast influence of a great purpose,—great, at least, to him,—he abandoned himself to habits from which it might have been supposed the mere delicacy of his organization would have availed to secure him. But when the ethereal portion of a man of genius is obscured, the earthly part assumes an influence the more uncontrollable, because the character is now thrown off the balance to which Providence had so nicely adjusted it, and which, in coarser natures, is adjusted by some other method. Owen Warland made proof of whatever show of bliss may be found in riot. He looked at the world through the golden medium of wine, and contemplated the visions that bubble up so gayly around the brim of the glass, and that people the air with shapes of pleasant madness, which so soon grow ghostly and forlorn. Even when this dismal and inevitable change had taken place, the young man might still have continued to quaff the cup of enchantments, though its vapor did but shroud life in gloom and fill the gloom with spectres that mocked at him. There was a certain irksomeness of spirit, which, being real, and the deepest sensation of which the artist was now conscious, was more intolerable than any fantastic miseries and horrors that the abuse of wine could summon up. In the latter case he could remember, even out of the midst of his trouble, that all was but a delusion; in the former, the heavy anguish was his actual life.

From this perilous state he was redeemed by an incident which more than one person witnessed, but of which the shrewdest could not explain or conjecture the operation on Owen Warland's mind. It was very simple. On a warm afternoon of spring, as the artist sat among his riotous companions with a glass of wine before him, a splendid butterfly flew in at the open window and fluttered about his head.

"Ah," exclaimed Owen, who had drank freely, "are you alive again, child of the sun and playmate of the summer breeze, after your dismal winter's nap? Then it is time for me to be at work!"

And, leaving his unemptied glass upon the table, he departed and was never known to sip another drop of wine.

And now, again, he resumed his wanderings in the woods and fields. It might be fancied that the bright butterfly, which had come so spirit-like into the window as Owen sat with the rude revellers, was indeed a spirit commissioned to recall him to the pure, ideal life that had so etherealized him among men. It might be fancied that he went forth to seek this spirit in its sunny haunts; for still, as in the summer time gone by, he was seen to steal gently up wherever a butterfly had alighted, and lose himself in contemplation of it. When it took flight his eyes followed the winged vision, as if its airy track would show the path to heaven. But what could be the purpose of the unseasonable toil, which was again resumed, as the watchman knew by the lines of lamplight through the crevices of Owen Warland's shutters? The towns-people had one comprehensive explanation of all these singularities. Owen Warland had gone mad! How universally efficacious—how satisfactory, too, and soothing to the injured sensibility of narrowness and dulness—is this easy method of accounting for whatever lies beyond the world's most ordinary scope! From St. Paul's days down to our poor little Artist of the Beautiful, the same talisman had been applied to the elucidation of all mysteries in the words or deeds of men who spoke or acted too wisely or too well. In Owen Warland's case the judgment of his towns-people may have been correct. Perhaps he was mad. The lack of sympathy—that contrast between himself and his neighbors which took away the restraint of example—was enough to make him so. Or possibly he had caught just so much of ethereal radiance as served to bewilder him, in an earthly sense, by its intermixture with the common day-light.

One evening, when the artist had returned from a customary ramble and had just thrown the lustre of his lamp on the delicate piece of work so often interrupted, but still taken up again, as if his fate were embodied in its mechanism, he was surprised by the entrance of old Peter Hovenden. Owen never met this man without a shrinking of the heart. Of all the world he was most terrible, by reason of a keen understanding which saw so distinctly what it did see, and disbelieved so uncompromisingly in what it could not see. On this occasion the old watchmaker had merely a gracious word or two to say.

"Owen, my lad," said he, "we must see you at my house to-morrow night."

The artist began to mutter some excuse.

"Oh, but it must be so," quoth Peter Hovenden, "for the sake of the days when you were one of the household. What, my boy! don't you know that my daughter Annie is engaged to Robert Danforth? We are making an entertainment, in our humble way, to celebrate the event."

"Ah!" said Owen.

That little monosyllable was all he uttered; its tone seemed cold and unconcerned to an ear like Peter Hovenden's; and yet there was in it the stifled outcry of the poor artist's heart, which he compressed within him like a man holding down an evil spirit. One slight outbreak, however, imperceptible to the old watchmaker, he allowed himself. Raising the instrument with which he was about to begin his work, he let it fall upon the little system of machinery that had, anew, cost him months of thought and toil. It was shattered by the stroke!

Owen Warland's story would have been no tolerable representation of the troubled life of those who strive to create the beautiful, if, amid all other thwarting influences, love had not interposed to steal the cunning from his hand. Outwardly he had been no ardent or enterprising lover; the career of his passion had confined its tumults and vicissitudes so entirely within the artist's imagination that Annie herself had scarcely more than a woman's intuitive perception of it; but, in Owen's view, it covered the whole field of his life. Forgetful of the time when she had shown herself incapable of any deep response, he had persisted in connecting all his dreams of artistical success with Annie's image; she was the visible shape in which the spiritual power that he worshipped, and on whose altar he hoped to lay a not unworthy offering, was made manifest to him. Of course he had deceived himself; there were no such attributes in Annie Hovenden as his imagination had endowed her with. She, in the aspect which she wore to his inward vision, was as much a creature of his own as the mysterious piece of mechanism would be were it ever realized. Had he become convinced of his mistake through the medium of successful love,—had he won Annie to his bosom, and there beheld her fade from angel into ordinary woman,—the disappointment might have driven him back, with concentrated energy, upon his sole remaining object. On the other hand, had he found Annie what he fancied, his lot would have been so rich in beauty that out of its mere redundancy he might have wrought the beautiful into many a worthier type than he had toiled for; but the guise in which his sorrow came to him, the sense that the angel of his life had been snatched away and given to a rude man of earth and iron, who could neither need nor appreciate her ministrations,—this was the very perversity of fate that makes human existence appear too absurd and contradictory to be the scene of one other hope or one other fear. There was nothing left for Owen Warland but to sit down like a man that had been stunned.

He went through a fit of illness. After his recovery his small and slender frame assumed an obtuser garniture of flesh than it had ever before worn. His thin cheeks became round; his delicate little hand, so spiritually fashioned to achieve fairy task-work, grew plumper than the hand of a thriving infant. His aspect had a childishness such as might have induced a stranger to pat him on the head—pausing, however, in the act, to wonder what manner of child was here. It was as if the spirit had gone out of him, leaving the body to flourish in a sort of vegetable existence. Not that Owen Warland was idiotic. He could talk, and not irrationally. Somewhat of a babbler, indeed, did people begin to think him; for he was apt to discourse at wearisome length of marvels of mechanism that he had read about in books, but which he had learned to consider as absolutely fabulous. Among them he enumerated the Man of Brass, constructed by Albertus Magnus, and the Brazen Head of Friar Bacon; and, coming down to later times, the automata of a little coach and horses, which it was pretended had been manufactured for the Dauphin of France; together with an insect that buzzed about the ear like a living fly, and yet was but a contrivance of minute steel springs. There was a story, too, of a duck that waddled, and quacked, and ate; though, had any honest citizen purchased it for dinner, he would have found himself cheated with the mere mechanical apparition of a duck.

"But all these accounts," said Owen Warland, "I am now satisfied are mere impositions."

Then, in a mysterious way, he would confess that he once thought differently. In his idle and dreamy days he had considered it possible, in a certain sense, to spiritualize machinery, and to combine with the new species of life and motion thus produced a beauty that should attain to the ideal which Nature has proposed to herself in all her creatures, but has never taken pains to realize. He seemed, however, to retain no very distinct perception either of the process of achieving this object or of the design itself.

"I have thrown it all aside now," he would say. "It was a dream such as young men are always mystifying themselves with. Now that I have acquired a little common sense, it makes me laugh to think of it."

Poor, poor and fallen Owen Warland! These were the symptoms that he had ceased to be an inhabitant of the better sphere that lies unseen around us. He had lost his faith in the invisible, and now prided himself, as such unfortunates invariably do, in the wisdom which rejected much that even his eye could see, and trusted confidently in nothing but what his hand could touch. This is the calamity of men whose spiritual part dies out of them and leaves the grosser understanding to assimilate them more and more to the things of which alone it can take cognizance; but in Owen Warland the spirit was not dead nor passed away; it only slept.

How it awoke again is not recorded. Perhaps the torpid slumber was broken by a convulsive pain. Perhaps, as in a former instance, the butterfly came and hovered about his head and reinspired him,—as indeed this creature of the sunshine had always a mysterious mission for the artist,—reinspired him with the former purpose of his life. Whether it were pain or happiness that thrilled through his veins, his first impulse was to thank Heaven for rendering him again the being of thought, imagination, and keenest sensibility that he had long ceased to be.

"Now for the task," said he. "Never did I feel such strength for it as now."

Yet, strong as he felt himself, he was incited to toil the more diligently by an anxiety lest death should surprise him in the midst of his labors. This anxiety, perhaps, is common to all men who set their hearts upon anything so high, in their own view of it, that life becomes of importance only as conditional to its accomplishment. So long as we love life for itself, we seldom dread the losing it. When we desire life for the attainment of an object, we recognize the frailty of its texture. But, side by side with this sense of insecurity, there is a vital faith in our invulnerability to the shaft of death while engaged in any task that seems assigned by Providence as our proper thing to do, and which the world would have cause to mourn for should we leave it unaccomplished. Can the philosopher, big with the inspiration of an idea that is to reform mankind, believe that he is to be beckoned from this sensible existence at the very instant when he is mustering his breath to speak the word of light? Should he perish so, the weary ages may pass away—the world's, whose life sand may fall, drop by drop—before another intellect is prepared to develop the truth that might have been uttered then. But history affords many an example where the most precious spirit, at any particular epoch manifested in human shape, has gone hence untimely, without space allowed him, so far as mortal judgment could discern, to perform his mission on the earth. The prophet dies, and the man of torpid heart and sluggish brain lives on. The poet leaves his song half sung, or finishes it, beyond the scope of mortal ears, in a celestial choir. The painter—as Allston did—leaves half his conception on the canvas to sadden us with its imperfect beauty, and goes to picture forth the whole, if it be no irreverence to say so, in the hues of heaven. But rather such incomplete designs of this life will be perfected nowhere. This so frequent abortion of man's dearest projects must be taken as a proof that the deeds of earth, however etherealized by piety or genius, are without value, except as exercises and manifestations of the spirit. In heaven, all ordinary thought is higher and more melodious than Milton's song. Then, would he add another verse to any strain that he had left unfinished here?

But to return to Owen Warland. It was his fortune, good or ill, to achieve the purpose of his life. Pass we over a long space of intense thought, yearning effort, minute toil, and wasting anxiety, succeeded by an instant of solitary triumph: let all this be imagined; and then behold the artist, on a winter evening, seeking admittance to Robert Danforth's fireside circle. There he found the man of iron, with his massive substance thoroughly warmed and attempered by domestic influences. And there was Annie, too, now transformed into a matron, with much of her husband's plain and sturdy nature, but imbued, as Owen Warland still believed, with a finer grace, that might enable her to be the interpreter between strength and beauty. It happened, likewise, that old Peter Hovenden was a guest this evening at his daughter's fireside, and it was his well-remembered expression of keen, cold criticism that first encountered the artist's glance.

"My old friend Owen!" cried Robert Danforth, starting up, and compressing the artist's delicate fingers within a hand that was accustomed to grip bars of iron. "This is kind and neighborly to come to us at last. I was afraid your perpetual motion had bewitched you out of the remembrance of old times."

"We are glad to see you," said Annie, while a blush reddened her matronly cheek. "It was not like a friend to stay from us so long."

"Well, Owen," inquired the old watchmaker, as his first greeting, "how comes on the beautiful? Have you created it at last?"

The artist did not immediately reply, being startled by the apparition of a young child of strength that was tumbling about on the carpet,—a little personage who had come mysteriously out of the infinite but with something so sturdy and real in his composition that he seemed moulded out of the densest substance which earth could supply. This hopeful infant crawled towards the newcomer, and setting himself on end, as Robert Danforth expressed the posture, stared at Owen with a look of such sagacious observation that the mother could not help exchanging a proud glance with her husband. But the artist was disturbed by the child's look, as imagining a resemblance between it and Peter Hovenden's habitual expression. He could have fancied that the old watchmaker was compressed into this baby shape, and looking out of those baby eyes, and repeating, as he now did, the malicious question:—

"The beautiful, Owen! How comes on the beautiful? Have you succeeded in creating the beautiful?"

"I have succeeded," replied the artist, with a momentary light of triumph in his eyes and a smile of sunshine, yet steeped in such depth of thought that it was almost sadness. "Yes, my friends, it is the truth. I have succeeded."

"Indeed!" cried Annie, a look of maiden mirthfulness peeping out of her face again. "And is it lawful, now, to inquire what the secret is?"

"Surely; it is to disclose it that I have come," answered Owen Warland. "You shall know, and see, and touch, and possess the secret! For, Annie,—if by that name I may still address the friend of my boyish years,—Annie, it is for your bridal gift that I have wrought this spiritualized mechanism, this harmony of motion, this mystery of beauty. It comes late, indeed; but it is as we go onward in life, when objects begin to lose their freshness of hue and our souls their delicacy of perception, that the spirit of beauty is most needed. If,—forgive me, Annie,—if you know how to value this gift, it can never come too late."

He produced, as he spoke, what seemed a jewel box. It was carved richly out of ebony by his own hand, and inlaid with a fanciful tracery of pearl, representing a boy in pursuit of a butterfly, which, elsewhere, had become a winged spirit, and was flying heavenward; while the boy, or youth, had found such efficacy in his strong desire that he ascended from earth to cloud, and from cloud to celestial atmosphere, to win the beautiful. This case of ebony the artist opened, and bade Annie place her finger on its edge. She did so, but almost screamed as a butterfly fluttered forth, and, alighting on her finger's tip, sat waving the ample magnificence of its purple and gold-speckled wings, as if in prelude to a flight. It is impossible to express by words the glory, the splendor, the delicate gorgeousness which were softened into the beauty of this object. Nature's ideal butterfly was here realized in all its perfection; not in the pattern of such faded insects as flit among earthly flowers, but of those which hover across the meads of paradise for child-angels and the spirits of departed infants to disport themselves with. The rich down was visible upon its wings; the lustre of its eyes seemed instinct with spirit. The firelight glimmered around this wonder—the candles gleamed upon it; but it glistened apparently by its own radiance, and illuminated the finger and outstretched hand on which it rested with a white gleam like that of precious stones. In its perfect beauty, the consideration of size was entirely lost. Had its wings overreached the firmament, the mind could not have been more filled or satisfied.

"Beautiful! beautiful!" exclaimed Annie. "Is it alive? Is it alive?"

"Alive? To be sure it is," answered her husband. "Do you suppose any mortal has skill enough to make a butterfly, or would put himself to the trouble of making one, when any child may catch a score of them in a summer's afternoon? Alive? Certainly! But this pretty box is undoubtedly of our friend Owen's manufacture; and really it does him credit."

At this moment the butterfly waved its wings anew, with a motion so absolutely lifelike that Annie was startled, and even awe-stricken; for, in spite of her husband's opinion, she could not satisfy herself whether it was indeed a living creature or a piece of wondrous mechanism.

"Is it alive?" she repeated, more earnestly than before.

"Judge for yourself," said Owen Warland, who stood gazing in her face with fixed attention.

The butterfly now flung itself upon the air, fluttered round Annie's head, and soared into a distant region of the parlor, still making itself perceptible to sight by the starry gleam in which the motion of its wings enveloped it. The infant on the floor followed its course with his sagacious little eyes. After flying about the room, it returned in a spiral curve and settled again on Annie's finger.

"But is it alive?" exclaimed she again; and the finger on which the gorgeous mystery had alighted was so tremulous that the butterfly was forced to balance himself with his wings. "Tell me if it be alive, or whether you created it."

"Wherefore ask who created it, so it be beautiful?" replied Owen Warland. "Alive? Yes, Annie; it may well be said to possess life, for it has absorbed my own being into itself; and in the secret of that butterfly, and in its beauty,—which is not merely outward, but deep as its whole system,—is represented the intellect, the imagination, the sensibility, the soul of an Artist of the Beautiful! Yes; I created it. But"—and here his countenance somewhat changed—"this butterfly is not now to me what it was when I beheld it afar off in the daydreams of my youth."

"Be it what it may, it is a pretty plaything," said the blacksmith, grinning with childlike delight. "I wonder whether it would condescend to alight on such a great clumsy finger as mine? Hold it hither, Annie."

By the artist's direction, Annie touched her finger's tip to that of her husband; and, after a momentary delay, the butterfly fluttered from one to the other. It preluded a second flight by a similar, yet not precisely the same, waving of wings as in the first experiment; then, ascending from the blacksmith's stalwart finger, it rose in a gradually enlarging curve to the ceiling, made one wide sweep around the room, and returned with an undulating movement to the point whence it had started.

"Well, that does beat all nature!" cried Robert Danforth, bestowing the heartiest praise that he could find expression for; and, indeed, had he paused there, a man of finer words and nicer perception could not easily have said more. "That goes beyond me, I confess. But what then? There is more real use in one downright blow of my sledge hammer than in the whole five years' labor that our friend Owen has wasted on this butterfly."

Here the child clapped his hands and made a great babble of indistinct utterance, apparently demanding that the butterfly should be given him for a plaything.

Owen Warland, meanwhile, glanced sidelong at Annie, to discover whether she sympathized in her husband's estimate of the comparative value of the beautiful and the practical. There was, amid all her kindness towards himself, amid all the wonder and admiration with which she contemplated the marvellous work of his hands and incarnation of his idea, a secret scorn—too secret, perhaps, for her own consciousness, and perceptible only to such intuitive discernment as that of the artist. But Owen, in the latter stages of his pursuit, had risen out of the region in which such a discovery might have been torture. He knew that the world, and Annie as the representative of the world, whatever praise might be bestowed, could never say the fitting word nor feel the fitting sentiment which should be the perfect recompense of an artist who, symbolizing a lofty moral by a material trifle,—converting what was earthly to spiritual gold,—had won the beautiful into his handiwork. Not at this latest moment was he to learn that the reward of all high performance must be sought within itself, or sought in vain. There was, however, a view of the matter which Annie and her husband, and even Peter Hovenden, might fully have understood, and which would have satisfied them that the toil of years had here been worthily bestowed. Owen Warland might have told them that this butterfly, this plaything, this bridal gift of a poor watchmaker to a blacksmith's wife, was, in truth, a gem of art that a monarch would have purchased with honors and abundant wealth, and have treasured it among the jewels of his kingdom as the most unique and wondrous of them all. But the artist smiled and kept the secret to himself.

"Father," said Annie, thinking that a word of praise from the old watchmaker might gratify his former apprentice, "do come and admire this pretty butterfly."

"Let us see," said Peter Hovenden, rising from his chair, with a sneer upon his face that always made people doubt, as he himself did, in everything but a material existence. "Here is my finger for it to alight upon. I shall understand it better when once I have touched it."

But, to the increased astonishment of Annie, when the tip of her father's finger was pressed against that of her husband, on which the butterfly still rested, the insect drooped its wings and seemed on the point of falling to the floor. Even the bright spots of gold upon its wings and body, unless her eyes deceived her, grew dim, and the glowing purple took a dusky hue, and the starry lustre that gleamed around the blacksmith's hand became faint and vanished.

"It is dying! it is dying!" cried Annie, in alarm.

"It has been delicately wrought," said the artist, calmly. "As I told you, it has imbibed a spiritual essence—call it magnetism, or what you will. In an atmosphere of doubt and mockery its exquisite susceptibility suffers torture, as does the soul of him who instilled his own life into it. It has already lost its beauty; in a few moments more its mechanism would be irreparably injured."

"Take away your hand, father!" entreated Annie, turning pale. "Here is my child; let it rest on his innocent hand. There, perhaps, its life will revive and its colors grow brighter than ever."

Her father, with an acrid smile, withdrew his finger. The butterfly then appeared to recover the power of voluntary motion, while its hues assumed much of their original lustre, and the gleam of starlight, which was its most ethereal attribute, again formed a halo round about it. At first, when transferred from Robert Danforth's hand to the small finger of the child, this radiance grew so powerful that it positively threw the little fellow's shadow back against the wall. He, meanwhile, extended his plump hand as he had seen his father and mother do, and watched the waving of the insect's wings with infantine delight. Nevertheless, there was a certain odd expression of sagacity that made Owen Warland feel as if here were old Peter Hovenden, partially, and but partially, redeemed from his hard scepticism into childish faith.

"How wise the little monkey looks!" whispered Robert Danforth to his wife.

"I never saw such a look on a child's face," answered Annie, admiring her own infant, and with good reason, far more than the artistic butterfly. "The darling knows more of the mystery than we do."

As if the butterfly, like the artist, were conscious of something not entirely congenial in the child's nature, it alternately sparkled and grew dim. At length it arose from the small hand of the infant with an airy motion that seemed to bear it upward without an effort, as if the ethereal instincts with which its master's spirit had endowed it impelled this fair vision involuntarily to a higher sphere. Had there been no obstruction, it might have soared into the sky and grown immortal. But its lustre gleamed upon the ceiling; the exquisite texture of its wings brushed against that earthly medium; and a sparkle or two, as of stardust, floated downward and lay glimmering on the carpet. Then the butterfly came fluttering down, and, instead of returning to the infant, was apparently attracted towards the artist's hand.

"Not so! not so!" murmured Owen Warland, as if his handiwork could have understood him. "Thou hast gone forth out of thy master's heart. There is no return for thee."

With a wavering movement, and emitting a tremulous radiance, the butterfly struggled, as it were, towards the infant, and was about to alight upon his finger; but while it still hovered in the air, the little child of strength, with his grandsire's sharp and shrewd expression in his face, made a snatch at the marvellous insect and compressed it in his hand. Annie screamed. Old Peter Hovenden burst into a cold and scornful laugh. The blacksmith, by main force, unclosed the infant's hand, and found within the palm a small heap of glittering fragments, whence the mystery of beauty had fled forever. And as for Owen Warland, he looked placidly at what seemed the ruin of his life's labor, and which was yet no ruin. He had caught a far other butterfly than this. When the artist rose high enough to achieve the beautiful, the symbol by which he made it perceptible to mortal senses became of little value in his eyes while his spirit possessed itself in the enjoyment of the reality.

4 · Aggression and Submission: War and Bureaucracy

A short while ago, Hannah Arendt aroused a storm of protest when she painted a portrait of Adolph Eichmann as someone who was the product of an impersonal bureaucratic machine rather than a lonely, sadistic monster. The hue and cry raised against her point of view reflected an honest public concern with the problems of personal responsibility, but it also reflected the public's need to find in Eichmann a scapegoat on whom to vent its anger and aggression. Miss Arendt's plea for understanding of the dangers of the bureaucratic mechanism was misunderstood in the same way that psychoanalysis is misunderstood. In its attempts to broaden the base of human understanding, society is torn by its desire for vengeance and its knowledge that increasing information tends to blur its definition of responsibility.

Miss Arendt's horrifying realization that bureaucratic institutions destroy the notion of personal responsibility by allowing the individual to displace his own guilt on to the machine should not have been so surprising. Orwell and Kafka had told us all about it years before. They understood how bureaucracy, by tacitly encouraging submission as well as displacement of guilt, creates a passive kind of hostility that allows a man to weep at the sight of blood while he is coldbloodedly pushing a button to destroy the world. This process, known as dissociation, lies behind a good deal of violent criminal behavior and provides protection for the ego under what would otherwise be an unbearable condition of stress.

On the other side of this bureaucratic coin is the institution of war, which encourages a destructive and active ex-

pression of aggression. War—any particular war—is always explicable in terms of economic, political or historical antecedents. Yet the unconscious sources of human aggression that apply to every war have seldom been examined by social scientists, who tend to rule out psychological explanations of war as reductionism. As with the subject of bureaucracy, writers and artists have been far less inhibited. Their troubled portrayals of sexual and unconscious sources of war have not been lost on readers who intuitively accept the truth about themselves as warlike and aggressive animals.

In exposing the unconscious motives of war, Alix Strachey is particularly concerned with the way in which the group encourages regression and allows the unresolved unconscious conflicts of the individual to emerge and express themselves in hostile action.

ALIX STRACHEY

The Group as a Regressive Force
FROM *The Unconscious Motives of War*

We are accustomed, quite rightly, to regard the wider society in which the individual lives as an essential factor in enabling him to overcome his infantile attitudes and attachments, by offering him objects and situations outside the narrow sphere of self and family. Thus we look on it as having an eminently progressive influence upon his mental development.

On the other hand, we have just learnt that it provides him with forms of expression for ego-dystonic attitudes which he cannot otherwise express except in pathological symptoms. Furthermore, these forms of expression are regularly resorted to by every individual in it, however normal. This was accounted for, among other things, by their being easier to use than private symptoms. Yet it is hard to believe that all normal people should have such strong dystonic attitudes as to make universal use of those public alternatives to them. It therefore almost seems as if a person's social environment not only provides him with such public symptoms but causes him to have a special need for them— causes him, in other words, to have something akin to a mental illness.

However this may be, it is certain that some kinds of society do have one effect which underlies most mental illnesses. This is that they set up regressive processes in the individuals who compose them. The most striking example of a regressively-acting society of this kind is to be found in the crowd. People who are closely collected together in large numbers tend to enter into a very different frame of mind from what they are in when they are alone or in the company of a few others. This fact is a commonplace and familiar to all. Everyone knows that a candidate for Parliamentary election must speak in very different accents to his prospective voters, according to whether he is addressing them from the hustings, or whether he is canvassing them singly or speaking to them in a small circle over the radio; and a man who has been at a mass-meeting often looks back with amazement at the thoughts and feelings that moved him at the time.

When an individual finds himself close together with a large number of other persons certain changes take place in his mind. In the first place this physical juxtaposition heightens his instinctual impulses and he becomes more excited. In the second place, he becomes more easily infected by the states of mind of those about him. This still further increases his excitations (since theirs, owing to their juxtaposition, are above the normal) as well as rendering him more easily excitable. It also implies an extensive identificatory introjection with his neighbours, so that he feels and thinks and wills as they do. Nor is an equal extension of identificatory projection lacking. The subject is not only inclined to feel (and be) like his fellows; he is inclined to feel and believe that they are like him. And the two processes between them help to give him an enormous sense of amplitude and assurance and of oneness with the rest of the crowd.

Furthermore, the inhibitory capacity of his ego is weakened, and he is much more liable to yield to his impulses. We see in Shakespeare's *Julius Caesar,* for instance, how readily the mob of angry Roman citizens take to violence and proceed to burn, loot and kill. Again, the ego's synthesizing powers are reduced, so that he lends himself more easily to his in any case heightened ambivalence. Once more we remember how the mob in *Julius Caesar* fluctuates violently between acclamation of Brutus as their country's liberator and condemnation of him as the murderer of its benefactor. A third effect is that the intellectual faculties of the ego undergo debasement and regress from the secondary processes to the primary ones. Here is a classical example in *Julius Caesar.* The crowd, thirsting for the blood of the conspirators, one of whom is called Cinna, come across a poet who happens also to have that name:

3rd Citizen. Your name, sir, truly?
Cinna. Truly, my name is Cinna.
2nd Citizen. Tear him to pieces; he is a conspirator.
Cinna. I am Cinna the poet, I am Cinna the poet.

4th Citizen. Tear him for his bad verses, tear him for his bad verses.
Cinna. I am not Cinna the conspirator.
2nd Citizen. It is no matter, his name's Cinna; pluck but his name out of
his heart, and turn him going.
3rd Citizen. Tear him, tear him . . . etc.

(Act iii, Scene 3)

Having the same name is enough to make two quite different people
the same in the eyes of the members of the mob.

Yet another effect is that the ego resumes a good deal of its ancient
narcissism and sense of omnipotence, so that the subject's self-regard is
very much enhanced and he feels grand and great and good; and this
belief he projects onto his fellows, so that they also seem grand and
great and good.

Nor does the super-ego escape regression. It, too, reverts once more
to the earlier and more primitive stages through which it has passed in
the course of its development. Indeed, it tends to shrink back into the
nothingness from which it came. As we see, the mob in *Julius Caesar*
has no compunction in looting and burning all it can lay hands on; and
it tears its victims to pieces without a thought.

But the same regressive process which causes a person to lose his
super-ego also causes him to feel the need once more for an external
authority to take its place. If they are together for any length of time,
the members of a crowd accordingly tend to look for someone who shall
dominate and guide them in virtue of his superior intelligence, resolution
and eloquence—a Brutus or a Mark Antony on however small a scale.
Or at any rate, they are very ready to accept such a person. They gladly
turn to him and set him up, or allow him to set himself up, over them
and direct their feelings, thoughts and actions. And now, too, it is not
difficult to detect in the figure of the leader the lineaments of their
childhood father-imago.

But his ascendancy is apt to be short-lived. In accordance with the
primary process they make easy displacements from object to object so
that the leader of the moment is always in danger of being superseded by
another. Then, too, we have to consider their ambivalence which makes
them liable to change their feelings from love to hatred (and *vice versa*)
and to take up an opposite side from the one they have just espoused.
The fickleness of crowds is proverbial. We see once more in *Julius
Caesar* how the mob gives up its allegiance to Brutus in favour of
Antony as quickly and frivolously as it had abandoned Caesar for
Brutus before. Nor is the crowd an enduring unit. It soon melts away; its

leaders, if any, disappear, and the individual who has formed part of it returns to his ordinary frame of mind.

There are, however, other collections of people which are not change-able and short-lived like crowds, but which yet exercise a considerable degree of regressive effect upon the minds of their members. These owe their stability and permanence to the fact that the spontaneous ties of feeling which arise between their constituents are increased and secured by artificial means.[1]

Freud was specially interested in one type of artificially organized group as being the most successful of all. This group exhibits two main external features. One is that it has a leader who possesses autocratic power over its members. The other is that its members all belong to the male sex.

To begin with the first feature. The fact that the rank-and-file mem-bers are in their leader's power and must obey him in everything tends to make them submissive to him in mind as well as in outward behav-iour. One reason for this is that being in his power takes them back to a childhood situation in which they had to obey their father (or their father-figures) without question and in which they also felt mentally dependent on him. Thus physical and mental submission became linked together. In addition, they felt awe of him and love for him as an omnipotent and (mainly) benevolent being; and these attitudes, too, are revived by the contemporary situation, so that their wish to please and obey their leader is further reinforced. Furthermore, in virtue of the massive identificatory introjections they make in respect of him as their father-figure, each sets up a considerable portion of super-ego which is modelled on him and his commands. Thus they come to have a common or 'group' super-ego which represents him and whose word is law. Fi-nally, such a common attitude to their leader promotes powerful ties or identification with one another. All this makes strongly for the stability and cohesion of the group.

As regards the second feature, that of the members being all males, this means in the first place that the libidinal ties which exist between them are of a homosexual kind, and this lends itself better to complete sublimation than does heterosexual libido (doubtless because it is neces-sary for the survival of the species that the latter should be resistant to complete de-sexualization). Unsublimated sexual love leads to one-to-one relationships of an exclusive kind and to situations of jealousy and anger between the members, which would tend to break up the group. In the second place, sameness of sex once more constitutes an important likeness between the members and thus furnishes a good soil for identificatory ties between them. Lastly, the sameness of sex between the rank and file and their leader assists them in making those identificatory introjections of him which are responsible for the setting up of a common super-ego in each. The reason why such monosexual groups should be composed of males rather than females is partly because, as we have seen, leaders are nearly always male persons, the properties of command and domination being for the most part masculine. In any case, in Freud's view women are less well fitted for making the necessary sublimation.[2]

We see then that the intra-group attachments thus set up in each member of the group are of three kinds: ties of mental dependence, ties of identification and libidinal ties.

Freud cites as the two most outstanding examples of organized groups of this kind the army and the (Roman Catholic) Church. Both have a supreme head invested with autocratic power: in the first case, the Commander-in-Chief, and in the second, Christ Himself, with the Pope as His earthly representative, and in both there is a rigid hierarchy of officers or priests, as the case may be, to consolidate the top leader's power and to bring it home to the rank and file. Both, too, consist only of men.

These two groups, moreover, strengthen their internal ties by many added means. To begin with, they increase the members' mental submissions to the leaders' will by repeated exactions of acts of external submission. This is seen in the many rituals and fixed hours and movements of devotion which the Church demands from its priesthood, and the constant drill and severe discipline to which soldiers are subjected—a discipline which is thus seen to have something more than the useful and necessary aim of making soldiers able to carry out orders promptly. In matters of external discipline, indeed, the army excels the Church; but to make up for this, the Church approaches the matter more directly as well and enjoins its members not only to obey their leader but to worship him. Such actions in common also directly strengthen the identificatory ties between the members, since it makes them alike in their demeanour (not to mention the fact that if it is carried out by large numbers of them close together, it increases those identificatory experiences which are more especially connected with crowd-mentality—and which perhaps belong to still earlier states of mind than those regressed to in group-mentality). Similarity of dress, too—the priest's cassock and the soldier's tunic—strengthen the identificatory ties between the members of each group, as well as between them and their leaders of every rank, in so far as the latter wear the same kind of uniform, though with suitable differences to mark their varying degree of superiority.

As we can see, it is not only the Roman Catholic Church and the Army which fulfil the necessary conditions for being a regressive group of the kind we have in mind. Other Churches, Christian or otherwise, also to a greater or lesser extent satisfy those requirements; and so do the other branches of the armed forces.

Moreover, there are collections of persons outside religious or military bodies which also qualify to be regarded as artificially-organized groups of a regressive kind, even if in a minor degree. We have only to think of our own Public Schools, with their hierarchy of headmaster, assistant masters and prefects under him, their quite considerable amount of discipline, their games and other actions in common, their distinctive dress and their exclusively male population; or of secret male societies—e.g. the Freemasons—with their implicit obedience to an often mysterious leader, their special rituals and signs, and so on.

The regressive operation of organized groups, moreover, is not limited to collections of people which exhibit the two external features so far described, even if those which do are the most marked type of them.

As regards the first feature, we find regressive groups in which the leader does not wield autocratic power—in which he must rule them according to law. Or the group may be inspired and held together by a cause rather than a person. Nevertheless, these differences are more seeming than real. If the group is founded on law, then that law and the makers of it are revered as the omnipotent father or at any rate the omnipotent ancestors; and if it is inspired by a cause, the cause assumes his place. (Yet those symbols of the great father are rarely as potent as a living representative, and the group is by that much less effective in its influence.) Lastly, if the group is democratic, it almost gains on the swings what it loses on the roundabouts. Whilst the parental authority in it is weakened, another ancient power is increased; for the members also admire in the leaders they have elected a projection of their own infantile sense of grandeur and omnipotence.[3]

As regards the second feature, certain groups which are not exclusively male are nevertheless regressive. Political parties such as the

Fascist or Communist parties, with their iron discipline and autocratic rule, are clearly of this type, yet they contain women as well as men members. (Though here there is no doubt that it is the men who are not only the leaders but who constitute the backbone of the group.) On the other hand, we know that some secret societies are exclusively made up of women and the same cannot be said of *them*. Then, too, we have co-educational boarding schools and boarding schools for girls only; and both these exhibit nearly as much group-spirit as do their purely masculine counterparts.

Even groups which are much more loosely organized than those described above, tend to cause some degree of regressive group-mentality in their members. Boy Scout and Girl Guide movements, sporting clubs, ordinary clubs, trade unions, women's institutes and local bodies of all sorts, whose members are not regimented to anything like the same degree as are the members of the Church or the armed forces or even Public Schools, do nevertheless develop a strong common spirit in which regressive features are not wanting. Even societies which exist for the sole purpose of promoting intellectual and progressive thought and whose organization is as loose and liberal as is consonant with its proper functioning are not entirely free from traces of group-regression. The amateur botanists of a country district, for instance, may form a local society for the sole purpose of reading papers to one another and conducting discussions about plant life. But they will soon develop some kind of *esprit de corps,* on however modest a scale, from the mere fact that they meet together for their discussions under the auspices of a president or a chairman and undertake expeditions in common in order to collect rare flowers. As a result, each member is inclined to think a little more highly of himself, his fellow botanists and his society and to feel a little more strongly on their behalf than he would otherwise do and than the facts warrant. This mild group-mentality tends also to manifest itself in small outward and concrete signs—signs which in their turn fortify it—as befits the proneness to symbolization and sensory regression which are some of its accompaniments. The local botanists, for instance, may celebrate their existence as members of their botanical society by wearing a distinctive badge in their coat lapels and by instituting an annual dinner with self-congratulatory speeches and toasts to their president.

Hardly less remarkable than the extent to which the member loves and overestimates his group and its leaders, is the extent to which he identifies himself with it and his fellow-members. A soldier, for instance, is as proud of a victory which his army has gained or as humiliated by a defeat it has suffered when he has not been in the battle as when he has been in it and has helped to win or lose it; and according as his fellow-soldiers who fought in it behaved in a brave or cowardly fashion on that occasion, so does he feel that he has behaved in a brave or cowardly fashion, even though he was not there at all. A worthless member of a first-rate school feels far superior to a meritorious member of a third-rate one; and the latter may, in his turn, accept his own inferiority in virtue of the inferiority of his school (unless, of course—as is quite likely—he refuses to recognize that his school *is* inferior).

Moreover, on the mental level to which he has regressed, he is very prone to personify his group. He thinks of it as something that can be born or can die, be sick or well, happy or unhappy, hurt or not hurt, brave or cowardly, clever or stupid, well- or ill-intentioned, and so on and so forth, instead of being something whose *members* can be born or die, happy or unhappy, etc. And more than this. In so far as he identifies himself with his group, he thinks of himself as participating in its supposed human qualities and vicissitudes. Thus, e.g., if a boy's Public School is an old one he not only tends to think of it as mature and wise, as an old man is; he tends to think of his schoolfellows and himself as mature and wise—or as more mature and wise than the inmates of a new school.

These unrealistic views of groups are not only held by the members of them. The ordinary outsider, too, is inclined to have them, though perhaps not so strongly. For after all, even as a private individual, he is not exempt from anthropomorphic attitudes and other forms of primitive thought. Thus, for instance, when we look at a collection of persons moving in various directions—as say in Piccadilly Circus any day of the week—we often get the totally false impression that the collection as such is *feeling* undecided in what direction to move, and that consequently each individual in it is undecided, when in fact each is going steadily on his way with a single purpose in mind.[4]

Organized groups not only engender group-mentality in each of its members while he is together with the rest of the group. Unlike crowd-formations, whose effect on the individual vanishes as soon as he leaves them—and which are in any case short-lived—they continue to influence his mind even when he is going about his ordinary business. But then, of course, it continues to have its external holds on him, so that he still feels that he belongs to it. Yet it can go on influencing him even after he has ceased to be a member of it (as we see in the case of old Public School boys or ex-Army men). Nevertheless its influence is not as strong then as it is when he is still a member of it. The group has yet more effect when he is together with other members of it—and the more of them, the stronger the effect is. And it is most powerful of all when he and his fellow-members are together not by chance but as a group, especially if they are taking part in one or other of the activities which help to consolidate and symbolize its existence. An ex-college man, for instance, is apt to be more offended by adverse outside criticism of his college tie than he is by adverse criticism of a private tie of his own. But he is not so much put out by it as he would be if he were still at college. And his resentment is still greater if he is with his co-collegiates, and greatest of all if he and they are on their way to a college celebration.

For this reason every group sees to it that its members shall not only be together a great deal but shall from time to time convene in a more formal manner to mark its existence and exalt its worth. Church festivals and processions, military tattoos and trooping the colours, college commemoration days, Communist or Nazi rallies—all these occasions help in their varying degrees to strengthen and perpetuate the group spirit of those concerned.

An organized social unit of the kind we have described does not permit the minds of its members to regress as far as does such an unorganized social unit as a crowd. It obliges them to inhibit many of their instinctual impulses and to sublimate others, and it provides them with a super-ego. Nevertheless, it does cause their minds to regress to a point at which they are unable to take a realistic view of their own group or of objects outside it, especially in relation to their group, or to make independent ethical judgments about them. Moreover, since the regressions that take place in a group are much more lasting than those which take place in a crowd, their effect is more serious. A member of a crowd in a killing mood only wants to tear its enemy to pieces while he is in that crowd; a member of a group like the *Mafia* is *always* in a killing mood towards its enemies. When the organized group is of a high standing this regressive effect is, however, very much obscured. In the first place, certain progressive influences do take place as well in the minds of its members. An illiterate peasant, for instance, may learn to read and write for the first time because he is sent to a school for making priests. In the second place, the members of a group are bound to accept the views of the leader of their group, however little they understand or appreciate them. If a leader is in favour of beneficent and enlightened behaviour, so are they. But though the first fact may operate progressively, it only does so within a limited sphere; and the second fact, however useful from an external point of view, can scarcely be called a progressive phenomenon in itself. An ignorant savage who believes that the world is round just because his white master tells him that it is round, is no more capable of realistic thinking than is an ignorant savage who believes it is flat because his own medicine man tells him that it is flat.

The regressive attitude which such groups engender in its members is apt, moreover, to impair their capacity to grasp difficult ideas or ideas that are at all abstract. Thus the ideas which they are taught by their leaders tend to become debased and to assume concrete and personal forms in their minds. It is, for instance, easier to worship an idol of God than a concept of Him. Indeed, good leaders know this and take care that the ideas they want to put over to their followers shall be clothed in sense-perceptual forms. The Church abounds in painted images and symbolic signs.

Moreover, the aims and ideals which the leader promulgates tend to be regarded by the rank and file not only as being put forward *by* him and thus acquiring great authority, but as being personified *in* him, or being a part of him (for that, of course, is how associations work in the unconscious). To most Nazis in Germany, for instance, it was not the pure doctrine of Nazism or even Nazism as put over to them by Hitler that captured their imagination, but Nazism-cum-Hitler; and the average Communist gives his allegiance not simply to Communism or the Communist idea but to it plus his idea of Marx, Lenin and Stalin, or, in some cases, to them alone.

This adds still more to the value and importance of these aims and ideals in the eyes of the members of the group. The leader is not slow to take advantage of this, and he magnifies his personality not only in order to keep the group in being and to maintain his place at the head of it, but to give the cause it stands for added force and virtue for his followers. Nazis, Communists and Fascists alike decorated every available place with more than life-size portraits of Hitler, Stalin, Lenin, Tito and Mussolini, as the case may be. This was done not merely as a spontaneous expression of feeling on the part of the members but by orders from above. The same can happen in the field of religious beliefs, too, where the subject's idea of God is not only enhanced by his membership of a Church congregation under a priesthood, but may to a greater or lesser extent become attached to that priesthood. In comparatively recent times, for instance, the Pope has, as head of the Roman

Catholic Church, officially taken on the attributes of Infallibility—an attribute which, one would have thought, could only belong to God.

The fact that group-mentality involves a strengthening of primitive attitudes of mind in the individual does not mean that it is altogether a bad thing. For such attitudes have great value in many respects. In the first place, they help to secure the happiness and well-being of the members of the group by encouraging in each feelings of pride in and devotion to his group which often alone may enable him to behave in an altruistic way in regard to his fellow members. It is only by believing rather more than is true in the value of his fellows, himself and his leader, in their oneness and in the immortal soul of his group, that he can summon up the necessary fortitude and self-sacrifice to put its interests before his own—and that he thinks it worth while. Furthermore, as has been said, the receptiveness and docility of mind which group-mentality engenders in the rank-and-file towards their leaders (and fellows) undoubtedly open their minds, within limits, to instruction and betterment, should the group or its leader chance to be a progressive and enlightened one. Then, again, the mental relaxation produced by regression is not only pleasurable and perhaps even healthful in itself, but may even enable the subject's mind to function more realistically and preconsciously in spheres of thought not connected with the group, or at times when his group mentality is not being activated, since it rests his mind and so gives it renewed vigour to work on higher levels. Then, too, group-thinking, may, like phantasying, drain off much of his wishful and unconscious modes of thought into permissible channels of discharge, so that they do not impede his realistic thinking in other fields. Furthermore, the individual gets a great sense of power and security from being in a group, partly because he feels protected by his omnipotent father once more, partly because his own sense of power is vastly expanded and partly because there is safety in numbers, both as a means of sharing guilt and being protected from external danger. These things give him and his fellows the requisite confidence to carry out dangerous but necessary actions—such as, say, fighting a bad fire, where the fire-brigade depends not only on its combined force and organization to master the fire but upon the heroism of its men.

As we know, too, instant and full execution of orders is often absolutely requisite for effective action; and this is not only a matter of skill and practice but of unquestioning and automatic obedience to authority which is the hall-mark of the group.

The *dis*value of regressive group-mentality, on the other hand, is considerable. In the first place, it induces an unrealistic state of mind in the subject on all matters connected with it, so that the ends he aims at in regard to it are often bad, from being mistaken, and the means he adopts to attain them are inexpedient. In the second place, it makes him indifferent to persons outside his group, since his libidinal impulses are mostly directed to persons within it, and most of his identifications are made with them. Nor has he any sense of duty or compunction about outsiders, since his group super-ego is not concerned with them. Indeed, if he happens to dislike them there is nothing to prevent his wanting to injure them and trying to do so, if he thinks it possible and safe.

This brings us to the third and perhaps the most serious objection to group-mentality. Much of the large amount of libido which a group-member expends upon his attachment to his leader and his fellow-members is got by withdrawing it from non-members, and that makes him not only indifferent to their welfare and happiness but actually desirous of their destruction and unhappiness. For, since his attitude to them is in any case bound to be to some extent ambivalent, such a withdrawal of libido increases the relative proportion of his destructive and hostile impulses towards them and removes another check upon them. These destructive impulses, moreover, are *positively* increased by the fact that he also increases the relative strength of his libidinal attitude to his co-members and his leader by deflecting the destructive side of his ambivalent attitude to them on to persons outside his group. On top of this, it must be remembered that members of regressive groups have actually more destructiveness in their mental composition than have individuals in their private capacity, from the very fact of having regressed to an earlier developmental stage.

Furthermore, the ties of mental dependence and of identification which the member forms as well with persons within his group detract from the strength of similar ties which he has formed with persons outside it. This, if it does not increase his *hostility* to the latter, does increase his *indifference*. And it decreases the efforts he makes to inhibit his hostility.

All this, it is obvious, makes groups that are powerful a serious potential danger to the outside world, and history is full of its struggles, sometimes successful sometimes not, to keep them in their place.

NOTES

[1] For what follows in this section, cf. Freud's book *Group Psychology and an Analysis of the Ego.*

² Cf. in this connection his *Civilization and Its Discontents,* pp. 73 ff.

³ It must be said that Freud lays much more emphasis on the member's filial attitude to his leader than on his, perhaps earlier, narcissistic attitude to his group, as a characteristic of regressive groups. But, as will be seen later, the group itself takes on a parental aspect for its members, so that they do have a filial attitude to it as well as a narcissistic one.—On the other hand, in a democracy the members have more power of individual choice over their own fate, and this encourages their realistic and preconscious activities and so makes them less liable to regress. . . .

⁴ Poets and imaginative writers, who are licensed to regress in phantasy, are, of course, entitled to speak of groups and crowds as a living entity—as a many-headed monster. But even the scientific approach to them is often distorted by such a view. Even the sociological term "group mind" seems sometimes to cover the concept, not of individual minds as they have been changed by being in a group—changed among other things, it is true, in the direction of becoming more alike—but of a single "collective" mind which informs the whole group.

Bruno Bettelheim's examination of the psychological dynamics that worked to destroy the individual's sense of identity in the concentration camp is hardly attractive. It points up the similarities between the large impersonal machinery created by the Nazis and the bureaucratic trappings of any apparently benign society. It suggests, as literature has before, that bureaucracy, by denying the individual an outlet for his hostile or aggressive feelings, hastens the process of disintegration and leads to dissociation and ego failure.

BRUNO BETTELHEIM

FROM *The Informed Heart*

REMOTE CONTROL

The vastness of the political system and its bureaucracy, and the bigness of most modern technological enterprises, now add still another factor—distance. Each one fosters personality disintegration because just at the point where man begins to feel he is losing control of his destiny and may be spurred to do something about it, he is offered a convenient excuse for evading the responsibility. Mass society is so complex that a man can justify his saying helplessly that he does not understand his role in the political or productive process. The trouble is that the justification does not help; it just lowers his own confidence in himself. His distance from the managers adds the often valid excuse that he is powerless to reach them, let alone influence anyone directly.

Without clear notions of these psychological phenomena, many Germans made use of them after the war when confronted with the horrors they supposedly consented to. They said (unless they disclaimed any knowledge of the horrors): "I was only a little man, what could I do?"[1] But if the excuse was heavily justified by reality, it marked another step toward personal disintegration. It was contrary to what we like to consider man's greatest pride: maintaining his independence in the face of outside pressure.

Significantly, similar statements were made by workers on the atomic bomb projects in denying their responsibility. The atomic bomb brought into relief some of the social and psychological problems people face in the mass state. Public reaction in the U.S. was first one of pride in the power of the state and its managers, with whom most citizens identified. On further thought the terrifying power of whoever owned the bomb roused anxiety in the individual and a feeling of utter helplessness. Since he could not cope with his anxiety, he turned to society and its managers for protection, willing to grant them even greater power in exchange for protection against the new danger. A battle then began between the rational control of emotional fear ("there's no protection from atomic death except world cooperation") and mechanisms of compensation that are aggressive in nature, namely, reliance on the managers' power to offer security ("let's use it first!").

The feeling of helplessness, of being "only a little man," just an object of manipulation, brings about a need for compensation. The child who depends on his parent for survival must believe in his parent's goodness because only then can he feel sure of being cared for. Critical or aggressive feelings toward the parent create guilt feelings because the child is so dependent to begin with. Similarly, the more powerless the individual becomes in the mass state, socially, economically, politically, the more important appear those who seem to hold the power; therefore the individual needs to believe that these powerful managers will look after him. Only in this belief lies his psychological security. Lack of justice, when experienced in reality, is then blamed on the ill will of the middleman— on the foreman in the factory or the straw boss.

Here, too, modern man finds himself in a strangely contradictory situation. While he sees himself as hopelessly enmeshed in, and at the mercy of the vast enterprise of modern society, there is no doubt in his mind that this, his society, is by far the most powerful known to man. The more powerful society grows, the more powerful (he rightfully feels) he should become, as a part of it. But actually the opposite is true, so that emotionally it adds insult to injury.

This might, in part, explain the anxiety and resentment many feel about nuclear power. Such a tremendous advance in science and technology should have given everyone a feeling of greater security and strength. Actually it has increased our feeling of being helplessly at the mercy of powers beyond our comprehension, or at least beyond our control. As an advance in making nature serve man it should have given us immense satisfaction, but what we enjoy is almost negligible compared to the vast new anxiety created. Once again, as society became so much more powerful, the citizen got the short end of it. With society wielding more power than ever, and himself more anxious than before, the individual must rely for his very survival on the wisdom of the managers of society.

Physical distance from the managers keeps a man from testing against reality his belief in their good will, a process that might prove disastrous to his sense of economic and social security. It also protects the pipe dream of managerial wisdom and correctness on which he bases his psychological security. This psychological process is as old as civilization. Throughout history, the conqueror's power has made men invest him with virtue, at times even to transfigure him into a demigod or hero. It seems almost inevitable as a mental process. The greater an individual's power over others, the greater the evil that might possibly originate with him. The greater the threat, the greater the need to deny it by believing in his virtue.

Distance which prevents reality testing of the manager's virtue was used to advantage in the Hitler mass state. The leader appeared in public only on great occasions and then surrounded by his guards, speaking to large masses. This put a double distance between him and the individual: the guards who were close to the leader, and the tremendous audience preventing personal contact.

Another kind of distance was also used for intimidation: distance in time. The masses waited hours for the leader to appear. During this time their tension was increased to an insufferable degree by demonstrations, exciting music and the sheer physical exhaustion of standing for hours. The leader's appearance and the ending of tension that followed, was experienced as the great emotional relief it actually was. The experience of the leader's appearance bringing relief and the end of tension left an impression of some inherent power he had for relieving stress. This inspired gratitude and a belief in his "magic" power over the individual.

Because the contents of his speech bore no relation to the relief from tension, any one of his speeches had the desired effect on those present. This divorcement of effect from content increased the belief in the leader's charisma. The shallowness and unexciting quality of Hitler's or Mussolini's speeches, when heard over the radio without exposure to the events that preceded them, was for most persons in stark contrast to the impact of the leader's appearance on the physically present audience. With no previous tension built up in the radio listener, the leader's presence brought no relief, and the speech fell flat.

Consciously or unconsciously, distance in time is used by the boss in our society who lets an inferior wait before seeing him. This impresses the person with the boss' power and his own inferiority. Conversely, seeing the inferior immediately helps to establish direct, personal contact on a friendly, equal footing. This example also shows the inner forces at work: the waiting person becomes tense and anxious as time passes. He cannot deal with the accumulating anxiety about seeing the manager, his feeling of impotence grows and weakens his position. Only the very secure person (or someone who does not care about the outcome of the meeting) can stand the tension without getting anxious, and then insecure. Thus the ability to "be oneself" in the managed society is, again, largely a matter of personal integration and not entirely dependent on the structure of society.

The demoralizing effect of using time instead of intrinsic merit for gaining security can also be recognized in how wage earners try to compensate psychologically. Although they know better, they try to counteract fears of losing a job in which they are easily replaceable, by referring to how long they've been working on it. Irreplaceability due to quality of performance, as in the craft shop, is replaced by the pseudo security of time. Stable inner security based on a conviction of knowledge and skill is replaced by a reliance on outer security that can be shattered at any moment.[2] ...

ANONYMITY

Effacing oneself was a defense which, more than any other, helped to produce the kind of childishly submissive, easily manipulated person the SS wanted. To remain inconspicuous, and therefore unnoticed, was one of the best means of surviving in the camp (as typified by the fate of the Hambers).

True compliance with all commands and prohibitions was impossible if one wanted to live. So the real necessity was to just not get caught. That this was not simply a solution worked out by prisoners, but one intended by the SS, was made very clear to everyone. Again and again every SS, from the camp commander down, warned: "Don't dare to be noticeable," or "Don't dare to come to my attention." To the once traditional qualities of the "good" child, that he should be seen and not heard (never talk back or express an opinion) was now added the further injunction that the prisoner should be even more child than the good one: in addition to not being heard he should also be unseen. That meant he had to be so much a part of the mass, so devoid of individuality, that at no time could he be distinguished from all others.

The occasions proving the usefulness of this total disappearance in the mass were legion. For example, during morning roll call a fight of one against all often began for the least visible positions in the parade ground formation. The reason was that the bad humor of block and room chiefs, or worse, of the SS, was directed at those most accessible. If prisoners could not stand rigidly at attention, the ones most likely to get the blows or kicks were those who could be reached without breaking up the formation. Flaws in the cleaning of shoes or uniforms were also easier to see and punish in the first, last, and side rows of the formation. One was more likely to escape harm when protected on all sides by other prisoners.

Nor was that the only reason for avoiding positions of exposure. Standing up front, one could not help but see what went on all over the parade ground. Here, there, and everywhere, one saw prisoner officials abusing and beating those who moved, fidgeted or were not perfectly in line; the SS following with the same or worse. For reasons already discussed it was not only safer if one just didn't see, it protected one against the helpless fury that welled up at having to watch the mistreatment.

Still another reason was that sometimes one had to remain on the parade grounds for hours: if the roll call was not correct, if winter darkness or dense fog kept the prisoners from going to work and they were forced to stand rigidly at attention. Those inside the formation were hard to check; they could afford to stand at ease, and even while away the time by talking.

There were also the terrors of being "noticed" in the daily slave market. Every morning, after roll call, unassigned prisoners ran fearfully across the parade grounds to join some larger group without a labor command on that day. Speed was imperative, because a tired prisoner shuffling along was sure to attract attention. On the assumption that he had been dropped from his previous command as an undesirable, he would be placed in the least desirable work gang. Since he was unfit and tired, he was "expendable," a "drag" on the camp, and might as well be "finished off." Chances of escaping such a fate were better if one could quickly disappear in the mass.

Invisibility was thus a primary rule of defense whatever the situation might be. The need to feel invisible reduced men to the behavior of animals who also do their best to remain unseen, or of children who screen their faces or try to shrink away when confronted with danger. Adopting this enforced anonymity was a successful defense against the real dangers of the camp. But it meant making deliberate efforts to give up individuality and initiative, qualities much needed for the constantly changing emergencies of the camp situation.

Truly making such attitudes one's own had still other advantages. Not having a will of one's own removed the chances for having to go against one's own desires, or else having to repress or deny them. Not having a distinct personality meant not having to hide it, not having to fear that at any moment it might assert itself and bring on destruction. Anonymity meant relative safety, but it also meant giving up one's own personality, though the body walked about for some time, and more safely. But let the situation arise needing vision, independence of action, decision-making, and the ones who had given up personality to safeguard the body were least able to preserve the body they had safeguarded at such loss to their humanity.

RUDE AWAKENING

Another important strain on integration was the problem of what to do with one's hostility. Psychologically this problem was far more complex than dealing with the hostility of others. Prisoners found themselves in an impossible state of severe irritation, if only because of a steady interference, by guards or other prisoners, with anything they may have wished to do. The result was a steady accumulation of great amounts of aggression. Even getting up in the morning may illustrate these relentless pressures toward destroying each man as a self-respecting person.

Out of their slumber each morning, prisoners were rudely awakened long before they were rested. At Dachau the morning sirens sounded as early as 3:15 in summer; in winter somewhat later. Then there was roughly 45 minutes for chores. This would seem adequate time, but the actuality of the concentration camp made it otherwise. From the moment the siren sounded, a mad scramble began, with prisoners fighting to get all personal and official tasks done within the time allotted.

This was one of many occasions when friendly cooperation between prisoners and help from block and room chiefs might have made all the difference in the world. Cooperation between a few friends, which existed in most units, was ineffectual against the ferocious disorder that reigned among the majority. In these frantic moments, newcomers were always in the way of old-timers, as were individuals who could not fit themselves into a rigid discipline.

Very few blocks managed to get through the morning period in an orderly fashion without tension, anxiety, fighting, beatings, all kinds of mutual aggravation. Relative peace reigned only in the blocks housing prisoners who had been inmates for years, and where rule was by decent block and room chiefs. The reason was that finishing all required tasks in the time allowed asked for great experience and skill in each prisoner; even a few slow or clumsy ones threw the whole process out of gear. That kind of skill was acquired only after hundreds of performances, and only by prisoners in good health. But no such conditions prevailed in the majority of the barracks.

The first experience of the new day was one that forcefully impressed on each prisoner that they existed to obey, that the rules laid down from above took precedence over all natural desire to care for their bodily needs. It was an experience that set prisoner against prisoner, making life unbearable, and all this without the SS having uttered a word. The SS achieved it by their insistence on a senseless order and cleanliness. The enforcement of absolute and irrational orderliness and cleanliness in the barracks was one of the worst tortures of camp life, partly because all prisoners were in constant dread of punishment if even one of their number proved deficient.

The two major tasks in the morning were to "build" one's bed (if any) and to clean one's locker. The first was such a difficult task that prisoners sometimes preferred to sleep on the floor sooner than risk destroying their well built beds by sleeping in them and then being unable to rebuild them in the morning. For this they risked discovery and punishment for violation of rules. But it took even a skillful and experienced prisoner ten to fifteen minutes to build his bed. Some prisoners never learned to do it, particularly some of the older ones who could not balance well standing on the edge of the lower bunk while building the upper one.

As soon as the siren sounded (before then no light could be turned on and therefore no beds could be built) the prisoners jumped out of bed and those sleeping in the top row began. They were pestered by those who slept below them not to deface their mattresses, though it was almost impossible to build the top bed without messing up the one below. Then they were urged to hurry so that the prisoner below might begin his own bed. This often led to long feuds between those who slept above and those below. The same was true for two adjacent beds, since a well built bed might easily be defaced by the person building the one next to it.

To build a bed correctly, the straw mattresses had to be so restuffed and fixed that they were flat as a table, while the sides had to form an absolute rectangle. Pillows, if any, had to be placed on top of the mattress and also fixed so as to form an absolute cube. Both the pillow cube and the mattress had to be covered with a blue and white checked coverlet. These checks were quite small but the cover had to be so placed that the checks were in perfect alignment, horizontally and vertically. To make things more difficult, not only had every single bed to be perfectly built, but the whole row of beds and mattresses had to be in perfect alignment. Some SS checked with yardsticks and levels to make sure that the beds were built correctly and the rectangles perfect; others shot their gun across the beds to see that they were absolutely flat.

If one prisoner's bed was not built to perfection, he was punished severely; if several beds in a barrack were found wanting, the entire unit suffered severely. Always to one's own fear of punishment was added the pressure of others who feared punishment if anyone else's bed or locker was imperfect. Thus, the building of beds was one more fear haunting the prisoner, because whether at work or at rest, he could never be sure that during the day somebody might not inadvertently or maliciously touch his bed so that a piece of dust would fall on it, or a row of squares be out of place and thus render him liable to punishment. Or he may have seen another prisoner build his bed poorly and been in fear that the unit might suffer.

Many a prisoner who never learned to build his bed had to pay every day with money, labor or food to those who were willing to make his bed in addition to their own. In general, because of the haste in performing all chores, prisoners in units not extremely well organized were always having to make choices as to which activities they were willing to skip or neglect.

This sort of pressure was just one more device forcing men to work with gearlike precision, like automatons, running one another with speed and efficiency. It permitted no thoughts of one's own, nor could one do things in the tempo and sequence of one's own volition. All activities were externally regulated to prevent any autonomy on the part of the prisoner.

To take a few minutes longer at washing usually meant losing the chance to brush one's teeth, drink the morning coffee, or use the latrine. Having to rebuild one's bed because one had failed at the first attempt nearly always meant going without washing and coffee.

No prisoner could use the toilet or washroom after the first half hour in the morning, nor was he usually permitted to use the latrines till hours later. So it was absolutely necessary to eliminate before leaving the barracks. An average of six to eight open toilets had to serve anywhere from 100 to 300 men, nearly all suffering from digestive ailments because of the camp fare. So prisoners who had just finished fighting one another over the building of beds, now exploded at those who seemed to be leisurely about sitting on the toilet. Nor did having to watch others eliminate increase their good will toward one another. And so began the new day.

Before the sun had risen, a fight of one against all had already taken place with its tensions, degradations, and depression. It was forced upon prisoners even before a guard had entered the camp in the morning. The distant, still invisible SS had already ground them into a mass of people, unable to act upon their anger, frustrated in their impotence.

NOTES

[1] Hans Fallada's book, *Little Man, What Now?* (*Kleiner Mann, was nun?*, Hamburg, 1932/1950) was widely read before the ascent of Hitler, and also presented as a movie. Even those who did not read it were familiar with the title which became a slogan of the pre-Hitler epoch. The story emphasized the individual's inability to decide his own fate, which was then to be decided by totalitarian control.

[2] This, of course, does not fully apply where seniority on the job does provide security through union contracts.

Like most of Ambrose Bierce's work, "The Horseman in the Sky" depends for its effect upon a surprise ending. Such tales intrigue readers, but sound intuition has never allowed them to be characterized as great art. Their shock endings do not allow the reader to deflect his anxiety onto a safely concealing symbol.

Whether or not this horrifying little tale is great art it does force us to recognize a basic truth about the nature of the unconscious conflict that is the source of war.

AMBROSE BIERCE

A Horseman in the Sky

One sunny afternoon in the autumn of the year 1861 a soldier lay in a clump of laurel by the side of a road in western Virginia. He lay at full length upon his stomach, his feet resting upon the toes, his head upon the left forearm. His extended right hand loosely grasped his rifle. But for the somewhat methodical disposition of his limbs and a slight rhythmic movement of the cartridge box at the back of his belt, he might have been thought to be dead. He was asleep at his post of duty. But if detected he would be dead shortly afterward, death being the just and legal penalty of his crime.

The clump of laurel in which the criminal lay was in the angle of a road which, after ascending southward, a steep acclivity to that point turned sharply to the west, running along the summit for perhaps one hundred yards. There it turned southward again and went zigzagging downward through the forest. At the salient of that second angle was a large flat rock, jutting out northward, overlooking the deep valley from which the road ascended. The rock capped a high cliff; a stone dropped from its outer edge would have fallen sheer downward one thousand feet to the tops of the pines. The angle where the soldier lay was on another spur of the same cliff. Had he been awake he would have commanded a view, not only of the short arm of the road and the jutting rock, but of the entire profile of the cliff below it. It might well have made him giddy to look.

The country was wooded everywhere except at the bottom of the valley to the northward, where there was a small natural meadow, through which flowed a stream scarcely visible from the valley's rim. This open ground looked hardly larger than an ordinary dooryard, but was really several acres in extent. Its green was more vivid than that of the inclosing forest. Away beyond it rose a line of giant cliffs similar to those upon which we are supposed to stand in our survey of the savage scene, and through which the road had somehow made its climb to the summit. The configuration of the valley, indeed, was such that from this point of observation it seemed entirely shut in, and one could not but have wondered how the road which found a way out of it had found a way into it, and whence came and whither went the waters of the stream that parted the meadow two thousand feet below.

No country is so wild and difficult but men will make it a theater of war; concealed in the forest at the bottom of that military rattrap, in which half a hundred men in possession of the exits might have starved an army to submission, lay five regiments of Federal infantry. They had marched all the previous day and night and were resting. At nightfall they would take to the road again, climb to the place where their unfaithful sentinel now slept, and descending the other slope of the ridge, fall upon a camp of the enemy at about midnight. Their hope was to surprise it, for the road led to the rear of it. In case of failure, their position would be perilous in the extreme; and fail they surely would, should accident or vigilance apprise the enemy of the movement.

The sleeping sentinel in the clump of laurel was a young Virginian named Carter Druse. He was the son of wealthy parents, an only child, and had known such ease and cultivation and high living as wealth and taste were able to command in the mountain country of western Virginia. His home was but a few miles from where he now lay. One morning he had risen from the breakfast table and said quietly but gravely: "Father, a Union regiment has arrived at Grafton. I am going to join it."

The father lifted his leonine head, looked at the son a moment in silence, and replied: "Well, go, sir, and whatever may occur, do what you conceive to be your duty. Virginia, to which you are a traitor, must get on without you. Should we both live to the end of the war, we will speak further of the matter. Your mother, as the physician has informed you, is in a most critical condition; at the best she cannot be with us longer than a few weeks, but that time is precious. It would be better not to disturb her."

So Carter Druse, bowing reverently to his father, who returned the salute with a stately courtesy which masked a breaking heart, left the home of his childhood to go soldiering. By conscience and courage, by deeds of devotion and daring, he soon commended himself to his fellows and his officers; and it was to these qualities and to some knowledge of the country that he owed his selection for his present perilous duty at the extreme outpost. Nevertheless, fatigue had been stronger than resolution, and he had fallen asleep. What good or bad angel came in a dream to rouse him from his state of crime, who shall say? Without a movement, without a sound, in the profound silence and the languor of the late afternoon, some invisible messenger of fate touched with unsealing finger the eyes of his consciousness—whispered into the ear of his spirit the mysterious awakening word which no human lips ever have spoken, no human memory ever has recalled. He quietly raised his forehead from his arm and looked between the masking stems of the laurels, instinctively closing his right hand about the stock of his rifle.

His first feeling was a keen artistic delight. On a colossal pedestal, the cliff—motionless at the extreme edge of the capping rock and sharply outlined against the sky—was an equestrian statue of impressive dignity. The figure of the man sat the figure of the horse, straight and soldierly, but with the repose of a Grecian god carved in the marble which limits the suggestion of activity. The gray costume harmonized with its aerial background; the metal of accoutrement and caparison was softened and subdued by the shadow; the animal's skin had no points of high light. A carbine, strikingly foreshortened, lay across the pommel of the saddle, kept in place by the right hand grasping it at the "grip"; the left hand, holding the bridle rein, was invisible. In silhouette against the sky, the profile of the horse was cut with the sharpness of a cameo; it looked across the heights of air to the confronting cliffs beyond. The face of the rider, turned slightly away, showed only an outline of temple and beard; he was looking downward to the bottom of the valley. Magnified by its lift against the sky and by the soldier's testifying sense of the formidableness of a near enemy, the group appeared of heroic, almost colossal, size.

For an instant Druse had a strange, half-defined feeling that he had slept to the end of the war and was looking upon a noble work of art reared upon that commanding eminence to commemorate the deeds of an heroic past of which he had been an inglorious part. The feeling was dispelled by a slight movement of the group: the horse, without moving its feet, had drawn its body slightly backward from the verge; the man remained immobile as before. Broad awake and keenly alive to the significance of the situation, Druse now brought the butt of his rifle against his cheek by cautiously pushing the barrel forward through the bushes, cocked the piece, and glancing through the sights, covered a vital spot of the horseman's breast. A touch upon the trigger and all would have been well with Carter Druse. At that instant the horseman turned his head and looked in the direction of his concealed foeman—seemed to look into his very face, into his eyes, into his brave, compassionate heart.

Is it then so terrible to kill an enemy in war—an enemy who has surprised a secret vital to the safety of one's self and comrades—an enemy more formidable for his knowledge than all his army for its numbers? Carter Druse grew pale; he shook in every limb, turned faint, and saw the statuesque group before him as black figures, rising, falling, moving unsteadily in arcs of circles in a fiery sky. His hand fell away from his weapon, his head slowly dropped until his face rested on the leaves in which he lay. This courageous gentleman and hardy soldier was near swooning from intensity of emotion.

It was not for long; in another moment his face was raised from earth, his hands resumed their places on the rifle, his forefinger sought the trigger; mind, heart, and eyes were clear, conscience and reason sound. He could not hope to capture that enemy; to alarm him would but send him dashing to his camp with his fatal news. The duty of the soldier was plain: the man must be shot dead from ambush—without warning, without a moment's spiritual preparation, with never so much as an unspoken prayer, he must be sent to his account. But no—there is a hope; he may have discovered nothing—perhaps he is but admiring the sublimity of the landscape. If permitted, he may turn and ride carelessly away in the direction whence he came. Surely it will be possible to judge at the instant of his withdrawing whether he knows. It may well be that his fixity of attention—Druse turned his head and looked through the deeps of air downward, as from the surface to the bottom of a translucent sea. He saw creeping across the green meadow a sinuous line of figures of men and horses—some foolish commander was permitting the soldiers of his escort to water their beasts in the open, in plain view from a dozen summits!

Druse withdrew his eyes from the valley and fixed them again upon the group of man and horse in the sky, and again it was through the sights of his rifle. But this time his aim was at the horse. In his memory, as if they were a divine mandate, rang the words of his father at their parting: "Whatever may occur, do what you conceive to be your duty." He was calm now. His teeth were firmly but not rigidly closed; his nerves were as tranquil as a sleeping babe's—not a tremor affected any muscle of his body; his breathing, until suspended in the act of taking aim, was regular and slow. Duty had conquered; the spirit had said to the body: "Peace, be still." He fired.

An officer of the Federal force, who in a spirit of adventure or in quest of knowledge had left the hidden *bivouac* in the valley, and with aimless feet, had made his way to the lower edge of a small open space near the foot of the cliff, was considering what he had to gain by pushing his exploration further. At a distance of a quarter-mile before him, but apparently at a stone's throw, rose from its fringe of pines the gigantic face of rock, towering to so great a height above him that it made him giddy to look up to where its edge cut a sharp, rugged line against the sky. At some distance to his right it presented a clean, vertical profile against a background of blue sky to a point half the way down, and of distant hills, hardly less blue, thence to the tops of the trees at its base. Lifting his eyes to the dizzy altitude of its summit the officer saw an astonishing sight—a man on horseback riding down into the valley through the air!

Straight upright sat the rider, in military fashion, with a firm seat in the saddle, a strong clutch upon the rein to hold his charger from too impetuous a plunge. From his bare head his long hair streamed upward, waving like a plume. His hands were concealed in the cloud of the horse's lifted mane. The animal's body was as level as if every hoof-stroke encountered the resistant earth. Its motions were those of a wild gallop, but even as the officer looked they ceased, with all the legs thrown sharply forward as in the act of alighting from a leap. But this was a flight!

Filled with amazement and terror by this apparition of a horseman in the sky—half believing himself the chosen scribe of some new Apocalypse, the officer was overcome by the intensity of his emotions; his legs failed him and he fell. Almost at the same instant he heard a crashing sound in the trees—a sound that died without an echo—and all was still.

The officer rose to his feet, trembling. The familiar sensation of an abraded shin recalled his dazed faculties. Pulling himself together he ran rapidly, obliquely away from the cliff to a point distant from its foot;

thereabout he expected to find his man; and thereabout he naturally failed. In the fleeting instant of his vision his imagination had been so wrought upon by the apparent grace and ease and intention of the marvelous performance that it did not occur to him that the line of march of aerial cavalry is directly downward, and that he could find the objects of his search at the very foot of the cliff. A half hour later he returned to camp.

This officer was a wise man; he knew better than to tell an incredible truth. He said nothing of what he had seen. But when the commander asked him if in his scout he had learned anything of advantage to the expedition he answered:

"Yes, sir; there is no road leading down into this valley from the southward."

The commander, knowing better, smiled.

After firing his shot, private Carter Druse reloaded his rifle and resumed his watch. Ten minutes had hardly passed when a Federal sergeant crept cautiously to him on hands and knees. Druse neither turned his head nor looked at him, but lay without motion or sign of recognition.

"Did you fire?" the sergeant whispered.

"Yes."

"At what?"

"A horse. It was standing on yonder rock—pretty far out. You see it is no longer there. It went over the cliff." The man's face was white, but he showed no other sign of emotion. Having answered, he turned away his eyes and said no more. The sergeant did not understand.

"See here, Druse," he said, after a moment's silence, "it's no use making a mystery. I order you to report. Was there anybody on the horse?"

"Yes."

"Well?"

"My father."

The sergeant rose to his feet and walked away. "Good God!" he said.

It is a well-known psychoanalytic fact that love and death are often equated in the unconscious. The Russians, for example, refer to the orgasm as a "little death." A. E. Housman's deceptively sing-song poetry uses irony to smuggle a message about man's love affair with war and death past the watchful sentinels of the ego.

A. E. HOUSMAN

I Did Not Lose My Heart

I did not lose my heart in summer's even,
　　When roses to the moonrise burst apart:
When plumes were under heel and lead was flying,
　　In blood and smoke and flame I lost my heart.

I lost it to a soldier and a foeman,
　　A chap that did not kill me, but he tried;
That took the sabre straight and took it striking,
　　And laughed and kissed his hand to me and died.

All of Gogol's stories are intensely personal, emotionally charged sketches of psychological dissociation. Gogol's ability to turn horror into humor effectively disguises the truly terrifying content of his tales, and releases in laughter an enormous quantity of anxiety over the emergence of dangerous unconscious material.

In "The Nose" Gogol offers us not only an insight into an individual psychological disorder, but a brilliant description of what we might call the bureaucratic personality. The wretched hero transfers his unconscious fears and conflicts onto his nose, personified by bureaucratic trappings of status. Bureaucracy's encouragement of dissociation and the resultant disintegration of the ego are clearly symbolized in this alternately funny and terrifying tale.

NIKOLAI GOGOL

The Nose

1

An extraordinarily strange incident took place in Petersburg on the 25th of March. The barber, Ivan Yakovlevitch, who lives in the Voznesensky Prospect (his surname is lost, and nothing more appears even on his signboard, where a gentleman is depicted with his cheeks covered with soapsuds, together with an inscription "also lets blood")—the barber Ivan Yakovlevitch woke up rather early and was aware of a smell of hot bread. Raising himself in bed he saw his spouse, a rather portly lady who was very fond of drinking coffee, engaged in taking out of the oven some freshly-baked loaves.

"I won't have coffee to-day, Praskovya Osipovna," said Ivan Yakovlevitch; "instead I should like some hot bread with onion." (The fact is that Ivan Yakovlevitch would have liked both, but he knew that it was utterly impossible to ask for two things at once, for Praskovya Osipovna greatly disliked such caprices.)

"Let the fool have bread, so much the better for me," thought his spouse to herself; "there will be an extra cup of coffee left," and she flung one loaf on the table.

For the sake of propriety Ivan Yakovlevitch put a tail coat over his shirt, and, sitting down to the table, sprinkled with salt and prepared two onions, took a knife in his hand and, making a solemn face, set to work to cut the bread. After dividing the loaf into two halves he looked into the middle of it—and to his amazement saw there something that looked white. Ivan Yakovlevitch scooped at it carefully with his knife and felt it with his finger: "It's solid," he said to himself. "Whatever can it be?"

He thrust in his finger and drew it out—it was a nose! . . . Ivan Yakovlevitch's hand dropped with astonishment, he rubbed his eyes and felt it: it actually was a nose, and, what's more, it looked to him somehow familiar. A look of horror came into Ivan Yakovlevitch's face. But that horror was nothing to the indignation with which his wife was overcome.

"Where have you cut that nose off, you brute?" she cried wrathfully. "You scoundrel, you drunkard, I'll go the police myself to tell of you! You ruffian! Here I have heard from three men that when you are shaving them you pull at their noses till you almost tug them off."

But Ivan Yakovlevitch was more dead than alive: he perceived that the nose was no other than that of Kovalyov, the collegiate assessor, whom he shaved every Wednesday and Sunday.

"Stay, Praskovya Osipovna! I'll wrap it up in a rag and put it in a corner. Let it stay there for a bit; I'll return it later on."

"I won't hear of it! As though I would allow a stray nose to lie about in my room. You dried-up biscuit! To be sure, he can do nothing but sharpen his razors on the strop, but soon he won't be fit to do his duties at all, the gad-about, the good-for-nothing! As though I were going to answer to the police for you. . . . Oh, you sloven, you stupid blockhead. Away with it, away with it! Take it where you like! Don't let me set eyes on it again!"

Ivan Yakovlevitch stood as though utterly crushed. He thought and thought, and did not know what to think. "The devil only knows how it happened," he said at last, scratching behind his ear. "Did I come home drunk last night or not? I can't say for certain now. But from all signs and tokens it must be a thing quite unheard of, for bread is a thing that is baked, while a nose is something quite different. I can't make head or tail of it." Ivan Yakovlevitch sank into silence. The thought that the police might make a search there for the nose and throw the blame of it on him reduced him to complete prostration. Already the red collar, beautifully embroidered with silver, the sabre, hovered before his eyes, and he trembled all over. At last he got his breeches and his boots, pulled on these wretched objects, and, accompanied by the stern up-braidings of Praskovya Osipovna, wrapped the nose in a rag and went out into the street.

He wanted to thrust it out of sight somewhere, under a gate, or somehow accidentally to drop it and then turn off into a side street, but as ill-luck would have it he kept coming upon some one he knew, who would at once begin by asking: "Where are you going?" or "Whom are you going to shave so early?" so that Ivan Yakovlevitch could never find a good moment. Another time he really did drop it, but a sentry pointed to it with his halberd from a long way off, saying as he did so: "Pick it up, you have dropped something!" and Ivan Yakovlevitch was obliged to pick up the nose and put it in his pocket. He was overcome by despair, especially as the number of people in the street was continually increasing as the shops and stalls began to open.

He made up his mind to go to St. Isaac's Bridge in the hope of being able to fling it into the Neva. . . . But I am rather in fault for not having hitherto said anything about Ivan Yakovlevitch, a worthy man in many respects.

Ivan Yakovlevitch, like every self-respecting Russian workman, was a terrible drunkard, and though every day he shaved other people's chins, his own went for ever unshaven. Ivan Yakovlevitch's tail coat (he never wore any other shape) was piebald, that is, it was black dappled all over with brown and yellow and grey; the collar was shiny, and instead of three buttons there was only one hanging on a thread. Ivan Yakovlevitch was a great cynic, and when Kovalyov the collegiate asses-sor said to him while he was being shaved: "Your hands always stink, Ivan Yakovlevitch," the latter would reply with the question: "What should make them stink?" "I can't tell, my good man, but they do stink," the collegiate assessor would say, and, taking a pinch of snuff, Ivan Yakovlevitch lathered him for it on his cheeks and under his nose and behind his ears and under his beard—in fact wherever he chose.

The worthy citizen found himself by now on St. Isaac's Bridge. First of all he looked about him, then bent over the parapet as though to look under the bridge to see whether there were a great number of fish racing by, and stealthily flung in the rag with the nose. He felt as though with it a heavy weight had rolled off his back. Ivan Yakovlevitch actually grinned. Instead of going to shave the chins of government clerks, he repaired to an establishment bearing the inscription "Tea and refreshments" and asked for a glass of punch, when he suddenly observed at the end of the bridge a police inspector of respectable appearance with full whiskers, with a three-cornered hat and a sword. He turned cold, and meanwhile the inspector beckoned to him and said: "Come this way, my good man."

Ivan Yakovlevitch, knowing the etiquette, took off his hat some way off and, as he approached, said: "I wish your honour good health."

"No, no, old fellow, I am not 'your honour': tell me what you were about, standing on the bridge?"

"Upon my soul, sir, I was on my way to shave my customers, and I was only looking to see whether the current was running fast."

"That's a lie, that's a lie! You won't get off with that. Kindly answer!"

"I am ready to shave you, gracious sir, two or even three times a week with no conditions whatever," answered Ivan Yakovlevitch.

"No, my friend, that is nonsense; I have three barbers to shave me and they think it a great honour, too. But be so kind as to tell me what you were doing there?"

Ivan Yakovlevitch turned pale . . . but the incident is completely veiled in obscurity, and absolutely nothing is known of what happened next.

2

Kovalyov the collegiate assessor woke up early next morning and made the sound "brrrr . . ." with the lips as he always did when he woke up, though he could not himself have explained the reason for his doing so. Kovalyov stretched and asked for a little looking-glass that was standing on the table. He wanted to look at a pimple which had come out upon his nose on the previous evening, but to his great astonishment there was a completely flat space where his nose should have been. Kovalyov in a fright asked for some water and a towel to rub his eyes: there really was no nose. He began feeling with his hand, and pinched himself to see whether he was still asleep: it appeared that he was not asleep. The collegiate assessor jumped out of bed, he shook himself— there was still no nose. . . . He ordered his clothes to be given him at once and flew off straight to the head police-master.

But meanwhile we must say a word about Kovalyov in order that the reader may have some idea of what kind of collegiate assessor he was. Collegiate assessors who receive that title through learned diplomas cannot be compared with those who are created collegiate assessors in the Caucasus. They are two quite different species. The learned collegiate assessors . . . But Russia is such a wonderful country that, if you say a word about one collegiate assessor, all the collegiate assessors from Riga to Kamchatka would certainly take it to themselves; and it is the same, of course, with all grades and titles. Kovalyov was a collegiate assessor from the Caucasus. He had only been of that rank for the last two years, and so could not forget it for a moment; and to give himself greater weight and dignity he did not call himself simply collegiate assessor but always spoke of himself as a major. "Listen, my dear," he would usually say when he met in the street a woman selling shirt-fronts, "you go to my house; I live in Sadovoy Street; just ask, does Major Kovalyov live here? Any one will show you." If he met some prepossessing little baggage he would give her besides a secret instruction, adding: "You ask for Major Kovalyov's flat, my love." For this reason we will for the future speak of him as the major.

Major Kovalyov was in the habit of walking every day up and down the Nevsky Prospect. The collar of his shirt-front was always extremely clean and well starched. His whiskers were such as one may see nowadays on provincial and district surveyors, on architects and army doctors, also on those employed on special commissions and in general on all such men as have full ruddy cheeks and are very good hands at a game of boston: these whiskers start from the middle of the cheek and go straight up to the nose. Major Kovalyov used to wear a number of cornelian seals, some with crests on them and others on which were carved Wednesday, Thursday, Monday, and so on. Major Kovalyov had come to Petersburg on business, that is, to look for a post befitting his rank: if he were successful, the post of a vice-governor, and failing that the situation of an executive clerk in some prominent department. Major Kovalyov was not averse to matrimony, but only on condition he could find a bride with a fortune of two hundred thousand. And so the reader may judge for himself what was the major's position when he saw, instead of a nice-looking, well-proportioned nose, an extremely stupid level space.

As ill-luck would have it, not a cab was to be seen in the street, and he was obliged to walk, wrapping himself in his cloak and hiding his face in his handkerchief, as though his nose were bleeding. "But perhaps it was my imagination: it's impossible I could have been so silly as to lose my nose," he thought, and went into a confectioner's on purpose to look at himself in the looking-glass. Fortunately there was no one in the shop: some boys were sweeping the floor and putting all the chairs straight; others with sleepy faces were bringing in hot turnovers on trays: yesterday's papers covered with coffee stains were lying about on the tables and chairs. "Well, thank God, there is nobody here," he thought; "now I can look." He went timidly up to the mirror and looked. "What the devil's the meaning of it? how nasty!" he commented, spitting. "If only there had been something instead of a nose, but there is nothing! . . ."

Biting his lips, he went out of the confectioner's with annoyance, and resolved, contrary to his usual practice, not to look or smile at any one. All at once he stood as though rooted to the spot before the door of a house. Something inexplicable took place before his eyes: a carriage was stopping at the entrance; the carriage door flew open; a gentleman in uniform, bending down, sprang out and ran up the steps. What was the horror and at the same time amazement of Kovalyov when he recognised that this was his own nose! At this extraordinary spectacle it seemed to him that everything was heaving before his eyes; he felt that he could scarcely stand; but he made up his mind, come what may, to await the gentleman's return to the carriage, and he stood trembling all over as though in fever. Two minutes later the nose actually did come out. He was in a gold-laced uniform with a big stand-up collar; he had on chamois-leather breeches, at his side was a sword. From his plumed hat it might be gathered that he was of the rank of a civil councillor. Everything showed that he was going somewhere to pay a visit. He looked to both sides, called to the coachman to open the carriage door, got in and drove off.

Poor Kovalyov almost went out of his mind; he did not know what to think of such a strange occurrence. How was it possible for a nose—which had only yesterday been on his face and could neither drive nor walk—to be in uniform! He ran after the carriage, which luckily did not go far, but stopped before the entrance to the bazaar.

He hurried in that direction, made his way through a row of old beggar women with their faces tied up and two chinks in place of their eyes at whom he used to laugh so merrily. There were not many people about. Kovalyov felt so upset that he could not make up his mind what to do, and looked for the gentleman up and down the street; at last he saw him standing before a shop. The nose was hiding his face completely in a high stand-up collar and was surveying some goods in the shop window with the utmost attention.

"How am I to approach him?" thought Kovalyov. "One can see by everything—from his uniform, from his hat—that he is a civil council-lor. The devil only knows how to do it!"

He began by coughing at his side; but the nose never changed his position for a minute.

"Sir," said Kovalyov, inwardly forcing himself to speak confidently. "Sir. . . ."

"What do you want?" answered the nose, turning round.

"It seems . . . strange to me, sir. . . . You ought to know your proper place, and all at once I find you, where? . . . You will admit . . ."

"Excuse me, I cannot understand what you are talking about. . . . Explain."

"How am I to explain to him?" thought Kovalyov, and plucking up his courage he began: "Of course I . . . I am a major, by the way. For me to go about without a nose you must admit is improper. An old woman selling peeled oranges on Voskresensky Bridge may sit there without a nose; but having prospects of obtaining . . . and being besides acquainted with a great many ladies in the families of Tchehtarev the civil councillor and others . . . You can judge for yourself . . . I don't know, sir (at this point Major Kovalyov shrugged his shoulders) . . . excuse me . . . if you look at the matter in accordance with the principles of duty and honour . . . you can understand of yourself . . ."

"I don't understand a word," said the nose. "Explain it more satisfactorily."

"Sir," said Kovalyov, with a sense of his own dignity, "I don't know how to understand your words. The matter appears to me perfectly obvious . . . either you wish . . . Why, you are my own nose!"

The nose looked at the major and his eyebrows slightly quivered.

"You are mistaken, sir, I am an independent individual. Moreover, there can be no sort of close relations between us. I see, sir, from the buttons of your uniform, you must be serving in a different department." Saying this the nose turned away.

Kovalyov was utterly confused, not knowing what to do or even what to think. Meanwhile they heard the agreeable rustle of a lady's dress: an elderly lady was approaching, all decked out in lace, and with her a slim lady in a white dress which looked very charming on her slender figure, in a straw-coloured hat as light as a pastry puff. Behind them stood, opening his snuff-box, a tall footman with big whiskers and quite a dozen collars.

Kovalyov came nearer, pulled out the cambric collar of his shirt-front, arranged the seals on his gold watch-chain, and, smiling from side to side, turned his attention to the ethereal lady who, like a spring flower, faintly swayed forward and put her white hand with its half-transparent fingers to her brow. The smile on Kovalyov's face broadened when he saw under the hat her round, dazzling white chin and part of her cheek flushed with the hues of the first spring rose; but all at once he skipped away as though he had been scalded. He recollected that he had absolutely nothing on his face in place of a nose, and tears oozed from his eyes. He turned away to tell the gentleman in uniform straight out that he was only pretending to be a civil councillor, that he was a rogue and a scoundrel, and that he was nothing else than his own nose. . . . But the nose was no longer there; he had managed to gallop off, probably again to call on some one.

This reduced Kovalyov to despair. He went back and stood for a minute or two under the colonnade, carefully looking in all directions to see whether the nose was anywhere about. He remembered very well that there was a plume in his hat and gold lace on his uniform; but he had not noticed his greatcoat nor the colour of his carriage, nor his horses, nor even whether he had a footman behind him and if so in what livery. Moreover, such numbers of carriages were driving backwards and forwards and at such a speed that it was difficult even to distinguish them; and if he had distinguished one of them he would have had no means of stopping it. It was a lovely, sunny day. There were masses of people on the Nevsky; ladies were scattered like a perfect cataract of flowers all over the pavement from Politseysky to the Anitchkin Bridge. Here he saw coming towards him an upper-court councillor of his acquaintance whom he used to call "lieutenant-colonel," particularly if he were speaking to other people. There he saw Yaryzhkin, a head clerk in the senate, a great friend of his, who always lost points when he went eight at boston. And here was another major who had received the rank of assessor in the Caucasus, beckoning to him. . . .

"Ah, deuce take it," said Kovalyov. "Hi, cab! drive straight to the police-master's."

Kovalyov got into a cab and shouted to the driver:

"Drive like a house on fire."

"Is the police-master at home?" he cried, going into the entry.

"No," answered the porter, "he has only just gone out."

"Well, I declare!"

"Yes," added the porter, "and he has not been gone so long: if you had come but a tiny minute earlier you might have found him."

Kovalyov, still keeping the handkerchief over his face, got into the cab and shouted in a voice of despair: "Drive on."

"Where?" asked the cabman.

"Drive straight on!"

"How straight on? Here's the turning, is it to right or to left?"

This question pulled Kovalyov up and forced him to think again. In his position he ought first of all to address himself to the department of law and order, not because it had any direct connection with the police but because the intervention of the latter might be far more rapid than any help he could get in other departments. To seek satisfaction from the higher officials of the department in which the nose had announced himself as serving would have been injudicious, since from the nose's own answers he had been able to perceive that nothing was sacred to that man and that he might tell lies in this case too, just as he had lied in declaring that he had never seen him before. And so Kovalyov was on the point of telling the cabman to drive to the police station, when again the idea occurred to him that this rogue and scoundrel who had at their first meeting behaved in such a shameless way might seize the opportunity and slip out of the town—and then all his searches would be in vain, or might be prolonged, which God forbid, for a whole month. At last it seemed that Heaven itself directed him. He decided to go straight to a newspaper office and without loss of time to publish a circumstantial description of the nose, so that any one meeting it might at once present it to him or at least let him know where it was. And so, deciding upon this course, he told the cabman to drive to the newspaper office, and all the way never ceased pommelling him with his fist on the back, saying as he did so, "Quicker, you rascal; make haste, you knave!"

"Ugh, sir!" said the cabman, shaking his head and flicking with the reins at the horse, whose coat was as long as a lapdog's. At last the droshky stopped and Kovalyov ran panting into a little reception room where a grey-headed clerk in spectacles, wearing an old tailcoat, was sitting at a table and with a pen between his teeth was counting over some coppers he had before him.

"Who receives inquiries here?" cried Kovalyov. "Ah, good day!"

"I wish you good day," said the grey-headed clerk, raising his eyes for a moment and then dropping them again on the money lying in heaps on the table.

"I want to insert an advertisement . . ."

"Allow me to ask you to wait a minute," the clerk pronounced, with one hand noting a figure on the paper and with the finger of his left hand moving two beads on the reckoning board. A flunkey with braid on his livery and a rather clean appearance, which betrayed that he had at some time served in an aristocratic family, was standing at the table with a written paper in his hand and thought fit to display his social abilities: "Would you believe it, sir, that the little cur is not worth eighty kopecks; in fact I wouldn't give eight for it, but the countess is fond of it—my goodness, she is fond of it, and here she will give a hundred roubles to any one who finds it! To speak politely, as you and I are speaking now, people's tastes are quite incompatible: when a man's a sportsman then he'll keep a setter or a poodle; he won't mind giving five hundred or a thousand so long as it is a good dog."

The worthy clerk listened to this with a significant air, and at the same time was reckoning the number of letters in the advertisement brought him. Along the sides of the room stood a number of old women, shop-boys, and house-porters who had brought advertisements. In one it was announced that a coachman of sober habits was looking for a situation; in the next a second-hand carriage brought from Paris in 1814 was offered for sale; next a maid-servant, aged nineteen, experienced in laundry work and also competent to do other work, was looking for a situation; a strong droshky with only one spring broken was for sale; a spirited, young, dappled grey horse, only seventeen years old, for sale; a new consignment of turnip and radish seed from London; a summer villa with all conveniences, stabling for two horses, and a piece of land that might well be planted with fine birches and pine trees; there was also an appeal to those wishing to purchase old boot-soles, inviting such to come for the same every day between eight o'clock in the morning and three o'clock in the afternoon. The room in which all this company was assembled was a small one and the air in it was extremely thick, but the collegiate assessor Kobalyov was incapable of noticing the stench both because he kept his handkerchief over his face and because his nose was goodness knows where.

"Dear sir, allow me to ask you . . . my case is very urgent," he said at last impatiently.

"In a minute, in a minute! . . . Two roubles, forty-three kopecks! . . . This minute! One rouble and sixty-four kopecks!" said the grey-headed gentleman, flinging the old women and house-porters the various documents they had brought. "What can I do for you?" he said at last, turning to Kovalyov.

"I want to ask . . ." said Kovalyov. "Some robbery or trickery has occurred; I cannot make it out at all. I only want you to advertise that any one who brings me the scoundrel will receive a handsome reward."

"Allow me to ask what is your surname?"

"No, why put my surname? I cannot give it you! I have a large circle of acquaintances: Madame Tchehtarev, wife of a civil councillor, Pelageya Grigoryevna Podtatchin, widow of an officer . . . they will find out. God forbid! You can simply put: 'a collegiate assessor,' or better still, 'a person of major's rank.' "

"Is the runaway your house-serf, then?"

"A house-serf indeed! that would not be so great a piece of knavery! It's my nose . . . has run away from me . . . my own nose."

"H'm, what a strange surname! And is it a very large sum this Mr. Nosov has robbed you of?"

"Nosov! . . . you are on the wrong tack. It is my nose, my own nose that has disappeared, I don't know where. The devil wanted to have a joke at my expense."

"But in what way did it disappear? There is something I can't quite understand."

"And indeed, I can't tell you how it happened; the point is that now it is driving about the town, calling itself a civil councillor. And so I beg you to announce that any one who catches him must bring him at once to me as quickly as possible. Only think, really, how can I get on without such a conspicuous part of my person. It's not like a little toe, the loss of which I could hide in my boot and no one could say whether it was there or not. I go on Thursdays to Madame Tchehtarev's; Pelageya Grigoryevna Podtatchin, an officer's widow, and her very pretty daughter are great friends of mine; and you can judge for yourself what a fix I am in now. . . . I can't possibly show myself now. . . ."

The clerk pondered, a fact which was manifest from the way he compressed his lips.

"No, I can't put an advertisement like that in the paper," he said at last, after a long silence.

"What? Why not?"

"Well. The newspaper might lose its reputation. If every one is going to write that his nose has run away, why . . . As it is, they say we print lots of absurd things and false reports."

"But what is there absurd about this? I don't see anything absurd in it."

"You fancy there is nothing absurd in it? But last week, now, this was what happened. A government clerk came to me just as you have; he brought an advertisement, it came to two roubles seventy-three kopecks, and all the advertisement amounted to was that a poodle with a black coat had strayed. You wouldn't think that there was anything in that, would you? But it turned out to be a lampoon on some one: the poodle was the cashier of some department, I don't remember which."

"But I am not asking you to advertise about poodles but about my own nose; that is almost the same as about myself."

"No, such an advertisement I cannot insert."

"But since my nose really is lost!"

"If it is lost that is a matter for the doctor. They say there are people who can fit you with a nose of any shape you like. But I observe you must be a gentleman of merry disposition and are fond of having your joke."

"I swear as God is holy! If you like, since it has come to that, I will show you."

"I don't want to trouble you," said the clerk, taking a pinch of snuff. "However, if it is no trouble," he added, moved by curiosity, "it might be desirable to have a look."

The collegiate assessor took the handkerchief from his face. "It really is extremely strange," said the clerk, "the place is perfectly flat, like a freshly fried pancake. Yes, it's incredibly smooth."

"Will you dispute it now? You see for yourself I must advertise. I shall be particularly grateful to you and very glad this incident has given me the pleasure of your acquaintance."

The major, as may be seen, made up his mind on this occasion to resort to a little flattery.

"To print such an advertisement is, of course, not such a very great matter," said the clerk. "But I do not foresee any advantage to you from it. If you do want to, put it in the hands of some one with a skilful pen, describe it as a rare freak of nature, and publish the little article in the *Northern Bee*" (at this point he once more took a pinch of snuff) "for the benefit of youth" (at this moment he wiped his nose), "or anyway as a matter of general interest."

The collegiate assessor felt quite hopeless. He dropped his eyes and looked at the bottom of the paper where there was an announcement of an entertainment; his face was ready to break into a smile as he saw the name of a pretty actress, and his hand went to his pocket to feel whether he had a five-rouble note there, for an officer of his rank ought, in Kovalyov's opinion, to have a seat in the stalls; but the thought of his nose spoilt it all.

Even the clerk seemed touched by Kovalyov's difficult position. Desirous of relieving his distress in some way, he thought it befitting to express his sympathy in a few words: "I am really very much grieved that such an incident should have occurred to you. Wouldn't you like a pinch of snuff? it relieves headache and dissipates depression; even in intestinal trouble it is of use." Saying this the clerk offered Kovalyov his snuff-box, rather neatly opening the lid with a portrait of a lady in a hat on it.

This unpremeditated action drove Kovalyov out of all patience.

"I can't understand how you can think fit to make a joke of it," he said angrily; "don't you see that I am without just what I need for sniffing! The devil take your snuff! I can't bear the sight of it now, not merely your miserable Berezina stuff but even if you were to offer me rappee itself!" Saying this he walked out of the newspaper office, deeply mortified, and went in the direction of the local police superintendent.

Kovalyov walked in at the very moment when he was stretching and clearing his throat and saying: "Ah, I should enjoy a couple of hours' nap!" And so it might be foreseen that the collegiate assessor's visit was not very opportune. The police superintendent was a great patron of all arts and manufactures; but the paper note he preferred to everything. "That is a thing," he used to say, "there is nothing better than that thing; it does not ask for food, it takes up little space, there is always room for it in the pocket, and if you drop it, it does not break."

The police superintendent received Kovalyov rather coldly and said that after dinner was not the time to make an enquiry, that nature itself had ordained that man should rest a little after eating (the collegiate assessor could see from this that the sayings of the ancient sages were not unfamiliar to the local superintendent), and that a respectable man does not have his nose pulled off.

This was adding insult to injury. It must be said that Kovalyov was very easily offended. He could forgive anything whatever said about himself, but could never forgive insult to his rank or his calling. He was even of the opinion that any reference to officers of the higher ranks might be allowed to pass in stage plays, but that no attack ought to be made on those of a lower grade. The reception given him by the local superintendent so disconcerted him that he tossed his head and said with an air of dignity and a slight gesticulation of surprise: "I must observe that after observations so insulting on your part I can add nothing more . . ." and went out.

He went home hardly conscious of the ground under his feet. But now it was dusk. His lodgings seemed to him melancholy or rather utterly disgusting after all these unsuccessful efforts. Going into his entry he saw his valet, Ivan, lying on his dirty leather sofa; he was spitting on the ceiling and rather successfully aiming at the same spot. The nonchalance of his servant enraged him; he hit him on the forehead with his hat, saying: "You pig, you are always doing something stupid."

Ivan leapt up and rushed headlong to help him off with his cloak.

Going into his room, weary and dejected, the major threw himself into an easy chair, and at last, after several sighs, said:—

"My God, my God! Why has this misfortune befallen me? If I had lost an arm or a leg—anyway it would have been better; but without a nose a man is goodness knows what: neither fish nor fowl nor human being, good for nothing but to fling out of the window! And if only it had been cut off in battle or in a duel, or if I had been the cause of it myself, but, as it is, it is lost for no cause or reason, it is lost for nothing, absolutely nothing! But no, it cannot be," he added after a moment's thought; "it's incredible that a nose should be lost. It must be a dream or an illusion. Perhaps by some mistake I drank instead of water the vodka I use to rub my chin after shaving. Ivan, the fool, did not remove it and very likely I took it." To convince himself that he was not drunk, the major pinched himself so painfully that he shrieked. The pain completely convinced him that he was living and acting in real life. He slowly approached the looking-glass and at first screwed up his eyes with the idea that maybe his nose would appear in its proper place; but at the same minute sprang back, saying: "What a caricature."

It really was incomprehensible; if a button had been lost or a silver spoon or a watch or anything similar—but to have lost this, and in one's own flat too! . . . Thinking over all the circumstances, Major Kovalyov reached the supposition that what might be nearest the truth was that the person responsible for this could be no other than Madame Podtatchin, who wanted him to marry her daughter. He himself liked flirting with her, but avoided a definite engagement. When the mother had informed him directly that she wished for the marriage, he had slyly put her off with his compliments, saying that he was still young, that he must serve for five years so as to be exactly forty-two. And that Madame Podtatchin had therefore made up her mind, probably out of revenge, to ruin him, and had hired for the purpose some peasant witches, because it was impossible to suppose that the nose had been cut off in any way; no one had come into his room; the barber Ivan Yakovlevitch had shaved him on Wednesday, and all Wednesday and even all Thursday his nose had been all right—that he remembered and was quite certain about; besides, he would have felt pain, and there could have been no doubt that the wound could not have healed so soon and been as flat as a pancake. He formed various plans in his mind: either to summon Madame Podtatchin formally before the court or to go to her himself and tax her with it. These reflections were interrupted by a light which gleamed through all the cracks of the door and let him know that a candle had been lighted in the entry by Ivan. Soon Ivan himself appeared, holding it before him and lighting up the whole room. Kovalyov's first movement was to snatch up his handkerchief and cover the place where yesterday his nose had been, that his really stupid servant might not gape at the sight of anything so peculiar in his master.

Ivan had hardly time to retreat to his lair when there was the sound of an unfamiliar voice in the entry, pronouncing the words: "Does the collegiate assessor Kovalyov live here?"

"Come in, Major Kovalyov is here," said Kovalyov, jumping up hurriedly and opening the door.

There walked in a police officer of handsome appearance, with whiskers neither too fair nor too dark, and rather fat cheeks, the very one who at the beginning of our story was standing at the end of St. Isaac's Bridge.

"You have been pleased to lose your nose, sir?"

"That is so."

"It is now found."

"What are you saying?" cried Major Kovalyov. He could not speak for joy. He gazed open-eyed at the police officer standing before him, on whose full lips and cheeks the flickering light of the candle was brightly reflected. "How?"

"By a strange chance: he was caught almost on the road. He had already taken his seat in the diligence and was intending to go to Riga, and had already taken a passport in the name of a government clerk. And the strange thing is that I myself took him for a gentleman at first, but fortunately I had my spectacles with me and I soon saw that it was a nose. You know I am short-sighted. And if you stand before me I only see that you have a face, but I don't notice your nose or your beard or anything. My mother-in-law, that is my wife's mother, doesn't see anything either."

Kovalyov was beside himself with joy. "Where? Where? I'll run at once."

"Don't disturb yourself. Knowing that you were in need of it I brought it along with me. And the strange thing is that the man who has had the most to do with the affair is a rascal of a barber in the Voznesensky Street, who is now in custody. I have long suspected him of drunkenness and thieving, and only the day before yesterday he carried off a strip of buttons from one shop. Your nose is exactly as it was."

With this the police officer put his hand in his pocket and drew out the nose just as it was.

"That's it!" Kovalyov cried. "That's certainly it. You must have a cup of tea with me this evening."

"I should look upon it as a great pleasure, but I can't possibly manage it: I have to go from here to the penitentiary. . . . How the prices of all provisions are going up! . . . At home I have my mother-in-law, that is my wife's mother, and my children, the eldest particularly gives signs of great promise, he is a very intelligent child; but we have absolutely no means for his education. . . ."

For some time after the policeman's departure the collegiate assessor remained in a state of bewilderment, and it was only a few minutes later that he was capable of feeling and understanding again: he was reduced to such stupefaction by this unexpected good fortune. He took the recovered nose carefully in his two hands, holding them together like a cup, and once more examined it attentively.

"Yes, that's it, it's certainly it," said Major Kovalyov. "There's the pimple that came out on the left side yesterday." The major almost laughed aloud with joy.

But nothing in this world is of long duration, and so his joy was not so great the next moment; and the moment after, it was still less, and in the end he passed imperceptibly into his ordinary frame of mind, just as a circle on the water caused by a falling stone gradually passes away into the unbroken smoothness of the surface. Kovalyov began to think, and reflected that the business was not finished yet; the nose was found, but it had to be put on, fixed in its proper place.

"And what if it won't stick?" Asking himself this question, the major turned pale.

With a feeling of irrepressible terror he rushed to the table and moved the looking-glass forward that he might not put the nose on crooked. His hands trembled. Cautiously and circumspectly he replaced it in its former position. Oh horror, the nose would not stick on! . . . He put it to his lips, slightly warmed it with his breath, and again applied it to the flat space between his two cheeks; but nothing would make the nose keep on.

"Come, come, stick on, you fool!" he said to it; but the nose seemed made of wood and fell on the table with a strange sound as though it were a cork. The major's face worked convulsively.

"Is it possible that it won't grow on again?" But, however often he applied it to the proper place, the attempt was as unsuccessful as before.

He called Ivan and sent him for a doctor who tenanted the best flat on the first storey of the same house. The doctor was a handsome man, he had magnificent pitch-black whiskers, a fresh and healthy wife, ate fresh apples in the morning and kept his mouth extraordinarily clean, rinsing it out for nearly three-quarters of an hour every morning and cleaning his teeth with five different sorts of brushes. The doctor appeared immediately. Asking how long ago the trouble had occurred, he took Major Kovalyov by the chin and with his thumb gave him a flip on the spot where the nose had been, making the major jerk back his head so abruptly that he knocked the back of it against the wall. The doctor said that that did not matter, and, advising him to move a little away from the wall, he told him to bend his head round first to the right, and feeling the place where the nose had been, said, "H'm!" Then he told him to turn his head round to the left side and again said "H'm!" And in conclusion he gave him again a flip with his thumb, so that Major Kovalyov threw up his head like a horse when his teeth are being looked at. After making this experiment the doctor shook his head and said:—

"No, it's impossible. You had better stay as you are, for it may be made much worse. Of course, it might be stuck on; I could stick it on for you at once, if you like; but I assure you it would be worse for you."

"That's a nice thing to say! How can I stay without a nose?" said Kovalyov. "Things can't possibly be worse than now. It's simply beyond everything. Where can I show myself with such a caricature of a face? I have a good circle of acquaintances. Today, for instance, I ought to be at two evening parties. I know a great many people; Madame Tchehtarev, the wife of a civil councillor, Madame Podtatchin, an officer's widow . . . though after the way she has behaved, I'll have nothing more to do with her except through the police. Do me a favour," Kovalyov went on in a supplicating voice; "is there no means of sticking it on? Even if it were not neatly done, so long as it would keep on; I could even hold it on with my hand at critical moments. I wouldn't dance in any case for fear of a rash movement upsetting it. As for remuneration for your services, you may be assured that as far as my means allow . . ."

"Believe me," said the doctor, in a voice neither loud nor low but persuasive and magnetic, "that I never work from mercenary motives; that is opposed to my principles and my science. It is true that I accept a fee for my visits, but that is simply to avoid wounding my patients by refusing it. Of course I could replace your nose; but I assure you on my honour, since you do not believe my word, that it will be much worse for you. You had better wait for the action of nature itself. Wash it frequently with cold water, and I assure you that even without a nose you will be just as healthy as with one. And I advise you to put the nose in a bottle, in spirits or, better still, put two tablespoonfuls of sour vodka on it and heated vinegar—and then you might get quite a sum of money for it. I'd even take it myself, if you don't ask too much for it."

"No, no, I wouldn't sell it for anything," Major Kovalyov cried in despair; "I'd rather it were lost than that!"

"Excuse me!" said the doctor, bowing himself out, "I was trying to be of use to you. . . . Well, there is nothing for it! Anyway, you see that I have done my best." Saying this the doctor walked out of the room with a majestic air. Kovalyov did not notice his face, and, almost lost to consciousness, saw nothing but the cuffs of his clean and snow-white shirt peeping out from the sleeves of his black tail-coat.

Next day he decided, before lodging a complaint with the police, to write to Madame Podtatchin to see whether she would consent to return him what was needful without a struggle. The letter was as follows:—

DEAR MADAM,
>   ALEXANDRA GRIGORYEVNA.

I cannot understand this strange conduct on your part. You may rest assured that you will gain nothing by what you have done, and you will not get a step nearer forcing me to marry your daughter. Believe me, that business in regard to my nose is no secret, no more than it is that you and no other are the person chiefly responsible. The sudden parting of the same from its natural position, its flight and masquerading, at one time in the form of a government clerk and finally in its own shape, is nothing else than the consequence of the sorceries practised by you or by those who are versed in the same honourable arts as you are. For my part I consider it my duty to warn you, if the above-mentioned nose is not in its proper place to-day, I shall be obliged to resort to the assistance and protection of the law.

I have, however, with complete respect to you, the honour to be

>   Your respectful servant,
>   PLATON KOVALYOV.

DEAR SIR,
>   PLATON KUZMITCH!

Your letter greatly astonished me. I must frankly confess that I did not expect it, especially in regard to your unjust reproaches. I assure you I have never received the government clerk of whom you speak in my house, neither in masquerade nor in his own attire. It is true that

Filipp Ivanovitch Potantchikov has been to see me, and although, indeed, he is asking me for my daughter's hand and is a well conducted, sober man of great learning, I have never encouraged his hopes. You make some reference to your nose also. If you wish me to understand by that that you imagine that I meant to make a long nose at you, that is, to give you a formal refusal, I am surprised that you should speak of such a thing when, as you know perfectly well, I was quite of the opposite way of thinking, and if you are courting my daughter with a view to lawful matrimony I am ready to satisfy you immediately, seeing that has always been the object of my keenest desires, in the hope of which I remain always ready to be of service to you.

ALEXANDRA PODTATCHIN.

"No," said Kovalyov to himself after reading the letter, "she really is not to blame. It's impossible. The letter is written as it could not be written by any one guilty of a crime." The collegiate assessor was an expert on this subject, as he had been sent several times to the Caucasus to conduct investigations. "In what way, by what fate, has this happened? Only the devil could make it out!" he said at last, letting his hands fall to his sides.

Meanwhile the rumours of this strange occurrence were spreading all over the town, and of course not without especial additions. Just at that time the minds of all were particularly interested in the marvellous: experiments in the influence of magnetism had been attracting public attention only recently. Moreover, the story of the dancing chair in Konyushenny Street was still fresh, and so there is nothing to be surprised at in the fact that people were soon beginning to say that the nose of a collegiate assessor called Kovalyov was walking along the Nevsky Prospect at exactly three in the afternoon. Numbers of inquisitive people flocked there every day. Somebody said that the nose was in Yunker's shop—and near Yunker's there was such a crowd and such a crush that the police were actually obliged to intervene. One speculator, a man of dignified appearance with whiskers, who used to sell all sorts of cakes and tarts at the doors of the theatres, made purposely some very strong wooden benches, which he offered to the curious to stand on, for eighty kopecks each. One very worthy colonel left home earlier on account of it, and with a great deal of trouble made his way through the crowd; but to his great indignation, instead of the nose, he saw in the shop windows the usual woollen vest and a lithograph depicting a girl pulling up her stocking while a foppish young man, with a waist-coat with revers and a small beard, peeps at her from behind a tree; a picture which had been hanging in the same place for more than ten years. As he walked away he said with vexation: "How can people be led astray by such stupid and incredible stories!" Then rumour would have it that it was not on the Nevsky Prospect but in the Tavritchesky Park that Major Koval-yov's nose took its walks abroad; that it had been there for ever so long; that, even when Hozrev-Mirza used to live there, he was greatly surprised at this strange freak of nature. Several students from the Academy of Surgery made their way to the park. One worthy lady of high rank wrote a letter to the superintendent of the park asking him to show her children this rare phenomenon with, if possible, an explanation that should be edifying and instructive for the young.

All the gentlemen who invariably attend social gatherings and like to amuse the ladies were extremely thankful for all these events, for their stock of anecdotes was completely exhausted. A small group of worthy and well-intentioned persons were greatly displeased. One gentleman said with indignation that he could not understand how in the present enlightened age people could spread abroad these absurd inventions, and that he was surprised that the government took no notice of it. This gentleman, as may be seen, belonged to the number of those who would like the government to meddle in everything, even in their daily quarrels with their wives. After this . . . but here again the whole adventure is lost in fog, and what happened afterwards is absolutely unknown.

3

What is utterly nonsensical happens in the world. Sometimes there is not the slightest resemblance to truth about it: all at once that very nose which had been driving about the place in the form of a civil councillor, and had made such a stir in the town, turned up again as though nothing had happened, in its proper place, that is, precisely between the two cheeks of Major Kovalyov. This took place on the seventh of April. Waking up and casually glancing into the looking-glass, he sees—his nose! puts up his hands, actually his nose! "Aha!" said Kovalyov, and in his joy he almost danced a jig barefoot about his room; but the entrance of Ivan checked him. He ordered the latter to bring him water at once, and as he washed he glanced once more into the looking-glass—the nose! As he wiped himself with the towel he glanced again into the looking-glass—the nose!

"Look, Ivan, I fancy I have a pimple on my nose," he said, while he thought: "How dreadful if Ivan says 'No, indeed, sir, there's no pimple and, indeed, there is no nose either!' "

But Ivan said: "There is nothing, there is no pimple: your nose is quite clear!"

"Good, dash it all!" the major said to himself, and he snapped his fingers.

At that moment Ivan Yakovlevitch the barber peeped in at the door, but as timidly as a cat who has just been beaten for stealing the bacon.

"Tell me first: are your hands clean?" Kovalyov shouted to him while he was still some way off.

"Yes."

"You are lying!"

"Upon my word, they are clean, sir."

"Well, mind now."

Kovalyov sat down. Ivan Yakovlevitch covered him up with a towel, and in one instant with the aid of his brushes had smothered the whole of his beard and part of his cheek in cream, like that which is served at merchants' name-day parties.

"My eye!" Ivan Yakovlevitch said to himself, glancing at the nose and then turning his customer's head on the other side and looking at it sideways. "There it is, sure enough. What can it mean?" He went on pondering, and for a long while he gazed at the nose. At last, lightly, with a cautiousness which may well be imagined, he raised two fingers to take it by the tip. Such was Ivan Yakovlevitch's system.

"Now, now, now, mind!" cried Kovalyov. Ivan Yakovlevitch let his hands drop, and was flustered and confused as he had never been confused before. At last he began circumspectly tickling him with the razor under his beard, and, although it was difficult and not at all handy for him to shave without holding on to the olfactory portion of the face, yet he did at last somehow, pressing his rough thumb into his cheek and lower jaw, overcome all difficulties, and finish shaving him.

When it was all over, Kovalyov at once made haste to dress, took a cab, and drove to the confectioner's shop. Before he was inside the door he shouted: "Waiter, a cup of chocolate!" and at the same instant peeped at himself in the looking-glass. The nose was there. He turned round gaily and, with a satirical air, slightly screwing up his eyes, looked at two military men, one of whom had a nose hardly bigger than a waistcoat button. After that he set off for the office of the department, in which he was urging his claims to a post as vice-governor or, failing that, the post of an executive clerk. After crossing the waiting-room he glanced at the mirror; the nose was there. Then he drove to see another collegiate assessor or major, who was much given to making fun of people, and to whom he often said in reply to various sharp observations: "There you are, I know you, you are as sharp as a pin!" On the way he thought: "If even the major does not split with laughter when he sees me, then it is a sure sign that everything is in its place." But the sarcastic collegiate assessor said nothing. "Good, good, dash it all!" Kovalyov thought to himself. On the way he met Madame Podtatchin with her daughter; he was profuse in his bows to them and was greeted with exclamations of delight—so there could be nothing amiss with him, he thought. He conversed with them for a long time and, taking out his snuff-box, purposely put a pinch to each nostril while he said to himself: "So much for you, you petticoats, you hens! but I am not going to marry your daughter all the same. Just simply *par amour*—I daresay!"

And from that time forth Major Kovalyov promenaded about, as though nothing had happened, on the Nevsky Prospect, and at the theatres and everywhere. And the nose, too, as though nothing had happened, sat on his face without even a sign of coming off at the sides. And after this Major Kovalyov was always seen in a good humour, smiling, resolutely pursuing all the pretty ladies, and even on one occasion stopping before a shop in the Gostiny Dvor and buying the ribbon of some order, I cannot say with what object, since he was not himself a cavalier of any order.

So this is the strange event that occurred in the Northern capital of our spacious empire! Only now, on thinking it all over, we perceive that there is a great deal that is improbable in it. Apart from the fact that it certainly is strange for a nose supernaturally to leave its place and to appear in various places in the guise of a civil councillor—how was it that Kovalyov did not grasp that he could not advertise about his nose in a newspaper office? I do not mean to say that I should think it too expensive to advertise: that is nonsense, and I am by no means a mercenary person: but it is unseemly, awkward, not nice! And again: how did the nose come into the loaf, and how about Ivan Yakovlevitch himself? . . . no, that I cannot understand, I am absolutely unable to understand it! But what is stranger, what is more uncomprehensible than anything is that authors can choose such subjects. I confess that is quite beyond my grasp, it really is . . . No, no! I cannot understand it at all. In the first place, it is absolutely without profit to the fatherland; in the second place . . . but in the second place, too, there is no profit. I really do not know what to say of it. . . .

And yet, with all that, though of course one may admit the first point, the second and the third . . . may even . . . but there, are there not inconsequences everywhere?—and yet, when you think it over, there really is something in it. Whatever any one may say, such things do happen—not often, but they do happen.

5 · Outcasts:
The Diseased and Alienated

In writing Civilization and Its Discontents, *Sigmund Freud identified civilization with repression. His implication was obvious: people would be a lot happier if they could express their sexual and aggressive behavior directly. Man's animal nature cries out for such expression, but social needs force him to suppress his incestuous and parricidal desires. To protect itself even further, society forces men to feel guilty merely for thinking of acts that could rend the gossamer fabric of social organization.*

In Freud's view, man had to make the best of a bad bargain: either he repressed his destructive instincts in order to live in society, or he allowed his instinctual urges to surface and then lived forever in conflict with his world—or outcast from it—either as a neurotic, a psychotic or a criminal.

Psychoanalysts after Freud* altered this pessimistic and oversimplified view. Most psychoanalysts now recognize that man is not simply the victim of his environment but its maker as well. Both man and culture are in a constant state of flux, and each is being reformed by the other in a dynamic process that has equal potential for good or ill.

In our own society, the need for rapid and drastic change has superseded virtually all other human needs. The traditional norms by which human behavior was once established and controlled no longer work. The superego as well as the ego seem unable to integrate society's goals with individual strivings. The result has been a shift in psychological organization which was aptly described by David Riesman some years ago as the difference between the "inner-directed" and

*Even Freud himself intimated that this interpretation of human sexuality might not tell the whole story.

"other-directed" individual. It is pointless to go into the numerous historical factors that hastened this process in America, but it is in America that the process is most clearly outlined. Riesman's "other-directed" person is actually suffering from a weakened ego and super-ego structure. The rising incidence of the so-called schizophrenias (a catch-all term that describes several mental diseases characterized by ego-failure), the growing numbers of addicts, the rising crime rates, seem to suggest that the human psyche has been unable to find a substitute for the traditional methods that once molded and supported the human ego. Not only psychoanalysts but writers have noticed that highly industrialized societies seem to encourage greater and greater loss of ego. These literary and scientific visionaries see man's dilemma as a choice between two equally unpleasant alternatives: he may withdraw completely from the dialectic of life and succumb to a mindless anthill society, or he may allow his destructive instincts to break totally free of social restraint in the apocalypse of an atomic holocaust.

Today we are at a crossroads, groping for new answers presented by the problems of change, mobility, automation. We seek new social forms that might supply the ego supports we so sorely need. Largely, we are growing dependent on the psychoanalyst and his procedures to provide the necessary structure in which a person may successfully grow to maturity.

In this final portion of the book we examine some of our social illnesses. Most are simply reflections of the unresolved conflicts of each individual writ large against the background of Western history and culture. What is prejudice but self-hatred turned outward. What is one of the major causes of crime but the desire for punishment to expiate unconscious sins. What encourages addiction but the desire to escape conflicts that no current social institution is capable of resolving. What helps cause schizophrenia but human confusion over what one is expected to be, how one is expected to behave, what role one is expected to fill.

Finally we must ask the crucial question: whether the social attitudes that we have developed towards all those who flounder in the contradictory expressions offered by our society have not served to foster and support exactly the alienation they were designed to prevent. Is it possible that all the mental disease, the crime, the addiction that we see around us are positive attempts made by human beings in stress to re-integrate failing egos, to prevent death at any cost? If this proves to be so, then the need for a change in attitude is mandatory.

This volume concludes with a parable about two sheep. It is neither a pleasant nor particularly reassuring tale. Its cry for help mirrors the malaise of our century. Its conclusions affirm once more the dubious value of that bit of apple eaten in the Garden of Eden. To be sure, our living sheep is caught in the treadmill of the compulsion to repeat and repeat the event that has turned life to dust. In his blindness our sheep cannot see the possibility of escape from this eternal and horrifying wheel of mental illness. He has not yet learned that true self-awareness, the gift of psychoanalysis, teaches us to navigate the dark corridors of the unconscious, to face death and to fulfil, in the end, all the potentials offered by life.

Study of certain kinds of criminal behavior reveals that the criminal's principal motivation is a desire for punishment. Like the neurotic who punishes himself over and over for crimes he has not even committed, the criminal seeks expiation of his guilt at the hands of society. In dealing with such criminals society might do better to react with kindness rather than punishment, because punishment serves to reduce moral inhibitions by relieving guilt and it encourages the very behavior it would like to prevent.

FRANZ ALEXANDER AND HUGO STAUB

Psychoanalytic Theory and Criminal Psychology
FROM *The Criminal, the Judge, and the Public*

As has been stated, the psychological understanding of crime and of the criminal is based primarily on the data obtained from our psychoanalytical knowledge of the neuroses; before beginning the special consideration of our problem we shall, therefore, state briefly the principles of the general theory of the neuroses.

The fact that we learn to understand crime through the understanding of the neuroses is an anachronism not infrequently found in the history of science; the neurosis presents the intrapsychic inheritance and parody of primitive criminality; in other words, the criminal act can be understood through the study of the psychic fossils of man. Is not a neurosis of a civilized man a sort of living out of his primitive anti-social tendencies, this living out having been pushed out of reality into the domain of psychic life? From the standpoint of its psychological content and structure it presents a true reproduction of primitive, prehistoric penal traditions. Crime and punishment is *the* meaning of a psychoneurosis, except that all this takes place not in real life but in the unconscious world of phantasy, and is represented by the neurotic symptoms. The study of a neurosis yields unconscious material which makes it possible for us to reconstruct not only the spirit of primitive justice—the talion principle, but also the nature of the primitive social problems, *i.e.*, the primitive crime of incest and murder of the father and even the primitive punishment—castration.

The medical man whose studies have been confined to purely biological facts receives a remarkable, and at first a rather strange, set of impressions when he gains his first acquaintance with the psychoanalytic theory of the neuroses; he suddenly discovers that these diseases are described in terms to which natural sciences are not accustomed; he finds that the descriptions are couched partly in literary terms, partly in the language of a jurist and that they are based on a number of criminological concepts. He will read, for instance, about the Œdipus complex, the content of which embraces the primitive crime of murder of the father and incest with the mother; he will hear about castration anxiety, *i.e.*, the fear of that singular punishment which represents the deepest fundamental source of all our human renunciations in favor of a social order; this same anxiety is the primary condition of the general structural development of our psychic apparatus, that divides our psychological functions into conscious and unconscious. He will also hear of the *sense of guilt* and *expiation*, of *sacrifice* and *penance*, of *bribery*, of the *severity* of certain unconscious psychic agencies, of the *need for punishment* and the *compulsion to confess* one's sins.

The medical man studied and learned all about the bones and muscle system of the human body; he learned about blood circulation and the physico-chemical processes of the human body; he learned to consider the body as a complicated heating machine—and suddenly he finds that psychoanalysis leads him into a sort of court room where the most primitive spirit of primitive races, or children, rules supreme; he suddenly learns that this singular court is deeply imbedded into the unconscious of the human personality. Psychoanalysis then assures him that many neurotic symptoms, which frequently appear in the form of physical symptoms and which he always thought are due to physico-chemical disturbances in the body, are due to those singular intrapsychic processes which we have just sketched; he also learns that these symptoms present a secret gratification of forbidden anti-social tendencies and that these symptoms, the pain and the discomfort of a neurosis, present at the very same time the punishment for these transgressions. Thus, a peculiar metamorphosis must take place; the medical man in order to understand and to cure certain diseases had to go through a thorough training in biology, chemistry, etc., now he suddenly faces the necessity of becoming a criminologist; he has to gain an understanding of criminal psychology, and delve deeply into the spirit of a remarkably primitive, barbarian penal code, the chief subject matter of which is murder, incest, and castration. Thus, the road from the psychoanalytical theory of the neuroses to the court room appears to us much shorter than the road to anatomy and physiology of the brain or to the physical chemistry of bodily processes.

The psychoneurotic symptom consists either of physiologically useless deficiencies and disturbances of innervations, or of psychologically meaningless, and groundless psychic reactions.

The first group of physical symptoms which are psychically conditioned, such as vomiting, constipation, difficulties in breathing, cramps, paralyses, or the psychologically conditioned blindness, deafness, abnormalities of sensation, or lack of sensations in various parts of the body are called by psychoanalysis *conversion symptoms,* and are most characteristic of *hysteria.* They are the expression of unconscious psychic processes, which, like all neurotic symptoms, partly serve as a gratification of forbidden impulses and partly play the rôle of self-injury as a punishment for the forbidden gratification.

Disturbances of purely psychological nature such as fears, inhibitions, depressions, self-accusations, all founded not on reality of fact, but on intrapsychic conflicts, also the unfounded changes of mood and apparently meaningless compulsions which appear foreign to the conscious personality—all these symptoms have proved through psychoanalysis to be the result of the play of unconscious forces generated by repressed instinctual demands and inner moral reaction against them. These disturbances comprise the symptomatology of *anxiety neuroses, phobias, compulsion neuroses* and *manic-depressive states.* As to the multiform morbid pictures of psychoses, *i.e.,* the pathological falsification of inner (psychic) and outer reality by means of delusions, hallucinations, and even complete disorientation, and a resulting complete withdrawal of all interests in, and all relationships to, the outside world—all these symptoms acquire a definite meaning only if we think of them as psychological regressions to primitive forms of thinking and feeling.

Psychiatry was well acquainted with this whole mass of pathological psychic reactions: the purely external manifestations of these illnesses were described many times and arranged in numerous systems; however, the meaning and significance of these symptoms remained unknown till Freud propounded psychoanalysis. The discovery of unconscious mental processes and of the psychoanalytic technique for the study of these processes offered at once a clue to many mysteries which dwelt until then in the field of medical psychology. In the history of science one is able to find but few examples of such a sudden growth of a branch of scientific knowledge; in a very short time it explored successfully and in many respects even conquered a region which until then seemed so obscure and impenetrable. As a result of therapeutic efforts and by means of the technique of free associations and of dream interpretation, and as a result of the understanding of the affective relationship between physician and patient, a new anatomy and physiology of the human mind was created. When toward the close of the Middle Ages the *inside of the human body* stopped being taboo and dissections were finally permitted, the founding of the science of anatomy was carried out within a comparatively short time. In our day we overcame a similar resistance to looking *inside* the human psyche, *i.e.,* the unconscious part of *our personality;* this made it possible to gain knowledge of the structure of the human Ego in a comparatively shorter time. The neurotic symptom, be it the purely physical conversion symptom or the purely psychological symptom, acquired a meaning as soon as the unconscious motives which they were covering up were discovered. The incomprehensible, seemingly meaningless and useless symptom, like the seemingly meaningless dream can be understood as the product of interplay between two psychodynamic forces, the product of repressed wishes which the conscious personality rejects, and of the reaction against them on the part of the socially adjusted part of our personality. A symptom is, therefore, a compromise between the repressing and the repressed forces.

Psychoanalysis succeeded at first in uncovering the unconscious anti-social content of symptoms; this content was described in general terms as a combination of sexual drives and hostile impulses which were directed against the various members of the family, chiefly the parents. It took two decades of psychoanalytical research to prove conclusively that the Œdipus complex presented the chief unconscious psychological content of neurotic symptoms. It was found that all those psychological undercurrents which the adult person usually represses are affectively connected with the Œdipus situation of early childhood; these psychic currents, after they are repressed, continue in the unconscious, tied as with a navel cord to the infantile Œdipus complex.

The first investigations dealt mainly with the unconscious repressed psychological content. However, the *repressing forces, i.e.,* the reaction of the Ego to these forbidden ideas were not so well known. In a general way it was known that there exists in every individual a tendency to cover up the real meaning of our unconscious ideas by means of the mechanisms of dream and symptom formation; this tendency was generally recognized as a defense reaction on the part of the Ego. The first concept was that of two mutually antagonistic forces; the unconscious containing the primitive anti-social tendencies and the conscious Ego, *i.e.,* the socially and ethically minded part of our personality. In other words, our Ego and our *instinctual* life, *i.e.,* the *unconscious* and the *conscious* were considered as the two opposite poles of our personality. The manifest dream content and the neurotic symptom were considered as the expression of the repressed, which was clad in a harmless, unintelligible form in order not to disturb the socially fastidious, conscious Ego.

This first presentation, crude as it was, proved fundamentally true; yet it soon became clear that this simple formula failed to describe fully the reaction between the Ego and the repressed. Soon after he published his first communications regarding hysterical symptoms, Freud saw clearly that the neurotic symptom presents not only the disguised Ego-alien wish, but also a tendency directed against the Ego itself, an ethical element, a sort of self-punishment. If the symptoms were nothing more than a disguised gratification, then it would be impossible to understand why the neurotic suffers, why he complains that he is not well, or in general why a neurotic symptom should be unpleasant. Many neurotic states, such as the deep depressive states, for instance, show a great deal of suffering; they also show definitely the tendency to self-punishment; in severe cases it leads to self-destruction. The recognition of the feminine masochistic (homosexual) gratification, which permits a person's turning against his own self does not appear to be sufficient to explain this phenomenon, although such an erotic (masochistic) admixture is not only always present, but at times plays the main role in depressions. These observations on the self-punishment and suffering of neurotics gradually brought forth a sufficient amount of evidence which led Freud to assume the existence of an unconscious need for punishment; it remains unconscious and is most intimately bound with the ethico-social part of the Ego, that is, the Super-Ego.

To cite a definite example of how deeply seated this inner need for suffering is, we may mention the following well-known clinical fact; many neurotic patients begin to feel subjectively worse as soon as they sense a slight improvement in their symptoms or even at the very beginning of the analytical treatment; they then develop severe anxiety states and at times even a weird drive for self-destruction; one could observe clearly in such patients how they cling with at least the same persistency to the suffering as they clung to the gratification which the symptoms usually provide. It is the immanent sense of guilt which apparently comes from the gratification alien to the Ego that forces the neurotic individual to carry his cross. One of the writers definitely established that neurotic suffering is one of the fundamental conditions of unconscious gratification.[1]

An observation made by Freud on manic-depressive patients could be applied to the general theory of symptom formation. Freud stated that frequent alternations of manic and depressive states in the same individual depend upon an alternation of unlimited gratification of unconscious wishes with unconscious self-punishment. The unbridled gratification of forbidden wishes which takes place in a manic attack causes an accumulation of feelings of guilt and the need for punishment; the satisfaction of the latter relieves one from this feeling of guilt. This need for punishment dominates the picture of a depression which follows a manic attack. The suffering, as a result of self-inflicted punishment, the unbridled raging of conscience in an attack of depression leads into a fresh manic attack in which, as in a revolution, the instincts too severely restricted in the depression break through with renewed vigor of self-assertion.

The very same individual who, while in a severe depression was constantly playing with the idea of suicide, may in a manic attack become dangerous to the lives of others.

When viewed in the light of the fundamental conditions leading to the development of a neurosis, the relationship which exists between the gratification of an unconscious wish and the subsequent reactive need of suffering, could be summarized as follows:

Each gratification of a repressed wish obtained through a symptom arouses an unconscious *anxiety before one's own conscience, i.e.,* an anxiety experienced by the Ego in face of the socially adapted part of it, the Super-Ego, which latter is to a great extent also unconscious. This anxiety is the intrapsychic continuation of the child's fear of the older person who brought him up; it is an internalization of the infantile fear of punishment and the fear of losing the affection of others. It is, in other words, the same anxiety which the child once had when facing the adult mentor; the individual carries over this anxiety into adulthood and experiences it when facing his conscience; the latter we shall recall, developed as an inner representative of the parents, with whom the child identified itself. This is seen with particular clearness in cases of depression, who couch their pathological self-reproaches in the same words that were used by their parents reprimanding them in childhood.

The gratification of forbidden wishes, even if carried out in a disguised form of meaningless symptoms, arouses a fear of the Super-Ego. *The need for punishment* is a direct result of this unconscious anxiety. The various types of self-punishment and suffering have this dynamic significance: they tend to raise the pressure of the inhibiting conscience and thus open the way for a subsequent free gratification of forbidden wishes. The spirit of that criminal code which claims that punishment expiates a crime is thus made eternally active in the psychology of the neurosis; the neurotic Ego makes one step further in this logical causal chain; it considers the imposed punishment as a moral justification, as a license to indulge in new gratifications of forbidden wishes.

In the light of these considerations certain observations which did not seem clear before or which were not quite in accord with the general theory, could be explained. Disguising the unconscious meaning of symptoms is apparently not a satisfactory means to obviate a moral protest and to avoid the neurotic anxiety. If this disguise were sufficient for the escape from one's own conscience, then the self-punishing tendencies and the suffering accompanying a neurosis would prove superfluous and unintelligible. Moreover, the theory based merely on the mechanisms of covering up one's unconscious tendencies would totally fail to explain certain phobic states of inhibition. In these states, the patients anxiously try to avoid performing simple harmless things such as walking in the street, riding on a train, writing, etc.; all this because these simple activities have for them an unconscious symbolic sexual meaning; this unconscious meaning is so deeply hidden in the manifest act that one cannot see it; why then should certain neurotics react to such things with so much anxiety? Mere disguise in such cases is apparently of little help; it is the judgment of the Super-Ego that continues to generate anxiety. On the other hand, in such phobic states one does not find, as a rule, the usual "self-punishment technique" or "the bribery maneuver" which, through suffering, tend to disarm the inhibiting Super-Ego. That is apparently the reason why one finds in these cases of phobias that the usual unconscious gratifications are also absent; the illness consists of a direct inhibition, which is brought on by anxiety. On the other hand, the majority of the obsessional neurotics show such a high degree of development of the "bribery policy" that even the most forbidden unconscious trends, like murder and incest, appear in consciousness undisguised; these patients acquire their freedom of thought through formal self-control and self-restriction, like overpunctiliousness, exaggerated conscientiousness in small things, and through painful compulsions to wash constantly and to perform all sorts of neurotic ceremonies, which represent an exaggeration of the orders given to them in childhood by those who trained them in cleanliness, orderliness, etc.

Thus it may be said that the general condition of every neurotic symptom formation is the satisfaction of one's own moral demands, by means of unconscious self-punishment; this satisfaction is combined with the concealment of the sense of the repressed wishes. While this disguise aims to conceal the real unconscious meaning of the symptom from the *conscious* part of the personality, the *unconscious* moral inhibitions find themselves disarmed by virtue of the fact that the need for punishment is also gratified.

Thus the structure and the content of every neurosis stands out as a partial repetition of the primary event of the primitive society, *i.e.,* the first primitive crime and punishment; all this is internalized and deeply buried in the unconscious. Crime and punishment may appear to-day as changed both in form and content, but the deeply emotional connection with the principle of considering the punishment as an atonement is still highly effective even to-day. Anyone who is acquainted with the practical administration of justice to-day knows very well that the attempts of modern justice to consider punishment as a factor in prevention of crime are hardly more than of purely theoretical importance.

In the courtroom to-day, as of yore, we find that the principle of atonement is still the dominating principle; anyone who commits a crime must suffer a punishment proportionate to the severity of the crime; the establishement of the degree of punishment as well as the gravity of the crime is, strictly speaking, still not a matter of scientific knowledge, but a matter of feeling.

It is possible that as an individual, man of to-day may have progressed a little ahead of the spirit of primitive man, but as a social being, as seen in the function of his Super-Ego and also in many of his public institutions, particularly in the spirit of his justice, he continues to remain on the level of primitive society.

Thus it would appear that the criminal and the law, taken together, as a social phenomenon, perform the same task together as the neurotic does alone, by means of his psychic reactions and symptoms; to wit, crime and atonement. There is another parallel between the two; the neurotic utilizes the atonement (the suffering) as a license for his transgression (symptom formation). In the case of a number of criminals, whom we designate as neurotic criminals, punishment frequently serves the purpose only of lifting their moral inhibitions. The forthcoming punishment or the sentence already served is for the neurotic criminal the necessary condition for the performance of his transgressions, in particular for the repetition of his crimes. In cases of such criminals the most effective mode of treatment would prove the one which Victor Hugo imagined in *Les Miserables,* in the case of the priest who was attacked by a robber. The priest, instead of imposing punishment, which the criminal unconsciously hoped to obtain, responded to the crime with kind deeds. This mode of action, we believe, would prove in the cases under consideration a much more effective preventive method than any form of punishment; for punishment results in little more than the fact that the criminal experiences a sense of relief; it gives him a sense of having expiated his sins and thus reduces his inhibitions; kindness, on the contrary, would increase still further the inhibitory power of his Super-Ego, which is fundamentally so excessively strong in a neurotic criminal.

NOTE

[1] Alexander—*Psychoanalysis of the Total Personality.*

In examining the relationship between Buddhism and catatonia Dr. Franz Alexander has illuminated a phenomenon that occurred in America twenty years after his piece first appeared. The devotion of the "Beats" to a particular form of Buddhism seems to indicate a profound alienation expressed not in rebellion but in the desire to escape from involvement, a desire for complete oblivion and loss of ego.

FRANZ ALEXANDER

Buddhistic Training as an Artificial Catatonia

When I review the subject matter of this paper I find that I could just as accurately have announced as its title "The Psychic Meaning of Biological Occurrences," instead of the reverse, as I have done. This reciprocal relation forms my thesis, the consistent elaboration of which is my task today, namely: that psychic processes have a biological validity just as biological processes have a psychic one. Today, however, I do not wish to prove this principle upon the basis of individual analytical experience, but rather to turn to the understanding of a definite mental condition. I, therefore, do not start upon the same deductive path which philosophy has always traveled in order to penetrate its fundamental problem, the connection between body and mind. The solutions of the problem by the philosophers have been not a little varied and even at present are not uniform. For example, in the radical materialistic conception of Vogt thoughts are regarded as products of brain secretion, whereas the idealism of Berkeley completely denied the existence of the material world and regarded it as an appearance, as mere mental content. Only one of the philosophical solutions interests us especially. I refer to the identity theory of Spinoza which for the first time expressed the idea that mental events are at the same time physical, and vice versa. "Ordo et connexio idearum idem est ac ordo et connexio rerum." The solution of Spinoza is so simple and matter of fact. It is the metaphysical egg of Columbus, and one can only wonder how it is that, after long wanderings through labyrinths of epistemological speculation it was left for Schopenhauer alone to reiterate the thought of Spinoza, albeit in a new form, modified by the theory of evolution. However, it is probably not accidental, and shows us the trend of development, that Spinoza designates his first principle, his *causa sui,* whose Janus head is at one and the same time body and mind, by a physical expression, "Substance," whereas Schopenhauer equates it with the psychological phenomenon of "Will." Actually the dynamic conception of force, of power, is the only one which is common to physical and psychological experience.

Physics and biology have shown that, aided by a scientific method, one can learn more of this *"causa sui,"* while the attempt of psychology to discover anything of value by direct introspective means for a long time remained without success. Freud first pointed the way through the discovery of free association and the art of interpretation, which extends the circle of consciousness inward and makes it possible for us by way of immediate knowledge to understand biological happenings. In this way the metaphysical concept of will receives a scientific content in the concept of instinct and establishes a connection with biology.

One kind of introspective knowledge was known to Indian philosophy in a remarkable form long before the discovery of the psychoanalytical method. Just as psychoanalysis, in order to understand the unconscious, prescribes a certain mental condition which eliminates the occurrence of conscious criticism, so the Buddhistic doctrine of self-absorption worked out a psychotechnique in order to turn "knowing" from the outer world inward, and through this to achieve the emotionless condition of Nirvana. With this, I come to my task of today: namely, to elucidate the self-absorption phenomena of Buddha upon the basis of the principle of the identity of biological and psychological processes. From our present psychoanalytical knowledge it is clear that Buddhistic self-absorption is a libidinal, narcissistic turning of the urge for knowing inward, a sort of artificial schizophrenia with complete withdrawal of libidinal interest from the outside world. The catatonic conditions of the Hindu ascetics in self-absorption prove quite clearly the correctness of this contention. The mastery of the world is given up and there remains as an exclusive goal of the libido the mastery of self. In the older pre-Buddha Yogi practice the aim is clearly a mastery of the body, while the absorption of Buddha is directed toward the psychic personality, *i.e.,* the ego. We know, however, that in Hindu fakirs the connection of the conscious will with the depth of bodily processes is never completely successful. They carry out their wonderful performances in the Yogi absorption, which, in contrast to the Buddhistic practice, takes place in a condition of autohypnosis. They are undeniably capable of quite extraordinary feats; they can consciously regulate, even though incompletely, fundamental physiological functons, otherwise inaccessible to the will, or at least they can consciously initiate a regulating interference. Let us repeat this again and see what it means: to regulate physiological processes consciously. It means nothing else than an increase in analytical ability, a longed for but never mentioned goal of psychoanalytical science: the exploration, perhaps the cure, of organic illness through the expansion of the regulatory activity of consciousness to the physical libido which governs the coördination of cells. Up to now, a conscious mastery of the object-libido, which lies nearer to consciousness, is the successful result of analytical research. Unquestionably the next step is the therapy of the narcissistic neuroses, and after this the investigations of organic illness of the neuroses of the cell bodies, the organs—and last the investigation of the regressive phenomena of cell functions; I mean by this, tumors.

The Yoga self-absorption, however, has no therapeutic goal; the mastery of the body is an end in itself. Likewise, in Buddhistic self-absorption the turning of the perceptive consciousness inward is an end in itself, a narcissistic-masochistic affair, shown by the fact that the way to it leads through asceticism. Psychoanalysis turns inward in order to help the instincts to accommodate themselves to reality; it wishes to effect an alliance between consciousness and instinct, in order to make experience with the outer world useful to the instincts. The Buddhistic theory sets itself an easier task: it eliminates reality and attempts to turn the entire instinctual life away from the world, inward, towards itself.

Freud expressed the difference between the artist and the neurotic thus: The artist, in contrast to the neurotic, establishes contact with reality by a phantasy satisfaction of his libido, and to this extent acts socially. In this sense self-absorption is a kind of narcissistic neurosis and psychoanalysis is its scientific counterpart. I should like to try and show you that this neurosis, through its incomparable depths of narcissistic regression, has an especial meaning for us, and deserves our attention.

In what does the Nihilistic theory of Gatama Buddha consist, and what influence has it upon his disciples, who follow his teaching?

The common factor in the various Indian self-absorption methods is the goal-conscious, systematic withdrawal of all libidinal interest from the outer world, and the attempt to dispose narcissistically of all such freed quantities of libido. The important and interesting thing for us is that in self-absorption the intellectual functions are also drawn in. Even in Buddha's teaching the chief accent falls upon this inward perception. "Where there is no self-absorption there is no wisdom, and no wisdom where there is no self-absorption, and he who has both self-absorption and wisdom is near to Nirvana," says Buddha.[1]

The actual mental absorption is introduced by a general ascetic training, which consists in a systematic suppression of all emotional life. The chief conditions are freedom from hatred, ceasing to desire property, denial of all fleshly pleasures, and sexual continence. Analytically regarded, this means that not only every genital but also every sadistic, oral-erotic, and anal-erotic outlet must be closed, in order to lead the libido to the ego, in its most primitive functions. The external means of accomplishing these demands consist in isolation, a peaceful composure of the body, and the observation and regulation of breathing. It is clear why breathing plays this especial rôle. It is the only constant periodical function which is accessible to the conscious will. After this ascetic preparation the first mental absorption sets in, which leads to Nirvana through the four steps of Jhana. The first Jhana step consists in a turning aside from the variety of external perceptions and inner imagination, and in the limitation of phantasy activity—concentration of thought upon a single theme. The objects of these meditations are different, yet are exclusively such as tend to depreciate the world and life in its entirety, meditations on the brevity and futility of human existence. Gradually these meditations pass over to increasingly gloomy observations of the hideousness and impurity of the human body, death, and the corruption of the flesh. These observations are bound with feelings of lively disgust with the body. The melancholic coloring is the chief feature of these sadistic, self-directed self-observations, the first stage of absorption, as emphasized by Heiler, in his research into religions. "In this phase of absorption the cosmic picture of the meditating monk is amazingly simplified, the entire world still only the inscrutable symbol of universal metaphysical evil . . . deep sorrow shakes the meditator, bitter contempt of the world fills him, . . . all these transitory worldly desires and wishes die." It is thus that Heiler describes this phase of absorption, which, in the light of our clinical psychoanalytical knowledge, is exceedingly clear and especially interesting, inasmuch as it presents an experimentally induced melancholia. It is caused through the world, with all its multiplicity ceasing to be a libido-object, after every worldly interest is artificially withdrawn, during the ascetic preparatory training, and now the entire withdrawn libido is directed to the individual's body. This assumes the rôle previously taken by the world and becomes the sole object. The libidinal interest of the ego is, at this stage, purely sadistic. The passionate frenzy against itself does not differ in any way from the well known clinical picture of melancholia. This condition is, however, far removed from the desired goal of absorption. The monk still feels disgust with his own body, and even this feeling must be conquered. If the conquest of disgust is successful, then the sadistic attitude towards the body will be replaced by a positive attitude. To put it clearly, the barrier erected during individual development, the feeling of disgust, the dam which is to protect the libido from narcissistic regression, is broken down and the entire libido, which until now found an outlet only in its sadistic component, streams back into the large reservoir of the ego. After the barrier of disgust is broken down no inhibiting factor is there to stop the transformation of object-libido into narcissistic libido, that is, to stop the regression of libido into primary form, self-love. This phase of positive attitude towards the ego is described in the Buddha text in the following words: "In this condition the monk is like a pool, fed from a source within himself, which has no outlet, neither to the east, nor to the west, north, nor south, and which also is not replenished by rain from time to time. This pool is fed from the cool stream of water within itself, with cool water streamed through, filled and flooded entirely, so that no single corner of the pool remains unsaturated: just so does the Bikkhu drink from his physical body, fills and saturates himself completely from all sides with the joy and pleasurable feelings born out of the depths of absorption, so that not the smallest particle remains unsaturated." This is the second Jhana step. I think no analyst can more fittingly describe the condition of narcissism than is done in this text, if we substitute the word "libido" for "stream of water." For this reason this description seems to me especially interesting and important, because it is the description of a condition which we have only theoretically reconstructed and named "narcissism." The person's own body and, indeed, his entire body, becomes his sole object. This feeling of pleasure, a consummate voluptuousness of all organs, tissues, and cells, a pleasure completely freed from the genitals, an orgasm diffused through the whole body, is a condition which we ascribe to the schizophrenic in his catatonic ecstasy. We can consider the Buddhistic wording an introspective description of the mental situation during catatonia. This text justifies me methodologically in regarding Buddhistic absorption and Nirvana as psychological documents rather than as products of metaphysical speculation. Freud's conception of the development of object-libido from ego-libido is confirmed, point for point, in the artificial regression of absorption, and becomes an experimental truth. Furthermore, Freud's melancholia mechanism receives substantiation by the finding in the preceding melancholy stage of Jhana, which occurs when the world as object is lost, becomes sadistically depreciated, and when this sadism turns against the ego, which again recaptures its former developmental object-rôle from the outer world. The narcissistic step corresponds to the next further regression in that the barriers of disgust are broken down and the whole organism is flooded with positive libido. Perhaps the only new thing that we learn from this is in what sense a schizophrenic regression is deeper than one in melancholia. The deeper regression in schizophrenia comes about when the sadistic investment of the ego is replaced by a positive one. The protective rôle played by disgust, the disappearance of which is an old and well known symptom of schizophrenia, comes clearly to expression: the conquest of disgust is the precondition for entering the second step of Jhana. Hate, disgust of the body protects against love and is employed in the construction of the ego system in the form of feelings of disgust. If, then, schizophrenic regression corresponds to the narcissistic phase of individual development, melancholia must correspond to that post-narcissistic stage in which a critical agency is set up for the purpose of fighting the narcissism of the ego, which negatively invests the nucleus of the ego. In the self-accusations of the melancholic we hear the voice of the strict educator, whose criticisms and punishments are a pattern for a negative attitude of the ego against itself.

We have thus far seen that absorption systematically reverses the direction which development took in a constructive path, and then strives to demolish the entire physical and psychic personality. We may well be curious to learn where this repressive path can still lead, after the stage of narcissistic orgasm.

The third step of Jhana consists in a constant diminution of the feeling of pleasure of the second stage with a gradual transition into apathy. The narcissistic orgasm of the entire body is followed by a state of detumescence. The fourth stage is the condition of complete mental emptiness and uniformity. "Exalted above pleasure and pain, free from love and hate, indifferent to joy and sorrow, indifferent toward the whole world, toward Gods and Men, even toward himself, the monk lingers on the heights of *sancta-indifferentia*, on the threshold of Nirvana." Thus

Heiler describes the last step of absorption. It is not difficult for us to recognize in this condition the last stage of schizophrenia, schizophrenic dementia, but it *is* difficult to evaluate and establish to which period of individual development it corresponds. According to Heiler, this condition is only quantitatively different from that of Nirvana; Nirvana means only its intensification.

We have several ways of approaching the analytical understanding of this state. First of all, physical behavior. Complete immobility with scarcely perceptible breathing; a limitation of metabolism, a kind of trance. In the final condition of the older autohypnotic Yoga absorption this physical effect is much more striking than in the Nirvana of the Buddhistic absorption. The unbelievable miracles of the fakirs, which seem to mock at all physiology, take place in this autohypnotic state of Yoga practice. When we consider these miracles, we are struck by the remarkably stereotyped position of the body. Crouched together, the extremities folded up, with the head down, hanging from a tree, and similar things. Yet the greatest miracle is allowing oneself to be buried alive. It is not our province here to determine to what extent the stubbornly repeated rumors of forty-day burials rest upon truth. Sufficient other acts have been proven and the remarkable capacity of the fakir to influence his physiological function, even metabolism, has been established.

We are chiefly interested in the meaning of these customs, the meaning of which is involuntarily forced upon the analytical eye. Immobility, a remarkably uncomfortable position of the body, restriction, indeed almost cessation of breathing, burial. The sense is clear, a regression to the condition before birth, immobility, being folded together, without breathing, lying in the mother. The end-effects of Yoga practice which Buddha employed, only spiritualized, makes it very probable that the end condition of his absorption, Nirvana, likewise means the deepest regression to the condition of intra-uterine life, the more so since the physical characteristics are the same, immobility, being folded together, breathlessness,—think of a Buddha statue. Nirvana is the condition in the mother's womb. "Without perception, without wishes, the peace in which there is no death nor being reborn, no Here, no Beyond, only an intermediate kingdom, that is even the end of sorrow," says Heiler.

But the intra-uterine meaning of Nirvana will be much more obvious if we regard its psychic content and follow Buddha step by step through the four stages of Jhana into Nirvana. Here our analytical interest begins. The absorption was until now purely affective, yet Buddha promises his disciples knowledge, which is the true goal of absorption. Parallel with the physical and affective absorption runs the intellectual, the perception of the concealed connections of existence in the self to be attained by turning all intellectual power inwards. In the fourth stage of Jhana, Buddha recognized the eternal law of Karma, the cycles of eternal reincarnation. In birth, Buddha sees the cause of the three-fold evils, age, sickness, and death. In the legend of the young prince who thrice sets forth upon a journey, Buddha explains to his followers the cause of his religious strivings, the cause of which leads him to turn away from the world, back into his innermost being. On first venturing forth, the young prince is induced to return by the sight of a helpless old man; at the second, the sight of sick people who are wallowing in their own excrements, and the third time by a funeral procession. The conquest of age, sickness, and death is the expressed goal of Buddhistic teaching and we may rightly call it a narcissistic religion in opposition to the transference religion, Christianity, which attempts to regulate the social life of humanity in its affective relation. We can even express it more forcibly. The aims of Buddhistic teaching are therapeutic, the conquest of age, sickness, and death. Their way is that of regression through introversion, and their cure Nirvana, the conquest, or nullification of birth. In his legend of the three-fold exodus, Buddha three times curses birth: "Oh, shame, say I, of birth, that at birth age appears, sickness appears, death appears."[2] The cause of the three-fold evil is birth, the cosmic law reincarnation, and Nirvana means its conquest. "In Nirvana the power is annihilated which leads to existence, no longer is there reincarnation —'says Buddha,' Man has regressed; sunk back into pure Being which is nothing but itself."[3]

I hope that I have succeeded in making it seem probable to you that the end goal of Buddhistic absorption is an attempt at psychological and physical regression to the condition of intra-uterine life. We saw the introspective description of the different steps of the regressive absorption scale which correspond to the various steps of individual development, that the way to Nirvana can be likened to a cinema film which is turning in the reverse direction. Beginning by liberating the libido from the world, and leading through melancholy and then through the narcissistic catatonic phase, it finally attains the apparent alibidinous condition of Nirvana, the intra-uterine state. We can understand this regression in the light of the libido theory until we reach the narcissistic phase. Analytical understanding is an equation which expresses the relation of the ego to the libido. The equation of the melancholy phase runs: sadistic investment of the ego as object; the equation of the narcissistic phase: positive investment of the ego as object. The question which remains open, according to the libido-ego equation of Nirvana, is that of the intra-uterine condition, which, according to the description in the Buddhistic texts, appears to be alibidinous. The difference between object and subject vanishes, says Heiler in regard to this state. "The Complete has sunk back into pure Being, which is nothing but itself." Thus says Buddha. A distinction between subject and object is truly necessary to an understanding of the libido concept, and even the narcissistic libido takes the ego itself as object. This apparently alibidinous condition of Nirvana, pure existence, can be nothing other than the most complete restriction of the ego impulses and of the libido, one such as Freud assumes for single-celled protozoa, or, like the original narcissism of the sperm cells which, according to his conception, were purely narcissistic.[4] According to this, the sensation of Nirvana would be identical with the complete coincidence of ego impulses and libido. This assertion, however, is a biological theory. What can that have to do with psychological sensation?

First of all, the intra-uterine state is not a single moment in time, but comprises the developmental period from the fertilized cell up to the time of birth. In which phase of intra-uterine life does Buddha discover the conquest of the cycle of reincarnations, the sinking back into pure existence? Indeed, where does Buddhistic regression really end?

We could easily form a picture of the melancholy phase of absorption. We found the description of the second stage of Jhana an excellent presentation of narcissism in the classical sense. In this state we could even recognize the catatonic ecstasy of schizophrenia. The psychological meaning of Nirvana, the sensation of the condition in the mother's womb, is difficult to imagine. That this condition is meant is entirely clear. Buddha himself calls it the conquest of birth, the conquest of eternal reincarnation. What does the expression "eternal rebirth" actually mean? For this we must seek some solution. One might easily get the impression that these statements about Nirvana are pure metaphysical conceptions, the fruit of some type of philosophical speculation. Yet we can at once discard this assumption. All other phases of absorption were psychological conditions and the path to them led through systematic, chronologically exact workings of the personality. The psychotechnique of Buddha made it possible voluntarily to trace this regressive path. The Yoga practice makes possible the physiological miracle, the voluntary restriction of metabolism; the absorption theory of Buddha produces a complete psychic regression. We are justified in assuming that the end state of this regression corresponds to a psychic experience as nearly related to the intra-uterine condition as narcissistic absorption is to the actual narcissistic period of individual development. Yet I have a still more weighty proof that Nirvana really is a psychological regression to the intra-uterine state, more precisely into a condition whose libido-ego equation is identical with that of the embryological period, a proof which I have withheld until now. I refer to the interpretation of Buddha's "salvation knowledge" in the fourth state of Jhana, which makes possible the entrance to Nirvana, the knowledge of the eternal repetition of rebirth. The meaning of these laws, the central core of Buddhism, can be understood in its deepest meaning only in the light of psychoanalytical interpretation. However, the philosopher Ziegler comes very near to this in his interpretations. Let us turn to his profound work, "The Eternal Buddha."

According to Ziegler, the whole way to self-absorption through the four steps of Jhana serves to free psychic processes from every tone of emotion, pleasurable as well as painful. All the painful feelings of the first state and all the pleasurable ones of the second stage of Jhana which could induce the worshipper to persist at one of the stages must be overcome. Only in the fourth stage, when thought is cleansed of every pleasurable or painful undercurrent, can the liberating recollection of the reincarnations enter. We analysts are also acquainted with two kinds of resistance in our patients: those which depend upon unpleasurable affects and those tenacious defenders of the borders of narcissism which are based upon a tendency to persist in a pleasurable condition. The absorption scale corresponds to the chronological path of a well conducted analysis. In conquering the melancholy phase the unpleasurable resistance is overcome and only then in the second stage ensues the conquest of narcissism.

Permit me to repeat the therapeutic meaning of the four-fold absorption in Ziegler's words: "In the same measure, as the monk becomes more absorbed within himself, and the sources of each external experience are dammed up upon which we Occidentals are accustomed to base almost all our knowledge, and surely all our science,—in just the same measure sources hitherto unknown to him begin to well up within him, the very distant whispering murmur of which his unusually sharpened ear ever more clearly perceives. He who has become strong in four-fold self-absorption has actually tempered and annealed for himself a new sense, which he can use as a drill is used by a geologist. Grown wise in himself and of himself—this monk is able above all things to recollect himself. This knowledge is recollection, and indeed in distinction and opposition to mere memory, is to be understood throughout as *anamnesis* in distinction and opposition to mere *mneme*. . . . That the ascetic shall remember most veridically and vividly all the circumstances of his life down to the least detail is the most important outcome of the four Jhanani; that is the first relatively holy wisdom." I leave it to you to draw the parallel with psychoanalysis.

Shall we believe that the pious monk who followed Buddha's prescriptions was capable of such recollections? In the three first Jhana stages we saw that in case he did not recollect, he reënacted, formed transitory symptoms in Ferenczi's sense, a passing melancholia, a passing schizophrenia; he repeated the stages of his earlier development. It is theoretically conceivable that in the affectless, resistance-free fourth state conscious memories arise. But how far this remembered knowledge, as Buddha calls it, goes is hard to establish. If we may believe Buddha, it goes very far. He halts not at all at the threshold of individual existence but passes over into a continuous state of regression. Let us hear what Buddha says of the condition of the fourth stage: "In such a zealous state of mind, refined, cleansed, purified, free of dross, supple, pliant, steadfast, invulnerable, I directed the heart toward recollected knowledge of previous forms of existence. I recollected many different forms of existence as if one life, then two lives, then three, then four, then five, then ten, then twenty—then a thousand, a hundred thousand, then times when many worlds were created, then times when many worlds declined, then times when many worlds arose—vanished."[5]

The meaning of those regressive recollections of all forms of existence, of all reincarnations until there is no more rebirth, until rebirth is finally dug out by the roots, until man is annihilated, can no longer remain in doubt. The regressive absorption, the turning of the film of life in a reverse direction, goes further, goes beyond birth and passes all stages of intra-uterine life, and unrolls embryological development, which is nothing other than a short repetition of all forms of life in the geological rise and fall of many worlds of early times since the first birth. The question previously put, Where does the Buddhistic regression end? can now be answered. Absorption goes back to the beginning of embryonic development.

I am perfectly aware of how improbable this sounds. Yet if you have followed me along the regressive path of absorption perhaps you will not deny that this path, which is a chronologically true demolition of ontogenetic development, finally leads to a primitive condition where ego impulses and libido completely merge, similar to the state which we can assume, according to Freud, to obtain for the germ cell. We know that neurotic symptoms make use of archaic forms of expression; it is really then only a quantitative question as to how old this form is. Whether it arises from the extra- or intra-uterine condition is no fundamental matter. In the form of action, of repetition, every regression is thinkable, and I hope I have made it probable that the condition of Nirvana in Indian ascetics who have mastered the regression technique and whose entire libido through years of practice is withdrawn in this introverted narcissistic direction, can be expressed as a libido-ego equation which is identical with that of the germ cell. But Nirvana means not alone a complete regression to the beginning of development, but at the same time a knowledge. The clairvoyant knowledge of eternal reincarnation, the recollection of all forms of life, all geological periods, which Buddha perceived after going through the fourth step of Jhana, is nothing more than our fundamental biogenetic law, except that Buddha discovered it by a completely different approach. He knew this law experientially by reliving in his affective regression, his embryological existence. The difficulty we cannot resolve is how consciousness, or, as Buddha maintains, memory, can follow this deep regression so far. Here we meet our most difficult problem, whose solution is hardly possible, and which I shall in no way undertake. Nevertheless, permit me to point out that we meet the same problem daily in analytical practice and that just this commonplaceness explains why we have accustomed ourselves not to think about it.

This problem begins with Freud's thesis, that the neurotic is always right. Our entire analytical striving rests upon this truth . . . that we listen to the neurotic and seek to trace a meaning in his symptoms. Freud's statement really means that the *unconscious* is always right. Now the above problem is brought somewhat nearer if we reformulate the sentence, "the unconscious is always right," more pretentiously: The unconscious knows everything—knows all that concerns the inner world. Ignorance of that which is within first begins with the Censorship. We find this thesis proven every day. The unconscious knows the "primal scene," knows of the amniotic fluid, and knows the fact of fertilization. Freud shows that it is unnecessary, in order to understand the knowledge of the unconscious, always to search for actual observations or even for early phantasies. He predicates the conception of inherent phantasies and with this predicates a phylogenetic knowledge. This knowledge is a sort of recollection. And as the memory of living matter is unlimited—in embryonic development are repeated even the occurrences of primeval times—so also the recollective knowledge of the unconscious is unlimited in time. The deepest layer of the unconscious cannot be other than the psychic reflection of those early biological events which we group together in the designation embryological development. Upon this deepest layer, which we can designate as phylogenetic knowledge, Buddha strikes in his regressive absorption. For this embryological period a capacity for unlimited recollection is characteristic. Biologically regarded, it *is* nothing else but recollection. And yet it remains a riddle, this discovering of biogenetic law by introspective means, the discovery, or rather the direct experiencing of it. This deepest layer of the unconscious, which is pure recollection, is furtherest of all from consciousness, and with Buddha this is said to become conscious!

We can hardly picture that the recollected knowledge of Buddha retraces and psychologically reproduces embryological development. We know what a piece of work it is to make a neurotic symptom, and archaic regression, conscious, even aided by the entire stock of our analytical experience. It seems implied that Buddha, while in his schizophrenic regression, presents a symptom, interprets it at the same time, and in this way substitutes memory for repetition. Yet if we deny this there then remains only the other possibility, that Buddha found this law not by subjective means, but by the usual kind of objective knowledge, and then phantasied this into its theoretically correct place in the scale of absorption. The truth may be midway between these extremes. The dogma of rebirth is contained in the old Indian Atman. It is in the form of a theory of the transmigration of souls, a primitive intuitive presentiment of the theory of evolution, but in part, perhaps chiefly based upon the objective observation of death, birth, and of the similarities between men and beasts, and representing a deductive conclusion from such observation. We may also be dealing with a sort of "fausse reconnaissance," as Heiler assumes, without recognizing the deeper meaning of that term. Heiler says: "We Occidentals can with difficulty picture to ourselves this anamnesis, this memory retrospect of previous existences. We can, however, psychologically understand how a person all whose desires and strivings focus on a flight from the painful recurrences of birth, in moments of highest spiritual tension, might, by a sort of fausse reconnaissance process, take the visual images which arise to be memories of previous reincarnation." But through Freud we know the deeper meaning of "fausse reconnaissance." We recognize something which we know unconsciously, which we have repressed, or which is present in us as unconscious knowledge. The emerging phantasy pictures, in Heiler's explanation, arise from the unconscious. They enter during the repetition of embryological development, similar to a dream, or a free association, and are the last tributaries of the unconscious to surge into consciousness. However this may be, it is clear that Buddha has in some manner experienced the fundamental biogenetic law; his experience has not alone biological but also geological validity. Yet this subjective experience is contained in every kind of knowledge, also in our seemingly purely objective type of knowledge of the outside world. Every intuitive comprehension of a truth, if it is accompanied by the subjective feeling of its being a discovery, or of having self-evidence, is a kind of fausse reconnaissance, a recognition of one's own self mirrored in the outside world. The connections within the self are just the same as in the external world—the self is only a special part of reality. "Ordo et connexio idearum idem est ac ordo et connexio rerum." And now I am again at my point of departure. I did not wish to prove the reciprocal validity of biological and psychological occurrences, but to use this concept to illuminate the phenomena of Buddha's self-absorption. The oldest problem in philosophy reappears in this individual case. Yet all our sense of wonder vanishes if we accept Spinoza's solution. There are two roads to all knowledge. One can experience the world as an object, or experience it directly, know it endopsychically. If the methods of both forms of knowing are correct, then they must lead to the same result, and this is the only true control. Indian culture has brought the subjective method of self-submersion to completion, while our occidental culture fosters the method of objective knowledge. Only in psychoanalysis do the two methods meet. Here I recall a statement of Groddeck that human intelligence is nothing but the stupidity acquired through repression.[6] I should like to amplify this sentence to the effect that in a certain sense our entire consciousness is based on such a relative stupidity upon ignorance of that which is within. We leave the regulation of our instinctual life to more primitive processes and agencies than our critical consciousness such as conscience, the consciousness of guilt. The regulation of deeper biological happenings is left to agencies which lie still further from consciousness and whose existence we are only beginning to appreciate.[7] With this stupidity in regard to our inner life we gain our knowledge of the external world. This freedom comes from inner processes, which take place automatically without the necessity of conscious interference and permits us to direct all our attention toward the world.

When Buddha announced his absorption theory a number of auto-hypnotic absorption methods, which one knows as Yoga practice, had already been discovered. Seeking the truth, Buddha had at first chosen autohypnotic absorption and later discarded it as not leading to his goal. His main methodological discovery was that absorption must take place under completely conscious circumstances in order to reach Nirvana. I will not again point out the striking similarity between the analytical method and the doctrine of Buddha. The overcoming of affective resist-ance and of narcissism, so that one is able to recollect instead of repeat the extension of consciousness in a regressive direction toward the past, this is the doctrine common to Freud and Buddha. Can we regard as accidental this remarkable repetition in the history of both spiritual creations whose founders both at first attempted to use hypnosis, which they found at hand as prescientific practice? And was it also accidental that both then arrived at the conclusion that the chief and really difficult task is to establish the connection with consciousness?

Yet there remains an insurmountable difference between the two doc-trines, deeply founded within the difference between Indian and European culture. Buddhistic absorption goes much deeper in the direc-tion of regression, yet it must pay dearly for this depth. Through this it allows the entire outside world to pass into oblivion, conquers the self, but loses the world thereby. The objective of psychoanalysis is more pretentious, it strives to conquer self without losing the outside world. The Buddhistic doctrine is more asocial; we find in the causes of absorp-tion only biological factors such as age, sickness, and death, but no so-cial factors such as the Oedipus complex. The world is given up, and the cure consists in regression to the condition where ego and libido, no longer driven by outer necessity, reach their ultimate boundaries. Buddha does not seek an adjustment to the world, as psychoanalysis seeks to achieve a new compromise, to establish a new boundary be-tween ego and libido, adjusted to reality. This asocial feature of his doctrine also spelt its end, which came with a tragic crash. The Neobud-dhists overlook this failure if they expect from his doctrine a new salva-tion.[8]

Buddha denies himself the eternal life, which he has achieved through the conquest of death, by the entrance to Nirvana. Here is the first contradiction in the completely self-contained Nirvana philosophy. Buddha, voluntarily parting from life, directs the following words to his favorite pupil, Ananda: "If to thee though, Ananda, the Perfect One has given an important sign, an important suggestion, thou hast not been able to see it, hast not prayed for the Perfect One . . . may the Exalted persist throughout the ages, may the Welcome One exist throughout the ages, for the good of many, for the healing of many, out of pity for the world, for the use, welfare and succour of gods, and men. Hadst thou, Ananda, prayed for the Perfect One, so had thy words been twice unheeded, the third time answered. For this reason thou hast overlooked it, hast missed it."[9] Here we see, heavily shrouded, in the dark background, the Oedipus complex, the father conflict. Buddha departs, because his followers have not understood him, because he has remained alone, because even his favorite pupil, Ananda, does not seek to keep him from going. This incomprehensible "not asking to remain" means nothing other than an unresolved father conflict. According to Oldenburg, the silence of Ananda is explained by saying that the death god, Mara, had confused his reason.[10] Yet Buddha understands Ananda's silence. He does not want to believe what he sees, and hints to Ananda that he expects from him a request to remain. But Ananda remains silent and Buddha departs. The attempt to eliminate reality completely has failed. He begins his analysis at a point which lies behind the Oedipus complex. He begins where we leave off, at the narcissistic boundary, at the borders of the organic.

And thus he instructs his disciples. He must go because his followers under the pressure of the unconquered father complex desire his departure. Buddha has not analyzed but repressed the object transference. Had he remained consistent, he would never have been able to announce his doctrine.[11] He completely withdrew from the world, yet one thread he left unsevered—his spiritual connection with his disciples. Here it is that he receives his mortal blow. He denied the world, and the denied world revenged itself upon him in the form of the unconscious parricidal wishes of his followers.

NOTES

[1] Heiler, "Die Buddhistische Versenkung." Munich, 1922.

[2] Leopold Ziegler, "Der ewige Buddho," Darmstadt, 1922.

[3] *Ibid.*, Heiler, p. 40.

[4] Freud, "Janseits des Lustprinzips," 2d edition, 1922 (English edition, "Beyond the Pleasure Principle," 1922).

[5] "Die Reden Gotamo Buddhos," from the collection Majjhimanikajo des Pali Kanons, translated by Karl Eugen Neumann, Vol. I, Munich, 1922. R. Piper & Co.

[6] Groddeck, "Ueber den Symbolisierungezwang." Imago, Vol. VIII, p. 72, 1922.

[7] One thinks of the "ego-memory-system" of Ferenczi (Psychoanalytical Observations on Tic. International Journal of Psycho-Analysis, VII, 1921).

[8] I think first of Leopold Ziegler.

[9] *Ibid.*, Ziegler, 1. c., pp. 159–160.

[10] Oldenburg, "Buddha; sein Leben, sein Lehre, seine Gemeinde," p. 356. Gottasche Buchhandlung, Stuttgart–Berlin, 1921.

[11] Buddha actually doubted whether he should keep his teachings to himself or announce them to mankind (Oldenburg, 1. c., p. 159). Nowhere in the Buddhistic literature has sufficient account been taken of the deep contradiction between the absorption doctrine and Buddha's practical ethics, so far as I am able to follow. The goal of absorption, Nirvana, is a complete asocial condition and is difficult to combine with ethical precepts.

Psychoanalysis has long sought to learn what kind of personality or what kind of events are likely to lead to addictions of any kind. Karl Menninger suggests that the source of the addict's problem is a thwarted eroticism. A tendency towards homosexuality, great fear of the mother and a terror of castration characterize the alcoholic. The alcoholic, like the drug addict, ironically accomplishes his own destruction by using the very device that helps him relieve the anxiety aroused by his fear of destruction.

KARL MENNINGER

Alcohol Addiction

FROM *Man Against Himself*

Only a few years ago, were a psychiatrist to approach the subject of alcohol, it would be assumed immediately that he would deal chiefly with the celebrated syndrome, delirium tremens. As a student at Harvard Medical School twenty years ago, I was minutely instructed, along with my classmates, in the details of differential diagnosis that would distinguish delirium tremens from a half dozen other psychotic pictures that somewhat resembled it. And this is all I learned of alcohol and its function in the disruption of mental health.

Today, in the active practice of psychiatry, with patients before my eyes daily, including many whom alcohol has ruined or nearly ruined, I have not seen three cases of delirium tremens in as many years. Not that this affliction has disappeared from the earth, for in the wards of public hospitals or behind the bars of city jails new cases are, I am sure, admitted daily.[1] But they do not interest psychiatrists now so much as those cases which give a better opportunity to discover why they drink rather than the results of their drinking.

I do not think this represents any change in the effects of alcohol on the human being. I think, rather, that it is the best possible illustration of the change in emphasis, interest, and concept in psychiatry. Once we looked curiously—and, to be sure, tenderly and humanely as well—at the end-results of men whose brains were finally reacting in a dramatic spectacle to a cumulative over-dose of poison. Those inestimably more numerous persons whose self-poisoning produced symptoms less vividly tinctured with hallucinations and terrors were regarded as sociological—not psychiatric—problems. The psychology of the man impelled to ruin himself by self-poisoning, in spite of disaster, remorse, and resolutions to abandon it, some way or other escaped the consideration of the psychiatrists and was left to the clergy, the social workers, the prohibitionists, or to the devil.

Drunkenness is as old as Noah, but drunkenness is not alcohol addiction. Many become drunk who never become addicts. Furthermore, an occasional alcoholic addict is seen who is never, or rarely, "drunk" in the popular sense (because he is partially intoxicated all the time, and the effects are concealed for want of a comparative background). It is not my intention to discuss the function of alcohol in the life of a normal person, or the amenities of social drinking. There is much to indicate that in our civilization alcohol has a very useful function to perform, and may be a source of increased happiness and decreased hostilities.

But there remains the phenomenon of self-destruction by irresistible addiction to repeated, excessive drinking of alcohol.[2] Everyone knows examples of this—individuals who suffer from what seems to be an irresistible impulse to throw away all obligations and opportunities and bring their house of cards tumbling about their heads by getting drunk. Every social worker could testify to homes filled with bitterness and despair because of an addiction to alcohol on the part of a father, husband, son, or even a mother. Furthermore, every psychiatrist (and others, too, of course) could, with the author, cite case after case of prominent and formerly successful men, together with many others who are potentially successful, whose lives are literally ruined in this peculiar way. I say "peculiar" because it is paradoxical that a substance which gives and has for centuries given pleasure, relief, and stimulation to man, should, for a few, become an instrument of self-destruction.

Someone may be tempted here to make a jocular response, that if, indeed, it be self-destruction, it is at least a pleasant form of it. With this no one intimately acquainted with the suffering of an alcoholic addict or his family could agree. Funny it may seem to the casual observer, but to the drinker's family and ultimately to him, too, it is a tragedy past jocularity.

Yet, at the same time, there is a little truth in that joke. It is an example of what has been called "gallows humor"—as in the case of the condemned man who remarked, on the way to his execution, "This is certainly going to be a lesson to me."

Since it is true that alcohol has the quality of giving some degree of relief from the pain of facing reality and also from other psychic pain resulting from emotional conflicts, to the extent that it is sought for the purpose of relieving pain, the use of alcohol can be regarded as an attempt at self-cure. Some alcoholics recognize this but many others cannot be persuaded that their periodic bouts are more than jolly little affairs which, for all they may end in a rather untidy and tiresome mess, with a few disappointments all around, no one should hold against them. This wish to be treated like a child and to have one's most serious aggressions overlooked is very characteristic of the type of personality which finds excessive indulgence in alcohol so irresistible.

This leads us to wonder what type of personality or what predisposing experiences in any personality lead to the election of this kind of suicide. . . .

Let us begin with the more superficial aspects. "Alcoholics" are almost invariably jolly, sociable, talkative fellows who make themselves very popular, who indeed seem *obliged* to make themselves well liked and are very skillful at doing so. It takes very little penetration to discover, however, that this inordinate wish to be loved which compels them to be at such pains to be charming and to win popularity in one circle or another bespeaks a great underlying feeling of insecurity, a feeling which must constantly be denied, compensated for, or anesthetized.

From clinical experience also we know that such feelings of insecurity and inferiority depend less upon actual reality comparisons than upon unconscious, "irrational" reasons—generally feelings of great frustration and rage, and the fear and guilt which the rage induces. All this is, of course, now unconscious. But once it was *fully* conscious, only too conscious. In fact, a supplementary function of the alcohol-drinking is the further repression of such feelings and memories which threaten to emerge, to become again conscious. Such individuals, as children, have endured bitter disappointment, *unforgettable* disappointment, *unforgivable* disappointment! They feel, with justification, that they have been betrayed, and their entire subsequent life is a prolonged, disguised reaction to this feeling.

It is true that every child meets with disappointment and frustration; this is inevitable in the nature of reality. We are born into a world where we must change from directing our existence according to the pleasure principle to a program of directing our existence according to a reality principle which we discover by painful testing, step by step. We all had to be weaned, we all had to give up our dependence on our parents, we all had to relinquish our belief in Santa Claus. In this respect, then, the alcoholic probably does not suffer in childhood anything qualitatively different from what the rest of us suffer, but apparently there is a quantitative difference. In the case of the alcoholic the disappointment has actually been greater than he could bear. It was so great that it definitely affected his personality development so that in certain respects he remains all his life what we call an "oral character." We have already referred to this in the discussion of melancholia; I shall only repeat that an oral character is one characterized by conspicuous residua of the stage of psychological development in which the child's attitude toward the world was determined by his wish to take it in through the mouth and to destroy with his mouth anything which resisted his demands.

Drinking (in the sense in which we are now using it) is a typical infantile revenge reaction. In the first place, it is performed with the mouth; in the second place, it places a fictitiously high value upon the magical virtues of the substance desired; more important still, its practical aggressive values are indirect. An adult reaction of revenge would be more directly aggressive. For example, a mature person, angry for good reason at his father, would state the issue and discontinue further dealings instead of grieving and embittering his father by debauches. But the alcoholic cannot risk giving up the love objects to which he clings, angry and resentful as he may feel toward them, consciously or unconsciously. Furthermore, like all neurotics he confuses his friends and his (theoretical) enemies and treats those whom he thinks he loves as if they were identical with those whom he hates or whom he *once* hated. Thus, the alcoholic suffers at the same time from the wish to destroy his love-objects and the fear that he will lose them. He also fears the consequences of the aggressions which he is constantly impelled to make against them and from which he deters himself only by fierce internal restraint which in time accumulates to the point of leading him to seek a form of anesthetization which indirectly achieves the very aggressions and other consequences which he so feared he would succumb to.

In this strong ambivalence of the alcoholic, this conflictual and confusing attitude of love and hate, one sees an epitome and therefore a partial explanation of the nature of the great disappointment which he once suffered. Rather than derive it logically, let me depend again on empirical observations. We have noted time after time in those cases which have been subjected to penetrating anamnestic and psychological investigations that the parents of alcoholics increased the inevitable disappointment of the child tremendously by artificial, however unintentional, means. Apparently they did this usually by leading the child to expect more gratification than they were prepared to give or than reality made it possible to give. A few examples of this will illustrate specifically what I mean. The mother of one alcoholic nursed her child until he was nearly three years old because she herself was so fond of the experience; she then became desperate because of the difficulty she encountered in weaning him and achieved her aim finally by painting her breasts with stove blacking in order to frighten and repel the child. The mother of another alcoholic made of her child a pet and darling, almost ignoring the other children, a role which naturally had to be relinquished when he grew a little older. The father of still another alcoholic habitually did such things as this: he sent his son to the corner drug store repeatedly for cigars and household supplies, instructing him to say to the clerk only the magic words, "Charge it." One day the son used this same formula to obtain some candy, seeing nothing wrong in extending his knowledge to this new need. When his father learned of it he whipped the boy severely to the child's astonishment and resentment. Still another father encouraged his son to work and develop a savings account; then he, the father, appropriated the account.

This inconsistency in attitude toward the child bespeaks an ambivalence on the parents' part and explains why these patients are so often described by their friends and relatives as "spoiled"; "a spoiled child that never grew up," and similar expressions which imply reproach to both the "child" and his parents. Such appellations are partially correct, but err in the assumption that such children are "spoiled" by having been given too much love. I doubt very much if any child is ever spoiled by too much love. What passes for excessive "love" on the part of the parents is often only thinly disguised hate or guilt, and this fact is perceived by the child, if not by the neighbors. Over-solicitous, over-protective mothers and fathers who bestow large gifts to avoid the necessity of spending time and thought on the child; parents who exploit, promote, or smother their children with their own personalities, for the gratification of their own narcissism, cannot be said to be "loving" their children however much they themselves may think so. And for all these aggressions against him the child will certainly some day, perhaps at great cost to himself, take full and terrible revenge.

All this theory becomes very much more understandable when studied in a particular case:

Jonathan Richardson was the son of one of the most distinguished men in the United States in his generation and in his particular field. We saw him—the patient—first at the age of thirty-five. The preceding fifteen years of his life had consisted of a dismal series of failures and the decimation of an opportunity for a career such as is offered to few men. The ostensible cause of all his failure was alcohol; indeed, the tragedy of his life was of just the sort which those opposed to the sale and use of alcohol use as an example with telling effect.

He was a very handsome man both in feature and in figure. He had perfect manners and good, if not superior, intelligence. These things, with his family's prestige and money, combined to make him exceedingly popular wherever he went. He had been a leading socialite, a prominent athlete, and a popular leader in the student body of the large and well-known eastern university to which he was sent. Nor did he carry his popularity with a bad grace; he was not arrogant, snobbish, or ostentatious. Indeed, his only fault during the earlier years of his life might be said to have lain in a certain passive acceptance of his good fortune rather than any energetic effort to gain it or make the best of it. He did not drink at all during his freshman year.

He left the university, where his father thought he was not working hard enough, and went to another school to obtain training in his father's business specialty in order to be equipped to take over the large responsibilities that would devolve upon him as the ultimate head of the firm—his father's great ambition for him. But here he showed a strange reaction to his opportunities which no one could understand. It was first a lack of enthusiasm about the work and later an out-and-out aversion to it. Finally, in spite of what seemed to be a conscientious effort, he failed completely in all the subjects related to the professional course.

It was in connection with this failure that he began drinking. Repeatedly, on nights when he should have been studying, he would go out for a few hours' relaxation and end up by becoming dead-drunk, and would then miss his classes the next day. In desperation his father insisted that he transfer to still another school but here the same thing happened. He had decided by now that he did not want to go into his father's business, that he had no interest in it or liking for it, that the apparently great opportunity meant nothing to him. His father could out-argue him and he would always admit that his father was probably right and then lapse into silence and (at the first opportunity) into another drunken spree.

He had some talent for drawing and pled that he be allowed to cultivate this talent, but his father thought it ridiculous that a son with his opportunities in the business world should dabble in art, for which, moreover, he seemed to have at best only a mediocre gift.

Then several things happened almost simultaneously: The World War broke out, and disregarding the opportunity for advancement which his father's prestige would have given him, he enlisted as a private and worked his own way up to the rank of commissioned officer. He married a beautiful woman and one who subsequently turned out to be as intelligent, levelheaded, and patient as she was beautiful. At that time, however, she was the cause of repeated penalization for him because he would absent himself from the army without leave in order to see her. He continued to drink surreptitiously and after his discharge more than ever.

The father in the meantime had become fully reconciled to the fact that his son would never come into his business and was anxious only to have him stop drinking and get into some work at which he would be self-supporting. During the next ten years he financed project after project, lending the son thousands of dollars, setting him up in one business after another, only to have him make a failure of every one of them. In each case the failure would be of the same character. There would be a burst of enthusiasm, an initial spurt of hard work, the establishment of many contacts, a period of good will and popularity and the promise of success, then increasing disappointments of customers on account of absences from the store (drinking), increasing drinking, and decreasing sales, the latter causing discouragement and thus more drinking, the whole thing ending up in bankruptcy, arrest and threatened or actual imprisonment, sudden disappearance, or some other dramatic finale. Throughout all this he would preserve an amiable, conciliatory, earnest manner that had the effect of convincing everyone that surely he had repented all his dissolute ways and had turned the corner toward reform.

"I have thrown away everything," he would say. "I have broken my mother's heart, turned down the best business opportunity a man ever had, wasted my youth, neglected opportunities for education, encumbered myself with the responsibilities of a loving wife and children whom I can't support, and what have I got out of it? Nothing! A lot of drunken brawls which I didn't even enjoy at the time."

Now to look into the psychology of this boy's drinking. He had what we feel to be the typical set-up for alcoholism. He had a powerful, money-bestowing, but vacillating (i.e., ambivalent) father; he had an indulgent and undiscriminating (therefore also ambivalent) mother; he had a sister whom the parents definitely preferred.

A word of explanation about these. The father, whom every son unconsciously strives to emulate, was in this instance on a very high pinnacle. This alone made a difficulty for the boy, because the greatness of his father seemed to him to be unattainable. But added to this was the fact that the father used his position cruelly. He was high and mighty with his son, at times savage with him, and at other times sentimental to the point of being maudlin. A consistently harsh father gives his son something to fight against. A father who, as this one, ridicules and humiliates the son with sarcasm until he leaves the table sobbing, and at other times boasts of him to others in his presence and overwhelms him with gifts, excites terrific antagonism and at the same time inspires its suppression. The son is not only embittered by the harshness but fore-stalled by the occasional kindness from normal attempts at retaliation.

Another resentment of this son against the father was the father's preference for the sister. Normal as this may have been on the part of the father, it aroused in the son—as it always does—unconscious envy of the feminine position because the father's attitude toward her was more consistently kind. The normal solution of the emotional conflict caused by this family set-up would be for the boy to turn toward his mother for such help as he needed during his growing years and then graduate from the family to more hospitable and less conflictual fields. But there are certain difficulties about this. The wives of such superior men as this boy's father are apt to have their own private neuroses, a very common one being the tendency to turn from the husband to the son as a love-object. This leads to further complications; it overwhelms the son with love from a source which either tends in the direction of keeping him a spoiled child who need make no manly effort to win love, or increases his fear of the powerful father in whose domain he is trespassing. One might say that such boys, incensed at being slighted by their fathers and by the preference shown their sisters (or someone else), turn toward the mothers for affection inordinately, but because of the fear of the powerful father, accept this love from her only in the infantile mode and remain sucklings.

Exactly this happened in the patient I have been describing. How it was reflected in later life can be clearly seen in the brief history of him given above. The boy was forced by his feelings of inferiority toward his father, his envy of the sister, and his oral dependence upon the mother into the acceptance of an extremely passive role in life. All the characteristics of the typical alcoholic which I described above can be related to his essential passivity and the wish to win love from people by excessive friendliness and essential subservience rather than by masculine achievement. But while passive in method, alcoholics are by no means lacking in aggressiveness.[3] Indeed, they use their passivity in the most aggressive way against those who thwart them. It is for this reason that alcoholism so often develops or increases to a pathological degree shortly after marriage. The predisposed individual seeks more maternal gratification from the wife than the average or normal woman is prepared to give, characteristically accuses her of not being affectionate enough, and is himself reluctant to assume his masculine responsibilities toward her. The result of this feeling of thwarting is a return to the bottle which serves at the same time as a gratification to him and as an aggression against her.

In the case of Jonathan Richardson, it will be recalled that the drinking began before marriage at a time when the father insisted upon a change in universities. He wanted the son to follow in his business. This the son could not do for many reasons. It implied an undesired identification with his father. Moreover, it would have put him in an unendurable position of comparison and rivalry with his father of whom he was so afraid. (It is characteristic of oral characters that they are poor winners and poor losers; they cannot bear to do either and hence usually sidestep competitive activities of all sorts.) Jonathan wanted rather to be an artist, another feminine identification (no aspersion upon artists is intended; I refer now to art as *he* conceived of it, which was in imitation of his mother). In this his father tried to thwart him and he tried in turn to thwart his father's ambition for him. He did so, however, in the way characteristic of alcoholics. He went through the motions of trying to comply with his father's wishes and appeared to fail only through succumbing to the temptation of drink (which is symbolically equivalent to the childhood retreat to his mother).

There is one other element in this case not invariably characteristic of alcoholics but very common. That is the fact that the patient's father himself drank very heavily. The older psychiatrists regarded this as a very important point because they considered alcoholism to be an hereditary trait. Of course, scarcely any scientist believes so today, although it is still a popular theory. Alcoholism cannot possibly be an hereditary trait, but for a father to be alcoholic is an easy way for the son to learn *how* to effect the retaliation he later feels compelled to inflict. Many alcoholics, as everyone knows, have parents distinguished for their sobriety and self-restraint. Of course, in such homes the alcoholism of the son carries the greater power as a weapon.

Such a case illustrates as well as any one case can some of the various psychological functions of alcohol addiction. What strikes some as most apparent in such cases is the feeling of inferiority which the alcoholism seems to relieve; many people have made this observation introspectively and the case just cited seems to be a good example of it. However, one should remember that such a great sense of inferiority usually depends upon guilt feelings arising from envy and hostility. The mild elation which releases inhibitions after a few drinks of an alcoholic beverage cannot be compared directly with the feelings of a person addicted to alcohol. For one thing, the alcoholic never stops in the stage where such feelings of release can be advantageously enjoyed but carries the drinking to a point where these feelings are annulled, and usually to a point where his behavior is such as to actually increase rather than decrease his social or intellectual disability or "inferiority." This, plus the most casual observation of the behavior of such individuals, is sufficient to convince anyone of the unconsciously aggressive function of the drinking. It would seem scarcely necessary to prove this point; everyone is familiar with the obnoxious behavior of drunken boors at parties, public gatherings, and in private life. Alcoholic patients give psychiatric hospitals more trouble than any others, not because of any consistent disagreeableness or belligerency but rather because of the contrast between their superficial attitude of amiable, courteous compliance and the petty grumbling and occasional impulsive and unexpected obstreperousness which any denial of their incessant importunacy evokes. They simply cannot endure the privations incident to life in a real world (or even in the specially modified world of the sanitarium). Indeed, an alcoholic may be considered as beginning to "get well" when he discovers that getting drunk is not the only way in which he habitually makes himself disagreeable. William Seabrook[4] in his amazingly candid account of his experiences while under treatment for alcoholism describes this faithfully and accurately. For anyone interested in the problem this book is an indispensable source of material in spite of the fact that what the author may have regarded as a deep psychological study of himself was quite obviously interrupted at a relatively superficial stage, at least so far as the recorded account goes.

I have stated that the inferiority feelings of the alcoholic frequently arise from a sense of guilt. In some individuals this consciously precedes the drinking but in the majority of instances it is often erroneously ascribed (by them and by some physicians) to the physiological effects of the drinking (hangover, katzenjammer, etc.). But this sense of guilt pertains not so much to the immediate aggressiveness implicit in the drinking as to the fundamental aggressiveness back of it, the partially but never successfully repressed hostility which, I believe, is one of the chief determinants of the alcoholic neurosis. This is apparent in some cases only after considerable study but in others, as in one now to be cited, it strikes one immediately.

This was a thoughtful, intelligent young fellow of twenty-three who looked and acted as if he were thirty and who, after outstanding success in the preparatory school from which he graduated with honors, was dismissed from the university on account of excessive drinking. Subsequent to this he lost position after position on account of drinking and dissipation with women. He came to the clinic in a serious frame of mind, determined that he must get help or face the consequences of becoming a hopeless drunkard. He was the more thoughtful and earnest about it because his father had recently died, throwing considerable responsibility upon his shoulders as well as increasing feelings of remorse which had never been entirely absent but which, on the other hand, had never been effective in inhibiting his drinking.

He was considerably disturbed by recurrent dreams of being in the penitentiary. He recalled that shortly after his father's death he had been awakened several times by a nightmare in which he saw his father's corpse arise from the dead, angry and threatening. His father, a successful, intelligent, far-seeing man, had been greatly disappointed in this son, and had been stern and reproachful with him. The patient admitted that he could not escape the conviction that his drinking had so distressed the father as to have actually been a contributing factor in causing his death. This explains the patient's nightmare dream and penitentiary dream. "I realize I killed my father," said he; "small wonder I dream of going to the penitentiary."

The patient continued to dream of being hanged or put in the penitentiary which disturbed him so much that he would get drunk and then remorseful again. "I am nothing but a drunken bum and a degenerate," he said. "Let me drink myself to death. I am not worth saving."

He broke off his treatment and left the institution (toward which, however, he retained the kindliest feelings) in a determined effort to carry out this intention of self-destruction. He continued to drink, became involved in an automobile accident in which a man *was* killed (as in his "prophetic" dream) and he was actually put on trial for manslaughter (also conforming to his dreams) but was acquitted.

He went to another psychoanalyst for a while but again broke off the treatment and entered business, in which he was moderately successful. He had meanwhile discontinued drinking as the result of his fright in connection with the automobile accident but in its place he suffered now from an array of almost paralyzing neurotic symptoms, fears, anxieties, inhibitions, physical symptoms, and morbid ideas. The substitution of one type of neurosis for another is here strikingly illustrated.

This case also demonstrates the rather typical sexual pattern in alcoholism relating the aggressiveness and guilt-feelings to the erotic value of the drinking. The terrific sense of guilt with reference to the father, the almost studied provocativeness toward him combined with a deep attraction to him led to a conflict between his wish for passive erotic dependence upon him, and his rejection of this wish. It is almost axiomatic that alcoholics in spite of a great show of heterosexual activity, have secretly a great fear of women and of heterosexuality in general, apparently regarding it as fraught with much danger. They often realize that they do not possess normal sexual powers or interests, frankly avowing that it is not sexual gratification they seek from women so much as affection, care, love—by which they mean maternal solicitude. This, ultimately, the normal wife rebels against giving to a grown man supposedly her protector and master. The outcome is inevitable. The patient then assumes a grieved or contemptuous or utilitarian or even consciously hostile attitude toward her and all women and turns toward men with a mixture of friendly and provocative behavior, with temporary jollity and popularity but ultimate misery and personal loss. At the same time that he is drinking with boon companions who appear to be substitutes for his father, he is defying and grieving his real father and rejecting his real mother or her substitute. This, in turn, gives rise to remorse which leads to self-depreciation and self-injury. Meanwhile the exasperated wife considers or applies for divorce. Immediately, the little-boy husband rushes back to her with tears, prayers, and promises to which she very likely succumbs and the whole cycle begins again.

The self-destructive consequences of alcoholism which are so obvious would seem to be in part incidental, that is, they are the untoward consequences of self-administered efforts at obtaining relief from internal dangers. As soon as these internal dangers threaten the destruction of the individual by his own impulses, alcoholism is chosen or substituted as a kind of lesser self-destruction serving to avert a greater self-destruction.

We have commented that the same problem faces many if not all people and the same solution is also available to everyone. The question is, what particular problems obsess the potential alcoholic and why is this particular method chosen by him to solve them. The cases recited illustrate some of the conditioning experiences which favor the development of the alcoholic's emotional problems and also favor this method of attempted solution. They relate to the thwarting of the early oral receptive cravings of these individuals, i.e., their need of love and the fearful resentments which these thwartings create with a corresponding anticipation of punishment or annihilation as the consequence of indulging or even fantasying these retaliations.

The alcoholism solves the problem neatly because it enables the individual to carry out these retaliations and aggressions, often against the very person toward whom they were originally directed; in addition, however, it incurs liability for a certain amount of punishment which is not so dreadful as that feared under the original circumstances.

Furthermore, it supplies the oral love—*symbolically,* in the form of a precious liquor taken by mouth, the "mother's milk" which was so much craved; and *actually,* in the form of conviviality and sentimentality which accompany social drinking. To be sure, this sometimes seems to be a substitute for heterosexual object love, but the alcoholic, like all oral characters, is not very discriminating between the sexes. Indeed, his chief resentment may be against women rather than men on account of thwarting propensities ascribed to his mother so that he discriminates against them, not so much on account of their sex, as on account of their similarity to her, i.e., not so much on a sexual basis as on a personal basis. Many alcoholics indulge in homosexual (or in heterosexual) relations only when they are drunk but these various facts confirm our proposition that all forms of self-destruction are partially (incompletely) eroticized, i.e., used as a source of pleasure.

The general problems of treatment I have consistently deferred for special consideration in the final section. Alcohol addiction is, however, such a widespread affliction and one in which present modes of treatment are so notoriously inadequate that I have thought it worthwhile to insert a brief summary of the treatment methods indicated by the conception of it as a form of self-destruction as outlined above.

Given this view of the problem of alcohol addiction, one can see that the general principles of its successful treatment must necessarily follow very different lines from those based upon the old conception that it represents a bad habit or an unfortunate inheritance. The effective treatment of alcohol addiction is, of course, the treatment of that which impels it. This means the gradual elimination of the tendency of over-reaction to frustration, and the progressive relief of those deep, inner feelings of anxiety, insecurity, and of childlike expectation and resentment which so regularly determine it.

Inasmuch, however, as the persistence of these traits represents a definite character deformity of very long standing, the modified results of childhood injuries, the accomplishment of their elimination implies a complete and thoroughgoing reconstruction of the entire personality.

So far as I know, there is only one treatment technique which even attempts to accomplish this, and that is psychoanalysis. I do not say that alcoholism cannot be cured by any other means. I have seen it happen in one instance as the result of a prolonged vigil of several years in a lonely spot by a very intelligent and determined man; I have known it to occur as the result of religious conversion; and I am sure it is occasionally possible in not too severe cases as the result of psychiatric conferences and counsel. We all know that "cure" is occasionally accomplished as the result of substituting another neurosis for the alcoholism; alcoholics, for example, sometimes cease to be alcoholics and become hypochondriacs or religious fanatics. And, finally, in justice to the facts, one must add that it sometimes happens suddenly following intense emotional experiences and also following apparently trivial incidents; the explanation of the metamorphosis in these cases remains entirely obscure.

But, on the other hand, I have never seen an alcoholic addict cured by confinement alone, even though alcohol is withdrawn completely during that period. This applies to long-time commitments as well as short-time "cures." I have talked to superintendents of numerous state hospitals where alcoholics have been treated and their observations have been the same as mine. In fact, one of our friends, who is the superintendent of such an institution, has recently refused to approve the admission of any more alcoholics to his hospital, not because of any scientific disinterest in them, but because of his conviction that residence in a state hospital is a state expense which accomplishes nothing for them or for the state.

It is not difficult to see why such treatment does not change the character or allay the underlying desires. Just as soon as the alcoholic is released he is once more exposed to the same opportunities for relief with just as much inner distress clamoring to be relieved.

To bring about the character revision necessary to relieve alcohol addiction requires psychological "surgery," i.e., psychoanalysis. *Theoretically,* it is the treatment of choice. *Practically,* there are many serious difficulties in the way. In the first place, psychoanalytic treatment cannot be accomplished in a few months. It is a typical alcoholic fantasy that the reconstruction of a character which has been thirty-odd years in forming (or, rather, deforming) can be accomplished in three, six, or even twelve months. The treatment of alcohol addiction, like the treatment of tuberculosis, is a long-time affair. This means that it is expensive in money as well as time. This is unfortunate but it is true. To encourage relatives or patients to believe that a few weeks or months are likely to bring about a fundamental change (with or without analysis) is only to disappoint them with certain failure.

Furthermore, most persons addicted to alcohol are too "far gone," too far removed from loyalty to the reality principle, to be treated by psychoanalysis under the ordinary circumstances. In other words, they must be treated in a specially adapted environment and for practical purposes this means that they must be confined, and opportunities for alcohol removed from immediate availability. Provision for increasing freedom, as their general behavior justifies it, is implicit in this plan. The proper direction of the aggressive tendencies as they become more and more direct and less and less circumvented by the neurotic inhibitions can be made to contribute to the therapeutic effectiveness of the treatment régime. Athletic and competitive tendencies are encouraged, and as soon as possible business or other sublimated aggressions engaged in.

Hence, confinement, *plus* psychoanalysis, *plus* the proper direction of the increasing capacity for externally directed aggressions constitute in our opinion and experience the best program of therapy for this affliction. Even this is not always successful but by means of it a few individuals have been cured and have stayed cured, not only of drinking but of the infantilism which accompanies it and the character deformities which produce it. This cannot be said, so far as I know, of any other treatment of alcohol addiction at the present time.

SUMMARY

Alcohol addiction, then, can be considered a form of self-destruction used to avert a greater self-destruction, deriving from elements of aggressiveness excited by thwarting, ungratified eroticism, and the feeling of a need for punishment from a sense of guilt related to the aggressiveness. Its further quality is that in a practical sense the self-destruction is accomplished *in spite of* and at the same time *by means of* the very device used by the sufferer to relieve his pain and avert this feared destruction.

NOTES

[1] "Dr. Karl M. Bowman, director of the department of psychiatry of Bellevue Hospital, New York City, in a recent address at the New York Academy of Medicine discussed the need of more effective means for the treatment of chronic alcoholics. He stated that at Bellevue Hospital his department was treating 1,000 cases of alcoholism a month and pointed out the fact that temporary treatment or fines or other jail sentences would not cure these inebriates. He recommended the establishment of State institutions for long-term treatment of chronic drunkards and psychopathic alcoholics. Mild cases of alcoholism should be treated by shorter periods of hospital care. He called attention to the fact that at present only those alcoholics whose families can afford to pay for private hospital treatment are receiving proper attention." (*Mental Hygiene News*, N.Y., Jan., 1937.)

[2] Addiction to drugs is psychologically similar, but differs in that all narcotic habituation is socially taboo, while alcohol ingestion is socially approved and hence immensely more dangerous and frequent as a basis of addiction.

[3] It is a common error to think of passivity as the opposite of aggressiveness. Passivity is often very aggressive in intention and effect.

[4] Seabrook, William, *Asylum*, Harcourt, Brace, 1935.

Writers have continually stressed the sexual and aggressive roots of prejudice, but social scientists have been slow to fully comprehend the role played by minorities, acting as scapegoats, in deflecting the unconscious hatred of the majority away from itself and onto another more helpless object.

MARTIN REISER

On Origins of Hatred Toward Negroes

There exists at the present time, as there has in the past, wide-spread feelings of hostility toward the Negro. Many explanations have been advanced in the attempt to account for this state of affairs, but a large proportion of these reasons seem to fall within the category of rationalization. These include explanations of a cultural, economic, or educational nature which do not adequately account for the extreme emotional nature of the conflict.

One of the first steps in trying to reach an understanding of a problem is to uncover and identify the contributing factors. In this instance, many of the underlying causes are unconscious and are not readily accessible to conscious scrutiny. But applying psychoanalytic means of speculation, perhaps we can shed a ray of light on this ubiquitous problem. Much of the enmity in regard to Negroes seems to be directed toward males. This is partly due to the fact that women in particular often feel attracted to men of a racially more primitive type and the unconscious jealousy that the perception of this attraction causes in men of the women's own race leads to brutality and violence.[1] In this connection, it is easier to assume aggression by Negro men than to admit the unpleasant possibility that Negro men may be sexually attractive to white women.[2] Many of the abhorred characteristics commonly attributed to Negroes are contrary to the facts. The beliefs that they have huge genitals, are oversexed, and especially prone to assault are unfounded. In fact, studies show that broken homes, dependency, and

980

fear create a passivity and impotence in Negro males to a very large extent.[3]

The dictionary[4] reveals that *Negro* comes from the Spanish *negro,* meaning black. This derives from the Latin *Niger,* which is akin to the Greek *Anigros,* meaning unclean or base. Negro, then, means a black man and some meanings accorded black are: darkness, dirty, menacing, hostile and foreboding, devoid of moral light or goodness, outrageously wicked, evil or harmful as a result of sorcery or magic involving forbidden practices, proscribed, banned or boycotted.

It is interesting that practically all of these meanings are expressions of conscious feeling toward the Negro. But what of the unconscious meaning? Words often derive their emotional content from experiences during childhood development.[5] The affect connected with these experiences is later projected outward onto specific objects in the environment and labeled so that it can be bound in the objects and controlled. We see this operating in primitive peoples where natural elements are anthropomorphized and imbued with supernatural powers. They then see the cause of most troubles as evil spirits and now can either gain their favor or escape from them.[6]

There seems to be in each individual's development a phase which corresponds to that animistic stage in the primitive and remnants of this stage are retained and can be reactivated.[7] These primitive, animistic ways of dealing with impulses in terms of the environment are largely determined by psychobiological development. Conflicts which arise during the various psychosexual stages of development are repressed and only their derivatives are allowed into consciousness. Perhaps we can trace some of these conflicts and try to discover the connection they might have with the current question.

During the oral stage of psychosexual development, part objects and later whole objects are internalized. Objects yielding pleasure are felt to be "good," and objects producing unpleasure are felt to be "bad." Because night is the time when the good mother and the good breast disappear, producing unpleasure, night is felt to be "bad." Night is also the time when the child is isolated from his parents, and they engage in mysterious frightening activity. This connection of darkness retains in the unconscious its association with incestuous wishes. This seems to be the prototype of "bad" in association with darkness and the connection with frustration, anxiety and hostility which result.

In the anal stage, toilet training is stressed and feces are objects of importance. The child is taught that feces are dirty and his original liking and pride for this body material turns to disgust. Because the fecal stick produces analerotic pleasure and because there is also gratification in giving or withholding this anal gift, some of the pleasure-feelings associated with feces are retained and the result is ambivalence over this "black" substance. Magical thinking predominates at this time and thoughts are equated with deeds. But sexual or hostile wishes are also felt to be dangerous and are considered thought-crimes which precipitate guilt feelings, anxiety and repression. All of these feelings are closely related on the basis of the cloaca theory. Since magical thinking is in close proximity to the "black" feces, omnipotence of thought can be experienced as a kind of sorcery or black magic.

During the phallic phase of development, the Oedipus Complex is in bloom. Incestuous impulses, homoerotic feelings and masturbation are felt to be dirty and menacing by the harsh superego. These forbidden impulses must be kept safely confined to the "black pit" of the unconscious. These conflicts are strongly repressed during the latency period but at puberty there is a revivification of psychic conflicts because of the maturation of the sex glands. The ego of the adolescent must now cope with the increased instinctual impulses.[8] These confined urges exert pressure and to relieve this turgidity, projection is commonly utilized. In individuals where ambivalence is especially marked, tension is eased, particularly from the hostile portion of the dammed-up impulses by detaching the affect from the self and applying it to others.[9]

Along with externalization of the taboo feelings is the need to bind the affect in a suitable object so that the object can then safely be treated with the hostility originally connected with the repressed impulses. It is at this time that the Negro is strongly cathected as the external symbol of the feared inner wishes.

Jones[10] has described in detail the process whereby a repressed sexual wish is replaced by fear and morbid anxiety. Three changes occur to the original wish: 1. love changes to sadism, 2. the event is feared rather than desired, and 3. the person to whom the wish relates is replaced by an unknown being. "The presence of the sadistic feature increases the difficulty of distinguishing the element of love and hate, of sexuality and hostility." Jones emphasized the oedipal nature of these wishes in producing the terrifying symbols in nightmares.

Negroes are suitable external symbols because of the association of sex and violence with black. The Negro is dark and mysterious, distant yet childlike and human. But the projected "dark" impulses are taboo and so colored people are also forbidden.[11]

It seems that homoerotic impulses are particularly difficult to accept in one's self, so they are deeply repressed. Reaction-formation occurs and the idea becomes, "I do not love him, I hate him." This is similar to what happens in relation to Negroes. The conflict is externalized and complementary projection is used. "The reason I hate him is that he hates me. He is after me." The next step in this involved mechanism is displacement and generalization. "It isn't only he that hates me and is against me, but it is the Negro (Jewish or Communistic) group that is after me." These can be seen as substitute sexual symbols or as handy, socially-sanctioned scapegoats who account for the feeling that someone is persecuting.[12]

After the establishment of a scapegoat for feelings and impulses experienced as dangerous, comes the further elaboration resulting from group psychology which leads to our present cultural situation. In order to lessen individual guilt feelings, people in a society take a scapegoat in common so that the guilt can be shared by the group. The group superego is less severe than is the individual one and there is also added strength in the forming of a group ego. Giving the formula for the libidinal constitution of groups, Freud[13] says, "A primary group of this kind is a number of individuals who have substituted one and the same object for their ego ideal and have consequently identified themselves with one another in their ego."

We now begin to see what has led to the present state of affairs. Negroes have become the external representatives of the individual's own taboo unconscious impulses. But behind the taboo is the desire. The strength of the fear is, then, a measure of the force of the hidden wish. The Negro can also represent symbolically specific repressed impulses generating conflict in the individual. The intensity of the specific representation is determined by the degree and level of fixation. Because the Negro represents externally the "black" contents of the feared unconscious, he is a convenient target for most of the punitive measures which the person would ordinarily impose on himself. The need for whites to maintain superiority over the Negro is analogous to the ego's need to remain in control of the id.

That the Negro represents unconscious conflicts has been amply demonstrated in the psychoanalysis of individuals as well as in the analysis of dreams. This "prejudice" seems to be fairly universal, varying, of course, with the intensity of individual intrapsychic conflict and the suitability of the Negro as a scapegoat. It includes Negroes themselves for the reasons already given and also because of the reinforcement from other racial groups, as well as the tendency to identify with the aggressor in dissociating from an onerous situation.

Because these highly emotional attitudes toward Negroes are unconsciously determined psychobiologically, it would seem to be an unrealistic aspiration to expect dramatic change, whether by revolution or by evolution. What might be hoped for is the gradual enlightenment of the individual through increased self-understanding so that the need for the current type of defensive measure diminishes. "The fateful question of the human species seems to me to be whether and to what extent the cultural process developed in it will succeed in mastering the derangements of communal life caused by the human instinct of aggression and self-destruction."[14]

REFERENCES

[1] FLUGEL, J. C. *The Psychoanalytic Study of the Family.* London: Hogarth Press, 1957, p. 114.

[2] DOLLARD, J. *Caste and Class in a Southern Town.* N.Y.: Doubleday, 1957, p. 170.

[3] KARDINER, A. and OVESEY, L. *The Mark of Oppression.* N.Y.: Norton, 1951.

[4] *Webster New International Dictionary* (Unabridged), 2nd Edition. Springfield, Mass.: Merriam Co., 1957.

[5] FERENCZI, S. On Obscene Words. *Selected Papers, Vol. I.* N.Y.: Basic Books, 1950.

[6] FRASER, J. G. *The Golden Bough.* N.Y.: Macmillan Co., 1958, p. 634.

[7] FREUD, S. The Uncanny. *Collected Papers, Vol. 4.* London: Hogarth Press, 1953, p. 394.

[8] REISER, M. A Note on the Analysis of the "Elvis Presley" Phenomenon. *The American Imago,* Vol. 15, No. 1, 1958, p. 97.

[9] REIK, T. *Ritual.* N.Y.: Farrar, Straus, 1946, p. 49.

[10] JONES, E. *On the Nightmare.* N.Y.: Liveright, 1951.

[11] ALLPORT, G. *The Nature of Prejudice.* N.Y.: Doubleday, 1958, p. 351.

[12] *Ibid.,* p. 395.

[13] FREUD, S. *Group Psychology and the Analysis of the Ego.* N.Y.: Liveright, 1949, p. 80.

[14] FREUD, S. *Civilization and Its Discontents.* London: Hogarth Press, 1955, p. 144.

*The inability to replace a neurotic behavior pattern with a
more flexible one may be an important source of anxiety.
Frieda Fromm-Reichmann summarizes several psychoanalytic
theories about anxiety and herself relates anxiety to a sense
of psychological death. Unable to grow emotionally, people
suffering from such anxiety often attempt to dispel their feeling of being dead by indulging in intense and frequently
violent emotional experiences, such as acts of delinquency and
the use of drugs or alcohol.*

FRIEDA FROMM-REICHMANN

Psychiatric Aspects of Anxiety

The most unpleasant and at the same time the most universal experience, except loneliness, is anxiety. We observe both healthy and mentally disturbed people doing everything possible to ward off anxiety or to
keep it from awareness.

Mentally disturbed people try to dispel anxiety by developing mental
symptoms. In fact as first stated by Freud, mental symptoms are at the
same time both the expression of unbearable anxiety and the means of
warding it off.[7] In other words mental symptoms and mental illness can
be understood simultaneously as the outcome of anxiety and as a defense against it. Mental illness can be understood as a person's response
to unbearable anxiety. Therefore, anxiety constitutes an essential problem in psychotherapy.

This holds true even though we consider anxiety to be an experience
by no means limited to the mentally disturbed. As initially stated, we
realize that anxiety in its milder forms is a universal human phenomenon. Philosophers and psychologists have known and advanced this
knowledge for a long time. In their eagerness to be great helpers and
healers, psychiatrists have been and are still partly inclined to overlook
the difference between what may be called the normal anxieties of the
emotionally healthy and the neurotic or psychotic excess anxiety which
should be subject to psychotherapy. For a long time, psychiatrists and
psychotherapists have also overlooked the fact that anxiety not only has
negative, disintegrative facets but also some positive, constructive ones.

985

As we set out to clarify the philosophy of psychotherapy regarding neurotic and psychotic anxieties, we must keep these two aspects of anxiety clearly in mind.

Anxiety, as we know, shows in a great variety of ways. Subjectively it may be experienced as a most unpleasant interference with thinking processes and concentration, as a diffuse, vague and frequently object-less feeling of apprehension or as a discomforting feeling of uncertainty and helplessness. As it arises in its milder forms, it may show objectively by a shift in tone of voice, and/or tempo of speech, by a change of posture, gesture and motion, also by the anxious person's intellectual or emotional preoccupation or blocking of communication. In people who are even more anxious, anxiety manifests itself psychologically in more or less marked degrees of paralysis of thought and action. The well-known physical manifestations that may be caused by anxiety are symptoms of a hyperactive sympathetic system such as change of turgor, perspiration, tremor, sensation of a lump in the throat, sinking abdominal sensations, diarrhea, vomiting, changes in pupilar reactions, in heart beat, pulse rate, and respiration. If anxiety-states become so severe that the anxiety-stricken person cannot handle them, mental symptoms and mental illness are the final outcome.

In the rare cases when anxiety is so severe that all these expressions of it and all defenses against it fail to bring relief, panic or terror may be the outcome. Panic, as defined by H. S. Sullivan, is an extreme concentration of attention and the direction of all available energy toward only one goal—escape, swift flight from internal dangers which are poorly envisaged, and in the case of failure to escape, by a temporary disintegration of personality with random destructive tendencies against oneself and others. Also according to Sullivan, terror is anxiety of a cosmic quality in the face of a primitively conceived threat of danger. The terror-stricken person feels himself to be alone among deadly menaces, more or less blindly fighting for his survival against dreadful odds.[21,22] Fortunately, terror and panic are short-lived. The organism produces quick defenses against the devastating influence which panic or terror of prolonged duration would exert. John Vassos' empathic pictorial work on Phobia (which, incidentally, is dedicated to H. S. Sullivan) should be mentioned here as an impressive contribution to the understanding of terror and panic.[26]

In contrast to these various forms of anxiety, fear is a useful, rational kind of fright elicited by realistic external dangers. To be described presently, and in contrast to fear, are the dangers from within, which elicit anxiety.

What is anxiety in terms of its conceptions in dynamic psychiatry? Freud says in "The Problems of Anxiety," that anxiety is felt by a person at the realization of formerly repressed inacceptable drives and wishes; his anxiety is with regard to loss of love and punishment, i.e., along the lines of Freud's libidinal concepts, castration-fear.[7]

We need not go into the discussion of Freud's older explanation of anxiety as the result of repressed sexual desires,[4] because he rejected it himself in "The Problems of Anxiety."

Sullivan shares with Freud the concept of the anxiety-arousing power of inacceptable thoughts, feelings, drives, wishes, and actions. But in the framework of his interpersonal conceptions he sees these forbidden inner experiences as interpersonal ones, not as instinctual drives per se; also the expected punishment is not seen as castration-fear. Rather, it is experienced by the anxious person as the anticipated disapproval, i.e., loss of love, from the significant people of his early life, from whom he has originally learned to discriminate between acceptable and inacceptable drives, attitudes, and actions. Later on this fear of disapproval may be transferred from the original significant people who trained and educated the anxious person to their emotional successors. Guilt feelings, separately described by other authors, are obviously inherent in Sullivan's conception of anxiety.[21,22,23,24]

This disapproval by the significant people of one's early life, to which both Freud and Sullivan refer, is vital enough to account for severe anxieties, because the infant and the young child are dependent upon the early important people for fulfillment of their basic needs. The infant's survival depends upon the loving care he is given by the mothering ones of his infancy.

Nearly all psychological concepts of anxiety have, in common with Freud and Sullivan, this one basic conception: that anxiety is tied up with the inner danger of inacceptable thoughts, feelings, wishes, or drives which elicit the expectation of loss of love and approval or of punishment. No matter how much these conceptions may differ in their explanatory details and regardless of whether or not this aspect of anxiety is explicitly mentioned in these conceptions, it is a viewpoint now commonly shared.

Let me quote a few outstanding representatives of various psychiatric schools of thinking. Rank speaks of separation anxiety which people first experience at birth and subsequently throughout their lives, present at all phases of personality-development and individuation, from weaning, i.e., separation from mother's breast, to separation from one's fellow men, by death.[18]

Adler uses his concept of inferiority feelings where other authors speak of anxiety. He asserts that these inferiority feelings can be overcome by people only in affirmation and strengthening of their social bonds with society, by enforcing the sense of belonging to a social group.[1]

Horney emphasizes the central significance of the interrelatedness between anxiety and hostility—anticipated in others and sensed in the anxious person himself; here again anxiety is seen as being tied up with the fear of disruption of one's interpersonal relationships.[15]

Poulson, Berdyaev, Halmos, Kardiner, Riesman and other social psychologists find the source of man's anxiety in his psychological isolation, his alienation from his own self and from his fellow men. They consider this the common fate of man in modern society, irrespective of his state of emotional health.[3,8,14,16,19] A poetic version of this viewpoint may be found in Auden's "Age of Anxiety."[2]

Goldstein's conception of anxiety as being the subjective experience of a danger to existence in the face of failure may also imply anxiety regarding loss of love and recognition by those who recognize the anxious person's failure.[11,12]

The same holds true for Rollo May's definition of anxiety as "the apprehension set off by a threat to some value which the individual holds essential to his existence as a personality."[17] Again this concept implies the fear of losing interpersonal recognition or acceptance since this could be tied up with the loss of essential values in the life of the individual. I will return later to the discussion of some other aspects of the conceptions of these authors. At this point I am primarily interested in demonstrating the ubiquitously implied acceptance of the concept that anxiety is connected with anticipated fear of punishment and disapproval, withdrawal of love, disruption of interpersonal relationships, isolation, or separation.

This conception of anxiety as the expression of the anticipated loss of love and approval, or separation, social isolation, or disruption of one's interpersonal relationships implies its close psychological affinity to loneliness. In fact, I believe that many of the emotional states to which psychiatrists refer as anxiety actually are states of loneliness or fear of loneliness.

Now I wish to return to the discussion of the psychodynamics of anxiety. According to Sullivan, the infant and child's need for love and approval and the anxiety connected with rejection and disapproval are utilized by the significant adults in handling the necessary early processes which are designed to train the infant and child for his interpersonal adjustment, his socialization and acculturalization. Out of this educative process evolves the part of human personality which Sullivan has called "self-system." This self-system operates in the service of people to obtain satisfacton without incurring too much anxiety. In the process of establishing the self-system certain infantile trends must be barred from awareness, dissociated. If they break into awareness, anxiety will reappear because the structure of the self-system, the nature of which tends toward rigid maintenance of its protective status quo, is threatened with change. The defensiveness against change makes for the danger of personal rigidity, which in turn increases the potentialities for further anxiety.[21,22] This anxiety connected with change is eternally in conflict with man's general innate tendencies toward growth, toward the change which is implied and particularly with the innate motivation of mental patients toward health. One of the great responsibilities of the psychotherapist is to help patients face and overcome this conflict constructively.[9]

I would like to offer an additional explanatory concept about the factors which make people expect punishment, disapproval and loss of love and which has helped me to understand better than I did previously the psychological significance of the anxieties of people in general and of mental patients in particular. Let us ask again: what do people disapprove of most gravely in themselves, i.e., which trends in themselves do they expect will bring the most severe disapproval on the part of the significant people in their lives? Are there other significant causes for the anxiety-arousing anticipation of disapproval and isolation in addition to those we have quoted? Let me offer the following hypothetical answer.

It is a well-known psychological fact that a person will misvalue the significant people of his childhood to the extent to which his early interpersonal tie-ups remain unresolved. If these early interpersonal patterns stand uncorrected, people will distort the image of various people whom they meet in the course of their lives. They may or may not dimly sense that they do so, but they will not recognize the interpersonal misconceptions of their early childhood as the root of the distortions of their interpersonal relationships.

An adult person who finds himself compulsively appraising other people inadequately, incorrectly evaluating their reactions, acting upon and responding to them in line with these misconceptions in terms of early patterns of living, may many times become semi-aware of his erroneous judgment and behavior. However, he may feel inadequate and helpless in his dim wish or attempt to change and correct his judgment and his emotional reactions because he is unaware of their unconscious roots, the unmodified fixations to the patterns of interpersonal relationships which he acquired in his early years. This helplessness in the face of the need to change anachronistic, distorted patterns of interpersonal relationships meets with self-disapproval and discontent; it interferes with the innate tendency to self-realization; it produces deep insecurity in people and meets with the anticipated disapproval of others; thus, it is the expression of anxiety and it produces further anxiety. Goldstein could demonstrate this type of anxiety in his brain-injured patients. When they were faced with a simple task which they could not accomplish for reasons unknown to them, stemming from their neurological brain injury, they became the prey of an abject feeling of helplessness, of nothingness, or a "catastrophic reaction," as Goldstein has called it.[11,12]

The hypothesis is offered that mentally disturbed people frequently develop a "catastrophic reaction," anxiety, in response to their compulsively determined inability to change their distorted, immature patterns of interpersonal relationships. This task may be set by the demands of their own conscience or by the actual or assumed demands of their elders or friends. This helplessness in the presence of the need to envision and to relate oneself adequately to other people, i.e., in accordance with one's chronological age and with one's psychological reality without full awareness of its causes, is most frightening, for more than one reason. It elicits a general feeling of helplessness and paralysis. It means that the person concerned is living in an unreal psychological world and that he feels he is in danger of pulling the people of his environment actually or in fantasy into the same threatening abyss of unreality. Being unable to successfully avail himself of the possibility of using new means of evaluating people and of relating himself meaningfully to them amounts to being blocked in the utilization of learning processes which serve growth and change. This absence of growth and change is tantamount to psychological stagnation and emotional sterility, i.e., psychological death.[10] In other words, the repetition-compulsion to follow early patterns of interpersonal evaluation and relatedness and the inability to learn to replace them by new patterns, deprives a person of the freedom to live and move about in the world of psychological reality which should be his, deprives him of the freedom for self-realization and conveys feelings of stagnation and sterility, hence the fear of psychological death, of Tillich's "not being," or Goldstein's "nothingness."[11,12,25]

By "self-realization" I mean (to repeat a definition I have previously given[9] a person's use of his talents, skills and powers to his satisfaction within the realm of his own freely established realistic set of values. Furthermore, I mean the uninhibited ability of patients to reach out for and to find fulfillment of their needs for satisfaction and security, as far as it can be obtained, without interfering with the laws and customs which protect the needs of their fellow-men. Goldstein's "self-actualization," Fromm's "productive character," Whitehorn's "mature personality" and the "self-affirmation" of the existentialists are formulations of the same concept.[8,11,27] In the classical psychoanalytic literature insufficient attention has been given so far to the concept of self-realization as a great source, if not the greatest source, of human fulfillment. Freud has referred to it in his teachings on secondary narcissism and ego-ideal formation, but he has dealt more with the investigation of the origin of the phenomenon than with the elaboration on the psychological significance of the end-product, mature self-realization.[5,6]

The lack of freedom for self-realization and the feeling of stagnation and "nothingness" that goes with it, this sense of psychological death, seems to me to be at the root of many people's anxiety. To repeat, they cling to infantile interpersonal patterns, and as a result feel helpless without really knowing why. They are unable to grow emotionally, to develop or change. They are not able to think, feel, and act according to their chronological age. They live anachronously in a deadening emotional rut where they compulsively continue to distort their interpersonal images of new people whom they meet, and to misvalue the interpersonal reactions and behavior of these people along the line of the conceptions gained in their unresolved interpersonal childhood contacts.

Example: A young woman, Anna, went to see her older friend and confidant, Mr. N., whom she trusted unequivocally. Anna asked him to contact certain significant people in her family and explain to them some facts about her life which she felt would be of immeasurable value for them and for her in the general family picture. Mr. N. assured Anna of his complete willingness to do this and when Anna left him she was confident that Mr. N. would take care of the situation with understanding and skill. For valid rational reasons, which are beside the point of our discussion, Mr. N. decided later not to meet the members of the family and have a talk with them along the lines suggested by Anna. He did not have an opportunity to discuss this with her. When Anna found out about it a few days later, she felt deep resentment against Mr. N. and developed a spell of severe anxiety. Why? She felt that her friend had not accepted her appraisal of the total situation nor given it serious consideration. She also felt he had treated her the same way her parents had always done; to judge everything the little girl suggested or offered for consideration as not being worthy of serious thought on their part, "little girls are too emotional." Anna realized though, that her resentment against Mr. N., whom she felt had betrayed her and had not taken her suggestion seriously was, somehow, unfounded and sensed dimly that he might well have fallen down on their agreement for valid, rational reasons. However, she felt completely incapable of overcoming her resentment and her severe spell of anxiety lasted for hours. The semi-awareness she had about the irrationality of her anxiety and resentment did not help any until, by psychoanalytic investigation, she finally discovered the reasons, of which she had been unaware. Then she recognized that her resentment was due to a distortion of the present situation between her and Mr. N., in the light of the unresolved interpersonal pattern of living with the parents of her childhood ("little girl"—"too emotional"—judgment and suggestions deserve no consideration).

Jurgen Ruesch's interesting new concept of anxiety which he gained from observation and investigation of people under stress, fits into this context. He says that anxiety arises as a result of overstimulation which cannot be discharged by action.[20] The anxious people who have been described are barred from discharging tension by action, from converting anxiety into euphoria because they live in a state of "not-being," or "nothingness."

The anxiety-producing aspects of people's unresolved early tie-ups and involvements, of which they are only partially aware, receive additional reinforcement because so many of these anxiety-producing aspects are experienced as forbidden and elicit anxiety connected guilt feelings. Love for the parent of the opposite sex and competitive hatred of the parent of the same sex should be mentioned here as the most outstanding example of such anxiety and guilt-evoking psychological constellations.

The resolution of such early tie-ups with the parents of one's childhood, which I have implicitly recommended as a preventive against anxiety, should not be confused with manifestations of a child's outwardly breaking away from his parents. Children who succeed in breaking away from their parents early may experience increased anxiety, since this emerging independence of a child meets with a sense of loss on the part of the parents, hence frequently with their disapproval of the child.

The psychology of masturbation is illustrative of our last statement. There has been much discussion about the following question: Why are there so many children who never have been exposed to any warning against masturbation and many adults who intellectually do not consider masturbation forbidden or dangerous and yet there are practically no people who masturbate without feeling guilty and anxious about it? How can we explain this fact? I believe that guilt eliciting masturbatory fantasies are only partly, if at all, responsible. Many cases of masturbatory feelings of guilt and anxiety seem to be connected with the fact that masturbation represents a child's first act of independence from his parents or others who have raised and mothered him. He needs his elders for the fulfillment of all his basic needs; getting food and fresh air and for being kept clean and getting fresh clothes and bedding. Masturbation is the only pleasure he can obtain without their help. As such, it constitutes an act of breaking away from one's parents, for which the child feels guilty and anxious regardless of the permissive or non-permissive attitude of the elders towards the act of masturbation per se.

It has been stated that practically no one in this culture gets ideally rid of his early interpersonal tie-ups and the resulting interpersonal problems. In other words, almost no one is entirely prepared to face the anxiety-provoking dangers of his present life, fully undistorted by interpersonal entanglements with the "ghosts of his past" and with full command of his adult emotional equipment. As Grinker puts it, in his research on "Anxiety and Psychosomatic Transactions": "The stimulus" (which arouses anxiety) "must be perceived in the light of inner expectation originating at an early and particularly helpless time in the organism's history, to be dangerous to its protective attachments and hence to his existence," i.e., to have the power to produce anxiety.[13]

REFERENCES

[1] ADLER, ALFRED. *The Neurotic Constitution.* Translated by Bernard Glueck. New York: Moffat, Yard & Co., 1917.

[2] AUDEN, W. H. *The Age of Anxiety.* New York: Random House, 1946.

[3] BERDYAEV, NICHOLAS. *Solitude and Society.* London: 1938.

[4] FREUD, SIGMUND. *A General Introduction to Psychoanalysis.* New York: Liveright, 1935; Garden City Publ. Co., 1943. (Chapter on Anxiety)

[5] FREUD, SIGMUND. "On Narcissism: An Introduction," in *Collected Papers,* IV. London: Hogarth Press, 1946. Pp. 30–59.

[6] FREUD, SIGMUND. *The Ego and the Id.* London: Hogarth Press, 1935.

[7] FREUD, SIGMUND. *Problems of Anxiety.* New York: Norton, 1936.

[8] FROMM, ERICH. *Man for Himself.* New York: Rinehart, 1947.

[9] FROMM-REICHMANN, FRIEDA. *Principles of Intensive Psychotherapy.* Chicago: University of Chicago Press, 1950.

[10] FROMM-REICHMANN, FRIEDA. "Psychoanalysis and Dynamic Psychotherapy. Similarities and Differences," *Journal of the American Psychoanalytic Association,* II (1954), 711–21.

[11] GOLDSTEIN, KURT. *Human Nature in the Light of Psychopathology.* Cambridge: Harvard University Press, 1940.

[12] GOLDSTEIN, KURT. *The Organism.* New York: American Book Co., 1939.

[13] GRINKER, ROY R. *Psychosomatic Research.* New York: Norton, 1953.

[14] HALMOS, PAUL. *Solitude and Privacy.* New York: Philosophical Library, 1953.

[15] HORNEY, KAREN. *New Ways in Psychoanalysis.* New York: Norton, 1939.

[16] KARDINER, ABRAM. *The Psychological Frontiers of Society.* New York: Columbia University Press, 1945.

[17] MAY, ROLLO. *The Meaning of Anxiety.* New York: Ronald Press, 1951.

[18] RANK, OTTO. *Will Therapy and Truth and Reality.* New York: Knopf, 1945.

[19] RIESMAN, DAVID. *The Lonely Crowd.* New Haven, Yale University Press, 1950.

[20] RUESCH, JURGEN. "The Interpersonal Communication of Anxiety," *Symposium of Stress* (Wash., D.C.: Walter Reed Army Medical Center, 1953), 154–64.

[21] SULLIVAN, H. S. *Conceptions of Modern Psychiatry.* Wash., D.C.: The Wm. Alanson White Found., 1947. New Edition, New York: Norton, 1953.

[22] SULLIVAN, H. S. *The Interpersonal Theory of Psychiatry.* New York: Norton, 1953.

[23] SULLIVAN, H. S. "The Meaning of Anxiety in Psychiatry and in Life," *Psychiatry,* XI (1948), 1–13.

[24] SULLIVAN, H. S. "The Theory of Anxiety and the Nature of Psychotherapy," *Psychiatry,* XII (1949), 3–12.

[25] TILLICH, PAUL. *The Courage To Be.* New Haven: Yale University Press, 1952.

[26] VASSOS, JOHN. *Phobia.* New York: Covici-Friede, 1931.

[27] WEIGERT, EDITH. "Existentialism and Its Relation to Psychotherapy," *Psychiatry,* XII (1949), 399–412.

Bruno Bettelheim's ability to guide people through the complexities of psychoanalytic theory and make them see for themselves is truly remarkable. In "I'm Somebody Else," a worried mother learns how confusion in a child's identity may result from a parent's unconscious conflict and the consequent inability to offer reassurance and support for the child's ego development.

This particular kind of confusion seems oddly American, a reflection of the fluid nature of a society that provides us with few traditional guidelines into which we might channel feelings of guilt, fear and inadequacy. The fluidity once reflected largely in the rapidly and continually changing landscape of America may be mirrored today in the prevalence of ego failure in children.

BRUNO BETTELHEIM

I'm Somebody Else

FROM *Dialogues With Mothers*

DR. B.: Well, Christmas is over. It's a big time in your child's life and in yours too, but not always an easy one. I trust you've all weathered it successfully. Yes? [*Nodding to a mother*] Go ahead.

MOTHER: I have a question, Dr. Bettelheim. My little girl is two and a half and I have another girl three months old. During the summer my older girl began to pretend she was different animals. One day she would be a mouse and would go around squeaking all day. Then after the baby came she wasn't anything for a while. But about six weeks ago she took on the identity of the little girl next door. It started out that she was Kathy—that's the little girl's name. I was Kathy's mother, and our baby was supposed to be Brian—that's the name of the little girl's baby brother. And she insists very firmly that we have to call her Kathy, and our baby has to be referred to as a boy, and be called Brian. Now all this time I've just been playing along with her and calling her by those names. But I'm just wondering how long it's going to go on.

DR. B.: For as long as you go along with it. And if it were just a question of humoring her, there wouldn't be anything wrong with it. But while many children, when they're a little past two, say they don't like their names, if she can play for a whole day at being an animal, she's intelligent enough and can express herself well enough to be able to tell you why she wants to be called by a different name. Have you asked her that?

MOTHER: No, I haven't. I don't know if she understands, or how much of it, when you ask, "Why?" She herself has just started asking about "Why."

DR. B.: Now look. To convey to you that she wants to be called Kathy and that she wants her baby sister to be called by a certain name calls for quite a vocabulary. This vocabulary she couldn't have acquired and used intelligently without understanding the "Why" of it.

MOTHER: No. What I mean is, sometimes I've asked her "Why" about other things, and she doesn't seem to understand.[1]

DR. B.: That's strange . . .

MOTHER: Well . . . but I was just wondering about her insisting on the baby being a boy.

DR. B.: Okay, let's look for a moment at what we can do if we don't understand what a child is up to. This is of general interest. If a child does something that doesn't make sense, or that we don't understand, but that we want to understand, what's always a good way of finding out? One possibility is to play along with the notion of the child and see where it leads us. That's what this mother is doing, but it's gotten her nowhere. What else can we do?

SECOND MOTHER: Well, she started out by wanting to be called by the name of a friend of hers.

DR. B.: That's going over the facts we already know; that's not finding out the cause.

SECOND MOTHER: Well, she could talk to her.

DR. B.: Sure, but the mother's already done that. What else can you do if you don't understand strange behavior in your child?

THIRD MOTHER: Go and ask somebody. That's why we come to you!

DR. B.: Yes, but I'm not always so conveniently around.

FOURTH MOTHER: I'd ask myself, when would I act this way.

DR. B.: Exactly! But why do you say it so hesitantly? So often when you give the wrong answer you're very forceful, but with the right answer you're hesitant. We just don't trust ourselves enough to believe we have the answers right in us, if we just dared to look into ourselves. But that's where we have to look for all the difficult answers. All right, so the first thing I ask myself when there's strange behavior I don't understand is: "When would I do this; and if I do so, why would I do it?"

MOTHER: Well, my first thought was that she didn't want to be herself any more.

DR. B.: Exactly! So what *did* you do? What did you show her through your behavior?

MOTHER: Well, I asked somebody else.

DR. B.: That's a possibility. Let's have an experiment and ask someone else right now. We have many good-looking men and women here tonight. What if I wanted to be as good-looking as they are? What would I do? Would I change my name to one of theirs?

FOURTH MOTHER: No, you should be encouraged to be yourself.

DR. B.: Exactly! It's not a question of who I want to be, or what you'd like to be. There's no way out, my girl . . . there's no way out; we just have got to be what we are!

MOTHER: You mean, I should just let her suffer it out?

DR. B.: That's right! She's stuck with herself, with her own name, with the baby sister! And so are you. Well, let's not call it "stuck," though she may feel it that way. We can give it a much pleasanter name. What I'm driving at is that you're the mother and should know better. Yet by entering this play, you not only enforce her idea that she can be somebody else, that she can change the sex of her brothers or sisters, that she can pretend she has different parents, but that you agree that all this would be nice. Do you think that's right?

MOTHER: Well, this is what I did. You know her real name is Pat, and the baby is Karen. So when I'd talk to her I would talk to her as Pat and the baby as Karen, and she'd keep correcting me—that she was Kathy and the baby was Brian, and she would get real mad about it.

DR. B.: Of course! Who wouldn't like to change at will? If I thought I could change at will and somebody interfered with me, I'd get mad, too!

MOTHER: Yes, but the other thing I thought about was—at this two-and-a-half-year-old stage, when they're so domineering, I thought they should be humored as much as they can. So I was torn between the two things!

DR. B.: The two-and-a-half-year-old is supposed to be humored?

MOTHER: Well . . . that's what I read.

DR. B.: And you don't want to be humored?

MOTHER: Sure, everybody wants to be humored!

DR. B.: All right! Then why talk about the two-and-a-half-year-old as somebody who wants to be humored?

MOTHER: Oh, I don't mean it particularly, but I thought that was an age . . .

DR. B.: But it's true for all ages . . . that we want to be humored. The question is: how do we want to be humored? And does it do us any good to be humored in this particular way? Do you really think—if you dreamed of being the most beautiful woman in the world—do you really think it would be of service to you if everybody humored you in that idea?

MOTHER: No, of course not.

DR. B.: Then why should it be any different for your two-and-a-half-year-old? So the real problem is: when should you humor her and when not. And how can you humor her? How do we all want to be humored? But let's drop these generalities and get back to your little girl. Why do you think she started the game?

MOTHER: Because she wanted attention.

DR. B.: So do we all. But you and I still wouldn't know what she wanted. Let's not go through that again. It's a fascinating topic, but . . .

SECOND MOTHER: Because of the new baby, I think.

DR. B.: Maybe, but we shouldn't shove everything off on the new baby. It's a first guess, and a very reasonable one, but I've seen it misfire. Mommy's suddenly interested in something else. It needn't be the new baby, but the new baby is a wonderful excuse.

MOTHER: You mean it could have been something else? But it happened at about the time the baby was six weeks old.

DR. B.: But she started with the animals before that.

MOTHER: Oh . . . yes. The animals were before the baby came.

DR. B.: Yes. So why should we assume it was the baby? It started when you were pregnant, and maybe there was less time to play with her. In any case, we've made progress. We no longer say that the child just wants to be humored, which would be pushing it all on the poor child. Let's say instead that something is suddenly missing in life, and that the child, in her own childish way, is trying to make up for the deficiency. You see, I'm not worried about your child. What she did was quite reasonable in terms of the means a two-and-a-half-year-old can muster for coping with a difficult situation. What worries me is that you fell for it instead of presenting her with a reasonable way out. You could have told her, "You can pretend to be a mouse if you like, or a lion, or to be Kathy for a little while. But it's a pretend game, because you can't be Kathy, and particularly, you cannot change the sex of the baby." Because that's one of the greatest fears of young children anyway—that sex can be changed at will. So by humoring her, by joining her so seriously, you may have increased her anxiety instead of concentrating on making it less desirable for her to be Kathy.

Now, how you do that is another story. That we have to investigate in terms of what you can do for your child at the moment, and that may be harder. But at the least you have to insist on your and her and the baby's true name and sex, on who her real parents are, and so forth.

MOTHER: She's even insisted I was Kathy's mommy.

DR. B.: Sure. Because if you're Kathy's mommy, pretty soon she's Kathy herself. Do you feel that this answers your question?

MOTHER: Well, I'm wondering. Do you think I should just do it real suddenly? Tomorrow, when she starts to pretend again . . .

DR. B.: Yes, I think you should stop right away. That doesn't mean you should forcefully forbid her her fantasies. But you can quietly tell her who you are and who she is. On the other hand, you have no right to stop her game unless you have some plan about how you're going to close the gap she was trying to fill by this living in a make-believe world. To take away the game without filling the need for it is just no good. It'll only force her to invent something different and maybe more devious.

MOTHER: What do you mean? Showing her why she did it?

DR. B.: No, that you cannot do. All you can do is to continue your explanation till she gets her fill of it, but without getting angry or upset. Say that she is she, you are you, and the baby is Karen. She'll get so bored by it she'll invent another game, but a more realistic one. On the other hand, I think you should play with her a good deal, spend a lot of time with her, and maybe your husband could help—so that the wish to be somebody else will subside because she'll enjoy being herself so much more.

MOTHER: Well, we do try. We spend lots of time with her . . .

DR. B.: That's fine. You do that, and let's see what happens.

[*One month later*]

MOTHER: I want to tell you about the results of some suggestions you offered. Remember when I told you about my little girl who adopted another name, and one for the baby too?

DR. B.: Oh, yes. I wanted to hear about what happened.

MOTHER: Well, the next morning we started out by calling her Pat, and she said "No," she was Kathy. So we told her, "No," she was Pat. This happened several times, and then it was dropped. We just continued to call her Pat and she didn't say anything. Then a little later in the morning I said something about Karen, the baby, and she said, "No, the baby is Brian." So I said, "No, she's Karen."

DR. B.: Good for you!

MOTHER: Well, and you also said I should ask her "Why," and at the time I didn't think she would understand and she didn't. I said, "Why do you think Karen is Brian?" and she said, "Because he's a boy!" and I said, "Well, why do you think she's a boy?" and she said, "Because he's a boy," and that was her only answer.[2] So I said, "Well, no, honey, you know she's a girl, and her name is Karen," and we went over that several times and then she dropped it and everything was fine after that. I also announced to my husband when I came home that there wasn't going to be any more cooking or baking or cleaning; that I was just going to spend my days with the children for a while. Well, I didn't go so far as to have sandwiches at every meal, but as far as dinner went, we just had what was very simple and I would just wait till he got home to fix it.

DR. B.: And he hasn't lost any appreciable weight?

MOTHER: Oh, no! And after that, everything was fine as far as the names were concerned. Yesterday, at two different times when she was unhappy about something, and I called her Pat, she tried to tell me she was Kathy. So I just told her again she was Pat.

DR. B.: So you see now that it was all a reaction to being unhappy.

MOTHER: Very definitely! And anyhow, since then her behavior's improved very much. She's much happier, and she hasn't at all gone back to the other names. In fact, it got to the point where I couldn't even call her my little pumpkin because she'd say, "No, I'm Pat!"

DR. B.: That'll teach you!

MOTHER: Anyhow, it's been working out very well!

DR. B.: Well, that's very gratifying. But don't fool yourself; if you hadn't spent more time with your child, just insisting on the names wouldn't have done it. The one without the other wouldn't have worked.

MOTHER: Oh, yes, I know it. But I'd fallen into this pattern of not spending much time with her, and I hadn't realized it until you spoke about it. Then I could see very clearly what I'd been doing. Oh, yes . . .

and the other thing she's started, since all this happened, is that she's suddenly started going to the toilet having her B.M.'s in the toilet.

DR. B.: Well, since we've achieved such a miracle cure . . .

MOTHER: No, really. It's not a miracle. It's just what should be.

DR. B.: Well, believe me, to do what we should do in bringing children up in this world of ours sometimes seems little short of a miracle!

NOTES

[1] A frequent and understandable error of parents. They ask their young child to explain things he does without plan or inner motive. The young child does not know what is meant, or how *he* can explain what to him is self-evident or in no need of thought or explanation. But the same child, when beset by deep needs to which he has found a solution (in this case, by changing identity), can well explain the situation because here he is deeply involved. Just because a young child cannot explain to us, or even understand our question, when *we* are curious and involved but he is not, we must not therefore assume that he cannot do so when he *is* deeply curious and involved.

[2] In view of my comment in note 1, I might add here that this is exactly the type of explanation one might hope for in such a young child. She tells us that she wanted the names changed because she did not want a baby sister, but would have liked having a baby brother. He, being of the other sex, would have threatened her identity less, including her identity as a girl, or so it may have seemed to her. Thus unbeknownst to the mother, her answer, "Because he's a boy," irrational as it sounds on an intellectual level, is a correct answer in terms of her emotional needs.

The connection between asthma and a child's fear of being absorbed by his mother is made beautifully clear in this short excerpt. It explains as well the intensity of Marcel Proust's relationship with his mother; Proust, too, was an asthmatic.

DOROTHY W. BARUCH

FROM *One Little Boy*

In his last session Kenneth had declared anger but he had not brought much of it out. He had wheezed on and off since and was wheezing when he came in the next time. He announced, however, that he had discovered that his grasshopper could hop. Could it burrow, too? Into the ground? "Do grasshoppers have holes there that belong to them for burrowing purposes?"

He had been at a miniature golf course in his neighborhood the day before. "We had fun! There was me and Brad and Gene. He's a boy in the neighborhood."

Ken broke off and drew his eyebrows together. "Brad got two holes in one. He's good! I hope he doesn't improve any more!"

Then Ken went back to thinking about holes. During the golf game he'd wondered what went on down in those holes. And in holes like Hamburger dug into in the ground or like Hamburger's nose went into inside a person's ear. What's inside? "What do you see if you go exploring?"

"It sounds as if you'd like to explore?"

He smiled secretively.

"How about an exploring game?" I suggested.

"Or an exploring picture."

"O.K."

He put the finger paint on thickly, a pinkish red-earth color. "Here I go!"

His index finger slithered up through the thick paint.

I made no comment but I noted that he was exploring up a hole and not down into one.

"This hole first. A smelly hole, this one. Like when your finger goes into the ear . . ."

"Or?"

"Or into the big job hole."

He wiggled his finger back and forth through the thickish paint in a small zig-zag path. "Up. Up. Up. Finger, finger, finger, finger.

"And now," he announced, "he goes into the other hole with his head." His own head made a butting kind of motion. "It's bigger and it's dark. But he crawls in." His whole hand and wrist and arm slid through the paint, making a pathway upward.

"Can he see anything?" I asked.

"Yes. *I* see all kinds of things. I go up a little way and I see a couple of balls. Bigger than anything. They start rolling at me. They want to push me out.

"And then I go a little farther and I see something that looks like a fish. A great big one. And it wants me out.

"And I go a little farther and I meet a monkey. It wants to push me out, too. But *it* doesn't matter. It's a silly thing that makes a lot of chatter and doesn't really count.

"And I go a little farther and I come to the baby." His smile was of quiet depths. He did not move; just sat with his hand curved and relaxed on the center of the warm earth-pink.

But presently, as though opening his eyes from sleep into waking, he moved his hands in circular motion. "The baby starts moving and rolling around and wraps all around me and we roll around together like wrestling. You can hardly tell which is which."

"You and the baby seem to be one?"

"Uhuh, we are."

So, he was that baby. This much was clear, as was also the monkey. He had used practically the same words about his brother the session before. The fish was strangely reminiscent of father's great fish of which he had spoken from time to time. And the balls a bit further down than father's fish? One might hazard a guess.

His hand commenced rotating more quickly in an orgiastic gathering of speed. Faster and faster. He was breathing freely but hard as if in travail. And presently, "It's time now, baby, for you to get out."

His hand turned and shoved downward, inching its way.

"Unghh. Unghh. It's hard work," he groaned. "They push and pull me. Everybody's trying to get me out."

He came near the edge of the paper and there his hand began scrabbling back and forth, back and forth, scraping and pushing, until finally with clawing fingers spread wide, he shoved with a gigantic heave out over the edge, ripping the paper with his nails.

"I tore her to pieces, I did it so hard."

And with a great sigh of exhaustion, "There now! I'm out."

He sat back, still breathing freely but hard, gradually quieting. Tired and pensive he sat there until presently he murmured to himself, wonderingly, "About ten years ago I was in there . . ."

More quietness. And finally, wistful and uncertain, as if he were decrying hesitance on entering untrod country, "I'm not in there; I'm glad I'm out. I'm never going back in . . ." He left the finished sentence in mid-air as if it were unfinished and turned his eyes to meet mine.

To me he had shown the terrible struggle he'd had in the tortuous effort of birth. To me he was now showing the small, whispered protest against the more than half-wish to not-be, to repose, to return.

He needed to rest for a moment. But not for too long. Not for long enough to sink into regret and yearning for what was forever past. Not long enough to forget the small sparkle of forward wishing with which he'd commenced.

Could I help him hold to the glimpse he had had that the smaller wish was truly the bigger?

"Yes," I said, hoping he could sense that I knew with him, in the heritage of being human, the pull of giving up to that other wish that had been wrapping him in its promise of peace. "You're all through being in there with the whole of you. That's over, Ken. But you were just beginning with the wish to have a part of you do the exploring."

He stared at me, very sober. For a moment. Then he smiled and a chuckle escaped him. He nodded eagerly and confided, "A part of me, yes. And it won't be my hand."

The notion that mental disturbances may evoke physical symptoms is not a new one. Yet despite the pioneering work done in the fields of psychosomatic medicine, the tendency to regard body and mind as separate entities still exist. The following article attempts to analyze some of the emotional characteristics of the ulcer patient. Its bearing on the Huysmans story is obvious.

FLANDERS DUNBAR

FROM *Mind and Body*

There is more to the ulcer personality than his conflict over dependence. Once the digestive tract has started to acquire a sore spot, other emotions can contribute to the progress of the disease. Anger, fear, hostility and resentment are the most common, but any serious emotional shock stimulates the ulcer-forming or ulcer-irritating process.

Popular speech has linked these emotions to the stomach in dozens of picturesque phrases. We say we hate so-and-so's guts, or we admire the guts displayed in an act of bravery, or we go to the guts of a question. We can't stomach injustice or hypocrisy or somebody's manners. We refuse to swallow an insult. Our style is cramped. We propose to digest a problem. We abase ourselves when in the wrong with an expression of our willingness to eat crow or humble pie. We choke on all sorts of feelings, and it is a fact that a good many of them can give us the sensation of having a lump in the throat, just as more intense emotions can cause a more severe physical upset of the stomach.

Every ulcer patient illustrates the truth of some of these sayings. Walter S—— proved the aptness of most of them. As the oldest of three children he had always, he said, regarded himself as sort of responsible for his younger brother and sister. They were not very practical people, he explained, and were likely to get into all sorts of trouble if left to themselves. Their parents? Well, of course the father had always provided well enough, but both mother and father were impractical, too. They needed guidance.

At first, Walter gave the impression of being the sole prop of the whole family. Actually he had never contributed to the support of any of its members because they did not need it. He was always seeking to "make things easier" for his parents by urging them to tell him what they needed, but they seemed quite content to live modestly on Mr. S—'s little retirement income. Walter had not so much as seen his sister for years, but he knew she had four children and a husband who did not make much money, so he thought he ought to do something for them. The only trouble was that they wouldn't take anything. His brother was in even easier circumstances than Walter himself.

The family had been a close-knit one, as Walter described it. But he felt a little apart from it. His mother had a great many interests outside the home—clubs, the suffrage movement, study courses—and he was sure she liked his younger brother better anyway. Walter thought that was fitting; the youngest as the most helpless should be the favorite. His father naturally, he said, preferred the daughter. The boy had been competently cared for as far as his physical needs went, but he had had little further attention in the home. He remembered being told that he had colic all the time. One of his earliest recollections was of crawling up on a sofa to put his arms around his mother affectionately, only to be brushed aside without anger because she was reading. The indifference, he said, made more impression on him than a blow would have done.

There was no ulcer history that he knew of in the family, but his mother had complained frequently of minor digestive disorders. His father and his sister had suffered from asthma and hay fever, and at seventy his father was told that he had a mild heart condition and ought to take it easy. Walter could not remember that his mother, now sixty-five, had ever been seriously ill except for a vague and protracted siege some years before which he assumed had been related to her menopause. He himself, in addition to the usual childhood diseases, had been through an appendectomy and a long bout of pneumonia during successive summers in his teens. He remembered them vividly, he said, because they had spoiled his holidays.

Walter had left college in the last half of his senior year in order to get married. A friend of the family had offered him a place in a small but thriving business, and it seemed a wonderful opportunity to become independent of his parents. The job paid enough to support a wife if they were careful, and the girl was willing. Walter was just twenty-one, and plunged into the work of being head of a household with a great deal of energy. Within a few years he had been made a partner in the business, had two children and was quite generally regarded as a highly successful young fellow.

By the time he was thirty, he began to have mild stomach trouble. At first he thought he got it from eating irregularly in the course of business trips, but when he stayed home for months at a time and stuck to rather simple food, the attacks grew even more frequent. They were not, however, unbearable, and so he did not bother to consult medical advice. He saved that for a few years later, and then he went to see a doctor because he had had a series of bad colds and sore throats. He did not mention his stomach upsets, considering them unworthy of serious attention. He was advised to have his tonsils removed and did so. Thereafter he was free of what he considered major troubles for several years.

Finally, however, the pains in his stomach grew too much for him. He went back to the physician, and ulcer was readily diagnosed. Diet and avoidance of worry were prescribed. The first was easy—Walter confined his meals to milk and eggs and mush—but the second was beyond his powers. He really had nothing much to worry about superficially, and often his personal life was so uneventful that he was reduced to worrying about the iniquities of the government, the decay of politics in our time and the state of the world in general. His ulcer gave him a good deal of pain, but there were intervals when he was almost unaware of it. Curiously enough, he was nearly always free from serious discomfort when he was on his business trips; his worst attacks were saved for the privacy of the home.

On several occasions, his ulcer was so bad that he went away for rest cures. These always did him a lot of good. He threw aside business responsibility, family responsibility and care, forgot about the people he didn't like and allowed himself to be taken care of in every way.

The vacation from his dislikes was particularly important. While not a man given to outbursts of temper, Walter had developed a collection of pet hates, anxieties and fears. He had become a confirmed pessimist, and the world being what it is he was frequently confirmed in his gloomy predictions.

At the same time, Walter was no bitter misanthrope shunning his fellows. He liked cards and parties and gatherings at which his business associates met for wassail and jubilee, even though he no longer took part in the wassail. He was popular enough, telling a story well and willing to listen, too.

He was forty-five when he was advised that surgery was the only hope for him, but he was advised at the same time that there are psychic factors about an ulcer which he ought to investigate. He decided to investigate both, but his ulcer was so far advanced that there was nothing for it but to operate. Psychotherapy, except for helping put him in a better frame of mind to undergo the operation, came later.

Walter began, after some rapport with the physician had been established by talking freely of his feeling of responsibility for his father, mother, sister and brother. His mother did foolish things—taking trips and buying clothes or furniture which she couldn't afford—and his father did nothing to stop her. That angered and worried him. His sister failed to ask his advice, although she knew he was ready to give it to her, and he gloomily predicted that his bachelor brother was too irresponsible to come to any good end. He himself, he confided, was the only practical one of the lot.

It was pretty plain that his relationship with his mother had been one of resentment because she was not sufficiently dependent upon him and dissatisfaction because he had never been able to get himself babied. It was equally plain that neither of these sentiments was understood by him in the least. And still more plain was the fact that his curious reticence about his wife and children was based on an even more disturbing emotional conflict.

As the case eventually developed, it appeared that when he married her his wife had all the mannerisms of the helpless and fluttering female who was seeking to attach herself to his strength for protection. But as their married life settled into domestic routine, she showed a certain aggressiveness which was mainly directed toward furthering his career. She was a nagger, in short. Walter had to work pretty hard to keep himself believing that he held the upper hand in the more obvious areas of family decision. He could not relax for a moment and sink into the role of the pampered husband if he was to retain his self-respect. But he had a very obvious yearning to play that role. The degree to which he repressed it was measured by the intensity of his ulcer pains.

"Sometimes," he said, "I get so mad at that woman I have to get out for a while. But she adores me really, and there isn't anything I can do to change her."

It would have done Walter no good to have changed her. It was himself he had to change. Peace, and freedom from any recurrence of his ulcer, came to him when he finally understood that it was in his own emotional conflict that his troubles originated.

Classical psychology has tended to look upon mental illness as the symptom of disintegration of the ego. Karl Menninger has another point of view: mental disease is an attempt made by the organism to defend itself against extinction. Treated as a process instead of an entity, a period of mental illness might actually serve to help the individual achieve a higher degree of ego integration.

KARL MENNINGER

Prevention, Endurance, and Transcendence

FROM *The Vital Balance*

SYNOPSIS: *From the traditional viewpoint, much is gained by providing ever more effective therapies for mental illness. But the goals of psychiatry must go beyond cure to prevention. With this emphasis, psychiatry becomes deeply involved in the well and the sick, in social structure, mores, attitudes, and values. A broad reappraisal of the health-illness continuum in that context also has implications for the goals of treatment. These need no longer be confined to a reinstatement of the status quo ante ("recovery" in the popular sense), but might push forward toward the development of new potentialities and transcendence of previous levels of vital balance to a state of being "weller than well."*

We have rounded the circle. . . . We proposed taking a look at the psychiatry of yesterday and then the psychiatry of today, with a glance into the possibilities of psychiatry for tomorrow. We outlined diagnosis in a new key, viewing human beings as in a constant process of adaptation, subject to occasional major derailments. Estimating the severity and reversibility of these derailments, we said, and determining how and why they occur, might enable us to plan logical and effective intervention.

We continued then with a discussion of *organization;* after dipping deep into *dysorganization* and describing that in many phases, we returned at last to *reorganization;* i.e., to recovery and reconstitution. We described the human organization interacting with the environmental organization, noting particularly the individual's motives and his ways of coping with interferences in their expression. We described the psychological machinery for dealing with them, leaving an elaboration of the physiological machinery to colleagues versed in that area.

When the stress of adjustment reaches a certain height, we said, numerous emergency relief devices are summoned, like the firemen and police in a city. Their efforts become apparent to the outside world in diverse forms of altered behavior which often is disruptive and uncomfortable. But its purpose is essentially salvaging. It endeavors to effect a compromise between self-destructive and self-preservative forces. A strategic retreat is made under the shelter of the "symptoms." When they have done their work and served their purpose, when shifts in the balance of determining factors have resulted in a reduction of tension, the emergency measures disappear and the customary life mode is resumed.

For the pathologist and the pessimist such excursions constitute illness; for the therapist and the optimist they represent a lowering of the level of optimal degrees of healthiness. Illness and recovery are but two aspects of the same process. "As a man develops a disease, so begins at the same time a fight between the disease and the counter striving life, which seeks incessantly to overcome the new enemy . . . The moment of disease is at the same time the moment of healing."[1]

Our theory regards the two aspects of the process as representing the dominance of one or the other of the two polar drives of the personality, which are in a continuous and infinitely varied state of conflict, fusion, and defusion. The aggressive and self-destructive forces are constantly opposed by constructive, integrative, and reintegrative ones. From these derive both the automatic healing measures within the organism and the search for the assistance of benevolent and useful features of the environment, including the physician. The goal of therapeutic intervention is the expediting of the upward trend of the illness-recovery process. To accomplish this the positive factors must be identified as well as the negative or pathogenic factors, the former to be supported and the latter combated.

Psychiatric treatment has evolved through many stages—extrusion; ostracism; torture; execution; studied neglect; dreary maintenance; kindly care; mechanical, surgical, and electrical assaults of various kinds; an infinite assortment of chemical alteratives, sedatives, and stimulants; and varied programs of work therapy, play therapy, music therapy, psychotherapy. The long era of therapeutic nihilism was terminated by the discovery of arsphenamine and of psychoanalysis.

With the new knowledge came new hope. As our eyes were opened to the power of the malignant forces in the environment and to those within the personality, we had begun to find ways of combating both. New treatment methods and philosophies evolved. Young people of both sexes began to turn in increasing numbers to the acquiring of various skills in the service of assisting the recovery of the mentally ill. These workers brought to the task also the force of their personalities, their affections, their faith in psychiatry, their hopeful confidence that better things were possible.

With this great wave of faith, hope, and dedication, combined with scientific and professional growth, psychiatry ascended into hitherto untouched heights. On the one hand, mental illness was recognized and officially declared by the organized medical profession to be "the number-one health problem of our country." On the other hand, the application of new methods and a new spirit revolutionized psychiatric hospitals and changed the expectations for recovery from mental illness from very low to very high. True, there remain many cases of stubborn chronicity, especially in the partially disabled, but it is now common knowledge that the vast majority of hospitalized patients recover and return home within a few weeks or months of admission. (This assumes a modern and properly operated psychiatric hospital.)

The success of psychiatric treatment has had two paradoxical consequences. One of these was the great increase in the numbers of those seeking help. Many sufferers who had resigned themselves or who had been resigned by their relatives to despair, and many others previously not considered amenable to psychiatric treatment began to seek it. Couples in marital discord, confused schoolchildren whose potentialities were obviously greater than their achievement, misunderstood or misunderstanding employees whose joy in work had become replaced with bitterness and inefficiency, clergymen and teachers dissatisfied and frustrated in their profession, offenders whose criminal acts did not get them what they sought—all these and many other individuals began coming to psychiatrists. And although the psychiatrists have gradually surrounded themselves with many therapeutic assistants, treatment case loads continued to mount far more rapidly than additional psychiatrists could be trained.

Thus the success of psychiatry also aroused the long-cherished and wistfully protected notion of *prevention*. Better than treatment, better even than diagnosis, would be the diminution of the incidence of need. Not that anyone expects the vicissitudes and sorrow of life to disappear: accidents will continue to happen, aggressions will continue to erupt, wounds will continue to be inflicted. But might not something be done to mitigate the severity of the reaction or the frequency of the *severe* reaction? Does the knowledge of what things men cannot bear, or of what they bear only with the greatest difficulty, or of how their ability to bear stresses becomes impaired—could this knowledge give us a basis for improving life conditions and hence life itself?

Many so-intended social programs have been offered, but those in charge of public affairs, who give careful ear to public-health measures of other sorts—concerning food and water and sewage—are not inclined to take seriously the practical measures proposed for the insurance of mental health. Psychiatrists plead the importance of security and affection in early mother-child relationships, better schools, better teachers, better playgrounds and more of them. But school-board members still are inclined to regard such measures as too expensive or irrelevant. Our government still separates thousands of (Indian) children from mothers by force at an early age and consigns them to educational factories at long distances from their homes on the basis that learning English and arithmetic is more important than learning to love and to feel secure.

No one disputes the theoretical importance of stable family life, fidelity in marriage, kindness to children, and such pleasant things, but they are not thought of generally as basic to mental health. Our divorce rate rises, the battered-child syndrome appears ever more frequently, racial intolerance and bitterness increase. Psychiatrists plead for wilderness areas, not for the preservation of beauty but for the preservation of mental health. What happens? Certain commercial interests protest and one stubborn politician blocks the efforts of years with impunity. Art galleries, museums, concert halls, gymnasiums, and facilities for outdoor recreation are commended as contributing to mental health, but it is a handful of angels who keep such things going.

All these measures have been proposed time and time again; many of them have been tried—are being tried—if often halfheartedly. No one really knows what a "total push" social reform of this kind might accomplish. It would be certain to receive the denunciation of politicians and hardheaded "realists" who consider such measures luxuries to be earned by the public "if it *really* wants them" but certainly not to be providently cast before—well, not swine but "unappreciative masses." The objectors have a point; if the masses are unappreciative, if the individuals *in* the mass cannot do their part in obtaining such bonanzas, these well-intended provisions become just that—bonanzas. They do not prevent mental ill health; they further it.

On the other hand, whenever I hear economic Tories raising this point in the course of a debate on the promotion of mental health, I am reminded of the intransigent British Parliament which in one century lost the American colonies through dogged adherence to a legal principle, and in the following century let the doctrine of *laissez faire* hypnotize them into contributing to the death by starving of two million of their citizens in Ireland, lest by governmental intervention they break the economic principle and save some lives.[2]

We have daily cause to remember that even in this best and certainly most prosperous of all countries, in this best or at least best-known of all possible worlds, there is too much sorrow and too much suffering, there is too much evidence of personal and social disorganization, there is too much mental ill health. The crime rate increases steadily; vandalism spreads; suicides multiply; neighborhoods decay; hospitals remain crowded; unemployment, strikes and other labor difficulties bespeak unrest and frustration in employment and industry. Science suggests this need not be.

An old Talmudic version of the Golden Rule reads "Love thy neighbor, he *is* thyself." We must try to protect our neighbor to protect ourselves; we must endeavor to prevent his mental illness, and our own. Too many of our neighbors still need food, a few clothes, a few hours of rest from exhausting labor. But along with sustenance and garments and shelter—indeed, to learn to share these necessities of life—we must find better techniques for living together, and for living closer together, as we are going to have to. We must find better ways of joining together in mutual satisfactions and for mutual benefit, while yet retaining our individuality, our personal identity, and our inescapable personal responsibility.

We must discover better methods of controlling dangerous impulses, both within ourselves and in some other drivers whose brakes are defective. Our innate aggressiveness and destructiveness have been so infinitely multiplied in power and potential consequence by recent physical and chemical discoveries that their control has become the most important problem in the world. All of us now living are threatened, constantly and imminently.

If these things that we have been saying were known to all teachers, would our schoolrooms improve? If they were known to all school-board members, would our teachers improve? If they were known to all employers, would work losses recede and profits rise? If they were known to labor leaders, would work satisfaction increase and industrial strife diminish? If they were known to clergymen, would religion move into new roles of importance and meaning? Would this be an effective approach to prevention?

No one has shown conclusively that good results would follow. This is a faith of ours rather than proved knowledge. But we have seen many small demonstrations in The Menninger Foundation, during seminar courses to industrialists, clergymen, and physicians. We see in many of these groups the surprising phenomenon of a sudden lifting of horizons, an enlightenment, an "improvement" in the mental health of people who weren't sick! The meaning of human life, of all human behavior, of "sickness" and "health" may suddenly change.

"We have gained a new concept of man!" exclaimed two clergymen near the end of one such session. "A changed concept of man requires a changed concept of God; and if of God, then of all our world, too." Many industrialists and executives have expressed similar sentiments in other words. This is more than a simple "learning experience" (although it is *that*, too). It is an internal reorganization resulting from a shaking up, a new insight, even a bit of travail and perplexity, but it enables further advance.

And what does psychiatry offer toward the alleviation of the dreadful predicament? Should we be hesitant to contribute to world thinking what we know of human nature? Is one of our colleagues wrong to suggest that perhaps it is "not an extravagant speculation that mental hospitals will be a nucleus of future progress in man's understanding of man, for they are natural centers for study and research in human relations and will not be overlooked indefinitely"?[3]

We psychiatrists are familiar with this in another setting, that of clinical practice. Not infrequently we observe that a patient who is in a phase of recovery from what may have been a rather long illness shows continued improvement, past the point of his former "normal" state of existence. He not only gets well, to use the vernacular; he gets as well as he was, and then he continues to improve still further. He increases his productivity, he expands his life and its horizons. He develops new talents, new powers, new effectiveness. He becomes, one might say, "weller than well."

WELLER THAN WELL

Of course this doesn't always happen, nor does it happen often enough. But that it happens at all—and every experienced psychiatrist has seen it—this fact should alert us to latent possibilities, just as the bobbing lid of his mother's teakettle caught Watt's attention and curiosity. What could it mean? It violates our conventional medical expectations, so perhaps it is often overlooked and occurs more often than we know. It may contain a clue for both better prevention and better treatment.

Abraham Lincoln is a famous example of this. Many people do not know of his several attacks of severe mental illness. His law partner, Stuart, described him as a "hopeless victim of melancholy." His future wife's relatives considered him "insane."[4] According to one version, on his wedding day all preparations were in order and the guests assembled, but Lincoln didn't appear. He was found in his room in deep dejection, obsessed with ideas of unworthiness, hopelessness, and guilt.

Prior to his illness Lincoln was an honest but undistinguished lawyer whose failures were more conspicuous than his successes. This was when he was considered well—*before* his mental illness made its appearance. What he became and achieved *after* his illness is part of our great national heritage.

John Stuart Mill, to take a less well-known example, suffered an attack of mental illness in 1826, when he was twenty years old, in which he was obsessed with the thought that even if he could have everything he wanted he would still not be happy. "Although 'suicidal' for many months," writes Szasz, "[Mill] 'recovered' from this turmoil, which some might call a 'depression,' and underwent a process of profound personality reorganization. There is no way of telling how Mill managed to reorganize himself, nor was this apparently clear to him. But of the result, he could inform us."[5]

Mill wrote: "The experiences of this period had two very marked effects on my opinions and character. In the first place, they led me to adopt a theory of life, very unlike that on which I had before acted, and having much in common with what at that time I certainly had never heard of, the anti-self-consciousness theory of Carlyle. I never, indeed, wavered in the conviction that happiness is the test of all rules of conduct, and the end of life. But I now thought that this end was only to be attained by not making it the direct end. Those only are happy (I thought) who have their minds fixed on some object other than their own happiness; on the happiness of others, on the improvement of mankind, even on some art or pursuit, followed not as a means, but as itself an ideal end. Aiming thus at something else, they find happiness by the way."[6]

Another example, most poignant to physicians, psychiatrists, psychologists, is none other than William James, who also became a great man only after he had been a very sick man. He was described as physically frail at nineteen; at twenty-three he had many presumably psychosomatic symptoms (eyes and stomach); at twenty-five he dropped his medical studies because of his health and took many treatments in Europe. He was depressed and entertained suicidal thoughts. "He awoke every morning with a horrible dread. For months he was unable to go into the dark alone . . . he wondered how other people could live so unconscious of the 'pit of insecurity beneath the surface of life.' "

"The world owes a great deal to these personal misfortunes," wrote Norman Cameron. "James was thrown heavily upon his own resources; his incapacities and frustrations at such a time gave him an intense and intimate appreciation of the deepest philosophical and religious problems; his illness clearly 'developed and deepened the bed in which the stream of his philosophic life was to flow.' "[7]

This is a man who thereafter became one of the greatest scientists who has ever lived, certainly the greatest psychologist and perhaps the greatest philosopher that America has produced. He transcended his illness to become "weller than well."

Many other examples could be given. Indeed, from friends who heard us discuss this have come numerous suggestions, records, and illustrative biographies; especially from my friend Rudolph Treuenfels. Max Weber had written a few minor books prior to a severe depression at fifty, from which he emerged to write his masterpiece, *The Protestant Ethic and the Spirit of Capitalism.* Conrad Ferdinand Meyer was a Swiss poet whose best work followed an illness, according to one authority. Ignatius Loyola is believed by some to have experienced a severe mental illness between his undistinguished military career and his subsequent very distinguished religious period.

Transcendence of illness is something the public does not ordinarily envision. In his goodheartedness the man of the street is glad to be told that someone with a mental illness is being properly cared for or is, perhaps, even getting better. He reads with pleasure in his local newspaper that "the friends of John Smith will be happy to learn that the hospital doctors report him to be improving and he will be glad to receive letters." He may even declare with confidence that he believes that old John Smith may yet get back on the job and be just about as good as ever. But it is still hard for him to believe that people like John Smith can ever really "be the same again" or be free from the suspicion of lurking susceptibility to irrationality. This uninformed attitude leads to a cruel stigmatization which is diminishing, but which is still present in the minds of too many good people. And as for the illness experience representing a growth, a blessing, a gateway, so to speak, into a life of greater mental healthiness—this seems almost inconceivable.

The authors of this book hope for nothing more than that mental illness and recovery may be seen in this wider, deeper view. Please believe that from a total of seventy years of work with psychiatric patients we are not unaware that some do not get as well as we would wish, that some long remain susceptible to losses of equilibrium and temporary recessions. We well know how difficult it is, sometimes, for sufferers to get well—even with all the help that we can muster. But we also know that transcendence does occur. And perhaps it is not an exception but a natural consequence of new insights and new concepts of treatment!

Transcendence might happen oftener if we could more frankly acknowledge the possibility of its occurrence, expect it, and hope for it, even though we are bound to be often disappointed. Doctors occasionally see indisputable evidences of it even in medical conditions. People who have tuberculosis in younger life often become very healthy and resistant to all infections subsequently. The famous world-record miler, Glen Cunningham, suffered as a child from burns on both legs so severe that it was predicted he would never recover sufficiently even to walk.[8]

No one who saw Helen Keller at the age of six could have guessed what she was to become at sixteen, or be at sixty (and eighty-three). The little college in Kansas which turned down the application of George Washington Carver had no inkling of the genius contained in the humble, shabby Negro boy, or it might have stretched its snobbish admission rules; when Christy Brown's mother observed her speechless, spastic child drawing in the dust of the floor with his toe, not even she could imagine that the little "imbecile" would become an author and an artist. These examples may be trite and well known to many, but the reader can be certain that there are thousands of unknown examples who have not been discovered or who have not yet written about their experiences.[9]

This chapter, written to recapitulate and round off the message of the book, may now itself need recapitulating. It can all be said to be an answer to the question put earlier, What difference does it make?

What difference does it make how we see psychiatry? Are we better off in viewing mental illness not in the old ways but as a process, as an episode of disequilibration, a degree of temporary disorganization in a life course? What difference does it make if, instead of carefully fitting these conditions with proper names and classifying them in lists of diseases, we think of them as representing one kind of human vicissitude to which we are all subject and for which some of us stand by to offer first aid in emergencies?

It makes the difference, we propose, that the new view justifies hope; an attitude of hopefulness in turn favorably affects the unfavorable condition.

This is a point of view in psychiatry which has rapidly grown along with the rapid growth of psychiatry itself in scope and in popularity. People rush for help. With and without adequate diagnosis, they are receiving many treatments and many cures, which is what one would expect. We have even begun to speak earnestly of prevention—not only to speak of it, which has often been done before, but to relate it to sociological and educational and recreational programs as a new justification for these latter. And, we have said, perhaps education, education as to the very facts we have reviewed in this book, is itself the most potent preventive measure.

What we cannot prevent we must deal with, especially the extreme and disabling attacks of mental illness which are so costly to the individual and to those about him. For these we should provide first of all accurate diagnosis, not a synthetic name for the pathology but an analysis of the factors which have combined to produce it, the internal factors and the external factors. Such a diagnosis permits us to recommend treatment measures likely to be effective.

Being realistic, we know that in spite of the best diagnosis and the best treatment some patients will not recover. This is a minority, but of all people we psychiatrists should be the last to ignore a minority. And there are some who in spite of everything will continue to need our sympathy, our patience, and our help in the hope that some vestige of inner strength will sustain them in their necessity for brave, but tortured, endurance.

Meanwhile, most of us will be dealing more promptly with our own bouts of mental illness, or getting effective help if we need it. Life resumed goes on as before, almost as well as before, sometimes even better.

But, of course, illness is not the *only* way to learn. The aspiration to improve oneself, to become "weller than well," to reach out constantly toward a more nearly perfect way of life—is this the virtue and the blessing of only a few fortunate ones? Is it given only to geniuses, or is it something latent in all of us, too easily stifled? If one reflects on the one hand how opportunities are daily discarded by millions in favor of escapism, intoxication, and chronic suicide, one tends to answer the question one way; when one observes, on the other hand, the unswerving efforts to obtain an education, acquire knowledge, improve character, and better the world in many ways, which are demonstrated by many an illustrious example, and by many unknown heroes and heroines,[10] one tends to answer the question another way.

Benjamin Franklin, that great American genius, inventor, thinker, and statesman, worked conscientiously and systematically all his life toward enhancing his mental health, toward becoming weller than well. As he later recorded it, he early

> conceived the arduous project of arrival at moral perfection. . . . But I soon found I had undertaken a task of more difficulty than I had imagined. While my care was employ'd in guarding against one fault, I was often surprised by another; habit took the advantage of inattention; inclination was sometimes too strong for reason. I concluded, at length, that the mere speculative conviction that it was our interest to be completely virtuous, was not sufficient to prevent our slipping; and that the contrary habit must be broken, and good ones acquired and established, before we can have any dependence on a steady, uniform rectitude of conduct. For this purpose I therefore contriv'd the following method. . . . I made a little book, in which I allotted a page for each of the virtues. I rul'd each page with red ink, so as to have seven columns, one for each day of the week, marking each column with a letter for the day. I cross'd these columns with thirteen red lines, marking the beginning of each line with the first letter of one of the virtues, on which line, and in its proper column, I might mark, by a little black spot, every fault I found upon examination to have been committed respecting that virtue upon that day.

The thirteen virtues Franklin listed were: Temperance, Silence, Order, Resolution, Frugality, Industry, Sincerity, Justice, Moderation, Cleanliness, Tranquillity, Chastity, and Humility. He determined to give a week's strict attention to each of the virtues successively, going "thro' a course in thirteen weeks, and four courses in a year."

> I was surpris'd [he wrote] to find myself so much fuller of faults than I had imagined; but I had the satisfaction of seeing them diminish . . . After a while I went thro' one course only in a year, and after-

ward only one in several years . . . but I always carried my little book with me.

Something that pretended to be reason, was every now and then suggesting to me that such extreme nicety as I exacted of myself might be a kind of foppery in morals, which, if it were known, would make me ridiculous; that a perfect character might be attended with the inconvenience of being envied and hated; and that a benevolent man should allow a few faults in himself, to keep his friends in countenance.

. . . But, on the whole, tho' I never arrived at the perfection I had been so ambitious of obtaining, but fell far short of it, yet I was, by the endeavour, a better and a happier man that I otherwise should have been if I had not attempted it; . . .

It may be well my posterity should be informed that to this little artifice, with the blessing of God, their ancestor ow'd the constant felicity of his life, down to his 79th year, in which this is written.[11]

There are no doubt many colleagues who will see in such self-correction and programming not so much a "foppery in morals" as something psychopathological for which, no doubt, an impressive psychiatric designation can be found: compulsivity, narcissism, masochism. These words do not well describe, in my opinion; and they surely do not condemn. The self-discipline and aspiration of that magnificent character stand out resplendently. Not only was he the "better and happier man" for his pains, but so may thousands of others be who catch the inspiration for self-improvement and self-realization, and who possess the humility to work at it and think about it, "alert with noble discontent" down to their seventy-ninth year!

Doctors have traditionally concentrated upon pathology to the neglect of potentialities and assets to be exploited. Conceiving it to be the doctor's first business to relieve the patient's pain, align his broken bones, prescribe a cathartic, psychiatrists have too much followed this medical tradition. But mental health and its achievement must include *in the doctor* a vision of continued growth, the continuing discovery and realization of new potentialities.

"The potentialities of development in human souls," wrote William James sixty years ago, "are unfathomable. So many who seemed irretrievably hardened have in point of fact been softened, converted, regenerated, in ways that amazed the subjects even more than they surprised the spectators, that we can never be sure in advance of any man that his salvation by way of love is hopeless. We have no right to speak of human crocodiles and boa-constrictors as of fixedly incurable things. We know not the complexities of personality, the smouldering emotional fires, the other facets of the character-polyhedron, the resources of the subliminal region."[12]

Transcendence of illness is not only an individual goal, but it may be seen as a collective striving as well, the thrust of human evolution. Our colleague, Gardner Murphy, puts it this way:

Human potentialities are given by the action of that which sleeps within us upon the unformed potentialities of the world. . . . We are provided with a complex set of organic equipment, and if it is not allowed to function, something happens to us, just as in using it we find joy. If we have tissues within us which through learning and thinking develop and enrich us, we shall in the same way find joy both in the new and in the old activities and in the process of learning and thinking. If thinking becomes a group-supported activity, we may, like the Athenians, foregather just to think, as the Icelanders foregather to play chess, or the Germans to make music. In the long run, the use of the brain, if not pre-empted entirely by the sheer process of keeping alive or keeping up with the Joneses, leads, over the centuries, to more and more exquisite cultural products. Those, according to my thesis, which supervene after ten generations of cumulative thought are just as directly and fundamentally an expression of human nature as breathing or eating. Because man has this rich potentiality for sensory, motor, intellectual experience, and has to combine all this in fresh acts of cultural creativeness, he is doing nothing more than realizing these potentialities when he writes *Macbeth* or flies a plane at Kitty Hawk. And it is not only human to invent oneself out of one world into another; it is also human to keep moving toward a destination which is not set within man's present nature but keeps changing as the nature of his environment changes. The bio-cultural reality keeps rolling up on itself.[13]

With the message of these magnificent words we draw our book to a close. We have covered a variety of themes and we have used many words and many pages to do so. But through them all has run this thread; implicit in the eloquence of William James and Ernest Southard and Gardner Murphy, it is a message which can also be put in more prosaic terms; it can even be conveyed in the language of gesture and feeling, without words. It is the assertion of hope, of faith in every individual's potential for growth and development and self-transcendence. It is a declaration of love for and of belief in one's fellow creatures.

In one form or another, each of the authors has tried to say some of these things before. This message was implicit, for example, when Martin Mayman wrote some years ago:

> Inner unrest, even turmoil, need not signify only illness, it may often signal incipient change for the better. Not all disequilibria are unhealthy; instability may indicate a condition still in flux whose direction of change may remain uncertain until a new integration is reached. Even in relatively healthy persons there will be periods or circumstances in which positive striving may be mistaken for wasteful inner strife.
>
> Certainly, unrest holds out at least the prospect of a change for the better, unlike the stagnation which often characterizes those patients who seem to have settled into a state of illness, who almost recoil from the prospect of change, who live their lives almost as if they were keeping themselves in a kind of protective custody, carefully putting off situations which might open up new experiences and new growth. A relatively healthy ego often welcomes (even invites) disturbance in its equilibrium; people seek stimulation and challenge, as recent experiments have shown.[14]

It was this same thought which Paul Pruyser had in mind when, tongue in cheek, he asked, "Is mental health possible?" and then answered the question by suggesting that

> mental health should be seen not as a state of rest nor as homeostatic return to a previous condition, but as a realization of values which can only be achieved through becoming as opposed to "being." Earlier we spoke of "heterostasis" and indicated how strained the traditional language of science becomes when it tries to deal with goals, strivings, purposes, expectations and the realization of potentialities. Yet we cannot evade the issue that, psychologically speaking, living is worth its cost only when it entails progressive order, increased awareness of the complexities of reality, deepened wisdom and enlarged experience. And these, we submit, may well be the product of the suffering and temporary defeat represented by a phase of illness.[15]

And it is a message which the third author of the trio would offer as his *l'envoi*, in words employed a few years ago to describe a patient's frame of mind at the termination of treatment:

> . . . Although it is true that his expectations were not met, his gains were *beyond* his expectations! He had learned to live, to love and to

live, to love and to be loved and therein to live. This was his great gain.

Learning this simple thing, and recognizing it to be a universal principle, of which his own personal experience is but an example, represents a beginning constructive identification of himself with the universe, with reality, with other people. No one ever gets as much love as he wants, no one gives as much love as he might. Choices can be made but choice involves the assumption of responsibility and the necessity for renunciation. But life is for living and this he has gained the courage to accept.[16]

The three of us, too, subscribe to those great lines of William James: *"Will you or won't you* have it so? is the most probing question we are ever asked. We are asked it every hour of the day, and about the largest as well as the smallest, the most theoretical as well as the most practical things. We answer by *consents* or *non-consents* and not by words. What wonder that these dumb responses should seem our deepest organs of communication with the nature of things! What wonder if the effort demanded by them be the measure of our worth as men!"[17]

It is this philosophy, this view of human life, and this understanding of mental illness and psychiatry which we want most to leave with our readers—those who know about mental illness, those who think they know nothing about it, those who have experienced and recovered from it, and those who are perhaps at this moment passing through the valley of the shadow.

We would especially impart this viewpoint to those distressed regarding a friend or relative. It is a frightening and heartbreaking experience to see the "alienation" of one we thought we knew, and it is perhaps natural to fear the worst. This horror, mixed with sorrow, anger, and guilt feelings, may be involuntary and irresistible—for a moment. But an informed intelligence, while soft-voiced, as Freud remarked, is fortunately persistent. For even though we grant the contradictory and presently inexplicable fact of cancer, and the less dramatic but no less malignant nature of some other afflictions, we do not recede from our position that the mentally ill usually recover. Mental illness is a curable condition and the mentally ill *can* be cured. The hopeless patient is a myth.

In the past ten years my brother, Doctor Will, has spoken earnestly to the legislatures of many states—Oklahoma, Ohio, Pennsylvania, Kentucky, Michigan, California, Iowa, Minnesota, Oregon, Tennessee, Texas, Wyoming, Maryland, West Virginia, North Dakota, Colorado,

Alabama, Arizona, Vermont, Washington, and South Carolina. The legislators have listened attentively; they have risen to acclaim his words. In many instances they have acted upon them.

What has he told these legislators? Simply that mental illness is our pre-eminent health problem in America, that the mentally ill can be helped, that most of them can be cured, that it is less expensive and more humane to treat them scientifically than to confine them despairingly. The percentage of people helped and the rapidity of their recovery are directly proportionate to the extent to which modern concepts of psychiatric treatment are entertained and applied. This has been re-demonstrated in the Topeka Veterans Administration Hospital and the Topeka State Hospital for the past twenty years.[18]

This is the "news" my brother has taken to legislators and others. He has not been alone in spreading this gospel; it has other eloquent spokesmen. Yet over 80 per cent of the state hospitals of our country still fail to offer any treatment at all to the patients assigned to them and confined in them![19]

This is hard for us to understand. It is hard to understand how Massachusetts in 1850 and scores of other states since then could have let a magnificent demonstration like that of Woodward, Todd, Brigham, Bell, Butler, Ray, Stedman, and Kirkbride sink into oblivion and desuetude while thousands of patients who undoubtedly could have been cured dragged out their weary lives in the dismal wards of state hospitals. Many still do.

Why is the public so willing to retain its pessimism and cling to the ancient superstition that mental illness is incurable? Why does not every heartbroken father whose son's career has been suddenly interrupted by mental illness, or every grieving mother, every saddened wife—why do not these dear relatives (and their name is legion) join together to move mountains, if necessary, in order to insure help for their loved ones?

Do people inwardly believe, still, that the mentally ill are damned and that is the end of it? Is this the negative of William James' "will to believe," a will *not* to believe? Is this incredulity born of an innate pessimism or of a fear of seeming gullible? Or is it perchance a refusal to take the responsibility which acceptance of the facts implies?

For we *can* help them. We *must* help them. They need help—that is what their illness means, no matter how disguised. It is a cry for our assistance, and we must know how to answer. We cannot plead ignorance, for we know how to do it. It is not our helplessness that has deterred us so long, but our hopelessness.

The injunction of Isaiah to "Comfort my people" rests heavily upon psychiatrists. For they must point the way, not yielding to the discouragement of asking, "Who hath believed our report?" Because *we* know that, depending upon how the particular mental illness is understood and reacted to—by the patient and by the relatives and by the community and *by the medical profession*—the future may be brighter than anything the past has held.

Where there is life there is, usually, hope. Earlier we considered giving this book the title *Where There Is Life*. But we felt that in one sense the implication was misleading; it was as if to say that *only while* there is life is there hope, that hope is sustained by life. Our point is rather that life is sustained by hope—that where there is hope there is life!

Life is more than permutations in the DNA molecule as the Fifth Symphony is more than vibrating air. And mental illness is more than an aggregate of errors in body physics and chemistry. It is a universal human experience which has a salvage function in maintaining the vital balance.

NOTES

¹ DIETL, JOSEPH. Quoted by Max Neuburger in *The Doctrine of the Healing Power of Nature Throughout the Course of Time*. New York: Boyd, 1932.

² WOODHAM-SMITH, CECIL. *The Great Hunger*. Boston: Houghton, Mifflin, 1963.

³ BOCKOVEN, J. SANBOURNE. "Moral Treatment in American Psychiatry." *J. Nerv. and Ment. Dis.* 124:293–321, 1956.

⁴ CLARK, L. PIERCE. "A Psychologic Study of Abraham Lincoln." *Psa. Rev.* 8:1–21, 1921.

⁵ SZASZ, THOMAS A. "Human Nature and Psychotherapy." *Comprehensive Psychiat.* 3:268–283, 1962.

⁶ MILL, JOHN S. *Autobiography*. New York: Columbia University, 1960. Mill went on: "The enjoyments of life (such was not my theory) are sufficient to make it a pleasant thing, when they are taken *en passant*, without being made a principal object. Once make them so, and they are immediately felt to be insufficient. They will not bear a scrutinizing examination. Ask yourself whether you are happy, and you cease to be so. The only chance is to treat, not happiness, but some end external to it, as the purpose of life. Let your self-consciousness, your scrutiny, your self-interrogation, exhaust themselves on that; and if otherwise fortunately circumstanced you will inhale happiness with the air you breathe, without dwelling on it or thinking about it, without either forestalling it in imagination, or putting it to flight by fatal questioning. This theory now becomes the basis of my philosophy of life. And I still hold to it as the best theory for all those who have but a moderate degree of sensibility and of capacity for enjoyment; that is, for the great majority of mankind."

⁷ CAMERON, NORMAN. *William James*. Madison: University of Wisconsin, 1942.

⁸ But doctors are apt to look upon these as exceptions. A recent book of radio

talks by a doctor whom I do not know concerns itself with "high-level wellness," an exhortation for "maximizing the potential of which the individual is capable, within the environment where he is functioning." Surely there is nothing wrong with this aspiration, but doctors will be suspicious if not supercilious. (Dunn, Halbert L. *High Level Wellness*. Arlington, Va.: R. W. Beatty Co., 1962.)

9 But many have. I would especially commend *Very Much Alive* by Terry Mc-Adam, *Greet the Man* by Harold Wilke, *My Left Foot* by Christy Brown, *Born That Way* by Earl R. Carlson, *If a Man Be Mad*, by Harold Maine, and *None So Blind* by Bernice Clifton. In *Minds That Came Back* (New York: Lippincott, 1961), Dr. Walter Alvarez has collected data on seventy-five recovered patients, some of whom illustrate our point, and in an appendix lists annotated autobiographies by many people—"cripples," "paranoiacs," "epileptics," alcoholics, drug addicts, sexual deviants, tramps, prisoners, blind-deaf people, lepers, and others.

10 MENNINGER, FLO V. *Days of My Life*. New York: Richard R. Smith, 1940.

11 DUNFORD, KATHERINE. "Benjamin Franklin's Bold and Arduous Project." *ETC*. 19:335–340, 1962.

12 JAMES, WILLIAM. *The Varieties of Religious Experience*. New York: Longmans, 1902.

13 MURPHY, GARDNER. *Human Potentialities*. New York: Basic Books, 1958.

14 MAYMAN, MARTIN. "Ego Strength and the Potential for Recovery from Mental Illness." *Festschrift for Gardner Murphy*. New York: Harper, 1960.

15 PRUYSER, PAUL. "Is Mental Health Possible?" *Bull. Menninger Clin.* 22:58–66, 1958.

16 MENNINGER, KARL. *Theory of Psychoanalytic Technique*. New York: Basic Books, 1958.

17 JAMES, WILLIAM. *The Will to Believe*. New York: Longmans, 1903.

18 This demonstration began before introduction of ataractic drugs.

19 These are the figures of the study of the Joint Commission on Mental Illness and Health (1961).

"I Look Out for Ed Wolfe" is a fascinating and accurate psychological portrait of the outcast. The hero is an orphan and a Jew, and thus doubly alienated, and doubly guilty for the death of his parents and of his God. To protect himself from his own aggressions, he must turn his guilt into hatred. Expiation arrives in the form of a woman, a Negro girl, who momentarily forgives him. The repetition of an Oedipal situation needs no comment. The tangled relationship of white with Negro which this story explores reinforces psychological belief in the sexual nature of prejudice. The recognition that kindness, not punishment, may provide the answer to hatred reiterates the plea made earlier by Doctors Staub and Alexander.*

STANLEY ELKIN

I Look Out for Ed Wolfe

He was an orphan, and, to himself, he seemed like one, looked like one. His orphan's features were as true of himself as are their pale, pinched faces to the blind. At twenty-seven he was a neat, thin young man in white shirts and light suits with lintless pockets. Something about him suggested the ruthless isolation, the hard self-sufficiency of the orphaned, the peculiar dignity of men seen eating alone in restaurants on national holidays. Yet it was this perhaps which shamed him chiefly, for there was a suggestion, too, that his impregnability was a myth, a smell not of the furnished room which he did not inhabit, but of the three-room apartment on a good street which he did. The very excellence of his taste, conditioned by need and lack, lent to him the odd, maidenly primness of the lonely.

He saved the photographs of strangers and imprisoned them behind clear plastic windows in his wallet. In the sound of his own voice he detected the accent of the night school and the correspondence course, and nothing of the fat, sunny ring of the world's casually afternooned.

1027

He strove against himself, a supererogatory enemy, and sought by a kind of helpless abrasion, as one rubs wood, the gleaming self beneath. An orphan's thinness, he thought, was no accident.

Returning from lunch he entered the office building where he worked. It was an old building, squat and gargoyled, brightly patched where sandblasters had once worked and then quit before they had finished. He entered the lobby, which smelled always of disinfectant, and walked past the wide, dirty glass of the cigarette and candy counter to the single elevator, as thickly barred as a cell.

The building was an outlaw. Low rents and a downtown address and the landlord's indifference had brought together from the peripheries of business and professionalism a strange band of entrepreneurs and visionaries, men desperately but imaginatively failing: an eye doctor who corrected vision by massage; a radio evangelist; a black-belt judo champion; a self-help organization for crippled veterans; dealers in pornographic books, in paper flowers, in fireworks, in plastic jewelry, in the artificial, in the artfully made, in the imitated, in the copied, in the stolen, the unreal, the perversion, the plastic, the *schlack*.

On the sixth floor the elevator opened and the young man, Ed Wolfe, stepped out.

He passed the Association for the Indians, passed Plasti-Pens, passed *Coffin & Tombstone*, passed Soldier Toys, passed Prayer-a-Day. He walked by the opened door of C. Morris Brut, Chiropractor, and saw him, alone, standing at a mad attention, framed in the arching golden nimbus of his inverted name on the window, squeezing handballs.

He looked quickly away but Dr. Brut saw him and came toward him, putting the handballs in his shirt pocket where they bulged awkwardly. He held him by the elbow. Ed Wolfe looked at the yellowing tile beneath his feet, infinitely diamonded, chipped, the floor of a public toilet, and saw Dr. Brut's dusty shoes. He stared sadly at the jagged, broken glass of the mail chute.

"Ed Wolfe, take care of yourself," Dr. Brut said.

"Right."

"Regard your posture in life. A tall man like yourself looks terrible when he slumps. Don't be a *schlump*. It's no good for the organs."

"I'll watch it."

"When the organs get out of line the man begins to die."

"I know."

"You say so. How many guys make promises. Brains in the brain-pan. Balls in the strap. The bastards downtown." He meant doctors in hospitals, in clinics, on boards, nonorphans with M.D. degrees and special license plates and respectable patients who had Blue Cross, charts, died in clean hospital rooms. They were the bastards downtown, his personal New Deal, his neighborhood Wall Street banker. A disease cartel. "They won't tell you. The white bread kills you. The cigarettes. The whiskey. The sneakers. The high heels. They won't tell you. Me, *I'll* tell you."

"I appreciate it."

"Wise guy. Punk. I'm a friend. I give a father's advice."

"I'm an orphan."

"I'll adopt you."

"I'm late to work."

"We'll open a clinic. 'C. Morris Brut and Adopted Son.' "

"It's something to think about."

"Poetry," Dr. Brut said and walked back to his office, his posture stiff, awkward, a man in a million who knew how to hold himself.

Ed Wolfe went on to his own office. He walked in. The sad-faced telephone girl was saying. "Cornucopia Finance Corporation." She pulled the wire out of the board and slipped her headset around her neck where it hung like a delicate horse collar. "Mr. La Meck wants to see you. But don't go in yet. He's talking to somebody."

He went toward his desk at one end of the big main office. Standing, fists on the desk, he turned to the girl. "What happened to my call cards?"

"Mr. La Meck took them," the girl said.

"Give me the carbons," Ed Wolfe said. "I've got to make some calls."

She looked embarrassed. The face went through a weird change, the sadness taking on an impossible burden of shame so that she seemed massively tragic, like a hit-and-run driver. "I'll get them," she said, moving out of the chair heavily. Ed Wolfe thought of Dr. Brut.

He took the carbons and fanned them out on the desk. He picked one in an intense, random gesture like someone drawing a number on a public stage. He dialed rapidly.

As the phone buzzed brokenly in his ear he felt the old excitement. Someone at the other end greeted him sleepily.

"Mr. Flay? This is Ed Wolfe at Cornucopia Finance." (Can you cope, can you cope? he hummed to himself.)

"Who?"

"Ed Wolfe. I've got an unpleasant duty," he began pleasantly. "You've skipped two payments."

"I didn't skip nothing. I called the girl. She said it was okay."

"That was three months ago. She meant it was all right to miss a few days. Listen, Mr. Flay, we've got that call recorded, too. Nothing gets by."

"I'm a little short."

"Grow."

"I couldn't help it," the man said. Ed Wolfe didn't like the cringing tone. Petulance and anger he could meet with his own petulance, his own anger. But guilt would have to be met with his own guilt and that, here, was irrelevant.

"Don't con me, Flay. You're a trouble-maker. What are you, Flay, a Polish person? Flay isn't a Polish name, but your address . . ."

"What's that?"

"What are you? Are you Polish?"

"What's that to you? What difference does it make?" That was more like it, Ed Wolfe thought warmly.

"That's what you are, Flay. You're a Pole. It's guys like you who give your race a bad name. Half our bugouts are Polish persons."

"Listen. You can't . . ."

He began to shout. "*You* listen. You wanted the car. The refrigerator. The chintzy furniture. The sectional you saw in the funny papers. And we paid for it, right?"

"Listen. The money I owe is one thing, the way . . ."

"We paid for it, right?"

"That doesn't . . ."

"Right? Right?"

"Yes, you . . ."

"Okay. You're in trouble, Warsaw. You're in terrible trouble. It means a lien. A judgment. We've got lawyers. You've got nothing. We'll pull the furniture the hell out of there. The car. Everything."

"Wait," he said. "Listen, my brother-in-law . . ."

Ed Wolfe broke in sharply. "He's got some money?"

"I don't know. A little. I don't know."

"Get it. If you're short, grow. This is America."

"I don't know if he'll let me have it."

"Steal it. This is America. Goodbye."

"Wait a minute. Please."

"That's it. There are other Polish persons on my list. This time it was just a friendly warning. Cornucopia wants its money. Cornucopia. Can you cope? Can you cope? Just a friendly warning, Polish-American. Next time we come with the lawyers and the machine guns. Am I making myself clear?"

"I'll try to get it to you."

Ed Wolfe hung up. He pulled a handkerchief from his drawer and wiped his face. His chest was heaving. He took another call card. The girl came by and stood beside his desk. "Mr. La Meck can see you now," she mourned.

"Later. I'm calling." The number was already ringing.

"Please, Mr. Wolfe."

"Later, I said. In a minute." The girl went away. "Hello. Let me speak with your husband, madam. I am Ed Wolfe of Cornucopia Finance. He can't cope. Your husband can't cope."

The woman said something, made an excuse. "Put him on, goddamn it. We know he's out of work. Nothing gets by. Nothing." There was a hand on the receiver beside his own, the wide male fingers pink and vaguely perfumed, the nails manicured. For a moment he struggled with it fitfully, as though the hand itself were all he had to contend with. He recognized La Meck and let go. La Meck pulled the phone quickly toward his mouth and spoke softly into it, words of apology, some ingenious excuse Ed Wolfe couldn't hear. He put the receiver down beside the phone itself and Ed Wolfe picked it up and returned it to its cradle.

"Ed," La Meck said, "come into the office with me."

Ed Wolfe followed La Meck, his eyes on La Meck's behind.

La Meck stopped at his office door. Looking around he shook his head sadly and Ed Wolfe nodded in agreement. La Meck let Ed Wolfe pass in first. While La Meck stood, Ed Wolfe could discern a kind of sadness in his slouch, but once La Meck was seated behind his desk he seemed restored, once again certain of the world's soundness. "All right," La Meck began, "I won't lie to you."

Lie to me. Lie to me, Ed Wolfe prayed silently.

"You're in here for me to fire you. You're not being laid off. I'm not going to tell you that I think you'd be happier someplace else, that the collection business isn't your game, that profits don't justify our keeping you around. Profits are terrific, and if collection isn't your game it's because you haven't got a game. As far as your being happier someplace else, that's bullshit. You're not supposed to be happy. It isn't in the cards for you. You're a fall-guy type, God bless you, and though I like you personally I've got no use for you in my office."

I'd like to get you on the other end of a telephone someday, Ed Wolfe thought miserably.

"Don't ask me for a reference," La Meck said. "I couldn't give you one."

"No, no," Ed Wolfe said. "I wouldn't ask you for a reference." A helpless civility was all he was capable of. If you're going to suffer, *suffer*, he told himself.

"Look," La Meck said, his tone changing, shifting from brutality to compassion as though there were no difference between the two, "you've got a kind of quality, a real feeling for collection. I'm frank to tell you, when you first came to work for us I figured you wouldn't last. I put you on the phones because I wanted you to see the toughest part first. A lot of people can't do it. You take a guy who's down and bury him deeper. It's heart-wringing work. But you, you were amazing. An artist. You had a real thing for the deadbeat soul, I thought. But we started to get complaints, and I had to warn you. Didn't I warn you? I should have suspected something when the delinquent accounts started to turn over again. It was like rancid butter turning sweet. So I don't say this to knock your technique. Your technique's terrific. With you around we could have laid off the lawyers. But Ed, you're a gangster. A gangster."

That's it, Ed Wolfe thought. I'm a gangster. Babyface Wolfe at nobody's door.

"Well," La Meck said, "I guess we owe you some money."

"Two weeks' pay," Ed Wolfe said.

"And two weeks' pay in lieu of notice," La Meck said grandly.

"And a week's pay for my vacation."

"You haven't been here a year," La Meck said.

"It would have been a year in another month. I've earned the vacation."

"What the hell," La Meck said. "A week's pay for vacation."

La Meck figured on a pad and tearing off a sheet handed it to Ed Wolfe. "Does that check with your figures?" he asked.

Ed Wolfe, who had no figures, was amazed to see that his check was so large. Leaving off the deductions he made $92.73 a week. Five $92.73's was evidently $463.65. It was a lot of money. "That seems to be right," he told La Meck.

La Meck gave him a check and Ed Wolfe got up. Already it was as though he had never worked there. When La Meck handed him the check he almost couldn't think what it was for. It was as if there should have been a photographer there to record the ceremony. ORPHAN AWARDED CHECK BY BUSINESSMAN.

"Goodbye, Mr. La Meck," he said. "It has been an interesting association," he added foolishly.

"Goodbye, Ed," La Meck answered, putting his arm around Ed

Wolfe's shoulders and leading him to the door. "I'm sorry it had to end this way." He shook Ed Wolfe's hand seriously and looked into his eyes. He had a hard grip.

Quantity and quality, Ed Wolfe thought.

"One thing, Ed. Watch yourself. Your mistake here was that you took the job too seriously. You hated the chiselers."

No, no, I loved them, he thought.

"You've got to watch it. Don't love. Don't hate. That's the secret. Detachment and caution. Look out for Ed Wolfe."

"I'll watch out for him," he said giddily and in a moment he was out of La Meck's office, and the main office, and the elevator, and the building itself, loose in the world, as cautious and as detached as La Meck would want him.

He took the car from the parking lot, handing the attendant the two dollars. The man gave him fifty cents back. "That's right," Ed Wolfe said, "it's only two o'clock." He put the half dollar in his pocket, and, on an impulse, took out his wallet. He had twelve dollars. He counted his change. Eighty-two cents. With his finger, on the dusty dashboard, he added $12.82 to $463.65. He had $476.47. Does that check with your figures? he asked himself and drove into the crowded traffic.

Proceeding slowly, past his old building, past garages, past bar and grills, past second-rate hotels, he followed the traffic further downtown. He drove into the deepest part of the city, down and downtown to the bottom, the foundation, the city's navel. He watched the shoppers and tourists and messengers and men with appointments. He was tranquil, serene. It was something he would be content to do forever. He could use his check to buy gas, to take his meals at drive-in restaurants, to pay tolls. It would be a pleasant life, a great life, and he contemplated it thoughtfully. To drive at fifteen or twenty miles an hour through eternity, stopping at stoplights and signs, pulling over to the curb at the sound of sirens and the sight of funerals, obeying all traffic laws, making obedience to them his very code. Ed Wolfe, the Flying Dutchman, the Wandering Jew, the Off and Running Orphan, "Look Out for Ed Wolfe," a ghostly wailing down the city's corridors. What would be bad? he thought.

In the morning, out of habit, he dressed himself in a white shirt and light suit. Before he went downstairs he saw that his check and his twelve dollars were still in his wallet. Carefully he counted the eighty-two cents that he had placed on the dresser the night before, put the coins in his pocket, and went downstairs to his car.

Something green had been shoved under the wiper blade on the driver's side.

YOUR CAR WILL NEVER BE WORTH MORE THAN IT IS WORTH RIGHT NOW! WHY WAIT FOR DEPRECIATION TO MAKE YOU AUTOMOTIVELY BANKRUPT? I WILL BUY THIS CAR AND PAY YOU CASH! I WILL NOT CHEAT YOU!

Ed Wolfe considered his car thoughtfully a moment and got in. He drove that day through the city playing the car radio softly. He heard the news each hour and each half hour. He listened to Arthur Godfrey far away and in another world. He heard Bing Crosby's ancient voice, and thought sadly, Depreciation. When his tank was almost empty he thought wearily of having to have it filled and could see himself, bored and discontented behind the bug-stained glass, forced into a patience he did not feel, having to decide whether to take the Green Stamps the attendant tried to extend. Put money in your purse, Ed Wolfe, he thought. Cash! he thought with passion.

He went to the address on the circular.

He drove up onto the gravel lot but remained in his car. In a moment a man came out of a small wooden shack and walked toward Ed Wolfe's car. If he was appraising it he gave no sign. He stood at the side of the automobile and waited while Ed Wolfe got out.

"Look around," the man said. "No pennants, no strings of electric light." He saw the advertisement in Ed Wolfe's hand. "I ran the ad off on my brother-in-law's mimeograph. My kid stole the paper from his school."

Ed Wolfe looked at him.

"The place looks like a goddamn parking lot. When the snow starts falling I get rid of the cars and move the Christmas trees right onto it. No overhead. That's the beauty of a volume business."

Ed Wolfe looked pointedly at the nearly empty lot.

"That's right," the man said. "It's slow. I'm giving the policy one more chance. Then I cheat the public just like everybody else. You're just in time. Come on, I'll show you a beautiful car."

"I want to sell my car," Ed Wolfe said.

"Sure, sure," the man said. "You want to trade with me. I give top allowances. I play fair."

"I want you to buy my car."

The man looked at him closely. "What do you want? You want me to go into the office and put on the ten-gallon hat? It's my only overhead so I guess you're entitled to see it. You're paying for it. I put on this big frigging hat, see, and I become Texas Willie Waxelman, the Mad Cowboy. If that's what you want, I can get it in a minute."

It was incredible, Ed Wolfe thought. There were bastards everywhere who hated other bastards downtown everywhere. "I don't want to trade my car in," Ed Wolfe said. "I want to sell it. I, too, want to reduce my inventory."

The man smiled sadly. "You want me to buy *your* car. You run in and put on the hat. I'm an automobile *salesman*, kid."

"No, you're not," Ed Wolfe said. "I was with Cornucopia Finance. We handled your paper. You're an automobile *buyer*. Your business is in buying up four- and five-year-old cars like mine from people who need dough fast and then auctioning them off to the trade."

The man turned away and Ed Wolfe followed him. Inside the shack the man said, "I'll give you two hundred."

"I need six hundred," Ed Wolfe said.

"I'll lend you the hat. Hold up a goddamn stagecoach."

"Give me five."

"I'll give you two fifty and we'll part friends."

"Four hundred and fifty."

"Three hundred. Here," the man said, reaching his hand into an open safe and taking out three sheaves of thick, banded bills. He held the money out to Ed Wolfe. "Go ahead, count it."

Absently Ed Wolfe took the money. The bills were stiff, like money in a teller's drawer, their value as decorous and untapped as a sheet of postage stamps. He held the money, pleased by its weight. "Tens and fives," he said, grinning.

"You bet," the man said, taking the money back. "You want to sell your car?"

"Yes," Ed Wolfe said. "Give me the money," he said hoarsely.

He had been to the bank, had stood in the patient, slow, money-conscious line, had presented his formidable check to the impassive teller, hoping the four hundred and sixty-three dollars and sixty-five cents she counted out would seem his week's salary to the man who waited behind him. Fool, he thought, it will seem two weeks' pay and two weeks in lieu of notice and a week for vacation for the hell of it, the three-week margin of an orphan.

"Thank you," the teller said, already looking beyond Ed Wolfe to the man behind him.

"Wait," Ed Wolfe said. "Here." He handed her a white withdrawal slip.

She took it impatiently and walked to a file. "You're closing your savings account?" she asked loudly.

"Yes," Ed Wolfe answered, embarrassed.

"I'll have a cashier's check made out for this."

"No, no," Ed Wolfe said desperately. "Give me cash."

"Sir, we make out a cashier's check and cash it for you," the teller explained.

"Oh," Ed Wolfe said. "I see."

When the teller had given him the two hundred fourteen dollars and twenty-three cents, he went to the next window where he made out a check for $38.91. It was what he had in his checking account.

On Ed Wolfe's kitchen table was a thousand dollars. That day he had spent a dollar and ninety cents. He had twenty-seven dollars and seventy-one cents in his pocket. For expenses. "For attrition," he said aloud. "The cost of living. For streetcars and newspapers and half gallons of milk and loaves of white bread. For the movies. For a cup of coffee." He went to his pantry. He counted the cans and packages, the boxes and bottles. "The three weeks again," he said. "The orphan's nutritional margin." He looked in his icebox. In the freezer he poked around among white packages of frozen meat. He looked brightly into the vegetable tray. A whole lettuce. Five tomatoes. Several slices of cucumber. Browning celery. On another shelf four bananas. Three and a half apples. A cut pineapple. Some grapes, loose and collapsing darkly in a white bowl. A quarter pound of butter. A few eggs. Another egg, broken last week, congealing in a blue dish. Things in plastic bowls, in jars, forgotten, faintly mysterious left-overs, faintly rotten, vaguely futured, equivocal garbage. He closed the door, feeling a draft. "Really," he said, "it's quite cozy." He looked at the thousand dollars on the kitchen table. "It's not enough," he said. "It's not enough," he shouted. "It's not enough to be cautious on. La Meck, you bastard, detachment comes higher, what do you think? You think it's cheap?" He raged against himself. It was the way he used to speak to people on the telephone. "Wake up. Orphan! Jerk! Wake up. It costs to be detached."

He moved solidly through the small apartment and lay down on his bed with his shoes still on, putting his hands behind his head luxuriously. It's marvelous, he thought. Tomorrow I'll buy a trench coat. I'll take my meals in piano bars. He lighted a cigarette. "I'll never smile again," he sang, smiling. "All right, Eddie, play it again," he said. "Mistuh Wuf, you don' wan' ta heah dat ol' song no maw. You know whut it do to you. She ain' wuth it, Mistuh Wuf." He nodded. "Again, Eddie." Eddie played his black ass off. "The way I see it, Eddie," he said, taking a long, sad drink of warm Scotch, "there are orphans and there are orphans." The overhead fan chuffed slowly, stirring the potted palmetto leaves.

He sat up in the bed, grinding his heels across the sheets. "There are orphans and there are orphans," he said. "I'll move. I'll liquidate. I'll sell out."

He went to the phone and called his landlady and made an appointment to see her.

It was a time of ruthless parting from his things, but there was no bitterness in it. He was a born salesman, he told himself. A disposer, a natural dumper. He administered severance. As detached as a funeral director, what he had learned was to say goodbye. It was a talent of a sort. And he had never felt quite so interested. He supposed he was doing what he had been meant for, what, perhaps, everyone was meant for. He sold and sold, each day spinning off, reeling off little pieces of himself, like controlled explosions of the sun. Now his life was a series of speeches, of nearly earnest pitches. What he remembered of the day was what he had said. What others said to him, or even whether they spoke at all, he was unsure of.

Tuesday he told his landlady, "Buy my furniture. It's new. It's good stuff. It's expensive. You can forget about that. Put it out of your mind. I want to sell it. I'll show you bills for over seven hundred dollars. Forget the bills. Consider my character. Consider the man. Only the man. That's how to get your bargains. Examine, Examine. I could tell you about inner springs; I could talk to you of leather. But I won't. I don't. I smoke, but I'm careful. I can show you the ashtrays. You won't find cigarette holes in *my* tables. Examine. I drink. I'm a drinker. I drink. But I hold it. You won't find alcohol stains. May I be frank? I make love. Again, I could show you the bills. But I'm cautious. My sheets are virginal, white.

"Two hundred fifty dollars, landlady. Sit on that sofa. That chair. Buy my furniture. Rent the apartment furnished. Deduct what you pay from your taxes. Collect additional rents. Realize enormous profits. Wallow in gravy. Get it, landlady? Get it? Just two hundred fifty dollars. Don't disclose the figure or my name. I want to remain anonymous."

He took her into his bedroom. "The piece of resistance, landlady. What you're really buying is the bedroom stuff. I'm selling you your own bare floor. What charm. Charm? Elegance. Elegance! I throw in the living-room rug. That I throw in. You have to take that or it's no deal. Give me cash and I move tomorrow."

Wednesday he said, "I heard you buy books. That must be interesting. And sad. It must be very sad. A man who loves books doesn't like to sell them. It would be the last thing. Excuse me. I've got no right to talk to you this way. You buy books and I've got books to sell. There. It's business now. As it should be. My library—" He smiled helplessly. "Excuse me. Such a grand name. Library." He began again slowly. "My books, my books are in there. Look them over. I'm afraid my taste has been rather eclectic. You see, my education has not been formal. There are over eleven hundred. Of course many are paperbacks. Well, you can see that. I feel as if I'm selling my mind."

The book buyer gave Ed Wolfe one hundred twenty dollars for his mind.

On Thursday he wrote a letter:

American Annuity & Life Insurance Company
Suite 410
Lipton-Hill Building
2007 Bevero Street, S.W.
Boston 19, Massachusetts

Dear Sirs,

I am writing in regard to Policy Number 593-000-34-78, a $5,000, twenty-year annuity held by Edward Wolfe of the address below.

Although only four payments having been made, sixteen years remain before the policy matures, I find I must make application for the immediate return of my payments and cancel the policy.

I have read the "In event of cancellation" clause in my policy, and realize that I am entitled to only a flat three percent interest on the "total paid-in amount of the partial amortizement." Your records will show that I have made four payments of $198.45 each. If your figures check with mine this would come to $793.80. Adding three percent interest to the amount ($23.81), your company owes me $817.61.

Your prompt attention to my request would be gratefully appreciated, although I feel, frankly, as though I were selling my future.

On Monday someone came to buy his record collection. "What do you want to hear? I'll put something comfortable on while we talk. What do you like? Here, try this. Go ahead, put it on the machine. By the edges, man. By the edges! I feel as if I'm selling my throat. Never mind about that. Dig the sounds. Orphans up from Orleans singing the news of chain gangs to café society. You can smell the freight trains, man. Recorded during actual performance. You can hear the ice cubes clinkin' in the glasses, the waiters picking up their tips. I have jazz. Folk. Classical. Broadway. Spoken Word. Spoken Word, man! I feel as though I'm selling my ears. The stuff lives in my heart or I wouldn't sell. I have a one-price throat, one-price ears. Sixty dollars for the noise the world makes, man. But remember. I'll be watching. By the edges. Only by the edges!"

On Friday he went to a pawnshop in a Checker Cab.

"You? You buy gold? You buy clothes? You buy Hawaiian guitars? You buy pistols for resale to suicides? I wouldn't have recognized you. Where's the skullcap, the garters around the sleeves? The cigar I wouldn't ask you about. You look like everybody. I don't know what to say. I'm stuck. I don't know how to deal with you. I was going to tell you something sordid, you know? You know what I mean? Okay, I'll give you facts.

"The fact is, I'm the average man. That's what the fact is. Eleven shirts, 15 neck, 34 sleeve. Six slacks, 32 waist. Five suits at 38 long. Shoes 10-C. A 7½ hat. You know something? Those marginal restaurants where you can never remember whether they'll let you in without a jacket? Well the jackets they lend you in those places always fit me. That's the kind of guy you're dealing with. You can have confidence. Look at the clothes. Feel the material. And there's one thing about me. I'm fastidious. Fastidious. Immaculate. You think I'd be clumsy. A fall guy falls down, right? There's not a mark on the clothes. Inside? Inside it's another story. I don't speak of inside. Inside it's all Band-Aids, plaster, iodine, sticky stuff for burns. But outside—fastidiousness, immaculation, reality! My clothes will fly off your racks. I promise. I feel as if I'm selling my skin. Does that check with your figures?

"So now you know. It's me, Ed Wolfe. Ed Wolfe, the orphan? I lived in the orphanage for sixteen years. They gave me a name. It was a Jewish orphanage so they gave me a Jewish name. Almost. That is they couldn't know for sure themselves so they kept it deliberately vague. I'm a foundling. A lostling. Who needs it, right? Who the hell needs it? I'm at loose ends, pawnbroker. I'm at loose ends out of looser beginnings. I need the money to stay alive. All you can give me.

"Here's a good watch. Here's a bad one. For good times and bad. That's life, right? You can sell them as a package deal. Here are radios. I'll miss the radios. A phonograph. Automatic. Three speeds. Two speakers. The politic bastard shuts itself off. And a pressure cooker. It's valueless to me, frankly. No pressure. I can live only on cold meals. Spartan. Spartan.

"I feel as if I'm selling—this is the last of it, I have no more things—I feel as if I'm selling my things."

On Saturday he called the phone company: "Operator? Let me speak to your supervisor, please.

"Supervisor? Supervisor, I am Ed Wolfe, your subscriber at TErrace 7-3572. There is nothing wrong with the service. The service has been excellent. No one calls, but you can have nothing to do with that. However, I must cancel. I find that I no longer have any need of a telephone. Please connect me with the business office.

"Business office? Business office, this is Ed Wolfe. My telephone number is TErrace 7-3572. I am closing my account with you. When the service was first installed I had to surrender a twenty-five-dollars deposit to your company. It was understood that the deposit was to be refunded when our connection with each other had been terminated. Disconnect me. Deduct what I owe on my current account from my deposit and refund the rest immediately. Business office, I feel as if I'm selling my mouth."

When he had nothing left to sell, when that was finally that, he stayed until he had finished all the food and then moved from his old apartment into a small, thinly furnished room. He took with him a single carton of clothing—the suit, the few shirts, the socks, the pajamas, the underwear and overcoat he did not sell. It was in preparing this carton that he discovered the hangers. There were hundreds of them. His own. Previous tenants'. Hundreds. In each closet on rods, in dark, dark corners was this anonymous residue of all their lives. He unpacked his carton and put the hangers inside. They made a weight. He took them to the pawnshop and demanded a dollar for them. They were worth, he argued, more. In an A&P he got another carton free and went back to repack his clothes.

At the new place the landlord gave him his key.

"You got anything else?" the landlord asked. "I could give you a hand."

"No," he said. "Nothing."

Following the landlord up the deep stairs he was conscious of the $2,479.03 he had packed into the pockets of the suit and shirts and pajamas and overcoat inside the carton. It was like carrying a community of economically viable dolls.

When the landlord left him he opened the carton and gathered all his money together. In fading light he reviewed the figures he had entered in the pages of an old spiral notebook:

Pay	$463.65
Cash	12.82
Car	300.00
Savings	214.23
Checking	38.91
Furniture (& bedding)	250.00
Books	120.00
Insurance	817.61
Records	60.00
Pawned:	
Clothes	$110.00
2 watches	18.00
2 radios	12.00
Phonograph	35.00
Pressure Cooker	6.00
Phone deposit (less bill)	19.81
Hangers	1.00
Total	$2,479.03

So, he thought, that was what he was worth. That was the going rate for orphans in a wicked world. Something under $2,500. He took his pencil and lined through all the nouns on his list. He tore the list carefully from top to bottom and crumpled the half which inventoried his ex-possessions. Then he crumpled the other half.

He went to the window and pushed the loose, broken shade. He opened the window and set both lists on the ledge. He made a ring of his forefinger and thumb and flicked the paper balls into the street. "Look out for Ed Wolfe," he said softly.

In six weeks the season changed. The afternoons failed. The steam failed. He was as unafraid of the dark as he had been of the sunlight. He longed for a special grief, to be touched by anguish or terror, but when he saw the others in the street, in the cafeteria, in the theatre, in the hallway, on the stairs, at the newsstand, in the basement rushing their fouled linen from basket to machine, he stood, as indifferent to their errand, their appetite, their joy, their greeting, their effort, their curiosity, their grime, as he was to his own. No envy wrenched him, no despair unhoped him, but gradually, he became restless.

He began to spend, not recklessly so much as indifferently. At first he was able to recall for weeks what he spent on a given day. It was his way of telling time. Now he had difficulty remembering and could tell how much his life was costing only by subtracting what he had left from his original two thousand four hundred seventy-nine dollars and three cents. In eleven weeks he had spent six hundred seventy-seven dollars and thirty-four cents. It was almost three times more than he had planned. He became panicky. He had come to think of his money as his life. Spending it was the abrasion again, the old habit of self-buffing to come to the thing beneath. He could not draw infinitely on his credit. It was limited. Limited. He checked his figures. He had eighteen hundred and one dollars, sixty-nine cents. He warned himself, "Rothschild, child. Rockefeller, feller. Look out, Ed Wolfe. Look out."

He argued with his landlord, won a five-dollar reduction in his rent. He was constantly hungry, wore clothes stingily, realized an odd reassurance in his thin pain, his vague fetidness. He surrendered his dimes, his quarters, his half-dollars in a kind of sober anger. In seven weeks he spent only one hundred thirty dollars, fifty-one cents. He checked his figures. He had sixteen hundred seventy-one dollars, eighteen cents. He had spent almost twice what he had anticipated. "It's all right," he said. "I've reversed the trend. I can catch up." He held the money in his hand. He could smell his soiled underwear. "Nah, nah," he said. "It's not enough."

It was not enough, it was not enough, it was not enough. He had painted himself into a corner. Death by *cul-de-sac*. He had nothing left to sell, the born salesman. The born champion, long-distance, Ed Wolfe of a salesman, and he lay in his room winded, wounded, wondering where his next pitch was coming from, at one with the ages.

He put on his suit, took his sixteen hundred seventy-one dollars and eighteen cents and went down into the street. It was a warm night. He would walk downtown. The ice which just days before had covered the sidewalk was dissolved to slush. In darkness he walked through a thawing, melting world. There was, on the edge of the air, something, the warm, moist odor of the change of the season. He was, despite himself, touched. "I'll take a bus," he threatened. "I'll take a bus and close the windows and ride over the wheel."

He had dinner and some drinks in a hotel. When he finished he was feeling pretty good. He didn't want to go back. He looked at the bills thick in his wallet and went over to the desk clerk. "Where's the action?" he whispered. The clerk looked at him, startled. He went over to the bell captain. "Where's the action?" he asked and gave the man a dollar. He winked. The man stared at him helplessly.

"Sir?" the bell captain said, looking at the dollar.

Ed Wolfe nudged him in his gold buttons. He winked again. "Nice town you got here," he said expansively. "I'm a salesman, you understand, and this is new territory for me. Now if I were in Beantown or Philly or L.A. or Vegas or Big D or Frisco or Cincy, why I'd know what was what. I'd be okay, you know what I mean?" He winked once more. "Keep the buck, kid," he said. "Keep it, keep it," he said, walking off.

In the lobby a man sat in a deep chair, *The Wall Street Journal* opened widely across his face. "Where's the action?" Ed Wolfe said, peering over the top of the paper into the crown of the man's hat.

"What's that?" the man asked.

Ed Wolfe, surprised, saw that the man was a Negro.

"What's that?" the man repeated, vaguely nervous. Embarrassed, Ed Wolfe watched him guiltily, as though he had been caught in an act of bigotry.

"I thought you were someone else," he said lamely. The man smiled and lifted the paper to his face. Ed Wolfe stood before the man's opened paper, conscious of mildly teetering. He felt lousy, awkward, complicatedly irritated and ashamed, the mere act of hurting someone's feelings suddenly the most that could be held against him. It came to him how completely he had failed to make himself felt. "Look out for Ed Wolfe, indeed," he said aloud. The man lowered his paper. "Some of my best friends are Comanches," Ed Wolfe said. "Can I buy you a drink?"

"No," the man said.

"Resistance, eh?" Ed Wolfe said. "That's good. Resistance is good. A deal closed without resistance is no deal. Let me introduce myself. I'm Ed Wolfe. What's your name?"

"Please, I'm not bothering anybody. Leave me alone."

"Why?" Ed Wolfe asked.

The man stared at him and Ed Wolfe sat suddenly down beside him. "I won't press it," he said generously. "Where's the action? Where is it?

Fold the paper, man. You're playing somebody else's gig." He leaned across the space between them and took the man by the arm. He pulled at him gently, awed by his own boldness. It was the first time since he had shaken hands with La Meck that he had touched anyone physically. What he was risking surprised and puzzled him. In all those months to have touched only two people, to have touched even two people! To feel their life, even, as now, through the unyielding wool of clothing, was disturbing. He was unused to it, frightened and oddly moved. The man, bewildered, looked at Ed Wolfe timidly and allowed himself to be taken toward the cocktail lounge.

They took a table near the bar. There, in the alcoholic dark, within earshot of the easy banter of the regulars, Ed Wolfe seated the Negro and then himself. He looked around the room and listened for a moment. He turned back to the Negro. Smoothly boozy, he pledged the man's health when the girl brought their drinks. He drank stolidly, abstractedly. Coming to life briefly, he indicated the men and women around them, their sun-tans apparent even in the dark. "Pilots," he said. "All of them. Airline pilots. The girls are all stewardesses and the pilots lay them." He ordered more drinks. He did not like liquor and liberally poured ginger ale into his bourbon. He ordered more drinks and forgot the ginger ale. *"Goyim,"* he said. "White *goyim*. American *goyim*." He stared at the Negro. "These are the people, man. The mothered and fathered people." He leaned across the table. "Little Orphan Annie, what the hell kind of an orphan is that with all her millions and her white American *goyim* friends to bail her out?"

He watched them narrowly, drunkenly. He had seen them before—in good motels, in airports, in bars—and he wondered about them, seeing them, he supposed, as Negroes or children of the poor must have seen him when he had had his car and driven sometimes through slums. They were removed, aloof—he meant it—a different breed. He turned and saw the Negro and could not think for a moment what the man could have been doing there. The Negro slouched in his chair, his great white eyes hooded. "You want to hang around here?" Ed Wolfe asked him.

"It's your party," the man said.

"Then let's go someplace else," Ed Wolfe said. "I get nervous here."

"I know a place," the Negro said.

"You know a place. You're a stranger here."

"No, man," the Negro said. "This is my hometown. I come down here sometimes just to sit in the lobby and read the newspapers. It looks good, you know what I mean? It looks good for the race."

"The *Wall Street Journal?* You're kidding Ed Wolfe. Watch that."

"No," the Negro said. "Honest."

"I'll be damned," Ed Wolfe said. "I come for the same reasons."

"Yeah," the Negro said. "No shit."

"Sure, the same reasons." He laughed. "Let's get out of here." He tried to stand, but fell back again in his chair. "Hey, help me up," he said loudly. The Negro got up and came around to Ed Wolfe's side of the table. Leaning over, he raised him to his feet. Some of the others in the room looked at them curiously. "It's all right," Ed Wolfe said. "He's my man. I take him with me everywhere. It looks good for the race." With their arms around each other's shoulders they stumbled out of the room and through the lobby.

In the street Ed Wolfe leaned against the building and the Negro hailed a cab, the dark left hand shooting up boldly, the long black body stretching forward, raised on tiptoes, the head turned sharply along the left shoulder. Ed Wolfe knew he had never done it before. The Negro came up beside Ed Wolfe and guided him toward the curb. Holding the door open he shoved him into the cab with his left hand. Ed Wolfe lurched against the cushioned seat awkwardly. The Negro gave the driver an address and the cab moved off. Ed Wolfe reached for the window handle and rolled it down rapidly. He shoved his head out the window of the taxi and smiled and waved at the people along the curb.

"Hey, man. Close the window," the Negro said after a moment. "Close the window. The cops, the cops."

Ed Wolfe lay his head along the edge of the taxi window and looked up at the Negro who was leaning over him and smiling and seemed trying to tell him something.

"Where we going, man?" he asked.

"We're there," the Negro said, sliding along the seat toward the door.

"One ninety-five," the driver said.

"It's your party," Ed Wolfe told the Negro, waving away responsibility.

The Negro looked disappointed, but reached into his pocket to pull out his wallet.

Did he see what I had on me? Ed Wolfe wondered anxiously. Jerk, drunk, you'll be rolled. They'll cut your throat and then they'll leave your skin in an alley. Be careful.

"Come on, Ed," the Negro said. He took him by the arm and got him out of the taxi.

Fake. Fake, Ed Wolfe thought. Murderer. Nigger. Razor man.

The Negro pulled Ed Wolfe toward a doorway. "You'll meet my friends," he said.

"Yeah, yeah," Ed Wolfe said. "I've heard so much about them."

"Hold it a second," the Negro said. He went up to the window and pressed his ear against the opaque glass.

Ed Wolfe watched him without making a move.

"Here's the place," the Negro said proudly.

"Sure," Ed Wolfe said. "Sure it is."

"Come on, man," the Negro urged him.

"I'm coming, I'm coming," Ed Wolfe mumbled, "but my head is bending low."

The Negro took out a ring of keys, selected one, and put it in the door. Ed Wolfe followed him through.

"Hey, Oliver," somebody called. "Hey, baby, it's Oliver. Oliver looks good. He looks *good*."

"Hello, Mopiani," the Negro said to a short black man.

"How is stuff, Oliver?" Mopiani said to him.

"How's the market?" a man next to Mopiani asked with a laugh.

"Ain't no mahket, baby. It's a *sto'*," somebody else said.

A woman stopped, looked at Ed Wolfe for a moment, and asked: "Who's the ofay, Oliver?"

"That's Oliver's broker, baby."

"Oliver's broker looks good," Mopiani said. "He looks *good*."

"This is my friend, Mr. Ed Wolfe," Oliver told them.

"Hey, there," Mopiani said.

"Charmed," Ed Wolfe said.

"How's it going, man," a Negro said indifferently.

"Delighted," Ed Wolfe said.

He let Oliver lead him to a table.

"I'll get the drinks, Ed," Oliver said, leaving him.

Ed Wolfe looked at the room glumly. People were drinking steadily, gaily. They kept their bottles under their chairs in paper bags. Ed Wolfe watched a man take a bag from beneath his chair, raise it, and twist the open end of the bag carefully around the neck of the bottle so that it resembled a bottle of champagne swaddled in its toweling. The man poured into his glass grandly. At the dark far end of the room some musicians were playing and three or four couples danced dreamily in front of them. He watched the musicians closely and was vaguely reminded of the airline pilots.

In a few minutes Oliver returned with a paper bag and some glasses.

A girl was with him. "Mary Roberta, Ed Wolfe," he said, very pleased. Ed Wolfe stood up clumsily and the girl nodded.

"No more ice," Oliver explained.

"What the hell," Ed Wolfe said.

Mary Roberta sat down and Oliver pushed her chair up to the table. She sat with her hands in her lap and Oliver pushed her as though she were a cripple.

"Real nice little place here, Ollie," Ed Wolfe said.

"Oh, it's just the club," Oliver said.

"Real nice," Ed Wolfe said.

Oliver opened the bottle and poured liquor in their glasses and put the paper bag under his chair. Oliver raised his glass. Ed Wolfe touched it lamely with his own and leaned back, drinking. When he put it down empty, Oliver filled it again from the paper bag. He drank sluggishly, like one falling asleep, and listened, numbed, to Oliver and the girl. His glass never seemed to be empty anymore. He drank steadily but the liquor seemed to remain at the same level in the glass. He was conscious that someone else had joined them at the table. "Oliver's broker looks good," he heard somebody say. Mopiani. Warm and drowsy and gently detached, he listened, feeling as he had in barbershops, having his hair cut, conscious of the barber, unseen behind him, touching his hair and scalp with his warm fingers. "You see Bert? He looks good," Mopiani was saying.

With great effort Ed Wolfe shifted in his chair, turning to the girl.

"Thought you were giving out on us, Ed," Oliver said. "That's it. That's it."

The girl sat with her hands folded in her lap.

"Mary Roberta," Ed Wolfe said.

"Uh huh," the girl said.

"Mary Roberta."

"Yes," the girl said. "That's right."

"You want to dance?" Ed Wolfe asked.

"All right," she said. "I guess so."

"That's it, that's it," Oliver said. "Stir yourself."

He got up clumsily, cautiously, like one standing in a stalled Ferris wheel, and went around behind her chair, pulling it far back from the table with the girl in it. He took her warm, bare arm and moved toward the dancers. Mopiani passed them with a bottle. "Looks good, looks good," Mopiani said approvingly. He pulled her against him to let Mopiani pass, tightening the grip of his pale hand on her brown arm. A muscle leaped beneath the girl's smooth skin, filling his palm. At the edge of the dance floor Ed Wolfe leaned forward into the girl's arms and they moved slowly, thickly across the floor. He held the girl close, conscious of her weight, the life beneath her body, just under her skin. Sick, he remembered a jumping bean he had held once in his palm, awed and frightened by the invisible life, jerking and hysterical, inside the stony shell. The girl moved with him in the music, Ed Wolfe astonished by the burden of her life. He stumbled away from her deliberately. Grinning, he moved ungently back against her. "Look out for Ed Wolfe," he crooned.

The girl stiffened and held him away from her, dancing self-consciously. Ed Wolfe, brooding, tried to concentrate on the lost rhythm. They danced in silence for a while.

"What do you do?" she asked him finally.

"I'm a salesman," he told her gloomily.

"Door to door?"

"Floor to ceiling. Wall to wall."

"Too much," she said.

"I'm a pusher," he said, suddenly angry. She looked frightened. "But I'm not hooked myself. It's a weakness in my character. I can't get hooked. Ach, what would you *goyim* know about it?"

"Take it easy," she said. "What's the matter with you? Do you want to sit down?"

"I can't push sitting down," he said.

"Hey," she said, "don't talk so loud."

"Boy," he said, "you black Protestants. What's that song you people sing?"

"Come on," she said.

"Sometimes I feel like a motherless child," he sang roughly. The other dancers watched him nervously. "That's our national anthem, man," he said to a couple that had stopped dancing to look at him. "That's our song, sweethearts," he said, looking around him. "All right, mine then. I'm an orphan."

"Oh, come on," the girl said, exasperated, "an orphan. A grown man."

He pulled away from her. The band stopped playing "Hell," he said loudly, "from the beginning. Orphan. Bachelor. Widower. Only child. All my names scorn me. I'm a survivor. I'm a goddamned survivor, that's what." The other couples crowded around him now. People got up from their tables. He could see them, on tiptoes, stretching their necks over the heads of the dancers. No, he thought. No, no. Detachment and caution. The La Meck Plan. They'll kill you. They'll kill you and kill you. He edged away from them, moving carefully backward against the bandstand. People pushed forward onto the dance floor to watch him. He could hear their questions, could see heads darting from behind backs and suddenly appearing over shoulders as they strained to get a look at him.

He grabbed Mary Roberta's hand, pulling her to him fiercely. He pulled and pushed her up onto the bandstand and then climbed up beside her. The trumpet player, bewildered, made room for him. "Tell you what I'm going to do," he shouted over their heads. "Tell you what I'm going to do."

Everyone was listening to him now.

"Tell you what I'm going to do," he began again.

Quietly they waited for him to go on.

"I don't *know* what I'm going to do," he shouted. "I don't *know* what I'm going to do. Isn't that a hell of a note?

"Isn't it?" he demanded.

"Brothers and sisters," he shouted, "and as an only child bachelor orphan I used the term playfully you understand. Brothers and sisters, I tell you what I'm *not* going to do. I'm no consumer. Nobody's death can make me that. I won't consume. I mean it's a question of identity, right? Closer, come up closer, buddies. You don't want to miss any of this."

"Oliver's broker looks good up there. Mary Roberta looks good. She looks good," Mopiani said below him.

"Right, Mopiani. She looks good, she looks *good*," Ed Wolfe called loudly. "So I tell you what I'm going to do. What am I bid? What am I bid for this fine strong wench? Daughter of a chief, masters. Dear dark daughter of a dead dinge chief. Look at those arms. Those arms, those arms. What am I bid?"

They looked at him, astonished.

"What am I bid?" he demanded. "Reluctant, masters? Reluctant masters, masters? Say, what's the matter with you darkies? Come on, what am I bid?" He turned to the girl. "No one wants you, honey," he said. "Folks, folks, I'd buy her myself, but I've already told you. I'm not a consumer. Please forgive me, miss."

He heard them shifting uncomfortably.

"Look," he said patiently, "the management had asked me to remind you that this is a living human being. This is the real thing, the genuine article, the goods. Oh, I told them I wasn't the right man for this job. As an orphan I have no conviction about the product. Now you should have seen me in my old job. I could be rough. Rough. I hurt people. Can you imagine? I actually caused them pain. I mean, what the hell, I was an orphan. I *could* hurt people. An orphan doesn't have to bother with love. An orphan's like a nigger in that respect. Emancipated. But you people are another problem entirely. That's why I came here tonight. There are parents among you. I can feel it. There's even a sense of parents behind those parents. My God, don't any of you folks ever die? So what's holding us up? We're not making any money. Come on, what am I bid?"

"Shut up, mister." The voice was raised hollowly someplace in the back of the crowd.

Ed Wolfe could not see the owner of the voice.

"He's not in," Ed Wolfe said.

"Shut up. What right you got to come down here and speak to us like that?"

"He's not in, I tell you. I'm his brother."

"You're a guest. A guest got no call to talk like that."

"He's out. I'm his father. He didn't tell me and I don't know when he'll be back."

"You can't make fun of us," the voice said.

"He isn't here. I'm his son."

"Bring that girl down off that stage!"

"Speaking," Ed Wolfe said.

"Let go of that girl!" someone called angrily.

The girl moved closer to him.

"She's mine," Ed Wolfe said. "I danced with her."

"Get her down from there!"

"Okay," he said giddily. "Okay. All right." He let go of the girl's hand and pulled out his wallet. The girl did not move. He took out the bills and dropped the wallet to the floor.

"Damned drunk!" someone shouted.

"That white man's crazy," someone else said.

"Here," Ed Wolfe said. "There's over sixteen hundred dollars here," he yelled, waving the money. It was, for him, like holding so much paper. "I'll start the bidding. I hear over sixteen hundred dollars once. I hear over sixteen hundred dollars twice. I hear it three times. Sold! A deal's a deal," he cried, flinging the money high over their heads. He saw them reach helplessly, noiselessly toward the bills, heard distinctly the sound of paper tearing.

He faced the girl. "Goodbye," he said.

She reached forward, taking his hand.

"Goodbye," he said again, "I'm leaving."

She held his, squeezing it. He looked down at the luxuriant brown hand, seeing beneath it the fine articulation of bones, the rich sudden rush of muscle. Inside her own he saw, indifferently, his own pale hand, lifeless and serene, still and infinitely free.

Although fascination with the Beat movement in America seems to have subsided to a degree, the implications of the Beat phenomenon have yet to be measured. We have some clues to the aim of the Beat in Dr. Alexander's article that appears earlier. Jack Kerouac himself tells us how the Beat's involvement with noise and motion and pointless sexual activity complements the uses of Zen in helping the Beat achieve complete and utter oblivion.

JACK KEROUAC

FROM *The Dharma Bums*

But the next night, about midnight, Coughlin and I and Alvah got together and decided to buy a big gallon jug of Burgundy and go bust in on Japhy in his shack.

"What's he doing tonight?" I asked.

"Oh," says Coughlin, "probably studying, probably screwing, we'll go see." We bought the jug on Shattuck Avenue way down and went over and once more I saw his pitiful English bicycle on the lawn. "Japhy travels around on that bicycle with his little knapsack on his back all up and down Berkeley all day," said Coughlin. "He used to do the same thing at Reed College in Oregon. He was a regular fixture up there. Then we'd throw big wine parties and have girls and end up jumping out of windows and playing Joe College pranks all up and down town."

"Gee, he's strange," said Alvah, biting his lip, in a mood of marvel, and Alvah himself was making a careful interested study of our strange noisy-quiet friend. We came in the little door again, Japhy looked up from his crosslegged study over a book, American poetry this time, glasses on, and said nothing but "Ah" in a strangely cultured tone. We took off our shoes and padded across the little five feet of straw to sit by him, but I was last with my shoes off, and had the jug in my hand, which I turned to show him from across the shack, and from his crosslegged position Japhy suddenly roared "Yaaaaah!" and leaped up into the air and straight across the room to me, landing on his feet in a fencing position with a sudden dagger in his hand the tip of it just barely stabbing the glass of the bottle with a small distinct "clink." It was the most amazing leap I ever saw in my life, except by nutty acrobats, much like a mountain goat, which he was, it turned out. Also it reminded me of a Japanese Samurai warrior—the yelling roar, the leap, the position, and his expression of comic wrath his eyes bulging and making a big funny face at me. I had the feeling it was really a complaint against our breaking in on his studies and against wine itself which would get him drunk and make him miss his planned evening of reading. But without further ado he uncapped the bottle himself and took a big slug and we all sat crosslegged and spent four hours screaming news at one another, one of the funniest nights. Some of it went like this:

Japhy: Well, Coughlin, you old fart, what you been doin?

Coughlin: Nothin.

Alvah: What are all these strange books here? Hm, Pound, do you like Pound?

Japhy: Except for the fact that that old fartface flubbed up the name of Li Po by calling him by his Japanese name and all such famous twaddle, he was all right—in fact he's my favorite poet.

Ray: Pound? Who wants to make a favorite poet out of that pretentious nut?

Japhy: Have some more wine, Smith, you're not making sense. Who is your favorite poet, Alvah?

Ray: Why don't somebody ask me *my* favorite poet, I know more about poetry than all of you put together.

Japhy: Is that true?

Alvah: It might be. Haven't you seen Ray's new book of poems he just wrote in Mexico—"the wheel of the quivering meat conception turns in the void expelling tics, porcupines, elephants, people, stardusts, fools, nonsense . . ."

Ray: That's not it!

Japhy: Speaking of meat, have you read the new poem of . . .

Etc., Etc., then finally disintegrating into a wild talkfest and yellfest and finally songfest with people rolling on the floor in laughter and ending with Alvah and Coughlin and I going staggering up the quiet college street arm in arm singing "Eli Eli" at the top of our voices and dropping the empty jug right at our feet in a crash of glass, as Japhy laughed from his little door. But we'd made him miss his evening of study and I felt bad about that, till the following night when he suddenly appeared at our little cottage with a pretty girl and came in and told her to take her clothes off, which she did at once.

This was in keeping with Japhy's theories about women and love-making. I forgot to mention that the day the rock artist had called on him in the late afternoon, a girl had come right after, a blonde in rubber boots and a Tibetan coat with wooden buttons, and in the general talk she'd inquired about our plan to climb Mount Matterhorn and said "Can I come with ya?" as she was a bit of a mountainclimber herself.

"Shore," said Japhy, in his funny voice he used for joking, a big loud deep imitation of a lumberjack he knew in the Northwest, a ranger actually, old Burnie Byers, "shore, come on with us and we'll all screw ya at ten thousand feet" and the way he said it was so funny and casual, and in fact serious, that the girl wasn't shocked at all but somewhat pleased. In this same spirit he'd now brought this girl Princess to our cottage, it was about eight o'clock at night, dark, Alvah and I were quietly sipping tea and reading poems or typing poems at the typewriter and two bicycles came in the yard: Japhy on his, Princess on hers. Princess had gray eyes and yellow hair and was very beautiful and only twenty. I must say one thing about her, she was sex mad and man mad, so there wasn't much of a problem in persuading her to play yabyum. "Don't you know about yabyum, Smith?" said Japhy in his big booming voice striding in in his boots holding Princess's hand. "Princess and I come here to show ya, boy."

"Suits me," said I, "whatever it is." Also I'd known Princess before and had been mad about her, in the City, about a year ago. It was just another wild coincidence that she had happened to meet Japhy and fallen in love with him and madly too, she'd do anything he said. Whenever people dropped in to visit us at the cottage I'd always put my red bandana over the little wall lamp and put out the ceiling light to make a nice cool red dim scene to sit and drink wine and talk in. I did this, and went to get the bottle out of the kitchen and couldn't believe my eyes when I saw Japhy and Alvah taking their clothes off and throwing them every whichaway and I looked and Princess was stark naked, her skin white as snow when the red sun hits it at dusk, in the dim red light. "What the hell," I said.

"Here's what yabyum is, Smith," said Japhy, and he sat crosslegged on the pillow on the floor and motioned to Princess, who came over and sat down on him facing him with her arms about his neck and they sat like that saying nothing for a while. Japhy wasn't at all nervous and embarrassed and just sat there in perfect form just as he was supposed to do. "This is what they do in the temples of Tibet. It's a holy ceremony, it's done just like this in front of chanting priests. People pray and recite Om Mani Pahdme Hum, which means Amen the Thunderbolt in the Dark Void. I'm the thunderbolt and Princess is the dark void, you see."

"But what's she thinking?" I yelled almost in despair, I'd had such idealistic longings for that girl in that past year and had conscience-stricken hours wondering if I should seduce her because she was so young and all.

"Oh this is lovely," said Princess. "Come on and try it."

"But I can't sit crosslegged like that." Japhy was sitting in the full lotus position, it's called, with both ankles over both thighs. Alvah was sitting on the mattress trying to yank his ankles over his thighs to do it. Finally Japhy's legs began to hurt and they just tumbled over on the mattress where both Alvah and Japhy began to explore the territory. I still couldn't believe it.

"Take your clothes off and join in, Smith!" But on top of all that, the feelings about Princess, I'd also gone through an entire year of celibacy based on my feeling that lust was the direct cause of birth which was the direct cause of suffering and death and I had really no lie come to a point where I regarded lust as offensive and even cruel.

"Pretty girls make graves," was my saying, whenever I'd had to turn my head around involuntarily to stare at the incomparable pretties of Indian Mexico. And the absence of active lust in me had also given me a new peaceful life that I was enjoying a great deal. But this was too much. I was still afraid to take my clothes off; also I never like to do that in front of more than one person, especially with men around. But Japhy didn't give a goddamn hoot and holler about any of this and pretty soon he was making Princess happy and then Alvah had a turn (with his big serious eyes staring in the dim light, and him reading poems a minute ago). So I said "How about me startin to work on her arm?"

"Go ahead, great." Which I did, lying down on the floor with all my clothes on and kissing her hand, then her wrist, then up, to her body, as she laughed and almost cried with delight everybody everywhere working on her. All the peaceful celibacy of my Buddhism was going down the drain. "Smith, I distrust any kind of Buddhism or *any* kinda philosophy or social system that puts down sex," said Japhy quite scholarly now that he was done and sitting naked crosslegged rolling himself a

Bull Durham cigarette (which he did as part of his "simplicity" life). It ended up with everybody naked and finally making gay pots of coffee in the kitchen and Princess on the kitchen floor naked with her knees clasped in her arms, lying on her side, just for nothing, just to do it, then finally she and I took a warm bath together in the bathtub and could hear Alvah and Japhy discussing Zen Free Love Lunacy orgies in the other room.

"Hey Princess we'll do this every Thursday night, hey?" yelled Japhy. "It'll be a regular function."

"Yeah," yelled Princess from the bathtub. I'm telling you she was actually glad to do all this and told me "You know, I feel like I'm the mother of all things and I have to take care of my little children."

"You're such a young pretty thing yourself."

"But I'm the old mother of earth. I'm a Bodhisattva." She was just a little off her nut but when I heard her say "Bodhisattva" I realized she wanted to be a big Buddhist like Japhy and being a girl the only way she could express it was this way, which had its traditional roots in the yabyum ceremony of Tibetan Buddhism, so everything was fine.

Alvah was immensely pleased and was all for the idea of "every Thursday night" and so was I by now.

"Alvah, Princess says she's a Bodhisattva."

"Of course she is."

"She says she's the mother of all of us."

"The Bodhisattva women of Tibet and parts of ancient India," said Japhy, "were taken and used as holy concubines in temples and sometimes in ritual caves and would get to lay up a stock of merit and they meditated too. All of them, men and women, they'd meditate, fast, have balls like this, go back to eating, drinking, talking, hike around, live in viharas in the rainy season and outdoors in the dry, there was no question of what to do about sex which is what I always liked about Oriental religion. And what I always dug about the Indians in our country . . . You know when I was a little kid in Oregon I didn't feel that I was an American at all, with all that suburban ideal and sex repression and general dreary newspaper gray censorship of all our real human values but and when I discovered Buddhism and all I suddenly felt that I had lived in a previous lifetime innumerable ages ago and now because of faults and sins in that lifetime I was being degraded to a more grievous domain of existence and my karma was to be born in America where nobody has any fun or believes in anything, especially freedom. That's why I was always sympathetic to freedom movements, too, like anarchism in the Northwest, the oldtime heroes of Everett Massacre and all. . . ." It ended up with long earnest discussions about all these subjects and finally Princess got dressed and went home with Japhy on their bicycles and Alvah and I sat facing each other in the dim red light.

"But you know, Ray, Japhy is really sharp—he's really the wildest craziest sharpest cat we've ever met. And what I love about him is he's the big hero of the West Coast, do you realize I've been out here for two years now and hadn't met anybody worth knowing really or anybody with any truly illuminated intelligence and was giving up hope for the West Coast? Besides all the background he has, in Oriental scholarship, Pound, taking peyote and seeing visions, his mountainclimbing and bhikkuing, wow, Japhy Ryder is a great new hero of American culture."

"He's mad!" I agreed. "And other things I like about him, his quiet sad moments when he don't say much. . . ."

"Gee, I wonder what will happen to him in the end."

"I think he'll end up like Han Shan living alone in the mountains and writing poems on the walls of cliffs, or chanting them to crowds outside his cave."

"Or maybe he'll go to Hollywood and be a movie star, you know he said that the other day, he said 'Alvah you know I've never thought of going to the movies and becoming a star, I can do anything you know, I haven't tried that yet,' and I believe him, he *can* do anything. Did you see the way he had Princess all wrapped around him?"

"Aye indeed" and later that night as Alvah slept I sat under the tree in the yard and looked up at the stars or closed my eyes to meditate and tried to quiet myself down back to my normal self.

Alvah couldn't sleep and came out and lay flat on his back in the grass looking up at the sky, and said "Big steamy clouds going by in the dark up there, it makes me realize we live on an actual planet."

"Close your eyes and you'll see more than that."

"Oh I don't know what you mean by all that!" he said pettishly. He was always being bugged by my little lectures on Samadhi ecstasy, which is the state you reach when you stop everything and stop your mind and you actually with your eyes closed see a kind of eternal multiswarm of electrical Power of some kind ululating in place of just pitiful images and forms of objects, which are, after all, imaginary. And if you don't believe me come back in a billion years and deny it. For what is time? "Don't you think it's much more interesting just to be like Japhy and have girls and studies and good times and really be doing something, than all this silly sitting under trees?"

"Nope," I said, and meant it, and I knew Japhy would agree with me. "All Japhy's doing is amusing himself in the void."

"I don't think so."

"I bet he is. I'm going mountainclimbing with him next week and find out and tell you."

"Well" (sigh), "as for me, I'm just going to go on being Alvah Goldbook and to hell with all this Buddhist bullshit."

"You'll be sorry some day. Why don't you ever understand what I'm trying to tell you: it's with your six senses that you're fooled into believing not only that you have six senses, but that you contact an actual outside world with them. If it wasn't for your eyes, you wouldn't see me. If it wasn't for your ears, you wouldn't hear that airplane. If it wasn't for your nose, you wouldn't smell the midnight mint. If it wasn't for your tongue taster, you wouldn't taste the difference between A and B. If it wasn't for your body, you wouldn't feel Princess. There is no me, no airplane, no mind, no Princess, no nothing, you for krissakes do you want to go on being fooled every damn minute of your life?"

"Yes, that's all I want, I thank God that something has come out of nothing."

"Well, I got news for you, it's the other way around nothing has come out of something, and that something is Dharmakaya, the body of the True Meaning, and that nothing is this and all this twaddle and talk. I'm going to bed."

"Well sometimes I see a flash of illumination in what you're trying to say but believe me I get more of a satori out of Princess than out of words."

"It's a satori of your foolish flesh, you lecher."

"I know my redeemer liveth."

"What redeemer and what liveth?"

"Oh let's cut this out and just live!"

"Balls, when I thought like you, Alvah, I was just as miserable and graspy as you are now. All you want to do is run out there and get laid and get beat up and get screwed up and get old and sick and banged around by samsara, you fucking eternal meat of comeback you you'll deserve it too, I'll say."

"That's not nice. Everybody's tearful and trying to live with what they got. Your Buddhism has made you mean Ray and makes you even afraid to take your clothes off for a simple healthy orgy."

"Well, I did finally, didn't I?"

"But you were coming on so hincty about—Oh let's forget it."

Alvah went to bed and I sat and closed my eyes and thought "This thinking has stopped" but because I had to think it no thinking had stopped, but there did come over me a wave of gladness to know that all this perturbation was just a dream already ended and I didn't have to worry because I wasn't "I" and I prayed that God, or Tathagata, would give me enough time and enough sense and strength to be able to tell people what I knew (as I can't even do properly now) so they'd know what I know and not despair so much. The old tree brooded over me silently, a living thing. I heard a mouse snoring in the garden weeds. The rooftops of Berkeley looked like pitiful living meat sheltering grieving phantoms from the eternality of the heavens which they feared to face. By the time I went to bed I wasn't taken in by no Princess or no desire for no Princess and nobody's disapproval and I felt glad and slept well.

*Poe's symbolism in "The Black Cat" conceals the fear and
dependency upon women and the terror of castration and
impotence that characterize the alcoholic.*

EDGAR ALLAN POE

The Black Cat

For the most wild, yet most homely narrative which I am about to
pen, I neither expect nor solicit belief. Mad indeed would I be to expect
it, in a case where my very senses reject their own evidence. Yet, mad
am I not—and very surely do I not dream. But to-morrow I die, and today I would unburden my soul. My immediate purpose is to place before
the world, plainly, succinctly and without comment a series of mere
household events. In their consequences, these events have terrified—
have tortured—have destroyed me. Yet I will not attempt to expound
them. To me they have presented little but horror, to many they will
seem less terrible than baroques. Hereafter, perhaps, some intellect may
be found which will reduce my phantasm to the commonplace—some
intellect more calm, more logical, and far less excitable than my own,
which will perceive in the circumstances I detail with awe nothing more
than an ordinary succession of very natural causes and effects.

From my infancy I was noted for the docility and humanity of my
disposition. My tenderness of heart was even so conspicuous as to make
me the jest of my companions. I was especially fond of animals, and was
indulged by my parents with a great variety of pets. With these I spent
most of my time, and never was so happy as when feeding and caressing
them. This peculiarity of character grew with my growth, and in my
manhood I derived from it one of my principal sources of pleasure. To
those who have cherished an affection for a faithful and sagacious dog, I
need hardly be at the trouble of explaining the nature or the intensity of
the gratification thus derivable. There is something in the unselfish and
self-sacrificing love of a brute, which goes directly to the heart of him
who has had frequent occasion to test the paltry friendship and gossamer fidelity of mere Man.

1060

I married early, and was happy to find in my wife a disposition not uncongenial with my own. Observing my partiality for domestic pets she lost no opportunity of procuring those of the most agreeable kind. We had birds, goldfish, a fine dog, rabbits, a small monkey and a cat.

This latter was a remarkably large and beautiful animal, entirely black, and sagacious to an astonishing degree. In speaking of his intelligence, my wife, who at heart was not a little tinctured with superstition, made frequent allusion to the ancient popular notion, which regarded all black cats as witches in disguise. Not that she was ever serious upon this point—and I mention the matter at all for no better reason than that it happens, just now, to be remembered.

Pluto—this was the cat's name—was my favorite pet and playmate. I alone fed him, and he attended me wherever I went about the house. It was even with difficulty that I could prevent him from following me through the streets.

Our friendship lasted, in this manner, for several years, during which my general temperament and character—through the instrumentality of the fiend Intemperance—had (I blush to confess it) experienced a radical alteration for the worse. I grew, day by day, more moody, more irritable, more regardless of the feelings of others. I suffered myself to use intemperate language to my wife. At length I even offered her personal violence. My pets, of course, were made to feel the change in my disposition. I not only neglected them, but ill-used them. For Pluto, however, I still retained sufficient regard to restrain me from maltreating him, as I made no scruple of maltreating the rabbits, the monkey or even the dog, when by accident or through affection they came in my way. But my disease grew upon me—for what disease is like alcohol! And at length even Pluto, who was now becoming old, and consequently somewhat peevish—even Pluto began to experience the effects of my ill-temper.

One night, returning home much intoxicated from one of my haunts about town, I fancied that the cat avoided my presence. I seized him, when, in his fright at my violence, he inflicted a slight wound upon my hand with his teeth. The fury of a demon instantly possessed me. I knew myself no longer. My original soul seemed, at once, to take its flight from my body; and a more than fiendish malevolence, gin-nurtured, thrilled every fiber of my frame. I took from my waistcoat pocket a penknife, opened it, grasped the poor beast by the throat, and deliberately cut one of its eyes from the socket! I blush, I burn, I shudder while I pen the damnable atrocity.

When reason returned with the morning—when I had slept off the fumes of the night's debauch—I experienced a sentiment half of horror, half of remorse, for the crime of which I had been guilty; but it was, at best, a feeble and equivocal feeling, and the soul remained untouched. I again plunged into excess, and soon drowned in wine all memory of the deed.

In the meantime the cat slowly recovered The socket of the lost eye presented, it is true, a frightful appearance, but he no longer appeared to suffer any pain. He went about the house as usual, but, as might be expected, fled in extreme terror at my approach. I had so much of my old heart left as to be at first grieved by this evident dislike on the part of a creature which had once so loved me. But this feeling soon gave place to irritation. And then came, as if to my final and irrevocable overthrow, the spirit of perverseness. Of this spirit philosophy takes no account. Yet I am not more sure that my soul lives than I am that perverseness is one of the primitive impulses of the human heart—one of the indivisible primary faculties or sentiments which give direction to the character of man. Who has not, hundreds of times, found himself committing a vile or silly action, for no other reason than because he knows he should not? Have we not a perpetual inclination, in the teeth of our best judgment, to violate that which is Law, merely because we understand it to be such? This spirit of perverseness, I say, came to my final overthrow. It was this unfathomable longing of the soul to vex itself—to offer violence to its own nature—to do wrong for the wrong's sake only—that urged me to continue and finally to consummate the injury I had inflicted upon the unoffending brute. One morning, in cold blood, I slipped a noose about its neck, and hung it to the limb of a tree; hung it with the tears streaming from my eyes and the bitterest remorse at my heart; hung it because I knew that it had loved me, and because I felt it had given me no offense; hung it because I knew that in so doing I was committing a sin—a deadly sin that would so jeopardize my immortal soul as to place it, if such a thing were possible—even beyond the reach of the infinite mercy of the most merciful and most terrible God.

On the night of the day on which this cruel deed was done, I was aroused from sleep by the cry of "fire!" The curtains of my bed were in flames. The whole house was blazing. It was with great difficulty that my wife, a servant and myself made our escape from the conflagration. The destruction was complete. My entire worldly wealth was swallowed up, and I resigned myself thenceforward to despair.

I am above the weakness of seeking to establish a sequence of cause and effect between the disaster and the atrocity. But I am detailing a chain of facts, and wish not to leave even a possible link imperfect. On the day succeeding the fire I visited the ruins. The walls, with one exception, had fallen in. This exception was found in a compartment wall, not very thick, which stood about the middle of the house, and against which had rested the head of my bed. The plastering had here, in great measure, resisted the action of the fire—a fact which I attributed to its having been recently spread. About this wall a dense crowd were collected, and many persons seemed to be examining a particular portion of it with very minute and eager attention. The words "strange!" "singular!" and other similar expressions excited my curiosity. I approached and saw, as if graven in bas-relief upon the white surface, the figure of a gigantic cat. The impression was given with an accuracy truly marvelous. There was a rope about the animal's neck.

When I first beheld this apparition—for I could scarcely regard it as less—my wonder and my terror were extreme. But at length reflection came to my aid. The cat, I remembered, had been hung in a garden adjacent to the house. Upon the alarm of fire this garden had been immediately filled by the crowd—by some one of whom the animal must have been cut from the tree and thrown through an open window into my chamber. This had probably been done with the view of arousing me from sleep. The falling of other walls had compressed the victim of my cruelty into the substance of the freshly spread plaster, the lime of which with the flames, and the ammonia from the carcass, had then accomplished the portraiture as I saw it.

Although I thus readily accounted to my reason, if not altogether to my conscience, for the startling fact just detailed, it did not the less fail to make a deep impression upon my fancy. For months I could not rid myself of the phantasm of the cat; and, during this period, there came back into my spirit a half sentiment that seemed, but was not, remorse. I went so far as to regret the loss of the animal, and to look about me, among the vile haunts which I now habitually frequented, for another pet of the same species and of somewhat similar appearance, with which to supply its place.

One night as I sat, half stupefied, in a den of more than infamy, my attention was suddenly drawn to some black object, reposing upon the head of one of the immense hogsheads of gin, or of rum, which constituted the chief furniture of the apartment. I had been looking steadily at the top of this hogshead for some minutes, and what now caused me surprise was the fact that I had not sooner perceived the object there-upon. I approached it and touched it with my hand. It was a black cat—a very large one—fully as large as Pluto, and closely resembling him in every respect, but only Pluto had not a white hair upon any portion of his body; but this cat had a large, although indefinite, splotch of white, covering nearly the whole region of the breast.

Upon my touching him he immediately arose, purred loudly, rubbed against my hand, and appeared delighted with my notice. This, then, was the very creature of which I was in search. I at once offered to purchase it of the landlord; but this person made no claim to it—knew nothing of it—had never seen it before.

I continued my caresses, and when I prepared to go home the animal evinced a disposition to accompany me. I permitted it to do so, occa-sionally stooping and patting it as I proceeded. When it reached the house it domesticated itself at once, and became immediately a great favorite with my wife.

For my own part, I soon found a dislike to it arising within me. This was just the reverse of what I had anticipated; but—I know not how or why it was—its evident fondness for myself rather disgusted and annoyed me. By slow degrees these feelings of disgust and annoy-ance rose into the bitterness of hatred. I avoided the creature; a certain sense of shame, and the remembrance of my former deed of cruelty, preventing me from physically abusing it. I did not, for some weeks, strike, or otherwise violently ill use it; but gradually—very gradually—I came to look upon it with unutterable loathing, and to flee silently from its odious presence, as from the breath of a pestilence.

What added, no doubt, to my hatred of the beast, was the discovery, on the morning after I brought it home, that, like Pluto, it also had been deprived of one of its eyes. This circumstance, however, only endeared it to my wife, who, as I have already said, possessed, in a high degree, that humanity of feeling which had once been my distinguishing trait, and the source of many of my simplest and purest pleasures.

With my aversion to this cat, however, its partiality for myself seemed to increase. It followed my footsteps with a pertinacity which it would be difficult to make the reader comprehend. Whenever I sat it would crouch beneath my chair or spring upon my knees, covering me with its loathsome caresses. If I arose to walk it would get between my feet, and thus nearly throw me down, or, fastening its long and sharp claws in my dress, clamber, in this manner, to my breast. At such times, although I longed to destroy it with a blow, I was yet withheld from so doing, partly by a memory of my former crime, but chiefly—let me confess it at once—by absolute dread of the beast.

This dread was not exactly a dread of physical evil—and yet I should be at a loss how otherwise to define it. I am almost ashamed to own—yes, even in this felon's cell, I am almost ashamed to own—that the terror and horror with which the animal inspired me had been heightened by one of the merest chimeras it would be possible to conceive. My wife had called my attention more than once, to the character of the mark of white hair, of which I have spoken, and which constituted the sole visible difference between the strange beast and the one I had destroyed. The reader will remember that this mark, although large, had been originally very indefinite; but, by slow degrees—degrees nearly imperceptible, and which for a long time my reason struggled to reject as fanciful—it had, at length, assumed a rigorous distinctness of outline. It was now the representation of an object that I shudder to name—and for this, above all, I loathed and dreaded, and would have rid myself of the monster had I dared—it was now I say the image of a hideous, of a ghastly thing—of the gallows. Oh, mournful and terrible engine of horror and of crime—of agony and of death!

And now was I indeed wretched beyond the wretchedness of mere humanity. And a brute beast, whose fellow I had contemptuously destroyed—a brute beast to work out for me—for me, a man, fashioned in the image of the High God—so much of insufferable woe. Alas! neither by day nor night knew I the blessing of rest any more. During the former the creature left me no moment alone, and in the latter I started hourly from dreams of unutterable fear, to find the hot breath of the thing upon my face, and its vast weight—an incarnate nightmare that I had no power to shake off—incumbent eternally upon my heart.

Beneath the pressure of torments such as these the feeble remnants of the good within me succumbed. Evil thoughts became my sole intimates —the darkest and most evil of thoughts. The moodiness of my usual temper increased to hatred of all things and of all mankind; while, from the sudden, frequent and ungovernable outbursts of a fury to which I now blindly abandoned myself, my uncomplaining wife, alas! was the most usual and the most patient of sufferers.

One day she accompanied me upon some household errand into the cellar of the old building, which our poverty compelled us to inhabit. The cat followed me down the steep stairs, and, nearly throwing me headlong, exasperated me to madness. Uplifting an axe, and forgetting, in my wrath, the childish dread which had hitherto stayed my hand, I aimed a blow at the animal which, of course, would have proved instantly fatal had it descended as I wished. But this blow was arrested by the hand of my wife. Goaded, by the interference, into a rage more than demoniacal, I withdrew my arm from her grasp, and buried the ax in her brain. She fell dead upon the spot, without a groan.

This hideous murder accomplished, I set myself forthwith, and with entire deliberation, to the task of concealing the body. I knew that I could not remove it from the house, either by day or by night, without the risk of being observed by the neighbors. Many projects entered my mind. At one period I thought of cutting the corpse into minute fragments and destroying them by fire. At another I resolved to dig a grave for it in the floor of the cellar. Again, I deliberated about casting it into the well in the yard—about packing it in a box, as if merchandise, with the usual arrangements, and so getting a porter to take it from the house. Finally I hit upon what I considered a far better expedient than either of these. I determined to wall it up in the cellar—as the monks of the middle ages are recorded to have walled up their victims.

For a purpose such as this the cellar was well adapted. Its walls were loosely constructed, and had lately been plastered throughout with a rough plaster, which the dampness of the atmosphere had prevented from hardening. Moreover, in one of the walls was a projection, caused by a false chimney, or fireplace, that had been filled up, and made to resemble the rest of the cellar. I made no doubt that I could readily displace the bricks at this point, insert the corpse, and wall the whole up as before, so that no eye could detect anything suspicious.

And in this calculation I was not deceived. By means of a crowbar I easily dislodged the bricks, and, having carefully deposited the body against the inner wall, I propped it in that position, while, with little trouble, I relaid the whole structure as it originally stood. Having procured mortar, sand and hair with every possible precaution, I prepared a plaster which could not be distinguished from the old, and with this I very carefully went over the new brickwork. When I had finished I felt satisfied that all was right. The wall did not present the slightest appearance of having been disturbed. The rubbish on the floor was picked up with the minutest care. I looked around triumphantly and said to myself, "Here, at least, then, my labor has not been in vain."

My next step was to look for the beast which had been the cause of so much wretchedness, for I had at length firmly resolved to put it to death. Had I been able to meet with it at the moment there could have been no doubt of its fate; but it appeared that the crafty animal had been alarmed at the violence of my previous anger and forebore to present itself in my present mood. It is impossible to describe or to imagine the deep, the blissful sense of relief which the absence of the detested creature occasioned in my bosom. It did not make its appearance during the night—and thus, for one night at least since its introduction into the house, I soundly and tranquilly slept—aye, slept, even with the burden of murder upon my soul!

The second and the third day passed, and still my tormentor came not. Once again I breathed as a free man. The monster, in terror, had fled the premises forever! I should behold it no more! My happiness was supreme! The guilt of my dark deed disturbed me but little. Some few inquiries had been made, but these had been readily answered. Even a search had been instituted—but, of course, nothing was to be discovered. I looked upon my future felicity as secured.

Upon the fourth day of the assassination a party of the police came very unexpectedly into the house and proceeded again to make a rigorous investigation of the premises. Secure, however, in the inscrutability of my place of concealment, I felt no embarrassment whatever. The officers bade me accompany them in their search. They left no nook or corner unexplored. At length, for the third or fourth time, they descended into the cellar. I quivered not in a muscle. My heart beat as calmly as that of one who slumbers in innocence. I walked the cellar from end to end. I folded my arms upon my bosom and roamed easily to and fro. The police were thoroughly satisfied and prepared to depart. The glee at my heart was too strong to be restrained. I burned to say but one word, by way of triumph, and to render doubly sure their assurance of my guiltlessness.

"Gentlemen," I said at last, as the party ascended the steps, "I delight to have allayed your suspicions. I wish you all health and a little more courtesy. By the by, gentlemen, this—this is a very well constructed house." (In the rabid desire to say something easily I scarcely knew what I uttered at all.) "I may say an excellently well constructed house. These walls—are you going, gentlemen?—these walls are solidly put together;" and here, through the mere frenzy of bravado, I rapped heavily, with a cane which I held in my hand, upon that very portion of the brickwork behind which stood the corpse of the wife of my bosom.

But may God shield and deliver me from the fangs of the Arch Fiend! No sooner had the reverberation of my blows sunk into silence than I was answered by a voice from within the tomb!—by a cry, at first muffled and broken, like the sobbing of a child, and then quickly swelling into one long, loud and continuous scream, utterly anomalous and inhuman—a howl!—a wailing shriek, half of horror and half of triumph, such as might have arisen only out of hell, conjointly from the throats of the damned in their agony and of the demons that exult in the damnation.

Of my own thoughts it is folly to speak. Swooning, I staggered to the opposite wall. For an instant the party upon the stairs remained motionless, through extremity of terror and of awe. In the next a dozen stout arms were toiling at the wall. It fell bodily. The corpse, already getting decayed and clotted with gore, stood erect before the eyes of the spectators. Upon its head, with red, extended mouth and solitary eye of fire, sat the hideous beast whose craft had seduced me into murder, and whose informing voice had consigned me to the hangman. I had walled the monster up within the tomb!

*"The Vigilante" makes perfectly clear the intimate rela-
tionship between sexual frustration and prejudice. In the
lynching of a Negro the white man finds release from his
sexual tensions and convinces himself of his own superiority.*

JOHN STEINBECK

The Vigilante

The great surge of emotion, the milling and shouting of the people fell
gradually to silence in the town park. A crowd of people still stood
under the elm trees, vaguely lighted by a blue street light two blocks
away. A tired quiet settled on the people; some members of the mob
began to sneak away into the darkness. The park lawn was cut to pieces
by the feet of the crowd.

Mike knew it was all over. He could feel the let-down in himself. He
was as heavily weary as though he had gone without sleep for several
nights, but it was a dreamlike weariness, a gray comfortable weariness.
He pulled his cap down over his eyes and moved away, but before
leaving the park he turned for one last look.

In the center of the mob someone had lighted a twisted newspaper
and was holding it up. Mike could see how the flame curled about the
feet of the grey naked body hanging from the elm tree. It seemed curious
to him that negroes turn a bluish grey when they are dead. The burning
newspaper lighted the heads of the up-looking men, silent men and
fixed; they didn't move their eyes from the hanged man.

Mike felt a little irritation at whoever it was who was trying to burn
the body. He turned to a man who stood beside him in the near-dark-
ness. "That don't do no good," he said.

The man moved away without replying.

The newspaper torch went out, leaving the park almost black by
contrast. But immediately another twisted paper was lighted and held up
against the feet. Mike moved to another watching man. "That don't do
no good," he repeated. "He's dead now. They can't hurt him none."

1069

The second man grunted but did not look away from the flaming paper. "It's a good job," he said. "This'll save the county a lot of money and no sneaky lawyers getting in."

"That's what I say," Mike agreed. "No sneaky lawyers. But it don't do no good to try to burn him."

The man continued staring toward the flame. "Well, it can't do much harm, either."

Mike filled his eyes with the scene. He felt that he was dull. He wasn't seeing enough of it. Here was a thing he would want to remember later so he could tell about it, but the dull tiredness seemed to cut the sharpness off the picture. His brain told him this was a terrible and important affair, but his eyes and his feelings didn't agree. It was just ordinary. Half an hour before, when he had been howling with the mob and fighting for a chance to help pull on the rope, then his chest had been so full that he had found he was crying. But now everything was dead, everything unreal; the dark mob was made up of stiff lay-figures. In the flamelight the faces were as expressionless as wood. Mike felt the stiffness, the unreality in himself, too. He turned away at last and walked out of the park.

The moment he left the outskirts of the mob a cold loneliness fell upon him. He walked quickly along the street wishing that some other man might be walking beside him. The wide street was deserted, empty, as unreal as the park had been. The two steel lines of the car tracks stretched glimmering away down the street under the electroliers, and the dark store windows reflected the midnight globes.

A gentle pain began to make itself felt in Mike's chest. He felt with his fingers; the muscles were sore. Then he remembered. He was in the front line of the mob when it rushed the closed jail door. A driving line forty men deep had crashed Mike against the door like the head of a ram. He had hardly felt it then, and even now the pain seemed to have the dull quality of loneliness.

Two blocks ahead the burning neon word BEER hung over the sidewalk. Mike hurried toward it. He hoped there would be people there, and talk, to remove this silence; and he hoped the men wouldn't have been to the lynching.

The bartender was alone in his little bar, a small, middle-aged man with a melancholy moustache and an expression like an aged mouse, wise and unkempt and fearful.

He nodded quickly as Mike came in. "You look like you been walking in your sleep," he said.

Mike regarded him with wonder. "That's just how I feel, too, like I been walking in my sleep."

"Well, I can give you a shot if you want."

Mike hesitated. "No—I'm kind of thirsty. I'll take a beer. . . . Was you there?"

The little man nodded his mouse-like head again. "Right at the last, after he was all up and it was all over. I figured a lot of the fellas would be thirsty, so I came back and opened up. Nobody but you so far. Maybe I was wrong."

"They might be along later," said Mike. "There's a lot of them still in the park. They cooled off, though. Some of them trying to burn him with newspapers. That don't do no good."

"Not a bit of good," said the little bartender. He twitched his thin moustache.

Mike knocked a few grains of celery salt into his beer and took a long drink. "That's good," he said. "I'm kind of dragged out."

The bartender leaned close to him over the bar, his eyes were bright. "Was you there all the time—to the jail and everything?"

Mike drank again and then looked through his beer and watched the beads of bubbles rising from the grains of salt in the bottom of the glass. "Everything," he said. "I was one of the first in the jail, and I helped pull on the rope. There's times when citizens got to take the law in their own hands. Sneaky lawyer comes along and gets some fiend out of it."

The mousy head jerked up and down. "You God-dam' right," he said. "Lawyers can get them out of anything. I guess the nigger was guilty all right."

"Oh, sure! Somebody said he even confessed."

The head came close over the bar again. "How did it start, mister? I was only there after it was all over, and then I only stayed a minute and then came back to open up in case any of the fellas might want a glass of beer."

Mike drained his glass and pushed it out to be filled. "Well, of course everybody knew it was going to happen. I was in a bar across from the jail. Been there all afternoon. A guy came in and says, 'What are we waiting for?' So we went across the street, and a lot more guys was there and a lot more come. We all stood there and yelled. Then the sheriff come out and made a speech, but we yelled him down. A guy with a twenty-two rifle went along the street and shot out the street lights. Well, then we rushed the jail doors and bust them. The sheriff wasn't going to do nothing. It wouldn't do him no good to shoot a lot of honest men to save a nigger fiend."

"And election coming on, too," the bartender put in.

"Well, the sheriff started yelling, 'Get the right man, boys, for Christ's sake get the right man. He's in the fourth cell down.'

"It was kind of pitiful," Mike said slowly. "The other prisoners was so scared. We could see them through the bars. I never seen such faces."

The bartender excitedly poured himself a small glass of whiskey and poured it down. "Can't blame 'em much. Suppose you was in for thirty days and a lynch mob came through. You'd be scared they'd get the wrong man."

"That's what I say. It was kind of pitiful. Well, we got to the nigger's cell. He just stood stiff with his eyes closed like he was dead drunk. One of the guys slugged him down and he got up, and then somebody else socked him and he went over and hit his head on the cement floor." Mike leaned over the bar and tapped the polished wood with his forefinger. " 'Course this is only my idea, but I think that killed him. Because I helped get his clothes off, and he never made a wiggle, and when we strung him up he didn't jerk around none. No, sir. I think he was dead all the time, after that second guy smacked him."

"Well, it's all the same in the end."

"No, it ain't. You like to do the thing right. He had it coming to him, and he should have got it." Mike reached into his trousers pocket and brought out a piece of torn blue denim. "That's a piece of the pants he had on."

The bartender bent close and inspected the cloth. He jerked his head up at Mike. "I'll give you a buck for it."

"Oh no, you won't!"

"All right. I'll give you two bucks for half of it."

Mike looked suspiciously at him. "What you want it for?"

"Here! Give me your glass! Have a beer on me. I'll pin it up on the wall with a little card under it. The fellas that come in will like to look at it."

Mike haggled the piece of cloth in two with his pocket knife and accepted two silver dollars from the bartender.

"I know a show card writer," the little man said. "Comes in every day. He'll print me up a nice little card to go under it." He looked wary. "Think the sheriff will arrest anybody?"

" 'Course not. What's he want to start any trouble for? There was a lot of votes in that crowd tonight. Soon as they all go away, the sheriff will come and cut the nigger down and clean up some."

The bartender looked toward the door. "I guess I was wrong about the fellas wanting a drink. It's getting late."

"I guess I'll get along home. I feel tired."

"If you go south, I'll close up and walk a ways with you. I live on south Eighth."

"Why, that's only two blocks from my house. I live on south Sixth. You must go right past my house. Funny I never saw you around."

The bartender washed Mike's glass and took off the long apron. He put on his hat and coat, walked to the door and switched off the red neon sign and the house lights. For a moment the two men stood on the sidewalk looking back toward the park. The city was silent. There was no sound from the park. A policeman walked along a block away, turning his flash into the store windows.

"You see?" said Mike. "Just like nothing happened."

"Well, if the fellas wanted a glass of beer they must have gone some-place else."

"That's what I told you," said Mike.

They swung along the empty street and turned south, out of the business district. "My name's Welch," the bartender said. "I only been in this town about two years."

The loneliness had fallen on Mike again. "It's funny—" he said, and then, "I was born right in this town, right in the house I live in now. I got a wife but no kids. Both of us born right in this town. Everybody knows us."

They walked on for a few blocks. The stores dropped behind and the nice houses with bushy gardens and cut lawns lined the street. The tall shade trees were shadowed on the sidewalk by the street lights. Two night dogs went slowly by, smelling at each other.

Welch said softly—"I wonder what kind of a fella he was—the nigger, I mean."

Mike answered out of his loneliness. "The papers all said he was a fiend. I read all the papers. That's what they all said."

"Yes, I read them, too. But it makes you wonder about him. I've known some pretty nice niggers."

Mike turned his head and spoke protestingly. "Well, I've knew some dam' fine niggers myself. I've worked right 'longside some niggers and they was as nice as any white man you could want to meet.—But not no fiends."

His vehemence silenced little Welch for a moment. Then he said, "You couldn't tell, I guess, what kind of a fella he was?"

"No—he just stood there stiff, with his mouth shut and his eyes tight closed and his hands right down at his sides. And then one of the guys smacked him. It's my idea he was dead when we took him out."

Welch sidled close on the walk. "Nice gardens along here. Must take a lot of money to keep them up." He walked even closer, so that his shoulder touched Mike's arm. "I never been to a lynching. How's it make you feel—afterwards?"

Mike shied away from the contact. "It don't make you feel nothing." He put down his head and increased his pace. The little bartender had nearly to trot to keep up. The street lights were fewer. It was darker and safer. Mike burst out, "Makes you feel kind of cut off and tired, but kind of satisfied, too. Like you done a good job—but tired and kind of sleepy." He slowed his steps. "Look, there's a light in the kitchen. That's where I live. My old lady's waiting up for me." He stopped in front of his little house.

Welch stood nervously beside him. "Come into my place when you want a glass of beer—or a shot. Open till midnight. I treat my friends right." He scampered away like an aged mouse.

Mike called. "Good night."

He walked around the side of his house and went in the back door. His thin, petulant wife was sitting by the open gas oven warming herself. She turned complaining eyes on Mike where he stood in the doorway.

The her eyes widened and hung on his face. "You been with a woman," she said hoarsely. "What woman you been with?"

Mike laughed. "You think you're pretty slick, don't you? You're a slick one, ain't you? What makes you think I been with a woman?"

She said fiercely, "You think I can't tell by the look on your face that you been with a woman?"

"All right," said Mike. "If you're so slick and know-it-all, I won't tell you nothing. You can just wait for the morning paper."

He saw doubt come into the dissatisfied eyes. "Was it the nigger?" she asked. "Did they get the nigger? Everybody said they was going to."

"Find out for yourself if you're so slick. I ain't going to tell you nothing."

He walked through the kitchen and went into the bathroom. A little mirror hung on the wall. Mike took off his cap and looked at his face. "By God, she was right," he thought. "That's just exactly how I do feel."

Although no one is sure of what causes childhood schizo-phrenia, psychoanalysts have often observed that mothers of these ego-less children often act unconsciously as if their children were invisible. Like the witch in the story, the spell of invisibility is cast so that the mother may keep the child to herself. Ability to express their sexual and aggressive feel-ings is often the first sign of any improvement in the reality testing of such children. Interestingly, the little boy in this tale gains his freedom and identity the moment he makes his hatred and aggression known.

RAY BRADBURY

Invisible Boy

She took the great iron spoon and the mummified frog and gave it a bash and made dust of it, and talked to the dust while she ground it in her stony fists quickly. Her beady gray bird-eyes flickered at the cabin. Each time she looked, a head in the small thin window ducked as if she'd fired off a shotgun.

"Charlie!" cried Old Lady. "You come outa there! I'm fixing a lizard magic to unlock that rusty door! You come out now and I won't make the earth shake or the trees go up in fire or the sun set at high noon!"

The only sound was the warm mountain light on the high turpentine trees, a tufted squirrel chittering around and around on a green-furred log, the ants moving in a fine brown line at Old Lady's bare, blue-veined feet.

"You been starving in there two days, darn you!" she panted, chiming the spoon against a flat rock, causing the plump gray miracle bag to swing at her waist. Sweating sour, she rose and marched at the cabin, bearing the pulverized flesh. "Come out, now!" She flicked a pinch of powder inside the lock. "All right, I'll come get you!" she wheezed.

She spun the knob with one walnut-colored hand, first one way, then the other. "O Lord," she intoned, "fling this door wide!"

When nothing flung, she added yet another philter and held her breath. Her long blue untidy skirt rustled as she peered into her bag of darkness to see if she had any scaly monsters there, any charm finer than the frog she'd killed months ago for such a crisis as this.

She heard Charlie breathing against the door. His folks had pranced off into some Ozark town early this week, leaving him, and he'd run almost six miles to Old Lady for company—she was by way of being an aunt or cousin or some such, and he didn't mind her fashions.

But then, two days ago, Old Lady, having gotten used to the boy around, decided to keep him for convenient company. She pricked her thin shoulder bone, drew out three blood pearls, spat wet over her right elbow, tromped on a crunch-cricket, and at the same instant clawed her left hand at Charlie, crying, "My son you are, you are my son, for all eternity!"

Charlie, bounding like a startled hare, had crashed off into the bush, heading for home.

But Old Lady, skittering quick as a gingham lizard, cornered him in a dead end, and Charlie holed up in this old hermit's cabin and wouldn't come out, no matter how she whammed door, window, or knothole with amber-colored fist or trounced her ritual fires, explaining to him that he was certainly her son *now*, all right.

"Charlie, you *there*?" she asked, cutting holes in the door planks with her bright little slippery eyes.

"I'm all of me here," he replied finally, very tired.

Maybe he would fall out on the ground any moment. She wrestled the knob hopefully. Perhaps a pinch too much frog powder had grated the lock wrong. She always overdid or underdid her miracles, she mused angrily, never doing them just *exact*, Devil take it!

"Charlie, I only wants someone to night-prattle to, someone to warm hands with at the fire. Someone to fetch kindling for me mornings, and fight off the spunks that come creeping of early fogs! I ain't got no fetchings on you for myself, son, just for your company." She smacked her lips. "Tell you what, Charles, you come out and I *teach* you things!"

"What things?" he suspicioned.

"Teach you how to buy cheap, sell high. Catch a snow weasel, cut off its head, carry it warm in your hind pocket. There!"

"Aw," said Charlie.

She made haste. "Teach you to make yourself shotproof. So if anyone bangs at you with a gun, nothing happens."

When Charlie stayed silent, she gave him the secret in a high fluttering whisper. "Dig and stitch mouse-ear roots on Friday during full moon, and wear 'em around your neck in a white silk."

"You're *crazy*," Charlie said.

"Teach you how to stop blood or make animals stand frozen or make blind horses see, all them things I'll teach you! Teach you to cure a swelled-up cow and unbewitch a goat. Show you how to make yourself invisible!"

"Oh," said Charlie.

Old Lady's heart beat like a Salvation tambourine.

The knob turned from the other side.

"You," said Charlie, "are funning me."

"No, I'm not," exclaimed Old Lady. "Oh, Charlie, why, I'll make you like a window, see right through you. Why, child, you'll be surprised!"

"Real invisible?"

"Real invisible!"

"You won't fetch onto me if I walk out?"

"Won't touch a bristle of you, son."

"Well," he drawled reluctantly, "all right."

The door opened. Charlie stood in his bare feet, head down, chin against chest. "Make me invisible," he said.

"First we got to catch us a bat," said Old Lady. "Start lookin'!"

She gave him some jerky beef for his hunger and watched him climb a tree. He went high up and high up and it was nice seeing him there and it was nice having him here and all about after so many years alone with nothing to say good morning to but bird-droppings and silvery snail tracks.

Pretty soon a bat with a broken wing fluttered down out of the tree. Old Lady snatched it up, beating warm and shrieking between its porcelain white teeth, and Charlie dropped down after it, hand upon clenched hand, yelling.

That night, with the moon nibbling at the spiced pine cones, Old Lady extracted a long silver needle from under her wide blue dress. Gumming her excitement and secret anticipation, she sighted up the dead bat and held the cold needle steady-steady.

She had long ago realized that her miracles, despite all perspirations and salts and sulphurs, failed. But she had always dreamt that one day the miracles might start functioning, might spring up in crimson flowers and silver stars to prove that God had forgiven her for her pink body and her pink thoughts and her warm body and her warm thoughts as a young miss. But so far God had made no sign and said no word, but nobody knew this except Old Lady.

"Ready?" she asked Charlie, who crouched cross-kneed, wrapping his pretty legs in long goose-pimpled arms, his mouth open, making teeth. "Ready," he whispered, shivering.

"There!" She plunged the needle deep in the bat's right eye. "So!"

"Oh!" screamed Charlie, wadding up his face.

"Now I wrap it in gingham, and here, put it in your pocket, keep it there, bat and all. Go on!"

He pocketed the charm.

"Charlie!" she shrieked fearfully. "Charlie, where *are* you? I can't *see* you, child!"

"Here!" He jumped so the light ran in red streaks up his body. "I'm here, Old Lady!" He stared wildly at his arms, legs, chest, and toes. "I'm here!"

Her eyes looked as if they were watching a thousand fireflies crisscrossing each other in the wild night air.

"Charlie, oh, you went *fast*! Quick as a hummingbird! Oh, Charlie, come *back* to me!"

"But I'm *here*!" he wailed.

"Where?"

"By the fire, the fire! And—and I can see myself. I'm not invisible at all!"

Old Lady rocked on her lean flanks. "Course you can see *you*! Every invisible person knows himself. Otherwise, how could you eat, walk, or get around places? Charlie, touch me. Touch me so I *know* you."

Uneasily he put out a hand.

She pretended to jerk, startled, at his touch. *"Ah!"*

"You mean to say you can't *find* me?" he asked. "Truly?"

"Not the least half rump of you!"

She found a tree to stare at, and stared at it with shining eyes, careful not to glance at him. "Why, I sure *did* a trick *that* time!" She sighed with wonder. "Whooeee. Quickest invisible I *ever* made! Charlie. Charlie, how you *feel*?"

"Like creek water—all stirred."

"You'll settle."

Then after a pause she added. "Well, what you going to do now, Charlie, since you're invisible?"

All sorts of things shot through his brain, she could tell. Adventures stood up and danced like hell-fire in his eyes, and his mouth, just hanging, told what it meant to be a boy who imagined himself like the mountain winds. In a cold dream he said, "I'll run across wheat fields, climb snow mountains, steal white chickens off'n farms. I'll pick pink pigs when they ain't looking. I'll pinch pretty girls' legs when they sleep, snap their garters in schoolrooms." Charlie looked at Old Lady, and from the shiny tips of her eyes she saw something wicked shape his face. "And other things I'll do, I'll do, I will," he said.

"Don't try nothing on me," warned Old Lady. "I'm brittle as spring ice and I don't take handling." Then: "What about your folks?"

"My folks?"

"You can't fetch yourself home looking like that. Scare the inside ribbons out of them. Your mother'd faint straight back like timber falling. Think they want you about the house to stumble over and your ma have to call you every three minutes, even though you're in the room next her elbow?"

Charlie had not considered it. He sort of simmered down and whispered out a little "Gosh" and felt of his long bones carefully.

"You'll be mighty lonesome. People looking through you like a water glass, people knocking you aside because they don't reckon you to be underfoot. And women, Charlie, *women*——"

He swallowed. "What about women?"

"No woman will be giving you a second stare. And no woman wants to be kissed by a boy's mouth they can't even *find*!"

Charlie dug his bare toe in the soil contemplatively. He pouted. "Well, I'll stay invisible, anyway, for a spell. I'll have me some fun. I'll just be pretty careful, is all. I'll stay out from in front of wagons and horses and Pa. Pa shoots at the nariest sound." Charlie blinked. "Why, with me invisible, someday Pa might just up and fill me with buckshot, thinkin' I was a hill squirrel in the dooryard. Oh . . ."

Old Lady nodded at a tree. "That's likely."

"Well," he decided slowly, "I'll stay invisible for tonight, and tomorrow you can fix me back all whole again, Old Lady."

"Now if that ain't just like a critter, always wanting to be what he can't be," remarked Old Lady to a beetle on a log.

"What you mean?" said Charlie.

"Why," she explained, "it was real hard work, fixing you up. It'll take a little *time* for it to wear off. Like a coat of paint wears off, boy."

"You!" he cried. "You did this to me! Now you make me back, you make me seeable!"

"Hush," she said. "It'll wear off, a hand or a foot at a time."

"How'll it look, me around the hills with just one hand showing!"

"Like a five-winged bird hopping on the stones and bramble."

"Or a foot showing!"

"Like a small pink rabbit jumping thicket."

"Or my head floating!"

"Like a hairy balloon at the carnival!"

"How long before I'm *whole*?" he asked.

She deliberated that it might pretty well be an entire year.

He groaned. He began to sob and bite his lips and make fists.

"You magicked me, you did this, you did this thing to me. Now I won't be able to run home!"

She winked. "But you *can* stay here, child, stay on with me real comfort-like, and I'll keep you fat and saucy."

He flung it out: "You did this on purpose! You mean old hag, you want to keep me here!"

He ran off through the shrubs on the instant.

"Charlie, come back!"

No answer but the pattern of his feet on the soft dark turf, and his wet choking cry which passed swiftly off and away.

She waited and then kindled herself a fire. "He'll be back," she whispered. And thinking inward on herself, she said, "And now I'll have me my company through spring and into late summer. Then, when I'm tired of him and want a silence, I'll send him home."

Charlie returned noiselessly with the first gray of dawn, gliding over the rimed turf to where Old Lady sprawled like a bleached stick before the scattered ashes.

He sat on some creek pebbles and stared at her.

She didn't dare look at him or beyond. He had made no sound, so how could she know he was anywhere about? She couldn't.

He sat there, tear marks on his cheeks.

Pretending to be just waking—but she had found no sleep from one end of the night to the other—Old Lady stood up, grunting and yawning, and turned in a circle to the dawn.

"Charlie?"

Her eyes passed from pines to soil, to sky, to the far hills. She called out his name, over and over again, and she felt like staring plumb straight at him, but she stopped herself. "Charlie? Oh, Charles!" she called, and heard the echoes say the very same.

He sat, beginning to grin a bit, suddenly, knowing he was close to her, yet she must feel alone. Perhaps he felt the growing of a secret power, perhaps he felt secure from the world, certainly he was *pleased* with his invisibility.

She said aloud, "Now where *can* that boy be? If he only made a noise so I could tell just where he is, maybe I'd fry him a breakfast."

She prepared the morning victuals, irritated at his continuous quiet. She sizzled bacon on a hickory stick. "The smell of it will draw his nose," she muttered.

While her back was turned he swiped all the frying bacon and devoured it tastily.

She whirled, crying out, "Lord!"

She eyed the clearing suspiciously. "Charlie, that you?"

Charlie wiped his mouth clean on his wrists.

She trotted about the clearing, making like she was trying to locate him. Finally, with a clever thought, acting blind, she headed straight for him, groping. "Charlie, where *are* you?"

A lightning streak, he evaded her, bobbing, ducking.

It took all her will power not to give chase; but you can't chase invisible boys, so she sat down, scowling, sputtering, and tried to fry more bacon. But every fresh strip she cut he would steal bubbling off the fire and run away far. Finally, cheeks burning, she cried, "I know where you are! Right *there*! I hear you run!" She pointed to one side of *him*, not too accurate. He ran again. "Now you're there!" she shouted. "There, and there!" pointing to all the places he was in the next five minutes. "I hear you press a grass blade, knock a flower, snap a twig. I got fine shell ears, delicate as roses. They can hear the stars moving!"

Silently he galloped off among the pines, his voice trailing back, "Can't hear me when I'm set on a rock. I'll just *set*!"

All day he sat on an observatory rock in the clear wind, motionless and sucking his tongue.

Old Lady gathered wood in the deep forest, feeling his eyes weaseling on her spine. She wanted to babble: "Oh, I see you, I see you! I was only fooling about invisible boys! You're right there!" But she swallowed her gall and gummed it tight.

The following morning he did the spiteful things. He began leaping from behind trees. He made toad-faces, frog-faces, spider-faces at her, clenching down his lips with his fingers, popping his raw eyes, pushing up his nostrils so you could peer in and see his brain thinking.

Once she dropped her kindling. She pretended it was a blue jay startled her.

He made a motion as if to strangle her.

She trembled a little.

He made another move as if to bang her shins and spit on her cheek.

These motions she bore without a lid-flicker or a mouth-twitch.

He stuck out his tongue, making strange bad noises. He wiggled his loose ears so she wanted to laugh, and finally she did laugh and explained it away quickly by saying, "Sat on a salamander! Whew, how it poked!"

By high noon the whole madness boiled to a terrible peak.

For it was at that exact hour that Charlie came racing down the valley stark boy-naked!

Old Lady nearly fell flat with shock!

"Charlie!" she almost cried.

Charlie raced naked up one side of a hill and naked down the other—naked as day, naked as the moon, raw as the sun and a newborn chick, his feet shimmering and rushing like the wings of a low-skimming hummingbird.

Old Lady's tongue locked in her mouth. What could she say? Charlie, go dress? For *shame*? *Stop* that? *Could* she? Oh, Charlie, Charlie, God! Could she say that now? *Well*?

Upon the big rock, she witnessed him dancing up and down, naked as the day of his birth, stomping bare feet, smacking his hands on his knees and sucking in and out his white stomach like blowing and deflating a circus balloon.

She shut her eyes tight and prayed.

After three hours of this she pleaded, "Charlie, Charlie, come here! I got something to *tell* you!"

Like a fallen leaf he came, dressed again, praise the Lord.

"Charlie," she said, looking at the pine trees, "I see your right toe. *There* it is."

"You do?" he said.

"Yes," she said very sadly. "There it is like a horny toad on the grass. And there, up there's your left ear hanging on the air like a pink butterfly."

Charlie danced. "I'm forming in, I'm forming in!"

Old Lady nodded. "Here comes your ankle!"

"Gimme *both* my feet!" ordered Charlie.

"You got 'em."

"How about my hands?"

"I see one crawling on your knee like a daddy longlegs."

"How about the other one?"

"It's crawling too."

"I got a body?"

"Shaping up fine."

"I'll need my head to go home, Old Lady."

To go home, she thought wearily. "No!" she said, stubborn and angry. "No, you ain't got no head. No head at all," she cried. She'd leave that to the very last. "No head, no head," she insisted.

"No head?" he wailed.

"Yes, oh my God, yes, yes, you got your blamed head!" she snapped, giving up. "Now, fetch me back my bat with the needle in his eye!"

He flung it at her. "Haaaa-yoooo!" His yelling went all up the valley, and long after he had run toward home she heard his echoes, racing.

Then she plucked up her kindling with a great dry weariness and started back toward her shack, sighing, talking. And Charlie followed her all the way, *really* invisible now, so she couldn't see him, just hear him, like a pine cone dropping or a deep underground stream trickling, or a squirrel clambering a bough; and over the fire at twilight she and Charlie sat, him so invisible, and her feeding him bacon he wouldn't take, so she ate it herself, and then she fixed some magic and fell asleep with Charlie, made out of sticks and rags and pebbles, but still warm and her very own son, slumbering and nice in her shaking mother arms . . . and they talked about golden things in drowsy voices until dawn made the fire slowly, slowly wither out. . . .

"Mrs. Razor" is a classic tale that reflects exactly the confusion voiced by Dr. Bettelheim's mother. The parents' willingness to accept the child's fantasy, their actual participation in it serves to convince the child of its reality and does not answer her anguished cry for help.

JAMES STILL

Mrs. Razor

"We'll have to do something about that child," Father said. We sat in the kitchen, eating our supper, though day held and the chickens had not yet gone to roost in the gilly trees. Elvy was crying behind the stove, and her throat was raw with sobbing. Morg and I paused, bread in hand, and glanced over our shoulders. The firebox of the Cincinnati stove winked, the iron flowers of the oven throbbed with heat. Mother tipped a finger to her lips, motioning Father to hush. Father's voice lifted:—

"I figure a small thrashing would make her leave off this foolish notion."

Elvy was six years old. She was married, to hear her tell it, and had three children and a lazy shuck of a husband who cared not a mite for his own and left his family to live upon her kin. The thought had grown into truth in her mind. I could play at being Brother Hemp Leckett, climb onto a chopblock and preach to the fowls; or I could be Round George Harks, riding the creeks, killing all who crossed my path; I could be any man body. Morg couldn't make-believe; he was just Morg. But Elvy had imagined herself old and thrown away by a husband, and she kept believing.

"A day will come," Elvy told us, "when my man's going to get killed down dead, the way he's living." She spoke hard of her husband and was a shrew of a wife who thought only of her children; she was as busy with her young as a hen with biddies. It was a dog's life she led, washing rags of clothes, sewing with a straw needle, singing by the half hour to cradled arms, and keeping an eye sharp for gypsies. She jerked at loose garments and fastened and pinned, as Mother did to us.

Once we spied her in the grape arbor making to put a jacket on a baby that wouldn't hold still. She slapped the air, saying, "Hold up, young'un!" Morg stared, half believing. Later she claimed her children were stolen. It wasn't by the dark people. Her husband had taken them —she didn't know where. For days she sat pale and small, minced her victuals, and fretted in her sleep. She had wept, "My man's the meanest critter ever was. Old Scratch is bound to get him."

And now Elvy's husband was dead. She had run to Mother to tell this thing, the news having come in an unknown way. She waited dry-eyed and shocked until Father rode in from the fields in middle afternoon and she met him at the barn gate to choke out her loss.

"We've got to haste to Biggety Creek and fetch my chaps ere the gypsies come," she grieved. "They're left alone."

"Doornail dead?" Father had asked, smiling to hear Biggety Creek named, the Nowhere Place he had told us of once at table: Biggety Creek where heads are the size of water buckets, where noses are turned up like old shoes, women wear skillets for hats, and men screw their breeches on, and where people are so proper they eat with little fingers pointing, and one pea at a time. Father rarely missed a chance to preach us a sermon.

"We've got to haste," Elvy pled.

"Do you know the road to Biggety Creek?"

Elvy nodded.

Father keened his eyes to see what manner of chap was his own, his face lengthening and his patience wearing thin. He grabbed his hat off and clapped it angrily against his leg; he strode into the barn, fed the mules, and came to the house with Elvy tagging after and weeping.

"Fix an early supper," he told Mother.

Father's jaws were set as he drew his chair to the table. The day was still so bright the wall bore a shadow of the unkindled lamp. Elvy had hidden behind the stove, lying on the cat's pallet, crying. "Come and eat your victuals," Mother begged, for her idea was to humor children and let them grow out of their notions. But Elvy would not.

2

We knew Father's hand itched for a hickory switch. Disobedience angered him quicker than anything. Yet he only looked worried. The summer long he had teased Elvy, trying to shake her belief. Once while shaving he had asked, "What ever made you marry that lump of a husband, won't come home, never furnishes a cent?" Morg and I stood by to spread the leftover lather on our faces and scrape it off with a kitchen knife. "I say it's past strange I've not met my own son-in-law. I hunger to shake his hand and welcome him to the family, ask him to sit down to our board and stick his feet under."

Father had glanced slyly at Elvy. "What's his name? Upon my honor I haven't been told."

Elvy looked up. Her eyes glassed in thought. "He's called Razor."

"Given name or family?"

"Just Razor."

"Ask him to come," Father urged in mock seriousness. "Invite him up for Sunday dinner."

Elvy had promised that her husband would come. She had Mother fry a chicken, the dish he liked best, claiming the gizzard was his chosen morsel. Nothing less than the flax tablecloth was good enough, and she gathered spiderwort blossoms for the centerpiece. An extra chair was placed, and we waited; we waited noon through, until one o'clock. Then she told us confidentially, "Go ahead and eat. Razor allus was slow as Jim Christmas." She carried a bowl of soup behind the Cincinnati stove to feed her children. In the evening she explained, "I've learnt why my man stayed away. He hain't got a red cent to his pocket and he's scared o' being lawed for not supporting his chaps."

Father had replied, "I need help—need a workhand to grub corn ground. A dollar a day I'll pay, greenback on the barrel top. I want a feller with lard in his elbows and willing to work. Fighting sourwood sprouts is like going to war. If Razor has got the measure of the job, I'll hire him and promise not to law."

"I ought never to a-took him for a husband," Elvy confessed. "When first I married he was smart as ants. Now he's turned so lazy he won't even fasten his gallus buckles. He's slouchy and no 'count."

"Humm," Father had grunted, eyeing Morg and me, the way our clothes hung on us. "Sloth works on a feller," he preached. "It grows roots. He'll start letting his sleeves flare and shirttail go hang. One day he gets too sorry to bend and lace his shoes, and it's a *swarp, swarp* every step. A time comes he'll not latch the top button of his breeches— ah, when a man turns his potty out, he's beyond cure."

"That's Razor all over," Elvy had said.

Father's teasing had done no good. As we sat at supper that late afternoon, listening to Elvy sob behind the stove, Morg began to stare into his plate and could eat no more. He believed Elvy. Tears hung on his chin.

Father's face tightened, half in anger, half in dismay. He lifted his hands in defeat. "Hell's bangers!" he blurted.

I whispered to Morg, "Razor is a lie-tale." Morg's tears fell thicker. I spoke small into his ear, "Act it's not so," but Morg could never make-like.

Father suddenly thrust back his chair. "Hurry and get ready," he ordered, "the whole push of you. We're going to Biggety Creek." His voice was as dry as a stick.

Elvy's sobbing hushed. Morg blinked. The room became so quiet I could hear flames eating wood in the firebox. Father arose and made long-legged strides toward the barn to harness the mules.

We mounted the wagon, Father and Mother to the spring seat, Elvy settling between; I stood with Morg behind the seat. Dusk was creeping out of the hollows. Chickens walked toward the gilly trees, flew to their roosts, sleepy and quarrelsome. Father gathered the reins and angled the whip to start the mules. "Now, which way?" he asked Elvy. She pointed ahead and we rode off.

The light faded. Night came. The shapes of trees and fences were lost and there were only the wise eyes of the mules to pick the road when the ground had melted and the sky was gone. Elvy nodded fitfully, trying to keep awake. We traveled six miles before Father turned back.

Among all the brilliant passages in Remembrance of Things Past *one, describing Proust's earliest recollection of his mother, stands out with singular luminosity. This passage appears both at the beginning and the end of the book to clarify the author's growing understanding of his symbolic conquest of his mother and of the guilt that his conquest evoked.*

MARCEL PROUST

FROM *Swann's Way*

I knew very well that my brain was a rich mineral basin where there was a vast area of extremely varied precious deposits. But would I have time to exploit them? I was the only person able to do this, for two reasons: with my death there would disappear, not only the one miner able to extract the minerals but the deposit itself; now, when I returned home presently, a collision between the auto I took and another would suffice to destroy my body and to force my mind to abandon my new ideas for all time. And, by a strange coincidence, this rational fear of danger was developing in me at a time when the idea of death had been for only a short while a matter of indifference to me. The fear of ceasing to be myself had formerly caused me horror and especially with each new love that came to me—for Gilberte, for Albertine—because I could not endure the idea that one day he who loved them would exist no longer, which would be a sort of death. But, after this fear had recurred many times, it was naturally transmitted into a confident serenity.

While the idea of death had thus in those days cast a shadow over love for me, for a long time now the remembrance of love had aided me to contemplate death without fear, for I understood that it was no new thing to die but that, on the contrary, I had already died many times since childhood. To take the most recent period—had I not clung to Albertine even more than to life itself? Could I at that time have conceived of myself without my love for her continuing to form part of me?

Now, I no longer loved her; I was not the person who used to love her
but a different person who did not love her; I had ceased to love her
when I had become another person. But I did not suffer on account of
having become this other person and having ceased to love Albertine;
and, assuredly, some day no longer to have my body could in no wise
appear to me as sad a thing as formerly had seemed to me the idea of
some day no longer loving Albertine. And yet how unimportant it now
appeared to me not to love her any more. These successive deaths, so
dreaded by the 'me' they were to obliterate, but so gentle and inconse-
quential once they had become a fact and when he who had feared them
was no longer there to feel them, had a while before made me realise
how unintelligent it would be to be afraid of death. And it was now,
shortly after I had become indifferent to death, that I was beginning
anew to fear it—under another form, it is true, and not for myself but
for my book, to the full flowering of which this life, menaced by so
many dangers, was, at least for a while, indispensable. Victor Hugo said,

Il faut que l'herbe pousse et que les enfants meurent.

But I say that it is the cruel law of art that human beings should die and
that we ourselves must die after exhausting the gamut of suffering so
that the grass, not of oblivion but of eternal life, may grow, the thick
grass of fecund works of art, on which future generations will come and
gaily have their 'picnic lunch,' without a thought for those who sleep
beneath. I said 'external dangers,' but there are internal dangers also. If
I escaped an accident from without, who knows whether I might not be
prevented from making full use of this merciful favour through some
mischance occurring within myself, some internal catastrophe, some
cerebral accident, before the months had passed that were needed for
the writing of this book?

Even the cerebral accident was not necessary. Some symptoms—
indicated to me by a peculiar mental void and a tendency to forget
things and have them come back to me only by accident, just as, when
you are putting certain objects in order, you come across one you had
forgotten and had not even thought to look for—made me feel like a
miser whose broken treasure chest had allowed his riches to slip away
one by one.

When I should return home presently through the Champs-Elysées,
what guarantee had I that I would not be struck with the same malady
as was my grandmother one afternoon when she had come there with
me for a stroll which was to be her last, without her suspecting it,

unconscious, as are we all, that the minute-hand now stands over the very point where the spring will be released to strike the hour? Possibly the fear of having already consumed almost the entire minute which precedes the first stroke of the hour and during which the stroke is making ready to fall, possibly the fear that it was about to be set in motion in my brain, was a sort of obscure sense of what was going to happen, a reflexion in the consciousness, so to speak, of the precarious condition of the brain, the arteries of which are about to give way—which is no more impossible than the sudden conviction of approaching death which many a wounded man has so clearly that, although he has retained his mental lucidity and both the physician and his own desire to live seek to deceive him, he says, foreseeing what is going to happen, "I am going to die, I am ready," and he writes his farewell to his wife.

This obscure sense of what was going to happen was conveyed to me by the strange thing which occurred before I had begun my book and which befell me in a manner I would never have expected. When I went out one evening, my friends thought me looking better than before; they expressed surprise that my hair was still black. But three times I nearly fell as I went down the stairs. I was away only two hours and yet, when I got home, I felt as if I had no memory, no power to think, no strength, no life at all. If someone had come to see me, to proclaim me king, to lay hold of me, to arrest me, I would have let them do to me whatever they wished without uttering a word or opening my eyes, like the people crossing the Caspian Sea who are taken with the worst form of seasickness and do not even make a feeble gesture of resistance when they are told they are going to be thrown overboard. Strictly speaking, I had no particular illness but I felt as though I had become incapable of anything, as frequently happens to an old man who, active the day before, breaks his hip or has an attack of indigestion and may for some time to come lead a bedridden existence which is only a more or less long preparation for the now inevitable end. One of my various selves—the one who used to go to those barbaric banquets called formal dinners, where for the white-shirted men and the semi-nude, feather-bedecked women values are so reversed that anyone who does not come, after accepting the invitation, or does not arrive until the roast is being served, commits a more reprehensible act than the immoral conduct discussed so lightly in the course of the dinner along with recent deaths, and where death or serious illness are the only excuses for not coming (and then only provided you notify your hostess of your dying condition in time for her to invite a fourteenth person)—that self within me had kept his society scruples and lost his memory. My other self, on the contrary, the one who had reached a clear conception of his task, had not forgotten. I had received an invitation from Mme. Molé and had learned that Mme. Sazerat's son was dead. I made up my mind to waste in sending apologies to Mme. Molé and condolences to Mme. Sazerat one of those hours after which, my tongue paralysed, as was the case with my grandmother during her last illness, I would no longer be able to utter a word or even swallow some milk. But a few minutes later I had forgotten that I was to do this. Fortunate forgetfulness, as the remembrance of my work was vigilant and would employ in laying the first foundations the hour of extra existence which had thus reverted to me. Unluckily, as I took up a notebook to start writing, Mme. Molé's card of invitation slipped in front of me. Straightway my forgetful self which, however, took precedence over the other, as happens with all scrupulous barbarians who attend formal dinners, pushed the notebook aside and wrote to Mme. Molé—who, by the way, would doubtless have thought very highly of me for it, had she learned that I had put my reply to her invitation ahead of my architectural labours. Suddenly a remark in my reply reminded me that Mme. Sazerat had lost her son; I wrote to her also. Then, having sacrificed a real duty to the fictitious obligation of shewing myself courteous and sympathetic, I fell back exhausted, closed my eyes and for a week I merely vegetated. And yet, while all my useless duties to which I was ready to sacrifice the real one went out of my head in a few minutes, the idea of the thing I was to construct did not leave me for an instant. I knew not whether it would be a church in which the true believers would be able little by little to learn some truths and discover some harmonies, the great, comprehensive plan, or would stand, forever unvisited, on the summit of an island, like a druid monument. But I had decided to devote to it all my strength, which was leaving me slowly, as though reluctant and wishing to allow me time, having completed the outer structure, to close the funereal door. Soon I was able to shew a few sketches. No one understood a word. Even those who were favourable to my conception of the truths which I intended later to carve within the temple congratulated me on having discovered them with a microscope when I had, on the contrary, used a telescope to perceive things which, it is true, were very small but situated afar off and each of them a world in itself. Whereas I had sought great laws, they called me one who grubs for petty details. Moreover, what was the use of my undertaking it? I had had a certain facility as a young man and Bergotte had declared my schoolboy writings 'perfect';[1] but instead of working, I had lived in idleness, in the dissipation of a life of pleasure, amid sickness, care of my health and strange humours, and I was taking up my work on the eve of my death, with no knowledge of my craft. I no longer felt equal to facing either my obligations to human beings or my duties to my thought and work—still less to both. As for the former, my task was somewhat simplified by my habit of forgetting the letters I had to write. The loss of my memory aided me a little by cutting out some of my obligations; my work filled their place. But suddenly at the end of a month the association of ideas brought back my memory, together with my remorse, and I was crushed with a sense of my own impotence. I was astonished to find myself indifferent to the criticism made of me but the truth is that, from the day when my legs had trembled so as I descended the stairs, I had become indifferent to everything; I craved nothing now but rest, while waiting for the long rest that would eventually come. My unconcern over the approval of the élite of my own time was not due to the expectation that my work would not receive until after my death the admiration which it seemed to me to deserve. Those who came after me might think what they wished. I was just as little concerned about that. In reality, if I thought of my work and not at all of the letters to be answered, this was no longer because I recognised any great difference in importance between the two objects, as I had done in the days of my idleness and then in the time of my active work up to the evening when I was obliged to seize hold of the railing of the staircase. The organization of my memory and my preoccupations was closely bound up with my work, perhaps because, whereas the letters were forgotten immediately after being received, the idea of my work was in my mind, always the same, in a perpetual state of development. But it also had become irksome to me. It was to me like a son whose dying mother must still take upon herself the fatigue of looking after him between injections and cuppings. Possibly she still loves him but she now knows it only through the exhausting obligation she is under to take care of him. In me the powers of the writer were no longer equal to the inconsiderate demands of the work. Since that day on the staircase, nothing concerning the social world, no happiness, whether it came from the unfriendliness of people, the progress of my work, the hope of fame, any longer penetrated to my consciousness except as such a pale ray of sunlight that it no longer had the power to warm me, put life into me, give me any desire whatsoever; and even at that, wan though it was, it was still too dazzling for my eyes and I preferred to close them and turn my head toward the wall. It seems to me, as far as I was able to feel the movement of my lips, that

I must have had an imperceptible little smile at one corner of my mouth when a lady wrote me, "I was *surprised* not to get a reply to my letter." Nevertheless, that reminded me of the letter and I answered her. In order that I might not be thought an ingrate, I tried to place my present courtesy on a par with the courtesy people might have had for me. And I was crushed under the superhumanly wearisome burdens of life which I imposed upon my existence as it ebbed to its agonising close.

This idea of death took up its permanent abode within me as does love for a woman. Not that I loved death, I detested it. But, doubtless because I had pondered over it from time to time as over a woman one does not yet love, now the thought of it adhered to the deepest stratum of my brain so completely that I could not turn my attention to anything without first relating it to the idea of death and, even if I was not occupied with anything but was in a state of complete repose, the idea of death was with me as continuously as the idea of myself. I do not think that, on the day I became half-dead, it was the accompanying symptoms, such as my inability to descend the staircase, to recall a name, to get up, which gave rise, even by an unconscious process of reasoning, to the idea of death, the idea that I was already nearly dead, but rather that all this had come at the same time, that inevitably the great mirror of the mind was reflecting a new reality. And yet I did not see how one could pass without warning from the ills I was enduring to actual death. But then I thought of others, of all those who die every day without the hiatus between their illness and their death seeming to us extraordinary. I even thought it was only because I saw them from within (still more than through the consequent disappointment of my hopes) that certain ailments did not appear to me fatal when considered singly, although I believed in my death, just as those who are the most firmly convinced that their term has come are nevertheless easily persuaded that, if they cannot pronounce certain words, it has nothing to do with a stroke or an attack of aphasia, but comes from a fatigue of the tongue, from a nervous affection akin to stammering or from exhaustion consequent upon an attack of indigestion.

As for me, it was something quite other than a dying man's farewell to his wife which I had to write, something long and addressed to more than one person. Long to write! Only in the daytime, at best, might I try to sleep. If I worked, it would be only at night. But I should need many nights, possibly a hundred, possibly a thousand. And I would live in the anxiety of not knowing whether the master of my destiny, less indulgent than the Sultan Sheriar, when I interrupted my story in the morning, would permit me to take up the continuation of it the following evening. Not that I intended to reproduce in any respect the *Arabian Nights,* any more than the *Mémoires of Saint-Simon,* which likewise were written at night, any more than any of the books I had loved so deeply that, superstitiously devoted to them as to the women I loved, I could not, in my childish *naïveté,* imagine without horror a book that might be different from them. But like Elstir and Chardin, one cannot reproduce what one loves without abandoning it. Doubtless my books also, like my earthly being, would finally some day die. But one must resign oneself to the idea of death. One accepts the idea that in ten years one's self, and in a hundred years one's books, will no longer exist. Eternal existence is not promised to books any more than to men. It might be a book as long as the *Arabian Nights* but entirely different. It is quite true that, when one is enamoured of a book, one would like to create something exactly like it but one must sacrifice one's love of the moment and think, not of one's predilection but of a truth which does not ask our preferences and forbids us to give them a thought. And it is only by following this truth that one happens occasionally to come upon what one abandoned and, even while keeping them out of one's mind, to write the *Arabian Nights* or the *Mémoires of Saint-Simon* of another period. But had I still time? Was it not too late?

In any event, if I still had the strength to accomplish my work, I realised that the nature of the circumstances which today, even during the progress of this reception at the Princesse de Guermantes', had given me at one and the same time the idea of my work and the fear of not being able to carry it out would assuredly before all else imprint upon it the form I had once dimly sensed in the church at Combray, during certain days which had deeply influenced me, a form which usually remains invisible to us, the form of Time. This dimension of Time which I had once vaguely felt in the church at Combray I would try to make continually perceptible in a transcription of human life necessarily very different from that conveyed to us by our deceptive senses. There are, it is true—this was proven to me, as has been seen, by sundry episodes in this narrative—many other errors of our senses which distort for us the true aspect of this world. But after all, in the more accurate transcription which I would do my utmost to give, I would at least be able not to change the location of sounds, to take care not to detach them from their cause, with which the intelligence retroactively associates them— although to make rain hum in the middle of a room and our boiling *tisane* come down in torrents in the courtyard cannot, when all is said and done, be more disconcerting than what artists have so often done in representing as very near us or very far away, according as the laws of perspective, the intensity of the colours and the illusion of the first glance make them appear to us, a sail or a mountain peak which our reason will later move, sometimes an enormous distance, farther away or nearer to us.

I might, although this error is more serious, continue, as is customary, to assign features to the countenance of a passing woman character, whereas, in place of the nose, cheeks and chin, there should at the very most be a vacant space on which would play the light of our desires. And even if I did not have the leisure for that far more important matter, namely, to prepare the hundred masks that needs must be attached to a single face—even if one would merely portray it according to the various pairs of eyes that look at it and the meanings they read into its features and, in the case of one and the same pair of eyes, according to the hope and fear (or, on the contrary, the love and confidence) which over so many years hide the changes due to age; even, moreover, if I did not (although my liaison with Albertine sufficed to prove to me that otherwise all is spurious and deceitful) undertake to represent certain persons, not outwardly but as they exist within us, where their slightest acts may induce fatal disturbances, and did not undertake also to vary the lighting from the subjective sky according to the variations in pressure of our sensitiveness or according to the serenity of our confidence, which makes an object seem so small, whereas the mere shadow of a risk instantly multiplies its size; even if I could not introduce these changes and many others (the necessity for which, if one desires to paint things as they really are, has become apparent in the course of this narrative) into the transcription of a universe which required to be entirely redrawn, at any rate I would not fail, above all else, to describe man as having the length, not of his body but of his years, which he must drag about with him from place to place, an ever increasing burden which overcomes him in the end. Moreover, everyone realises that we occupy a steadily growing place in Time and this universality could not fail to rejoice me, since it was truth, the truth vaguely sensed by each, which I must seek to make clear to all. Not only is everyone conscious that we occupy a place in Time, but this place even the most simple-minded person measures approximately, just as he would measure the place we occupy in space. True, the measuring is often incorrect, but the fact that it was considered possible shews that age was thought of as something measurable.

I also asked myself, "Not only have I still time, but am I going to be able to complete my work?" By forcing me, like a stern spiritual adviser, to declare myself dead to the world, illness had done me a great service —for, if the grain of wheat die not after it hath been sown, it will abide alone; but if it die, it will bear much fruit—and after indolence had protected me from my facility in writing, ill health was perhaps going to save me from my indolence; but this same illness had exhausted my mental faculties and (as I had noticed long before, when I ceased to love Albertine) also the power of my memory. But recreating through the memory impressions which must then be plumbed to their depths, brought into the light and transformed into intellectual equivalents, was this not one of the prerequisites, almost the very essence, of a work of art such as I had conceived it in the library a few moments ago? Ah, if only I still had the mental power that was intact on that evening the memory of which I evoked when my eye fell on *François le Champi*! It was that evening, when my mother abdicated her authority, which marked the commencement of the waning of my will power and my health, as well as the beginning of my grandmother's lingering death. Everything was predetermined from the moment when, unable any longer to endure the idea of waiting until the morning to press a kiss upon my mother's face, I made up my mind, jumped out of bed and, in my nightshirt, went and sat by the window through which the moonlight came, until I heard M. Swann leave. My parents had accompanied him to the door; I heard the door open, the bell tinkle and the door shut again. Even at this moment, in the mansion of the Prince de Guermantes, I heard the sound of my parents' footsteps as they accompanied M. Swann and the reverberating, ferruginous, interminable, sharp, jangling tinkle of the little bell which announced to me that at last M. Swann had gone and Mamma was going to come upstairs—I heard these sounds again, the very identical sounds themselves, although situated so far back in the past. Then, thinking over all the events that necessarily ranged themselves between the moment when I heard those sounds and the Guermantes reception, I was startled at the thought that it was, indeed, this bell which was still tinkling within me and that I could in no wise change its sharp janglings, since, having forgotten just how they died away, to recapture it and hear it distinctly, I was forced to close my ears to the sound of the conversations the masks were carrying on around me. To endeavour to listen to it from nearby, I had to descend again into my own consciousness. It must be, then, that this tinkling was still there and also, between it and the present moment, all the infinitely unrolling past which I had been unconsciously carrying within me. When the bell tinkled, I was already in existence and, since that night, for me to have been able to hear the sound again, there must have been no break of continuity, not a moment of rest for me, no cessation of existence, of thought, of consciousness of myself, since this distant moment still clung to me and I could recapture it, go back to it, merely by descending more deeply within myself. It was this conception of time as incarnate, of past years as still close held within us, which I was now determined to bring out into such bold relief in my book. And it is because they thus contain all the hours of days gone by that human bodies can do such injury to those who love them, because they contain so many past memories, joys and desires, already effaced for them but so cruel for one who contemplates and carries back in the domain of Time the cherished body of which he is jealous, jealous even to the point of desiring its destruction. For after death Time withdraws from the body, and the memories—so pale and insignificant—are effaced from her who no longer exists, and soon will be from him whom they still torture, and the memories themselves will perish in the end when the desire of a living body is no longer there to keep them alive.

There came over me a feeling of profound fatigue at the realisation that all this long stretch of time not only had been uninterruptedly lived, thought, secreted by me, that it was my life, my very self, but also that I must, every minute of my life, keep it closely by me, that it upheld me, that I was perched on its dizzying summit, that I could not move without carrying it about with me.

The date when I heard the sound—so distant and yet so deep within me—of the little bell in the garden at Combray was a landmark I did not know I had available in this enormous dimension of Time. My head swam to see so many years below me, and yet within me, as if I were thousands of leagues in height.

I now understood why it was that the Duc de Guermantes, whom, as I looked at him sitting in a chair, I marvelled to find shewing his age so little, although he had so many more years than I beneath him, as soon as he rose and tried to stand erect, had tottered on trembling limbs (like those of aged archbishops who have nothing solid on them except their metallic cross, with the young divinity students flocking assiduously about them) and had wavered as he made his way along the difficult summit of his eighty-three years, as if men were perched on giant stilts, sometimes taller than church spires, constantly growing and finally rendering their progress so difficult and perilous that they suddenly fall.

I was alarmed that mine were already so tall beneath my feet; it did not seem as if I should have the strength to carry much longer attached to me that past which already extended so far down and which I was bearing so painfully within me! If, at least, there were granted me time enough to complete my work, I would not fail to stamp it with the seal of that Time the understanding of which was this day so forcibly impressing itself upon me, and I would therein describe men—even should that give them the semblance of monstrous creatures—as occupying in Time a place far more considerable than the so restricted one allotted them in space, a place, on the contrary, extending boundlessly since, giant-like, reaching far back into the years, they touch simultaneously epochs of their lives—with countless intervening days between—so widely separated from one another in Time.

NOTE

1 Allusion to the author's first book, *Les Plaisirs et les Jours*. (Note in the French edition.)

Like the Marquis de Sade, Huysmans allowed his imagination free rein, never censoring any of the perverse ideas that thrust themselves upon him in what were probably onanistic sexual fantasies. In this almost clinical description of a man with a gastric disturbance, Huysmans not only indicates the intimate relationship between mind and body but exhibits his understanding of the unconscious source of the disease by having the man cure himself with a symbolic punishment. In rejecting all food taken by mouth and feeding himself solely with enemas, Des Esseintes manages to circumvent a profound fear of aggression and its resultant guilt. The implications of the cure—a desire to return to the womb—indicate a rather severe regression, and the physician in the story is astute enough to recognize that Des Esseintes may be suffering from a serious mental illness.

J. K. HUYSMANS

FROM *Against the Grain*

After blazing up like a fire of straw, his enthusiasm for the "digester" was extinguished with a like rapidity. Soothed for the time being, his dyspepsia began again; presently, this over-stimulating essence of nourishment brought on such an irritation of the bowels that Des Esseintes was obliged to drop its use with all possible speed.

The complaint resumed its course, hitherto unknown symptoms going with it. First nightmares, hallucinations of smell, disturbances of vision, a hacking cough, coming on at a fixed hour with the regularity of clockwork, a beating of the arteries and heart accompanied by cold sweats; then, delusions of hearing, all the mischiefs, in fact, that mark the last stage of the malady.

Eaten up by a burning fever, Des Esseintes would suddenly hear the sound of running water, the buzz of wasps; then these noises would melt into a single one resembling the whirring of a lathe; then this would grow shriller and thinner, changing finally into the silvery tinkle of a bell.

Then he would feel his maddened brain wafted away on waves of music, rolling among the billows of harmony familiar to his boyhood. The chants he had learned from the Jesuit Fathers recurred to him, recalling the college, the college chapel, where they had echoed; then the hallucination would pass on to the olfactory and visual organs, wrapping them in the vapour of incense and the gloom of a sanctuary dimly lit through painted windows under lofty vaults.

Among the Fathers, the rites of religion were performed with great pomp and ceremony; an excellent organist and a noteworthy choir made these spiritual exercises an artistic delight, to the great end of edification. The organist was a lover of the old masters, and on days of festival he would select one of Palestrina's or Orlando Lasso's masses, Marcello's psalms, Handel's oratorios, Sebastian Bach's motets, would play in preference to the sensuous, facile compilations of Father Lambillotte so much favoured by the average priest, certain "Laudi spirituali" of the sixteenth century whose stately beauty had many a time fascinated Des Esseintes.

But above all, he had experienced ineffable pleasures in listening to the "plain-song," which the organist had kept up in spite of modern prejudices.

This form, now looked down upon as an effete and Gothic type of the Christian liturgy, as an antiquarian curiosity, as a relic of barbarous centuries, was the life-word of the ancient Church, the very spirit of the Middle Ages; it was the prayer of all time set to music in tones modulated in accord with the aspirations of the soul, the never-ceasing hymn of praise that had risen for hundreds of years to the throne of the Most High.

This traditional melody was the only one that, with its mighty unison, its solemn, massive harmonies, like blocks of ashlar, could fitly go with the old basilicas and fill their romanesque vaults, of which it seemed the emanation and the living voice.

How many times had not Des Esseintes been entranced and mastered by an irresistible awe when the "Christus factus est" of the Gregorian chant had swelled up in the nave whose pillars trembled amid the floating clouds of incense, or when the rolling bass of the "De profundis" groaned forth, mournful as a stifled sob, poignant as a despairing cry of mankind bewailing its mortal destiny, imploring the tender mercy of its Saviour.

In comparison with this magnificent plain-song, created by the genius of the Church, impersonal, anonymous as the organ itself, whose inventor is unknown, all other religious music seemed to him secular, profane. At bottom, in all the works of Jomelli and Porpora, of Carissimi and Durante, in the most admirable conceptions of Handel and Bach, there was no real renunciation of popular triumph, no sacrifice of artistic success, no abdication of human pride listening to itself at prayer; at best, in those imposing masses of Lesueur's performed at Saint-Roch was the true religious style renewed, grave and august, making some approach to the unadorned nudity, the austere majesty of the old plain-song.

Since those days, utterly revolted by pretentious works like the *Stabat mater* of Rossini or the similar compositions of Pergolese, disgusted with all this intrusion of worldly art into the liturgical sanctum, Des Esseintes had held aloof altogether from these equivocal productions tolerated by an indulgent Mother Church.

In fact, this fatal complacence, due partly to the greed for offertories, partly to a supposed attraction the music exercised on the faithful, had led directly to abuses,—airs borrowed from Italian operas, trivial cavatinas, unseemly quadrilles, performed with full orchestral accompaniment in the churches transformed into fine ladies' boudoirs, entrusted to theatre actors who bellowed aloft under the roof while down below the women fought a pitched battle of fine clothes with one another and quivered with soft emotion to hear the heroes of the opera whose wanton tones defiled the sacred notes of the organ!

For years now he had positively refused to take part in these pious entertainments, resting satisfied with his memories of childhood, regretting even having heard sundry *Te Deums* by great masters, for did he not remember that admirable *Te Deum* of the plain-song, that hymn so simple and grandiose, composed by some Saint, a St. Ambrose or a St. Hilary, who, lacking the complicated resources of an orchestra, failing the mechanical music of modern music, displayed an ardent faith, a delirious joy, the essence of the soul of all humanity expressed in burning, trustful, almost heavenly accents?

In any case, Des Esseintes' ideas on music were in flagrant contradiction with the theories he professed as to the other arts. In religious music, he really cared only for the monastic music of the Middle Ages, that ascetic music that acted instinctively on the nerves, like certain pages of the old Christian Latinity; besides, he admitted it himself, he was incapable of understanding the artful devices contemporary masters

might have been able to introduce into Catholic art. The truth is, he had
not studied music with the same passionate ardour he had applied to
painting and to literature. He could play the piano like any other
amateur, had come, after many fumblings, to be competent to read a
score; but he knew nothing of harmony or the technique needful for
really appreciating lights and shades of expression, for understanding
nice points, for entering, with proper comprehension, into refinements
and elaborations.

Then, on another side, secular music is a promiscuous art which one
cannot enjoy at home and alone, as one reads a book; to taste it, he
must needs have mixed with that inevitable public that crowds to theatres and besieges the *Cirque d'hiver* where, under a broiling sun, in an
atmosphere as muggy as a wash-house, you see a man with the look of a
carpenter bawling a remoulade and massacring disconnected bits of
Wagner to the huge delight of an ignorant crowd!

He had never had the courage to plunge into this bath of promiscuity
in order to hear Berlioz; some fragments of whom had nevertheless won
his admiration by their high-wrought passion and abounding fire, while
he realized with no less perspicacity that there was not a scene, not a
phrase in any opera of the mighty Wagner that could be detached from
its context without ruining it.

The scraps thus cut from the whole and served up at a concert lost all
meaning, all sense, for, like the chapters in a book that mutually complete each other and all concur to bring about the same conclusion, the
same final effect, his melodies were used by Wagner to define the character of his personages, to incarnate their thoughts, to express their
motives, visible or secret, and their ingenious and persistent repetitions
were only intelligible for an audience which followed the subject from its
first opening and watched the characters grow little by little more clearly
defined, observed them develop in surroundings from which they could
not be separated without seeing them perish like branches severed from
a tree.

So Des Esseintes thought, convinced that of all the horde of melo-
maniacs who every Sunday fell into ecstasies on the benches, twenty at
most knew the score the musicians were massacring, when the box-
openers were kind enough to hold their tongues and let the orchestra be
heard.

The circumstance also being remembered that the intelligent patriot-
ism of the French nation forbade the production of an opera of Wagner's at a Paris theatre, there was nothing left for the curious amateur

who is unskilled in the arcana of music and cannot or will not travel to Bayreuth, save to stay at home, and that was the reasonable course Des Esceintes had adopted.

On another side, more popular, easier music and detached morceaux taken from the old-fashioned operas scarcely appealed to him; the trivial tunes of Auber and Boïeldieu, of Adam and Flotow, and the commonplaces of musical rhetoric favoured by Ambroise Thomas, Bazin and their like repelled him just as much as the antiquated sentimentalities and cheap graces of the Italian composers. He had therefore resolutely refused to have anything to do with music, and for all the years this renunciation lasted, he found nothing to look back upon with any pleasure save a few chamber concerts at which he had heard Beethoven and above all Schumann and Schubert, who had stimulated his nerves as keenly as the most telling and tragical poems of Edgar Allan Poe.

Certain settings for the violoncello by Schumann had left him positively panting with emotion, gasping for breath under the stress of hysteria; but it was chiefly Schubert's *lieder* that had stirred him to the depths, lifted him out of himself, then prostrated him as after a wasteful outpouring of nervous fluid, after a mystic debauch of soul.

This music thrilled him to the very marrow, driving back an infinity of forgotten griefs, of old vexations, on a heart amazed to contain so many confused miseries and obscure sorrows. This music of desolation, crying from the deepest depths of being, terrified, while fascinating him. Never, without nervous tears rising to his eyes, had he been able to repeat the "Young Girl's Plaints," for in this *lamento* there was something more than heart-broken, something despairing that tore his entrails, something recalling the end of love's dream in a dismal landscape.

Every time they came back to his lips, these exquisite and funereal laments called up before his fancy a lonely place beyond the city boundaries, a beggarly, forsaken locality, where noiselessly, in the distance, lines of poor folks, harassed by life's wretchedness, filed away, bent double, into the gloom of twilight, while, meantime, he himself, full of bitterness, overflowing with disgust, felt himself standing alone, all alone in the midst of weeping Nature, overborne by an unspeakable melancholy, by an obstinate distress, the mysterious intensity of which brooked no consolation, no comparison, no respite. Like a passing bell, the despairing air haunted his brain now that he lay in bed, enfeebled by fever and tormented by an anxiety the more implacable because he could no longer discover its cause. Eventually he surrendered himself to the current, let himself be swept away by the torrent of the music, suddenly barred for a brief minute by the plain-song of the psalms that rose with its long-drawn bass notes in his head, whose temples seemed bruised and battered by the clappers of a hundred bells.

One morning, however, these noises fell quiet; he was in better possession of his faculties and asked the servant to hand him a mirror. He hardly knew himself; his face was earthen in hue, the lips dry and swollen, the tongue furrowed, the skin wrinkled; his straggling hair and beard, which his man had not trimmed since the beginning of his illness, added to the horror of the sunken cheeks and staring, watery eyes that burned with a feverish brightness in this death's-head bristling with unkempt hair.

Worse than his weakness, worse than his irrepressible fits of vomiting which rejected every attempt at taking food, worse than the wasting from which he suffered, this disfigurement of face alarmed him. He thought he was done for; then, in spite of the exhaustion that crushed him down, the fierce energy of a man at bay brought him to a sitting posture in his bed, lent him strength to write a letter to his Paris doctor and order his servant to go instantly to find him and bring him back with him, cost what it might, the same day.

In an instant, he passed from the most absolute despair to the most comforting hope. The physician in question was a noted specialist, renowned for the cure of nervous disorders; "he must before now have cured more obstinate and more dangerous cases than mine," Des Esseintes told himself; "not a doubt of it, I shall be set up again in a few days' time." But presently again this over-confidence was followed by a feeling of utter disenchantment; no matter how learned and how perspicacious they may be, doctors really know nothing about nervous disease, the very cause of which they cannot tell. Like all the rest, he would prescribe the everlasting oxide of zinc and quinine, bromide of potassium and valerian; "and who can say," he went on to himself, clinging to the last twig of hope, "if the reason why these remedies have hitherto failed me is not simply because I have not known how to employ them in proper doses."

Despite everything, this waiting for expected relief gave him new life; but presently a fresh dread assailed him,—suppose the doctor should not be in town or should decline to disturb his arrangements; then came yet another panic lest his servant should have failed to find him at all. This threw him into the depths of despair. His mind began to fail again, jumping, moment by moment, from the most inordinate hopefulness to the most baseless apprehension, exaggerating both his chances of sudden recovery and his fears of immediate danger. Hour after hour slipped by, and a time arrived when, despairing and exhausted, convinced the doctor would never come, he told himself over and over again in impotent anger that, if only he had seen to it in time, he would undoubtedly have been saved; then after a while, his rage with his servant, his indignation at the doctor's delay, abated, and he began to cherish a bitter vexation against himself instead, blaming his own procrastination in having waited so long before sending for help, persuading himself that he would have been perfectly well by now, if, even the night before only, he had provided himself with good, strong medicines and proper nursing.

Gradually these alternate paroxysms of hope and fear that tormented his half-delirious brain grew milder, as these repeated panics wore down his strength. He dropped into a sleep of exhaustion broken by incoherent dreams, a kind of coma interrupted by periods of wakefulness too brief for consciousness to be regained. He had finally lost all notion of what he wished and what he feared so completely that he was merely bewildered, and felt neither surprise nor satisfaction, when suddenly the doctor made his appearance in the room.

The servant no doubt had informed him of the manner of life Des Esseintes led and of various symptoms he had himself been in a position to notice since the day when he had picked up his master by the window where he lay, felled by the violence of his perfumes, for he asked the patient very few questions, knowing indeed his antecedents for many years past. But he examined and sounded him and carefully scrutinized the urine, in which certain white streaks told him the secret of one of the chief determining causes of his nervous collapse. He wrote a prescription and took his leave without a word, saying he would come again.

His visit comforted Des Esseintes, albeit he was alarmed at the doctor's silence and besought his servant not to hide the truth from him any longer.

The man assured him the doctor had showed no signs of anxiety and, suspicious as he was, Des Esseintes could detect no tokens whatever of prevarication or falsehood in the old man's calm face.

Then his thoughts grew more cheerful; indeed the pain had stopped and the feebleness he had experienced in every limb had merged into a sort of agreeable languor, a feeling of placid content at once vague and slowly progressive. Then he was at once astonished and pleased to find his bedside table unlittered with drugs and medicine bottles, and a pale smile hovered over his lips when finally his servant brought him a nourishing enema compounded with peptone, and informed his master that he was to repeat the little operation three times every twenty-four hours.

The thing was successfully carried out, and Des Esseintes could not help secretly congratulating himself on the event which was the coping stone, the crowning triumph, in a sort, of the life he had contrived for himself; his predilection for the artificial had now, and that without any initiative on his part, attained its supreme fulfilment! A man could hardly go farther; nourishment thus absorbed was surely the last aberration from the natural that could be committed.

"What a delicious thing," he said to himself, "it would be if one could, once restored to full health, go on with the same simple régime. What a saving of time, what a radical deliverance from the repugnance meat inspires in people who have lost their appetite! what a definite and final release from the lassitude that invariably results from the necessarily limited choice of viands! what a vigorous protest against the degrading sin of gluttony! last but not least, what a direct insult cast in the face of old Mother Nature, whose never varying exigencies would be for ever nullified!"

In this vein, he went on talking to himself under his breath. Why, it would be easy enough to sharpen one's appetite by swallowing a strong aperient, then when one could truly tell oneself: "Come, what hour is it now? seems to me it must be high time to sit down to dinner, I have a wolf in my stomach," the table would be laid by depositing the noble instrument on the cloth,—and lo! before you had time so much as to say grace, the troublesome and vulgar task of eating would be suppressed.

Some days later, the man handed his master an enema altogether different in colour and smell from the peptone suppositories.

"Why, it's not the same!" exclaimed Des Esseintes, looking with consternation at the liquid poured into the apparatus. He demanded the menu as he might have done in a restaurant and unfolding the physician's prescription, he read out—

> Cod-liver oil . . . . 20 grammes
> Beef-tea 200   "
> Burgundy 200   "
> Yolk of one egg . . . .

He sat pensive. He had never succeeded, on account of the ruined state of his stomach, in taking a serious interest in the art of cookery; now he was surprised to find himself all of a sudden pondering over combinations of *a posteriori* gourmandise! Then a grotesque notion shot across his brain. Perhaps the doctor had imagined his patient's abnormal palate was wearied by this time of the flavour of peptone; perhaps, like a skilful chef, he had wished to vary the savour of the foods administered, to prevent the monotony of the dishes leading to a complete loss of appetite. Once started on this train of thought, Des Esseintes busied himself in composing novel recipes, contriving dinners for fast days and Fridays, strengthening the dose of cod-liver oil and wine, while striking out the beef-tea as being meat and therefore expressly forbidden by the Church. But, before very long, the necessity disappeared of deliberating about these nourishing liquids, for the doctor managed little by little to overcome the nausea and gave him, to be swallowed by the ordinary channel, a syrup of punch mixed with powdered meat and having a vague aroma of cocoa about it that was grateful to his genuine mouth.

Weeks passed and the stomach at last consented to act; occasionally fits of nausea still recurred, which, however, ginger beer and Rivière's anti-emetic draught were effectual in subduing. Eventually, little by little the organs recovered with the help of the pepsines, and ordinary foods were digested. Strength returned and Des Esseintes was able to stand on his feet and try to walk about his bedroom, leaning on a stick and holding on to the furniture. Instead of being pleased with this success, he forgot all his past sufferings, was irritated by the length of his convalescence, and upbraided the doctor for protracting it in this slow fashion. True, sundry ineffectual experiments had delayed matters; no better than quinine did the stomach tolerate iron, even when mitigated by the addition of laudanum, and these drugs had to be replaced by preparations of arsenic; this after a fortnight had been lost in useless efforts, as Des Esseintes noted with no small impatience.

At last, the moment was reached when he could remain up for whole afternoons at a time and walk about his rooms without assistance. Then his working-room began to get on his nerves; defects to which custom had blinded his eyes now struck him forcibly on his coming back to the room after his long absence. The colours chosen to be seen by lamplight seemed to him discordant under the glare of daylight; he thought how best to alter them and spent hours in contriving artificial harmonies of hues, hybrid combinations of cloths and leathers.

"Without a doubt I am on the highroad to health," he told himself, as he noted the return of his former pre-occupations and old predilections.

One morning, as he was gazing at his orange and blue walls, dreaming of ideal hangings made out of stoles of the Greek Church, of gold-fringed Russian dalmatics, of brocaded copes patterned with Slavonic lettering, adorned with precious stones from the Urals and rows of pearls, the doctor came in and, noting what his patient's eyes were looking at, questioned him.

Then Des Esseintes told him of his unrealizable ideals and began to plan out new experiments in colour, to speak of novel combinations and contrasts of hues that he meant to contrive, when the physician soused a sudden douche of cold water over his head, declaring in the most peremptory fashion that, come what might, it would not be in that house he could put his projects into execution.

Then, without giving him time to recover breath, he announced that so far he had only attacked the most urgent necessity, the re-establishment of the digestive functions, but that now he must deal with the nervous derangements which were by no means mitigated and would require for their cure years of regimen and careful living. He concluded with the ultimatum that, before trying any course of cure, before beginning any sort of hydropathic treatment,—impracticable in any case at Fontenay,—he was bound to abandon this solitary existence, to return to Paris and take part again in the common life of men; in a word, endeavour to find diversions the same as other people.

"But they don't divert *me*, the pleasures other people enjoy," protested Des Esseintes, indignantly.

Without discussing the question, the doctor simply assured his hearer that this radical change of life which he ordered was in his opinion a matter of life and death, of restored health or insanity followed at short notice by tuberculosis.

"Then it is a case either of death or deportation!" cried Des Esseintes, in exasperation.

The physician, who was imbued with all the prejudices of a man of the world, only smiled and made for the door without vouchsafing an answer.

*Janet Frame's uncanny perceptions of the unconscious are
frequently disguised by allegory. The simple story that follows embodies an attitude towards disease that in some
respects echoes that of Menninger. In Frame's view, those
who have not suffered the terror of mental illness, are de-
luding themselves. Unaware of the unconscious they do not
know their enemy and go heedless to the grave.*

*While Menninger offers hope for use of mental illness to
effect its own cure, Frame is not nearly so optimistic. Her
sheep, crippled by anxiety and fear, manages to survive but
his life seems little more than a bleak and meaningless passage through time.*

JANET FRAME

Two Sheep

Two sheep were traveling to the saleyards. The first sheep knew that
after they had been sold their destination was the slaughterhouse at the
freezing works. The second sheep did not know of their fate. They were
being driven with the rest of the flock along a hot dusty valley road
where the surrounding hills leaned in a sun-scorched wilderness of rock,
tussock and old rabbit warrens. They moved slowly, for the drover in his
trap was in no hurry, and had even taken one of the dogs to sit beside
him while the other scrambled from side to side of the flock, guiding
them.

"I think," said the first sheep who was aware of their approaching
death, "that the sun has never shone so warm on my fleece, nor, from
what I see with my small sheep's eye, has the sky seemed so flawless,
without seams or tucks or cracks or blemishes."

"You are crazy," said the second sheep who did not know of their
approaching death. "The sun is warm, yes, but how hot and dusty and
heavy my wool feels! It is a burden to go trotting along this oven shelf.
It seems our journey will never end."

1109

"How fresh and juicy the grass appears on the hill!" the first sheep exclaimed. "And not a hawk in the sky!"

"I think," replied the second sheep, "that something has blinded you. Just look up in the sky and see those three hawks waiting to swoop and attack us!"

They trotted on further through the valley road. Now and again the second sheep stumbled.

"I feel so tired," he said. "I wonder how much longer we must walk on and on through this hot dusty valley?"

But the first sheep walked nimbly and his wool felt light upon him as if he had just been shorn. He could have gamboled like a lamb in August.

"I still think," he said, "that today is the most wonderful day I have known. I do not feel that the road is hot and dusty. I do not notice the stones and grit that you complain of. To me the hills have never seemed so green and enticing, the sun has never seemed so warm and comforting. I believe that I could walk through this valley forever, and never feel tired or hungry or thirsty."

"Whatever has come over you?" the second sheep asked crossly. "Here we are, trotting along hour after hour, and soon we shall stand in our pens in the saleyards while the sun leans over us with its branding irons and our overcoats are such a burden that they drag us to the floor of our pen where we are almost trampled to death by the so dainty feet of our fellow sheep. A fine life that is. It would not surprise me if after we are sold we are taken in trucks to the freezing works and killed in cold blood. But," he added, comforting himself, "that is not likely to happen. Oh no, that could never happen! I have it on authority that even when they are trampled by their fellows, sheep do not die. The tales we hear from time to time are but malicious rumors, and those vivid dreams which strike us in the night as we sleep on the sheltered hills, they are but illusions. Do you not agree?" he asked the first sheep.

They were turning now from the valley road, and the saleyards were in sight, while drawn up in the siding on the rusty railway lines, the red trucks stood waiting, spattered inside with sheep and cattle dirt and with white chalk marks, in cipher, on the outside. And still the first sheep did not reveal to his companion that they were being driven to certain death.

When they were jostled inside their pen the first sheep gave an exclamation of delight.

"What a pleasant little house they have let to us! I have never seen such smart red-painted bars, and such foursquare corners. And look at the elegant stairway which we will climb to enter those red caravans for our seaside holiday!"

"You make me tired," the second sheep said. "We are standing inside a dirty pen, nothing more, and I cannot move my feet in their nicely polished black shoes but I tread upon the dirt left by sheep which have been imprisoned here before us. In fact I have never been so badly treated in all my life!" And the second sheep began to cry. Just then a kind elderly sheep jostled through the flock and began to comfort him.

"You have been frightening your companion, I suppose," she said angrily to the first sheep. "You have been telling horrible tales of our fate. Some sheep never know when to keep things to themselves. There was no need to tell your companion the truth, that we are being led to certain death!"

But the first sheep did not answer. He was thinking that the sun had never blessed him with so much warmth, that no crowded pen had ever seemed so comfortable and luxurious. Then suddenly he was taken by surprise and hustled out a little gate and up the ramp into the waiting truck, and suddenly too the sun shone in its true colors, battering him about the head with gigantic burning bars, while the hawks congregated above, sizzling the sky with their wings, and a pall of dust clung to the barren used-up hills, and everywhere was commotion, pushing, struggling, bleating, trampling.

"This must be death," he thought, and he began to struggle and cry out.

The second sheep, having at last learned that he would meet his fate at the freezing works, stood unperturbed now in the truck with his nose against the wall and his eyes looking through the slits.

"You are right," he said to the first sheep. "The hill has never seemed so green, the sun has never been warmer, and this truck with its neat red walls is a mansion where I would happily spend the rest of my days."

But the first sheep did not answer. He had seen the approach of death. He could hide from it no longer. He had given up the struggle and was lying exhausted in a corner of the truck. And when the truck arrived at its destination, the freezing works, the man whose duty it was to unload the sheep noticed the first lying so still in the corner that he believed it was dead.

"We can't have dead sheep," he said. "How can you kill a dead sheep?"

So he heaved the first sheep out of the door of the truck onto the rusty railway line.

"I'll move it away later," he said to himself. "Meanwhile here goes with this lot."

And while he was so busy moving the flock, the first sheep, recovering, sprang up and trotted away along the line, out the gate of the freezing works, up the road, along another road, until he saw a flock being driven before him.

"I will join the flock," he said. "No one will notice, and I shall be safe."

While the drover was not looking, the first sheep hurried in among the flock and was soon trotting along with them until they came to a hot dusty road through a valley where the hills leaned in a sun-scorched wilderness of rock, tussock, and old rabbit warrens.

By now he was feeling very tired. He spoke for the first time to his new companions.

"What a hot dusty road," he said. "How uncomfortable the heat is, and the sun seems to be striking me for its own burning purposes."

The sheep walking beside him looked surprised.

"It is a wonderful day," he exclaimed. "The sun is warmer than I have ever known it, the hills glow green with luscious grass, and there is not a hawk in the sky to threaten us!"

"You mean," the first sheep replied slyly, "that you are on your way to the saleyards, and then to the freezing works to be killed."

The other sheep gave a bleat of surprise.

"How did you guess?" he asked.

"Oh," said the first sheep wisely, "I know the code. And because I know the code I shall go around in circles all my life, not knowing whether to think that the hills are bare or whether they are green, whether the hawks are scarce or plentiful, whether the sun is friend or foe. For the rest of my life I shall not speak another word. I shall trot along the hot dusty valleys where the hills are both barren and lush with spring grass.

"What shall I do but keep silent?"

And so it happened, and over and over again the first sheep escaped death, and rejoined the flock of sheep who were traveling to the freezing works. He is still alive today. If you notice him in a flock, being driven along a hot dusty road, you will be able to distinguish him by his timidity, his uncertainty, the frenzied expression in his eyes when he tries, in his condemned silence, to discover whether the sky is at last free from hawks, or whether they circle in twos and threes above him, waiting to kill him.